The Adolescent

The Adolescent

Development, Relationships, and Culture

NINTH EDITION

F. Philip Rice

University of Maine

Allyn and Bacon

Boston ■ London ■ Toronto ■ Sydney ■ Tokyo ■ Singapore

Vice President, Editor in Chief, Social Sciences: Sean W. Wakely
Senior Editor: Carolyn O. Merrill
Editorial Assistant: Amy Goldmacher
Director of Field Marketing: Joyce Nilsen
Editorial-Production Administrator: Annette Joseph
Editorial-Production Coordinator: Susan Freese
Editorial-Production Service: TKM Productions
Text Design: Denise Hoffman, Glenview Studios
Composition Buyer: Linda Cox
Photo Researcher: Laurie Frankenthaler
Electronic Composition: Omegatype Typography, Inc.
Art Studio: Precision Graphics
Manufacturing Buyer: Megan Cochran
Cover Administrator: Linda Knowles
Cover Designer: Studio Nine

Library of Congress Cataloging-in-Publication Data
Rice, F. Philip
   The adolescent: development, relationships, and culture /F.
   Philip Rice—9th ed.
       p.   cm
   Includes bibliographical references and index.
   ISBN 0-205-27617-2
   1. Youth—United States—Social conditions. 2. Adolescent
   psychology—United States. 3. Adolescence. I. Title.
   HQ796.R543   1998
   305.235—dc21   98-5164
                                                      CIP

Printed in the United States of America

10 9 8 7 6 5 4 3 2 1   VHP   03 02 01 00 99 98

Photo credits continue on page 518, which constitutes a continuation of the copyright page.

BRIEF CONTENTS

CONTENTS

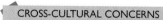

PREFACE

Judging by the positive response from professors and students alike during the past 24 years, this book has been recognized as one of the most important texts on adolescent psychology. Acceptance has continued to grow over the life span of the book because the text has been kept as current as possible. It was also one of the first books to offer extensive diversity coverage. With each new edition, every chapter is updated—new topics are added and outdated ones are deleted. The aim has always been to produce a text that combines academic excellence with popular acceptance, as comprehensively and interestingly as possible.

I am absolutely delighted at the positive comments I have received and am grateful for the helpful suggestions that continue to be made. Based on that feedback, many important changes and new features have been added to this ninth edition.

Basic Outline The organization of the text is as follows:

Part One: Adolescence Three major chapters are included in Part One: Adolescents in Social Context, Adolescents in Theoretical Context, and Adolescents in Ethnic Context. Chapter 1, all of which is new, places adolescent development, relationships, and culture in a social context and discusses the revolutionary changes in society and how they affect the lives of adolescents. Six changes are discussed: the computer revolution, the materialistic revolution, the education revolution, the family revolution, the sexual revolution, and the violence revolution. Chapter 2 places adolescence in a theoretical context and discusses the multidisciplinary views of adolescence. Chapter 3, which places adolescence in an ethnic context, includes seven major groups: adolescents of low socioeconomic status, African Americans, Mexican Americans, Puerto Ricans, Native Americans, Chinese Americans, and Southeast Asian Americans.

Part Two: Physical This part has two chapters of great interest to students: Sexual Maturation and Physical Growth as well as The Body Image.

Part Three: Intellectual The two subjects covered in Part Three are Cognitive Growth and Change as well as Intelligence, Information Processing, and Decision Making.

Part Four: Psychosexual The all-important topics of Gender, Self-Concept, Self-Esteem, Ethnicity, and Identity are discussed. Sexual Values, Behavior, and Education are also included in Part Four.

Part Five: Social Coverage of social development includes three major chapters: Adolescent Society, Culture, and Subculture; Social Development, Relationships, Dating, Nonmarital Cohabitation, and Marriage; and Development of Moral Judgment, Character, Values, Beliefs, and Behavior.

Part Six: Familial The subject of Adolescents and Their Families is found in Part Six, along with a chapter on Divorced, Parent-Absent, and Blended Families.

Part Seven: Educational and Vocational Education and School covers developments during the 1990s, including discussion of private versus public schools. Work and Vocation is the second chapter in this part.

Part Eight: Psychosocial Problems Adolescent Alienation, as expressed through running away, suicide, and juvenile delinquency, is discussed in this section, along with a chapter on Substance Abuse, Addiction, and Dependency.

New Topics Topics that have been revised or are new to this edition include the following:

Impact of growing up in high-risk, crime-infested neighborhoods

Educational and vocational achievement of adolescents from different ethnic groups

Preparing girls for menstruation

Trends in Scholastic Assessment Test (SAT) scores

Economic hardship and adolescent self-esteem

Elaboration of identity statuses

Parental ethnic acculturation

Unwanted sexual aggression

Human immunodeficiency virus (HIV) prevention

Teen pregnancy: incidence, cause, pregnancy resolution, and teen fathers

Problems of adolescent mothers

Sources of sex information

Extracurricular activities and adolescent popularity

Importance of telephones in the lives of adolescents

Music videos

Nonmarital cohabitation: attitudes of different ethnic groups, incidence, effects on marriage, premarital childbearing

How adolescents gain prestige

Leisure activities and early dating experiences

Modes of making moral decisions

Impact of TV viewing

Adolescent-parent communication

Corporal punishment

Cross-cultural concepts of what is a "bad" kid

Sexual abuse

Family types and their effects on adolescents: intact, first-marriage family; divorced, single-parent family; stepfamily; and single-mother family

Child custody

Dropping out of school

Employment opportunities

Problems of adolescent runaways

Trends in adolescent drug abuse

New References   Information from over 200 new journal articles has been incorporated into this edition. These articles were published in the mid-1990s.

Boxes   Three different types of boxed features appear in this edition, including many new topics and examples. *Personal Issues* discusses topics of individual interest to students. *Cross-Cultural Con-*cerns shows comparisons between different racial and ethnic groups on a wide variety of subjects. *Highlight* continues the discussion of current research issues of special interest. Together, these boxed features add variety and interest to the text.

New Visuals   An exciting new look for the text—including new photographs, graphs, charts, and tables—enhances the learning process and makes this edition as visually appealing as possible.

Other important features, highly praised by adopters of the book, have been retained from previous editions. These features include:

Broad Research Base   The discussions are substantiated with over 1,400 citations, most of which are original research studies; however, the emphasis in the text is on discussing the subjects, not summarizing one research study after another.

Pedagogical Aids   This book has been written with the teaching-learning process in mind. Each chapter begins with a detailed outline. Key terms appear in text in bold type and are defined as margin features on or near the same page where first mentioned; they appear again in the Glossary at the end of the book and at the end of each chapter that first introduces them. Each chapter includes a detailed, numbered Summary. Thought Questions at the end of each chapter may be used in class discussions or in essay assignments. The Suggested Reading list that concludes each chapter enables students and instructors to do extra reading on topics, as desired. A completely revised Instructor's Manual, including test questions, is available for teachers. A unique and helpful feature is the italicizing of key phrases. This allows students to review the most important thoughts without having to underline or highlight with a marker.

Eclectic Orientation   This text presents not one theory of adolescence but many, discussing the contributions, strengths, and weaknesses of each.

Comprehensive Coverage   The book is as comprehensive as possible within the confines of one text. The adolescent is discussed within the context of contemporary society. Material includes both theory and life experiences of adolescents and discusses physical, intellectual, emotional, psychosexual, social, familial, educational, and vocational aspects of adolescent development and behavior. It also reviews psychosocial problems of adolescents.

Adolescents in Contemporary Society How modern society and social forces shape the lives of adolescents today is an important topic. Adolescents are discussed in social, theoretical, and ethnic contexts, not as though they were isolated from the social forces around them.

Cultural Diversity Adolescents are not all alike, any more so than are adults. A wide variety of ethnic, racial, and cultural groups are discussed.

Adolescent Society and Culture This book includes not only adolescent development and relationships but also group life and culture. Subjects include cultural versus subcultural societies, dress, social activities, and group life in and out of school. The importance of the automobile, telephone, and music in the life of adolescents is also emphasized.

Gender Issues and Concerns Gender issues are raised in relation to a wide range of topics: physical attributes and body image, cognitive abilities and intelligence, eating disorders, social development and dating, sexual values and behavior, education, work and vocation, and others.

Personal Applications The Thought Questions at the end of each chapter are designed to bring out student attitudes, feelings, and responses to the subjects discussed. Students are encouraged to reflect on their own adolescent years, to talk about adolescents they know (either their own friends or children), and to react in a critical way to the issues discussed.

Acknowledgments

I gratefully acknowledge the special help of the following people, who provided valuable guidance in writing and producing this book: at Allyn and Bacon, Carolyn Merrill, Senior Editor, and her assistant, Amy Goldmacher, and at TKM Productions, Lynda Griffiths.

I would also like to thank the following individuals, who reviewed this book at various stages and offered useful suggestions:

Victor Broderick,
Ferris State University

Darlene DeMarie-Dreblow,
Muskingum College

Mary Ann Drake,
Mercer University

Cynthia A. Edwards,
Meredith College

Roger Gaddis,
Gardner-Webb University

Brenda Grubb,
Mississippi Delta State University

Jennifer Kerpelman,
University of North Carolina–Greensboro

Pamela Manners,
Troy State University

Frederic Medway,
University of South Carolina

Karla Miley,
Black Hawk College

Carol L. Patrick,
Southern Illinois University–Carbondale

Larry D. Pound,
St. John Fisher College

Robert W. Read,
Salem State College

Nicholas Santilli,
John Carroll University

Robert E. Schell,
State University of New York–Oswego

Samuel Snyder,
North Carolina State University

Debra C. Steckler,
Mary Washington College

Ignatius J. Toner,
University of North Carolina–Charlotte

I

Adolescents in Social Context

The word *adolescence* comes from the Latin verb *adolescere*, which means "to grow" or "to grow to maturity." Adolescence is the period of growth between childhood and adulthood. The transition from one stage to the other is gradual and uncertain, and the time span is not the same for every person, but most adolescents eventually become mature adults. In this sense, adolescence is likened to a bridge between childhood and adulthood over which individuals must pass before they take their places as mature, responsible, creative adults.

Maturity is that state at which a person is considered fully developed physically, emotionally, socially, intellectually, and spiritually. The balance of all these characteristics is not always achieved, however. A person may be mature physically but not emotionally. Conversely, there are some individuals who are intellectually quite mature but have not attained full spiritual and moral growth.

Puberty can be used in a fairly narrow sense to denote only that age when a person first becomes sexually capable of having children. In a broader sense (and the sense in which it is used in this book), puberty denotes the several years during which physical changes relative to sexual maturation are taking place: those years during which the mature primary and secondary sexual characteristics develop. Generally, the first two years of puberty are spent in preparing the body for reproduction, and the last two years are spent in

> **adolescence** the period of growth from childhood to maturity.
>
> **maturity** the time in life when one becomes an adult physically, emotionally, socially, intellectually, and spiritually.
>
> **puberty** the whole period during which a person reaches sexual maturity and becomes capable of reproduction.

completing it. The first part of puberty overlaps childhood and adolescence, and the last part coincides with the first several years of adolescence.

Pubescence is used synonymously with *puberty* to denote the whole period during which sexual maturation takes place. Literally, it means becoming hairy or downy, describing one of the important physical changes that occur during puberty. So a *pubescent* child is one who is arriving at or has arrived at puberty.

The term **teenager,** in a strict sense, means only those in the teen years: 13 to 19 years of age. However, because children (especially girls) sometimes mature physically before 13 years of age, there are some discrepancies. An 11-year-old girl may look and act like a teenager, but a 15-year-old boy, if not yet sexually mature, may still act and look like a child. The term *preteen* is sometimes used to describe individuals who have entered puberty but are not yet in the teen years.

The word *teenager* is of fairly recent origin. It first appeared in the *Readers' Guide to Periodical Literature* in the 1943–1945 issue. Subsequently, the term has become popular in the lay vocabulary. It is a word to which many youths used to object because of its negative emotional connotations: wild, delinquent, incorrigible, and immoral. Margaret Mead, the noted anthropologist, objected to the term because it is too restrictive in terms of age (13 to 19 years). She objected to it for emotional reasons also. There are many different types of teenagers: scholarly, intellectual teenagers; cool, street-smart teenagers; and lethargic, unmotivated teenagers. In this book, the designation *adolescent* is preferred over the term *teenager.*

The word **juvenile** is generally used in a legal sense to signify one who is not yet considered an adult in the eyes of the law, in most states anyone up to 18 years of age. The legal rights of 18-year-olds are confusing, however, for they vary from state to state. The Twenty-Sixth Amendment gave them the right to vote, and in some areas they are called for jury duty. They may obtain credit in their own names at some stores or banks, but at others they have to obtain cosigners, even though they are legally responsible for their own debts. Many landlords still require parents of 18-year-olds to cosign leases. In Colorado, 18-year-olds can sign some contracts but not others and they can marry without parental consent; they do not attain full legal rights until age 21. The net result is confusion. When do adolescents fully become adults? Some teens feel they have to wait too many years to "get into the club." *Early adolescence* is usually considered to be 11 to 14 years of age, and *middle or late adolescence* is delineated as 15 to 19 years. This is a helpful way of distinguishing which part of adolescence one is talking about (Sherrod, Haggerty, and Featherman, 1993).

There are various approaches to the study of adolescents. The first is the *biological* approach, which discusses the process of sexual maturation and physical growth that take place at puberty. It involves the maturation and functions of the male and female organs, the development of secondary sexual characteristics, and the growth trends in height and weight that take place during pubescence. Along with these are such issues as health concerns relating to nutrition, weight, physical attractiveness, and the adolescents' emotional reactions to the changes that take place in their bodies. We will focus on the biological approach in Part II of this book (Chapters 4 and 5).

The second approach to the study of adolescents is the *cognitive* approach, which deals with two aspects: (1) the qualitative changes that take place in the way adolescents think and (2) the quantitative changes that take place in intelligence and information processing. Of concern also is the effect that cognitive changes have on the adolescent's personality and behavior. Such topics as intelligence quotients (IQs), Scholastic Assessment Test (SAT) scores, memory ability, thinking, problem solving, and decision making are discussed along with the adolescent's education and schooling. We will take up the cognitive approach in Part III (Chapters 6 and 7).

The third approach to the study of adolescents is the *psychosexual* approach, which deals with the development of emotions and of the self, including the development of self-concept, self-esteem, gender, and identity. It is concerned also with mental health, emotional disorders, and the effects of stress on the adolescent. Sexual values, behavior, and education are usually included under this approach. We will examine the psychosexual approach in Part IV (Chapters 8 and 9).

The fourth approach to the study of adolescents is the *social* approach. This broad approach includes social development, relationships, dating, and the development of moral judgment, character, values, beliefs, and behavior. Included also is a consideration of adolescent society, culture, and subculture. Parent-adolescent relationships are examined together with the influence of various types of family structure on adolescent development. Adolescents from divorced, parent-absent, and blended families face a variety of unique problems, which are analyzed. How modern society and social forces shape the lives of adolescents today is an important focus. There are significant differences among adolescents from different ethnic, racial, and cultural groups. Some of these differences are highlighted and comparisons made. Finally, psychosocial problems such as juvenile delinquency, running away, adolescent suicide, and substance abuse are included in the category of social development of adolescents. We will focus on the social approach in much of the rest of the book—Parts I, V, VI, VII, and VIII (Chapters 1 through 3 and 10 through 18).

The emphasis in this book is on an *eclectic approach* to the study of adolescents—that is, the approach is interdisciplinary, emphasizing not one aspect of adolescent development but all of them, recognizing that no single approach contains all the facts. As such, the contributions of biologists, psychologists, educators, sociologists, anthropologists, and medical personnel are all important. If we are to get a complete view of adolescents, we must stand in different places and look at adolescents from different perspectives.

Our Society in Revolution

The society in which adolescents grow up has an important influence on their development, relationships, adjustments, and problems. The expectations of the society mold their personalities, influence their roles, and guide their futures. The structure and functions of the society either help them fulfill their needs or create new problems by stimulating further tension and frustration. Because adolescents are social beings who are part of a larger society, we need to understand this social order and some of the ways it influences them.

Let's consider six important influences on today's adolescents: the computer revolution, the materialistic revolution, the education revolution, the family revolution, the sexual revolution, and the violence revolution.

The Computer Revolution

Adolescents today live in a society undergoing rapid technological changes. In fact, these changes may be so great as to be called a *revolution,* which the dictionary defines as a radical and profound change in society and the social structure. Probably no other society has so revered technological innovation while placing little restraint on it than that of the United States. Since the turn of the century, Americans have witnessed unprecedented advances: the introduction of electricity, radio, television, automobiles, airplanes, nuclear energy, rocketry, computers, lasers, robots, and satellite communication.

Of all these changes, none has had as profound an effect as the introduction of the computer. The first computers were less powerful than today's personal computers (PCs) yet occupied whole rooms and cost millions of dollars. It's easy to forget that the first personal computer was introduced in 1980. Since that time, the use of computers has skyrocketed. About half of all U.S. workers today use computers on the job. In a recent year, 28 percent of students were using computers at home, and over 60 percent were using computers at school. Amazing as it may seem, about 27 percent of prekindergarten and kindergarten students were using computers at school (U.S. Bureau of the Census, 1996).

There are several good explanations of why the use of computers continues to increase. One reason is that the cost has steadily declined, making computers more affordable to the general population. Another reason is that computers are much smaller and faster today. Desktop computers can store hundreds of thousands of pages of text,

pubescence   the whole period during which physical changes related to sexual maturation take place.

teenager   in a strict sense, includes only the teen years: ages 13 to 19.

juvenile   one who is not yet considered an adult in the eyes of the law.

assist in buying the groceries, make sales presentations to clients miles away, keep personal schedules, check electronic mail (e-mail), yet take up less space than a small television set.

The Internet

One of the most important reasons for using the computer has been the introduction of the **Internet.** Some 25,000 interconnected networks made up of several hundred thousand host computers and their servers span the globe, ready to exchange information and allow you to connect with people all over the world.

The researchers who created the Internet needed a safe way to store and communicate sensitive government information in the event of a nuclear war. The solution was a network that lacked a central computer to store its billions of bytes of information or to direct the actions of remote computers. Each computer site on the network stands alone but is also interconnected to the others. Thus, the destruction of one site (in the event of war) would not prevent the free interchange of information or destroy the data stored at other sites.

Today, the result is a decentralized network of data stored on thousands of computers that make up the network or that speak a common language. If a particular computer breaks, the rest of the computers connected to the network can use any number of other connections to maintain their link.

Conservative estimates put more than 100 million users on the Internet by the year 2000 (Carlson, 1996). The Internet is open 24 hours a day, 365 days a year. It's a way to meet people; find adventure; share ideas and experiences; look for a job, a date, or a mate; ask questions; or give advice. The information resources of thousands of universities, government agencies, and researchers are at your fingertips. It's like a shopping mall that never closes where you can shop for everything from automobiles to food. It's cyberspace: the final frontier. Cyberspace has no borders or defined boundaries; it is a system where you can go to meet people, communicate, learn, explore, and get information. Cyberspace is the place for those who connect to each other electronically to share their thoughts and feelings (Benedickt, 1991).

Once online, you can have private and group conversations, join in lively discussions with nationally known experts, play online games, browse through the articles of hundreds of periodicals and online magazines, go on a shopping spree, make flight or hotel reservations, or track investments with the latest stock market quotes and investment advice.

In addition to its communication role, each of the hundreds of thousands of Internet servers resembles a mini-library. Each server maintains its own information (or database), catalogs that information, and decides what to store and what to discard. The Internet is analogous to a library, but there is no card catalog for this library. More accurately, each server stores information without indexing or cross-referencing the entire database. To find a particular topic, there are numerous programs called *search engines* that allow you to search the vast depth of the database simply by typing in the topic word or words and hitting the Enter key.

The World Wide Web

The *World Wide Web* was developed in 1992 by a group of Swiss scientists. The web has been primarily responsible for the explosion of Internet users in the past several years. If you log on to the Internet using a software product called a *browser,* you can point and click your way through the catalogs of art and science museums, bookstores, corporate advertisements, personal home pages, and thousands of online shopping malls. The splendor of the *National Geographic* may come to life on the screen, complete with still photographs as well as sound and video clips.

Computers in the classroom serve a wide variety of purposes, from teaching phonics and reading skills to unlocking the wonders of science by analyzing the temperature and viscosity of a liquid in chemistry class. It is no wonder that students are excited about what they can do with computers. The world is virtually at their fingertips (Carlson, 1996).

Inappropriate Materials

Many parents are not aware that a wide range of inappropriate materials are available on the Internet. Sexually explicit materials include photographs and motion videos of singles, couples, and groups involved in various sex acts. Some pho-

One of the most important reasons for using a computer is to connect to the World Wide Web via the Internet. Using a browser, such as the one shown here, you can find a myriad of useful resources.

tographic and artistic materials contain examples of bestiality and pedophilia. Fictional and nonfictional accounts of sexual encounters may include incest, group sex, or bondage. Users can find personal ads of individuals seeking same-sex and opposite-sex partners for extramarital affairs and one-night stands. Catalogs for sexual devices and clothing as well as advertisements for pay-for-service organizations ranging from phone sex to escort services are also offered. There's nothing on the Internet that isn't available in other places, but the Internet is not as controllable and thus online materials are more accessible to adolescents and children than some other sources.

Violent and destructive materials are also included on the Internet. Recipes for bombs, booby traps, and other destructive devices can be found. There has been at least one example of an adolescent who found an Internet recipe for a bomb similar to that used in Oklahoma City in 1995 and purchased materials at the local hardware store with the intent of seeing if it worked. The Internet may also contain information on drugs and drug users' devices. Radical activist groups also provide materials on the Internet. Such materials may come from neo-Nazi groups or state militia organizations or include information on gang-related activity. Users can also find information on cults and other organizations that teach witchcraft and satanic rituals.

The Internet provides potential for adults to prey on children. Numerous cases have been cited in the media of child pornographers who lured boys and girls into compromising situations by posing as persons other than themselves. Parents and lawmakers have sought to pass legislation that would help protect their children from these kinds of exposures (Carlson, 1996). The Communications Decency Act was passed into law in February 1996. Within days, several civil rights organizations challenged the law on the grounds that it violates the First Amendment. The court overturned the law, and the Department of Justice has promised appeals to the United States Supreme Court, if necessary.

Effects

Just what effects the computer revolution will have on children and adolescents is not completely clear. Certainly, there are untold benefits. Adolescents have knowledge at their fingertips like never before. They have the potential to be the best-informed generation the United States has ever produced. The negative effects, however, are troublesome. A large number of research studies have measured the effects of pornography on children and adolescents. The *Final Report of the Attorney General's Commission on Pornography* (McManus,

Internet thousands of interconnected computer networks that span the globe, allowing the exchange of information.

World Wide Web a system whereby users can connect to the Internet by use of software that gives information on specific subjects.

1986, p. xviii) issued this consensus on five major conclusions:

1. Children and adolescents who participate in the production of pornographic materials experience adverse and enduring effects.
2. The prolonged use of pornography increases a person's belief that less customary sexual practices are common.
3. Pornography that portrays sexual aggression as pleasurable for the victim increases a person's acceptance of the use of coercion in sexual relations.
4. Acceptance of coercive sexuality appears to be related to sexual aggression.
5. In laboratory settings that measure short-term effects of exposure to violent pornography, subjects increase the punitive behavior toward women.

The extensive use of computers also has some other possible effects on adolescents and children. Many youths spend hours a day playing games and browsing through the Internet, searching for various kinds of materials. In fact, many parents now complain that their children are using their computers for more time each day than they used to spend watching television. Some computer addicts live an isolated existence. Communication with other human beings, including those in their own households, has declined. The Internet begins to serve as their new community, the electronic village as their hometown. Some primary relationships on a face-to-face basis have been superseded by computer relationships (Pipher, 1996).

Another interesting result of the computer revolution is that a technology gap has been created between children and their parents. Many parents don't understand computers and are afraid of them. As a result of these parents' slow assimilation of computer knowledge, the technology gap has widened. More and more adults are accepting computer technology, however, and are beginning to overcome their fears.

The Materialistic Revolution

In general, adolescents are growing up in a materialistic society, and this has had a profound effect on them and the families with whom they live.

Earnings, Income, and Real Dollars

Let's consider some basic facts: The average hourly wage for selected workers has risen from $6.66 per hour in 1980 to $11.44 per hour in 1995. But when inflation is taken into account and these wages are reported in constant (1982) dollars, real wages were $7.78 in 1980 and $7.40 in 1995, representing a decrease of 38 cents per hour. If we look only at income in constant dollars, we discover that the median income of families declined from $40,087 in 1990 to $38,782 in 1994 (U.S. Bureau of the Census, 1996, p. 466). If we look at the income of families in minority groups, we see that the situation is even worse.

Another result of the decrease in real wages has been the number of people who live below the poverty level (U.S. Bureau of the Census, 1996, p. 472). In 1994, 21 percent of all children in the United States lived below the poverty level; when we look at minority groups, however, we discover that 43 percent of all African American children and 41 percent of all Hispanic children lived below the poverty level.

In the meantime, costs are continuing to rise. In 1970, the median sales price of existing one-family homes was $23,000; in 1995, that same house sold for $112,900. The price of automobiles also continues to skyrocket. The average price of a new vehicle has increased by 33 percent during the last 10 years (U.S. Bureau of the Census, 1996, p. 630).

Multiple Jobholders and Overtime Work

It is quite obvious that many families in the United States are unable to keep up with the increase in the cost of living. This has resulted in several changes in employment. Some workers today are multiple jobholders, working a primary full-time job and a secondary part-time job; others have two full-time jobs. Over 6 percent of employed Americans are multiple jobholders (U.S. Bureau of the Census, 1996, p. 403). Other people work overtime to earn more money. In 1995, 32 percent of all workers worked over 40 hours a week; 8.5 percent of these people worked more than 60 hours. Obviously, working this number of hours cuts down on the amount of time workers can spend with their families and children. As one wife said,

"When my husband is giving 80 hours a week to his job, what is there left for me?" (author's counseling notes).

Working Women

Another indicator of attempting to keep up with the high cost of living is the increase in the number of women, even women with young children, who are working outside the home. In 1995, 70 percent of all married women worked outside the home. Some 76 percent of married women with children 6 to 17 years of age worked outside the home, as did 64 percent of all married women with children under age 6. Increasing employment for mothers has intensified the demand for child care. In some cases, the adolescents or older children in the family are expected to take over childrearing duties while their parents are at work.

Adolescent Employment

An additional solution for the differences between expenses and income is for adolescents to work. The proportion of high school students who work has been rising steadily. Generally speaking, working students have had the support of parents, teachers, and social scientists. The conventional wisdom seems to argue that working is actually good for students. With the blessing of society, then, American youths have gone to work. Among high school seniors, one of three male students works at least 20 hours a week, and one of four female students does the same (Bachman, Johnston, and O'Malley, 1987).

Some authorities, however, are beginning to feel that *many adolescents are devoting too much time to jobs and not enough to school* (Pritchard, Myers, and Cassidy, 1989). It is not unusual for a 16-year-old to earn $250 a week and spend the entire sum on car expenses, tickets to concerts, clothing, and tapes or CDs. These spending patterns fail to prepare adolescents for adult self-sufficiency.

One of the most highly contested issues in the study of adolescent work is whether extensive part-time employment threatens youngsters' schooling. One study examined the relationship between school-year employment and adjustment of approximately 1,800 high school sophomores and juniors from nine high schools in Wisconsin

The number of adolescents who hold part-time jobs has been rising steadily. An after-school job often conflicts with schoolwork and responsibilities at home, especially if the job takes more than 20 hours per week.

and California (Steinberg, Fegley, and Dornbusch, 1993). Analysis indicated that entering the labor force and, in particular, taking on a job of more than 20 hours weekly diminished youngsters' investment in school, increased delinquency and drug use, and increased autonomy from parental control. Adolescents who enter the labor force—and especially those who work more than 20 hours weekly—are less academically inclined and poorer students to begin with than their peers who do not work. This study indicates that working appears to make a bad situation worse, lowering educational expectations, adversely affecting school behaviors (specifically, time on homework and class attendance), and souring the school-related attitudes of students who are already achieving less and are more negative toward school than are their peers. Working long hours also tends to increase school misconduct and provides further evidence for the contention that employment weakens adolescents' attachments to formal education.

Working does not always erode students' grades, however, despite its negative impact on class attendance, homework performance, and attitudes toward school. This is due to the fact that many working adolescents are able to maintain and protect their grade-point average by choosing easier teachers, selecting less challenging courses, or cheating on class tests and assignments. As in previous studies, the researchers found that working is also associated with higher rates of deviance. Specifically, taking on a job for more than 20 hours weekly leads to more delinquency and substance abuse. The reason is that the adolescent has more discretionary income with which to purchase drugs and alcohol. In addition, working tends to lead to further independence from parents, at least as indexed by a measure of family decision making. Whether this effect should be viewed in a positive or negative light cannot be determined on the basis of the results reported by the researchers.

Other research indicated positive correlations between the intensity of adolescent work and problem behaviors (Bachman and Schulenberg, 1993). Work intensity appears to reduce the likelihood of getting sufficient sleep, eating breakfast, exercising, and having a satisfactory amount of leisure time, the lack of which contributes to problem behavior on the part of adolescents. Problem behaviors may include increased use of cigarettes, alcohol, and other drugs; trouble with the police; victimization; and arguments with parents. This same study indicated that satisfaction with life, enjoyment of leisure activities, and the degree of self-esteem all decreased as the number of hours worked per week increased (Bachman and Schulenberg, 1993).

It is important to understand, however, that when the number of hours adolescents work is restricted, there are some positive correlates of employment for them. Boys and girls whose hours of work are severely limited express higher levels of well being. There is also less substance abuse and school problem behavior (Mortimer, Finch, Shanahan, and Ryu, 1992).

Advertising and Consumption

The mass media are partly responsible for creating a generation of consuming adolescents.

Today's children have been surrounded, as no other generation before, by messages in newspapers and magazines, and on radio and television, urging the purchase of the newest antiperspirant, breakfast food, or shampoo. In 1994, 99 percent of U.S. households owned televisions and radios; 79 percent of U.S. households had videocassette recorders (VCRs); and 23 percent of U.S. households had personal computers. Some 27 million PCs were in U.S. homes in 1994 (U.S. Bureau of the Census, 1996).

Today's youths constitute a huge consumers' market. The increasing wealth of this age group has caused more and more businesses to cater directly to youths. Clothes, cosmetics, automobiles, CDs and tapes, pagers, stereos, skis, snowmobiles, motorcycles, magazines, grooming aids, sports equipment, cigarettes, and thousands of other items are given the hard sell to attract the dollars of increasing numbers of adolescents.

A major segment of the youth culture has become a status-conscious, prestige-seeking culture. In general, youths have become concerned about themselves—how best to get good jobs and satisfy their own material needs. The emphasis is on earning a big salary and winning the struggle for status, position, and material advancement.

Families that have not been able to keep up with the struggle for money, status, and prestige seem poorer than ever (Lipsitz, 1991). As a result, adolescents in those families often feel abandoned and rejected. Youths who come from extremely poor families (at least 14 percent of the population) are more likely to be nonjoiners in school activities, are seldom elected to positions of prestige, and often seek status through antisocial behavior (U.S. Bureau of the Census, 1996). These youths struggle for identity and sometimes become problems because they find an identity that middle-class society rejects.

Some middle-class and upper-middle-class youths have rebelled against the overemphasis on materialism and seem to want the other extreme. These adolescents are more content with very few material possessions, emphasizing instead relationships with other people and with the world of nature. A minority have joined groups that are openly rebelling against what they feel are hypocritical, superficial, and false values, and undesirable priorities and goals of society.

The Education Revolution

Expanding technology and social complexity have increased the need for higher education and thus lengthened the period of adolescent dependency. It is vital that adolescents graduate from high school and college if they are to get well-paying jobs. If U.S. adolescents wish to be competitive with their peers and other technological nations, they must spend more days and years in school, put in more hours doing homework, and tackle more complex information. It is imperative that they devote more time to learning new technological skills (DeSantis and Youniss, 1991). This essential increase in education means that the period of dependency on parents has lengthened. From 1970 to 1995, the proportion of young people in the United States between the ages of 18 and 24 living at home increased by 13 percent (U.S. Bureau of the Census, 1996). The result has been delayed independence and maturity of these young people (Chance, 1988).

Educational Attainment

Considerable progress has been made in educating students through high school age. In 1995, 82 percent of the population age 25 and older had completed four years or more of high school. This figure represents 83 percent of Whites, 74 percent of African Americans, and 54 percent of Hispanics. The percentages of students who have completed high school have almost doubled in the past 25 years. The record has not been so successful in educating those who have had four or more years of college, however. In 1995, 23 percent of people age 25 and older had completed four or more years of college. This number represents 24 percent of Whites but only 13 percent of African Americans and about 7 percent of Hispanics. Still, the percentage of students of all races who have completed four years or more of college has nearly tripled since 1960 (U.S. Bureau of the Census, 1996; see Figure 1.1). There is still a long way to go, however.

Part of the problem of raising higher educational levels is the rapid increase in costs. In 1995, the average fee for tuition and room and board in public four-year colleges was over $7,000 per year. This does not include the costs for books, lab fees, and personal expenses for students. In private colleges, the average fee for tuition and room and board was $21,010 per year. Fees at some of the elite private colleges are considerably more than that. This presents an increasing problem to students who want to go on to higher education but cannot afford it. In 1995, the average annual student loan was over $3,000. Many students are repaying their loans years after they graduate from college (U.S. Bureau of the Census, 1996, p. 186).

Adult Education

One encouraging trend in the education revolution is the increased participation in adult education. In 1995, some 40 percent of adults were enrolled in at least one course in adult education. Almost half of the people age 25 to 54 were participants in adult education. Most adult students cited that their primary reason for taking a course was to advance in their jobs. However, a number of them also took a course for personal or social reasons or to fulfill requirements for a degree. Adults who missed out on higher education when they were younger are now realizing the importance of increasing their education if they are going to qualify for better jobs. As of 1996, 15.2 percent of U.S. adults have earned bachelor's degrees and 7.8 percent of U.S. adults have earned advance degrees (U.S. Bureau of the Census, 1996, p. 160).

Early Intervention

One remarkable change in the emphasis on public education has been the increase in early intervention programs for young children. Nursery schools have grown in popularity. For example, during 1994, 47 percent of 3- and 4-year-olds were enrolled in some type of nursery school (U.S. Bureau of the Census, 1996, p. 197). This figure does not include the 5-year-olds enrolled in kindergarten.

Intervention through remedial programs can increase the educational achievement of young children and have lasting results. The general consensus is that high-quality programs for children who are economically deprived especially can have lasting and valuable effects. The best example comes from research on Head Start programs, which were designed to help disadvantaged preschool students do better in school as

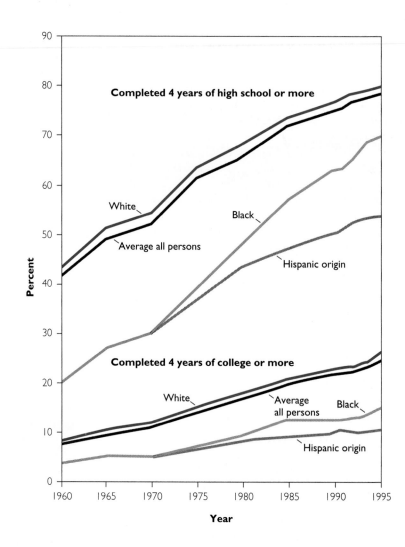

FIGURE 1.1   Educational Attainment by Race and Hispanic Origin: 1960 to 1995 (for persons 25 years old and over)

Source: U.S. Bureau of the Census, *Statistical Abstract of the United States, 1996* (Washington, DC: U.S. Government Printing Office, 1996), p. 150.

they grew older (Lee, Brooks-Gunn, Schnur, and Liaw, 1990). An 18-year study followed the progress of 123 children beginning when they were 3 and 4 years of age in Perry Elementary School in Ypsilanti, Michigan. Results showed that those children who had been in the Head Start program scored higher in reading, math, and language achievement than children in a control group. Head Start children showed fewer delinquent and antisocial tendencies as they got older. If Head Start programs are well funded, the teachers are confident that children in the programs will show (1) improved intellectual performance during early childhood, (2) better scholastic placement and improved scholastic achievement during elementary school, (3) a lower rate of adolescent delinquency, and (4) higher rates of both gradua-

tion from high school and employment at age 19 (Schweinhart and Weikert, 1985, p. 547).

An important part of Head Start is the involvement of parents—that is, giving them information and training in child development and care. Parent-focused programs appear to provide a particularly efficient strategy for intervention efforts (Seitz and Apfel, 1994).

Embracing the New Technology

The most exciting change in education is happening as teachers warm up to computers and introduce new uses for them. Educators across the nation continue to embrace the new electronic technologies that are available. Many are developing dynamic lesson plans that include significant uses of online resources outside the classroom for research in the development of background materials. In addition to using computers for research, many teachers employ computers in science classrooms as test equipment, in foreign-language labs for interactive work with students in other countries, in field trips to the countries students are studying, in math labs to model complex mathematical equations, and in the administrative offices for more traditional office applications. Students can send e-mail messages worldwide in minutes to correspond with those in other lands. In Internet relay chats, individuals can participate in live, interactive discussions via the keyboard. The changes that have been made in education over the past 25 years have been significant and inspiring but none will have more effect on educational processes than classroom computers.

The Family Revolution

Changes in Family Function

Like many other social institutions, families in the United States are undergoing some important changes. Traditionally, people were married for economic security, to provide goods and services for one another, to attain social status, and to reproduce and raise children. The traditional role of the family was an *instrumental role:* The family existed to meet the expectations of society. Modern views of the family tend to emphasize not only the instrumental role but also the role in fulfilling personal needs for emotional security and companionship. Today, people marry to satisfy their own emotional needs. This is the *expressive role* of the family.

In today's industrial society, the majority of people live in large urban centers. As a rule, neighbors remain strangers and it becomes harder for people to find friendships and emotional support. Affectional needs may not be met. Many individuals feel alone and isolated, even though surrounded by millions of people. In such an impersonal society, it becomes more important to find intimacy, a sense of belonging, and emotional security in the family itself. Achievement of intimacy is one of the major goals of life, according to Erikson (1968). In a highly impersonal society,

where emotional isolation is frequent, developing a close relationship with others is vital to one's identity and security (Rice, 1996).

This emphasis on personal relationships has placed more burden on the family unit. When people establish a family for love, companionship, and emotional security, but do not find fulfillment, they become disappointed and experience feelings of failure and frustration. This is one reason for the high rate of divorce in the United States. Rather than stay together for the sake of the family, couples often separate if their personal needs and expectations are not met.

Romantic Love

Adolescents today have grown up in a time where the fulfillment of romantic love and companionship are considered to be the primary functions of getting married. Romantic love stimulates very strong emotions and intense feelings. There is also a strong feeling of sexual attraction and a desire for physical contact. Romantic love is sometimes accompanied by idealization and adoration. When passion is strong, the relationship eclipses all else and lovers may find themselves in a wildly emotional state, with obsessive thoughts of each other. There is no question that romanticism plays a significant role in attraction and the decision to marry.

If romantic love is emphasized as the only criteria for marriage, however, the marriage can become dysfunctional. Feelings and intense emotion are not accurate indicators of the suitability for marriage. People can fall in love with emotionally insecure, unstable, irresponsible, hostile individuals. If romantic love leads to a high degree of idealization, adolescents (and adults) can make completely wrong decisions about whom to marry. Romantic love becomes dysfunctional if it blinds a couple from reality. This is, no doubt, one of the reasons for the country's high divorce rate. Youths get married before they know one another or they

---

instrumental role   a role that emphasizes meeting physical needs.

expressive role   a role that emphasizes fulfilling emotional needs.

get married while they are in the superromantic idealized state. Romantic love is not a sound basis for marriage under these circumstances.

The Rise of the Democratic Family

Throughout most of our nation's history, the American family was patriarchal, with the father considered as head of the household, having authority over and responsibility for other members of the family. As head of the household and owner of the property, his wife and children were expected to reside with him or near his family, according to his choice. One characteristic of the traditional patriarchal family was a clear-cut distinction between the husband's and the wife's role in the family. The husband was the breadwinner and was usually responsible for clearly defined chores that were considered "man's work." The wife was responsible for "woman's work," such as housecleaning, cooking, sewing, childrearing, and other responsibilities. Children were expected to be submissive and obedient to their parents and to follow their directions, including assuming a considerable responsibility in the performance of family chores.

Gradually, a more democratic form of the family evolved. This change came about for several reasons. First, the rise of the feminist movement brought some economic power and freedom to women. Women gained the power to own property and to borrow money. Also, increasing educational opportunities for women and the gradual increase in the percentage of married women working outside the home encouraged the adoption of more egalitarian sex roles in the family. As more wives earned incomes, more husbands were asked to take on greater responsibilities for homemaking and child care. The general trend was toward a more equal voice in decision making and a more equitable distribution of family responsibility. Third, the demand for equality of sexual expression resulted from the recognition of the sexual capabilities of women. With such recognition, marriages could be based on the mutual exchange of love and affection. The development of efficient contraceptives also freed women from unwanted pregnancies and enabled them to have personal lives of their own as well as social lives with their husbands.

The Rise of the Child-Centered Family

The child-study movement after World War II catalyzed the development of the child-centered family. No longer was the focus on what a child could do to serve his or her family, but rather a matter of what the family could contribute to the total development of the child. The rights and needs of children as important members of the family were emphasized. As children matured, they demanded a greater voice in family decision making, which sometimes led to rebelliousness against their parents. Adults complained that their children were ill-mannered, defiant, and disobedient. Some parents tried to become more authoritarian; others were overly permissive. The wisest ones, however, were those who tended to achieve a compromise between freedom and responsibility of their children.

Further Changes in Marriage and Parenthood

Trends in marriage and parenthood have changed over the last few decades. The marriage rate has declined, the age at which people marry has gone up, and the number of children per family has decreased.

Marriage Rates   As you can see in Figure 1.2, the marriage rate declined to an all-time low in 1960, rose in 1970 and 1980, and has since been declining (U.S. Bureau of the Census, 1996, p. 104).

Age at Marriage   One of the most important trends in the changing family has been the increase in the age of when people first marry. The median age at first marriage was 26.5 years for men and 23.9 years for women in 1993. This rate represents an increase since the 1950s. Furthermore, the gap in median age of marriage for men and women has narrowed substantially to about a two-year difference. The reasons for the trend to delay marriage probably include an increase in premarital sex, more opportunities for higher education, and an increase in nonmarital cohabitation (Cooney and Hogan, 1991; Miller and Heaton, 1991). This trend is significant because those who wait until their mid- to late twenties to marry have a greater chance of marital success

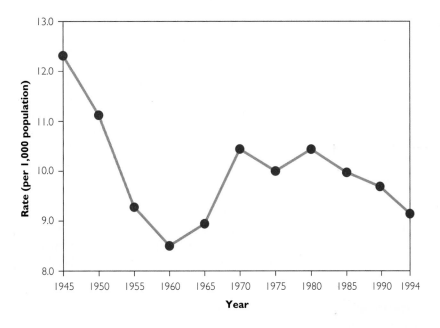

FIGURE 1.2   Marriage Rate per 1,000 Population

Source: U.S. Bureau of the Census, *Statistical Abstract of the United States, 1989* (Washington, DC: U.S. Government Printing Office, 1989) and U.S. Bureau of the Census, *Statistical Abstract of the United States, 1996* (Washington, DC: U.S. Government Printing Office, 1996), p. 104.

than those who wed earlier. The delay of marriage has also resulted in a marked increase in unmarried young adults in the population. More than one-third of the men and one-fourth of the women in the United States have not married by 30 years of age. This is due partly to a decline in negative attitudes toward remaining single.

Family Size   Declining birth rates since 1965 have resulted in smaller families. The average number of people per family was 3.67 in 1960, 3.19 in 1985, and 2.65 in 1995. Some 51 percent of families in 1995 had no children of their own under 18 years of age. An additional 20 percent of families had only one child of their own at home who was under 18 years of age. These figures seem almost incredible: An amazing 71 percent of U.S. families had one or no children under age 18 living at home. These figures reflect the fact that women in the United States are having fewer children. At the beginning of the twentieth century, the average married woman had five children. Today, the average number of total births to an ever-married woman between the age of 15 to 55 has declined to 1.8 (U.S. Bureau of the Census, 1996).

There are several advantages for adolescents who come from smaller families. Parents are more likely to give sufficient attention and care to each child. Adolescents who come from small families also have a greater opportunity to continue their higher education, since parents' resources are more available to them. The important consideration is whether the children who are born into the family are wanted and are there by choice rather than chance. The timing of parenthood affects the way parents fulfill their roles as fathers and mothers. The psychological impact on the parents are lessened considerably if parenthood is chosen and welcomed. Not surprisingly, unwanted children are more likely to be neglected and abused (Cooney, Pedersen, Indelicato, and Paklovitz, 1993).

Nonmarital Cohabitation

Another significant change in marriage trends in the United States is the increase in the number of couples who cohabit before marriage. According to the government definition referred to as *Persons of the Opposite Sex Sharing Living Quarters* (*POSSLQ*), there were 3,661,000 unmarried cohabiting couples in the United States in 1994. This represents a 130 percent increase since 1980 (U.S. Bureau of the Census, 1996). About 35 percent of these couples had some children under 15 years of age living in the households. Approximately 21 percent of all the cohabiting couples were under age 25. A complete discussion of nonmarital cohabitation is found in Chapter 11 of this book.

Suffice it to say for now that there is no evidence that premarital cohabitation weeds out incompatible couples and prepares people for successful marriage (Schoen and Weinick, 1993). One national survey reported that couples who had cohabited before marriage reported lower-quality marriages, lower commitment to the institution of marriage, more individualistic views of marriage (women only), and a greater likelihood of divorce than couples who had not cohabited. These consequences were generally more likely for those who had cohabited for longer periods before marriage (Thomson and Colella, 1992). DeMaris and Rao (1992) found that cohabiting prior to marriage, regardless of the nature of that cohabitation, is associated with an enhanced risk of later marital disillusion.

Divorce

The divorce rate in the United States has been declining slightly since 1980 (U.S. Bureau of the Census, 1996, p. 104; see Figure 1.3). In spite of this direction, the United States has the highest divorce rate of any country. About one-half of the marriages of couples age 25 to 40 years will end in divorce (Norton and Moorman, 1987). Nearly two out of three of these divorces involve children. The high divorce and separation rate, plus a rise in out-of-wedlock births, means that over one-half of all children who were born in the 1980s and 1990s will spend a considerable amount of time living with only one parent (Hofferth, 1985). This usually means less contact with and support from their natural fathers. If parents remarry, the children have the added task of learning to live with a stepparent.

Reactions of Children   A growing number of clinicians emphasize that children perceive divorce as a major, negative event that stimulates painful emotions, confusion, and uncertainty. Some clinicians feel that the majority of children regain psychological equilibrium in a year or so and resume a normal curve of growth and development. Other researchers feel that for a significant portion of children, the upheaval in their lives will interfere in wholesome social-emotional growth. This view is substantiated by Judith Wallerstein in a 15-year study of 60 divorced families, in-

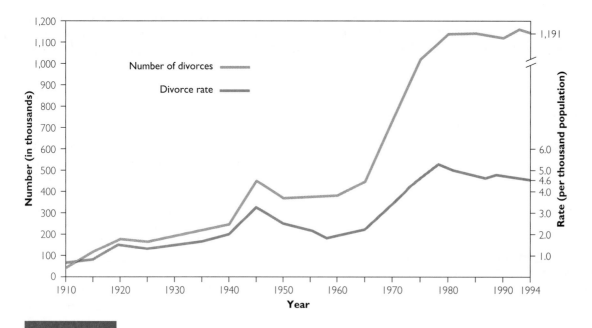

FIGURE 1.3   Number of Divorces and Divorce Rates: 1910 to 1994

Source: U.S. Bureau of the Census, *Statistical Abstract of the United States, 1996* (Washington, DC: U.S. Government Printing Office, 1996), p. 104.

volving 131 children, living in Marin County, California (Wallerstein and Blakeslee, 1989). Wallerstein found that 10 years after divorce, one-half of the women and one-third of the men were still so angry at their former spouses that this anger colored their relationships with their children. The children felt that they had been abandoned (usually by the father), that they were denied basic security with which to grow, and that they lost their childhood by feeling compelled to assume responsibilities for their parents' well-being. Half the children entered adulthood as underachieving, self-deprecating young men and women. High levels of alcohol abuse, promiscuity, and delinquency showed up 10 to 15 years after the divorce (Wallerstein and Blakeslee, 1989).

Wallerstein's sample came from an affluent area during years of rapid social change in the United States. There was no control group with which to compare findings, nor was a study done of how tension prior to divorce affected children. So whether these findings can be applied to other children from divorced families is not certain.

Coming from a divorced home has differential effects on adolescents (Wallerstein and Kelly, 1980). Some adolescents blame themselves and feel guilty and upset about the divorce. However, the effect of divorce can be positive if it ends turmoil and upset in the family. Some adolescents whose parents have been divorced report that parental conflict and tension beforehand was more stressful than the divorce itself. These adolescents report fear of physical violence, social embarrassment because of parental strife, upset over financial hardships, and anxiety and confusion regarding successive separations and reconciliations of parents. In such cases, divorce comes almost as a relief from years of strife. Thus, parental separation does not always result in traumatic experiences for children (Baydar, 1988).

When upset and conflict exist in the family of the adolescent, whether the parents divorce or remain unhappily married, the effect is disturbing (Demo and Acock, 1988). One study showed that boys from subsequently divorcing homes showed a decline in academic functioning prior to their parents' divorce (McCombs and Forehand, 1989). Girls from subsequently divorcing families showed a decline in academic functioning that began prior to divorce and continued beyond the time of

Continuing conflict between parents creates an upsetting home environment. If divorce occurs, there is often relief for the adolescent, since the source of tension is reduced.

divorce (Neighbors, Forehand, and Armistead, 1992).

The overall effect of divorce depends on the conditions of the divorce and on the events before and after it. When there is little fighting between parents during and after the divorce, when the separation is amicable, and when the children have free access to both parents and a lot of support from parents, siblings, and friends, upset is kept to a minimum.

Children have a variety of adjustments to make when their parents divorce. They must adjust to the absence of one parent, often one on whom they depended deeply for affection and for help. One teenage girl remarked, "The hardest thing for me was to get used to living without my father. I never really realized how much I needed him until he left" (author's counseling notes). Older children may also be required to assume more responsibility for family functioning: cooking, housekeeping, caring for younger siblings, even earning money to support the family. This adjustment is usually a maturing experience. Some children, used to having everything, have a hard time realizing that money is short and that

Divorce and Remarriage

The Virginia Longitudinal Study of Divorce and Remarriage was conducted over an 11-year period. Children and families in the divorce group, as originally planned, were studied at 2 months, 1 year, and 2 years after divorce. A 6-year postdivorce follow-up when the children were 10 years old and an 11-year follow-up when they were 15 years old were added.

A partial summary of the findings is as follows:

1. In the first year after divorce, in comparison with children in nondivorced families, both boys and girls showed more anxious, demanding, noncompliant, aggressive, and dependent behavior with peers and adults. These problems were present in the home and school, increased over the first year, and declined in the second year as children adjusted to their new home situations.
2. By 2 years after the divorce, young girls in the divorced families showed no more problems in social and emotional development than those in nondivorced families. Although the behavior of boys in the divorced families improved, they still exhibited more problems in the home and in school than did children from nondivorced families, and these were still present when they were 15 years of age.
3. By age 10, girls in divorced families, especially early-maturing girls who associated with older peers, were showing an increasing number of problems. By age 15, both boys and girls in divorced families and in remarried families, in comparison with those in nondivorced families, were exhibiting more externalizing and internalizing behavior and problems in social competence and in school.
4. After remarriage, both boys and girls were initially resistant to the entrance of a stepfather. They ex-

hibited less prosocial behavior and showed more externalizing and internalizing behavior than children in nondivorced families.
5. If the remarriage occurred when the child was 8 years of age or younger, and if it was at least 2 years beyond the time of divorce, by age 10 boys in stepfamilies with a warm, supportive, authoritative stepfather were showing no more problems than boys in nondivorced families. In addition, they exhibited fewer problems, especially in externalizing behavior, than did boys whose divorced mothers did not remarry.
6. Although preadolescent girls also were adapting to the remarriage, even 2 years after the transition they were showing more externalizing behavior than were girls with either nondivorced parents or with a divorced, nonremarried mother. If the remarriage occurred when children were 9 years of age or older, higher levels of problem behavior and little adaptation to the marriage by either boys or girls had occurred by age 15.

Dysfunctional marriages, divorce, and remarriage involve an increase in challenges and risks in the adjustment of family members. Marital transitions are often difficult experiences for both parents and children. Even as adults, many offspring of divorced parents still view their parents' divorce as traumatic. In spite of these unhappy memories and experiences, most go on to lead capable and fulfilling lives. It is the diversity rather than the inevitability of outcomes that is notable in response to divorce and remarriage (Hetherington, 1993).

they can't buy the clothes and other things they used to.

Special adjustments are necessary, of course, when the parent caring for the children begins to date again and become emotionally involved with another person. The children must then learn to share their parent with another adult. If the parent remarries, as the majority do, the children are

confronted with readjustment to a stepparent and perhaps stepsiblings.

The Sexual Revolution

The sexual revolution is characterized by significant changes in sexual attitudes and behavior.

Actually, the sexual revolution has both positive and negative characteristics. Let's begin with the positives and then proceed to the negatives.

Development of Scientific Knowledge of Sexual Functioning

For years, scientists have studied the human body and how it functions, and researchers have studied the various body systems. Somehow, though, a scientific study of the sexual response system was considered off limits. Much attention was devoted to human reproduction but little to sexual arousal, response, and expression.

This all changed when the research team of Masters and Johnson began to observe the physical details of human sexual arousal in the laboratory. For the first time, reports were given on the physiological changes in human sexual response that occur under sexual stimulation. Since the pioneering work of Masters and Johnson (1966), other clinicians have made significant contributions to the field (Kaplan, 1979).

This knowledge of the sexual response system enables individuals to understand better the stages of sexual response. In turn, this increased understanding may enhance the pleasure of sexual relationships and help solve many sexual problems. Knowing exactly what is to take place, medical personnel are now able to assist individuals in dealing with problems of sexual dysfunction. The study of the human sexual response system also exploded some sexual myths, one of which was that human females are not really sexual beings and are not able to respond sexually like males. Researchers have found that the phases of sexual response in females are similar to those of males and that females have as great a capacity for sexual enjoyment as do males. This fact tended to free females from the harmful philosophy that sex is a woman's duty and a man's pleasure. Today, women and men are now seen as equals in their sexual responsiveness.

Treatment of Sexual Dysfunction

Scientific knowledge has enabled medical authorities to understand the causes of sexual dysfunction and how to treat it, which is considered a major medical breakthrough. Countless millions of individuals have not been able to express themselves sexually because of some problem or another. Now, with proper treatment, most people can enjoy normal sexual relationships. Problems such as orgasm dysfunction and inhibited sexual desire in both men and women; premature ejaculation, erectile dysfunction, and ejaculatory inhibition in men; and painful intercourse (dyspareunia) and vaginismus in women are treatable sexual functions.

Development of Contraceptives

Numerous birth control measures have been developed, including hormones, chemicals and spermicides, intrauterine devices (IUDs), condoms, diaphragms, vaginal sponges, and new sterilization techniques. The development of contraceptives freed women from the burden of bearing one child after the other, and enabled couples to plan their families rather than having them by chance. Such measures have enhanced the health of mothers and babies, strengthened the functioning of the family, and given women other life-style choices.

Willingness to Deal with Unwanted Sexual Behavior

In recent years, people have become more willing to discuss openly problems of sexual harassment, various types of unwanted sexual behavior, and the issue of rape and violence against women. Women who used to suffer the pain and humiliation of rape in silence are now coming forth to confront their aggressors. The sexual abuse of children is also finally being faced and dealt with in a more helpful and healthful manner. Although our society still has a long way to go in reducing the incidence of sexual abuse of women and children, much progress has been made. This is certainly one of the more positive aspects of the sexual revolution.

Flexibility of Gender Roles

Due in part to the sexual revolution, gender roles are undergoing some drastic changes. Traditionally, society defined what was meant by *femininity* and *masculinity*. People were stereotyped and pressured to live up to certain roles according to their genders. These gender-role stereotypes placed limitations on the relationships that people were capable of forming and on career and personal achievements. Today, gender roles in the family are becoming more flexible and men and women are interchanging roles. Similarly, housekeeping and child-care roles have expanded to include both sexes. Gender roles regarding choice of vocation have also changed, so that many women now occupy positions of leadership that were formerly reserved for men.

Openness of Sexual Discussion

As people have learned to accept their human sexuality, they have generally been more willing to discuss the subject of sex with their children and with other adults. More parents are doing a better job of sex education at home than did previous generations.

Negative Characteristics of the Sexual Revolution

Unfortunately, the more open sexual topics have become, the more opportunity there is for this freedom to be abused. The media expose children to sexual images and violent materials before they learn to ride tricycles. Toddlers and youngsters are not emotionally ready for sexual scenes or for the scenes or reports of sadistic sexual murders of children. Children have scant protection from sexual messages that 20 years ago would have been taboo for grown-ups. Adolescents are certainly affected by watching sexually explicit materials on television and in the movies. It is hardly uncommon to hear of parents' reports of their 12-year-old children attending parties where the children experiment sexually as part of the party games. A girl from Kansas said, "In fifth grade, my friends and I decided we would have sex with boys. Now we can't get our reputations back. Now we're sluts of the school." Another girl remarked, "It's confusing, you're pressured to have sex but when you do, you're a whore" (Pipher, 1996).

Greater Permissiveness of Premarital Sexual Behavior

Researchers have noticed significant changes in premarital sexual attitudes and behavior over the last 40 years. Not only are youths more likely to have premarital intercourse but the age of their initial intercourse is years younger than in the recent past. The latest research indicates that half of all African American men have had intercourse by age 15, half of all Hispanic men by age 16½, and half of all White men by age 17. Half of all African American women have had intercourse by age 17, and half of all White and Hispanic women have had intercourse by age 18 (Michael, Gagnon, Laumann, and Kolata, 1994).

Nonmarital Pregnancy

Greater permissiveness of premarital sexual behavior has led to an epidemic of unwed teen pregnancies. The number of pregnancies is estimated to be over one million each year among women less than 20 years of age. Almost 400,000 of the babies are born out of wedlock (U.S. Bureau of the Census, 1996). Today, about 96 percent of unwed mothers decide to keep their babies. From most points of view, motherhood for the young, unmarried, teenage girl is a tragedy (Ohannesian and Crockett, 1993). The unwed teenage mother who decides to keep her baby may become entangled in a self-destructive cycle consisting of failure to finish school, repeated pregnancies, inability to establish a stable family life, and dependence on others for support (Hanson, 1992).

Sexually Transmitted Diseases and AIDS

One of the most important consequences of the sexual revolution is the rapid spread of sexually transmitted diseases (STDs). In today's world, gonorrhea is more common than chicken pox, measles, mumps, whooping cough, tetanus, rubella, tuberculosis, and trichinosis combined. The incidents of acquired immune deficiency syndrome (AIDS) has begun to decline, but of the 71,547 cases of AIDS reported in the United States in 1995, some 16 percent were among children and young people from 13 to 29 years of age (U.S. Bureau of the Census, 1996, p. 142).

Confusion about Sex

Adolescents are more and more confused about their sexuality. They are encouraged to learn about and discuss it, and some are stimulated to sexual arousal, but they are not quite certain how and if they should express their sexuality when they are confronted with the danger of contracting AIDS and dying in the process. Sex has been demystified, which may be a good thing, but it is also being marketed, which is not a good thing. Adolescents have moved from viewing sex as forbidden and terrifying to seeing sex as accessible and interesting but still terrifying. Sex education and counseling are needed more than ever.

The Violence Revolution

Another social change taking place is reflected in the increase of violence.

Violent Crime

From 1984 to 1994, violent crime—which includes murder, forcible rape, robbery, and aggravated assault—increased some 46 percent. Of the total number of murder victims in 1994, 11½ percent were under 18 years of age. The largest percentage of rape and sexual assault victims in 1994 were girls 16 to 19 years of age. Over half of all victims of rape and sexual assault were relatives or acquaintances of the offender.

Violence in Society

Not only are greater percentages of adolescents involved in violent crime but all of them have been exposed year after year to physical violence and disturbances in the world: the murder or attempted assassination of national leaders, the bombing of embassies, terrorism on a global scale, and war in over a dozen countries. Television and the press have provided constant exposure to violence. The mass media have created an age of instant news—television viewers share in the experi-

A greater percentage of adolescents have become involved in violent crime in recent years. This 14-year-old is accused of opening fire inside a Kentucky school, killing three classmates and wounding five others.

ence of starving Africans, terrorist bombings, wars, and massive earthquakes (Schroeder, Gaier, and Holdnack, 1993). Today's youths have not just heard about killings; they have seen them in the nightly news. They have been bombarded with sensory information that affects emotions and feelings as well as cognitive perceptions. As a result of this constant exposure to violence, many adolescents become insensitive to the violence that goes on around them, and they begin to feel that violence is a necessary and accepted part of their lives.

Violence in the Home

Part of the violence in today's world may be traced back to violence in the home. Adolescents who are

Computer Games

Many parents and youth leaders have become disturbed at the level of violence found in video and computer games. One advertisement of a computer game titled "Quake" uses the following descriptive phrases:

"The vanguard of a terrifying new level of aversive technology."
"Quake overwhelms the senses."
"Quake is the biggest, baddest, bloodiest, and most atmospheric three-D action game ever conceived." (*P.C. Games*, 1997, p. 1)

Another advertisement for a computer game called "Myth" describes the game's realism:

"Real physics, real terrain, real weather, real lightning."
"Rocks and heads will roll downhill; blood will stain the landscape. An adjustable camera will let you see every bit of this fully three-D world so you can revel in the gore." (*P.C. Games*, 1997, p. 30)

For a game called "Reloaded," the ad describes "flesh-seeking missiles that cook victims to perfection.

Every kill is finger-licking good. Twelve mission-based, blood-soaked worlds demanding non-stop violence and mental marauding." There are insane weapons of mass terror, including "blood bath tidal waves" and "multi-player mayhem."

Still another ad is for a computer game titled "Deus." The goal of the game is to save the scientific community from terrorists. The obstacles are 40 predators, 5 lunatic terrorists, and other mind-bending puzzles. The strategy is to "Kill. Eat. Kill. Sleep. Kill. Tend wounds. Kill. Amputation is just what the doctor ordered." Another part of the advertisement states, "On second thought, maybe you shouldn't have skinned her babies. If he only had a heart, then you could rip it out" (*P.C. Games*, 1997, p. 1).

Just what total effect these kinds of games have on children and adolescents requires further research. At present, however, studies indicate that children and adolescents who are exposed to violence are influenced by that violence and are more likely to act violently themselves (Bandura, 1973).

---

brought up in violent families where spouse abuse and child abuse are common tend to become abusive parents and mates themselves. Youths generally model the marital aggression that they witness in their homes. Children who observe their fathers hitting their mothers are more likely to be perpetrators as well as victims of severe marital aggression. The greater the frequency of violence, the greater the chance that the young victims will grow up to be violent parents or partners. Moreover, teenagers who are exposed to violence are more likely to use violence against their parents. A man who is involved in dating violence is likely to have been severely abused by his father (Alexander, Moore, and Alexander, 1991).

Violent Deaths

The most disturbing development in recent years relates to adolescent mortality factors. When young people die, most die violent deaths: Among adolescents age 15 to 24 who die, 77 percent die violently. Death from accidents, suicides, and homicides has exceeded disease as the leading cause of death for youths (U.S. Bureau of the Census, 1996). Some 51 percent of violent deaths of adolescents involve car accidents. Young people are the only age group in the United States that has not enjoyed improved health status over the past 30 years; the reason is the increase in violent deaths (U.S. Bureau of the Census, 1996).

HIGHLIGHT

Teens Who Kill

One form of intrafamilial violence that is attracting more attention is child-to-parent violence. *Parricide,* the killing of one's mother or father, is becoming increasingly publicized, although it remains relatively infrequent. Most of the research emphasizes a common theme: Parricide is often a response to a long-standing child-abuse problem. Typically, the child who kills his or her parent is 16 to 18 years old and from a White middle-class family. In most cases, a bizarre, neurotic relationship exists between the assassin and the victim, in which the parent-victim mistreats the child excessively and pushes him or her to the point of explosive violence. Dispatching the tormentor can be seen as an act of sanity, a last-resort effort at self-preservation (Toufexis, 1992).

More difficult to understand is the violence of young teenagers against younger children, seemingly without reason. Recently, a 13-year-old Maine boy was indicted for bludgeoning to death a 3-year-old boy in his neighborhood. In Indiana, four teenage girls doused 12-year-old Sandra Shrer with gasoline and burned her alive because she was trying to "steal" the friendship of another girl. Henry James, 19, opened fire into a passing car on a Washington-area interstate because he felt like "busting somebody." The somebody turned out to be a 32-year-old woman driving home from work. It seems that in some communities, every teenager has a gun. When everyone has a gun, every argument carries the potential for deadly violence (Traver, 1992).

SUMMARY

1. *Adolescence* is the period of growth between childhood and adulthood. Such words as *maturity, puberty, pubescence, teenager, juvenile,* and *youth* describe related concepts. Adolescence is sometimes divided into early adolescence (ages 11 to 14) and middle or late adolescence (ages 15 to 19).

2. The various approaches to the study of adolescents are the biological approach, the cognitive approach, the psychosexual approach, and the social approach.

3. This book takes an eclectic approach, emphasizing an interdisciplinary philosophy.

4. The society in which an adolescent grows up has an important influence on development, relationships, adjustments, and behavior. In order to understand adolescents, it is important to understand this society.

5. Today, our society is undergoing radical and profound change, so it may be labeled a *society in revolution.*

6. Six aspects of our society in revolution are the computer revolution, the materialistic revolution, the education revolution, the family revolution, the sexual revolution, and the violence revolution.

7. No social change has had as powerful an influence as the rapid rise in the use of computers. Sales and use have skyrocketed as computers have become cheaper, smaller, more powerful, faster, and easier to use.

8. One of the important reasons for the increase in knowledge has been the introduction of the Internet, which literally puts the world at our fingertips.

9. The development of the World Wide Web has placed vast stores of knowledge at our disposal.

10. Unfortunately, many materials that are inappropriate for children and adolescents have also become available on the Internet: pornography, bomb recipes and destructive devices, and information on neo-Nazis, gang-related activities, drugs, and cults, witchcraft, and satanic rituals.

11. Adolescents who have been exposed to sexual violence are more likely to act violently.

12. Adolescents who spend long periods of time with their computers are substituting electronic relationships and isolation for person-to-person contacts.

13. Our society is undergoing a materialistic revolution where real wages have not caught up with the cost of living, necessitating some workers to work overtime or at two jobs.

14. More married women with children are forced to work outside the home.

15. Some adolescents spend too much time working, thereby neglecting their schoolwork.
16. Advertising has created a generation of consuming adolescents who want instant gratification.
17. Those who are not able to keep up with the struggle for money are poorer than ever, with large numbers living below the poverty level.
18. Education has undergone many changes.
19. Increasing technology has increased the need for higher education and lengthened the period of adolescent dependency.
20. Greater percentages of students are graduating from high school, but many more need to go on to college.
21. More adults are enrolling in adult education classes.
22. Early intervention programs for preschoolers are needed to increase the educational achievement of children.
23. More schools are embracing the new technology made available by computers.
24. The family is undergoing revolutionary changes.
25. The instrumental role of the family has been partly replaced by the expressive role, so that most people marry for love and emotional fulfillment.
26. Romantic love, if overidealized and not based on reality, becomes dysfunctional as a basis for marital choice, resulting in many disappointments, a high rate of failure, and divorce.
27. The modern family has become more child centered and more democratic, with greater equality.
28. Marriage rates are declining, the age at marriage is increasing, and the number of children in the family is decreasing, all of which seem to be beneficial.
29. Nonmarital cohabitation is increasing, but it does not result in greater marital success overall.
30. The divorce rate is declining slowly.
31. The effect of divorce on children is variable, depending on the atmosphere in which children are living before and after the divorce.
32. Special adjustments are necessary in remarriages.
33. Our society is undergoing a sexual revolution.
34. The sexual revolution has brought many positive developments as well as negative ones.
35. Nonmarital pregnancy and the transmission of STDs and AIDS are among the most serious consequences of unprotected sex.
36. Our society is experiencing a violence revolution with an increase in violent crime, violence in society, violence in the home, and violent deaths.
37. Some authorities are concerned about the increase of violence in the media and on computers.

KEY TERMS

adolescence **1**	juvenile **2**	teenager **2**
expressive role **11**	maturity **1**	World Wide Web **4**
instrumental role **11**	puberty **1**	
Internet **4**	pubescence **2**	

THOUGHT QUESTIONS

1. Did you learn to operate computers at school? If not, where? Do you have a personal computer at home? What has been the effect of computers on society? What do you personally use a computer for?
2. Do you believe some subjects and materials on the computer are inappropriate for children? Support your answer. Should parents control what their children see on the Internet? If yes, how? If no, why not?
3. How has the Internet affected people's lives?
4. "We live in a very materialistic society." Do you agree or disagree with this statement? Explain your answer.
5. If your boss asked you to work a 60-hour week on a regular basis, what would you say? Be specific in your answer.
6. What is the effect on children when both parents work full time outside the home?
7. Should the amount of time a full-time student works be limited to 20 hours a week or less? Explain you answer.

8. In what ways does advertising affect consumer buying habits?
9. How can the country assure that more students will go on to college?
10. Have you ever taken an adult education class? If yes, describe your experiences and discuss how the class affected you.
11. Give your opinion on the effects of nursery school education on 2- and 3-year-old children.
12. How does the family of today differ from that of your parents? What do you think of the changes?
13. Have you been romantically in love? If yes, describe your experiences and discuss whether those experiences were or would be a sound basis for marriage.
14. Describe the family in which you were brought up.
15. Have you been involved in a nonmarital cohabitation? If yes, discuss your experiences. If no, why not?
16. "We are going through a sexual revolution." Do you agree or disagree with this statement? Explain your answer. Is this a good thing to happen or a bad thing?
17. Do you believe this country is experiencing a a violence revolution? Support your answer.
18. Do you think adolescents have too many or too few adult privileges? Explain your opinion.

19. What are some effects on the adolescent and on parents of the prolongation of the period of dependency of adolescents?
20. What do you think about adolescents holding part-time jobs after school?
21. What have been the most important social changes during the years you've been growing up? How have these changes affected your life?
22. What is the evidence that today's youths have become very materialistic?
23. What is the effect on adolescents of living in a poverty-stricken family?
24. In what ways have television, radio, movies, computers, and other mass media influenced your outlook on life and society? In what ways have they influenced your own personality and emotional security?
25. Do you think there is any relationship between violence on television and acts of violence in the lives of young people? Explain your answer.
26. What are some possible effects on adolescents when parents get divorced?
27. What are some of the problems of being raised by a stepparent?

SUGGESTED READING

Benedikt, M. (1991). *Cyberspace: First Steps.* Cambridge, MA: MIT Press.

Carlson, M. (1996). *Childproof Internet: A Parent's Guide to Safe and Secure Online Access.* New York: Mis Press.

Graff, H. J. (1995). *Conflicting Paths: Growing Up in America.* Cambridge, MA: Harvard University Press.

Michael, R. T., Gagnon, J. H., Laumann, E. O., and Kolata, G. (1994). *Sex in America.* Boston: Little, Brown.

Pipher, M. (1996). *The Shelter of Each Other: Rebuilding Our Families.* New York: Grosset/Putnam Books.

Salzman, M., and Pondiscio, R. (1995). *Kids On-Line: 150 Ways for Kids to Surf the 'Net for Fun and Information.* New York: Avon Books.

Steinberg, L., with Steinberg, W. (1994). *Crossing Paths: How Your Child's Adolescence Triggers Your Own Crisis.* New York: Simon & Schuster.

Straus, M. B. (1994). *Violence in the Lives of Adolescents.* New York: W. W. Norton.

U.S. Department of Justice, Attorney General's Commission on Pornography. (1986). *Final Report of Attorney General's Commission on Pornography.* Washington, DC: U.S. Government Printing Office.

2

Biological View of Adolescence
Arnold Gesell: Spiral Growth Patterns

Psychoanalytical Views of Adolescence
Sigmund Freud
Anna Freud

Psychosocial Views of Adolescence
Erik Erikson: Ego Identity
Robert Havighurst: Developmental Tasks
Kurt Lewin: Field Theory

Cognitive Views of Adolescence
Jean Piaget: Cognitive Development
Robert Selman: Social Cognition

Ecological View of Adolescence
Urie Bronfenbrenner: An Ecological Model

Social-Cognitive Learning View of Adolescence
Albert Bandura: Social Learning Theory
Social-Cognitive Theory

Anthropological Views of Adolescence
Margaret Mead and Ruth Benedict
Extended Adolescence versus Early Adulthood

PERSONAL ISSUES
When Do They Become Adults?

Cultural Continuity versus Discontinuity
Storm and Stress versus Cultural Conditioning
Cross-Cultural Views on Parent-Adolescent Relations

Adolescents in Theoretical Context

Another way to answer the question, What is adolescence? (from Chapter 1), is to look at adolescence from different points of view. In this book, we will draw on the studies of biologists, psychiatrists, psychologists, ecologists, sociologists, social psychologists, and anthropologists. This chapter will begin by surveying the views of a few representative and influential scholars from these disciplines. Later on, we will revisit some of these views as we take a closer look at various aspects of adolescence. By understanding different viewpoints, we gain a truer, more complete picture.

Biological View of Adolescence

A strictly *biological view* of adolescence emphasizes this period as one of physical and sexual matura-

tion during which important growth changes take place in the child's body. Any biological definition outlines in detail these physical, sexual, and physiological changes; their reasons (when known); and their consequences.

The biological view also emphasizes biogenetic factors as the primary cause of any behavioral and psychological change in the adolescent. Growth and behavior are under the control of internal maturational forces, leaving little room for environmental influences. Development occurs in an almost inevitable, universal pattern, regardless of the sociocultural environment.

Arnold Gesell:
Spiral Growth Patterns

Arnold Gesell (1880–1961) is known for observations of human development from birth to adolescence that he and his staff made at the Yale Clinic of Child Development and later at the Gesell Institute of Child Development. His best-known book on adolescence is *Youth: The Years from Ten to Sixteen* (Gesell and Ames, 1956). Gesell was a student of G. Stanley Hall's and learned much from him.

Gesell was interested in the behavioral manifestations of development and personality. He observed the actions and behavior of children and youths at different ages and constructed descriptive summaries of the stages and cycles of development. In his summaries, he described what he felt were the norms of behavior in their chronological sequences.

Gesell's theory is essentially a *biologically oriented theory*, suggesting that maturation is mediated by genes and biology that determine the order of appearance of behavioral traits and developmental trends. Thus, abilities and skills appear without the influence of special training or practice (Thelen and Adolph, 1992). This concept implies a sort of biological determinism that prevents teachers and parents from doing any-

thing to influence human development. Because maturation is regarded as a natural ripening process, it is assumed that time alone will solve most of the minor problems that arise in raising children. Difficulties and deviations will be outgrown, claimed Gesell, so parents were advised against emotional methods of discipline (Gesell and Ames, 1956).

Gesell did try to allow for individual differences, accepting that each child is born unique, with his or her own "genetic factors or individual constitution and innate maturation sequences" (Gesell and Ames, 1956, p. 22). But he emphasized that "acculturation can never transcend maturation" because maturation is of primary importance. In spite of accepting individual differences and the influence of environment on individual development, Gesell nevertheless considered many of the principles, trends, and sequences to be universal among humans. This concept partly contradicts the findings of cultural anthropology and social and educational psychology, which emphasize significant, culturally determined individual differences (Gesell and Ames, 1956, p. 41).

Although Gesell tried to emphasize that changes are gradual and overlap, his descriptions often indicate profound and sudden changes from one age to the next. He emphasized also that development is not only upward but also spiral,

Although Gesell's theory implied a sort of biological determinism, he did allow for individual differences, accepting that each child is unique and will develop at his or her own pace. Parents and teachers need to be aware of this variation in maturation.

characterized by both upward and downward changes that cause some repetition at different ages. For example, both the 11- and 15-year-old are generally rebellious and quarrelsome, whereas the 12- and 16-year-old are fairly stable.

One of the chief criticisms of Gesell's work concerns his sample. He drew his conclusions from boys and girls of favorable socioeconomic status in New Haven, Connecticut. He contended that such a homogenous sample would not lead to false generalizations. However, even when only physical factors are considered, children differ so greatly in the level and timing of growth that it is difficult to establish norms for any age level. Nevertheless, Gesell's books were used by thousands of parents and exerted tremendous influence on childrearing practices during the 1940s and 1950s. The books were considered the "child-development bibles" for many students and teachers during those years.

Psychoanalytical Views of Adolescence

Sigmund Freud was a Viennese physician who became interested in neurology, the study of the brain, and nervous disorders. He was the originator of psychoanalytical theory. His daughter, Anna, applied Freud's theory to adolescents.

Sigmund Freud

Sigmund Freud (1856–1939) was not greatly involved with theories on adolescence, for he considered the early years of a child's life to be the formative ones. He did, however, deal briefly with adolescence in his *Three Essays on the Theory of Sexuality* (Freud, 1953b). He described adolescence as a period of sexual excitement, anxiety, and sometimes personality disturbance. According to Freud, puberty is the culmination of a series of changes destined to give infantile sexual life its final, normal form. During the period of infancy, when pleasure is linked with oral activities (the *oral stage*), children employ a sexual object outside their own bodies: their mother's breasts. From this object, they derive physical satisfaction, warmth, pleasure, and security. While the mother feeds her infants, she also cuddles, caresses, kisses,

and rocks them (Freud, 1953a [published after Freud's death]).

Gradually, children's pleasures become autoerotic; that is, children begin to derive pleasure and satisfaction from activities that they can carry on by themselves. As they give up sucking at their mother's breasts, they find they can still derive pleasure from other oral activities. They learn to feed themselves, for example. At around age 2 or 3, much concern and pleasure center on anal activities and elimination (the *anal stage*). This period is followed by a developing interest in their own bodies and in the examination of their sex organs during the *phallic stage* (ages 4 and 5) of development.

During the next period, which Freud termed the *latency stage* (roughly from 6 years of age to puberty), children's sexual interests are not as intense, and they continue to relate to other people who help them and who satisfy their needs for love. Their source of pleasure gradually shifts from self to other people. They become more interested in cultivating the friendship of others, especially those of the same sex.

At puberty (the *genital stage*), this process of "object finding" is brought to completion. Along

---

oral stage the first psychosexual stage in Sigmund Freud's theory of development: from birth to one year, during which the child's chief source of pleasure and satisfaction comes from oral activity.

anal stage the second psychosexual stage in Sigmund Freud's theory of development: the second year of life, during which the child seeks pleasure and satisfaction through anal activity and the elimination of waste.

phallic stage the third psychosexual stage in Sigmund Freud's theory of development: from about the fourth to the sixth year, during which the genital area is the chief source of pleasure and satisfaction.

latency stage the fourth psychosexual stage in Sigmund Freud's theory of development: from about 6 to 12 years of age, during which sexual interests remain hidden while the child concentrates on school and other activities.

genital stage the last psychosexual stage in Sigmund Freud's theory of development, during which sexual urges result in seeking other persons as sexual objects to relieve sexual tension.

with maturation of the external and internal sexual organs comes a strong desire to resolve the sexual tension that follows. This resolution demands a love object; therefore, Freud theorized, adolescents are drawn to a member of the opposite sex who can resolve their tensions.

Freud emphasized two important elements of the sexual aim at adolescence, and with these some differences between men and women. One element is *physical and sensual.* In men, this aim consists of the desire to produce sexual products, accompanied by physical pleasure. In women, the desire for physical satisfaction and the release of sexual tension is still there but without the discharge of physical products. This desire in women was historically more repressed than in men, for the inhibitions to sexuality (shame, disgust, etc.) were developed earlier and more intensely in girls than in boys. Although this trend of female inhibition continues today, much change has taken place as researchers continue to confirm a greater equality in sexual desire for both men and women.

The second element of the sexual aim at adolescence is *psychic;* it is the affectionate component, which is more pronounced in females and which is similar to the infant's expression of sexuality. In other words, the adolescent desires emotional satisfaction as well as physical release. This need for affection is especially prevalent in females, but satisfying the need is an important goal of all adolescent sexual striving. Freud also emphasized that a normal sexual life is assured only when there is a convergence of the affectionate and the sensual currents, both being directed toward the sexual object and sexual aim. The combined desire for true affection and for the release of sexual tension are the underlying normal needs that motivate the individual to seek out a love object.

An important part of the maturing process at adolescence is the loosening of the child's emotional ties with parents. During the process of development, children's sexual impulses are directed toward their parents, with the son being drawn toward his mother and the daughter toward her father. Freud also spoke of an oedipal situation at adolescence, when a boy may fall in love with his mother and desire to replace his father (i.e., he develops an Oedipus complex) and a young girl may fall in love with her father and desire to replace her mother (i.e., she develops an Electra complex) (Freud, 1925). However, a nat-

ural and socially reinforced barrier against incest restrains this expression of sexuality, so adolescents seek to loosen their connections with their families. As they overcome and repudiate their incestuous fantasies, adolescents also complete "one of the most painful, psychical achievements of the pubertal period . . . : detachment from parental authority" (Freud, 1953b, p. 227 [published after Freud's death]). This is done by withdrawing their affection from their parents and transferring it to their peers. This emotional loss is called the "mourning of separation" (Blos, 1979).

Subsequent theorists refer to the process of *individuation,* which involves a differentiation of an individual's behavior, feelings, judgments, and thoughts from those of parents. At the same time, the parent-child relationship moves toward growing cooperation, equality, and mutuality as the child becomes an autonomous person within the family context (Mazor and Enright, 1988).

Freud assumed that the object-choice process during adolescence must find its way to the opposite sex. There is a need to establish heterosexual friendships as one moves away from the homosexual attachments of childhood. Freud saw no harm in sentimental friendships with others of one's own sex, provided there is no permanent inversion or reversal of the sexual role and choice of the sexual object. Although reversal of sexual roles and sexual objects is frequent, Freud regarded the reversal as a deviation from normal sexual life, to be avoided if possible (Freud, 1953b).

The theory espoused by Freud, called *psychoanalytical theory,* emphasizes the importance of early childhood experiences and unconscious motivations in influencing behavior. Many instinctual urges and memories of traumatic experiences are repressed early in life. They are driven out of conscious awareness into the unconscious mind, where they continue to cause anxiety and conflict and to influence behavior.

Freud felt that sexual urges and aggressive instincts and drives are the primary determinants of behavior. The individual is motivated by the *pleasure principle,* the desire to achieve maximum pleasure and to avoid pain. However, sexual and aggressive instincts put people in direct conflict with social mores, especially during the Victorian era of Freud's time, when prudishness and social convention were emphasized. The conflict within the individual between these instinctual urges and societal expectations was considered to be the primary cause of emotional disturbances and illnesses.

Freud's psychosexual theory of development is limited in scope, with an overemphasis (according to some) on sexual motivations as the basis of behavior, and the resolution of psychosexual conflict as the key to healthy behavior. Freud developed this theory on the basis of treatment of adult patients, so the theory was not tested on children. In fact, much of Freud's ideas are not easily tested by research. Freud also had a very cynical view of human nature that certainly does not explain the motivations of countless millions who act out of genuine care and concern.

Anna Freud

Anna Freud (1895–1982), daughter of Sigmund Freud, was more concerned with the period of adolescence than her father was. She elaborated more on the process of adolescent development and the changes in the psychic structure of the child at puberty (Freud, 1946, 1958).

Adolescence was characterized by Anna Freud as a period of internal conflict, psychic disequilibrium, and erratic behavior. Adolescents are, on the one hand, egoistic, regarding themselves as the sole object of interest and the center of the universe, but, on the other hand, also capable of self-sacrifice and devotion. They form passionate love relations, only to break them off suddenly. They sometimes desire complete social involvement and group participation and at other times solitude. They oscillate between blind submission to and rebellion against authority. They are selfish and material minded but also full of lofty idealism. They are ascetic yet indulgent, inconsiderate of others yet touchy themselves. They swing between optimism and pessimism, between indefatigable enthusiasm and sluggishness and apathy (Freud, 1946).

The reasons for this conflicting behavior are the psychic disequilibrium and internal conflict that accompanies sexual maturation at puberty (Blos, 1979). At puberty, the most obvious change is an increase in the instinctual drives. This is due partly to sexual maturation, with its accompanying interest in genitalia and the increase of genital impulses. But the flare-up in instinctual drives at puberty also has a physical base not confined solely to the sexual life. Aggressive impulses are inten-

sified, hunger becomes voracious, and naughtiness sometimes erupts into criminal behavior. Oral and anal interests, long submerged, appear. Habits of cleanliness give way to grime and disorder. Modesty and sympathy are replaced by exhibitionism and brutality. Anna Freud compared this increase in instinctual forces at puberty to the similar condition of early infancy. Early infantile sexuality and rebellious aggression are "resuscitated" at puberty (Freud, 1946, p. 159).

The impulses to satisfy desires, according to the pleasure principle, referred to as the *id,* increase during adolescence. These instinctual urges present a direct challenge to the individual's ego and superego. By *ego,* Anna Freud meant the sum of those mental processes that aim to safeguard mental function. The ego is the evaluative, reasoning power of the individual. By *superego,* Anna Freud meant the ego-ideal and the conscience that result from the incorporation of the social values of the same-sex parent. Therefore, the renewed vigor of the instincts at adolescence directly challenges the reasoning abilities and the powers of conscience of the individual. The careful balance achieved between these psychic powers during latency is overthrown as open warfare breaks out between the id and superego. The ego, which previously has been able to enforce a truce, has as much trouble keeping the peace now as

---

individuation   the formation of personal identity by the development of the self as a unique person separate from parents and others.

psychoanalytical theory   Freud's theory that the structure of personality is composed of the id, ego, and superego, and that mental health depends on keeping the balance among them.

pleasure principle   the motivation of the id to seek pleasure and avoid pain, regardless of the consequences.

id   according to Sigmund Freud, those instinctual urges that a person seeks to satisfy according to the pleasure principle.

ego   according to Sigmund Freud, the rational mind that seeks to satisfy the id in keeping with reality.

superego   according to Sigmund Freud, that part of the mind that opposes the desires of the id by enforcing moral restrictions that have been learned to try to attain a goal of perfection.

does a weak-willed parent when confronted by two strong-willed children who are quarreling. If the ego allies itself completely with the id, "no trace will be left of the previous character of the individual and the entrance into adult life will be marked by a riot of uninhibited gratification of instinct" (Freud, 1946, p. 163). If the ego sides completely with the superego, the character of the individual of the latency period will declare itself once and for all. The id impulses will be confined within the narrow limits prescribed for the child, but a constant expenditure of psychic energy on anticathexes (emotionally charged activities), defense mechanisms, and emotional sympathy will be needed to hold these impulses in check.

Unless this id-ego-superego conflict is resolved at adolescence, the consequences can be emotionally devastating to the individual. Anna Freud discussed how the ego employs indiscriminately all the methods of defense (in psychological terms, the **defense mechanisms**) to win the battle. The ego represses, displaces, denies, and reverses the instincts and turns them against the self; it produces phobias and hysterical symptoms and builds anxiety by means of obsessional thinking and behavior. According to Anna Freud, the rise of asceticism and intellectualism at adolescence is a symptom of mistrust of all instinctual wishes. (See also the section on Piaget in Chapter 6.) The accentuation of neurotic symptoms and inhibitions during adolescence signals the partial success of the ego and superego but at the expense of the individual. Anna Freud did believe, however, that harmony among the id, ego, and superego is possible and does occur finally in most normal adolescents. This balance is achieved if the superego is sufficiently developed during the latent period—but does not inhibit the instincts too much, which would cause extreme guilt and anxiety—and if the ego is sufficiently strong and wise to mediate the conflict (Freud, 1946).

Psychosocial Views of Adolescence

Erik Erikson: Ego Identity

Erik Erikson (1902–1994) modified Sigmund Freud's theory of psychosexual development as a result of findings of modern sociopsychology and anthropology. He described eight stages of human development (Erikson, 1950, 1968, 1982). In each stage, the individual has a psychosocial task to master. The confrontation with each task produces conflict, with two possible outcomes. If the conflict is resolved successfully, a positive quality is built into the personality and further development takes place. If the conflict persists or is resolved unsatisfactorily, the ego is damaged because a negative quality is incorporated into it.

According to Erikson, the overall task of the individual is to acquire a *positive ego identity* as he or she moves from one stage to the next. The positive solution of the task, each with its negative counterpart, is listed here for each period (Erikson, 1950, 1959):

1. *Infancy:* Achieving trust versus mistrust
2. *Early childhood:* Achieving autonomy versus shame and doubt
3. *Play age:* Achieving initiative versus guilt
4. *School age:* Achieving industry versus inferiority
5. *Adolescence:* Achieving identity versus identity diffusion
6. *Young adult:* Achieving intimacy versus isolation
7. *Adulthood:* Achieving generativity versus stagnation
8. *Mature age:* Achieving ego integrity versus disgust and despair

We will focus here on the adolescent task of establishing ego identity. Erikson emphasized several aspects of this process.

Identity formation neither begins nor ends with adolescence. It is a lifelong process, largely unconscious to the individual. Its roots go back in childhood to the experience of mutuality between the mothering adult and mothered children. As children reach out to their first love objects, they begin to find self-realization coupled with mutual recognition. Their identity formations continue through a process of selection and assimilation of childhood identifications, which in turn depend on parental, peer, and societal identification of them as important persons. The community both molds and gives recognition to newly emerging individuals. In his or her successive and tentative

This adolescent has established a sense of personal identity, as defined by Erikson. It is obvious from the areas of interest shown here in his bedroom.

identifications, the child begins early to build up expectations of what it will be like to be older and what it will feel like to have been younger—expectations that become part of an identity as they are, step by step, verified in decisive experiences of psychosocial fittedness. Thus, the process of *identity formation* emerges as an evolving configuration gradually established by successive ego syntheses and resyntheses throughout childhood (Erikson, 1959).

Erikson emphasized that adolescence is a normative crisis, a normal phase of increased conflict, characterized by a fluctuation of ego strength. The experimenting individual becomes the victim of an identity consciousness that is the basis for the self-consciousness of youth. During this time, the individual must establish a sense of *personal identity* and avoid the dangers of *role diffusion* and *identity diffusion.* To establish identity requires individual effort in evaluating personal assets and liabilities and in learning how to use these to achieve a clearer concept of who one is and what one wants to become. Adolescents who are actively engaged in identity exploration are more likely to evidence a personality pattern characterized by self-doubt, confusion, disturbed thinking, impulsivity, conflict with parents and other authority figures, reduced ego strength, and increased physical symptoms (Kidwell, Dunham, Bacho, Pastorino, and Portes, 1995).

Seven Conflicts Erikson believed that during adolescence there must be an integration of all converging identity elements and a resolution of conflict, which he divided into seven major parts.

1. *Temporal perspective versus time confusion:* Gaining a sense of time and of the continuity of life is critical for the adolescent, who must coordinate the past and the future and form some concept of how long it takes people to achieve their life plans. It means learning to estimate and allocate his or her time. A true sense of time does not develop until relatively late in adolescence—at around age 15 or 16.

2. *Self-certainty versus self-consciousness:* This conflict involves developing self-confidence based on past experiences so that a person believes in himself or herself and feels that there is a reasonable chance of accomplishing future aims. To do this, adolescents go through a period of increasing self-awareness and self-consciousness, especially in relation to their physical self-images and social relationships. When development follows a relatively normal course, children acquire confidence

defense mechanisms according to Sigmund Freud, unrealistic strategies used by the ego to protect itself and to discharge tension.

in themselves and their abilities. They develop confidence in their ability to cope in the present and in anticipation of future success (Randolph and Dye, 1981).

3. *Role experimentation versus role fixation:* Adolescents have opportunities to try out the different roles they are to play in society. They can experiment with many different identities, personality characteristics, ways of talking and acting, ideas, goals, or types of relationships. Identity comes through opportunities for such experimentation. Those who have developed too much inner restraint and guilt, who have lost initiative, or who have prematurely experienced role fixation never really find out who they are (Erikson, 1968).

4. *Apprenticeship versus work paralysis:* Similarly, the adolescent has an opportunity to explore and try out different occupations before deciding on a vocation. The choice of job plays a large part in determining a person's identity (Erikson, 1968). Furthermore, a negative self-image in the form of inferiority feelings can prevent a person from mustering the necessary energy to succeed at school or on the job.

5. *Sexual polarization versus bisexual confusion:* Adolescents continue to attempt to define what it means to be "male" and "female." Erikson believed it is important that adolescents develop a clear identification with one sex or the other as a basis for future heterosexual intimacy and as a basis for a firm identity. Furthermore, he emphasized that for communities to function properly, men and women must be willing to assume their "proper roles"; sexual polarization, then, is necessary (Erikson, 1968). Much of present-day analysis (and some criticism) of Erikson relates to his emphasis on the need for sexual polarization.

6. *Leadership and followership versus authority confusion:* As adolescents expand their social horizons through schoolwork, social groups, and new friends, they begin to learn to take leadership responsibilities as well as how to follow others. At the same time, they discover there are competing claims on their allegiances. The state, employer, sweetheart, parents, and friends all make demands, with the result that adolescents experience confusion in relation to authority. To whom should they listen? Whom should they follow? To whom should they give their primary allegiance?

Sorting out the answers requires an examination of personal values and priorities.

7. *Ideological commitment versus confusion of values:* Construction of an ideology guides other aspects of behavior. Erikson (1968) referred to this struggle as the "search for fidelity." He emphasized that individuals need something to believe in or to follow (Logan, 1980).

If the individual is able to resolve these seven conflicts, a firm identity emerges. The crisis is past when he or she no longer has to question at every moment his or her own identity, when he or she has subordinated childhood identity and found a new self-identification (Erikson, 1950). Erikson acknowledged that finding an acceptable identity is much more difficult during a period of rapid social change because the older generation is no longer able to provide adequate role models for the younger generation.

Psychosocial Moratorium   One interesting aspect of Erikson's theory is his concept of adolescence as a ***psychosocial moratorium,*** a societally sanctioned intermediary period between childhood and adulthood, during which the individual through free role experimentation may find a niche in society (Erikson, 1959). Adolescence becomes a period of analyzing and trying various roles without the responsibility for assuming any one. Erikson acknowledged that the duration and intensity of adolescence vary in different societies, but that near the end of adolescence, a failure to establish identity results in deep suffering for the adolescent because of a diffusion of roles. Such role diffusion may be responsible for the appearance of previously latent psychological disturbances.

The adolescent who fails in the search for an identity will experience self-doubt, role diffusion, and role confusion; such an individual may indulge in a self-destructive, one-sided preoccupation or activity. He or she will likely be preoccupied with the opinions of others or may turn to the other extreme of no longer caring what others think. He or she may withdraw or turn to drugs or alcohol in order to relieve the anxiety that role diffusion creates. Ego diffusion and personality confusion can be observed in the chronic delinquent and in psychotic personality disorganization (Muuss, 1988b, p. 63).

Erikson emphasized that although the identity crisis is most pronounced at adolescence, a redefinition of one's ego identity may also take place at other periods of life—when individuals leave home, marry, become parents, get divorced, or change occupations, for example. The extent to which people are able to cope with these changes in identity is determined partly by the success with which they have first mastered the adolescent identity crises (Erikson, 1959).

Since Erikson introduced his theory, numerous research studies have validated, clarified, or questioned his ideas (particularly those related to female subjects) (Anderson and Fleming, 1986; Cote, 1986; Juhasz, 1982; Morgan and Farber, 1982; Newman and Newman, 1988; Onyehalu, 1981; Rosenthal, Gurney, and Moore, 1981).

Components of Identity Identity has many components (Rogow, Marcia, and Slugoski, 1983)—*physical, sexual, social, vocational, moral, ideological,* and *psychological* characteristics—that make up the total self (Grotevant, Thorbecke, and Meyer, 1982; Waterman, 1982). Thus, individuals may be identified by their physical appearance and traits, their gender as well as their sex roles, their social relationships and membership in groups, their vocations and work, their religious and political affiliations and ideologies, and their psychological adjustment and the extent of their personality synthesis. *Identity* may be described in terms of the *total concept of self*. It is personal because it is a sense of "I-ness," but it is also social, for it includes "we-ness," or one's collective identity. Adolescents who have positive identities have developed a sense of accepting themselves. Furthermore, identity development is associated with the development of intimacy. Adolescents are attracted to those with identity statuses similar to their own (Goldman, Rosenzweig, and Lutter, 1980). Identity achievement also helps in developing committed relationships: Intimacy alters identity—it helps people grow (Kacerguis and Adams, 1980).

Some adolescents adopt negative identities that are at odds with the cultural values of the community:

"Failure," "good-for-nothing," "juvenile delinquent," "hood," and "slacker" are labels the adult society commonly applies to certain adolescents.

In the absence of any indication of the possibilities of success or contribution to the society, the young person accepts these negative labels as his/her self-definition and proceeds to validate this identity by continuing to behave in ways that will strengthen it. (Newman and Newman, 1978b, p. 313)

Protinsky (1988) found that adolescents who exhibit behavioral problems score much lower on measures of general identity than those who do not have such problems.

Other adolescents will behave in ways to reduce the anxiety of uncertain or incomplete identities. Some will try to *escape* through such intense immediate experiences as drug abuse or wild parties. These emotional experiences temporarily blot out the search for identity. An adolescent may substitute a *temporary identity* by becoming a joiner, a goof-off, a clown, or a bully. Some will seek to *strengthen their identities* temporarily through vandalism, competitive sports, or popularity contests. The person who becomes a bigot or a superpatriot seeks to build a temporary "fortress identity." Ensuring a *meaningless identity* by engaging in fads is another possibility. For some youths, meaningless identities are better than no identities at all.

Some aspects of identity are more easily formed than others. Physical and sexual identities seem to be established earliest. Young adolescents become concerned with their body images before they become interested in choosing a vocation or examining their moral values and ideologies. Similarly, they must deal with their own sexual identities both before and after puberty.

Vocational, ideological, and moral identities are established more slowly (Logan, 1983). These identities depend on adolescents reaching the formal operation stage of cognitive growth and development that enables them to explore alternative ideas and courses of action. (The formal operation stage will be introduced in the next section and considered in detail in Chapter 6.) In addition, reformulation of these identities requires

---

psychosocial moratorium a socially sanctioned period between childhood and adulthood during which an individual is free to experiment to find a socially acceptable identity and role.

independence of thought. The exploration of occupational alternatives is the most immediate and concrete task as adolescents finish high school or enter college. Religious and political ideologies are usually examined during late adolescence, especially the college years, but identities in these areas may be in a state of flux for years (Cote and Levine, 1992).

Robert Havighurst: Developmental Tasks

In *Developmental Tasks and Education,* Robert Havighurst outlined what he feels are the major developmental tasks of adolescence (Havighurst, 1972). His developmental task theory is an eclectic one, combining previously developed concepts. It has been widely accepted and considered useful in discussing adolescent development and education.

Havighurst sought to develop a psychosocial theory of adolescence by combining consideration of individuals' needs with societal demands. What individuals need and society demands constitute the **developmental tasks.** They are the skills, knowledge, functions, and attitudes that individuals have to acquire at certain points in their lives through physical maturation, social expectations, and personal effort. Mastery of the tasks at each stage of development results in adjustment and preparation for the harder tasks ahead. Mastery of adolescent tasks results in maturity. Failure to master the adolescent tasks results in anxiety, social disapproval, and inability to function as a mature person.

According to Havighurst, there exists a teachable moment—a correct time for teaching any task. Some of the tasks arise out of biological changes, others from societal expectations at a given age or the individual's motivation at certain times to do particular things. Furthermore, developmental tasks differ from culture to culture, depending on the relative importance of biological, psychological, and cultural elements in determining the tasks. There are significant differences in developmental tasks in the upper, middle, and lower classes of the United States. Adolescents may face different tasks at different points in their lives (Klaczynski, 1990). Also, the demands and opportunities differ in various cultures, so that

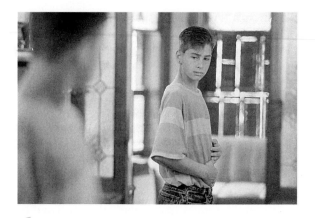

One of the major developmental tasks during the adolescent period, as defined by Havighurst, is accepting one's physique and using it effectively.

success is culturally defined, and the competencies required may differ (Ogbu, 1981).

Havighurst (1972) outlined eight major tasks during the adolescent period:

1. *Accepting one's physique and using the body effectively:* One characteristic of adolescents is their emerging, often extreme, self-consciousness about their physical selves as they reach sexual maturity. Adolescents need to accept their physiques and the pattern of growth of their own bodies, to learn to care for their bodies, and to use their bodies effectively in sports and athletics, recreation, work, and everyday tasks (Havighurst, 1972).

2. *Achieving new and more mature relations with age-mates of both sexes:* Adolescents must move from the same-sex interests and playmates of middle childhood to establish heterosexual friendships. Becoming an adult means also learning social skills and behaviors required in group life (Havighurst, 1972).

3. *Achieving a masculine or feminine social sex role:* What is a man? What is a woman? What are men and women supposed to look like? How should they behave? What are they supposed to be? Psychosexual social roles are established by each culture, but because masculine-feminine roles in Western culture have undergone rapid changes, part of the adolescent maturing process is to reexamine the changing sex roles of their culture and to decide what aspects they must adopt (Havighurst, 1972).

4. *Achieving emotional independence from parents and other adults:* Adolescents must develop understanding, affection, and respect without emotional dependence. Adolescents who are rebellious and in conflict with their parents and other adults need to develop a greater understanding of themselves and adults and the reasons for their conflict (Finkelstein and Gaier, 1983).

5. *Preparing for an economic career:* One of the primary goals of adolescents is to decide on a career, prepare for that career, and then become independent by earning their own living. Part of the task is to discover what they want out of life.

6. *Preparing for marriage and family life:* Patterns of marriage and family living are being readjusted to changing economic, social, and religious characteristics of society. The majority of youths desire a happy marriage and parenthood as one important goal in life and so they need to develop the positive attitudes, social skills, emotional maturity, and necessary understanding to make marriage work.

7. *Desiring and achieving socially responsible behavior:* This goal includes the development of a social ideology that takes into account societal values. The goal also includes participation in the adult life of the community and nation. Many adolescents are disturbed by the ethical quality of their society. Some become radical activists; others join the ranks of the uncommitted who refuse to act. These adolescents struggle to find their place in society in a way that gives meaning to their lives (Havighurst, 1972).

8. *Acquiring a set of values and an ethical system as a guide to behavior—developing an ideology:* This goal includes the development of a sociopolitico-ethical ideology and the adoption and application of meaningful values, morals, and ideals in one's personal life.

Havighurst feels that many modern youths have not been able to achieve identity and therefore suffer from aimlessness and uncertainty. He says that the way most youths (especially boys) achieved identity in the first half of the twentieth century was through selecting and preparing for an occupation; work was the whole axis of life. Now, he feels, with the emphasis on expressive values, nothing has replaced occupational choice

and preparation as the sure means of identity formation. Some adolescents, of course, would disagree; they would say that identity comes through a close, meaningful, loving relationship with another person, or persons, or through oneness with nature.

Kurt Lewin: Field Theory

Kurt Lewin's (1890–1947) theory of adolescent development is outlined in his article "Field Theory and Experiment in Social Psychology: Concepts and Methods" (1939). This field theory explains and describes the behavior of individual adolescents in specific situations.

Lewin's (1939) core concept is "that behavior (B) is a function (f) of the person (P) and of his environment (E)" (p. 34). To understand an adolescent's behavior, you must consider the individual's personality and the environment as interdependent factors. The sum total of all environmental and personal factors in interaction is called the life space (LSp) or the psychological space. Behavior is a function of the life space, $B = f (LSp)$, which includes physical-environmental, social, and psychological factors such as needs, motives, and goals, all of which influence behavior. Lewin's field theory integrates biological and environmental factors in behavior without trying to judge which has the greater influence.

Lewin compared the life space of a child with that of an adult. The child's life space is structured by what is forbidden and what is beyond his or her ability. As the child matures and becomes more capable, fewer restrictions are placed on freedom, so the life space expands into new regions and experiences. By the time the child reaches adolescence, more regions have become accessible, but it is unclear which ones the adolescent is supposed to enter. Thus, the life space remains undefined and unclear. The adult's space is considerably wider, but it is still bounded by activities beyond ability or forbidden by society. Figure 2.1 shows the life spaces of the child, adolescent, and adult.

developmental tasks   the skills, knowledge, functions, and attitudes that individuals have to acquire at certain points in their lives in order to function effectively as mature persons.

FIGURE 2.1 **Life Space of the Child, Adolescent, and Adult.** The actual activity regions are represented; accessible regions are gray; the inaccessible regions are color. *(a)* The *space of free movement* of the *child* includes regions 1–6, representing activities such as getting into the movies at children's rates and belonging to a boys' club. Regions 7–35 are not accessible, representing activities such as driving a car, writing checks for purchases, taking part in political activities, and performing adult occupations. *(b)* The *space of free movement* of the *adolescent* is greatly increased, including many regions that previously were not accessible to the child, such as smoking, returning home late, and driving a car (regions 7–9, 11–13, etc.). Certain regions accessible to the adult are clearly not accessible to the adolescent, such as voting (regions 10 and 16). Certain regions accessible to the child have already become inaccessible, such as getting into the movies at children's rates and behaving on a level that is too childish (region 1). The boundaries of these newly acquired portions of the space of free movement are only vaguely determined and are generally less clearly differentiated than for an adult. In such cases, the life space of the adolescent seems to be full of possibilities and, at the same time, uncertainties. *(c)* The *space of free movement* of the *adult* is considerably wider, although it, too, is bounded by regions of activities inaccessible to the adult, such as shooting enemies and entering activities beyond his or her social or intellectual capacity (regions 29–35, etc.). Some of the regions accessible to the child are not accessible to the adult, such as getting into the movies at children's rates and doing things that are socially taboo for an adult but permitted for a child (regions 1 and 5).

Source: K. Lewin, "Field Theory and Experiment in Social Psychology: Concepts and Methods," *American Journal of Sociology, 44* (1939): 868–897. Copyright © the University of Chicago Press. Used by permission of the University of Chicago Press.

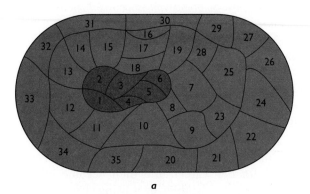

a

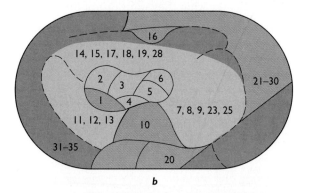

b

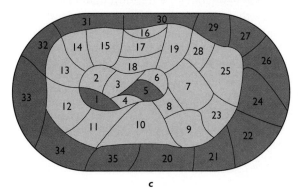

c

According to Lewin, adolescence is a period of transition during which group membership changes from childhood to adulthood. The adolescent belongs partly to the child group and partly to the adult group. Muuss (1988) wrote:

> Parents, teachers, and society reflect this lack of clearly defined group status; and their ambiguous feelings become obvious when they treat the adolescent at one time like a child and at another time like an adult. Difficulties arise because certain childish forms of behavior are no longer acceptable. At the same time some of the adult forms of behavior are not yet permitted either, or if they are permitted, they are new and strange to the adolescent. The adolescent is in a state of "social locomotion," moving into an unstructured social and psychological field. Goals are no longer clear, and the paths to them are ambiguous and full of uncertainties—the adolescent may no longer be certain that they even lead to the desired goals. (p. 147)*

*R. E. Muuss, *Theories of Adolescence,* 5th ed. (New York: McGraw-Hill, 1988). Copyright © 1988 McGraw-Hill Publishing Company. Quotations in this chapter are used by permission of the McGraw-Hill Companies.

This "lack of cognitive structures" helps explain uncertainty in adolescent behavior. Lewin referred to the adolescent as the "marginal man," represented in Figure 2.2 by the overlapping area (Ad) of the child region (C) and the adult region (A). Being a marginal man implies that the adolescent may at times act more like a child, often when he or she wants to avoid adult responsibilities; at other times, he or she acts more like an adult and requests adult privileges (Muuss, 1988, p. 169).

One of the strengths of Lewin's field theory is that it assumes both personality and cultural differences, so it allows for wide individual variations in behavior. It also allows for varying lengths of

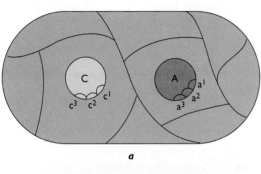

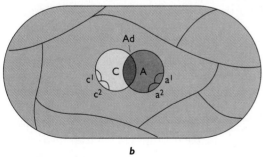

FIGURE 2.2 The Adolescent as a Marginal Man.
(*a*) During childhood and adulthood, the "adults" (A) and "children" (C) are viewed as relatively separated groups. The individual child (c^1, c^2) and the individual adult (a^1, a^2) are sure of their belonging to their respective groups.
(*b*) In adolescence, the adolescent is seen as belonging to a group (Ad) that can be viewed as an overlapping region of the children's (C) and the adults' (A) groups, belonging to both of them, or the adolescent is seen as standing between them, not belonging to either one.

Source: K. Lewin, "Field Theory and Experiment in Social Psychology: Concepts and Methods," *American Journal of Sociology, 44* (1939): 868–897. Copyright © the University of Chicago Press. Used by permission of the University of Chicago Press.

the adolescent period from culture to culture and from social class to social class within a culture (Muuss, 1988).

Cognitive Views of Adolescence

Cognition is the act or process of knowing. The emphasis is not on the process by which information is acquired but on the mental activity or thinking involved in understanding. Figure 2.3 presents an image of cognition. In this view, *S* represents all stimuli or observable effects that the adolescent experiences. *R* represents the adolescent's responses to these events. *C* is the thinking and mental activity that occurs between stimuli and response. In this view, cognition is all the unobservable events in the mind—all the processes, activities, and units. The study of cognitive development, then, is the study of how these mental processes change with age.

Jean Piaget: Cognitive Development

Jean Paul Piaget (1896–1980) was a Swiss psychologist who became interested in the growth of human cognitive development. More than anyone before him, Piaget changed people's conceptions and understandings of the cognitive resources of children. Piaget showed that from birth onward, intellectual competencies undergo continuous development that never ends (Beilin, 1992).

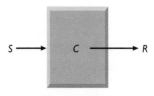

FIGURE 2.3 An Image of Cognition.
S = stimulus; *R* = response; *C* = cognition or mental activity.

cognition the act or process of knowing.

Piaget began his work in Alfred Binet's Paris laboratory, where modern intelligence tests originated. He disagreed with Binet's insistence that intelligence is fixed and innate and began to explore higher-level thought processes (Piaget and Inhelder, 1969). Piaget became more interested in how children reached conclusions than in whether their answers were correct. Instead of asking questions and scoring them right or wrong, Piaget questioned children to find the logic behind their answers. Through painstaking observation of his own, as well as other, children, he began to construct his theory of cognitive development (Piaget, 1950, 1967, 1971, 1972).

Piaget taught that *cognitive development* is the combined result of environmental influences and the maturation of the brain and nervous system. He used five terms to describe the dynamics of development. A *schema* represents the original patterns of thinking, or the mental structures that people use for dealing with what happens in the environment. For example, when children see something they want, they learn to reach out to grasp it. They form a schema that is needed in the situation.

Adaptation is including and adjusting to new information that increases a person's understanding. Adaptation takes place through two means: assimilation and accommodation. *Assimilation* means acquiring new information by using already existing structures in response to new environmental stimuli. *Accommodation* involves adjusting to new information by creating new structures to replace the old. For example, children may see dogs of various kinds (assimilation) and learn that some are safe to pet and others aren't (accommodation). As children acquire more and more information, they change their constructs and accommodate to the world differently.

Equilibrium involves achieving a balance between assimilation and accommodation. It means feeling comfortable, because the reality that a person experiences is compatible with what he or she has been taught to believe. *Disequilibrium* arises when there is dissonance between reality and a person's comprehension of it, when further accommodation is necessary. Children resolve the conflict by acquiring new ways of thinking so that what they understand agrees with what they observe. The desire for equilibrium becomes the motivation that pushes children through the stages of cognitive development. Piaget outlined four stages of cognitive development, which will be discussed next.

Sensorimotor Stage (Birth to 2 Years)   During the sensorimotor stage, children learn to coordinate physical motor actions with sensory experiences. Infants' senses of touch, hearing, vision, taste, and smell bring them into contact with objects exhibiting various properties. For instance, they learn to reach for a ball, move their arms and hands to pick up an object, and move their head and eyes to follow a moving object. The principal cognitive task during this period is called *the conquest of the object* (Elkind, 1970).

Preoperational Stage (2 to 7 Years)   During the preoperational stage, children acquire language and learn to use symbols that represent the environment. Preoperational children can deal with the world symbolically, but still cannot think logically. This is why Piaget (1967) labels this stage *the preoperational stage of thought*. Elkind (1970) labels the principal cognitive task during this period *the conquest of the symbol.*

Concrete Operational Stage (7 to 11 Years)   During the concrete operational stage, children show some capacity for logical reasoning, though it relates only to things actually experienced. They can form a number of mental operations. They can understand class-inclusion relationships, serialization (grouping objects by size or alphabetical order), hierarchical classifications, and the principles of symmetry and reciprocity (e.g., two sisters are sisters to each other). They can also understand the principle of conservation (e.g., pouring a liquid from a tall to a flat dish does not change the total volume of the liquid). The major cognitive task of this period is called *mastering classes, relations, and quantities* (Elkind, 1970).

Formal Operational Stage (11 Years and Older)   During the formal operational stage, adolescents move beyond concrete, actual experiences and begin to think in more logical, abstract terms. They are able to engage in introspection, thinking about their thoughts. They are able to use systematic, propositional logic in solving problems and drawing conclusions. They are also able to use inductive reasoning, bringing a number of facts together and constructing theories on the basis of these facts. Adolescents can also use deductive reasoning in scientifically testing and proving theories and can use algebraic symbols and metaphorical speech as symbols. Additionally, they can think beyond what is to what might be, projecting themselves into the future and planning for it.

We will discuss Piaget's stages of cognitive development in detail in Chapter 6.

Robert Selman: Social Cognition

Social cognition is the ability to understand social relationships. This ability elicits the understanding of others—their emotions, thoughts, intentions, social behavior, and general point of view. Social cognition is basic to all human relationships. Knowing what other people think and feel is necessary in getting along with them and in understanding them (Feldman and Ruble, 1988; Gnepp and Chilamkurti, 1988).

As the ability slowly develops, the question arises as to whether social knowledge and physical knowledge are gained in the same way. Certainly, much of both are acquired through observation, trial and error, exploration, direct firsthand experiences, and discovery. Gaining social knowledge, however, is more difficult. Physical knowledge is objective and factual; social knowledge is quite arbitrary, determined by a specific social situation, as well as by social, cultural, and even subcultural definitions and expectations. Because social rules are less uniform, less specific, and more situation dependent than physical phenomena, they are less predictable and more complicated to understand.

What is the relationship between other cognitive abilities, such as intellectual, moral, and social problem-solving skills? The person who has superior intellectual problem-solving skills does not necessarily have superior social problem-solving skills. An intellectually superior person may be socially inept, indicating that cognitive abilities involved in interpersonal relationships are not the same as those measured by a conventional IQ test. Social problem-solving skills may be learned or taught, separate from intellectual abilities. Shure and Spivak (1980) found that the improvement in social adjustment resulting from their interpersonal skills program was not a function of a child's level of intellectual functioning. Selman (1980)

concluded, "The development of social conceptions, reasoning, thought—social cognition—is distinct from, though not unrelated to, the development of nonsocial cognition." There is some evidence, however, that people who show superior ability in moral reasoning also show superior ability in social cognition (Muuss, 1982).

Social Role Taking One of the most useful models of social cognition is that of Robert Selman (1977, 1980), who has advanced a theory of *social role taking* (see Figure 2.4). To Selman, social role taking is the ability to understand the self and others as subjects, to react to others as to the self, and to react to the self's behavior from others' points of view. Selman's five stages of development are discussed next.

Stage 0: Egocentric undifferentiated stage (ages 3 to 6). Until about age 6, children cannot make a clear distinction between their own interpretation of a social situation and the point of view of another, nor can they understand that their own perception may not be correct. When asked how someone else feels in a particular situation, their responses reflect how *they* feel.

---

schema   the original patterns of thinking; the mental structures that people use for dealing with what happens in the environment.

adaptation   including and adjusting to new information that increases understanding.

assimilation   incorporating a feature of the environment into an existing mode or structure of thought.

accommodation   involves adjusting to new information by creating new structures to replace old.

equilibrium   according to Piaget, achieving a balance between schemas and accommodation.

social cognition   how people think and reason about their social world as they watch and interact with others; their understanding and ability to get along with other people.

social role taking   according to Selman, the social roles that individuals take on that reflect their understanding of themselves, their actions to others, and their abilities to understand others' points of view.

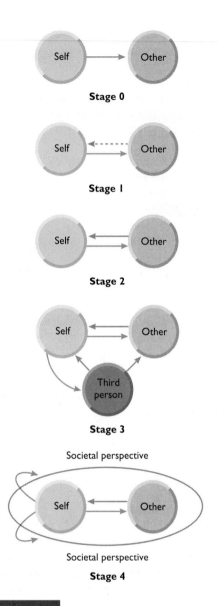

FIGURE 2.4   Selman's Five Stages of Social Role Taking

Source: R. E. Muuss, *Theories of Adolescence,* 5th ed. (New York: McGraw Hill, 1988), pp. 249, 251, 254, 256, 258. Copyright © 1988 McGraw Hill Publishing Company. Used by permission of the McGraw-Hill Companies.

Stage 1: Differential or subjective perspective-taking stage, or social-informational stage (ages 6 to 8). Children at this stage develop an awareness that others may have a different social perspective, but they have little understanding of the reasons for others' viewpoints (LeMare and Rubin, 1987). Children believe that if others had the same information, they would

feel as they do. However, they begin to distinguish between unintentional and intentional behavior and to consider the causes of actions (Miller and Aloise, 1989). They are capable of inferring other people's intentions, feelings, and thoughts, but they base their conclusions on physical observations that may not be correct, not realizing that people may hide their true feelings.

Stage 2: Self-reflective thinking or reciprocal perspective taking (ages 8 to 10). Preadolescents at stage 2 take the perspective of another individual. Preadolescents thus become capable of making inferences about the perspectives of others; they can reflect about their own behavior and their own motivation as seen from the perspective of another person.

This ability introduces an awareness that no single individual's social perspective is necessarily correct or valid in an absolute sense. In other words, another person's point of view may be as correct as one's own. Preadolescents think only within a two-person frame of reference—"I think; you think"—and cannot take a more general third-person perspective (Muuss, 1982, 1988b).

Stage 3: The third person or mutual perspective-taking stage (ages 10 to 12). Children can see their own perspectives, that of their partners, as well as that of a neutral third person. As third-person observers, they can see themselves as both object and actor (subject). They can understand a more generalized perspective that might be perceived by the majority of a group. Friendship now is viewed not as mutual back-scratching, but as a series of interactions over an extended period of time. Conflicts are seen as emerging from different personality characteristics (Muuss, 1982).

Stage 4: In-depth and societal perspective-taking stage (adolescence to adulthood). There are two distinguishing features of adolescents' conceptions of other people. First, they become aware that motives, actions, thoughts, and feelings are shaped by psychological factors. This notion of psychological determinants now includes the idea of the unconscious processes, although adolescents may not express this awareness in psychological terminology. Second, they begin to appreciate the fact that a personality is a system of traits, beliefs, values, and attitudes with its own developmental history.

During adolescence, the individual may move to a still higher and more abstract level of interpersonal perspective taking, which involves the coordination of all possible third-person perspectives—a societal perspective. The adolescent can conceptualize that each person can consider the shared point of view of the "generalized other"—that is, the social system—which, in turn, makes possible the accurate communication with an understanding of other people. Furthermore, the individual becomes aware of the idea that law and morality as a social system depends on the concept of consensual group perspective (Selman, 1980).

Selman has emphasized that not all adolescents or adults will reach stage 4 in social-cognitive development. Stage 4 corresponds to Piaget's level of formal operations in logical reasoning and to Kohlberg's conventional and postconventional stages of moral development (Selman, 1977, 1980). Selman's theory implies a movement away from limited concern with the cognitive side of learning toward an inclusion of interpersonal, social-cognitive awareness (Muuss, 1988).

Before we move on to consider ecological, psychosocial, and anthropological views of human development, let's summarize and compare the various stages of development outlined by some of the theorists we have discussed so far. Figure 2.5 compares the stages of Freud, Erikson, Piaget, and Selman. Notice which stages correspond to adolescence.

Ecological View of Adolescence

Adolescents do not develop in a vacuum. They develop within the multiple contexts of their families, communities, and countries. Adolescents are influenced by peers, relatives, and other adults with whom they come in contact, and by the religious organizations, schools, and groups to which they belong. They are also influenced by the media, the cultures in which they are growing up, national and community leaders, and world events. They are partly a product of environmental and social influences.

Urie Bronfenbrenner: An Ecological Model

Urie Bronfenbrenner (1979, 1987) developed an ecological model for understanding social influences. As you can see in Figure 2.6, social influences may be grouped into a series of systems extending beyond the adolescent. The adolescent is at the center of the systems.

The Microsystem The most immediate influences on the adolescent are within the *microsystem* and include those with whom he or she has immediate contact. For most adolescents, the immediate family is the primary microsystem, followed by friends and school. Other components of the microsystem are health services, religious groups, neighborhood play areas, and various social groups to which the adolescent belongs.

Microsystems change as the adolescent moves in and out of different social settings. For example, the adolescent may change schools, stop going to church or synagogue, drop out of some activities, and join others. In general, the peer microsystem increases in influence during adolescence, providing powerful social rewards in terms of acceptance, popularity, friendship, and status. The peer group may also exert negative influences, encouraging irresponsible sex, drug use, theft, gang membership, or cheating. A healthy microsystem offers positive learning and development that prepares the adolescent for success in adult life (Muuss, 1988).

The Mesosystem The *mesosystem* involves reciprocal relationships among microsystem settings. For example, what happens at school influences what happens at home and vice versa. An adolescent's social development is understood best when the influences from many sources are considered

microsystem includes those persons with whom the adolescent has immediate contact and who influence him or her.

mesosystem the reciprocal relationships among microsystem settings.

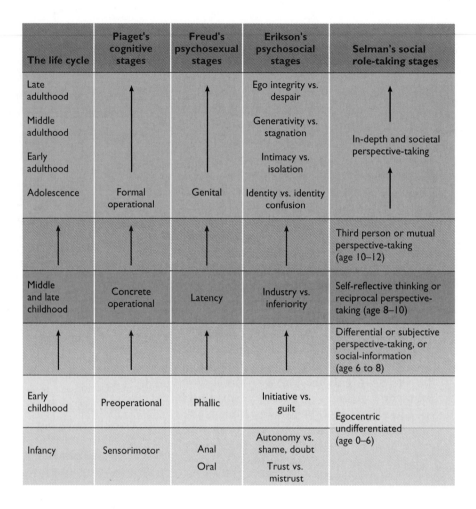

The life cycle	Piaget's cognitive stages	Freud's psychosexual stages	Erikson's psychosocial stages	Selman's social role-taking stages
Late adulthood			Ego integrity vs. despair	
Middle adulthood			Generativity vs. stagnation	In-depth and societal perspective-taking
Early adulthood			Intimacy vs. isolation	
Adolescence	Formal operational	Genital	Identity vs. identity confusion	
				Third person or mutual perspective-taking (age 10–12)
Middle and late childhood	Concrete operational	Latency	Industry vs. inferiority	Self-reflective thinking or reciprocal perspective-taking (age 8–10)
				Differential or subjective perspective-taking, or social-information (age 6 to 8)
Early childhood	Preoperational	Phallic	Initiative vs. guilt	Egocentric undifferentiated (age 0–6)
Infancy	Sensorimotor	Anal / Oral	Autonomy vs. shame, doubt / Trust vs. mistrust	

FIGURE 2.5
Comparison of Piaget's, Freud's, Erikson's, and Selman's Stages

in relation to each other. A mesosystem analysis would look at the frequency, quality, and influence of interactions, such as how family experiences are related to school adjustments, how family characteristics are related to peer pressures, or how church or synagogue attendance is related to intimacy with the opposite sex.

A microsystem and a mesosystem can reinforce each other or exert opposite influences. Trouble arises if basic values of the mesosystem and the microsystem diverge; the adolescent may feel overly stressed as different sets of values are sorted out.

The Exosystem The *exosystem* is composed of those settings in which the adolescent does not play an active role but that nevertheless influences him or her. For example, what happens to the parents at work influences the parents, and they, in turn, influence the adolescent's development. The parents' bosses determine the rate of pay,

work and vacation schedules, and the community in which the work will take place. If the company decides to move an employee, it affects the whole family. All of these factors influence the parents' relationships with their adolescent.

Similarly, community organizations affect the adolescent in many ways. For instance, the school board establishes the curriculum, the school calendar, and hires the teachers. The town government may open or close a youth center or a swimming pool. Those in the exosystem make decisions that affect the adolescent, whose parents are concerned that their adolescent's best interests are kept in mind.

The Macrosystem The *macrosystem* includes the ideologies, attitudes, mores, customs, and laws of a particular culture. It includes a core of educational, economic, religious, political, and social values. The macrosystem determines who is an

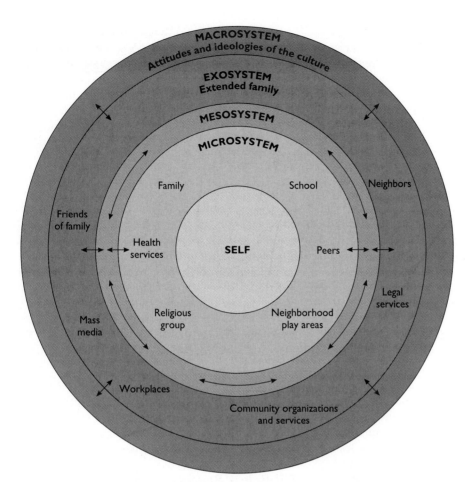

FIGURE 2.6
Bronfenbrenner's Ecological Model for Understanding Social Influences

Source: Data from Bronfenbrenner (1979).

adult and who is an adolescent. It sets standards of physical attractiveness and gender-role behavior, and influences health practices such as smoking. It also influences educational standards and relationships between the races.

Cultures may differ in various countries and in racial, ethnic, or socioeconomic groups. There are also differences within each group (Gutierrez, Sameroff, and Carrer, 1988). In Sweden, for example, it is against the law for parents to hit children, yet the practice is condoned by some groups in the United States. Middle-class parents in the United States often have different goals and philosophies of childrearing than do those in low-socioeconomic-status groups. Rural families may have different parenting values than urban families (Coleman, Ganong, Clark, and Madsen, 1989). These values and customs have differential effects on adolescents. In talking about social development, then, we have to discuss issues and concerns in the contexts in which adolescents are growing up.

Social-Cognitive Learning View of Adolescence

Social learning theory is concerned with the relationship between social and environmental factors and their influence on behavior.

Albert Bandura: Social Learning Theory

Albert Bandura, born in 1925, has been concerned with the application of social learning theory to

---

exosystem that part of an ecological system that includes settings in which the adolescent does not have an active role as a participant but that influence him or her nevertheless.

macrosystem the ideologies, attitudes, mores, customs, and laws of a particular culture that influence the individual.

adolescents. His view, outlined in a major book (Bandura, 1973), emphasizes that children learn through observing the behavior of others and by imitating this pattern—a process referred to as *modeling*. Modeling then becomes a socialization process by which habitual response patterns develop. As children grow, they imitate different models from their social environment. In many studies, parents are listed as the most significant adults in the lives of adolescents (Blyth, Hill, and Thiel, 1982; Galbo, 1983). Siblings are also mentioned as significant others, as are extended family members such as aunts and uncles. Nonrelated significant adults include ministers and youth ministers found within the church setting, teachers, and neighbors.

Different studies reveal varying results, however, depending on the group surveyed. In one study of 360 secondary school pupils in Scotland, 79 percent selected their parents as the most significant others in their lives, with 56 percent choosing mother and 23 percent choosing father. Sisters and brothers were chosen by 13 percent of young people, and other adults (mostly grandparents) were chosen by 8 percent of the sample (Hendry, Roberts, Glendinning, and Coleman, 1992). Adolescents from working-class families less frequently mention mothers or fathers. College-age adolescents often mention faculty members and friends as significant others in their lives (Galbo, 1984). When family influence declines, entertainment heroes and peers become increasingly important as models, especially in influencing verbal expressions, hairstyles, clothing, musical tastes, and basic social values.

Modeling and Aggressive Behavior   Bandura has investigated modeling and the development of aggressive behavior. He showed that when children watched unusually aggressive behavior in a real-life model or in a model in a film or cartoon, many of the children's responses were accurate imitations of the model's aggressive acts (Bandura, 1973). Similar results were found among high school students, young women, and male hospital attendants. This research has led to much concern about the effects on children and adolescents of watching aggressive behavior on movie and television screens: "Exposure to filmed aggression heightens aggressive reactions" (Bandura, 1973). This finding has been substantiated by others (Tooth, 1985).

Bandura showed that a number of factors in the home contribute to aggressive behavior of sons. Aggressive sons were encouraged to show aggression outside the home toward other children, to stand up for their rights, and to use their fists if needed. The fathers of aggressive boys seemed to get vicarious enjoyment from their sons' aggressive acts and were more permissive of their sons' sexual behavior.

The parents of aggressive boys were also more punitive when the aggressive behavior was directed toward them. They used more physical discipline, isolation, and deprivation of privileges, and less reasoning. The more the boys were punished physically at home for aggressive behavior, the more aggressive they became. Thus, they learned aggression by modeling the behavior of the punishing parent (Bandura, 1973).

The conscience development of aggressive boys differed from that of less aggressive sons. The behavior of the latter was controlled by guilt and internal avoidance. If the aggressive sons were inhibited at all, it was by fear of punishment rather than by guilt and internal controls. Because aggressive sons did not have as close relationships with their parents, especially with fathers, their conscience development suffered.

The Role of Reinforcement   Most social learning theorists emphasize the role of *reinforcement,* or the responses of others, in influencing future behavior. Bandura expands on this idea, speaking of *vicarious reinforcement* and *self-reinforcement.* Vicarious reinforcement consists of the positive or negative consequences that one observes others experiencing. Observing that others are rewarded for aggressive behavior increases the possibility that the observer will also show aggression. Bandura (1973) observed that self-reinforcement was as effective as external reinforcement in influencing behavior. Once the performance of a desired response pattern, such as shooting and making baskets with a basketball, acquired a positive value, adolescents could administer their own reinforcement by producing the baskets and then feeling good afterward. Adolescents who set reasonable goal levels of performance and reach that level feel proud and satisfied internally and become decreasingly dependent on parents, teachers, and bosses to give them rewards.

The work of social learning theorists is of great importance in explaining human behavior. It is especially important in emphasizing that *what adults do and the role models they represent are far more important in influencing adolescent behavior than what they say.* Teachers and parents can best encourage human decency, altruism, moral values, and a social conscience by exhibiting these virtues themselves.

Social-Cognitive Theory

In recent years, Bandura has expanded his social learning theory to include the role of cognition (Bandura, 1986, 1989). Rather than describing individuals as determined strictly by environmental influences, Bandura emphasized that they, in large measure, *determine their own destinies* by choosing their future environments as well as other goals they wish to pursue. People reflect on and regulate their own thoughts, feelings, and actions to achieve their goals. In short, the way they interpret environmental influences determines how they act. For example, consider again the behavior of aggressive boys. Research has shown that aggressive boys are biased in favor of attributing hostile intent to others in various situations (Dodge and Somberg, 1987). Aggressive boys are not careful in processing information that would help them to determine whether the intent of the action against them was hostile or benign. They pay less attention to information that would help them reach a more accurate inference about someone else's motives. Therefore, they are more likely to infer hostile intent when they come to conclusions quickly. In other words, it is not just what happens to these boys that determines the level of their aggression, but it is also the way they interpret others' intentions.

Social-cognitive theory emphasizes that individuals can actively control the events that affect their lives, rather than having to passively accept whatever the environment provides; they partially control the environment by the way they react to it. A placid, pleasant, easy-to-care-for adolescent may have a very positive influence on parents, encouraging them to act in a friendly, warm, and loving manner. However, an overactive, temperamental, hard-to-care-for adolescent who is easily upset may stimulate parents to be hostile, short-tempered, and rejecting. From this point of view, children—however involuntarily—are partly responsible for

creating their own environments. Because of individual differences, different people, at different developmental stages, interpret and act on their environments in differing ways that create different experiences for each person (Bandura, 1986).

Anthropological Views of Adolescence

The kinds of influences that mold the child depend on the culture in which the child grows up (Benedict, 1950; Mead, 1950, 1953).

Margaret Mead and Ruth Benedict

The theories of Margaret Mead (1901–1978), Ruth Benedict (1887–1948), and other cultural anthropologists have been called *cultural determinism* and *cultural relativism* because anthropologists emphasize the importance of the *social environment* in determining the personality development of the child. Because social institutions, economic patterns, habits, mores, rituals, and religious beliefs vary from society to society, culture is relative.

The later writings of Mead (1970, 1974) and others have undergone some modification: They

---

modeling   learning by observing and imitating the behavior of another.

reinforcement   positive reinforcements are influences that increase the probability that the preceding response will occur again. Negative reinforcements are influences that increase the probability that the preceding response will stop.

vicarious reinforcement   learning from observing the positive or negative consequences of another person's behavior.

self-reinforcement   the act of learners rewarding themselves for activities or responses that they consider of good quality.

cultural determinism   the influence of a particular culture in determining the personality and behavior of a developing individual.

cultural relativism   variations in social institutions, economic patterns, habits, mores, rituals, religious beliefs, and ways of life from one culture to another.

show some recognition of universal aspects of development (e.g., incest taboos) and more acknowledgment of the biological role in human development. Today, extreme positions are generally disregarded by both geneticists and anthropologists. They basically agree that a composite view that acknowledges both biogenetic factors and environmental forces comes closest to the truth. (For a critique of Mead, see Freeman, 1983.)

Extended Adolescence versus Early Adulthood

Anthropologists emphasize that the sociocultural milieu determines the direction of adolescence and strongly influences the degree to which adolescents are welcomed into the adult community. Achievement of adult status is not just the separation from parents but the establishment of personal identity and new roles into the community. In modern society, adolescence has become a prolonged stage of development: Its completion is imprecise and its privileges and responsibilities are often illogical and confused. This is in contrast to primitive societies, where puberty rites mark a definite and early introduction into adulthood (Comerci, 1989).

Research on adolescents has revealed that their feelings of satisfaction depend partly on having some control over their lives, being able to have choices, and taking responsibility for their own behavior (Ortman, 1988). This is exactly what

being an adult involves. This process is often delayed in modern industrial societies.

Cultural Continuity versus Discontinuity

Anthropologists challenge the basic truths of all age and stage theories of child and adolescent development (such as those of Freud, Erikson, Piaget, and Selman). Mead, for example, discovered that Samoan children follow a relatively continuous growth pattern, with no abrupt changes from one age to the other. They are not expected to behave one way as children, another way as adolescents, and yet another way as adults. Samoans never have to change abruptly their ways of thinking or acting; they do not have to unlearn as adults what they learned as children, so adolescence does not represent an abrupt change or transition from one pattern of behavior to another. This principle of *continuity of cultural conditioning* may be illustrated with three examples by Benedict (1938) and Mead (1950).

1. The responsible roles of children in primitive societies are contrasted with the nonresponsible roles of children in Western culture. Children in primitive societies learn responsibility quite early. Play and work often involve the same activity; for example, by "playing" with a bow and arrow, a boy learns to hunt. His adult hunting "work" is a continuation of his youthful hunting "play." In contrast,

PERSONAL ISSUES

When Do They Become Adults?

Researchers asked 113 adolescents, ranging in age from 13 to 19, with a mean age of 16.5 years, if and when they considered themselves to be adults. If they realized they were not yet adults, they were asked when they thought they would be.

Their responses were divided into two major categories. The first category contained *cognitive-related responses* and included such factors as reaching maturity, taking responsibility for their actions, and making their own decisions. The second category consisted of *event-*

related responses. Adolescents believed that to become adults, they had to be financially independent and have a job; get married and become a parent; move away from their parents' homes; reach a legal age to drive, drink, and vote; or graduate from high school or college.

The findings of this study were consistent with research suggesting that adulthood is an emerging process. This is a period of time (often in midadolescence) when youths begin to consider themselves adults—cognitively, emotionally, and behaviorally (Scheer, Unger, and Brown, 1996).

children in Western culture must assume drastically different roles as they grow up: They shift from nonresponsible play to responsible work and must do it rather suddenly.

2. The submissive role of children in Western culture is contrasted with the dominant role of children in primitive society. Children in Western culture must replace their childhood submission and adopt its opposite—dominance—as they become adults. Mead (1950) showed that Samoan children are not taught submission as children and then suddenly expected to become dominant when reaching adulthood. On the contrary, a 6- or 7-year-old Samoan girl dominates her younger siblings and in turn is dominated by the older ones. The older she gets, the more she dominates and disciplines others and the fewer there are to dominate her (the parents never try to dominate her). When she becomes an adult, she does not experience the dominance-submission conflict that the adolescent in Western society generally does.

3. The similarity of sex roles of children and adults in primitive cultures is contrasted with the dissimilar sex roles of children and adults in Western culture. Mead indicated that the Samoan girl experiences no real discontinuity of sex roles as she passes from childhood to adulthood. She has the opportunity to experiment and become familiar with sex with almost no taboos (except against incest). Therefore, by the time adulthood is reached, the Samoan female is able to assume a sexual role in marriage very easily. By contrast, in Western culture, infant sexuality is denied and adolescent sexuality is repressed; sex is considered sinful and dangerous. When adolescents mature sexually, they must unlearn those earlier attitudes and taboos and become sexually responsive adults.

Storm and Stress versus Cultural Conditioning

In showing the continuity of development of children in some cultures, in contrast to the discontinuity of development of children in Western culture, anthropologists and some psychologists (Roll, 1980) cast doubt on the universality of ages and stages of growth of children in all cultures. Only those societies that emphasize discontinuity of behavior (one type of behavior as a child, another as an adult) are described as "age-grade societies" (Benedict, 1938).

Anthropologists challenge the inevitability of the storm and stress of adolescence by minimizing the disturbance of physical changes and by emphasizing the interpretation of those changes. Menstruation is a case in point. One tribe may teach that the menstruating girl is a danger to the tribe (she may scare the game or dry up the well); another tribe may consider her condition a blessing (she could increase the food supply or the priest could obtain a blessing by touching her). A girl taught that menstruation is good will react and act differently than a girl who is taught that it is a curse. Therefore, the stress and strains of pubescent physical changes may be the result of certain cultural interpretations of those changes and not due to any inherent biological tendencies.

Cross-Cultural Views on Parent-Adolescent Relations

Anthropologists describe many conditions in Western culture that create a generation gap, but *they deny the inevitability of that gap* (Mead, 1974). Rapidity of social change, pluralistic value systems, and modern technology make the world appear too complex and too unpredictable to adolescents to provide them with a stable frame of reference. Furthermore, early physiological puberty and the need for prolonged education allow many years for the development and assimilation of a peer-group culture in which adolescent values, customs, and mores may be in conflict with those in the adult world (Finkelstein and Gaier, 1983).

Mead believed that close family ties should be loosened to give adolescents more freedom to make their own choices and live their own lives. By requiring less conformity and less dependency and by tolerating individual differences within the family, adolescent-parent conflict and tension can be minimized (Mead, 1950). Also, Mead wrote that youths can be accepted into adult society at younger ages. Gainful employment, even part time, would promote greater financial independence. Parenthood should be postponed, advocated Mead, but not necessarily sex or marriage. Adolescents should be given a greater voice in the social and political life of the community. These measures would eliminate some of the discontinuities of cultural conditioning of children growing up in Western society and would allow for a smoother, easier transition to adulthood.

SUMMARY

1. Each view discussed here has contributed to a better understanding of adolescence.
2. Gesell emphasized the importance of maturation in learning but he neglected environmental contributions to human growth.
3. Sigmund Freud made a significant contribution in his emphasis on early childhood experiences and unconscious motivations in influencing behavior. The desire to satisfy sexual instincts and psychic needs of affection are strong motivating factors in influencing adolescent behavior. Similarly, Freud's explanations of the need to release emotionally from parents, to establish heterosexual friendships with peers, and to find a love object for emotional fulfillment are helpful.
4. Anna Freud's emphasis on psychic drives and needs and on the psychic disequilibrium of adolescents helps us understand the causes of their erratic behavior.
5. Erikson's explanation of the adolescent's need for identity, its components, and the process by which the adolescent forms identity has had a marked influence on adolescent theory and research for over 40 years.
6. Havighurst's outline of developmental tasks is helpful to youths in discovering some of the things they need to accomplish to reach adulthood.
7. Lewin's field theory emphasizes adolescence as the bridge between childhood and adulthood and the role of both environmental and personal factors interacting with one another in shaping adolescent behavior.
8. Piaget was concerned about cognition, or the act or process of knowing. He emphasized not how much information is acquired, but the mental activity or thinking involved in developing understanding. He described the changes that take place in how children, adolescents, and adults think as they get older.
9. Selman emphasizes social cognition, the ability to understand social relationships, and the stages that people pass through in developing this ability. Selman's theory departs from a limited concern with cognitive learning and discusses the development of interpersonal social-cognitive awareness.
10. Bronfenbrenner's ecological view of adolescence emphasizes the importance of social influences on development in the context of the culture in which adolescents are being brought up.
11. Bandura's social learning theory is concerned with the relationship between social and environmental factors and their influence on behavior. He emphasizes the importance of modeling and reinforcement in the learning process. His later emphasis on cognitive factors in shaping the environment is an important contribution.
12. Mead and Benedict and other anthropologists provide evidence that there are few universal patterns of development. Cultural comparisons emphasize the positive and negative elements in each culture that aid or prevent the adolescent from becoming an adult.

KEY TERMS

accommodation **38**

adaptation **38**

anal stage **27**

assimilation **38**

cognition **37**

cultural determinism **45**

cultural relativism **45**

defense mechanisms **30**

developmental tasks **34**

ego **29**

equilibrium **38**

exosystem **42**

genital stage **27**

id **29**

individuation **28**

latency stage **27**

macrosystem **42**

mesosystem **41**

microsystem **41**

modeling **44**

oral stage **27**

phallic stage **27**

pleasure principle **28**

psychoanalytical theory 28

psychosocial moratorium **32**

reinforcement **44**

schema **38**

self-reinforcement **44**

social cognition **39**

social role taking **39**

superego **29**

vicarious reinforcement **44**

THOUGHT QUESTIONS

1. Which exerts the greater influence on adolescent development: heredity or environmental influences? Explain.
2. Give an example of adolescent behavior that is more under the influence of physical maturation than under environmental influences.
3. Is adolescence a period of storm and stress? Explain.
4. From a parent's point of view, what are the advantages and disadvantages of Gesell's view of child development?
5. What do you think of Sigmund Freud's point of view about development?
6. What do you think of Freud's point of view when he says that a normal sexual life is assured only when there is a convergence of the affectionate and the sensual components?
7. According to Freud, individuals are motivated primarily by the pleasure principle. What do you think of this idea?
8. Which ideas of Anna Freud do you consider most helpful in explaining the period of adolescence?
9. According to Anna Freud, what are the purposes of defense mechanisms?
10. What would you consider a healthy versus an unhealthy use of ego defense mechanisms?
11. Discuss one id-ego-superego conflict that might erupt during adolescence.
12. In what ways is adolescence a period of identity formation?
13. How do adolescents go about forming their identities? What happens if they cannot "find" themselves?
14. Is identity formation ever completed?
15. Can an individual find an identity without going through a psychosocial moratorium? Explain.
16. Can individuals experience more than one identity crisis in their lives? Explain.
17. Which component of identity is most easily formed?
18. Give specific examples of how adolescents adapt cognitively through assimilation and accommodation.
19. How can parents help children grow cognitively during the sensorimotor stage of development?
20. How does Selman's theory contribute to knowledge of how people can learn to understand and get along with one another?
21. Explain stage 0 of Selman's developmental view of social cognition.
22. Explain stage 4 of Selman's developmental view of social cognition.
23. In your opinion, which of the following microsystems exerted the greatest influence on you when you were an adolescent: parents, peers, church, or school? Explain.
24. What factors might determine how much influence the macrosystem has on an individual adolescent?
25. Give an example of a behavior pattern that adolescents have modeled after their parents.
26. What is your opinion of the influence of televised aggression on children and youths?
27. Should children and adolescents be restricted from watching some television programs because the programs are violent? Explain.
28. What are some of the factors in the home situation that contribute to the aggressive behavior of children and adolescents?
29. What might be the role of cognition in modifying aggressive behavior of children?
30. Which of the eight psychosocial tasks as outlined by Havighurst do you feel are the most difficult to achieve? Explain.
31. What does Lewin mean by "life space"?
32. In what ways is the adolescent the "marginal man," according to Lewin?
33. What should be done in our society to enable adolescents to bridge the gap between childhood and adulthood and to grow up faster?
34. Are there adult privileges given to adolescents that you feel should not be given? Are there privileges that are not given that should be? Explain.

SUGGESTED READING

Cote, J. E. (1994). *Adolescent Storm and Stress: An Evaluation of the Mead-Freeman Controversy.* Hillsdale, NJ: Erlbaum.

Tyson, P., and Tyson, R. L. (1990). *Psychoanalytic Theories of Development: An Integration.* New Haven, CT: Yale University Press.

Adolescents in Ethnic Context

One of the most common myths about adolescents is that they are all alike. Adolescents cannot be discussed as one homogenous group any more than any other age group. Not only do they come from a wide variety of ethnic and cultural backgrounds but also the environments in which they are raised are different, and the circumstances of their lives are quite varied.

Many sections of this book refer to cultural differences among adolescents. Differences between low-socioeconomic-status and middle-class adolescents are highlighted, as well as some differences between ethnic minorities and White adolescents. Unfortunately, much of the research with adolescents has been conducted with White, middle-class youths. Although these are the majority, they are not representative of all. So before we get into more detailed discussion of adolescence, let's look at the wide cultural diversity that exists among several representative minority groups.

We begin with low-socioeconomic-status adolescents of whatever race or national origin. The low-socioeconomic-status category cuts across

many ethnic boundaries, reaching into 11.6 percent of U.S. homes and affecting 14.5 percent of the population (U.S. Bureau of the Census, 1996). The discussion continues with a consideration of adolescents in six large ethnic-minority groups in the United States. Figure 3.1 shows the sizes of these groups. African Americans constitute the largest ethnic-minority group, with Mexican Americans composing the second largest. Puerto Rican Americans are the third largest minority, followed by Native Americans, Chinese Americans, and Asian Americans. In this book, discussion of Chinese Americans is representative of the total group of Asian Americans, although there are many differences among persons from different Asian countries. Southeast Asians, our newest immigrants, have special problems as refugees from war.

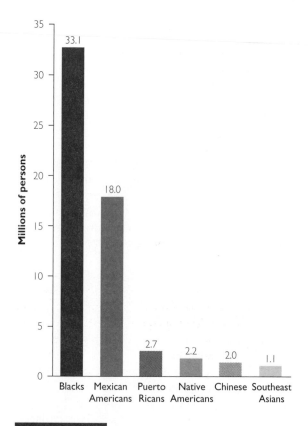

FIGURE 3.1   Size of Minority Groups in the United States (1995)

Source: U.S. Bureau of the Census, *Statistical Abstract of the United States, 1996* (Washington, DC: U.S. Government Printing Office, 1996).

Topics such as discrimination, segregation, housing, education, employment, and income are discussed. These factors can have considerable impact on the lives of adolescents. Parental and cultural values of Mexican American, Puerto Rican American, Native American, Chinese American, and Southeast Asian American adolescents are highlighted to show the difficulties in socialization and the cultural conflicts that beset youths of these minority groups.

A word of caution is in order as we begin. Even though we will be making general statements about various minority groups, all individuals within a minority group are not alike. Tremendous diversity exists within minority groups, just as it exists among minority groups and within the White middle-class majority. In describing minor-

ity groups, the intent is to provide the background for better understanding, *not* to create or reinforce stereotypes. You may even know individuals from these minority groups to whom these descriptions apply only partially, or perhaps not at all.

Adolescents of Low Socioeconomic Status

Various terms have been applied to youths who are of lower social classes and poor; among them are *disadvantaged, culturally deprived, educationally deprived, low socioeconomic status,* and *working class.* In this book, the term ***low socioeconomic status (low SES)*** is used because it refers to two important aspects of the living condition: low social class and status, including cultural deprivation, and low income. Note that not all youths of lower class are poor, nor are all low-income youths culturally deprived, even though the two aspects frequently go together. However, in this chapter, both lower social class and low income will be emphasized.

Low-socioeconomic-status adolescents grow up in 11.6 percent of U.S. families classified as poor (U.S. Bureau of the Census, 1996). Compared with the general population, they are more often from non-White families; have less education, fewer wage earners, and more female heads of household; and are from larger than average families. They reside more often in the South, in farm areas, or in cities and less often in rural nonfarm or suburban areas. By definition, these adolescents are also culturally deprived, with only limited access to leisure facilities, educational advantages, work opportunities, health and medical care, proper living conditions, and many of the values, attitudes, customs, institutions, and organizations characteristic of the large masses of middle-class Americans.

Socioeconomic status (SES) plays an important role in the lives of adolescents. Awareness of different levels of SES probably influences adolescents' self-perceptions as well as their perceptions of the external world. Children, adolescents, and adults learn their worth, in part, by comparing themselves with others. Also, their self-attitudes are influenced largely by the attitudes held by others toward them (Pearlman, 1995).

Limitations of Low Socioeconomic Status

Four important limitations are imposed on the lives of adolescents of low socioeconomic status.

Limited Alternatives Youths of low socioeconomic status have not been exposed to a variety of social and cultural settings. Vocationally, they have fewer opportunities. Poverty limits their educational and career attainments (Duncan and Rodgers, 1988). Socially, they are the nonjoiners, seldom going beyond the borders of kinship and neighborhood groups. Their limited experience and knowledge make it difficult to get out of or go beyond the narrow world in which they are growing up. Limited vision and experience restrict the possibilities and opportunities in their lives.

Helplessness, Powerlessness In the working world, the skills of low-socioeconomic-status adolescents are limited. They can exercise little autonomy or influence in improving their conditions, and they have little opportunity or knowledge to receive additional training. They are the most easily replaced workers. These youths have little political or social influence in their communities and, sometimes, inadequate legal protection of their rights as citizens.

Deprivation Adolescents of low socioeconomic status are aware of the affluence around them and the achievements of and benefits received by others. Their personal situations, however, make them constantly aware of their own abject status and "failure," resulting in bitterness, embarrassed withdrawal and isolation, or social deviation and rebellion.

Insecurity Low-socioeconomic-status individuals are at the mercy of life's unpredictable events: sickness, loss of work, injury, legal problems, school difficulties, family difficulties, and others. The lower their socioeconomic status, the more vulnerable they are to the stresses of life (Spencer, Dobbs, and Swanson, 1988). They strive just to provide themselves with the basic necessities of life and they never feel secure about their lives, in general.

Cycle of Poverty and Deprivation

The net effect of the limitations imposed on the lives of low-socioeconomic-status youths is to perpetuate poverty and cultural deprivation (Knapp and Shields, 1990). Figure 3.2 illustrates this cycle of poverty and cultural deprivation. The cycle begins at the top, with the low level of education. Moving clockwise, little education results in a low income, which results in a low level of living, which results in limited ability to manage or control the external environment. In fact, the adolescents are socialized to expect low education, a low level of living, and powerlessness. Their whole orientation perpetuates the life-style to which they have become accustomed.

Starting at the top of Figure 3.2 again and moving counterclockwise, the low level of education results in a low level of developed talent and ability and a low level of cultural experiences in the family. This, in turn, results in a narrow perception of the external world, which, along with the low level of living, contributes to limited ability to manage and control the environment. Because of discrimination and limitations imposed on them, parents, in one way or another, teach their children not to expect a very high income, level of living, or much education. Low-socioeconomic-status adolescents tend to be caught in a self-perpetuating cycle of poverty and cultural deprivation.

Low Level of Education

The ability to read and understand, to analyze situations and think critically about them, and to perform numerical calculations are important both to the individual and to society. Individuals with sound basic skills are more likely to attend and complete high school, perhaps go on to college, secure employment and higher wages, and live generally productive and happy lives. Individuals who are frustrated by deficiencies in their abilities to read and write are less likely to complete school, less likely to succeed in the labor market, and more likely to engage in behaviors

low socioeconomic status (low SES) those persons who are low social class and status, including cultural deprivation, and low income.

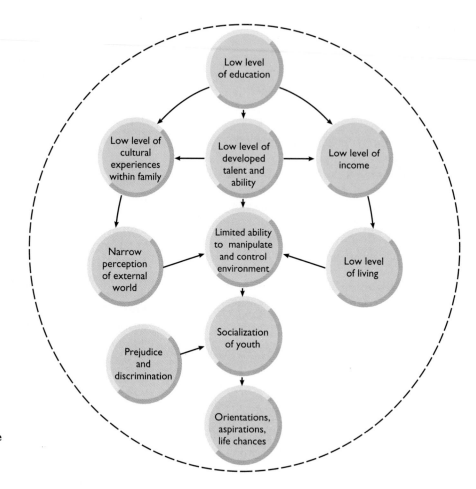

FIGURE 3.2 The Cycle of Poverty and Cultural Deprivation

with negative social consequences, such as teen pregnancy, welfare dependency, and crime.

Until recently, very little quantitative information was available about the specific nature or magnitude of the literacy problem. However, a National Assessment of Educational Progress (NAEP) studied by the Educational Testing Service (Johnson and Troppe, 1992) found that among 21- to 25-year-olds:

Only about three-quarters of Whites, two-fifths of Hispanics, and one-quarter of African Americans could locate information in a news article or in an almanac.

Only 25 percent of Whites, 7 percent of Hispanics, and 3 percent of African Americans could decipher a bus schedule.

Only two-fifths of Whites, one-fifth of Hispanics, and one-tenth of African Americans could directly determine the change

they were due from the purchase of a two-item restaurant meal.

This documented lack of basic skills required to perform adequately in society is an important challenge to our nation (Johnson and Troppe, 1992). Studies show that many of the differences between groups, such as between Whites and African Americans, are greatly reduced when the studies control for socioeconomic status.

Family Instability

Partly as a result of early marriages and economic struggles, low-socioeconomic-status families are much less stable than families of higher SES. The rates of divorce and separation increase as one goes down the socioeconomic scale (Rank, 1987). Illegitimacy rates also are higher among those of lower socioeconomic status, particularly among non-Whites. One reason is because they are more frequently sexually assaulted than are Whites. Another reason is that poorer pregnant teenagers are less likely to obtain abortions or to legitimate births through marriage. Entering into single parenthood at an early age bounds these individuals to poverty (Sullivan, 1993). Table 3.1 shows the birthrates of unmarried women of various ethnicities. These figures are of concern because they represent a large number of youths growing up without the benefit of a stable, two-parent family.

Female-Headed Households

Female-headed households are prevalent and persistent among the poor (Franklin, 1988). Research indicates that although a single-parent family may not be entirely disadvantaged (a father

may be a financial burden or a source of friction), the overall effects of the absence or only occasional presence of a father are detrimental to the emotional and social development of some adolescents. The difficulties appear in overdependence on the mother and lack of models in the development of masculine and feminine roles. There also may be more unsatisfactory peer-group relations and more feelings of inferiority and insecurity than among other youths. There is evidence that some adolescents react as if it is their fault that their fathers are absent. Sometimes, they have poor self-images and feel unlovable and self-derogating (Watson and Protinsky, 1988). These young people may see the love relationship between sexes as irregular and unstable. In addition, most young adults raised by single parents (primarily single mothers) tend to have lower educa-

TABLE 3.1   Birthrates of Unmarried Women

RACE AND HISPANIC ORIGIN	NUMBER OF BIRTHS (1,000)		BIRTHS TO UNMARRIED MOTHERS, PERCENT OF TOTAL	
	1990	1993	1990	1993
Total	4,158	4,000	26.6	31.0
White	3,290	3,150	16.9	23.6
Black	684	659	66.7	68.7
American Indian, Eskimo, Aleut	39	39	53.6	55.8
Asian and Pacific Islander[1]	142	153	(NA)	15.7
Filipino	26	30	15.9	17.7
Chinese	23	26	5.0	6.7
Japanese	9	9	9.6	10.0
Hawaiian	6	6	45.0	47.8
Hispanic origin[2]	595	654	36.7	40.0
Mexican	386	444	33.3	37.0
Puerto Rican	59	58	55.9	59.4
Cuban	11	12	18.2	21.0
Central and South American	83	92	41.2	45.2

NA Not Available

[1]Includes other races not shown separately.

[2]Hispanic persons may be of any race. Includes other types, not shown separately.

Source: U.S. National Center for Health Statistics, *Vital Statistics of the United States,* annual, *Monthly Vital Statistics Report* (Washington, DC: U.S. Government Printing Office, 1996/1997), and unpublished data.

tional, occupational, and economic attainment (Krein, 1986; Mueller and Cooper, 1986).

Two-Parent Families

Less attention has been paid to the poverty of children living in two-parent families, yet their economic deprivation is just as consequential for health, development, and future economic and social well-being. Economic instability and poverty are associated with well-documented negative effects on children. Poverty in childhood is linked with dropping out of school, low academic achievement, teenage pregnancy and childbearing, poor physical and mental health, delinquent behavior, and unemployment in adolescence and early adulthood. The longer children live in poverty, the poorer their cognitive development and social and emotional functioning become. The home environment, in particular, may play an important role in the process by which low income and economic stress affect child outcomes. Closer positive supervision and emotional support in the home improve children's socioemotional development, school performance, and self-worth, as well as prevent deviant behaviors. The role and behavior of parents may therefore mediate part of the disadvantage associated with low income (Harris and Marmer, 1996).

Working Mothers

Large numbers of low-socioeconomic-status mothers must work, even in intact families. A mother's part-time job apparently has a relatively stable and positive effect on girls from intact working-class families. What about mothers who work full time? Girls from these low-socioeconomic-status families often show strong affection for and strong dependency on the mother. They may show premature seriousness, somewhat more responsibility for housekeeping tasks than do adolescents of non-working mothers, and intense loyalty and strong emotional ties to the family. They are less likely to have stereotyped views of gender roles in the family than are daughters whose mothers do not work.

What is the effect of maternal employment on adolescent boys? The boys of part-time working mothers of the working-class group exhibit patterns that resemble those of the girls in this

group: They are generally active, responsible, and mature. However, the sons of full-time working mothers become more concerned with financial problems and may feel that their mother's working implies that something is wrong with the father as a provider. The father does not serve as an effective ideal, and the son less often chooses the father as a model. Some of these boys are rebellious toward adult authority and show signs of poor ego integration. They sometimes date heavily, which may reflect a lack of emotional security derived from the family. They do not have part-time jobs as often as other boys, nor do they have many organizational ties or leisure engagements.

Homelessness

A large number of the very poor are homeless. In some cities, there are two to four times as many low-income households as there are low-cost housing units available (Axelson and Dail, 1988). Because many of these families can't house or care for their adolescent children, some youths end up living on the streets, at least for a time (Bode, 1987). Some band together to live in abandoned buildings or apartments.

Homeless adolescents are subject to both physical and emotional stress. Many turn to prostitution, drug dealing, and other crimes in order to survive. A number are in need of psychiatric treatment. School performance is low due to lack of attendance or irregular attendance. Many homeless youths have multiple problems and they face a bleak future without some direct intervention (Hersch, 1988).

Childrearing Goals and Philosophies

Families of low socioeconomic status tend to be hierarchical, evidencing rigid parental relationships with adolescents. The parents are repeatedly seen as closed or inaccessible to the communication of adolescents. Parenting behavior is often affected by conditions of economic hardship. For example, assertive, harsh, and less supportive parenting behaviors are more likely to be employed in the context of economic hardship than in conditions of economic sufficiency (Abell, Clawson, Washing-

Many adolescents are homeless because their families cannot house or care for them, but some adolescents and their families find themselves living on the street together. This mother and daughter have been evicted from their city housing and are desperately seeking permission to stay at an emergency shelter.

ton, Bost, and Vaughn, 1996). The atmosphere is one of imperatives and absolutes, physical violence, and psychological distance, if not rejection, by the adults. Parent-child interaction patterns are rigid and oriented toward maintaining order, obedience, and discipline. The discipline—which is generally impulsive, harsh, and inconsistent—emphasizes physical punishment (even of adolescents) rather than verbal explanations and requests. As a group, adolescents from low-socioeconomic-status families report more problems with parents than do those from more privileged families.

Parents usually want to bring up their children to live decent, obedient, honest lives. They want their children to rise above them economically, and a good report card from school seems to promise upward movement. There is a great deal of concern over obedience, respect for adults, conformity to externally imposed standards, and staying out of trouble. Parents of low socioeconomic status are concerned with overt behavior, with the immediate situation, and not with what behavior means in terms of future development. Greater family control is exercised over adolescent daughters than sons, which is why many girls use marriage as an escape from their homes.

In large families, especially, parents seem to lack the time and will to control and give attention to their children as they get older. The mother may be preoccupied with a new baby, leaving the adolescents feeling left out and rejected. When problems arise with the adolescents, the parents feel hurt, bewildered, and powerless to remedy the situation. Frequently, the attitude of parents is, "We've done the best we could. You've made your bed; now you'll have to lie in it. There is nothing we can do." Their fatalistic attitude of accepting what comes is evident in the childrearing task.

Among low-socioeconomic-status youths, physical, social, and emotional emancipation from the family comes early and is often abrupt and psychologically premature. Adolescents do not yet feel ready or prepared to take their place in an adult world. Their social and emotional needs foster excessively dependent relationships with peers during the transition period from youth to adulthood.

Peer Orientation

Because adolescents from low-socioeconomic-status families tend to maintain weaker ties with parents than do youths from middle-class families, they form stronger, more lasting peer relationships. Those who report a low evaluation of parents and low self-esteem tend to be more peer oriented than those who have a high evaluation of parents (DiCindio et al., 1983). This may be so for at least two reasons.

Why Are Some People Poor?

The impact of poverty on the lives of adolescents is huge. The reasons for that poverty must be considered. Why are some people poor?

The following questionnaire will enable you to express your ideas. You can then compare your answers with those of a group of 220 undergraduates at the University of Canterbury in New Zealand (Stacey, Singer, and Ritchie, 1989).

INSTRUCTIONS

Circle the number by each reason that best expresses your opinion. In the scale below, a rating of 1 means you feel the reason is extremely important. A rating of 7 means you feel the reason is not important at all. Thus, the low numbers indicate high importance and the high numbers represent low importance, with 4 indicating moderate importance.

Internal Factors
Lack of effort and laziness	1 2 3 4 5 6 7
Poor money management	1 2 3 4 5 6 7
Lack of intelligence	1 2 3 4 5 6 7
Lack of physical attractiveness	1 2 3 4 5 6 7

Societal Factors
Economic and taxation systems are at fault	1 2 3 4 5 6 7
Salaries and wages are too low	1 2 3 4 5 6 7
Economic system does not create enough jobs	1 2 3 4 5 6 7
Financial system is prejudiced against them	1 2 3 4 5 6 7

Family Factors
Little money in the family	1 2 3 4 5 6 7
Little emphasis in the family on success	1 2 3 4 5 6 7
Family is unable to provide opportunities	1 2 3 4 5 6 7
Strain in family life	1 2 3 4 5 6 7

Luck
Bad luck	1 2 3 4 5 6 7
Factors beyond their control	1 2 3 4 5 6 7
Some persons are doomed to be poor	1 2 3 4 5 6 7
Unlucky in gambling, speculation, and taking chances	1 2 3 4 5 6 7

After filling out the questionnaire, add the numbers in each of the four categories and divide by four. This will give you the average score for each category. Compare your answer with the following:

Category	Average Score
Internal factors	4.70
Societal factors	3.63
Familial factors	3.40
Luck	4.75

Source: Adapted from B. G. Stacey, M. S. Singer, and G. Ritchie, "The Perception of Poverty and Wealth among Teenage University Students," *Adolescence,* 24 (1989): 193–207. Used by permission.

First, adolescents do not gain status through their familial identifications. The parents of these youths are not doctors, professors, or business executives. The adolescents, then, do not acquire status from the identity of their parents. In fact, they are keenly aware of their parents' lack of status in the community, and therefore their own lack of status. When a group in an achievement-oriented society cannot gain status in socially acceptable ways, then theft, extortion, narcotics, assault, sexual misconduct, vandalism, or other antisocial expressions may become the means of gaining status and recognition. The peer group replaces the family as the adolescent's primary reference group.

Second, low-socioeconomic-status adolescents become more peer oriented than parent oriented because of their need for security. In the ghetto, they need their gangs to protect lives; outside crime neighborhoods, they need their gangs for companionship, direction, and fulfillment.

Social Outcasts

Many adolescents of low socioeconomic status are socialized differently than middle-class youths. They have their own manner of dress, speech, and behavior. Those who seem loud, ill mannered, or aggressive are scorned by middle-class society. Those who withdraw, have low self-esteem, and are shy do not participate in many social functions and groups. In addition, inappropriate clothing and inadequate neatness and cleanliness invite criticism.

Ordinarily, school is an important part of the social world of adolescents, but prejudicial treatment by middle-class adults and students makes the low-socioeconomic-status adolescents social outcasts. They are likely to find themselves more and more socially isolated as they proceed through the grades, and, as a result, tend to seek friendships with out-of-school youths. Sometimes the association with other out-of-school youths influences adolescents to drop out of school.

Neighborhood Danger

Poverty is even more pernicious because of its association with a host of other social conditions, especially conditions that adolescents find in their neighborhoods. Many teens, as well as their families, are trapped in the inner cities and urban areas that are characterized by crime, violence, and a persistent sense of peril. Adolescents who live in these neighborhoods may be particularly likely to fall prey to their surrounding conditions and experience negative outcomes. Many, however, beat the odds. They avoid problem behavior, maintain high levels of physical and psychological well-being, graduate from high school, and move successfully into adult roles (Bowen and Chapman, 1996; Jarrett, 1995; Galbo and Demetrulias, 1996).

Mental Health

The lack of emotional security and lack of stability in low SES homes and particular patterns of childrearing lead to a high rate of psychological problems and mental illness among adolescents (see Special issue, 1988, p. 11). The incidence of schizophrenia, the most common psychosis of adolescents as well as adults, is significantly associated with social class. Furthermore, if they are hospitalized, low-socioeconomic-status adolescents are less likely to receive adequate treatment; are less often accepted for psychotherapy (partly due to a lower IQ level); are assigned less-skilled staff members; are treated for shorter periods with less intensive techniques; and are less likely to improve in psychotherapy.

African American Adolescents

Most Blacks have been in the United States for generations, having descended from enslaved Africans. There are also more recent arrivals from Haiti, Jamaica, and other places. Each of these groups has its own culture. Here, we will concentrate on African Americans.

Legacy of Discrimination

For generations, African American families, especially those of lower SES, were forced to assume an inferior role in order to get along in White society. In the past, getting along meant sitting in the back of the bus and avoiding all "Whites-only" restaurants, restrooms, recreational facilities, theaters, and playgrounds. African American parents had to teach their children the so-called Black role. As one mother bluntly put it, "You have to let them know before they get out of their own backyard." African American children left their homes for school at their peril if they had not learned where they could sit and what they could or could not do if they got hungry or thirsty. At 5 years old, just as surely as at 15 or 25 years old, they had to know their place. One of the important lessons to learn was that no matter how unjustly they were treated, they had to control anger and conceal hostility. They had to be subservient and polite in the face of provocation, and walk with their eyes straight ahead, unmoved by taunts and jeers. Above all, they had to ignore insults and never argue or get in a fight with a White person. Black parents felt that they had to use severe measures to instill fear in their children as their best protection, or White society would punish them more severely.

Richard Wright (1937) wrote of his "first lesson in how to live as a Negro." He was badly cut as a result of a fight with White boys who threw bottles at him and his friends.

> I sat brooding on my front steps, nursing my wound and waiting for my mother to come home from work. . . . I could just feel in my bones that she would understand. . . . I grabbed her hand and babbled out the whole story. She examined my wound, then slapped me.
>
> "How come yuh didn't hide?" she asked me. "How come yuh always fightin?"
>
> I was outraged and bawled. Between sobs I told her that I didn't have any trees or hedges to hide behind. . . .
>
> She grabbed a barrel stave, dragged me home, stripped me naked, and beat me till I had a fever of one hundred and two. She would smack my rump with the stave, and, while the skin was still smarting, impart to me gems of Jim Crow wisdom. I was never to throw cinders any more. . . . I was never, never under any conditions to fight white folks again. And they were absolutely right in clouting me with the broken milk bottle. (Wright, 1937)

Not all African American families used these means to protect their children from the wrath of Whites. Upper-class African American families told their children to avoid fights or brawls with Whites, not because it was dangerous but because it was beneath their social status. These families tried to isolate their children from racial discrimination as much as possible by outsegregating the White segregationists.

New Image

The image of Black people has changed greatly and continues to evolve. In the second half of the twentieth century, a series of sweeping judicial decisions that promised to desegregate Blacks and Whites contributed to the formation of a new image of Black people in the minds of Whites and Blacks alike. Changes were seen in the emergence of a significant Black middle class, the rise of political leadership among Blacks, enfranchisement, the regulation of fair employment practices, and efforts to discover their heritage and culture. With a new confidence and sense of security, young African Americans no longer give the impression that they feel inferior or are a helpless minority. More and more, African American adolescents are accepting the fact that they are human beings of worth, with a positive identity, united with each other in proclaiming their admission into the human race and into middle-class culture (Mboya, 1986).

Contemporary Segregation

On May 17, 1954, the U.S. Supreme Court overruled the principle of "separate but equal" oppor-

Multiple factors determine the level of self-esteem and self-image of African American adolescents. These include graduating from high school, positive relationships with their families, and family approval.

tunity in education (Merrit, 1983). In 1956, Dr. Martin Luther King, Jr., launched his passive resistance movement against the segregated bus system of Montgomery, Alabama. Although the court battles have been fought and won, there is still considerable disparity today between White and Black income, education, and other standards of living; segregation continues to be a fact of life.

Unequal Education

In spite of the legal efforts to ensure equal education for all citizens, African American adolescents still do not enjoy that privilege. In terms of the total number of years of schooling, young African Americans have almost caught up with Whites. If only those who are 25 years old and older are considered, the educational attainment of these young African Americans almost equals the attainment of Whites. Figure 3.3 shows the educational attainment of these two races in 1995. If quality of education is considered, however, African Americans still lag far behind Whites.

The level of academic attainment among African American adolescents depends on a number of factors, one of which is family income. Greater family financial resources is associated with more supportive and harmonious family interactions and with lower levels of interparental conflicts. These, in turn, have a positive influence on the academic success of the children in the family. Parents who have more education are more likely to participate in their children's school experiences. Thus, parental involvement in schooling, family interaction quality, and per-capita income all have effects on adolescents' development (Brody, Stoneman, and Flor, 1995).

Occupational Aspirations

In general, African American adolescents achieve lower grades and have higher dropout rates than do White students. Although there has been an increase in the number of African Americans reaching higher socioeconomic levels in recent decades, several authors have pointed out that the actual *percentage* has declined.

It must be emphasized that *not all African Americans have lower educational and vocational aspir-*

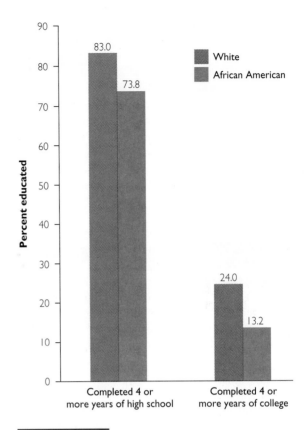

FIGURE 3.3   Educational Attainment, African Americans and Whites, Age 25 and Older

Source: U.S. Bureau of the Census, *Statistical Abstract of the United States, 1996* (Washington, DC: U.S. Government Printing Office, 1996).

ations than do Whites. One study of African American males and females enrolled in college revealed some interesting facts. The African Americans in this study expected to be making about $10,000 a year more at the age 35 than did the European American students. They also expected to attain a higher level of education, and the predicted probability of being successful was higher than that of Whites (Ganong, Coleman, Thompson, and Goodwin-Watkins, 1996).

The African Americans in this study clearly showed higher aspirations, but how their aspirations were formed is a matter of conjecture. Perhaps because societal views of what it means to be successful are rather constricted, intelligent young African Americans are often encouraged to aspire to status and wealth by becoming lawyers or doctors. This is the case whether the young person's abilities and interests are in those areas or not. Another explanation is that African American young adults view education as their main chance for successful careers—an access to the American Dream. African American students are aware of barriers they may face, and more perceive that education is a prerequisite to success. It may also be that some African Americans value success and education more and, as a result, they have greater expectations for themselves.

Desegregation Efforts

Because most African American adolescents live in segregated neighborhoods, there is little opportunity for interracial contact. Consequently, desegregation advocates of the 1960s and 1970s suggested that if students of different races were brought together in school, a "melting pot" effect would ensue, encouraging interethnic contact and the assimilation of middle-class values for minority students. The intent of school busing was to foster positive race relations between minority and majority groups and to offer equal educational opportunities for all students.

These efforts were only partially successful. Research has shown that some schools and communities are better equipped and willing to foster positive race relations than are others (Miller, 1989). Consequently, some students are more integrated than others, depending on the school. Offering minorities the same educational opportunities as majority students does not automatically ensure high levels of interracial contact or guarantee the quality of race relations (Miller, 1989). Also, researchers today are refocusing on the belief that maintaining a group's ethnicity and customs can serve as a vehicle in promoting self-confidence in that group's youths, and that taking pride in cultural heritage is preferred over losing identity and blending in to the "melting pot."

Unemployment Rates

When the unemployment rates (percent of civilian labor force) of non-White and White teenagers are compared, the differences are striking (Billingsley, 1988). As Figure 3.4 shows, African American teenagers have a far greater unemploy-

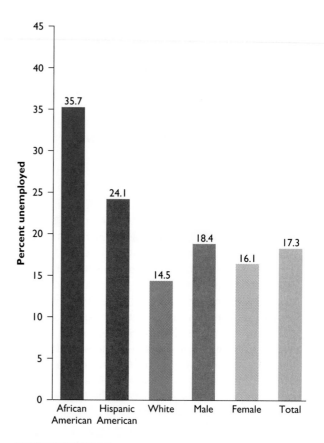

FIGURE 3.4   African American, Hispanic American, and White Unemployment Rates, Ages 16 to 19 (1995)

Source: U.S. Bureau of the Census, *Statistical Abstract of the United States, 1996* (Washington, DC: U.S. Government Printing Office, 1996).

ment rate than their White contemporaries. About one-third of African American teenagers were unemployed in 1995, leaving large numbers wandering the streets with nothing to do.

Income

In spite of the fact that the income of both Whites and African Americans has been increasing, the income gap between Whites and non-Whites has *widened,* not closed (U.S. Bureau of the Census, 1996). In every occupational category, African Americans are paid less than Whites for the same work. Unequal income, unequal education, segregation, and discrimination are still a reality.

Legally, African American adolescents should have equal rights with White youths; in actuality, complete equality is still a goal to be attained.

Adolescent Pregnancy

The incidence of unwed pregnancy among adolescents has skyrocketed since the 1960s (Murry, 1992). Teenage pregnancy among African Americans is especially high—higher than among any other racial or ethnic group in the United States (Pete and DeSantis, 1990). Black teenagers are more than twice as likely to give birth out of wedlock than are White teenagers (Rogers and Lee, 1992). Of the total African American babies born, 69 percent are born to unmarried mothers (U.S. Bureau of the Census, 1996).

Adolescent pregnancy affects the emotional, social, physical, and economic well-being of the teenage parent and child. Few of these young mothers consider the option of putting their babies up for adoption (Pete and DeSantis, 1990). Furthermore, there is a low level of demand for the formal adoption of infants in the African American community (Kalmuss, 1992). Since most of the girls are minors, marriage requires parental consent, which few parents feel they should give. As a consequence, the young women decide to care for their children as single parents, with whatever help they can get from their families (Mayfield-Brown, 1989). They usually continue living with their families.

Extended-kin networks are prevalent in the African American community. This has several effects. The supply of African American infants placed for formal adoption is reduced. Furthermore, the practice of extended-kin support reduces the costs associated with early childrearing for African American teenagers. For example, the greater likelihood that young African American women will reside with their own mothers after giving birth makes it easier for them to continue their schooling, which diminishes the educational and economic consequences of early childrearing for these women. The buffering function of the kin network, in turn, decreases the motivation for many young African American pregnant women to consider other pregnancy resolution options. Other researchers have noted that the supportive function of the kin network begins to break down

for these young mothers over time, particularly as they have additional children. African American teenage mothers of second-born children are much more likely to live in "mother-alone" families than are mothers of first-born children (Kalmuss, 1992).

Other research indicates that some African American pregnant adolescents have significantly lower total functional support—that is, lower emotional and tangible support—than do Whites. The reason is that the African American families generally have the least amount of support to give, even though the proportion of support provided by the families is greatest for this ethnic group (Koniak-Griffin, Lominska, and Brecht, 1993).

Some unwed adolescent fathers are willing to take some responsibility for parenting their children (Fernandez, Ruch-Ross, and Montague, 1993). This is more likely if the fathers have a good self-image, which enables them to be more psychologically prepared to handle fatherhood (Christmon, 1990). Obviously, their ability to contribute to the welfare of their child depends on economic circumstances. They are also influenced greatly by their own parents' attitudes toward involvement with the child (Marsiglio, 1989).

Many teenage pregnancies are accompanied by problems from the beginning (Franklin, 1988). These young women usually wait longer to get prenatal care than older women, who are usually better off financially. Pregnancy for African American teenagers is more likely to present medical complications than it is for adults (Pete and DeSantis, 1990). The percentage of babies with low birth weight is 14 percent among African Americans, compared with 7 percent among Whites (U.S. Bureau of the Census, 1996). Infant mortality rates are high. The mothers and their children suffer because of inadequate resources to care for the children properly. A greater percentage of African American children are raised below the poverty level than are those of any other ethnic or racial group—43 percent of Blacks, 16 percent of Whites, and 41 percent of Hispanics (U.S. Bureau of the Census, 1996).

Adolescent Mothers

Adolescent mothers and their children begin their lives together at an overwhelming disadvantage.

Females who become mothers during adolescence are more likely to drop out of school and to earn low wages, and are less likely to find stable employment and to marry, compared to women who bear children during their twenties. Poverty represents the greatest difficulty in parenting. Raising children in poverty often results in living in poor-quality neighborhoods with limited exposure to individuals who have achieved educationally and occupationally. Poverty and social isolation are also associated with greater incidents of punitive parenting behavior. For example, poor, single mothers are more likely to scold and hit their children.

Inadequate parenting among adolescent mothers has been attributed to poor childrearing skills and elevated stress. Increased stress experienced by young mothers may be attributed to the combined demands associated with adolescent development and, simultaneously, parenthood. Too often, the stress of parenting overwhelms adolescent mothers, resulting in their lashing out at their children. Haskett, Johnson, and Miller (1994) reported that approximately half of the adolescent mothers included in their study were at risk of abusing their children. Those at greatest risk were young adolescent mothers who tended to have limited social support (Mulsow and Murry, 1996).

Family Strengths

Many of the problems that beset the African American families are due to racial discrimination and the economic conditions under which many live (Crawley, 1988). These families struggle to survive against the backdrop of high unemployment, disproportionate numbers of poor, and retrenchment of social programs important to them (Crawley, 1988). However, African American families also show a number of positive characteristics that have enabled them to function and survive in a hostile social environment (Broman, 1988; Bryant and Coleman, 1988).

Strong Kinship Bonds   Extended families are common in many minority populations. African Americans, in general, are exposed to far more

HIGHLIGHT

Those Who Make It

In spite of prejudices and handicaps that they face, some Black adolescents achieve a high level of academic and social success. One study of rural Black adolescents from the Southeast showed that those who succeeded had several characteristics in common:

1. Close and supportive family networks with strong direction from parents.
2. Highly developed social network outside of family.
3. Strong identification with positive role models.
4. Active participation in school and church activities with limited activity in community activities.
5. Positive educational experiences, with school providing the major social outlet.
6. Strong future orientation based on realism.
7. High educational and occupational goals and expectations.
8. Moderate to highly conservative moral attitudes.
9. Strong religious convictions.
10. Positive but realistic view of self with the ability to accept responsibility for self and behavior, the ability to lead and follow, and an internal locus of control.
11. Well-developed outside interests although limited in scope.
12. Limited degree of Black consciousness or of racial identity (that is, race was not an important factor in their social interactions).
13. Well-developed views on the nature of success.

Source: C. C. Lee, "Successful Rural Black Adolescents: A Psychological Profile," *Adolescence, 20* (Spring 1985): 140. Reprinted by permission.

stress than Whites, but family members rely on one another for care, strength, and mutual support (Taylor, Casten, and Flickinger, 1993). According to one study, African American youths reported significantly higher levels of parental control and family intimacy. As a result, they described their friendships as somewhat less intimate, perceived less peer pressure, and reported a lower need for approval from peers than White youths in the sample (Giordano, Cernkovich, and DeMaris, 1993).

Favorable Attitude toward the Elderly   At all socioeconomic levels, African Americans have a more favorable attitude toward the elderly than do Whites. One reason for the high degree of respect for the elderly family members is the strong kinship bond just discussed.

Adaptable Roles   Husband-wife relationships in African American families are more egalitarian than in other races, with African American husbands sharing significantly in the performance of household tasks. Roles of all family members are flexible. For instance, an uncle or grandfather can assume the vacated position of a father or mother.

Strong Religious Orientation   Religion has been a source of solace for downtrodden people, as well as a vehicle for rebellion and social advancement. The African American church—through preaching and teaching, symbols, belief systems, and rituals—remains the glue that binds families and communities together. Young people who attend church have a relatively high level of faith and support that helps them deal with the stresses in their lives (McCreary, Slavin, and Berry, 1996).

Mexican American Adolescents

Mexican Americans are the second largest minority group in the United States. Adolescents 15 to 19 years of age constitute about 19 percent of the total Mexican American population, or over 1.6 million (U.S. Bureau of the Census, 1996). About 87 percent reside in Arizona, California, Colorado, New Mexico, and Texas; the vast majority live in California and Texas.

Various terms are used to describe Mexican Americans. The preferences vary by region, ranging from *Latin American* or *Latino* in Texas, *Spanish American* in New Mexico, *Mexican* in Arizona and eastern Colorado, to *Mexican American* and **Chicano** in California. The term *Chicano* is associated with working-class males who have been struggling for fair economic treatment. The term *Hispanic* refers to those in this minority group who speak Spanish. In this book, we will primarily use the term *Mexican American*.

Segregation and Housing

Mexican American youths, like White youths, are primarily urbanized: 79 percent live in urban areas. Many live in cities and go to work as migrant workers on farms. About 75 percent of all Mexican-Americans are segregated in residential ghettos called **colonias** or **barrios** (neighborhoods) (U.S. Bureau of the Census, 1996). Some Mexican Americans, however, such as those in Los Angeles, have been able to move to areas outside the central city.

Education

Many Mexican American children enter school without the kind of cognitive experiences on which successful school life depends. Often, they begin school at a grade level below their White peers. In addition, there is a language problem for some children whose parents do not speak English at home (Singh and Hernandez-Gantes, 1996). The restricted and authoritarian environment at home also discourages conversational facility in English, free thinking, and autonomy. Most Mexican American parents are concerned about their children's education, but the opportunities are limited. Schools in the barrios often are poorly funded, and the educational programs offered are inferior. Because the parents of many Hispanic students have very low educational levels, which, in turn, contribute to low socioeco-

Chicano (Chicana)   term for Mexican American.

colonias or barrios   colonies or districts of Spanish-speaking people.

nomic levels, it is difficult for them to advocate for their children's educational needs.

Another factor in the overall poor scholastic performance of Mexican American adolescents is the teacher. Some White teachers are hostile to Mexican American children, especially if they persist in speaking Spanish or if they speak with a considerable accent. The teachers often do not understand Spanish, Mexican American culture, or the sociocultural factors affecting the classroom behavior of the children.

Under these circumstances, it is not surprising that scholastic performance of Mexican American children is poorer than that of White children. Table 3.2 shows the percentage of Mexican Americans and Whites aged 25 and older with designated years of schooling. Segregation has been, and continues to be, a major obstacle to the attainment of equal educational opportunity for a substantial number of Hispanic students (DeBlassie and DeBlassie, 1996).

Partially as a result of low levels of education, Mexican American men and women are overrepresented in low-level jobs. These jobs are the most abundant and require low levels of training (Arbona and Novy, 1991). A comparison between academically successful and academically unsuccessful Mexican American high school students revealed that the unsuccessful group came from families that were larger, poorer, and more rural than the successful students' families. The successful group was found to score higher on modernism, to be more stably acculturated, to have a clearer sense of themselves, to have higher occupational aspirations and expectations, and tended to desire jobs with greater responsibility and stability than did the unsuccessful group (Manaster, Chan, and Safady, 1992).

Families

Mexican American families tend to be larger than White American ones, averaging one more child per family than Whites (Jorgensen and Adams, 1988). In general, children with more siblings have less chance of realizing their occupational aspirations than do those from smaller families. Mexican American boys with four or more siblings show as much as 10 points lower IQ than those with only one sibling.

Favoring Mexican American families is the fact that the marriages are much more stable than those of either Whites or African Americans. The greater stability holds true even when statistical allowances are made for differences in age, age at first marriage, education, and place of residence (Staples and Mirande, 1980). Apparently, the traditional, paternalistic Mexican American family is highly cohesive. The mother is especially close to the children and plays an important role in their care (Martinez, 1988). Extended families are common. There is some evidence, however, that the traditional emphasis on the family is beginning to decline. Mexican American women, who formerly found their major role to be that of wives and mothers, are increasingly going to work outside the home. This is particularly true among many college-educated wives and among those with preschool-aged children. What effect these changes will have on marital stability remains to be seen.

Socialization of Adolescents

Mexican American parents often emphasize some values that hinder the advancement of adolescents in an individualistic, highly competitive, materialistic society. An emphasis on family ties and dependency, authority, living in the present, and politeness are not conducive to independence, achievement, deferred gratification, and success. For example, the older son's role in the Mexican American family is an extension of that of the father: protector, orderer, and guardian of the younger children. Excessive family dependency

---

TABLE 3.2 Percentage of People Aged 25 or Older with Designated Years of Schooling (1994)

	Mexican Americans	Whites
Four or more years of college	6.3	22.4
Four years of high school	46.7	82

Source: U.S. Bureau of the Census, Department of Commerce, *Statistical Abstract of the United States, 1996* (Washington, DC: U.S. Government Printing Office, 1996).

Mexican American adolescents often enjoy the stability of traditional familial and cultural cohesiveness. This family is celebrating "Quincinera," the 15th birthday of their twin daughters.

hinders the development of initiative and autonomy, particularly when sons are overindulged and given much social freedom but little motivation to succeed in school or at work. Mexican American daughters are closely supervised and taught primarily to take their place in the home. The emphasis on honor and respectful conduct leads to extraordinary courtesy and politeness. Young people are taught to show respect, obedience, and humility. (In traditional homes, the answer to the parent's call is "*Mande usted*"—"At your command.")

In school or work, Mexican American adolescents are not prodded to take risks but to be careful not to bring shame on themselves or their families. They are inclined to adopt in wholesale fashion their parents' commitments to occupational and ideological choices and activities (Abraham, 1986). This is one reason why comparisons between Mexican American and White American adolescents show that the latter are much more competitive. Mexican Americans are concerned with personal gain but more often avoid competitive behavior. Furthermore, Mexican American children are not expected to defer gratification but to live in the present. Such an orientation is not conducive to upward mobility. The lack of independence training in the family, the negative self-identity of many Mexican American youths,

and the prejudicial treatment in the schools also interfere with achievement.

Heterosexual Relationships

When Mexican American males reach adolescence, they are expected to take an interest in females and to talk and act in the sexual sphere to demonstrate their virility. There are those girls who the males exploit for sexual purposes to prove their *machismo* (manhood) and those who they idealize and eventually marry. Dating is frowned on, but the practice is difficult to suppress in the United States. However, a matchmaker (*portador*) is still called into service when mate selection reaches a serious stage. Some youths prefer to bypass the elaborate ritual of courtship and the expenses of the wedding by eloping.

Sex Education

The importance of modesty is highly emphasized, especially for girls, who are not supposed to learn about sexual relations by either conversation or

---

machismo   Spanish term for maleness or manhood.

PERSONAL ISSUES

Stresses of Adolescent Mexican American Immigrants

Many Mexican American adolescents have only recently immigrated to the United States. A study of 244 immigrant adolescents in five schools in Los Angeles revealed the stresses that these youths faced when adjusting to their new environment (Zambrana and Silva-Palacios, 1989). The following table lists 24 sources of stress in rank order of decreasing stress. Items were scored on a 5-point Likert-type scale from 1, indicating not stressful, to 5, indicating extremely stressful.

The perceived stress items that ranked highest were related to family—parents going to the hospital, a family member arrested, leaving relatives and friends, and not enough money to pay bills. The second-highest-ranking group of stresses were related to language and ethnic dif-

ferences, especially at school—other kids making fun of the way you speak or dress, talking a different language, or calling you names because you are Hispanic and not born in the United States. Some of the students were pressured to speak Spanish at home, and were teased at home for not speaking Spanish well. Others were pressured to speak English at home.

Another source of stress is related to social adjustments—living in a crime-ridden neighborhood, being pressured to fight, moving to another neighborhood, and not having enough Hispanic friends. The more acculturated Mexican American adolescents become, the more susceptible they are to antisocial peer pressure (Wall, Power, and Arbona, 1993).

Mean Levels of Stressors on Mexican American Adolescents

Item	Mean Level	Item	Mean Level
Parents getting sick and going to hospital	3.9	Being called bad names because you were not born in the United States	2.7
Having a family member arrested	3.7	When other kids make fun of the way you dress	2.7
Father or mother drinking	3.4	Living in a house with many people	2.7
Living in poor neighborhood where there is crime	3.4	Not having enough Hispanic or Latino friends	2.6
Leaving relatives, friends behind when moving	3.3	When you speak in one language and your friends speak in another	2.6
Parents not making enough to pay bills	3.2	Being pressured to speak only Spanish at home	2.5
When other kids make fun of way you speak English	3.0	Being teased at home about not knowing how to speak Spanish well	2.4
Not understanding the teacher when he or she explains something in English	3.0	Being pressured to speak only English at home	2.3
Getting in trouble at school	3.0	Making new friends at school	2.2
When other kids (not Latino) talk about you	3.0	Having to take care of your brothers and sisters	2.2
Moving from one neighborhood to another	2.9	Having to go to church	2.1
Being pressured by friends to get into fights	2.8		
Being called bad names because you are Hispanic	2.8		

Source: R. E. Zambrana and V. Silva-Palacios, "Gender Differences in Stress among Mexican Immigrant Adolescents in Los Angeles, CA," *Journal of Adolescent Research, 4,* pp. 426–442, copyright © 1989 by Sage Publications. Reprinted by permission of Sage Publications, Inc.

experience. The result is a very low level of scientific knowledge about human sexuality (Scott et al., 1988). Mothers do not discuss sex, and many do not even discuss menstruation, with daughters.

The uninformed daughter is left on her own to learn about menstruation and sexual relations in marriage. As a result, the honeymoon period and early days of marriage are often upsetting and painful experiences for them. Because of the negative, repressive attitudes they learn, it is difficult for wives to care much about sex or enjoy it as much as their husbands do.

Such attitudes have resulted in a lower level of sexual intercourse among Mexican American adolescent girls than among non-Hispanic Whites. Pregnancy, however, is more common among Mexican American adolescents than among non-Hispanic Whites primarily because of the lack of use of adequate birth control measures (Remez, 1991). Mexican American adolescents are encouraged to preserve their virginity until marriage. This socialization partially explains the later age of first premarital sex of Mexican American adolescent women relative to their non-Hispanic White counterparts (Slonim-Nevo, 1992).

When unmarried Mexican American adolescent girls do get pregnant, they have more contact and receive more support from their extended families than do White adolescent mothers. They are also less likely to live alone and are more likely to live with a boyfriend or to marry and live with their spouse than are White adolescents. This is consistent with Mexican American familistic orientation, where the family is perceived as the center of emotional security (Codega, Pasley, and Kreutzer, 1990).

Sex education for Mexican American boys comes primarily from other male friends and from experience. Boys tell one another about and seek experiences with promiscuous girls and prostitutes who help them learn about the physical aspects of sex. In addition to being a high risk factor for sexually transmitted diseases such as the acquired immune deficiency syndrome (AIDS), such education is also negative and exploitative, for boys learn to use girls rather than to share companionship, love, and sex with them.

Puerto Rican Adolescents

In 1995, there were 2.7 million Puerto Ricans living in the United States. They represent the third largest minority group in the country (see Figure 3.1) (U.S. Bureau of the Census, 1996). About 69 percent of all Puerto Ricans in the United States live in the Northeast, with New York City having the largest population. The remaining 31 percent are scattered across the country. One-fifth of the Puerto Ricans are of adolescent age.

As United States citizens, Puerto Ricans may enter the country and travel freely within it. This fact, combined with overpopulation and much poverty on their island, contributed to a rapid immigration of Puerto Ricans to the mainland in the decades following World War II. In recent years, immigration has declined, however. In fact, more Puerto Ricans now emigrate from the mainland to the island than the other way around (Wright, 1990).

Adolescents constitute one-fifth of the U.S. Puerto Rican population. Most Puerto Rican families live in the Northeast.

Family Life

Puerto Ricans have a profound sense of family. Most women view motherhood as their central role. Their concept of motherhood is based on the female capacity to bear children and on the notion of *marianismo*, which presents the Virgin Mary as a role model. *Marianismo* implies that a woman finds her identity and derives her life's greatest satisfaction through motherhood.

Ideal family relations are described by two interrelating themes—family interdependence and family unity. Family interdependence fits within the Puerto Rican orientation to life, which stresses that the individual cannot do everything and still do it well. Older Puerto Rican women especially adhere strongly to the value of family interdependence. It influences patterns of mutual assistance with their children as well as expectations of support. The older women expect their adult children to take care of them during old age.

Family unity emphasizes the desirability of close and intimate kin ties—members get along well and keep in frequent contact during separations. Puerto Ricans believe that the greater the degree of unity in the family, the greater emphasis family members will place on interdependence and familial obligation.

In spite of their emphasis on family, Puerto Ricans have the highest rate of divorce and of female-headed households of any Hispanic group (Vega, 1990). The rates are almost as high as those of African Americans, who have the highest rates. In 1993, 53 percent of U.S. Puerto Rican families consisted of married couples, 41 percent were headed by female householders with no spouse present, and 6 percent were headed by male householders with no spouse present (U.S. Bureau of the Census, 1994).

A growing proportion of Puerto Rican children are born outside of formal marriages or of informal coresidential unions. Among children born into intact unions, an increasing number are the offspring of informal unions. Puerto Rican children face high and rising risks of experiencing family disruption during childhood. Among those who are born into single-parent families, the duration of time with the single mother is fairly brief, since very often the children must be cared for by someone else (Landale and Hauan, 1992).

The very high rate of births to unmarried mothers is one of the most important reasons for the high percentage of female householders with no spouse present (Fennelly, Cornwell, and Casper, 1992). In 1993, among Puerto Ricans in the United States, 59 percent of all live births were to unmarried mothers; 22 percent of all births were to teenage mothers (U.S. Bureau of the Census, 1996). Puerto Rican mothers have a greater risk than other Hispanic women of experiencing serious problems such as low-birth-weight infants and infant mortality (Klitsch, 1991).

What are the reasons for the high rate of marital disruption among Puerto Ricans? Puerto Rican women marry young, often because of premarital pregnancy, which is associated with a high probability of divorce (Frisbie, 1986). Living in a crowded metropolitan area results in higher probability of marital disruption. The increasing number of Puerto Rican women joining the labor force is an important factor contributing to the high divorce rate, because the women have increased economic independence and can therefore end unhappy marriages (Canabal, 1990). Immigration of whole families to the mainland presents problems of adjustment and acculturation of children, often causing additional strains on the family.

Puerto Ricans who were born and raised in Puerto Rico and who immigrate to the mainland generally establish modified patriarchal family structures (Cooney, Rogler, Hurrell, and Ortiz, 1982). Sex roles are segregated, as evidenced by gender-based terminology: *trabajo de hombre* (men's work) and *trabajo de mujer* (women's work). Puerto Ricans who are born, raised, and married in the United States are gradually establishing egalitarian roles (Rogler and Procidano, 1989). The upwardly mobile younger wives in New York City, for example, see egalitarian spouse relations as one component of marital satisfaction.

Education, Employment, and Income

The problems confronting Puerto Rican families are partly a result of the adverse economic and social conditions under which they live. In 1995, 39 percent of adult Puerto Ricans had less than 12 years of schooling. Only 11 percent had 4 years of college or more. Puerto Ricans had the highest rate (11 percent) of unemployment of all Hispanics (U.S. Bureau of the Census, 1996). As a consequence, income was low. The median family income in 1994 was $20,929—about 87 percent that of Hispanics in general. Some 36 percent of Puerto Ricans in the United States lived below the poverty level.

Research has indicated that low education is associated not only with low family income but also with high fertility rates and an increase in female-headed households (Moore and Pachon, 1985). The greater the educational attainment, the higher the marital stability. However, given the high poverty rate of female-headed families, Puerto Rican children risk experiencing sustained poverty during childhood (Landale and Hauan, 1992).

Implications for Adolescents

Considering the prevalence of single-parent households, Puerto Rican adolescents often lack appropriate parental role models with whom they can identify, and therefore they lack adaptive behaviors and values to imitate during adolescence. Identity formation among minority adolescents includes discovering, on a personal basis, what it means to be a member of a specific group. But characteristics of the group are changing or are often confusing (McLoyd, 1990). Puerto Rican adolescents experience an identity crisis compounded by strong intercultural and intergenerational conflicts. They experience conflict between the cultural values represented by their parents and the cultural values they experience on the city streets. They also face language and socioeconomic barriers to acculturation.

Many Puerto Rican youths are compelled to live in abject poverty, in the poorest slum areas of the city, where crime rates are astronomical, drug use is rampant, and good schools and quality education are scarce. They have to struggle just to survive on the streets. These realities are often the reason why many disillusioned families return to Puerto Rico. The problem these youths face have been linked to higher prevalence of mental disorders, anxiety and depression, drug and alcohol abuse, delinquency, and lower self-esteem, com-

pared with populations of African Americans and Whites (Costantino, Malgady, and Rogler, 1988).

Native American Adolescents

The number of Native Americans of all ages in the United States is dependent on the definition of what constitutes a Native American. At the present, the Bureau of Indian Affairs (BIA) defines *Native Americans* as those with one-fourth or more Native American blood. The latest census figures (1995) indicate that 2,242,000 persons identify themselves as Native Americans (U.S. Bureau of the Census Commerce, 1996). No one knows with certainty how many of these have at least one-fourth Native American ancestry. The Bureau is concerned primarily with those Native Americans living on or near land under some form of federal supervision. In 1995, this included approximately 808,000 people. This leaves over 1.4 million who have migrated off reservations or federal trust lands. The number of Native Americans living both on and off reservations continues to increase.

Of the total population of Native Americans, 43 percent live in the West and Southwest: Arizona, New Mexico, California, and Oklahoma (Utter, 1993). Arizona and Oklahoma represent two extremes in tribal representation. Arizona has the largest number of Native Americans, as well as the largest single tribe—the Navaho, who live on the largest reservation in the United States. Oklahoma, in contrast, has the largest number of tribes—about 60. This land was once Indian Territory, to which Native Americans from all over the country were moved when their tribal lands were coveted by Whites. Because these displaced Native Americans were newcomers living on land next to their White neighbors (who had also recently immigrated), most Oklahoma Native Americans lived among the general population, although there are some remote reservations in the state. In

---

marianismo in Puerto Rican society, the implication that a woman finds her greatest satisfaction through motherhood.

states such as New Mexico and the Dakotas, the majority of the Native American population is still today confined to original reservations. In other states—such as North Carolina, California, and New York—the majority either resisted movement to reservations or now live on land where government control has terminated. Table 3.3 shows the 1990 population of the largest reservations in the United States.

Since the beginning of World War II, there has been a rapid migration of Native Americans to urban areas. In 1940, only 7.2 percent of the total Native American population lived in cities; in 1990, the figure was 45 percent. This rapid migration was partly the result of youths leaving reservations during World War II to join the armed services, or of adults going to work in wartime factories. The government encouraged migration and offered assistance through a relocation program that sought to promote rapid integration into White American life. This relocation created many problems, however. A follow-up study revealed that 40 percent had returned to the reservation (Miller, 1980). Some returned because of dislike for the city; others went back because they could not cope with urban demands.

Native Americans in cities are not integrated but are an alienated, invisible minority group. Urbanization has increased their level of income, rate of employment, quality of housing, and perceived quality of life, but it has not been a panacea for poverty, discrimination, and alienation. For example, for Native Americans who already had problems with alcoholism or crime, moving to the city increased these problems. Many Native Americans leave for cities with the promise of better job opportunities, income, medical care, housing, environment, and more recreational opportunities. Sometimes, friends or relatives already in cities urge them to move. Many are unhappy and would return to the reservations if job opportunities were available there. The problem is twofold: lack of assimilation into the White culture and active discrimination against Native Americans in economic affairs and interpersonal relationships. Whites and Native Americans say they support assimilation, but Whites will not tolerate cultural differences, and Native Americans want to preserve traditional ways (Utter, 1993).

The federal relocation program and its effects highlight one of the major problems of contemporary Native American youths: the problem of cultural conflict between the way of life on reservations and the way of life in urban America. We will examine this conflict in greater detail in a later section.

Health and Standard of Living

Native Americans have the highest birthrate, the highest death rate, and the shortest life expectancy of any other group in the United States (Utter, 1993). On the one hand, they suffer more from hunger and malnutrition than does any other group in the United States. On the other hand, they are at a very high risk from obesity and diabetes, due primarily to patterns of eating and food preparation (Snow and Harris, 1989). Eating dis-

TABLE 3.3 Population of Largest Native American Reservations (1990)

Navajo (Ariz., N.M., Utah)	185,561	Rosebud (S.D.)	17,128	Zuni (N.M.)	8,244
Cherokee (Okla.)	87,059	Gila River (Ariz.)	11,700	Pawnee (Okla.)	2,229
Creek (Okla.)	56,244	Tohona O'odam (Ariz.)	16,531	Northern Pueblos (N.M.)	6,866
Choctaw (Okla.)	26,884	Turtle Mountain (N.D.)	12,312	Shawnee (Okla., Texas)	1,034
Pine Ridge (S.D.)	20,206	Hopi (Ariz.)	9,617	Blackfeet (Mont.)	2,129
Southern Pueblos (N.M.)	18,837	Standing Rock (N.D., S.D.)	10,306	Yakima (Wash.)	6,706
Chicksaw (Okla.)	12,364	Fort Apache (Ariz.)	8,726	Wind River (Wyo.)	4,935

Source: The Information Please Almanac. Copyright © 1991 by Houghton Mifflin Company. Reprinted by permission.

orders, particularly bulimia, are common among Native American girls (Snow and Harris, 1989).

Native American individuals are more likely than others to suffer and die from a variety of causes, including all types of accidents (2.3 times as likely), liver disease (3.4 times), diabetes (2.6 times), pneumonia and influenza (1.3 times), suicide (1.3 times), homicide (1.6 times), and tuberculosis (5 times) (Utter, 1993). Suicide is the leading cause of death among Native American youths 15 to 19 years old, with a rate five times the national average (LaFramboise and Bigfoot, 1988). The rate varies tremendously from tribe to tribe, however.

Interestingly enough, the rate of cardiovascular disease and cancer among Native Americans is lower than in the general population (Utter, 1993). Otitis media, or middle ear disease, is the leading identifiable disease among Native American children, resulting in hearing loss and delays in cognitive, psycholinguistic, and emotional development, which, in turn, lead to delays in grade placement, reading problems, and emotional difficulties (McShane, 1988).

Substance abuse, particularly alcoholism, is rampant in Native American culture, resulting in a very high rate of *fetal alcohol syndrome* (*FAS*) in babies of both adult and adolescent mothers (Backover, 1991). FAS is believed to be the leading cause of mental retardation in the United States (McShane, 1988). Even though the alcoholism rate among the Native American population as a whole is comparatively high, the fact remains that a relatively small minority of Native Americans are alcoholic. The very complex problem of alcoholism (or substance abuse) among Native Americans—as well as among others—goes well beyond simple comparisons of cold statistics (Erikson, 1991; Mitchell, O'Nell, Beals, Dick, Keane, and Manson, 1996).

AIDS is very much a concern for Native Americans. AIDS experts consider many Native American people to be at high risk of HIV infections because of unsafe sex habits, alcohol use and related poor judgment, intravenous drug use, and the intermigration between urban centers and Native American lands (Erikson, 1991). Statistics on the rate of human immunodeficiency virus (HIV) infections and full-blown AIDS among Native American people have, in the past, been sketchy and confusing. Research techniques are now improving.

Native Americans have one of the lowest standards of living of any minority group in the United States, with unemployment high and income low. Approximately 31 percent live below the poverty level (U.S. Bureau of the Census, 1996). Unemployment on some reservations runs as high as 80 to 90 percent. In most Native American communities, the pattern is one of bare subsistence, with the result that some of the worst slums in the United States are on reservations.

Economic Strides and Possibilities

Native American lands include many beautiful areas as well as very valuable ones. They contain much valuable timber, for example. In recent years, nearly 60 tribes obtained 25 to 100 percent of their nonfederal revenues from timber operations (Utter, 1993). Roughly 15 percent of natural gas reserves, 10 percent of total U.S. coal reserves, 33 percent of reserves of low-sulfur coal, 33 percent of strippable coal west of the Mississippi, and 60 percent of U.S. uranium reserves are under Native American lands.

During the twentieth century, periodic mismanagement or corruption within the Bureau of Indian Affairs, as well as within certain state and tribal agencies, resulted in the accumulative loss of hundreds of millions of dollars in tribal royalty revenues from oil and gas leases. Other mineral and related sources that are found in varying amounts within one or more reservations or Native American communities include gold, silver, copper, molybdenum, zeolite, phosphate, vanadium, sandstone, basalt, shale, sulfur, limestone, lead, zinc, peat, iron, clay, gypsum, volcanic cinders, sand, gravel, and building stone (Washburn, 1988). Some tribes have made marked progress in tapping the wealth of their lands and in developing sources of revenue (White, 1990).

The Choctaws in Mississippi have auto parts assembly plants and other businesses that make them the state's fifteenth largest employer. The Passamaquoddy and Penobscot tribes of Maine have invested a land-based claim settlement in land and money-making business investments. Native Americans are slowly regaining control of their own destinies (Wright, 1990).

Gaming Revenues

Only since the early 1980s has gaming (a euphemism for *gambling*) become a significant economic activity on Native American lands. Immediately following the expansion of gaming in these lands, conflicts arose among federal, state, and tribal governments as to what was legal and what was not—and who had jurisdiction. What resulted from the conflict was the *Indian Gaming Regulatory Act (IGRA)* of 1988. The stated multiple purposes of this act are (1) to provide a legislative basis for the operation and regulation of gaming by Native American tribes; (2) to establish a *National Indian Gaming Commission* as a federal agency to meet congressional concerns and protect gaming as a means of generating tribal revenue; (3) to promote economic development, self-sufficiency, and strong tribal governments; (4) to shield tribes from organized crime; and (5) to assure fairness to operators and players.

Three classes of gaming and related jurisdiction are treated by the IGRA. Class I includes social, traditional games in connection with tribal ceremonies, conferences, or celebrations. Class II gaming includes such things as bingo, lotto, pull tabs, punchboards, tip jars, and certain card games. Class III includes the usual casino games of baccarat, blackjack, roulette, and craps, as well as slot machines, video poker, horse and dog racing, and so forth. As of December 1992, 160 tribes were involved in class II or class III gaming of some kind (Gamerman, 1992; Dvorchak, 1992). Estimates of gross revenues for Native Americans from gaming for 1992 reached as high as several billion dollars. Even if net returns were on the low end of a reasonable 10 to 15 percent, the $300,000,000 would be more than 20 times the amount appropriated directly for the Bureau of Indian Affairs economic development program in fiscal year 1991. Not surprisingly, gaming will continue to play a major role in tribal economies (Utter, 1993).

Education

The record of Native American education is one of broken promises, inadequate resources, poor teachers, and, worst of all, the use of education as a tool to destroy a culture and a way of life. By the beginning of the twentieth century, the BIA was operating 147 reservation day schools, 81 reservation boarding schools, and 25 off-reservation boarding schools for Native Americans in various parts of the country as a part of the government's trust responsibility. However, the goal was complete assimilation. "Kill the Indian and Save the Man" was the motto. Regimentation, reading, writing, arithmetic, the manual trades, and home economics were drilled into the students.

Life at boarding schools was regimented as well. Estranged from family, under the rule of an alien culture, and unable to talk to teachers (who did not know dialects), academic performance was poor. As many as 75 percent of Native American children in boarding schools were far from home and had school-related social or emotional problems. About one-third of the children in these schools were physically disabled (McShane, 1988).

In addition, the BIA operated a number of day schools located on or near the reservations. These schools also presented problems. Physical facilities were notoriously inadequate, texts and supplies were scarce and outdated, and little money was available to hire competent staff. The schools conducted all classes in English, yet some of the children spoke little or no English. The dropout rate was very high.

At the secondary level, the school curriculum did not acknowledge ethnic diversity. A report on education in Native American schools in Alaska stated that "education which gives the Indian, Eskimo, and Aleut knowledge of—and therefore pride in—their historic and cultural heritage is non-existent" (Henninger and Esposito, 1971).

The Indian Education Act of 1972 (known as Title IV) resulted in some improvements. This legislation established funding for special bilingual and bicultural programs, culturally relevant teaching materials, proper training and hiring of counselors, and establishment of an Office of Indian Education in the U.S. Department of Education. Most importantly, the act required participation of Native Americans in the planning of all relevant educational projects (O'Brien, 1989).

Native American education has improved remarkably in the past 25 years or so. In the early 1990s, the BIA funded 180 education facilities, including 48 day schools, 39 on-reservation boarding schools, 5 off-reservation boarding schools, and 8 Bureau-operated dormitories that enable students to attend public schools. In addition, under the provisions of the Indian Self-Determination Act of 1975, the BIA has contracted with various tribes to operate more than 60 day schools, 11 on-reservation boarding schools, 1 off-reservation boarding school, and 6 dormitories. Enrollment in all of the schools and dormitories exceeds 40,000, or roughly 10 percent of the total Native American student population. The remainder of the student population attends regular public, private, or parochial schools.

The Bureau of Indian Affairs also provides support funding to many public school districts around the United States. Such financial support is designed to aid in the education of more than 225,000 eligible Native American students who attend public schools.

One hopeful sign of these opportunities is the rise in the number of Native American young people going to college. Two postsecondary schools are operated by the BIA. Haskell Indian Junior College, in Lawrence, Kansas, has an enrollment of about 800 students, and the Southwestern Indian Polytechnic Institute in Albuquerque, New Mexico, has more than 400 students.

Approximately 15,000 Native American BIA students receive scholarships each year to attend colleges and universities. Between 400 and 500 of these students are in law school and other graduate programs. Altogether, an estimated 70,000 Native American students are attending college. The BIA also provides funding for the operation of 22 tribally controlled community colleges, which have a combined enrollment of more than 7,000 students. Navajo Community College, on the Navajo Reservation in Arizona, and Sinte Gleska (Spotted Tail) University, on the Rosebud Reservation in South Dakota, are two of the better-known of these institutions (Utter, 1993).

Family Life

There is no such institution as a typical Native American family. There are only tribes, and family structure and values will differ from tribe to tribe. Despite the attempt to impose Western family models on them, various family forms still exist among the different tribal groups. Some families are *matrilineal* (with descent through the mother's line) (Keshna, 1980). For many Native Americans, the extended family is the basic unit for carrying out family functions. This is often true despite the absence of extended kin in the same household. Children may be raised by relatives residing in different, noncontiguous households. The existence of multiple households sharing family functions is quite common. Abuse and neglect among Native American children are very prevalent due to alcoholism and other problems. As a result, 25 to 35 percent of all Native American children are removed from their families and placed in foster homes (McShane, 1988).

Children

Most Native Americans view children as assets to the family. Children are taught that family and tribe are of the utmost importance. Grandmothers are very important; in fact, the aged, in general, are looked up to for wisdom and counsel. The aged occupy the important position of relating traditions, beliefs, and customs through the role of storyteller. Children are taught to be independent (there are no rigid schedules for eating and sleeping), to be patient and unassuming, to maintain a rather severe reserve rather than to show emotions. The ability to endure pain, hardship, hunger, and frustration is emphasized, as are bravery and courage.

Cultural Conflict

For years, official government policy adopted the assimilation model—that is, the ultimate goal of full acceptance of Native Americans in the U.S. society by the dominant group. However, that

---

matrilineal   descent through the mother's line.

For many Native American tribes, the extended family is the basic family structure. Elderly family members, especially the grandmother, are often teachers of traditions and customs.

acceptance was to come about as members of the minority group became more like members of the majority. Native Americans were considered heathens and savages, and so White Americans sought to civilize them so that they could find their acceptance into the dominant society (Williams, Himmel, Sjoberg, and Torrez, 1995).

Today, however, Native Americans are making a determined effort to retain and to teach their cultural values to their young people. Religion has always been important, but many practices were banned when the federal government conducted its 60-year (1870–1930) program of enforced enculturation ("The Denial of Indian Civil and Religious Rights," 1975).

Puberty rites or equivalent rites of passage are still practiced by some tribes and form part of religious rituals today. When the federal government banned all Native American assemblies from 1870 to 1930, except between July 1 and July 4, the Apache changed the individual rite that marked a girl's first menstruation to a group rite in which all girls who had come of age during the year participated. The mandatory rite marks a transition in status from childhood to adulthood and makes the young woman eligible for marriage. Navaho boys and girls go through a religious ceremony at about the time of appearance of secondary sex characteristics. Through this ceremony, they are introduced to full participation in ceremonial life.

Most important, Native American values are at variance with White American culture. The Native American is present oriented, not concerned about the future or with time. Whites are future oriented, concerned about time and planning ahead. Native Americans see human life as being in harmony with nature. Whites tend to seek conquest over nature. Native American life is group oriented, emphasizing cooperation, whereas Whites emphasize individualism and competition.

As a result of conflicting cultures, Native American youths today are faced with an identity crisis: whether to accommodate themselves to the White world and learn to compete in it or to retain traditional customs and values and live apart from the White world (Markstrom-Adams, 1990). Over 150 years of determined government effort has not succeeded in destroying Native American culture and society. Yet, the longer Native American youths are isolated, the greater their chances are of remaining the most deprived minority in the United States. Certainly one answer is to help all people appreciate and understand the values of Native American culture and the importance of preserving a rich heritage. The adolescent who is proud of being a Native American, as many are, and who is respected by White society, can contribute richly to a Western culture that prides itself on being culturally diverse.

Sadly, the original inhabitants of the United States have never been accepted as an important segment of the nation's life. As a consequence, most contemporary Native American youths suffer psychological strain under the impact of cultural change. Progress has been slow because these people are caught between two cultures and immobilized from going in either direction easily. The following poem, "Thoughts to Ponder," was written by Marie Ann Begay, a Navaho, a senior at Del Norte High School in Albuquerque, New Mexico:

> Sitting here
> A thought came into my mind
> Living in two worlds—
> That seems hard sometimes,
> Especially if you are an Indian.
> You feel like two persons
> Trying to struggle for something
> That you don't care about at times.
>
> I ask myself what I am doing here,
> But all odds add up to my own benefits
> And a look at the new side.
> Even though I should be
> Riding or running in the open countryside
> With the fresh clean air racing along with me,
> Seeing the rain fall in the distance
> And thunder that shakes the earth—
>
> But here I am sitting trying to get
> What I think is good for an Indian
> Who's trying to make it
> In the White Men's world and his own.

Chinese American Adolescents

There are about 2 million Chinese Americans in the United States. A minority of modern Chinese Americans are descendants of Chinese who immigrated to the United States during the period of open immigration from 1820 to 1882. After 1882, a series of exclusion acts were passed that restricted Asian immigration. As a result, for a number of years, more Chinese left than entered the United States. It was not until 1965 that the national origin quota system that discriminated against Asians was abolished. Now, each Asian country is given an equal quota of 20,000 immigrants yearly (McLeod, 1986). Since that time, Chinese have immigrated in large numbers according to their quotas on a first-come, first-served basis.

Traditionally, Chinese men entered the United States without their wives and children. Custom required that a man marry before he left China and that his wife remain in the house of her husband's parents. The man's duty was to send money to his patiently waiting family and to return home eventually. Frequently, years passed before he returned. Many hoped to earn enough to bring their families to the United States, but under the Immigration Act of 1882, no Chinese women, except a minority of exempt classes and wives of U.S. citizens, were permitted to enter. This restriction continued until 1943. As a result, Chinese men who remained in the United States were condemned to a life without intimate family relations. They often joined together in clans and secret societies that provided a sense of family and solidarity. Some engaged in gambling, opium smoking, and prostitution, and were stereotyped by White Americans as lowly, immoral, and dangerous. In 1930, there were four Chinese men to every Chinese woman in the United States. Today, the ratio is almost equal.

Family and Children

Well-educated Chinese Americans have lower rates of divorce, mental illness, and public assistance—and higher family income—than the general U.S. population (McLeod, 1986). In comparison to other minorities, Chinese Americans have more conservative sexual values, a lower fertility rate, fewer out-of-wedlock births, and more conservative attitudes toward the role of women.

Most Chinese Americans today have a strong sense of family ties. They feel a high sense of duty to family, responsibility for relatives, and self-blame when a young person fails to live up to expectations. A child who misbehaves brings shame to the family name.

Philosophies and methods of childrearing depend on the degree of acculturation of a minority group to the culture of the dominant group (Sodowsky, Lai, and Plake, 1991). Traditional approaches use authoritarian methods: a strict interpretation of good and bad behavior, the limitation of social interaction, firm discipline involving physical punishment, little verbal communication

Many Chinese American families emphasize the importance of intergenerational family ties. Even their adolescent children still place a great deal of emphasis on the family unit.

other than commands or scoldings, the expectation of obedience and conformity, and the absence of overt parental praise.

Americanized Chinese parents use different approaches. The parents are nurturing and they expose their children to more varied experiences than other minority families. They use more verbal praise, talk and joke more with their children, and give them more freedom and choice in decision making. Chinese mothers play a significant role in decision making and discipline in the family. They consider teaching to be an important part of their maternal role and routinely provide regular formal instruction to children at home.

Chinese children are taught that everyone has to work for the welfare of the family. They are given a great deal of responsibility and are assigned specific chores. Adolescents are responsible for supervising young children and for working around the house or in the family business. In spite of effects of acculturation, even second-generation Chinese youths still place a great deal of emphasis on the family as the most important

unit (Feldman, Mont-Reynaud, and Rosenthal, 1992).

In one study, regardless of the level of acculturation, adolescents emphasized the need for interpersonal affection in the family. The research indicated that Chinese American adolescents gave greater priority to parental expectations than to their own personal desires and situations (Yau and Smetna, 1993). The concern for maintaining Chinese identity in U.S. society was also clearly reflected in adolescents' psychological justifications: "I look like a Chinese. I am a Chinese." "It's the heritage." The responses demonstrate pride in their heritage, knowledge of Chinese culture, and unity within their families.

Youth

Traditionally, rebellion among Chinese youths was almost unknown. Respect for elders was so deeply ingrained that youths never questioned their parents' authority or broke rules to bring dishonor on their families. If parents forbade something, it was wrong.

Contemporary Chinese American youths are more vocal than previous generations, more inclined to speak out and to rebel against authority. As these youths became more dissociated from their parents, antisocial behavior increased (Chiu, Feldman, and Rosenthal, 1992). Young and newly arrived immigrants from Hong Kong and Taiwan, and American-born Chinese school dropouts became estranged from both Chinese American community leaders and White America. Many became involved in radical political protest and others in delinquent activity. Some adolescent gangs became tied to organized adult crime.

Education

Chinese Americans have always stressed the importance of education and hard work as the means of getting ahead. A study was conducted of the school performance of first- and second-generation Chinese American students and their Westernized peers in Australia and the United States. Results indicated that Chinese American high schoolers of both generations reported that they put more effort into school and reported higher grades than did their White American and

Australian peers. Family factors were associated with both high achievement and greater effort (Rosenthal and Feldman, 1991). The emphasis is on earning a good deal of money and gaining special status and prestige from such technical professions as engineering, pharmacy, and dentistry (Leong, 1991).

About 38 percent of today's Asian Americans who are 25 years or older have a bachelor's degree or higher—almost double the rate among White Americans (U.S. Bureau of the Census, 1996). So great is the drive for educational accomplishment that Asian Americans now outscore all other groups on college-entrance math exams and are well represented at the nation's top universities (McLeod, 1986).

The primary educational problem for Chinese youths, especially those not born in the United States, is to learn English. Youths are handicapped if they cannot communicate. Without English fluency, they are forced to remain within the confines of the Chinatown job market: in restaurants, garment factories, or low-level office jobs.

Prejudices

Racial prejudices are still important limiting factors in the lives of Chinese Americans. Some employers like to hire people of Chinese heritage because of their reputation of being hardworking and dependable. Often, however, the jobs are low paying. In seeking more desirable employment, many Chinese Americans feel they do not have an equal chance with White Americans. For example, a successful engineer may still be labeled a "Chinese engineer," whereas reference is almost never made to a German or Swedish engineer. Frequent reminders of their racial origin makes some Chinese Americans feel that they are not fully accepted as Americans. "In the past we had the coolie who slaved," said Tim Tso, president of the Organization of Chinese Americans of Northern Virginia. "Today we have the high-tech coolie" (McLeod, 1986).

Housing

Nowhere is racial discrimination more evident than in segregated housing. Large numbers of Chinese Americans are forced to live in the Chinatowns of San Francisco, Chicago, New York, and Boston. The social conditions in which some live are appalling. For instance, whole families live in run-down, overcrowded, cramped, rat- and roach-infested tenements owned by absentee landlords who charge high rents and have no interest in doing repairs.

Health

Partly because of superstitions, the more traditional Chinese Americans are reluctant to seek health care, because there are strong taboos against hospitals. One result is that the incidence of tuberculosis and many other diseases is higher among Chinese Americans than among White Americans. Local clinics, partly staffed by Chinese-speaking personnel, help to overcome reluctance to obtain care (Huang and Grachow, n.d.).

Women

The complexities of acculturation have produced many identity conflicts in Chinese Americans. Young Chinese American women are undergoing such a crisis. They seek equal opportunities and reject the traditional image of Asian women as docile, submissive dolls or exotic sex objects. They want equality of social and economic status but do not want to abandon their Chinese cultural heritage. Some resent being "too Americanized." Many second-generation Chinese Americans are ashamed of their heritage, but by the third generation, they make determined efforts to recapture and preserve it.

Southeast Asian American Adolescents

Southeast Asian adolescents, new to the United States, are confronted with three special types of stress: physiological and emotional upheavals as adolescents, social and psychological adjustments as refugees, and intercultural conflicts caused by the immense value-system differences between Asian and U.S. cultures (Lee, 1988). Many of these youths are faced with the difficult tasks of recovering from old wounds caused by the trauma of war, struggling with daily survival issues at home and in school, and establishing a new identity that is acceptable to their family members and to the host country (Lee and Chan, 1985).

Refugee Experience

The Southeast Asian refugee exodus from the countries of Vietnam, Cambodia (now Kampuchea), and Laos is one of the largest such movements in modern history. The total Southeast Asian refugee population in the United States was 1.1 million as of 1990. This group continues to grow (U.S. Bureau of the Census, 1996).

There have been two major waves of Southeast Asian refugee settlement in the United States: from 1975 to 1977 and from 1978 to the present. Major political, economic, and sociocultural differences exist between these two waves of refugees. The first group of refugees admitted to the United States was almost all Vietnamese. They were generally well-educated, young, urban dwellers, in good health, and in the company of family. The second wave of refugees included a much greater proportion of Hmong, Khmer, Lao, and Chinese-Vietnamese ethnic groups. They were generally less well educated, less literate, and of rural origin. Escape attempts from the countries of origin were typically long and traumatic (Kinze et al., 1984).

Many of those who suffered from the trauma of war were children and youths. Among the first wave of 130,000 refugees admitted to the United States in May 1975, 46 percent were younger than age 18, and 50 percent of those who entered between January and May 1982 were age 19 or younger (Office of Refugee Resettlement, 1982). A study of 40,000 Southeast Asian refugees in San Diego County (California) showed a very young population, with a median age of 18 years, with 44 percent under the age of 18. The study's age-sex structure is typical of that of populations of developing countries and reflects high dependency and fertility ratios (Rumbaut and Weeks, 1985).

Since Congress passed the Amerasian Homecoming Act in 1987, there has been a substantial increase in the number of immigrants born of American servicemen and Vietnamese women during the Vietnam War. Several thousand Amerasians (Asian Americans) and their families left Vietnam and Cambodia for resettlement. There are currently over 30 cluster sights of volunteer organizations in the United States used for placement and resettlement. Major research findings indicate that most newly arrived Amerasians experience acculturative stress, primarily in the areas of spoken English, employment, and limited

Despite the stress of acculturation, adolescents from Southeast Asian cultures benefit a great deal from the educational opportunities available to them, once they are away from the unrest in their homelands. They often become excellent students.

79% live in urbanized neighborhoods
↳ Mexican American adolescents

Comparison of Traditional Asian Values and Urban Industrial Values

Traditional Asian Values	Urban Industrial Values
Group/community emphasis	Individual emphasis
Extended family	Nuclear family/blended family
Interdependence	Independence
Person-to-person orientation	Person-to-object orientation
Past→present→future	Future→present→past
Age	Youth
Conformity/cooperation	Competition
Harmony with nature	Conquest over nature
Fatalism	Master of one's own fate
Logic of the heart	Logic of the mind
Balance	Change
Patience/modesty	Aggression/assertion
Pragmatic outlook	Theoretical outlook
Suppression of emotion	Expression of emotion
Rigidity of role and status	Flexibility of role and state
Eastern	*Western*

Source: E. Lee, "Cultural Factors in Working with Southeast Asian Refugee Adolescents," *Journal of Adolescence,* *11* (June 1988): 167–179. Reprinted by permission.

formal education (Nwadiora and McAdoo, 1996). In the next section, acculturation stress is discussed in greater detail.

Acculturation Stress

In spite of the large number of refugee children and youths, very limited studies have been conducted solely on the Southeast Asian American population. *Acculturation* is a multifaceted phenomenon composed of numerous dimensions and factors. The acculturation rate of Southeast Asian refugee adolescents is influenced by five different cultures that are in continuous interplay: (1) the Southeast Asian culture, (2) the U.S. culture, (3) the refugee culture, (4) the U.S. adolescent culture, and (5) the refugee adolescent culture.

Many Southeast Asian American adoles-cents are confronted with the traditional values from the old country, the contemporary values from the new country, and the transitional values that represent a mixture of some traditional and contemporary traits (Tobin and Friedman, 1984).

There are major differences between the traditional Asian values and the contemporary urban industrial values. The degree of acculturation of each individual refugee adolescent depends on the following variables: (1) years in the United States, (2) cultural compatibility of the country of origin and the "host community," (3) age at time of immigration, (4) language usage at home, (5) school environment, and (6) acculturation rate of parents and family members.

Acculturation stress is not solely induced by the process of acculturation but also by the difference perceived by their friends and family members. A Vietnamese adolescent girl may be perceived as "too Vietnamese" by her American friends, "too old-fashioned" by her Vietnamese peers, and "too American" by her parents. Her

American friends may expect her to go out after school, to date American boys, to drive a car, and to be more independent. Her parents may expect her to speak only Vietnamese at home, to take care of her grandparents and younger siblings after school, to clean the house, and to marry someone chosen by the family. Many such adolescents deal with the conflict by rejecting both the new and the old cultures and establishing a "third culture" with a combination of the two with their refugee experiences.

Life-Cycle Stress

Adolescents who are refugees and are from other cultures have special developmental tasks confronting them. Two issues are critical in adolescent development: *separation and individuation* and *identity* (Tobin and Friedman, 1984). It is important to assess each developmental task in the context of the refugee experience and the cultural experience of the world of Southeast Asians.

Separation and Individuation Adolescence is a period of separation and individuation. A second separation lies at the core of refugee experience. With no alternatives, to be a refugee is to be separated from family members, peers, community, and possessions. Individuation and separation are threatening issues for refugee adolescents and their families, as the adolescents' growing psychological autonomy and widening circle of activities and relationships are likely to reawaken painful memories of previous separation from their country (Tobin and Friedman, 1984). For many unaccompanied refugee adolescents, the premature physical separation from their family members does not diminish the psychological attachment to their parents. Many are struggling with conflicting feelings of resentment (being abandoned and unprotected) and gratitude (being chosen to come to the United States).

Southeast Asian refugee adolescents are additionally prone to doubts and guilt concerning the separation issue. Many came from traditional extended Asian families in which three or four generations lived together. Sons and daughters are expected to take care of their parents until they die. The adolescents' wishes of moving and living on their own like their American peers are in considerable conflict with their parents' expectations.

Identity Erikson describes the concept of identity versus role confusion in adolescents (Erikson, 1959). If identity is difficult for adolescents growing up in stable and protective societies, it is certainly much more so for refugee adolescents. Traumatic experiences—such as removal from they family homes and community, disintegration of the family unit, suspension of schooling, witnessing death and torture, competition for food due to starvation, and forced internment in labor camps—destroyed most of the physical and emotional connections they had. The process of escape also intensifies their awareness of change in self, others, and the outside world. The sudden recognition that life is dangerous and that others cannot always be trusted and loved ones cannot always be protected creates overpowering emotions of fear, rage, and shame.

For many refugee adolescents, constructing a new identity after their arrival in the United States is not easy. Many are forced to take on adult roles and take care of their family members. They may perceive themselves as older or more mature than their friends of the same age in the United States. They do not feel accepted or connected with the U.S. adolescent culture. In addition, because of racism, and the unpopularity of the Vietnam War in this country, Southeast Asian adolescents may try to avoid contacts with Americans. Furthermore, the refugee adolescents' experience of discontinuity with their own culture creates a new identity crisis—not so much because they came to this country from another culture as because the culture they came from may seem to them failed and irrelevant. All too often they feel that their culture of origin is their parents' culture, not their own. The greatest threat to identity in refugee adolescents, then, is not the feeling of belonging to two cultures but the feeling of belonging to none (Tobin and Friedman, 1984).

Family Stress

In comparison with other family life-cycle stages, families migrating when their children are adolescents may have more stress because they will have less time together as a unit before the children move out on their own. Thus, the family must struggle with multiple transitions and generational conflicts at once. In addition, the distance from the grandparental generation left behind may be particularly distressing as grandparents become ill, disappear, or die. The parents may experience severe stress in not being able to fulfill their obligation to their parents in the country of origin and to their adolescent children in the new country (McGoldrick, 1982).

Some major sources of family stress in Southeast Asian refugee families with adolescents are intergenerational conflicts and the trauma of war.

Intergenerational Conflicts   Disparity between the adolescents' and the parents' values and expectations often erupt into major conflicts. Southeast Asian parents expect their children to be quiet, obedient, polite, humble, hardworking, and respectful to them and other extended family members. Good sons and daughters are expected to take care of younger siblings and aged parents and to bring honor to the family. Such value orientation is not only different but very opposite to American values, which have strong emphasis on independence, self-reliance, assertiveness, open communication, and competition. Three major intergenerational conflicts deserve special attention:

1. *Conflicts concerning dating and marriage:* Many parents still insist on taking an active part in the choice and approval of dating and marital partners of their children. Many adolescents are being pressured to date and marry within their own ethnic group (Tobin and Friedman, 1984).

2. *Conflicts concerning career choices:* Some career plans of the children are expected and are acceptable and some are not. Parents highly value professional careers such as medicine, law, engineering, and so forth. They usually disapprove of nonprofessional jobs such as factory worker, sales, and careers in music or writing.

3. *Conflicts caused by role reversal:* Southeast Asian refugee adolescents usually are much more educated than their parents, who had little or no opportunity to attend school. In addition, many monolingual parents depend on their English-speaking adolescents as the "cultural brokers" to deal with the outside world. Such dependence can evoke anger and resentment on both parts and may lead to prolonged family stress.

Special Family Stress Resulting from the Trauma of War   Like the families of survivors of the Nazi holocaust, many families, especially the families from Cambodia, experienced tremendous suffering and losses. Managing rage, aggression, despair, guilt, and grief is an enormous problem for the survivors. Life during the war and the escape process did not afford them adequate opportunities for expression of these feelings. During the postmigration period, many express these repressed emotions in the form of physical ailments, nightmares, compulsive work, drug abuse, and physical abuse of family members. Parental fighting sometimes takes the form of uncontrollable rage, usually followed by outbursts of tears and self-pity. Adolescent children often feel the intense obligation to compensate for their parents' helplessness and sorrow.

Assessment of Strengths

Southeast Asian families arrive in the United States with many problems associated with their refugee experience. They also bring thousands of years of Asian culture and specific coping strategies in response to stress. Despite the hardships of the refugee experience, many refugees manage to endure and cope effectively without serious psychological problems. Family strengths—such as the support of extended family members and siblings, a powerful sense of obligation and self-sacrifice, the strong focus on educational achievement, the strong work ethic, and the loyalty of family members and friends—can be respected (Lee, 1982). Furthermore, religious beliefs in Buddhism provide strength to endure suffering caused by war and trauma.

The support system in the refugee community also plays an important role in determining the facility with which each family resolves transition. Many refugee youths are in frequent contact with community education and social service agencies. Being cut off from their families, villages, and countries, most Southeast Asian refugees feel an urgent need to cluster together and to form community organizations as secondary sources of security.

SUMMARY

1. This chapter describes seven groups of adolescents to illustrate the wide cultural diversity that exists among adolescents in this country: (a) those who are of low socioeconomic status of whatever race or national origin, (b) African Americans, (c) Mexican Americans, (d) Puerto Ricans, (e) Native Americans, (f) Chinese Americans, and (g) Southeast Asian Americans.

2. Low socioeconomic status cuts across ethnic boundaries, affecting almost 12 percent of U.S. families. Low-socioeconomic-status youths are both culturally deprived and with low income. There are four limitations on their lives: limited experience and opportunities; little autonomy or influence, which results in a sense of helplessness and powerlessness; feeling a sense of failure because of their status amid those who are more affluent; and feeling insecure, at the mercy of life's unpredictable events. The net effect of these limitations is to perpetuate a cycle of poverty and cultural deprivation.

3. Adolescents from low SES families often achieve only a low level of education; they therefore do not have the basic skills to function in life.

4. Low-socioeconomic-status families are more unstable, resulting in large numbers of female-headed households. Parents tend to be authoritarian, impulsive, harsh, and rigid in disciplining children, more concerned with overt behavior and keeping children out of trouble than with personality growth. Adolescents usually leave the family early; many are homeless, becoming dependent on peers as parental ties weaken. Many fall prey to the dangerous conditions in the crime-filled neighborhoods in which they are brought up. The fact that they are socialized differently—with their own language, manners, dress, and behavior—invites criticism from middle-class society.

5. African American adolescents are gradually overcoming the legacy of prejudices and discrimination against them. A series of legal decisions that promise equality have helped in this struggle. Nevertheless, many African Americans still live in segregated neighborhoods and have not achieved equality of education, rates of employment, and income, although some achieve a high level of success in spite of the handicaps they face. Unwed adolescent pregnancy among African Americans continues to be a major problem.

6. African American family strengths include strong kinship bonds, favorable attitudes toward the elderly, adaptable roles, and a strong religious orientation.

7. The majority of Mexican American adolescents live in urban areas in segregated ghettos called *colonias* or *barrios,* experiencing a high degree of social isolation from White society. In general, their scholastic achievement is below average, partly because of language problems, resulting in low-level jobs.

8. Mexican American families tend to be more stable than either White or African American families. Members of the extended family, including relatives and godparents, depend closely on one another for help. Accepting welfare is an admission of failure. The husband/father role is a difficult one. He alone must be the dominant, controlling figure in his family, the sole supporter (wives are discouraged from working outside the home), and responsible for protecting his honor and that of his wife and daughters. The father is expected to exercise his authority in a fair and just manner.

9. Mexican American men are allowed to have premarital and extramarital affairs, but women are to be chaste before marriage and faithful after marriage. Traditional families try to protect the virginity of their daughters, sometimes chaperoning them whenever they leave the house. Dating is discouraged. Sex education is inadequate. The Virgin Mother is the ideal, symbolizing purity and motherhood, which are highly prized. Motherhood is the most acceptable identity for women, which is why family planning is frowned on. The husband-wife bond is based on procreation and love, with little companionship. Most socializing occurs in same-sex groups.

10. Puerto Ricans have a strong sense of family, emphasizing family interdependence and family unity. In spite of this, Puerto Rican families in the United States have the highest rate of divorce and female-headed households of any Hispanic group. A growing proportion of children are born outside of formal marriage. Education and income levels are low.

11. Because of the frequency of single-parent households, many Puerto Rican adolescents lack appropriate parental role models. They experience an identity crisis compounded by intercultural and intergenerational conflicts. This, in turn, contributes to high rates of mental disorders, drug and alcohol abuse, delinquency, and lower self-esteem.

12. A little over half of the 2 million citizens who identify themselves as Native Americans live off reservations. Some 43 percent dwell in the western and southwestern part of the United States. Since World War II, large numbers have migrated to

urban areas, encouraged by the government, which has tried to promote enforced acculturation and rapid integration into White American life.

13. Native Americans are severely handicapped by discrimination. They are the most deprived minority in the United States, having the highest birthrate, the highest death rate, and the shortest life expectancy of any other group. They are afflicted with major diseases (except cardiovascular diseases and cancer) to a much greater degree than other Americans and suffer from hunger and malnutrition. They have a lower standard of living than any other minority group; 31 percent of Native Americans live below the poverty level. Much of the vast mineral resources on their lands remain untapped. Running gaming casinos has become a major source of income for some tribes.

14. Education of Native Americans—whether in boarding schools away from home, in day schools (supposedly near reservations), or in regular public schools with White children—is of improving quality. From the beginning, the government used education as a means of waging cultural war against the Native American. Today, many tribes participate in designing educational programs to meet their own needs, and an increasing number of Native American young people are going to college.

15. The primary problem is cultural conflict between the White world and Native American customs and ways. This conflict will not be resolved until both Whites and Native Americans develop a greater understanding and appreciation of Native American culture and the importance of preserving a rich heritage.

16. By tradition, Chinese men immigrated to the United States without their wives, expecting to rejoin them later. A series of expulsion acts restricting additional Asian immigration kept families separated, so for years there were many more Chinese men than women in the United States. Today, the ratio is almost equal.

17. Chinese Americans have a strong sense of duty to family. Their customs emphasize obedience to parents, with firm discipline and little verbal communication except commands or scoldings. Americanized parents are more nurturing, allowing more freedom in decision making. But as youths become disaffiliated from parents, antisocial behavior, including delinquency, increases.

18. Chinese Americans have always stressed the importance of education and making money. The primary educational problem is teaching English to Chinese young people. Racial prejudices are still important limiting factors in their lives.

19. Racial discrimination is most evident in segregated housing within the ghettos of the Chinese American communities. Taboos against hospitals prevent some from getting adequate health care. Chinese American girls and women have rejected the image of Asian women as docile, submissive dolls or as erotic sex objects and are striving for equal social and economic status without becoming too Americanized.

20. Southeast Asian American adolescents are a unique group because their families are refugees from war. As a unique group, they are in tumultuous transitions. They are recovering from the wounds of war, struggling with daily survival issues at home and in school, and establishing a new identity that is acceptable to their family members and to the host country. The stresses that they face include the difficulties of acculturation, because there are major differences between traditional Asian values and contemporary urban industrial values; life-cycle stresses as they seek to solve the problems of individuation and separation from parents; identity; and family stresses. Family stresses arise because of intergenerational conflicts caused by the disparity between adolescents' and parents' values. Conflicts arise over dating and marriage, career choices, and role reversal. Special family stresses are also the result of the trauma of war.

21. Strengths include years of Asian culture, family solidarity, religious beliefs, and the support system in the refugee community.

KEY TERMS

Chicano **65**

colonias or barrios **65**

low socioeconomic status (low SES) **52**

machismo **67**

marianismo **70**

matrilineal **75**

THOUGHT QUESTIONS

1. What do you think of the belief that people are poor because they are lazy? Explain.
2. How is it possible for adolescents from poor families to break the cycle of poverty and deprivation?
3. What are the primary reasons why some adolescents achieve only a low level of education?
4. Why are divorce rates higher among those of low-socioeconomic-status groups than among those of high-socioeconomic-status groups?
5. Can children growing up in a female-headed household be well adjusted? Explain.
6. Why do low-socioeconomic-status families tend to be rigid, use harsh physical discipline, and be imperative and absolute in their discipline of children?
7. What might be some of the differences in peer orientation of low socioeconomic status from those of higher socioeconomic status?
8. Do low-socioeconomic-status adolescents consider themselves social outcasts? Why or why not?
9. Describe the situation in question 8 in relationship to racial prejudices on this campus.
10. Is education the answer to the problems confronting the African American adolescent? Explain.
11. Do African Americans, as a group, have lower motivation to succeed vocationally than do Whites? Explain.
12. Since the law stated that African Americans must have equality of opportunity in education and employment, why is there still much discrepancy between the situations of African Americans and Whites?
13. Compare the attitudes toward teenage unwed pregnancy among African Americans and Whites.
14. What factors contribute to lower levels of education of Mexican American children?
15. What factors in the family relationships of Mexican Americans contribute to occupational success?
16. What factors contribute to occupational failure of adolescents from Mexican American families?
17. What do you think of the traditional Mexican American family? Discuss the aspects of which you approve and disapprove.
18. Compare the values that Mexican American parents teach their children with the values that White American parents teach their children. Which do you prefer and why?
19. What are the effects on Mexican American adolescents of teaching them double standards of sex education and behavior?
20. What are the primary strengths of the Puerto Rican family?
21. Despite their influence on the family, how do you account for the high rate of divorce in Puerto Rican families?
22. Why do Hispanic female adolescents have special problems with identity formation?
23. What factors contributed to the rapid migration of Native Americans to urban areas in the years following World War II?
24. Why are Native Americans the most deprived minority in the United States?
25. Describe some of the economic advances that Native Americans have made in recent years.
26. What do you think of Native Americans turning to gaming as a primary source of revenue?
27. Should Native American adolescents be taught the ways of Whites? Why or why not?
28. Why did the government use education to acculturate the Native Americans and to try to destroy their culture?
29. Describe some of the most important advances in Native American education in the past 25 years or so.
30. Is it possible to be a Native American in a White-dominated society? Why or why not?
31. What are the primary strengths of the Chinese American culture?
32. Describe a Chinese American family and/or student you know.
33. Why is delinquency on the increase among Chinese American adolescents?
34. Why do Chinese American youths excel in school?
35. Are there any Southeast Asian families in your community? What special problems do they face?
36. What is meant by *acculturation stress*?
37. What might be some traditional values of Southeast Asians that are in conflict with urban industrial values in the United States?
38. Describe what is meant by *life-cycle stress*.
39. What do you admire most about Southeast Asian culture?

SUGGESTED READING

Jacobson, C. K. (Ed.). (1995). *American Families: Issues in Race and Ethnicity*. New York: Garland.

Sotomayor, M. (Ed.). (1991). *Empowering Hispanic Families: A Critical Issue for the '90s*. Milwaukee, WI: Family Service of America.

Steinitz, V. A., and Solomon, E. R. (1987). *Starting Out: Class and Community in the Lives of Working-Class Youth*. Philadelphia: Temple University Press.

4

Sexual Maturation and Physical Growth

We have described adolescence as a period of sexual maturation and physical growth. Let's look more closely at this maturation and growth: what changes take place and why, when, and how they occur.

The Endocrine Glands and Hypothalamus

The endocrine glands (see Figure 4.1) secrete biochemical substances called *hormones* (meaning "I excite") directly into the bloodstream. The hormones bathe every cell of the body, but each also has target organs on which it acts specifically. The hormones act as an internal communication system, telling the different cells what to do and when to act.

Because of their importance in human sexuality, we will discuss three glands of the endocrine system: the pituitary gland, the gonads, and the adrenal glands. The closely related hypothalamic region of the brain plays a role in regulating the secretions of the pituitary, so we will discuss it here as well.

Pituitary Gland

The *pituitary gland* is a small gland—about one-half inch long, weighing less than half a gram—and is located in the skull at the base of the brain.

hormones biochemical substances secreted into the bloodstream by the endocrine glands that act as an internal communication system that tells the different cells what to do.

pituitary gland master gland of the body located at the base of the brain.

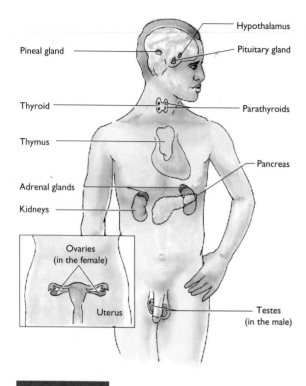

FIGURE 4.1   Some Major Glands of the Endocrine System. The endocrine system consists of glands that secrete chemicals called *hormones* directly into the bloodstream.

Source: S. A. Rathus, J. S. Nevid, and L. Fichner-Rathus, *Human Sexuality in a World of Diversity,* 3rd ed. (Boston: Allyn and Bacon, 1997), Figure 3.12, p. 85. Copyright © 1997 by Allyn and Bacon. Reprinted by permission.

It consists of three lobes: anterior, intermediary, and posterior. The anterior pituitary lobe is known as the master gland of the body, for it produces several hormones that control the action of the other glands.

One important pituitary hormone is the **human growth hormone (HGH),** also called the *somatotropic hormone (SH).* It affects the growth and shaping of the skeleton. An excess causes giantism; a deficiency causes dwarfism.

Gonadotropic hormones secreted by the anterior pituitary are so named because they influence the gonads, or sex glands. Two gonadotropic hormones, *follicle-stimulating hormone (FSH)* and *luteinizing hormone (LH),* are secreted to stimulate the growth of egg cells in the ovaries and sperm in the testes. FSH and LH in the female control the production and release of female sex hormones

by the ovary. LH in the male controls the production and release of male sex hormones by the testes (Rice, 1989).

In addition to growth hormones and gonadotropic hormones, the pituitary secretes another hormone, **luteotropic hormone (LTH),** containing the hormone *prolactin,* which stimulates the secretion of milk by the mammary glands of the breast.

Gonads

The *gonads,* or sex glands, secrete a number of sex hormones. The *ovaries* in the female secrete a whole group known as *estrogens* (meaning "producing mad desire") that stimulate the development of female sex characteristics such as breast development, the growth of pubic hair, and the distribution of fat on the body. These hormones also maintain the normal size and function of the uterus, its linings, and the vagina. In addition, estrogens maintain the normal condition and function of nasal and oral mucous membranes, control the growth of breast duct tissue, influence normal uterine contractions, and develop and maintain physical and mental health in other ways. By interacting with the pituitary, they control the production of various pituitary hormones. Studies have also shown that estrogens influence olfactory sensitivity, which is greatest midway between menstrual periods when estrogen levels are the highest (McCary and McCary, 1982).

A second female hormone, *progesterone,* is produced in the ovaries by a new cell growth called the *corpus luteum* (meaning "yellow body") for about 13 days following ovulation. The corpus luteum forms under the stimulus of LH from the pituitary, following the rupture of the ovum, or egg cell, from the ovarian follicle. If the ovum is not fertilized, the corpus luteum disintegrates, and the secretion of progesterone ceases until ovulation occurs again during the next cycle. If, however, the ovum is fertilized, and the corpus luteum does not degenerate, it continues to secrete progesterone and keep the *endometrium,* or uterine lining, ready to receive the fertilized egg. The corpus luteum continues to secrete progesterone for the first few months of pregnancy; after this time, the *placenta* takes over the task of secreting both estrogen and progesterone for the remainder of the pregnancy.

Progesterone is an extremely important hormone. It controls the length of the menstrual cycle from ovulation until the next menstruation. It is of primary importance in preparing the uterus for pregnancy and maintaining the pregnancy itself. A proper amount of progesterone is necessary to inhibit premature uterine contractions; it is often prescribed when there is a danger of spontaneous abortion. It also stimulates the mammary glands of the pregnant woman, causing enlargement of the breasts. In the nonpregnant female, it keeps breast tissue firm and healthy and reduces the possibility of painful menstruation, premenstrual tension, and other gynecological problems (McCary and McCary, 1982).

The *testes* in the male, under the stimulation of LH from the pituitary, begin the production of the male sex hormones, or *androgens.* One male hormone, *testosterone,* is responsible for the development and preservation of masculine secondary sexual characteristics—including facial and body hair, voice change, and muscular and skeletal development—and for the development of the other male sex organs—the seminal vesicles, prostate gland, epididymis, penis, and scrotum.

Note that the estrogens and androgens are found in both boys and girls but in negligible amounts prior to puberty. They are produced by the adrenals and the gonads in moderately increasing amounts during childhood. As the ovaries mature, the production of ovarian estrogens increases dramatically and begins to show the cyclic variation in level during various stages of the menstrual cycle. The level of androgens in the female's bloodstream increases only slightly. As the testes mature in the male, the production of testosterone increases dramatically, whereas the level of the estrogens in the male's bloodstream increases only slightly. Figure 4.2 shows the increases in hormones at puberty. It is the ratio of the levels of the male to female hormones that is partly responsible for development of male or female characteristics. An imbalance in the natural hormonal state in a growing child can produce deviations in primary and secondary sexual characteristics and affect the development of expected masculine or feminine physical traits. For example, a female with an excess of androgens may grow a mustache and body hair, develop masculine musculature and strength, develop an enlarged clitoris, or have other masculine characteristics. A male with an excess of estrogens or with an androgen deficiency may show decreased potency and sex drive and an enlargement of the breasts.

Adrenals

The *adrenal glands* are located just above the kidneys. In the female, they produce androgens

human growth hormone (HGH) a pituitary hormone that regulates body growth.

gonadotropic hormones hormones that are secreted by the pituitary and that influence the gonads, or sex glands.

follicle-stimulating hormone (FSH) a pituitary hormone that stimulates the maturation of the follicles and ova in the ovaries and of sperm in the testes.

luteinizing hormone (LH) a pituitary hormone that stimulates the development of the ovum and estrogen and progesterone in females and of sperm and testosterone in males.

luteotropic hormone (LTH) a pituitary hormone that contains the hormone prolactin, which stimulates mild production by the mammary glands of the female breast.

gonads the sex glands: testes and ovaries.

ovaries female gonads or sex glands that secrete estrogen and progesterone and produce mature egg cells.

estrogen feminizing hormone produced by the ovaries and, to some extent, by the adrenal glands.

progesterone a female sex hormone produced by the corpus luteum of the ovary.

corpus luteum a yellow body that grows from the ruptured follicle of the ovary and becomes an endocrine gland that secretes progesterone.

testes the male gonads that produce sperm and male sex hormones.

androgens a class of masculinizing sex hormones produced by the testes and, to a lesser extent, by the adrenals.

testosterone a masculinizing sex hormone produced by the testes and, to a lesser extent, by the adrenals.

adrenal glands ductless glands, located just above the kidneys, that secrete androgens and estrogens in both men and women, in addition to the glands' secretion of adrenaline.

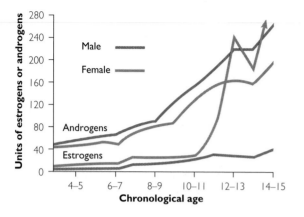

FIGURE 4.2   Hormone Secretion with Age

(masculinizing sex hormones) at low levels. The glands also secrete estrogen (feminizing sex hormones), partially replacing the loss of ovarian estrogen after menopause. In the male, the adrenals secrete both androgens and estrogens, with androgens produced in a greater amount (Rice, 1989).

Hypothalamus

The **hypothalamus** is a small area of the forebrain about the size of a marble. It is the motivational and emotional control center of the brain, regulating such functions as eating, drinking, hormonal production, menstrual cycles, pregnancy, lactation (milk production), and sexual response and behavior. It contains both the pleasure and pain centers connected with sexual response. Electrical stimulation of the hypothalamus can produce sexual thoughts and feelings. Stimulation of the hypothalamus in male rats can produce extraordinary sexual interest and performance.

We are most concerned here with the role of the hypothalamus in hormonal production and regulation. It produces a chemical called **gonadotropin-releasing hormone (GnRH)** to control the secretion of LH and FSH by the pituitary. Let's see how this works in men and women.

Sex Hormones in Males   The hypothalamus, pituitary gland, and testes function together in the male to control hormonal production. Under the influence of GnRH from the hypothalamus, the pituitary secretes FSH and LH. The follicle-stimulat-

ing hormone stimulates sperm growth in the testes **(spermatogenesis)**, as does LH. Without the luteinizing hormone, sperm production does not go beyond the second cell division and second stage of growth. However, the chief function of LH is to stimulate the testes to produce testosterone.

The level of testosterone is kept fairly constant by a phenomenon known as a *negative feedback loop* (see Figure 4.3). The GnRH stimulates the production of LH, which, in turn, stimulates secretion of testosterone. As the level of testosterone builds, the hypothalamus, sensitive to the amount of testosterone present, reduces the production of GnRH which, in turn, reduces the pro-

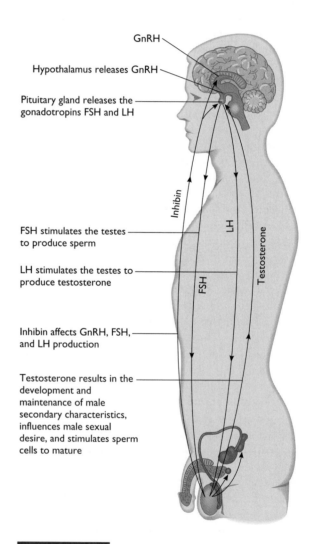

FIGURE 4.3   Negative Feedback Loops

duction of LH and testosterone. When the level of testosterone declines, the hypothalamus picks up this signal to increase secretion of GnRH, which stimulates greater production of LH and testosterone. The system acts much like a furnace with a thermostat to control the temperature of a room: An increase in temperature shuts the furnace down; a decrease turns it on.

An additional substance, *inhibin,* regulates FSH levels in another negative feedback loop (Hafez, 1980). Inhibin is produced by the testes or, perhaps, by the sperm themselves. As the level of inhibin builds, FSH production is suppressed, which results in a decline of sperm production. With the discovery of inhibin, researchers have shown considerable interest in the possibility of using it as a male contraceptive because it inhibits sperm production. Whether the idea is practical remains to be seen (Rice, 1989).

Sex Hormones in Females   The hypothalamus, pituitary gland, and ovaries also work together in a negative feedback loop to control hormonal production in females. The gonadotropin-releasing hormone from the hypothalamus stimulates the pituitary to produce FSH and LH. These hormones act on the ovary to stimulate the growth of follicles and egg cells and to stimulate the secretion of ovarian estrogen and progesterone. As the level of estrogen builds, it inhibits the production of GnRH, which, in turn, reduces the production of FSH (Rice, 1989).

The major difference between the hormonal systems of males and females is that the *level of testosterone in males is fairly constant, whereas estrogen and progesterone secretion is cyclic in females.* Estrogen and progesterone levels of females vary with different stages of the menstrual cycle, as we will see later in this chapter.

Maturation and Functions of Male Sex Organs

Figure 4.4 depicts the primary male sex organs: the testes, scrotum, epididymis, seminal vesicles, prostate gland, Cowper's glands, penis, vas deferens, and urethra. A number of important changes occur in these organs during adolescence. The growth of the testes and *scrotum* (the pouch of skin

containing the testes) accelerates, beginning at about age 11½, becoming fairly rapid by age 13½, and slowing thereafter. These ages are averages. Rapid growth may start between 9½ and 13½ years, ending between ages 13 and 17. During this time, the testes increase 2½ times in length and about 8½ times in weight. The *epididymis* is a system of ducts, running from the testes to the vas deferens, in which sperm mature and are stored. Before puberty, the epididymis is relatively large in comparison with the testes; after maturity, the epididymis is only about one-ninth the size of the testes.

Spermatogenesis

The most important change within the testes themselves is the development of mature sperm cells. This occurs when FSH and LH from the pituitary stimulate production and growth. The total process of spermatogenesis, from the time the primitive spermatogonium is formed until it grows into a mature sperm, is about 10 days (McCary and McCary, 1982).

Following spermatogenesis, the sperm migrate by contraction of the seminiferous tubules to reach the epididymis, where they may remain for as long as six weeks. Sperm are then transported by ciliary action through the epididymis into the

---

hypothalamus   a small area of the brain that controls motivation, emotion, pleasure, and pain in the body; that is, it controls eating, drinking, hormonal production, menstruation, pregnancy, lactation, and sexual response and behavior.

gonadotropin-releasing hormone (GnRH)   a hormone secreted by the hypothalamus that controls the production and release of FSH and LH from the pituitary.

spermatogenesis   the process by which sperm are developed.

inhibin   a hormone produced in the testes to regulate FSH secretion and sperm production.

scrotum   the pouch of skin containing the testes.

epididymis   a system of ducts, running from the testes to the vas deferens, in which sperm mature and are stored.

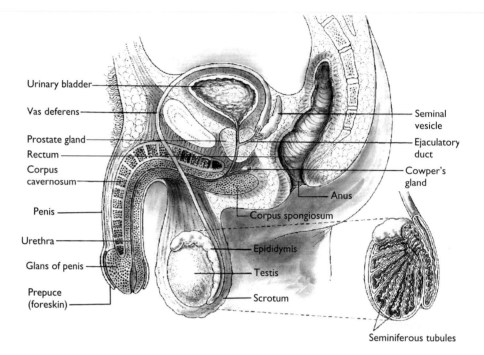

FIGURE 4.4   The Male Reproductive System.
The external male sex organs include the penis and the scrotum.

Source: S. A. Rathus, J. S. Nevid, and L. Fichner-Rathus, *Human Sexuality in a World of Diversity,* 3rd ed. (Boston: Allyn and Bacon, 1997), Figure 4.2, p. 103. Copyright © 1997 by Allyn and Bacon. Reprinted by permission.

vas deferens, where many are stored. There, they are conducted by ciliary action through the vas deferens, eventually reaching the **seminal vesicle** and **prostate gland.** It is here that they are made more mobile by the addition of the *seminal fluid,* passing with it through the **urethra** and out of the penis at each ejaculation. The seminal fluid—a highly alkaline, milky fluid—keeps the sperm alive, healthy, and mobile and serves as a vehicle for carrying the sperm out of the penis. About 70 percent of the seminal fluid comes from the seminal vesicles; the remaining 30 percent comes from the prostate glands (Spring-Mills and Hafez, 1980).

The Developing Penis

The **penis** doubles in length and girth during adolescence, with the most rapid growth taking place between ages 14 and 16. Genital growth usually takes 3 years to reach the adult stage, but some males complete this development in 1.8 years, and others take as many as 4.7 years. In the adult male, the flaccid (limp) penis averages from 3 to 4 inches in length and slightly over 1 inch in diameter. The tumescent (erect) penis, on the average, is 5½ to 6½ inches in length and 1½ inches in diameter; sizes vary tremendously from male to male (Gebhard and Johnson, 1979).

Adolescent boys are often concerned with the dimensions of their penis, for they associate masculinity and sexual capability with penis size. In fact, the size of the flaccid penis has little to do with the size of the erect penis, for the small penis enlarges much more in proportion to its size than does the large penis. Moreover, the size of the erect penis has little to do with sexual capability, for the vagina has few nerve endings, and female sexual excitation comes primarily from stimulation of the external genitalia. The degree of pleasure experienced by both the man and the woman has nothing to do with the size of the male organ.

The head of the penis (*glans penis*) is covered by a loose fold of skin, the *prepuce* or *foreskin,* often removed surgically through *circumcision* for hygienic or religious reasons. Circumcision is not an obligatory health measure today, as long as the foreskin can be retracted and the penis is kept clean. If the prepuce is not retracted and the glans washed, a cheeselike substance known as *smegma* collects, acting as a breeding ground for irritants and disease.

Erection of the penis is possible from infancy; it may be caused by tight clothing, local irritation, the need to urinate, or manual stimulation. Sigmund Freud was the first to acknowledge infant sexuality and the likelihood that the small boy

PERSONAL ISSUES

Use of Steroids by Athletes

Athletes sometimes take male hormones (testosterone; also called **anabolic steroids**) to increase their strength and endurance. Ever since several competitors were disqualified from the 1988 Olympics because of the illegal use of anabolic steroids, attention has focused on the use of these drugs by athletes of all ages. Fuller and LaFountain (1987) interviewed 50 athletes who admitted to steroid use. The athletes ranged in age from 15 to 45 years, with an average age of 19. No systematic differences between high school and college athletes were found. The athletes included weight lifters, football players, wrestlers, body builders, and track stars. These athletes justified use of the drugs because of the need to be competitive.

> We should be allowed to take them because all those other countries take them ... the women too. You have no choice if you want to compete in the big time. (Fuller and LaFountain, 1987, p. 971)

There is no question that steroids increase muscle mass, strength, and performance and reduce fat deposits and fluid retention by the body. They also increase hostility and aggression. Users gain an intense killer instinct. This hostility results in fights and arguments with others, increased sexual aggression, and beating up girlfriends or boyfriends when frustrated. Taking testosterone and

other steroids has been found to be a significant predictor of verbal and physical aggression as well as delinquent behavior problems in adolescent males. These substances also increase aggression in adolescent females (Halpern and Udry, 1992).

The most serious harm from anabolic steroids comes to various parts of the athlete's own body. The athlete can suffer damage to the heart, liver, reproductive system, and stomach as a result of taking anabolic steroids. Heart attacks, sterility, ulcers, and liver tumors are common in addition to psychological and emotional instability.

Many athletes are not concerned because they don't realize the harm, or they choose to deny the potential health problems.

> You can abuse anything. Even aspirin. I don't think there is any proven test that steroids really do hurt you. (Fuller and La Fountain, 1987, p. 972)

Other athletes place their performance above all health considerations.

> It gives me a chance to achieve for myself and I do all I can to make my body stronger.... If my coach says steroids will make me stronger I will use them. (Fuller and La Fountain, 1987, p. 974)

---

may gain pleasure from masturbation. In fact, young children sometimes masturbate to orgasm (Kinsey, Pomeroy, and Martin, 1948). However, ejaculation of semen does not occur prior to sexual maturity. (Chapter 9 provides information on masturbation during adolescence.)

Cowper's Glands

The *Cowper's glands,* which also mature during adolescence, secrete an alkaline fluid that lubricates and neutralizes the acidity of the urethra for easy and safe passage of the semen. This fluid may be observed at the opening of the glans during sexual excitement and before ejaculation. Because the fluid contains sperm in about 25 percent of cases examined, conception is possible whenever

vas deferens   the tubes running from the epididymis to the urethra that carry semen and sperm to the ejaculatory duct.

seminal vesicles   twin glands that secrete fluid into the vas deferens to enhance sperm viability.

prostate glands   two glands that secrete a portion of the seminal fluid.

urethra   the tube carrying the urine from the bladder to the outside; in males, it also carries the semen to the outside.

penis   the male organ for coitus and urination.

anabolic steroids   the masculinizing hormone testosterone taken by athletes to build muscle mass.

Cowper's glands   small twin glands that secrete a fluid to neutralize the acid environment of the urethra.

intercourse occurs, even if the male withdraws prior to ejaculation (McCary and McCary, 1982).

Nocturnal Emissions

Adolescent boys wonder and worry about *nocturnal emissions,* or so-called wet dreams. Kinsey and colleagues (1948) reported that almost 100 percent of men have erotic dreams, and about 83 percent of them have dreams that culminate in orgasm. These dreams occur most frequently among males in their teens and twenties, but about half of all married men continue to have them.

Research reveals that first ejaculation can be an upsetting experience (Adegoke, 1992). If nocturnal orgasms cause anxiety, adolescents should be reassured that such experiences are normal, that no harm comes from them, and that they should be accepted as part of a male's sexuality. Anxiety may be prevented if adolescents are prepared for nocturnal orgasms ahead of time (Paddack, 1987).

Mood Changes

There is substantial evidence that men go through cycles of mood that affect their behavior. However, there is no evidence that these cycles correspond to fluctuations in the levels of testosterone. So many factors—weather, health, fatigue, time of week, social happenings—affect mood fluctua-

tions that it is impossible to say they are based entirely on physiological changes. There is evidence of some correlation between high levels of testosterone and increased aggression (Ehrhardt and Meyer-Bahlburg, 1981). Advanced physical maturation in boys is modestly associated with positive moods, better attention, and more frequent reports of feeling strong. In addition, the strongest association between puberty and emotional experience was found with a specific feeling of being in love (Richards and Larson, 1993).

Maturation and Functions of Female Sex Organs

The primary internal female sex organs are the ovaries, fallopian tubes, uterus, and vagina. The external female sex organs are known collectively as the *vulva.* They are the mons veneris (mons pubis), the labia majora (major or large outer lips), the labia minora (small inner lips), the clitoris, and the *vestibule* (the cleft region enclosed by the labia minora). The *hymen* is a fold of connective tissue that partly closes the vagina in the virginal female. The ***Bartholin's glands,*** situated on either side of the vaginal orifice, secrete a drop or so of fluid during sexual excitement. Figure 4.5 depicts the female sexual organs.

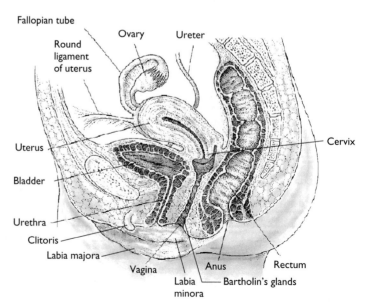

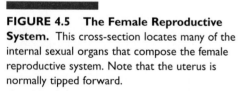

FIGURE 4.5   The Female Reproductive System. This cross-section locates many of the internal sexual organs that compose the female reproductive system. Note that the uterus is normally tipped forward.

Source: S. A. Rathus, J. S. Nevid, and L. Fichner-Rathus, *Human Sexuality in a World of Diversity,* 3rd ed. (Boston: Allyn and Bacon, 1997), Figure 3.3, p. 65. Copyright © 1997 by Allyn and Bacon. Reprinted by permission.

The Developing Vagina

The *vagina* matures at puberty in a number of ways. It increases in length and its mucous lining becomes thicker, becomes more elastic, and turns a deeper color. The Bartholin's glands begin to secrete their fluids, and the inner walls of the vagina change their secretion from the alkaline reaction of childhood to an acid reaction in adolescence.

Changes in the Vulva and Uterus

The *labia majora,* practically nonexistent in childhood, enlarge greatly, as do the *labia minora* and the *clitoris.* The *mons veneris* becomes more prominent through the development of a fatty pad.

A dramatic change also takes place in the *uterus,* which doubles in length, showing a straight-line increase during the period from 10 to 18 years of age. The uterus of the mature nonpregnant female is a hollow, thick-walled, muscular organ shaped like a pear, about 3 inches long, 2½ inches at the top and narrowing to a diameter of 1 inch at the cervix (McCary and McCary, 1982).

Ovarian Changes

The ovaries increase greatly in size and weight. They ordinarily show a fairly steady growth from birth to about 8 years of age. From age 8 to about the time of ovulation (age 12 or 13), the rate of growth accelerates somewhat, but the most rapid increase occurs after sexual maturity is reached. This is due, no doubt, to the maturation of the follicles within the ovary itself.

Every infant girl is born with about 400,000 follicles in each ovary. By puberty, this number has declined to about 80,000 in each ovary. Ordinarily, one follicle ripens into an ovum (egg) every 28 days for a period of about 38 years, which means that only about 495 ova ripen during the woman's reproductive years (McCary and McCary, 1982b). The *fallopian tubes* transport the ova from the ovaries to the uterus.

Menarche

On average, the adolescent girl begins her menstrual cycle at 12 to 13 years of age, although she may mature considerably earlier or later (9 to 18 years is an extreme range). *Menarche* (the onset of menstruation) usually does not occur until after maximum growth rates in height and weight have been achieved. Because of the superior nutrition and health care, girls start menstruating earlier today than in former generations. An increase in body fat may stimulate menarche; vigorous exercise tends to delay it (Stager, 1988).

The Menstrual Cycle

The menstrual cycle may vary in length from 20 to 40 days, averaging about 28 days. However, there is considerable difference in the length of the

---

nocturnal emissions   male ejaculation during sleep.

vulva   collective term referring to the external genitalia of the female.

vestibule   the opening cleft region enclosed by the labia minora.

hymen   the tissue partly covering the vaginal opening.

Bartholin's glands   glands on either side of the vaginal opening that secrete fluid during sexual arousal.

vagina   the canal from the cervix to the vulva that receives the penis during intercourse and acts as the birth canal through which the baby passes to the outside.

labia majora   major or large lips of tissue on either side of the vaginal opening.

labia minora   smaller lips or tissue on either side of the vagina.

clitoris   a small shaft containing erectile tissue, located above the vaginal and urethral openings, that is highly responsive to sexual stimulation.

mons veneris   mound of flesh (literally "mound of Venus") in the female located above the vagina, over which pubic hair grows.

uterus   the womb in which the baby grows and develops.

fallopian tubes   tubes that transport the ova from the ovaries to the uterus.

menarche   first menstruation.

cycle when different women are compared, and any one woman may show widespread variations. A regular cycle is quite rare.

The menstrual cycle has four phases: follicular or proliferative phase, ovulatory phase, luteal or secretory phase, and menstrual phase. As Figure 4.6 shows, hormones control the cycle. The *follicular phase* extends from just after menstruation until a follicle ripens (sometimes more than one follicle ripens) and an egg (or ovum) matures. During this phase, the pituitary secretes some LH but relatively higher levels of FSH. The follicle-stimulating hormone stimulates development of the follicles and one or more ova and induces the secretion of increasing levels of estrogen. When estrogen is at a peak, the hypothalamus acts on the pituitary to reduce the level of FSH and to secrete a surge of LH. The increased estrogen level results in a thickening of the inner lining of the uterus (the endometrium) to receive a possible fertilized egg.

Approximately 14 days before the onset of the next menstrual period, the spurt in LH production results in *ovulation,* during which a mature ovum erupts from its Graafian follicle and passes to the fallopian tube. The *ovulatory phase* is the shortest of the cycle.

The *luteal phase* follows ovulation and continues to the beginning of the next menstrual period. During the luteal phase, LH secretion from the pituitary stimulates growth of the follicle from which the ovum has erupted. This follicle develops into the corpus luteum, which secretes progesterone during the remainder of this phase.

During the *menstrual phase* (see Figures 4.6 and 4.7), the levels of estrogen and progesterone are at a minimum. This signals the hypothalamus to resume production of GnRH, which stimulates the pituitary to begin secretion of LH and FSH all over again.

One of the questions adolescents ask concerns the exact time ovulation occurs. Ordinarily, the time of ovulation is about 14 days before the onset of the next menstrual period, which would be on the 14th day of a 28-day cycle and on the 17th day of a 31-day cycle. However, there is some evidence to show that pregnancy may occur on any one day of the cycle, including during menstruation itself, and that some girls may ovulate more than once during a cycle, possibly due to the stimulus of sexual excitement itself. With the exact time of ovulation difficult to predict, *there is really no completely "safe" time during the month when a female cannot become pregnant.*

PERSONAL ISSUES

Stress and Pubertal Timing

Research has helped develop a new understanding of early menarche, especially regarding the role of environmental stress in the timing of puberty. The findings are as follows:

1. Compared with girls from intact families, those from divorced families have an earlier onset of menarche (Ellis, 1991).
2. Higher maternal reports of interparental conflict are significantly related to earlier menarche (Wierson, Long, and Forehand, 1993).
3. Family conflict predicts a somewhat earlier age of menarche.

4. Individuals who grow up under conditions of family stress (including family conflict, marital discord, and marital instability) experience behavioral and psychological problems that provoke earlier pubertal onset and reproductive readiness.

How do family stress and family conflict lead to early menarche? The researchers (Belsky, Steinberg, and Draper, 1991) propose that family conflict predisposes girls to lower metabolism and weight gain, triggering the early onset of menarche (Moffitt, Caspi, Belsky, and Silva, 1992).

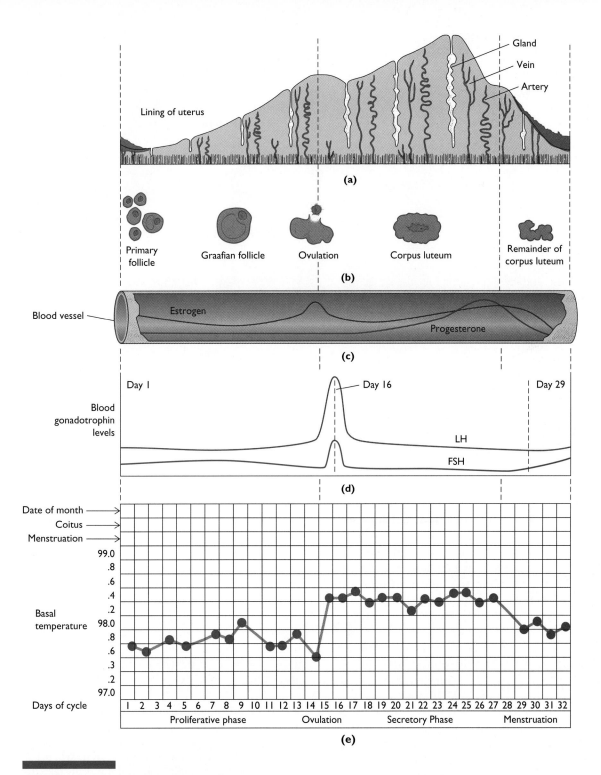

FIGURE 4.6 Some of the Changes That Occur during the Menstrual Cycle. This figure shows five categories of biological change: (*a*) changes in the development of the uterine lining (endometrium), (*b*) follicular changes, (*c*) changes in blood levels of ovarian hormones, (*d*) changes in blood levels of pituitary hormones, and (*e*) changes in basal temperature. Note the dip in temperature that is connected with ovulation.

Source: S. A. Rathus, J. S. Nevid, and L. Fichner-Rathus, *Human Sexuality in a World of Diversity,* 3rd ed. (Boston: Allyn and Bacon, 1997), Figure 3.14, p. 87. Copyright © 1997 by Allyn and Bacon. Reprinted by permission.

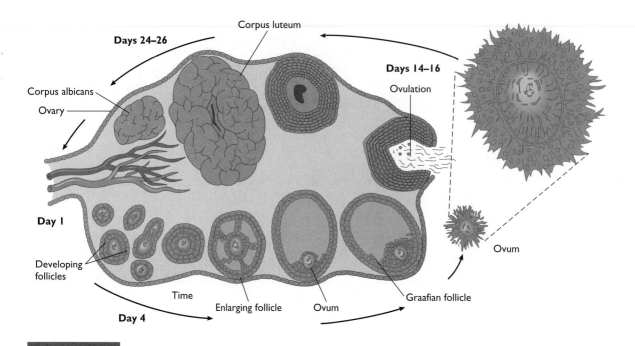

FIGURE 4.7 **Formation of the Corpus Luteum**

Source: J. W. Hole, *Human Anatomy and Physiology*, 4th ed. (New York: McGraw-Hill, 1987). Copyright © 1987 McGraw-Hill Publishing Company. Adapted by permission of the McGraw-Hill Companies.

A female may menstruate ***anovulatory*** (without ovulation) when her menstrual cycle begins, until the ovaries mature enough to discharge mature ova and until the endocrine glands secrete enough of their hormones to make ovulation possible. The first periods may be scanty and irregular, spaced at varying intervals until a rhythm is established. It is not uncommon for the flow to last only a day or so for the first few periods. Later, it may last from two to seven days, with the mean usually about five days. The total amount of blood lost averages 1.5 ounces (three tablespoonful). A normal range is from 1 to 5 ounces. Only part of the menstrual fluid is blood. The total discharge amounts to approximately one cupful (6 to 8 ounces) and is composed partly of mucus and broken-down cell tissue (McCary and McCary, 1982).

Menstrual Problems and Concerns

A study of 587 White girls in grades 6 through 9 from middle-class suburbs of Boston revealed two opposing attitudes toward menstruation (Stubbs, Rierdan, and Koff, 1989). Some girls held a set of beliefs about menstruation as something normal and acceptable. Others held a set of beliefs reflecting their worry and dislike of menstruation. Those who were early menstruaters were more likely to worry about menstruation than were their on-time peers. Apparently, the younger maturers had received less positive preparation that would have enabled them to accept the menstrual experience. Beginning menstruation can be a traumatic event for some girls who are not prepared ahead of time (Pillemer, Koff, Rhinehart, and Rierdan, 1987). One 16-year-old commented:

> I was very frightened of the sexual changes that occurred in my body. The first change I noticed was my menstrual period. I was very frightened of the blood; I didn't know why it occurred. When I finally asked my mother, she did not really take the time to explain it to me, so I didn't really know just why or how it happened. (Dreyfus, 1976, p. 43)

Other girls are able to accept menstruation in a natural way because they have been taught what to expect. One girl remarked:

I was aware of the changes that were going to take place in my body before they occurred. I was not really frightened of the changes in my body because I was told a lot about it by my next door neighbor and my mother. (Dreyfus, 1976, p. 42)

Generally, those who have been menstruating for some time have more positive attitudes about menstruation than do premenstrual young women (McGrory, 1990).

Some writers suggest that menarche should be a time of celebration and congratulations. For instance, Logan, Calder, and Cohen (1980) write:

Two elements of a tradition that seem most appropriate are a physical gesture such as a hug or a kiss and material token such as a present or a card. The physical gesture would convey a message of support and of acceptance of the body. . . . A material token has two advantages. First, a present is already an established form of celebration of life. Second, her major reaction to it can be private. She can come back to it and reflect on it when *she* feels comfortable. (p. 267)

Whether the adolescent girl experiences any menstrual problems will depend on both physical and emotional factors. Some research reports more conflict between mothers and daughters shortly after menarche (Holmbeck and Hill, 1991). Other research indicates increased emotional distance in parent-adolescent relationships shortly after the onset of pubertal development in girls, and especially in mother-adolescent dyads.

Almost all females experience variations of mood according to the stage of the menstrual cycle. For some women, the *premenstrual syndrome (PMS)* includes unpleasant physical changes and mood swings (Hopson and Rosenfeld, 1984). There is a physical basis for these fluctuations. Depression, hostility, anxiety, and emotional upset are more evident just before and during the menstrual period, when the female hormones are at their lowest levels. Feelings of joy are greatest midway between periods, when the estrogen level is at its highest.

Premenstrual symptoms do not always occur, and they vary from woman to woman. Some

---

anovulatory without ovulation.

premenstrual syndrome (PMS) typified by nervousness, irritability, anxiety, and unpleasant physical feelings and mood swings that occur just before menstruation.

HIGHLIGHT

Menstrual Irregularity in Athletes

Extensive research has established that amenorrhea, or irregular menstruation, is common in female athletes: ballet dancers, distance runners, swimmers, and others (Calabrese et al., 1983; Frisch et al., 1981; Baker et al., 1981). The current evidence, from both anecdotal and investigative sources, suggests that exercise-induced amenorrhea rapidly reverses once training is discontinued (Stager, 1984; Stager, Ritchie, and Robertshaw, 1984). When physical training is reduced or stopped, either as a result of a vacation or an injury, amenorrheic athletes report a resumption of normal menstrual cycles.

A study comparing former collegiate distance runners with current runners and sedentary controls showed that the former runners were similar to the control group in terms of the number of menses in the previous 12 months. Current runners reported significantly fewer menses than either of the other two groups. Further, the ex-athletes who experienced menstrual irregularity during training reported that the average (mean) time for resumption of normal menstruation was 1.7 months after training was terminated. No relationship was established between length of amenorrhea and the rate of resumption (Stager, Ritchie, and Robertshaw, 1984).

women are not bothered by PMS at all; others are bedridden. Keye (1983) reported that only 5 percent to 10 percent of the women in his study had premenstrual distress serious enough to interfere with functioning. Another research group that measured school grades found no effects of the menstrual cycle on academic performance (Walsh et al., 1981).

So many environmental factors can influence mood that it is a mistake to attribute all emotional fluctuations to female hormones. Both men and women experience biological and psychological cycles that depend on everything from the weather to personal relationships. Good and bad moods cannot be predicted solely on the basis of the time of month.

The young girl's attitudes and feelings about menstruation are also very important. It is important, therefore, that girls be prepared in a positive way for menstruation. The more knowledgeable they are prior to menarche, the more likely they will report a positive initial experience (Skandhan, Pandya, Skandhan, and Mehta, 1988). One study, however, did show that many of girls received considerable emotional shock from their first menstruation, whether or not they had been warned of its arrival (Adegoke, 1992).

Unfortunately, many girls are negatively conditioned even before menses (Amann-Gainotti, 1986). For example, one study of advertisements of menstrual products showed that the ads depicted menstruation as a "hygienic crisis" that is managed by an "effective security system" that affords protection and "peace of mind." Failure to provide adequate protection places the woman at risk for soiling, staining, embarrassment, and odor. Such ads encourage guilt and diminished self-esteem in the adolescent who experiences discomfort (Havens and Swenson, 1988).

There is a relationship between sociopsychological factors and menstrual distress. In general, women who have more liberal attitudes about the role of women in society experience less psychological stress that may manifest itself in menstrual difficulties. Women in therapy who are encouraged to understand and appreciate their female

PERSONAL ISSUES

Preparing Girls for Menstruation

Adolescent girls who are prepared for menstruation in a positive way are more likely to consider it a positive experience. Consider the following thoughts of ninth-grade girls.

[One] study asked adolescent girls who had been menstruating for one to three years how they would prepare younger girls for the event, and how they would advise parents to prepare their daughters. To this end, 157 9th-grade girls rated their own experience of menarche (in terms of preparation, initial response, parents' roles, and sources of information) and answered four open-ended questions. The girls emphasized the need for emotional support and assurance that menstruation was normal and healthy—not bad, frightening, or embarrassing. They stressed the pragmatics of menstrual hygiene and the subjective experience of menstruation (how it would actually feel), while downplaying the biological aspects and the link between menstruation and self-definition as a woman. Most girls had talked about menstruation with their mothers, but few had discussed it with their fathers. They saw mothers as critically important but often unable to meet their needs. Many girls felt uncomfortable talking about menstruation with fathers, wanting them to be supportive but silent; others believed that fathers should be excluded completely. Responses suggested several ways early preparation could be revised, including a shift in focus from the biology of menstruation to the more personal, subjective, and immediate aspects of the experience. Responses also supported a conceptualization of menstrual education as a long-term, continuous process, beginning well before menarche and continuing long after.

Source: E. Koff and K. Rierdan, "Preparing Girls for Menstruation: Recommendations from Adolescent Girls," *Adolescence, 30* (1995): 795–811.

roles report decreased menstrual symptomatology. Warm, supportive family and peer relations also may be conducive to less stressful menstrual cycles and to fewer physical difficulties, in general.

Some adolescent girls experience physical difficulties with their menstrual periods (Huffman, 1986). These physical problems usually fall into one of four categories. *Dysmenorrhea* is painful or difficult menstruation: menstrual cramps or abdominal pain, with or without other symptoms such as backache, headache, vomiting, fatigue, irritability, sensitivity of the genitals or breasts, pain in the legs, swelling of the ankles, or skin irritations such as pimples. *Menhorrhagia* is excessive bleeding due to physical or emotional factors (Altchek, 1988). *Amenorrhea* is absence of flow. This may be due to a physical cause, such as vigorous exercise that changes the percentage of body fat and alters hormonal secretion. It may also be caused by an endocrine disorder or a change of climate, overwork, emotional excitement, and other factors. *Metrorrhagia*—bleeding from the uterus at times other than during a menstrual period—is not common. It demands a medical checkup to determine physical and/or emotional causes.

Many questions arise concerning exercise, bathing, or swimming during the menstrual period. Exercise is not only possible but beneficial. Doctors may even prescribe certain exercises to relieve menstrual cramps. Bathing is desirable if the water is not too cold or hot; excessively cold water will stop the menstrual flow and sometimes cause cramps. Swimming is permissible if chilling or excessive fatigue is avoided. Authorities do not suggest forcing vigorous exercise during menstruation but emphasize that the continuation of normal professional and athletic activities during all phases of the menstrual cycle decreases the amount and intensity of menstrual discomfort.

Development of Secondary Sexual Characteristics

Sexual maturation at puberty includes development not only of the reproductive organs but also of secondary sex characteristics. These include the appearance of body hair, voice changes, the development of mature male and female body contours, and other minor changes.

Table 4.1 gives the sequence of development for boys and girls. The development of some of the primary sexual characteristics is also included to give a picture of the total sequence of development (primary characteristics are marked with an asterisk). The ages provided in the table are averages. Actual ages may extend several years before and after, with individual differences having a hereditary base (Akinboye, 1984; Westney, Jenkins, Butts, and Williams, 1984). Although the average girl matures about two years before the average boy, the rate of development is not always consistent. An early-maturing boy may be younger than a late-maturing girl. The mean age of menarche is 12.5; the mean age for first ejaculation of semen is 13.7. But it is untrue to refer to these ages as the norm. The age of sexual maturity extends over such a wide range (9 to 18 years is not unusual) that any ages within the range should be considered normal.

Generally speaking, the average age of sexual maturity has been decreasing over the years, primarily due to the better health care of today's generation of youth (Gilger, Geary, and Eisele, 1991). One study compared the physical development of boys and girls from rural Iowa with another sample from suburban Chicago. The boys and girls from rural Iowa matured at an earlier age than did those from suburban Chicago. One reason is that the rural Iowan adolescents were heavier in body weight. It is well known that diet and exercise can influence sexual maturation directly or indirectly through their effects on body weight. Because male and female adolescents in the rural Iowa sample were significantly heavier than their counterparts in the suburban Chicago sample, the rural Iowans were sexually mature earlier than those in Chicago (Robertson et al., 1992).

Males

The development of secondary sexual characteristics in boys is a gradual process. The beginning of pubic hair starts with sparse, straight hair at the base of the penis, and then the hair gradually becomes more profuse and curled, forming an inverse triangle and spreading up to the umbilicus. Figure 4.8 shows the developmental process

TABLE 4.1   Sequence of Development of Primary and Secondary Sexual Characteristics

Boys	Age Span		Girls
Beginning growth of testes, scrotum, pubic hair	11.5–13	10–11	Height spurt begins
Some pigmentation, nodulation of breasts (later disappears)			Slight growth of pubic hair
Height spurt begins			Breasts, nipples, elevated to form "bud" stage
Beginning growth of penis*			
Development of straight, pigmented pubic hair	13–16	11–14	Straight, pigmented pubic hair
Early voice changes			Some deepening of voice
Rapid growth of penis, testes, scrotum, prostate, seminal vesicles*			Rapid growth of vagina, ovaries, labia, uterus*
First ejaculation of semen*			Kinky pubic hair
Kinky pubic hair			Age of maximum growth
Age of maximum growth			Further enlargement, pigmentation, elevation of nipple, areola to form "primary breast"
Beginning growth of axillary hair			Menarche*
Rapid growth of axillary hair	16–18	14–16	Growth of axillary hair
Marked voice change			Filling out of breasts to form adult conformation, secondary breast stage
Growth of beard			
Indentation of frontal hairline			

*Primary sexual characteristics are marked with an asterisk.

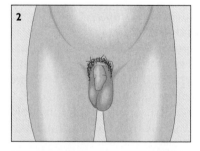
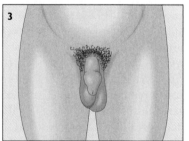
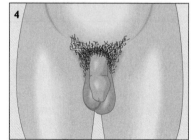
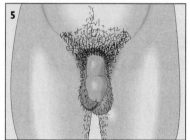

FIGURE 4.8   Stages of Pubic Hair Development in Adolescent Boys. Stages are (*1*) prepubertal (not shown) in which there is no true pubic hair; (*2*) sparse growth of downy hair mainly at base of penis; (*3*) pigmentation, coarsening, and curling with an increase in amount of hair; (*4*) adult hair, but limited in area; (*5*) adult hair with horizontal upper border and spread to thighs.

Source: Adapted from J. M. Tanner, *Growth at Adolescence,* 2d ed. (Oxford: Blackwell Scientific Publications, 1962), as reprinted in H. Katchadourian, *The Biology of Adolescence* (San Francisco: W. H. Freeman, 1977), p. 67.

(Katchadourian, 1977). Axillary (underarm) hair usually first appears about two years after the appearance of pubic hair, with the growth of the beard coming near the end of the total sequence, and the indentation of the hairline (this does not occur in girls) arriving as the final development. Muscular development, widening of the shoulders and chest, and other changes in body contours continue. Usually, a boy has reached 98 percent of his adult height by 17¼ years of age, plus or minus 10 months.

Changes in the boy's voice are due to the rapid growth of the larynx (the Adam's apple) and the lengthening of the vocal cords across it. The vocal cords nearly double in length, lowering the pitch one octave. Volume also increases, and the tonal quality is more pleasant. Roughness of tone and unexpected pitch changes may last until 16 or 18 years of age.

Before and during the period when sexual maturation takes place, some boys suffer what has been referred to as the *locker-room syndrome*. After physical education class, boys in middle school or junior high are herded into the showers, where they have to undress and bathe in front of others. The range in normal developmental rates is great enough so that some boys are completely underdeveloped and others are ahead of their classmates. The adolescent boy with little pubic or axillary hair, no noticeable beard, an underdeveloped penis, or a childlike body feels immature compared with his more fully developed friends. Those who have started to develop may feel self-conscious at their new sexual image. Involuntary erection in front of others is especially embarrassing, as is noticeable body odor. In fact, almost everything having to do with body development can become a source of embarrassment. The desire to avoid critical comments leads some boys to become excessively modest or withdrawn and to retreat from the world through daydreaming. Some boys become hostile and defensive, ready to argue or fight at the slightest provocation; others become daring show-offs, exhibiting bravado to hide their anxieties and their lack of self-confidence.

One of the most immediate results of sexual maturation is a developing preoccupation with sex. Attention becomes focused on sex, new sexual sensations, and the opposite sex. The greatest percentage of graffiti on the bathroom walls of ju-nior high schools is related to sex. Adolescent boys and girls spend a lot of time thinking or dreaming about sex, reading sex-oriented literature, and talking about the opposite sex.

These awakening sexual interests motivate adolescent boys to devote much time and attention to grooming and clothes, to body building and care, or to various attempts to attract the attention of girls. Some boys become preoccupied with finding girls who are sexually cooperative, available as outlets for sexual tension. Others turn their attention on themselves through masturbation. Still others partially sublimate their urges through sports, work, or other constructive outlets.

Quite typically, there is a wide variation in the strength of the sexual drive in adolescent boys, but most have to learn how to deal with their urges in socially acceptable ways. The developing male is usually able to adjust to these sexual changes and to come to grips with his feelings and urges only gradually. However, sex remains a problem for most adolescent boys until they develop satisfying relationships with girls. (See Chapter 9 on sexual behavior.)

Females

Development of pubic hair in girls is similar to the process that occurs with boys. On average, girls are 11.9 years of age when straight, pigmented pubic hair begins to grow, first along the labia, then, becoming more abundant and kinky, spreading over the mons in an inverse triangular pattern. By late adolescence, pubic hair spreads to the medial surface of the thighs. Figure 4.9 shows the developmental sequence (Katchadourian, 1977).

Facial hair of girls appears first as a slight down on the upper lip, then spreads to the upper part of the cheeks, and finally to the sides and lower border of the chin. The hair is less pigmented and of finer texture than that of men, but brunettes may have a darker, heavier down than blonds. Axillary hair grows about two years after pubic hair and is generally coarser and darker in brunettes than in blonds. Body hair, especially on the arms and legs, is the last to develop. Ordinarily, girls do not have noticeable hair on their chests, shoulders, or backs, except in cases of glandular disturbance.

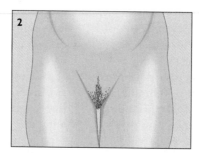
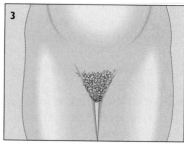
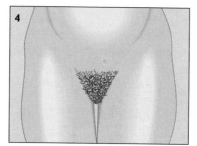
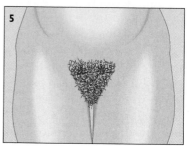

FIGURE 4.9   Stages of Pubic Hair Development in Adolescent Girls.
(*1*) Prepubertal (not shown) in which there is no true pubic hair; (*2*) sparse growth of downy hair mainly at sides of labia; (*3*) pigmentation, coarsening, and curling with an increase in the amount of hair; (*4*) adult hair, but limited in area; (*5*) adult hair with horizontal upper border.

Source: Adapted from J. M. Tanner, *Growth at Adolescence,* 2d ed. (Oxford: Blackwell Scientific Publishers, 1962), as reprinted in H. Katchadourian, *The Biology of Adolescence* (San Francisco: W. H. Freeman, 1977), p. 57.

PERSONAL ISSUES

Breast Concern

The adolescent girl's preoccupation with breast development and size is well illustrated in the following account:

> I was about six months younger than everyone else in my class.... I would sit in the bathtub and look at my breasts and know that any day now, any second now, they would start growing like everyone else's. They didn't. "I want to buy a bra," I said to my mother one night. "What for?" she asked.... "Why not use a Band-Aid instead?" she would say....
>
> I suppose that for most girls, breasts, brassieres, that entire thing, has more trauma, more to do with the coming of adolescence, with becoming a woman, than anything else....

> I started with a 28 AA bra.... My first brassiere came from Robinson's Department Store in Beverly Hills. I went there alone, shaking, positive they would look me over and smile and tell me to come back next year. An actual fitter took me into the dressing room and stood over me while I took off my blouse and tried the first one on. The little puffs stood out on my chest. "Lean over," said the fitter.... I leaned over, with the fleeting hope that my breasts would miraculously fall out of my body and into the puffs. Nothing.
>
> "Don't worry about it," said my friend Libby some months later, when things had not improved. "You'll get them after you're married."
>
> ...And I knew that no one would ever want to marry me. I had no breasts. I would never have breasts.

Source: N. Ephron, *Crazy Salad* (New York: Knopf, 1975), pp. 4–6.

One of the most noticeable changes in girls is the development of the breasts. It takes place in five stages:

1. *Prepubertal stage:* There is a flat appearance to the breasts.
2. *Bud stage:* Elevation, enlargement, and pigmentation of the nipple and surrounding areola begin, usually starting about two and one-half years before menarche.
3. *Primary stage:* An increase in the underlying fat surrounding the nipple and areola cause the areola to project in a mound above the level of the chest wall.
4. *Secondary or mature stage:* The mammary gland tissue develops, producing larger, rounder breasts. The areola recedes and is incorporated in the breast itself so that only the papilla (nipple) protrudes. This mature stage usually comes after menarche. Regardless of when development starts, it usually takes three years before the papilla projects out from the surrounding breast.
5. *Adult stage:* Development is complete.

Adolescent girls are concerned about the size and shape of their breasts. Some girls who are flat chested feel self-conscious because they are influenced by society's emphasis on full breasts as a mark of beauty and sexuality. Some adolescent girls go to the extremes of wearing padded bras and tight jerseys or sweaters, or even getting medical help to enlarge their breasts. Girls who have unusually large breasts are also self-conscious when they suffer unkind remarks and stares.

Also of concern to girls are the changes that take place in body contours. The most noticeable change other than breast development is the widening and rounding of the hips. This is due to the broadening of the pelvis and the increased deposit of fat in the subcutaneous tissue of this area. These changes occur over about an 18-month period, usually starting at about the same time that the first breast buds appear. During this period when girls are acquiring subcutaneous fat on their hips, boys seem to lose body fat across the hips. Girls stop growing in height, on average, at age 16¾, plus or minus 13 months.

There is some evidence that adolescent girls become more concerned than boys about the physical changes taking place in their bodies. The principal reason is that society places great emphasis on women's physiques. Women are rewarded in society for their appearance. It follows, therefore, that a girl will be concerned about her body fat because it helps her to determine whether she fits in socially and what her self-concept will be. The adolescent girl's concern is

Adolescence is a time of great change. The most obvious changes are physical, with the appearance of secondary sexual characteristics, growth spurts, weight changes, and changes in body proportions. The rate of these changes are variable, both within and between the sexes.

with meeting cultural standards of physical appearance and obtaining the approval of friends. As a consequence, glamour and popularity become important concerns.

Growth in Height and Weight

One of the earliest and most obvious physical changes of adolescence is the growth spurt that begins in early adolescence. This growth in height is accompanied by an increase in weight and changes in body proportion.

Growth Trends

As you can see in Figure 4.10, girls grow most in height and weight at approximately 12 years of age; boys grow most in height and weight at approximately age 14 (Tanner, 1962). Girls are usually shorter and lighter than boys during childhood; however, because they start to mature earlier, they are, on average, slightly taller than boys between ages 12 and 14 and heavier than boys between ages 10 and 14. Girls have reached 98 percent of their adult height at 16¾ years, but boys do not reach 98 percent of their adult height until 17¾ years. These rates vary for different individuals.

Determinants of Height

What determines the total mature height of an individual? A number of factors are believed to be important (Gertner, 1986), but one of the most important is heredity. Tall parents tend to have tall children; short parents tend to have short children. The most important environmental factor is nutrition. Children who are better nourished during the growth years become taller adults than those who are not nourished as well. Studies have shown that children from higher socioeconomic groups grow taller than those from poorer families. The reason is better nutrition—not income, job, or education. Depression and war can affect growth because they affect nutrition. For instance,

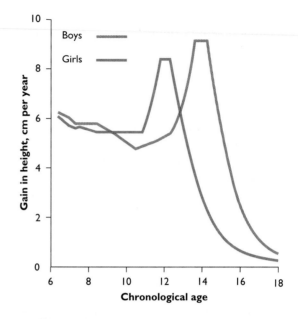

FIGURE 4.10   Increase in Height

Source: Adapted from J. M. Tanner, *Growth at Adolescence,* 2d ed. (Oxford: Blackwell Scientific Publishers, 1962), as reprinted in H. Katchadourian, *The Biology of Adolescence* (San Francisco: W. H. Freeman, 1977), p. 55.

during the last years of World War II and for several years thereafter, growth retardation of children was widespread.

The age when sexual maturation begins also affects the total height finally achieved. Boys and girls who are early maturers tend to be shorter as adults than those who are later maturers. Sexual maturation results in the secretion of sex hormones from the gonads; the hormones inhibit the pituitary from further production of human growth hormone. A later maturer has a longer time to grow before the sex hormones stop the pituitary from stimulating further growth.

Evidence indicates that the total process of growth is speeding up. Children and adolescents today experience the growth spurt earlier, grow faster, attain a greater total adult height, and attain this height earlier than did children and adolescents 100 years ago. The normal, healthy girl is ½ to 1 inch taller and reaches menarche 10 months earlier than her mother. Girls at the turn of the century reached their adult height at age 18 or 19; the average today has dropped to age 16. One researcher reported an increase in adult height of males of 2½ to 3½ inches during the last century. In 1880, males did not reach their final height until 23 to 25 years of age; today, their adult height is reached at age 18 (Tanner, 1968). The average height of U.S. sailors in the war of 1812 is estimated at 5 feet, 2 inches, which explains why the decks of the U.S.S. *Constitution* did not need to be more than 5 feet, 6 inches high.

Other dimensions, too, are larger today. The average male today wears a size 9 to 10B shoe; his grandfather wore a size 7. The seats of the famous La Scala opera house in Milan, Italy, constructed in 1776, were 18 inches wide; today, comfortable seats need to be 24 inches wide. These accelerated growth patterns, referred to as the *secular trend,* are beginning to taper off, at least in the United States and some other developed countries. Apparently, there is a limit to the ultimate size of human beings.

secular trend   the trend to mature sexually at earlier ages.

SUMMARY

1. Adolescence is a period of sexual maturation and physical growth. The changes that occur are triggered and controlled by the hypothalamus and endocrine glands that secrete hormones that stimulate and regulate the growth process.

2. The pituitary gland secretes HGH, the gonadotropic hormones FSH and LH, and LTH. FSH and LH stimulate the growth of egg cells in the ovaries, sperm in the testes, and the sex hormones. HGH affects the growth and shaping of the skeleton. LTH stimulates milk production by the mammary glands of the breast.

3. The ovaries secrete the hormones estrogen and progesterone. Estrogen stimulates the development of female sex characteristics and progesterone regulates the menstrual cycle and acts on the breasts.

4. The testes secrete the male hormone testosterone, which stimulates the development of male characteristics.

5. The adrenal glands secrete both androgens and estrogen.

6. The hypothalamus secretes GnRH, which controls the secretion of LH and FSH by the pituitary.

7. The level of testosterone and estrogen is regulated by negative feedback of these hormones, which tells the hypothalamus and gonads when enough of the hormones has been secreted.

8. Numerous changes occur in the male sex organs at puberty. The testes, scrotum, penis, prostate glands, and Cowper's glands enlarge. The testes increase the production of testosterone and begin the production of mature sperm (spermatogenesis).

9. Numerous changes occur in the female sex organs. The vagina, labia, clitoris, uterus, and Bartholin's glands enlarge and mature. The ovaries increase the secretion of estrogen and progesterone and begin the production of mature ova.

10. Menarche can become an upsetting event for girls who are not prepared for the menstrual cycle. Whether the adolescent girl experiences any menstrual problems will depend on physical and emotional factors.

11. Sexual maturation at puberty also includes the development of secondary sexual characteristics: in men, the appearance of pubic hair, the height spurt, voice changes, muscular development, and the growth of axillary hair, including the beard; in women, the appearance of pubic hair, breasts, the rounded female figure, and the growth spurt. Boys and girls can become self-conscious about their development, especially if they do not believe their growth is normal.

12. One of the earliest and most obvious physical changes of adolescence is the growth spurt that begins in early adolescence. The growth in height is accompanied by an increase in weight and changes in body proportion. Both heredity and

environmental factors determine the total mature height achieved. Also, the earlier sexual maturation occurs, the sooner the growth spurt slows down and stops.

13. Both boys and girls are maturing at younger ages than did those of previous generations. This secular trend is due primarily to better nutrition and health care.

KEY TERMS

THOUGHT QUESTIONS

1. Should female and male athletes be allowed to take testosterone to improve their abilities? What might be some of the effects?
2. Is it possible to tell if a man is virile by his build or the size of his genitals? Why or why not?
3. If you had a newborn baby boy, would you want to get him circumcised? Why or why not?
4. Explain why withdrawal is not a safe method of birth control, taking into account the action of the Cowper's glands.
5. Explain why there is no completely safe period of the month when a woman cannot get pregnant.
6. To men: When you had your first nocturnal emission, did you understand what was happening? Were you prepared for it? How did you feel?
7. To women: When you first started to menstruate, did you understand what was happening? Were you prepared for it? How did you feel?
8. Is PMS (premenstrual syndrome) primarily a psychological problem? Explain.
9. Why don't some female athletes menstruate?
10. Comment on the attitudes in U. S. society toward female breasts. What effect do these attitudes have on adolescent girls? Boys?
11. Is it possible to tell if a woman is sexually responsive by her figure? Why or why not?
12. When you were an adolescent, were you shorter or taller than your classmates? How did you feel? Explain.

SUGGESTED READING

Coles, R., and Stokes, T. (1985). *Sex and the American Teenager.* New York: Harper and Row.

Gullotta, T. P., Adams, G., and Montemayor, R. (Eds.). (1992). *Adolescent Sexuality.* Newbury Park, CA: Sage.

Rice, F. P. (1989). *Human Sexuality.* Dubuque, IA: William C. Brown.

5

The Body Image

The adolescent's emotional reactions to physical changes are as important as the changes themselves. Most adolescents become greatly concerned about body image: physical attractiveness, body type, body weight, and timing of their own development in relation to norms. In this chapter, we will discuss these and other health concerns along with two specific health problems: acne and nutrition.

The Body Beautiful

Physical Attractiveness

Physical attractiveness and body image have an important relationship to the adolescent's positive self-evaluation, popularity, and peer acceptance (Koff, Rierdan, and Stubbs, 1990). Physical attractiveness influences personality development, social relationships, and social behavior. Attractive adolescents are generally thought of in positive terms: warm, friendly, successful, and intelligent (Lerner, Delaney, Hess, Jovanovic, and von Eye, 1990). Partly as a result of differential treatment, attractive adolescents appear to have higher self-esteem and healthy personality attributes, are better adjusted socially, and possess a wider variety of interpersonal skills (Jovanovic, Lerner, and Lerner, 1989). In one study, physical attractiveness was significantly related to the self-esteem of both males and females (Thornton and Ryckman, 1991). In another study, adolescents who were ranked as physically attractive were also rated by teachers and by themselves as having better peer and parent relations than adolescents who were not considered as attractive (Lerner et al., 1991).

Body Types

Three body types have been identified: ectomorph, endomorph and mesomorph. Most people are a mixture rather than a pure type, but identifying the pure types helps considerably in any discussion of general body build. *Ectomorphs* are tall, long, thin, and narrow, with slender, bony, basketball-player builds. *Endomorphs* are at the other extreme, with soft, round, thick, heavy trunks and limbs, and wrestler-type builds. *Mesomorphs* fall between these two types. They have square, strong, well-muscled bodies, with medium-length limbs and wide shoulders. They represent the athletic type of build and participate in strenuous physical activity more frequently than the others.

Body proportions of each type change as individuals grow older. Adolescents tend to grow up before they grow out, so they may be long, slim "bean poles" before they round out. Their hands, feet, and limbs grow faster than the trunks of their bodies, so they may seem gangly, clumsy, and short-waisted. Parts of their faces, such as the nose or chin, may protrude from the relatively long heads until the flesh of the face fills in and the head becomes rounder. Gradually, however, the trunk lengthens, so that sitting height increases in relation to standing height. The waistline drops, the shoulders widen, the hips of the female broaden, and the body takes on a more mature appearance. The muscles of the limbs develop and flesh is added, so the hands and feet no longer seem out of proportion to the rest of the body.

When growth is complete, the body seems back in balance again.

Concepts of the Ideal

Adolescents are affected profoundly by the images of ideal body builds taught by their culture. Most adolescent boys and girls would prefer to be mesomorph types (Ogundari, 1985). Tall, skinny boys and girls are generally unhappy with themselves, as are short or fat adolescents. The female endomorph is especially miserable, for Western culture overemphasizes the slim, chic, well-proportioned feminine figure (Phelps et al., 1993). Weight and its distribution on the female body exert a powerful effect on women's evaluations of their bodies (Andersen and LeGrand, 1991). The desire for thinness has almost become an obsession among women in U.S. culture (Lundholm and Littrell, 1986). It is partly because of this obsession that anorexia nervosa and bulimia have become so common among adolescent girls (Cook, Reiley, Stallsmith, and Garretson, 1991; Grant and Fodor, 1986). If a girl does not have a slim figure, she is likely to be ignored by boys and less likely to have dates. It is hard to live with this type of social rejection. Self-esteem and self-satisfaction are closely related to acceptance and satisfaction with a physical self. Research shows a close association between a negative body image and

The soccer player in the middle illustrates the ectomorph body type—tall and thin with a slender, bony build. Most people are a mixture of the ectomorph, endomorph, and mesomorph body types.

depression in adolescent girls (Rierdan, Koff, and Stubbs, 1989).

Furthermore, research suggests that appearance anxiety in women is related to reported negative social experiences in childhood and early adolescence. These experiences may lead to childhood dissatisfactions and early adolescent appearances, which, in turn, are related to appearance anxiety in late adolescence and early adulthood (Keelan, Dion, and Dion, 1992).

Studies of males provide further evidence of the social importance of physical attractiveness and of possessing an average physique. Tall men with good builds are considered more attractive than short men. Men with muscular, mesomorphic body builds are more socially accepted than those with different builds. College-aged men with muscular builds are more likely to be socially easygoing and optimistic about interacting with others than endomorphs and ectomorphs (Tucker, 1983). In another study, adolescents who rated themselves as unattractive were also likely to describe themselves as lonely (Moore and Schultz, 1983).

Individual Body Characteristics

Adolescent girls in the sixth or seventh grade become conscious of particular signs of maturation, such as breast development. As adolescents mature, they turn their attention to other body features: hips, thighs, buttocks, noses, eyes, and teeth.

One study showed the importance of individual body characteristics in self-ratings of physical attractiveness by female and male college students (Lerner and Karabeneck, 1974). The mean age of women was 19.5 years and of men 20.4 years. These ratings, given in Table 5.1, show that both women and men felt that general appearance, face, body build, and teeth were important to physical attractiveness. Women also emphasized eyes, shape of legs, hips, waist, and chest. Men were not as concerned about these features but placed more emphasis on profile, height, neck, and shoulder width. Men and women were moderately but equally concerned about hair texture, nose, and mouth. Both were least concerned about ankles, ears, hair color, and arms. It is evident that these evaluations reflect cultural stereotypes of attractiveness.

TABLE 5.1 Mean Importance of Selected Body Characteristics for Own Physical Attractiveness for Males and Females

Body Characteristics	Female's Own Importance (N = 114)	Male's Own Importance (N = 70)
General appearance	1.3	1.5
Face	1.4	1.5
Facial complexion	1.6	1.8
Distribution of weight	1.7	2.0
Body build	1.7	1.9
Teeth	1.9	2.0
Eyes	1.9	2.4
Shape of legs	2.2	2.8
Hips	2.2	2.8
Hair texture	2.3	2.3
Waist	2.3	2.4
Chest	2.4	2.6
Nose	2.4	2.4
Mouth	2.4	2.4
Profile	2.5	2.3
Thighs	2.5	2.9
Height	2.9	2.7
Chin	3.1	2.8
Arms	3.1	3.0
Hair color	3.2	3.2
Width of shoulders	3.4	2.9
Ears	3.9	3.5
Ankles	4.1	4.2

Note: Respondents ranked characteristics on a scale of 1 to 5, from very important to very unimportant, respectively.

Source: R. M. Lerner and S. A. Karabeneck, "Physical Attractiveness, Body Attitudes, and Self-Concepts in Late Adolescents," *Journal of Youth and Adolescence,* 3 (1974): 307–316. Reprinted by permission.

ectomorph tall, slender body build.
endomorph short, heavy body build.
mesomorph medium, athletic body build.

The ideal masculine body image consists of being tall and having dark hair, broad shoulders, a slim waist, and well-proportioned arms and legs. Some adolescent boys, however, at least early in their development, look skinny, uncoordinated, out of proportion, and weak. Late developers are still short and childlike. Others are chubby, some with protruding breasts. Boys who deviate from the norm may be given hurtful nicknames ("Slim," "Stretch," "Fatso," etc.). The boy with the weak-looking build may spend hours working out to try to improve his build. The fat adolescent who is not able to diet successfully may withdraw from normal social contacts with girls and show marked symptoms of emotional maladjustment. So much emphasis is put on having an athletic build that the adolescent who is not able to conform feels extremely self-conscious and isolated.

Weight

Obesity

The body image of an adolescent is closely related to weight status (Fowler, 1989). Many adolescents worry about being overweight. One study of females from three junior high schools suggests that many adolescent girls appear to have concerns about body weight and dieting and have had concerns as early as elementary school age. More than 25 percent of the females reported that they had first dieted at age 12 or younger; 27 percent were on a diet at the time of the assessment. In addition, a significant number of these girls reported feeling depressed after overeating and were radically dieting as a form of weight control. Some reported experiencing what might be considered early manifestation of eating problems (Moreno and Thelen, 1995).

The causes of **obesity** are not a simple matter. Krieshok and Karpowitz (1988) divided the causes into two major categories: (1) physiological contributors and (2) psychological contributors.

Physiological Contributors to Obesity Physiological contributors may also be divided into the following three categories:

External Variables External variables may be regulated to some extent by the person. They include *food type and variety* and *activity level*. Obese adolescents do not necessarily eat more food, overall, but they prefer foods that are calorically dense and highly flavored (Keesey and Pawley, 1986). Furthermore, their physiological responses tend to encourage this consumption and do not become inhibited after the food is consumed. Specifically, after eating meals high in carbohydrates or sugars, insulin levels are elevated, which increases hunger and food consumption. In fact, just the

To an adolescent, physical attractiveness is very important. This seventh-grade adolescent is paying more attention to her physical attractiveness than to what is going on in the classroom.

sight and smell of foods can elevate the insulin level in obese people.

Activity level is another external variable related to excess fat accumulation. If exercise is moderate, the appetite is reduced somewhat, *metabolism* increases, and fat accumulation is decreased. If the activity level is low, fat accumulates because metabolism declines. Obese people have been found to be less active than people of normal weight. However, if exercise is too strenuous, the appetite increases. The body compensates for activity levels.

Internal Variables   Internal variables are also physiological variables that contribute to obesity. These are genetically controlled and cannot be changed by the person (except perhaps through surgery). There are differing opinions as to the strength of the genetic component. One suggestion is that endomorphs tend to have longer in-

testines than do ectomorphs, require more food before satiation, and allow more calories to be absorbed. This argument is substantiated by the fact that surgically shortening the intestine can increase weight loss (Powers, 1980).

Mediated Variables   Mediated variables are those over which the individual may have some regulation but not complete control. One such variable is the size or number of fat cells in the body. Everyone has fat cells, but overweight people have unusually large cells or more cells. Food type, variety, activity level, and genetic variables all affect the development of fat cells, but the cells are more

obesity   overweight; excessively fat.

metabolism   the rate at which the body utilizes food and oxygen.

HIGHLIGHT

Family Factors and Obesity

The beginnings of obesity may be found in the early relationships between parents and children (Brone and Fisher, 1988). The childhoods of many obese adolescents are characterized by intense parental involvement, overprotectiveness, and rigidity. Overprotectiveness involves an unusually high concern for the child's welfare. For example, in clinical interviews, parents frequently speak for their obese children or correct them when they attempt to speak for themselves. One father said he would not put his obese daughter on a diet because he would not permit her to be deprived of anything (Brone and Fisher, 1988).

One important manifestation of overprotectiveness is overfeeding. Furthermore, parents often show a hypochondriacal concern for the child's health. Outside interests and friends are many times seen as threats to the parent-child relationship. Obese adolescents often have difficulties in social relationships, so their family becomes a safe haven from the outside world (Doherty and Harkaway, 1990).

Parental frustrations and disappointments in their own lives often underlie the intense parental involve-

ments in the lives of obese adolescents. Obese adolescents are often from lower–socioeconomic-status families. Parents try to compensate by seeing that the child stays healthy and close to the family. Many obese adolescents emerge from childhood handicapped by feelings of ineffectiveness, dependency, and lack of direction.

Some of these adolescents rebel against their parents to try to increase separation from them. Although the obese child appears healthy and well cared for, he or she is a source of embarrassment to parents, who now urge him or her to reduce. One way the obese adolescent asserts independence is by rejecting the parents' pleas to reduce and by eating as a show of defiance (Brone and Fisher, 1988). Obesity, then, is a form of rebellion against parental control.

There seems to be some evidence that addictive eating is more common in adolescents whose parents are themselves addicted to alcohol, drugs, gambling, or overeating. Whether this is inherited or learned behavior is uncertain (Marston et al., 1988).

likely to be increased in number if excess weight is gained before the age of 12. This is why *eating habits developed before adolescence are important determinants of fat deposition on the body during adolescence* (Krieshok and Karpowitz, 1988). Also, people who have elevated numbers of fat cells may be limited in the amount of excess fat they are able to lose permanently.

Psychological Contributors to Obesity   Numerous psychological factors are also important contributors to obesity. For instance, eating is a greater positive reinforcement for obese people because they find it to be a more pleasurable activity than do people of normal weight. Jacobs and Wagnor (1984) found that the reinforcement values of spending time with friends and family were higher for obese people than for people of normal weight. For other people, eating is a negative reinforcement of disturbed emotions—that is, it can eliminate anxiety, depression, and upset. Oral activity becomes a means of finding security and release from tension (Heatherton, Herman, and Polivy, 1992).

For still other people, eating becomes a means of punishment. They have poor self-esteem or hate themselves. Weight gain becomes a way of reinforcing their own negative self-conceptions and proving they are right in feeling that way.

The most successful approaches to treating obesity recognize that it has many causes. Comprehensive examinations are necessary to detect genetic, metabolic, environmental, familial, and emotional factors. After reasons for obesity are diagnosed, proper medical and dietary treatments are instituted. If eating becomes an effort to relieve anxiety, therapy may be needed to deal with the emotional causes. One thing is certain: Weight-loss efforts are more successful when accompanied by a program of regular exercise (Gurin, 1989b).

Underweight

Underweight people burn more calories than they consume. Male adolescents particularly worry about being too skinny or "not having a good build." In one study of 568 adolescent males, over half were dissatisfied with their bodies, and 71 percent reported eating to gain weight (Fleischer and Read, 1982).

Eating Disorders

Sometimes the desire to be thin is carried to such an extreme that eating disorders develop. Two such disorders are discussed here: anorexia nervosa and bulimia.

Anorexia Nervosa

Anorexia nervosa is a life-threatening emotional disorder characterized by an obsession with food and weight. It is sometimes referred to as the *starvation sickness* or *dieter's disease.* The major symptoms are a constant preoccupation with food and dieting, body image disturbances (Mallick, Whipple, and Huerta, 1987; Muuss, 1985), excessive weight loss (15 percent or more of body weight), amnorrhea (cessation of menstrual period), hyperactivity (excessive exercise), moodiness, isolation, insecurity, helplessness, depression, and loneliness (American Psychiatric Association, 1987). Anorexia is also associated with numerous medical conditions: slow heartbeat, cardiac arrest (a frequent cause of death), low blood pressure, dehydration, hypothermia, electrolyte abnormalities, metabolic changes, constipation, and abdominal distress.

Once the illness has progressed, anorexics become thin and emaciated in appearance. They feel cold, even in warm weather. The body grows fine silky hair to conserve body heat. A potassium deficiency may cause malfunction of the kidneys. Researchers have also found brain abnormalities coupled with impaired mental performance and lessened reaction time and perception speed due to malnutrition.

Between 5 and 10 percent of anorexics die because of medical problems associated with malnutrition. Their obsession with dieting is combined with a compulsion to exercise, which leads to social isolation and withdrawal from family and friends. Hunger and fatigue are usually denied, and any attempt to interfere with the regime is angrily resisted. Anorexics are very difficult to treat (Grant and Fodor, 1984).

Anorexia is rare among males (Svec, 1987). Some 95 percent of anorexics are female, usually between the ages of 12 to 18. The disorder has become more common and now affects about 1 percent of all adolescent females. It has been showing up lately among all economic classes and wider

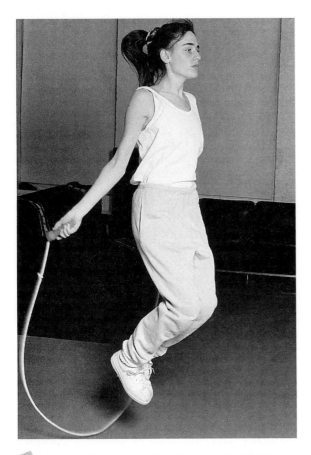

Among the symptoms associated with the life-threatening disorder of anorexia nervosa, which generally appears at puberty, are a constant preoccupation with food and dieting, a dangerous amount of weight loss, an excessive amount of exercise, and a distorted body image.

age groups. Some believe that more than half a million people are anorexic. This is due partly to intense pressure in U.S. culture to be thin (Stein and Reichert, 1990).

The fact that anorexia nervosa appears at puberty after the development of sexual characteristics suggests that sexual conflict is a central issue in the illness. Apparently, anxiety develops over feminine physiological changes. The girl's developing body symbolically demands coming to terms with her female sexual identification. She has the task of integrating her new body image with her concept of female sexual roles. If she cannot accept her female sexual identity, she seeks to repress her physical development to a stage of prepubertal development. She then actually distorts her body image through extreme weight loss and

takes on a slim, masculine appearance. She may become severely emaciated in appearance, removing all outward signs of her secondary sex characteristics. In addition, she stops menstruation (Jenkins, 1987). These efforts represent the youth's desperate attempt to halt her sexual development. Instead of progressing forward through adolescence, she follows a pathological deviation and regresses to a prepubertal stage of development.

Anorexics have a pervasive sense of inadequacy and distorted body images that often lead to depression. They have low self-esteem and high anxiety (Button, 1990), reflecting negative attitudes about physical attractiveness (Baird and Sights, 1986; Canals, Carbajo, Fernandez, Marti-Henneberg, and Domenech, 1996; Grant & Fodor, 1986). Hooker and Convisser (1983) explain that anorexics tend to separate their bodies from their person: "I see my body as something that drags along behind me." This split into a mind-body dichotomy is so complete that they literally do not know how they look (Seebach and Norris, 1989).

Adolescents with anorexia nervosa rarely look at themselves and, even when forced to, rarely perceive their body images accurately. They view their bodies with disgust, which is a projection of how they actually feel about themselves.

Anorexics often have disturbed relationships with their parents (Eisele, Hertsgaard, and Light, 1986). The families are usually rigid and overprotective with a hypochondriacal concern for the child's health (Brone and Fisher, 1988). Often, a power struggle develops between the adolescent girl and her parents, particularly with her mother (Levin, Adelson, Buchalter, and Bilcher, 1983, p. 54). This desire to guide and control becomes more evident as parental concern grows (Grigg and Friesen, 1989).

What are the various forms of treatment for anorexia nervosa? Medical treatment monitors the physical condition of the anorexic and tries to return her weight to the safe range. Behavior modification uses rewards and deprivation, contingent on eating behavior and weight gain. This

anorexia nervosa   an eating disorder characterized by an obsession with food and with being thin.

Five Theories about Causes of Anorexia

According to Muuss (1985, pp. 526–527), there are five theories that explain the possible causes of anorexia:

Social theory: The anorexic is brainwashed by a culture that emphasizes being slim, so she becomes obsessed with food and diets.

Psychosexual theory: The anorexic is unwilling to accept her role as a woman and her feminine sexuality. She fears sexual intimacy, so she uses the disorder to delay or regress her psychosexual development.

Family systems theory: The anorexic comes from a superficially good family that is overprotective and rigid, and whose members avoid conflict. This interferes with the adolescent's identity formation.

Biological theory: A disturbance in the hypothalamus triggers anorexic behavior.

Psychobiologic regression hypothesis: Once body weight drops below a critical level because of inadequate diet, neuroendocrine functions are impaired, which reverses the developmental changes of puberty. The girl regresses to a prepubertal stage of development.

may be successful in achieving weight gain but it does not deal effectively with more severe psychological problems. Family therapy seeks to solve underlying family interaction problems and to improve relationships with the anorexic (Dare, Eisler, Russell, and Szmukler, 1990). Individual psychodynamic approaches tries to help the individual resolve her emotional conflicts. Probably the most effective treatment combines medical and psychological approaches. The goals are to eliminate the anorexic symptoms and to enable the patient to feel and act as an independent person who likes herself, is confident about her capabilities, and is in control of her life. Accomplishing these goals may require long-term therapy.

Bulimia

Bulimia is a binge-purge syndrome. The name comes from the Greek *bous limos,* which means "ox hunger" (Ieit, 1985). The first cases of bulimia that appeared in the literature were in connection with anorexia nervosa (Casper, 1983). Some clinicians diagnosed bulimia as a subgroup of anorexia; however, since binge eating occurred in both obese and normal-weight individuals, bulimia was designated a separate eating disorder (American Psychiatric Association, 1987).

Bulimia is characterized by a compulsive and rapid consumption of large quantities of high-calorie food in a short period of time (Holleran, Pascale, and Fraley, 1988). One study of the frequency and duration of bingeing episodes among bulimic clients in an outpatient setting revealed an average of 13.7 hours spent in binge eating each week, with a range of 15 minutes to 8 hours for each episode (Mitchell, Pyle, and Eckert, 1981). Bingeing and purging may occur many times daily. Caloric consumption ranged from 1,200 to 11,500 calories per episode, with carbohydrates as the primary food. Many clients report losing the ability to perceive a sense of fullness. Episodes usually take place secretly, often in the afternoon or evening and sometimes at night. Induced vomiting is the usual aftermath of binge-eating episodes. Some bulimics use laxatives, diuretics, enemas, amphetamines, compulsive exercising, or fasting to offset the huge food intake.

Bulimics are unhappy with the appearance of their bodies and yearn to attain the thin shape glamorized by society (Brouwers, 1990). However, they lack control over eating.

The bulimic feels driven to consume food and, because of a concern about body size, to purge afterward. Binges usually follow periods of stress and are accompanied by anxiety, depressed mood (Brouwers, 1988), and self-deprecating thoughts during and after the episode (Ieit, 1985). The average age of bulimics is early 20s (Lachenmeyer and Muni-Brander, 1988), although the pattern is becoming more common in high school girls (Johnson et al., 1984; Van Thorre and Vogel, 1985).

Bulimics wish to be perfect yet they have a poor self-image, have a negative self-worth, are shy, and lack assertiveness (Holleran, Pascale, and Fraley, 1988). They are often preoccupied with fear of rejection in sexual relationships and with not being attractive enough (Van Thorre and Vogel, 1985). Also, they have traditional and exaggerated concepts of femininity that describe the ideal woman as accommodating, passive, and dependent.

Because of unrealistic standards and the drive for perfection, pressure builds up, which is relieved through lapses of control during binge-purge episodes. This is followed by feelings of shame and guilt, which contribute to the sense of low self-esteem and depression. Bulimics are often difficult to treat because they resist seeking help or they sabotage treatment.

The family situations of bulimics are similar to those of anorexics. Many of the families demonstrate the characteristics of enmeshment, overprotectiveness, perfectionism, and rigidity. They place a great deal of emphasis on attractiveness, physical fitness, achievement, and success (Roberto, 1986).

Some of the most promising treatment programs involve cognitive-behavioral approaches that help clients identify unrealistic and self-defeating cognitions and assumptions. Correcting these irrational beliefs is an essential step toward changing the bulimic's behavior.

Exercise

Adolescents as well as adults in the United States are in the midst of a nationwide fitness craze. Working out and staying in shape have become immensely popular. The trendiest clothes are active wear and different shoes for running, aerobics, and other sports. Every sizable community has its fitness centers, gyms, pools, tennis courts, and bike trails.

Benefits

People are finding that exercising is fun and beneficial in a variety of ways. One most obvious benefit is to *build physical fitness*. In one study, youths of all ages believed that frequent activity resulted in beneficial physical outcomes (Watkins, 1992). Exercise tones up the body system, builds muscles, strengthens the heart and lungs, and improves circulation. It also relieves nervous tension, depression, and anxiety.

A desire to *lose weight* motivates many adolescents to exercise. In a study of British adolescents, 24 percent of the 12-year-olds and 42 percent of the 14-year-olds reported exercising to lose weight (Davies and Furnham, 1986). Similarly, a study of 194 high school freshmen in the United States revealed that one-half of the normal-weight students and two-thirds of the heavy students exercised to control or lose weight (Desmond, Price, Gray, and O'Connell, 1986).

Exercise also *promotes psychological and mental health* (Carruth and Goldberg, 1990). Possessing a physically fit body that meets the cultural ideals of thinness and beauty can enhance body image and self-esteem (Mallick, Whipple, and Huerta, 1987). Exercise may improve self-esteem by promoting feelings of competence and mastery (Brown and Lawton, 1986).

The very fit feel significantly better about themselves than the less fit. One study of 229 female adolescents revealed that frequent vigorous exercise lessened the impact of stressful events (Brown and Lawton, 1986). Physical fitness also *improves intellectual performance* and the ability to perform a variety of mental tasks.

There is evidence that physical activity patterns developed in adolescence may continue into adulthood. A comparison of the physical activity levels of 453 young adult men, age 23 to 25, with their childhood fitness scores, revealed that those who were physically active as adults had better childhood physical fitness test scores than those who were not physically active (Dennison, Straus, Mellits, and Charney, 1988).

bulimia   an eating disorder characterized by binge-eating episodes and purging.

PERSONAL ISSUES

Exercise and Weight Loss

When you look at a standard calorie chart, it's hard to see how you can lose much weight through exercise. You have to walk at a normal pace for 2 hours or swim or ski for 1 hour to burn off 500 calories—the equivalent of one piece of pecan pie, or two pieces of chocolate cake, or 4½ ounces of sirloin steak. But working out does more than burn up calories while you're exercising. It gives you an "after burn." That is, it boosts your metabolism so that you're still using up calories for hours after your workout. Studies at the University of California at Davis showed that metabolism is still "revved up" 12 hours after a workout (Gurin, 1989a, 1989b).

Nutrition

Adults sometimes think that adolescents are constantly eating. The fact is, during the period of rapid growth, adolescents *need* greater quantities of food to take care of bodily requirements.

Digestion

The stomach increases in size and capacity in order to be able to digest the increased amounts of food eaten by adolescents. Research shows that the caloric requirement for girls may increase, on average, by 25 percent from ages 10 to 15 and then decrease slightly and level off. The caloric requirement for boys may increase, on average, by 90 percent from ages 10 to 19.

Importance of Nutrition

Development of proper eating habits during adolescence is extremely important to individual health. Attainment of maximum height, strength, and physical well-being depends on eating enough body-building foods. Bone, muscle, nerve, and other tissue growth requires good nutrition. National deficiencies are related to physical and mental retardation, reduced stamina, lower resistance to infection, premenstrual tension in girls, and emotional instability.

Adolescents are part of a national fitness craze. The benefits of exercising are many: physical fitness, losing weight, promoting good mental health, and improving intellectual performance. Hopefully these patterns will continue into adulthood.

Considerable attention has been given to the importance of good nutrition in pregnant teenage girls. Pregnancy during the teen years, when the adolescent mother's body is still in the formative stage, creates added physiological stress for the young girl. Her body makes increased nutritional requirements both for the growth of her body and for the development and subsequent feeding of her baby. Because many of these girls become pregnant out of wedlock, get very little or no prenatal care in the early stages of pregnancy, and show a depressed emotional state before and during pregnancy, they are poor obstetrical risks. Their babies may be born prematurely, have congenital defects, or lack the necessary nutrients to survive during the first days and months of life. Furthermore, these young mothers may be prone to such complications of pregnancy as toxemia (the presence of toxic substances in the blood) or eclampsia (convulsions).

Although many adults think that adolescents are constantly eating, many have inadequate diets, especially girls. Snacking and poor eating habits are two of the reasons.

Deficiencies

Most studies of nutrition during adolescence show that many adolescents have inadequate diets (Amos et al., 1989; U.S. Dept. of Agriculture and U.S. Dept. of Health and Human Services, 1985). Deficiencies may be summarized as follows:

1. Insufficient calcium (due primarily to an inadequate intake of milk)
2. Insufficient iron (especially true for girls)
3. Inadequate protein (usually true only for girls)
4. Insufficient vitamins, especially A and C (due primarily to lack of enough fresh vegetables and fruit in the diet)
5. Insufficient thiamine and riboflavin

Adolescent girls have nutritional deficiencies more often than boys. One reason for this deficit is that girls eat less and so are less likely to get the necessary nutrients (Newell, Hammig, Jurick, and Johnson, 1990). Another reason is that girls diet more often, depriving themselves of necessary nutrients. The additional need for some nutrients because of menstruation or pregnancy also imposes special problems.

Why do so many adolescents, both boys and girls, have inadequate diets? The reasons may be summarized as follows:

1. They *skip breakfast* because of lack of time in the morning, because they would rather sleep late, and for other reasons.

2. *Snacks,* which make up about one-fourth of the daily intake of food, *do not compensate for meals missed.* This is because snacks are primarily fats, carbohydrates, and sugars, and because the intake from snacks is not sufficient to make up for the food missed.

3. *Small quantities of foods are eaten,* especially of fruits, vegetables, milk, cheese, and meat. Girls usually need more eggs and whole-grain cereal than they eat. Also, girls who are dieting often develop nutritional deficiencies because of a low intake of food.

4. *Inadequate knowledge of nutrition* influences the development of poor nutrition practices. Many times, high school boys and girls know so little about nutrition that they cannot select a well-balanced meal in a cafeteria. Many adolescents need to reduce dietary fat and sugar (Read, Harveywebster, and Usinger-Lesquereux, 1988).

5. *Social pressures* may cause poor eating habits. Adolescents who adopt bizarre eating habits often reflect the ideas of their social or cultural group. Some ethnic groups are notorious for their poor nutritional habits,

regardless of the amount of money available to buy food.

6. *Troubled family relationships and personal adjustments* seem to accompany poor eating habits. Adolescents from broken or troubled homes may not have parents at home to cook for them or to see that they get an adequate diet. Those with emotional problems may have nervous stomachs, ulcers, or more complex reasons for not eating properly.

7. The *family is poor* and cannot afford to buy proper food. Altogether, about 12 percent of families in the United States are below the poverty level (U.S. Bureau of the Census, 1996).

Nutrition Education

Studies of food habits of adolescents reveal that many have already developed very negative dietary habits. A four-year health survey of 356 high school students from Illinois revealed that over half had an excess intake of red meat, saturated fats, and salt (Adeyanju, 1990). These habits, coupled with the fact that many students' families have a family history of heart disease or strokes, suggest the need for a health intervention program to reduce the risk of future cardiovascular disease.

Acne

At the onset of puberty, due to actions and reactions of the hormones of the body, the glands of the skin increase their activity. Often, this results in *acne.* Acne is a source of embarrassment to adolescents, often leading to self-consciousness and social withdrawal.

Skin Gland Development

Three kinds of skin glands can cause problems for the adolescent:

1. *Merocrine* sweat glands, distributed over most of the skin surfaces of the body
2. *Apocrine* sweat glands, located in the armpit, mammary, genital, and anal regions

3. *Sebaceous* glands, which are the oil-producing glands of the skin

During the adolescent years, the merocrine and apocrine sweat glands secrete a fatty substance with a pronounced odor that becomes more noticeable. The result is body odor. The sebaceous glands develop at a greater speed than the skin ducts through which they discharge their skin oils. As a result, the ducts may become plugged and turn black as the oil oxidizes and dries upon exposure to the air, creating a *blackhead.* At other times, the duct closes, forming *pustules* or *whiteheads.* Superficial acne is characterized by open blackheads or closed whiteheads. In deep acne, scarring is frequent.

Treatment

For less severe cases of acne, early treatment may prevent acne from becoming serious, either physically or psychologically. Adolescents need to keep the skin clean with a good soap (although many keep their skin clean and still have problems). Misconceptions about a relationship between acne and diet, athletics, or masturbation are common and should be corrected. Some cosmetics (especially greasy products or those containing isopropyl myristate) aggravate acne. Sunlight and some topical medications can aid superficial lesions. For more severe acne, however, oral tetracycline may be used to prevent scarring. Oral isotretinoin is sometimes used with patients when antibiotics are not successful, but it causes birth defects if the woman is pregnant, in addition to other side effects, so it is prescribed with caution (Berkow, 1987).

Victims of acne have receptors in their cells that accept the male androgens, which, in turn, stimulate the activity of the sebaceous glands. Some doctors counteract this activity by prescribing oral contraceptives that contain female estrogens. However, such pills work only on some patients, and undesirable side effects have made physicians more cautious.

Acne may be aggravated by tension and emotional upset that activate the skin glands. This is one reason why a tense adolescent may be more susceptible to acne than a calm one. In all cases, the adolescent should receive concerned, prompt treatment.

Early and Late Maturation

The effect of early or late physical maturation on both the psychological and social characteristics and adjustments of boys and girls has been the subject of intensive investigation. The results of these studies are important in understanding adolescents who differ from the norm in either the timing or the rate of their development (Collins and Propert, 1983) (see Figure 5.1).

Early-Maturing Boys

In boys, early maturation is associated with positive self-evaluations, whereas late maturation is generally associated with negative self-evaluations (Alsaker, 1992). Early-maturing boys are large for their age, stronger, more muscular, and better coordinated than late-maturing boys, so they enjoy a considerable athletic advantage. They are better able to excel in competitive sports and their athletic skills enhance their social prestige and position. They enjoy considerable social advantages in relation to their peers, participate more frequently in extracurricular activities in high school, and are often chosen for leadership roles. Early-maturing boys also tend to show more interest in girls and to be popular with them because of superior looks and more sophisticated social interests and skills. Early sexual maturation thrusts them into heterosexual relationships at an early age.

Adults, too, tend to favor early-maturing boys. Adults are more likely to rate them as more physically attractive, more masculine, better groomed, and more relaxed than late-maturing boys. Even more important, adults accept and treat early-maturing boys as more mature, able persons. The boys look older; the community therefore gives earlier recognition to their desires to assume adult roles and responsibilities. Thus, they are given privileges reserved for older people.

Note that this attitude of adults has some disadvantages as well as advantages. Adults tend to expect more of early-maturing boys and expect adult behavior and responsibilities. Early-maturing boys have less time to enjoy the freedom that comes with childhood. One adolescent boy remarked:

> I was tall and well developed by the time I was 13 years of age. People always thought I was 5 or 6

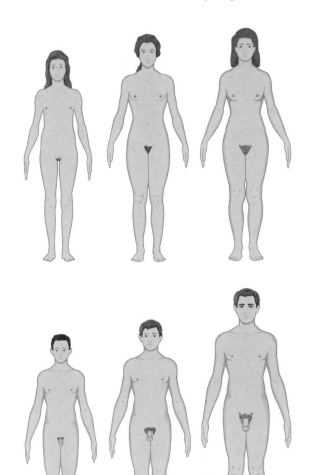

FIGURE 5.1   Variations in Pubescent Development. All three girls are 12¾ years and all three boys are 14¾ years of age but in different stages of puberty.

Source: Adapted from J. M. Tanner, *Scientific American* (Sept. 1973): 38.

years older than I really was. Consequently, they criticized me or made fun of me if I acted up or fooled around. "Don't be a kid, act your age," they

acne pimples on the skin caused by overactive sebaceous glands.

used to tell me. My Dad expected me to help out around the place. I had to go to work when I was only 15—I lied about my age to get the job. I never seemed to have time to have fun like the rest of the kids my age. (Author's counseling notes)

Late-Maturing Boys

Late-maturing boys suffer socially induced inferiority. A boy who has not reached puberty at age 15 may be 8 inches shorter and 30 pounds lighter than his early-maturing male friends. Accompanying this size difference are marked differences in body build, strength, and coordination. Because physical size and motor coordination play such an important role in social acceptance, late maturers develop negative self-perceptions and self-concepts. They are characterized as less attractive and popular; more restless, bossy, and rebellious against parents; and as having feelings of inadequacy, rejection, and dependency. They often be-

come self-conscious and some withdraw because of their social rejection.

Late maturers sometimes overcompensate by becoming overly dependent on others or overly eager for status and attention. At other times, they try to make up for their inadequacies by belittling, attacking, or ridiculing others or by using attention-getting devices. A typical example is the loud, daring show-off with a chip on his shoulder, ready to fight at the least provocation. The effects of these early negative social attitudes may persist into adulthood, long after physical differences and their social importance have disappeared. It has been found that most late-maturing boys delay adult psychological commitments such as marriage and are less secure in their vocational status because they earn less. In extreme cases of physical retardation caused by physiological factors, androgens are sometimes administered to hasten puberty, but social retardation may continue long afterward.

PERSONAL ISSUES

Late Maturation

In the following example, a 15-year-old boy, Stephen, adjusted to his late maturation by overconformity to rules on the one hand and by efforts to excel verbally and academically on the other. In relation to his parents, he was dependent, undercontrolled, rebellious, and childish.

> Stephen at fifteen was slight of build and had not as yet experienced any secondary sexual changes, such as body hair development, voice change, and the like. Always a good student, his application to his studies was far in excess of what was required and bordered on obsessional perfectionism. Indeed he had many features of the obsessive compulsive in his character structure, which had developed and continued from latency. He was punctilious, tidy, compliant, and fearful of authority. His strict re-

gard for the rules to which he adhered with almost a legalistic fanaticism made him a questionable asset in games with his peers. As would be expected, he veered away from athletic pursuits and found success and pleasure in such activities as the debating team. All his aggressiveness and competitiveness focused on verbal, intellectual pursuits and he delighted in fault-finding and one-upping both peers and teachers. But at home, he let his guard down, as it were, and was given to temper outbursts, demanding, whining behavior, and fierce rivalry with his brother, four years younger. . . . Stephen was thus still a latency child at fifteen, with no apparent heterosexual interests, his sexuality was limited to the crude locker room vulgarity more characteristic of the eleven-year-old.

Source: S. H. Shapiro, "Vicissitudes of Adolescence," in S. L. Cope (Ed.), *Behavior Pathology of Childhood and Adolescence* (New York: Basic Books, 1973), p. 95.

CROSS-CULTURAL CONCERNS

Early Development and Psychosexual Behavior of African American and Non-African American Adolescent Females

A study of a national sample of adolescent females aged 15 to 19 revealed that both African American and non-African American early-maturing girls were more likely to have experienced earlier dating and sexual activity than their late-maturing peers (Phinney, Jensen, Olsen, and Cundick, 1990). As a group, African Americans ex-perienced menarche and first intercourse at earlier ages than non-African Americans; dating and marriage were experienced at later ages. These racial differences are at-tributed to differing socialization patterns or cultural ex-pectations.

Early-Maturing Girls

A study on early-maturing girls found that early maturation was related significantly to poor body image and global negative self-evaluations in girls in the sixth and eighth grades (Alsaker, 1992). Early maturation in girls tends to have a negative effect during their elementary school years. A girl who is already physically mature in fifth or sixth grade is at some disadvantage because she is out of phase with the majority of her classmates. She is taller, more developed sexually, and tends to feel awkward and self-conscious because she is dif-ferent. For this reason, she enjoys less prestige at this age than do her prepubertal friends.

By junior high school, however, the early-ma-turing girl comes into her own socially. She begins to look more like a grown-up woman, is envied by other girls for her adult looks and clothes, starts to attract the attention of older boys, and begins dat-ing earlier than normal. This creates some prob-lems for her, however. Her parents begin to worry because of her precocious heterosexual interests and may try to limit her social desires and activi-ties. In fact, early maturation has been associated with increased sexual experience in young adoles-cent girls (Flannery, Rowe, and Gulley, 1993).

By the time early-maturing girls have reached 17 years of age, they have more positive self-concepts, score higher on total adjustment and family adjustment, and enjoy better personal rela-tions than do later maturers, although the net pos-itive effect of early maturation does not seem to be as pronounced for girls as for boys.

Late-Maturing Girls

Late-maturing girls are at a distinct social disad-vantage in junior high school and high school. They look like little girls and resent being treated as such. They are largely bypassed and overlooked in invitations to boy-girl parties and social events. Girls who experience menarche at ages 14 to 18 are especially late daters. As a consequence, late-maturing girls may be envious of their friends who are better developed. They are generally on the same level with normal-maturing boys and so have much in common with them as friends. However, they avoid large, mixed groups of boys and girls, and their activities reflect the interests of those of younger age groups with whom they spend their time. One advantage is that late-maturing girls do not experience the sharp criticism of parents and other adults as do girls who develop early. The chief disadvantage seems to be the temporary loss of social status because of their relative physical immaturity.

SUMMARY

1. Adolescents are concerned about body image: physical attractiveness, body-type concepts of the ideal, body weight, and timing of their own development in relation to what is considered normal. Adolescents who are physically attractive are treated in more positive ways, develop more positive self-perceptions and personalities, and are more popular and better adjusted socially.

2. The three body types are ectomorph, mesomorph, and endomorph. Mesomorphs with medium builds are preferred in both boys and girls. Those who are tall and skinny (ectomorphs) or short and fat (endomorphs) are viewed more negatively.

3. Adolescents are concerned about individual body characteristics: general appearance, face and complexion, weight and body build, and teeth. Girls are also concerned about the shape of their legs, breasts, and waist, and about their eyes. Boys worry about height, shoulders, profile, and neck. Boys and girls are equally concerned about hair texture, noses, and mouths and are less concerned about ankles, ears, hair color, and arms. Those who deviate from the norm may become self-conscious.

4. Adolescents worry about their weight. Obesity is not necessarily caused by overeating but by eating high-calorie foods and by underactivity. More calories are ingested than burned up. The most successful approach to treating obesity is a multifaceted one that considers it a multicausal problem. Underweight adolescents need to conserve energy and to increase their consumption of fattening foods.

5. Anorexia nervosa is a life-threatening emotional disorder characterized by an obsession with food and weight. Symptoms include constant preoccupation with food and dieting, body image disturbances, excess weight loss, amenorrhea, hyperactivity, moodiness, isolation, and strong feelings of insecurity, helplessness, depression, and loneliness. It is also associated with numerous medical conditions.

6. Anorexia is found primarily in teenage girls and usually appears at puberty. Anorexics often have disturbed relationships with their parents.

7. Bulimia is a binge-purge syndrome characterized by compulsive and rapid consumption of large quantities of high-calorie food, followed by efforts to purge the food.

8. Bulimics are unhappy with the appearance of their bodies, yet they are impulsive, lack control over eating, and are anxious and depressed with low self-esteem. They are perfectionists with unrealistic standards. Family relationships are usually disturbed, with parents who are overprotective, perfectionistic, and rigid.

9. Many U.S. adolescents have joined a nationwide fitness craze. Exercise is not only fun but physically and psychologically beneficial. Most adolescents participate in sports of some kind.

10. Nutrition is extremely important to individual health. Adolescents may suffer a variety of deficiencies: calcium, iron, protein, vitamins A and C, and thiamine and riboflavin. There are a number of reasons for deficiencies: Adolescents skip breakfast; snacks of junk food do not make up for meals missed; small quantities of food are eaten; inadequate knowledge of nutrition results in poor food selection; social pressures and troubled family relationships result in poor eating habits; or the family cannot afford to buy good food.

11. Nutrition education is useful in modifying the food habits of adolescents.

12. Adolescents worry about body odor and acne caused by the increased secretion of skin glands during puberty. Prompt attention and treatment of acne may prevent its becoming severe.

13. The timing of physical maturation is important. Some adolescents mature earlier or later than average, with a differential effect. Early-maturing boys enjoy athletic, social, and community advantages. There may be greater anxiety because of sudden pubertal changes, at least for a while, and more pressure to act older than their age. In general, however, early maturation for boys is an advantage. Late-maturing boys suffer socially induced inferiority, which may carry over into adulthood.

14. Girls who mature in elementary school tend to feel awkward and self-conscious because they look different. By junior high school, however, they begin to be envied by their peers for their adult looks. Early maturity results in precocious heterosexual interests, which may worry parents. Overall, however, by age 17, these girls have more positive self-concepts, are better adjusted, and enjoy better personal relations than late maturers. Late-maturing girls are at a distinct social disadvantage. They look like little girls, resent being treated as such, and are envious of their friends who have matured. These social advantages are temporary and may be overcome when maturation takes place.

KEY TERMS

acne **124**

anorexia nervosa **119**

bulimia **120**

ectomorph **114**

endomorph **114**

mesomorph **114**

metabolism **117**

obesity **116**

 THOUGHT QUESTIONS

1. Is it possible to have high self-esteem and only be of average physical attractiveness? Why or why not?
2. What characteristics do you consider most important in physical attractiveness? Which body features are most important? What can the adolescent who's not especially attractive do?
3. Have you ever been overweight or underweight? What has helped you?
4. Why is exercise absolutely necessary in weight-reduction efforts?
5. Have you ever known anyone who is anorexic? Describe the person and try to explain why you think the person became that way.
6. Have you ever known anyone who is bulimic? Describe the eating behavior of the person, something about the personality of the individual, and why you think the individual was bulimic.
7. Do you follow a regular routine of exercise? Why or why not? What prevents you from doing so if you do not?
8. Do you eat breakfast? Lunch? Why or why not?
9. What do nutritionists consider to be a balanced diet?
10. What helps most in the prevention and/or treatment of acne?
11. Did you mature earlier or later than your classmates? How did you feel? How did it affect you? What happened? What did you do?

 SUGGESTED READING

Cooper, P. J. (1995). *Bulimia Nervosa and Binge-Eating: A Guide to Recovery*. New York: New York University Press.

Fallon P., Katzman, N. A., and Wooley, S. C. (Eds.). (1994). *Feminist Perspectives on Eating Disorders*. New York: Guilford Press.

Kagawa-Singer, M., Katz, P. A., Taylor, D. A., and Vanderryn, J. H. M. (Eds.). (1996). *Health Issues for Minority Adolescents*. Lincoln: University of Nebraska Press.

Sandbek, T. J. (1993). *The Deadly Diet: Recovering from Anorexia and Bulimia*, 2nd ed. Oakland, CA: New Harbinger Publications.

Zraly, K., and Swift, D. (1992). *Overcoming Eating Disorders: Recovery from Anorexia, Bulimia, and Compulsive Overeating*. New York: Crossroads.

6

Cognitive Growth and Change

The word *cognition* literally means "the act of knowing or perceiving." So, in discussing the cognitive development of adolescents, we seek to discuss the process by which they grow in knowledge. More specifically, we will look at their ability to understand, think, and perceive, and to utilize these abilities in solving the practical problems of everyday living.

There are basically three approaches to this study of cognition. The first is the *Piagetian approach,* which emphasizes the qualitative changes in the way adolescents think. The second is the *information-processing approach,* which examines the progressive steps, actions, and operations that take place when the adolescent receives, perceives, remembers, thinks about, and utilizes information. The third approach is the *psychometric approach,* which measures quantitative changes in adolescent intelligence. The Piagetian approach is discussed in this chapter. A discussion of the information-processing approach and the psychometric approach is covered in Chapter 7.

Piaget's Stages of Cognitive Development

As we discovered in Chapter 3, Piaget divides cognitive development into four major stages (Overton and Byrnes, 1991; Overton and Montangero, 1991; Piaget 1950, 1967, 1971, 1972, 1980):

1. The sensorimotor stage is from birth to about age 2.
2. The preoperational stage is from about age 2 to age 7.
3. The concrete operational stage is from about age 7 to about age 11 or 12.
4. The formal operational stage is from age 11 or 12 on.

Berzonsky (1978) provided one of the best descriptions of Piaget's four stages:

> According to Piaget's theory, thought is internalized action. One initially acts overtly, i.e., one walks to the sink to get a drink of water. When one is thinking, however, the behavior is carried out covertly in one's mind, thought is thus internalized action. True directed thinking for Piaget is known as operations and involves internalized action that is reversible; i.e., one can mentally cancel out actions that have actually occurred. The type of operation that an individual is capable of using is the basis for naming the four stages. Sensorimotor operations are those carried out in action, not mentally. Preoperations deal with the internalization process; they are rigid rather than reversible. Concrete operations are internal actions which can be reversed but they involve actual behavior. Formal operations are not restricted to actual transformations of reality, they deal with abstractions which are independent of reality. (p. 279)

Let's look at each stage in more depth.

Sensorimotor Stage

During the *sensorimotor stage,* learning is related to the mastery of sensory-motor sequences. The infant moves from a self-centered, body-centered world to an object-centered world as the senses of vision, touch, taste, hearing, and smell bring him or her into contact with things having various properties and relationships to other objects. The child becomes intrigued with such simple motor activities as picking up objects, falling backward on a pillow, and blowing. Thinking, if any, occurs as a stimulus-response connection with the physical world without mediation, although the latter part of this period marks a transition to symbolic play, imitation, and representation of objects. Elkind (1967) labeled the principal cognitive task during this period the *conquest of the object.*

Preoperational Stage

The *preoperational stage* is the period when language is acquired. Children begin dealing with their world by learning and manipulating symbols, as well as through motor activity and direct interactions with the environment. Symbolic play, or *internalized imitation,* emerges. Elkind (1967) labeled the principal preoperational task the *conquest of the symbol.*

During this period, there is evidence of transductive reasoning rather than inductive or deductive reasoning. *Transductive reasoning* occurs when the child proceeds from particular to particular, without generalization, rather than from the particular to the general *(inductive reasoning)* or from the general to the particular *(deductive reasoning).* For example, the dog Fido jumps on you because he has in the past; Brownie will jump on you because he is frisky like Fido. Blackie, however, will

During Piaget's sensorimotor stage, children under 2 years old begin to move from a body-centered world to an object-centered world, where simple motor activities, such as picking up objects, become intriguing.

not jump on you because he is too big (but, in fact, he may). An error in judgment is made because the general concept that dogs jump on you is never developed.

At this stage, children sometimes make errors of *syncretism,* trying to link ideas that are not always related. For example, Mother had a baby the last time she went to the hospital, so the next time she goes to the hospital, you mistakenly expect Mother will bring home another baby.

Preoperational thinking is also *egocentric;* that is, children have difficulty understanding why someone else cannot see something in the same way they do. For example, you get upset when you cannot convince your parent not to wash your dirty rag doll. You gain security from it, and that is important to you, but to your parent, the important thing is that the doll is dirty.

Related to all the preceding characteristics is **centering,** which refers to children's tendencies to focus attention on one detail and their inability to shift attention to other aspects of a situation (Muuss, 1988b). For example, you may conclude there is more water in a shallow dish than in a glass because the dish is wider, even though you have already seen all the water poured from the glass into the dish (see Figure 6.1). You ignore the greater height of the glass and the demonstration of pouring.

As a result of their inability to maintain more than one relationship in their thinking at a time, children make errors of judgment, give inadequate or inconsistent explanations, show a lack of logical sequence in their arguments, and a lack of comprehension of constants. There is evidence of thinking but still an absence of operational thinking.

Concrete Operational Stage

During the *concrete operational stage,* children show a greater capacity for logical reasoning though still at a very concrete level. One of the reasons they can think more logically is that they are able to arrange objects into *hierarchical classifications* and comprehend *class inclusion relationships* (the inclusion of objects in different levels of the hierarchy at the same time). This gives children the ability to understand the relations of the parts to the whole, the whole to the parts, and the parts

to the parts. For example, suppose you are given a randomly organized array of blue and red squares and black and white circles. If you understand inclusion relationships, you discover there are two major collections (squares and circles) and two subtypes of each (blue versus red squares and black versus white circles). There is a hierarchy whose higher level is defined by shape and whose lower level is defined by color. This enables you to say that all squares are either blue or red; that there are more squares than blue squares; that there are more squares than red squares; that if the red squares are taken away, the blue ones are left; and so on.

Concrete operational children are capable also of *serialization,* or serial ordering. For example, in arranging animals, such as dogs and cats, into a hierarchy of classes, you might arrange dogs and cats into separate classes, and then dogs into further subdivisions, such as bulldogs and setters or perhaps according to color or size.

Children at this stage learn that different objects may be grouped by size, by alphabetical order, or by age, or that an object may simultaneously belong to more than one class. A child may

sensorimotor stage   the first stage of cognitive development, according to Piaget, lasting from birth to about 2 years of age.

preoperational stage   the second stage of cognitive development, according to Piaget, lasting from 2 to 7 years of age.

transductive reasoning   proceeding from particular to particular in thought, without making generalizations.

inductive reasoning   gathering individual items of information and putting them together to form hypotheses or conclusions.

deductive reasoning   beginning with an hypothesis or premise and breaking it down to see if it is true.

syncretism   the act of trying to link ideas together.

centering   the tendency of children to focus attention on one detail and their inability to shift attention to other aspects of the situation.

concrete operational stage   the third stage of cognitive development, according to Piaget, lasting from 7 to 11 or 12 years of age.

a   *b*

FIGURE 6.1 **Understanding the Principle of Conservation of Volume.** *(a)* The child agrees that glasses A and B have the same amount of water. *(b)* The water from B is poured into the dish. The child is unable to understand that glass A and the dish still have the same amount of water, because the dish appears broader even though it is shallower. The child is unable to retain one aspect (the amount) when another aspect changes (the height of the water column and the width of the column).

be a girl, a fourth-grader, an athlete, and a redhead, all at the same time. They learn that some relationships are *symmetrical,* or *reciprocal*—such as two brothers are brothers to each other. In dealing with numbers, children learn that different combinations of numbers make the same total and that *substitutions* may be made with the same result. In dealing with liquids and solids, they learn that a change in shape does not necessarily change volume or mass; the amount is conserved.

Piaget calls this stage the *concrete operational stage* of cognitive development because it involves concrete elements (objects, relations, or dimensions) and operations (such as addition or subtraction) as well as rules, or *properties,* that describe the way the operations may be performed. Elkind (1967) called the major cognitive task of this period *mastering classes, relations, and quantities.*

Muuss (1988b) summarizes four concrete operations the child is able to perform:

1. *Combinativity:* Two or more classes can be combined into one larger, more comprehensive class. For example, all men and all women equals all adults.
2. *Reversibility:* Every operation has an opposite operation that reverses it. Supraclasses can be taken apart, so that the effect of combining subclasses is reversed. All adults except all women equal all men. . . .
3. *Associativity:* The child whose operations have become associative can reach a goal in various ways . . . but the results obtained . . . remain the same. For example, (3 plus 6) plus 4 equals 13, and 6 plus (3 plus 4) equals 13.
4. *Identity or nullifiability:* An operation that is combined with its opposite becomes nullified. Illustrations . . . are: give 3 and take away 3 results in null. (p. 185)*

Conservation refers to the recognition that properties of things such as weight or volume are not altered by changing their container or shape.

Conservation tasks involve some manipulation of the shape of matter that does not alter the mass or volume of the matter (Piaget and Inhelder, 1969). A typical conservation problem is represented by the balls of clay in Figure 6.2. In this example, the child is asked to confirm that A and B are the same size. Then B is changed to B_1, then to B_2, then to B_3. The child is asked to compare A with B_1, then with B_2, and with B_3, each time stating whether A and B are still the same. Children in the preoperational stage are guided by the shapes they see. Children in the concrete operational stage preserve a recognition of the equality between A and B that transforms their physical shape.

It is important to remember that *the child's thinking is still linked to empirical reality* (Piaget, 1967). Children have made some progress toward extending their thoughts from the actual toward the potential (Elkind, 1970), but the starting point must still be real because concrete operational children can reason only about those things with which they have had direct, personal experience. When children have to start with any hypothetical or contrary-to-fact proposition, they have difficulty. Elkind (1967) also pointed out that one of the difficulties at this stage is that the child can deal with only two classes, relations, or quantitative dimensions at the same time. When more variables are present, the child flounders. This ability to consider more than two variables at once is achieved only during the formal operations stage that follows.

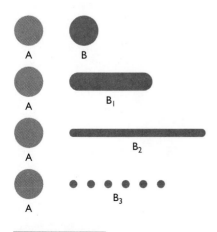

FIGURE 6.2   Conservation of Mass

Formal Operational Stage

The last stage of cognitive development, the *formal operational stage,* begins during early adolescence. Piaget subdivided the stage of formal operations further into substages III-A, almost full formal function (11 or 12 to 14 or 15 years), and III-B, full formal function (14 or 15 years and up). The division of the adolescent period at the age of 14 or 15 implies another restructuring and a disequilibrium, which then leads to a higher level of equilibrium and intellectual structure during late adolescence.

Substage III-A—the earlier substage, corresponding to early adolescence—appears to be a preparatory stage in which adolescents may make correct discoveries and handle certain formal operations. Their approach is still crude, however. They are not yet able to provide systematic and rigorous proof of their assertions. This substage has been titled *emergent formal operational thought.* At this time, adolescents are able to exhibit formal operations in some situations but not in others.

By the time adolescents reach substage III-B, they have become capable of formulating more elegant generalizations and advancing more inclusive laws. Most of all, they are now able to provide spontaneously more systematic proof for their assertions because they understand the importance of method of thought (Muuss, 1988b). This second substage is the true or consolidated stage of formal operational thought wherein the adolescent or adult demonstrates such thought across a variety of situations. Many adolescents and adults never truly reach the second substage. Most seem to remain fixated somewhat in substage III-A, often thinking formally only in situations with which they are familiar (Flavell, Miller, and Miller, 1993).

The attainment of formal operations is not an all-or-nothing proposition. Between the ages of 11 or 12 and 14 or 15, considerable modification, systemization, and formalization of thought processes can be observed. The complexity of the problems that the individual can handle increases

formal operational stage   the fourth stage of cognitive development, according to Piaget, during which people develop abstract thought independent of concrete objects.

substantially during these years and reaches an equilibrium after substage III-B has been attained (Muuss, 1988b). Some adolescents and adults never reach this formal operational stage because of limited intelligence or cultural deprivation.

Elkind (1967) called this final stage the *conquest of thought*. During this stage, the thinking of the adolescent begins to differ radically from that of the child (Piaget, 1972). The child has developed concrete operations and carried them out in classes, relations, or numbers, but their structure has never gone beyond the elementary level of logical "groupings" or additive and multiplicative numerical groups. The individual has never integrated them into a single, total system found in formal logic. Adolescents, however, are able to superimpose propositional logic on the logic of classes and relations. In other words, formal operations adolescents are able, through inductive reasoning, to systematize their ideas and deal critically with their own thinking to be able to construct theories about it. Furthermore, they can test these theories logically and scientifically, considering several variables, and are able to discover truth, scientifically, through deductive reasoning (Inhelder and Piaget, 1958). In this sense, adolescents are able to assume the role of scientists because they have the capacity to construct and test theories.

The difference between the way children approach problems and the logical, systematic approach of adolescents is given in the following example:

> E. A. Peel . . . asked children what they thought about the following event: "Only brave pilots are allowed to fly over high mountains. A fighter pilot flying over the Alps collided with an aerial cableway and cut a main cable, causing some cars to fall to the glacier below. Several people were killed." A child at the concrete-operational level answered: "I think the pilot was not very good at flying." A formal-operational child responded: "He was either not informed of the mountain railway on his route or he was flying too low. Also his flying compass may have been affected by something before or after take-off, thus setting him off course causing collision with the cable."
>
> The concrete-operational child assumes that if there was a collision the pilot was a bad pilot; the formal-operational child considers all the possibilities that might have caused the collision. The concrete-operational child adopts the hypothesis that seems most probable or likely to him. The formal-operational child constructs all possibilities and checks them out one by one. (Kohlberg and Gilligan, 1971, pp. 1061, 1062)

One of the experiments Piaget conducted, which led to discovering the strategies adolescents use in solving problems, involved a pendulum. The selected subjects were shown a pendulum suspended by a string (see Figure 6.3). The problem was to discover what factors would affect the oscil-

During Piaget's formal operational stage, which begins in early adolescence, thinking begins to differ radically from that of a child. The adolescent becomes able to construct theories and can test these theories using scientific methods.

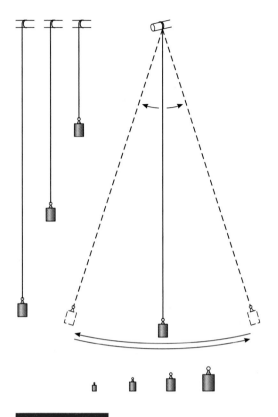

FIGURE 6.3   The Pendulum Problem. This simple pendulum consisting of a string, which can be shortened or lengthened, and a set of varying weights. The other variables that at first might be considered relevant are the height of the release point and the force of the push given by the subject.

Source: "The Pendulum Problem" from *The Growth of Logical Thinking: From Childhood to Adolescence* by Jean Piaget and Barbel Inhelder. Copyright © 1958 by Basic Books, Inc. Reprinted by permission of BasicBooks, a division of HarperCollins Publishers, Inc.

latory speed of the pendulum. The subjects were to investigate four possible effects: changing the length of the pendulum, changing its weight, releasing the pendulum from various heights, and starting the pendulum with various degrees of force. The subjects were allowed to solve the problem in any way they chose.

The adolescents showed three basic characteristics in their problem-solving behavior. First, they planned their investigations systematically. They began to test all possible causes for variation in the pendulum swings: long or short string, light or heavy weight, high or low heights, and various degrees of force of push. Second, they recorded the outcomes accurately and with little bias under the different experimental conditions. Third, they were able to draw logical conclusions.

For example, they observed that the height of drop and force had no effect on oscillatory speed. Believing that pendulum weight or length of string might be involved, they tried different combinations of weight with various combinations of string length, only to find that whatever the weight, the oscillation speed remained the same. They discovered, however, that changing the string length did alter the oscillation speed. They were able to conclude that pendulum length alone determined the speed of oscillation. Since this original experiment, the methods and results have been replicated by other researchers.

Younger subjects given the same problem may come up with the right answer by trial and error but they will not use systematic and scientific procedures or be able to give a logical explanation of the solution. Children tend to form conclusions that seem warranted by the facts. But often these conclusions are premature and false because the children have not considered all of the important facts and are not able to reason logically about them. Even when presented with contrary evidence, younger children tend to hold tenaciously to the initial hypothesis and try to make the circumstances fit these preconceived notions.

One characteristic of adolescents' thinking that these ideas suggest is the ability to be flexible. They can be quite versatile in their thoughts and in dealing with problems. They can also devise many interpretations of an observed outcome. Because they can anticipate many possibilities prior to an actual event, they are not surprised by unusual outcomes. They are not stuck with their preconceptions. In contrast, younger children are confused by atypical results inconsistent with their simple perceptions of events.

It has already been suggested that the preoperational child begins to utilize symbols. The formal operational adolescent, however, now begins to utilize a second symbol system: *a set of symbols for symbols.* For example, metaphorical speech or algebraic symbols are symbols of other words or numbers. The capacity to symbolize symbols makes the adolescent's thought much more flexible than the child's. Words can now carry double or triple meanings. Cartoons can represent a complete story that would otherwise have to be explained in words. It is no accident that algebra is not taught to elementary school children or that children have difficulty understanding political cartoons or religious symbols until approximately junior high age (Elkind, 1970).

Another important difference between concrete operational children and formal operations adolescents is that the latter are able to orient themselves toward what is abstract and not immediately present. They are able to escape the concrete present and think about the abstract and the possible. This facility enables adolescents to project themselves into the future, to distinguish present reality from possibility, and to think about what might be. Not only do adolescents have the capacity to accept and understand what is given but they also have the ability to conceive of what might be possible. Because they can construct ideas, they have the ability to elaborate on what they received, generating new or different ideas and thoughts. They become inventive, imaginative, and original in their thinking. Possibility dominates reality. "The adolescent is the person who commits himself to possibilities . . . who begins to build 'systems' or 'theories' in the largest sense of the term" (Baker, 1982). This ability to project themselves into the future has many important consequences for their lives.

In summary, formal thinking, according to Piaget, involves four major aspects: introspection (thinking about thought), abstract thinking (going beyond the real to what is possible), logical thinking (being able to consider all important facts and ideas and to form correct conclusions, such as the ability to determine cause and effect), and hypothetical reasoning (formulating hypotheses and examining the evidence for them, considering numerous variables).

Effects of Adolescent Thought on Personality and Behavior

What are the effects of adolescent thought on personality and behavior? Let's discuss this important question.

Idealism

As they become oriented to the adult world, adolescents' powers of reflective thinking enable them to evaluate what they learn (Schmidt and Davison, 1983). They become much more capable of moral reasoning. Furthermore, their ability to differentiate the possible from the real enables them to distinguish not only what the adult world is but also what it might be like, especially under ideal circumstances. This ability of adolescents to grasp what is and what might be makes them *idealistic*. They compare the possible with the actual, discover that the actual is less than ideal, and become critical observers of things as they are and ultracritical of adults.

For a while, some adolescents develop the equivalent of a *messianic complex*. In all modesty, they attribute to themselves essential roles in the salvation of humanity. They may make a pact with God, promising to serve Him without return but planning to play a decisive role in the cause they espouse (Piaget, 1967). They see themselves in a major effort to reform the world, usually in verbal discussions and for some, in group movements. Some adolescents get caught up in political idealism and become preoccupied with the utopian reconstruction of society. By late adolescence, their attention usually shifts from egocentrism to a newfound sociocentrism.

At the same time that adolescents become political idealists, they also become champions of the underdog. It is adolescents' own inner turmoil that accounts for their empathic capacities for the suffering of others. Due to their own insecure psychological positions, they can easily identify with the weak, the poor, and the oppressed victims of selfish society. Thus, the social injustices that they perceive mirror their own internal, individual struggles. Elkind (1967) has stated that young adolescents rebel primarily on a verbal level, doing little to work for humanitarian causes they espouse. Only later in adolescence do young people begin to tie their ideals to appropriate actions and to be more understanding, tolerant, and helpful.

Long-Term Values

The fundamental observable characteristic of adolescence is that the individual begins to take

Idealism in adolescents results from their newfound ability to distinguish between what is and what might be. They become champions of the underdog and often become involved in helping victims of society.

on adult roles. These include the tendency for adolescents to see themselves as equals with adults, to develop a life program, to be concerned with the future, and to have ideas about changing society. At first, the adolescent personality is highly egocentric, but the egocentricism is gradually broken down through a decentering process. Along with formal reasoning development comes the development of values with long-term implications rather than immediate gratification and goal satisfaction.

Hypocrisy

Because of the discrepancy between what they say and what they do, adolescents are sometimes accused of *hypocrisy.* Elkind (1978) gave two examples to illustrate this tendency. First, a teenage boy complains at great length about his brother going into his room and taking his things. He berates his father for not punishing the culprit; yet the same adolescent feels no compunction about going into his father's study, using his computer and calculator, and playing rock music on his father's stereo without asking. Second, a group of young people are involved in a "Walk for Water" drive, in which sponsors pay them for each mile walked. The money is for testing the water of Lake Ontario and for pollution control. Elkind described how pleased he was that these youths were not as

valueless and materialistic as they were sometimes described to be. The next day, however, a drive along the route the youths had walked revealed a roadside littered with fast-food wrappers and soft drink and beer cans. City workers had to be hired to clean up the mess. The question was: Did the cost of cleaning up amount to more money than was collected? Here was an example of hypocrisy at its finest. On the one hand, the youths objected to pollution, yet they were among the chief offenders in defacing their environment (Elkind, 1978).

The behavior of these adolescents was hypocritical to the extent that it revealed a discrepancy between idealism and behavior. But this assumes that they had the capacity to relate general theory to specific practice, which young adolescents are not necessarily able to do. Early adolescents have the capacity to formulate general principles, such as "Thou shalt not pollute," but lack the experience to see the application of these general rules to specific practice. This is due to intellectual immaturity rather than to a defect of character. Youths believe that if they can conceive and express high moral principles, then they have at-

hypocrisy discrepancy between what people say and do.

tained them, and nothing concrete need be done. This attitude confuses and upsets adults, who insist that ideals have to be worked for and cannot be attained instantly. This attitude is, in turn, considered cynical and hypocritical by youths (Elkind, 1978).

The ability of adolescents to think about themselves, their own thoughts, and society also leads to another manifestation of hypocrisy: pretending to be what they are not. They are expected to like school yet they rarely do. They are expected to conform to parental viewpoints and beliefs even when they do not agree with them. They are expected not to be hurt or angry but they really are. They are expected not to engage in behavior that will hurt or disappoint parents, so they do not dare talk to them. They are pressured not to be, not to feel, not to desire. They are expected to deny themselves and so they behave hypocritically. Their newly achieved capacity to envision what *should be* enables them to go beyond their real selves and to pretend to be what others expect them to be.

Creativity

Do we expect that adolescents who are capable of logical reasoning processes also be creative? *Creativity* is the process of becoming sensitive to problems (deficiencies, gaps in knowledge, missing elements, and disharmonies), identifying the difficulty (searching for solutions, making guesses, or formulating hypotheses about the deficiencies), then testing and retesting (possibly modifying) these hypotheses, and, finally, communicating the results.

However, investigations of the relationship of adolescent thinking processes with creative behavior suggest a negative relationship: Some adolescents become *less* creative, not more so. The reason is not that they are less capable of being creative; they have a greater potential than before. Actually, they are less creative because of the pressures on them—from both their peers and society in general—to conform. The price they pay for acceptance is conformity. As a result, they squelch their individuality and begin to dress, act, and think like others in groups to which they desire to belong. One study emphasized that adolescents who rate highest in self-trust (who believe in

themselves) are more willing to risk doing things that are imaginative and creative (Earl, 1987).

Pseudostupidity

Elkind (1978) pointed out that young adolescents also often demonstrate what he has called *pseudostupidity*, the tendency to approach problems at much too complex a level and fail, not because the tasks are difficult but because they are too simple. For example, an adolescent goes shopping to buy a pair of shoes and socks, but looks in the least obvious places. Another example is how youths try to solve a problem by holding a number of variables in mind at the same time yet they lack the capacity to assign priorities and to decide which choice is more appropriate. In other words, the ability to perform formal operations gives young adolescents the capacity to consider alternatives, but this new-found capacity is not completely under control. Thus, adolescents appear stupid because they are, in fact, bright but not yet experienced.

Egocentrism

Another effect of adolescents' intellectual transformation is their development of a new form of *egocentrism* (Vartanian and Powlishta, 1996; Hudson and Gray, 1986; deRosenroll, 1987). This egocentrism is manifested in two ways: through the development of what has been termed imaginary audience and personal fable ideations (Lapsley, FitzGerald, Rice, and Jackson, 1989).

As adolescents develop the capacity to think about their own thoughts, they become acutely aware of themselves, their person, and their ideas. As a result, they become egocentric, self-conscious, and introspective. They direct their thoughts toward themselves rather than toward others (Goossens, Seiffge-Krenke, and Marcoen, 1992). They become so concerned about themselves that they may conclude that others are equally obsessed with their appearance and behavior. "It is this belief that others are preoccupied with his appearance and behavior that constitutes the egocentrism of the adolescent" (Elkind, 1967, p. 1029). As a result, adolescents feel they are "on stage" much of the time. Thus, a great deal of their energy is spent "reacting to an *imaginary audience*" (Buis and Thompson, 1989).

HIGHLIGHT

Self-Consciousness under Pressure

In a cleverly designed experiment, the performances of children, adolescents, and adults in operating video games were measured when they did not know they were being observed and when an experimenter stood watching over their shoulder during the performance. While watching, the experimenter pointedly exhorted subjects to try to obtain the highest score they possibly could, reminding them they would have only one chance.

Children under 12 years old generally improved under audience pressure; adolescents from 14 to 19 years old showed substantial drops in performance; and adults aged 20 or older showed moderate drops in performance. This experiment suggests that self-consciousness is low in children, highest in adolescence, and intermediate or variable thereafter (Tice, Buder, and Baumeister, 1985).

The need to react to an imaginary audience helps account for the extreme self-consciousness of adolescents (Peterson and Roscoe, 1991). Whether in the lunchroom or on the bus going home, most youths feel that they are the center of attention. Sometimes, groups of adolescents react to this audience by loud and provocative behavior because they believe everyone is watching them.

Elkind (1967) also discussed what he termed *personal fable,* adolescents' beliefs in the uniqueness of their own experiences. Because of their imaginary audiences and their beliefs that they are important to so many people, adolescents come to regard themselves as special and unique. Some have a unique sense of their own immortality and invulnerability to harm (Dolcini et al., 1989). This may be why so many adolescents believe that unwanted pregnancies happen only to others, never to them.

Egocentrism may also be linked to adolescents' desires for social reform and to their efforts to assume adult roles (White, 1980). Not only do they try to adapt their egos to the social environment but they also try to adjust the environment to their egos. They begin to think how they might transform society. Inhelder and Piaget (1958) wrote:

> The adolescent goes through a phase in which he attributes an unlimited power to his own thoughts so that the dream of a glorious future or of transforming the world through ideas (even if this idealism takes a materialistic form) seems to be not only fantasy but also an effective action which in itself modifies the empirical world. This is obviously a form of cognitive egocentrism. (p. 345)

Daydreaming

One of the consequences of the ability of adolescents to think more and more about their thoughts and to go beyond reality is an increase in daydreaming. Gold and Henderson (1990) measured the frequency of daydreaming of intellectually gifted early adolescents, ages 10 to 16, during two consecutive summer programs and found a small but significant increase in daydreaming and visual imagery over this time period. This finding is in keeping with others that have shown that older gifted children report more positive, constructive use of daydreaming, more visual imagery, and higher levels of curiosity (Henderson and Gold, 1983).

At the same time that daydreaming and visual imagery increase, the content of the daydreams becomes more positive and constructive. Less

pseudostupidity the tendency to approach problems at much too complex a level and to fail, not because the tasks are difficult, but because they're too simple. Adolescents appear stupid but they are, in fact, bright but not yet experienced.

egocentricism the inability to take the perspective of another or to imagine the other person's point of view.

imaginary audience the adolescents' belief that others are constantly paying attention to them.

personal fable adolescents' belief that they are invulnerable and that their feelings are special and unique.

guilt and fear of failure in the dreams indicates that adolescents develop an increasing cognitive ability to deal with negative experiences (Gold and Henderson, 1990). Daydreams can serve a practical purpose in testing out alternative behavior and solutions to problems via the imagination.

Self-Concept

The capacity of adolescents to think about themselves is also necessary in the process of developing self-concepts and identities. In doing this, adolescents have to formulate a number of postulates about themselves, such as "I am physically attractive," "I'm smart in school," or "I'm popular." These postulates are based on a number of specifics, such as "I'm attractive because I have pretty hair." Because of formal operational thinking, they are able to entertain a number of simultaneous ideas and to test each one—for example, by asking a friend: "What do you think of my hair?" or "Do you think I have ugly hair?" Gradually, they begin to sort out what they feel is truth from error about themselves and to formulate total concepts of self.

Decentering and a Life Plan

The process of adopting adult roles, which is directly related to cognitive development, does not stop with egocentrism. Adolescents conceive of fantastic projects whose goals are self-assertion, imitation of adult models, and participation in circles that are actually closed. They follow paths that satisfy them for a time but are soon abandoned as they develop more cognitive objectivity and perspective. In other words, adolescents begin to cure themselves of their idealistic crises and to return to the reality that is the beginning of adulthood. Inhelder and Piaget (1958) emphasized that "the focal point of the decentering process is the entrance into the occupational world or the beginning of serious professional training. The adolescent becomes an adult when he undertakes a real job. It is then that he is transformed from an idealistic reformer into an achiever" (p. 346).

Piaget also referred to the importance of adolescent work in the community as a facilitator of human growth. He stated that work helps the adolescent meet the storm and stress of that period, as well as stimulates the development of social un-

derstanding and socially competent behavior. True integration into society comes when the adolescent reformer attempts to put his or her ideas to work. In this process, the ego is gradually decentered as the personality develops and begins to affirm a life plan and adopt a social role.

Critique of Piaget's Formal Operational Stage

Since Piaget formulated his concept of a formal operational stage of cognitive development, investigators have been examining various components of the formulation.

Age and Percentages

One question asked by investigators concerns the age at which formal operational thought replaces the concrete operational stage. Piaget (1972) himself advanced the possibility that in some circumstances, the appearance of formal operations may be delayed to 15 to 20 years of age and "that perhaps in extremely disadvantageous conditions, such a type of thought will never really take shape" (p. 7). Piaget (1971) acknowledged that social environment can accelerate or delay the onset of formal operations. In fact, fewer economically deprived adolescents achieve formal thought than do their more privileged counterparts, and there is a complete absence of formal operations among the mentally retarded. The absolute percentage of adolescents demonstrating formal operational thinking has usually been below 50 percent; when a larger proportion (around 60 percent) have shown formal thinking, they have been drawn from "gifted" samples or from older, more academic, college students.

It is important for adults, especially parents and teachers, to realize that not all same-aged adolescents are at the same stage of development (Flavell, 1992). Many have not yet achieved formal operations. These youths cannot yet understand reasoning that is above their level of comprehension; to ask them to make decisions among numerous alternatives or variables that cannot be grasped simultaneously is to ask them to do the impossible. A very few youths may make the transition to formal operations by age 10 or 11, but only about 40 percent have progressed beyond concrete operations by high school graduation (Bauman, 1978; Lapsley, 1990).

Test Criteria

The measured percentages of people reaching formal operational thinking depend partially on which criteria of formal thinking are used and the level of the tests employed. Piaget distinguishes between an easy level (III-A) and a more advanced level (III-B). One researcher, using Piaget's III-A level to measure the percentage of females achieving formal operational thinking, demonstrated that 32 percent of 11-year-old girls, 67 percent of college women, and 54 percent of adult women had reached that level. But when the more advanced III-B criteria were used in measurements, the percentages were 4 percent for girls, 23 percent for college students, and 17 percent for adults (Tomlinson-Keasey, 1972, p. 364).

In reviewing the research, Kuhn (1979) observed that only approximately 50 percent of the adult population actually attain the full stage of formal thinking (III-B). The formal operational stage, quite in contrast to the preceding childhood stages of Piaget's theory, may never be attained by a significant proportion of the general adolescent population. Piaget (1980) readily admitted that the subjects of his study were "from the better schools in Geneva" and that his conclusions were based on a "privileged population." In spite of evidence critical of his assumptions, he maintained that "all normal individuals are capable of reaching the level of formal operation" (Piaget, 1980, p. 75) as long as the environment provides the necessary cognitive stimulation. Although not all adolescents or adults reach the formal level, there is still a significant increase in the use of formal operational thinking during adolescence, especially between ages 11 and 15.

Beyond Formal Operations

Investigations of the Piagetian stage of formal operations suggest that progressive changes in thought structures may extend beyond the level of formal operations. The implication is that cognitive growth is continuous; there is no end point beyond which new structures may appear. Researchers continue to seek these new structures (Commons, Richards, and Kuhn, 1982).

Although the results of investigations are still tentative, there is some evidence that a fifth stage of development can be differentiated. It has been labeled a *problem-finding stage* (Arlin, 1975). This new stage characterizes creative thought, the envisioning of new questions, and the discovery of new problem-solving methods in thought. It represents an ability to discover problems not yet delineated, to formulate these problems, or to raise general questions for ill-defined problems.

---

problem-finding stage the fifth stage of cognitive development characterized by the ability to be creative, to discover, and to formulate problems.

◤ HIGHLIGHT

Gender Differences in Formal Operations

Piaget was concerned with fundamental questions of sequence and orderliness of cognitive changes and not with the variables that have always been of concern to the educational and developmental psychologist: individual differences, sex, socioeconomic level, IQ, reading level, and so forth. Piaget's theory has stimulated considerable research into sex differences on ability to solve Piagetian problems, especially on spatial processing tasks (Jamison and Signorella, 1980; Liben and Goldbeck, 1980;

Ray, Georgiou, and Ravizza, 1979). From childhood into early adulthood, males perform consistently better than females on Piagetian-type horizontal and vertical spatial tasks (judging the position of liquid in a tilted container and judging the position of plumb lines in an oblique context). Liben and Goldbeck (1980) concluded that sex differences persist (Plake, Kaplan, and Steinbrunn, 1986), but that these differences are due to differential social and educational influences in our society.

Not all subjects in the problem-solving stage should be characterized as having reached the problem-finding stage. In her research with college seniors, Arlin (1975) found that all subjects high in problem finding had reached formal operational thinking, but not all subjects who had reached formal thinking were high in problem finding. This fact demonstrates that sequencing was evident. In other words, formal operations had to be accomplished before individuals could move on to the next stage.

Maturation and Intelligence

To what extent does the *maturation* of the nervous system play a role in cognitive development? It is certain that maturation does play a part: The nervous system must be sufficiently developed for any real thought to take place. This is one reason why a greater percentage of older adolescents evidence formal thought than do younger adolescents.

In order to determine the relationship among maturation, intelligence, and cognition, Webb (1974) tested very bright (IQs of 160 and above) 6- to 11-year-old children to ascertain their levels of thinking. All subjects performed the concrete operational tasks easily, indicating that they were skilled in thinking at their developmental stage, but only four boys, age 10 and older, solved the formal thought problems, indicating that regardless of high intelligence, a degree of maturation interacting with experience is necessary for movement into the next stage of cognitive development.

Other things being equal, individuals of high IQ are more likely to develop formal thought sooner than those of low IQ, but it is the interaction of age and intelligence that contributes to cognitive ability. Cognitive development is influenced both by the *maturation of the nervous system (age)* and by the *level of intelligence.* Not all adolescents reach formal operations, but for those who do, not all reach it at the same age or to the same level for all tasks.

Culture and Environment

Cross-cultural studies have shown that formal thought is more dependent on social experience than is sensorimotor or concrete operational thought. The attainment of the first three Piagetian stages appears to be more or less universal, but

full attainment of formal thinking, even in college students and adults, is far from guaranteed. Adolescents from various cultural backgrounds show considerable variability in abstract reasoning abilities. Some cultures offer more opportunities to adolescents to develop abstract thinking than others, by providing a rich verbal environment and experiences that facilitate growth by exposure to problem-solving situations. Cultures that provide stimulating environments facilitate the acquisition of cognitive skills necessary to deal with the abstract world.

Social institutions such as the family and school accelerate or retard the development of formal operations. Factors such as maternal intelligence, sociodemographic status, and the quality of the home environment have been found to relate to children's cognitive development.

Parents who encourage exchanges of thoughts, ideational explorations, academic excellence, and the attainment of ambitious educational and occupational goals are fostering cognitive growth. Schools that encourage students to acquire abstract reasoning and develop problem-solving skills enhance cognitive development.

Aptitude

People have different aptitudes for solving various types of problems. For example, boys do significantly better than girls in solving conservation of volume tasks (Elkind, 1975). This must be interpreted as a matter of differential socialization and application of mental abilities, not as evidence of a difference in ability to do formal thinking. Girls, on the other hand, score much higher on tests of creative thinking (Milgram, 1978). Formal thinking, then, is not applied with equal facility to all types of tasks. One student may be able to apply formal reasoning to a science task, another to a problem with semantic content, and still another to a problem involving the processing of personal information. Students who have studied the sciences may do exceptionally well on some of the Piagetian formal thought tasks. (The pendulum experiment is commonly employed in physics classes.) Gallagher and Noppe (1976) wrote:

> According to Piaget, a lawyer may be formally operational with respect to law, whereas carpenters, mechanics, or locksmiths can reason deductively

Parents can create a rich and stimulating home environment that facilitates the development of cognitive skills necessary to deal with the abstract world.

about aspects of their particular trades. With this hypothesis in mind, it is possible that the persons most able to exhibit logical-mathematical reasoning while completing traditional tasks designed by Inhelder and Piaget are individuals associated with the sciences. Unfortunately, at present, there are few tasks devised to cap formal thought in specific content area. (p. 209)

Piaget did admit to differentiation in cognitive aptitude with increasing age, depending on interest, motivation, and environmental stimulation. Thus, some adolescents may show their operational skills in logic, mathematics, or physics; others may show it in literature, linguistics, or artistic endeavors; and still others in practical skills such as those performed by the carpenter, the locksmith, or the mechanic. However, in spite of this concern, it is important to keep in mind that Piaget's theory has been studied, tested, and developed in the adolescent age range primarily

with content material that came from science and mathematics. Piaget showed little concern with the question of how formal operations might manifest themselves in artistic and literary endeavors (Muuss, 1988b). Gardner (1973) even suggested that formal operations might actually interfere with artistic development.

Assuming that formal operations are manifested within the context of a particular aptitude, to get accurate measurement, it is necessary to isolate the superior aptitude of each individual and then to present a formal task congruent with that aptitude. No such individualized approach has been accomplished.

Motivation and Response

Caution should be exercised in using the results of formal operations tests to predict the scholastic behavior of adolescents. Test models describe what adolescents are *capable* of doing intellectually—not necessarily what they *will* do in a specific situation. Fatigue, boredom, or other factors affecting motivation may prevent adolescents from displaying full cognitive performance in any given situation. Also, Piaget's models are qualitative, not quantitative, measurements. They are used to describe thought problems and do not necessarily duplicate or predict in depth the performance of adolescents.

Role of School and Education

Let's review the number of ways that the development of abstract thinking and formal operations problem solving is encouraged. Experimental or problematic situations can be presented that allow students opportunities to observe, analyze possibilities, and draw inferences about perceived relationships.

Teachers who use authoritarian approaches rather than social interchange stifle real thinking. Discussion groups, problem-solving sessions, and science experiments are approaches that encourage the development of formal thinking and problem-solving abilities. Teachers must be prepared to handle group discussions and stimulate inter-

maturation the biological or generic components to development.

change and feedback. They must also be willing to give explicit help and encouragement and allow the necessary time for reasoning capacities to develop. Some students develop such abilities at a relatively slow pace. Piaget (1972) set forth two goals of education that incorporate this philosophy:

> The principal goal of education is to create men who are capable of doing new things, not simply of repeating what other generations have done—men who are creative, inventive, and discoverers. The second goal of education is to form minds which can be critical, can verify, and not accept everything they are offered.... We need pupils who are active, who learn early to find out by themselves, partly by their own spontaneous activity and partly through material we set up for them; who learn early to tell what is verifiable and what is simply the first idea to come to them. (p. 5)

SUMMARY

1. Piaget divides cognitive development into four major periods: the sensorimotor stage, the preoperational stage, the concrete operational stage, and the formal operational stage.
2. During the sensorimotor stage, children learn to master sensory-motor sequences.
3. The preoperational stage is the period during which language is acquired so that children can deal with the world by manipulating symbols.
4. During the concrete operational stage, children show a greater capacity for logical reasoning, but at a concrete level. They gain mastery over classes, relations, and quantities.
5. During the formal operational stage, children are able to use logic and abstract concepts independent of concrete objects. They become capable of introspection (thinking about thought), abstract thinking (going beyond the real to what is possible), logical thinking (being able to consider all important facts and ideas and to form correct conclusions), and hypothetical reasoning (formulating hypotheses and examining the evidence for them, considering numerous variables).
6. The ability to do formal thinking has several effects on adolescents' thoughts and behavior. The ability to grasp what is and to project what might be makes them idealistic rebels.
7. Individuals with formal reasoning ability are more likely to develop long-term values than those who have not reached this stage.
8. Because of the discrepancy between what they say and what they do, adolescents are sometimes accused of hypocrisy.
9. Adolescents are capable of being creative, but because of pressures on them to conform, they become less creative, not more so.
10. Sometimes adolescents demonstrate pseudostupidity—the tendency to approach problems at too complex a level.
11. Adolescents develop egocentrism as manifested by imaginary audience and personal fable ideations. They are very self-conscious and feel that they are on stage much of the time. Personal fable refers to the adolescents' belief in the uniqueness of their own experiences and their own vulnerability.
12. One of the consequences of the adolescents' ability to think about their thoughts is an increase in daydreaming and visual imagery. At the same time, the content of the daydreams becomes more positive and constructive, with less guilt and fear of failure.
13. Because they have reached formal operational thinking, adolescents begin to think about themselves and to develop an identity.
14. Intellectually gifted girls believe that smart students are the ones who succeed without putting forth much effort. They also believe that future success depends on being liked more than being talented.
15. As adolescents begin to cure themselves of their idealistic crises, they begin the decentering process. They enter into the occupational world or begin serious professional training to affirm a life plan and adopt a social role.
16. Not all adolescents reach formal operational thinking, and not all same-aged adolescents are at the same stage of development.
17. The percentage of adolescents reaching formal operational thinking depends partly on the criteria and tests used to measure the level of thought.
18. There is some evidence that a fifth stage of development can be differentiated: a problem-finding stage. This stage represents an ability to discover problems not yet delineated.
19. Cognitive development is influenced both by the maturation of the nervous system and the level of intelligence.
20. Sex differences in performance on Piagetian problems exist, especially in relation to spatial processing tasks.

21. Adolescents from various cultures show considerable variability in abstract reasoning abilities. Social institutions such as the family and school accelerate or retard the development of formal operations.
22. The amount of urbanization, literacy, and education all relate to formal thought development.
23. People have different aptitudes for solving various types of problems.

24. Piaget's tests are qualitative and not quantitative measurements. They are used to describe thinking processes, and do not necessarily duplicate or predict performance.
25. The school can play a role in developing formal operational thinking.

KEY TERMS

centering **133**

concrete operational stage **133**

deductive reasoning **132**

egocentrism **140**

formal operational stage **135**

hypocrisy **139**

imaginary audience **140**

inductive reasoning **132**

maturation **144**

personal fable **141**

preoperational stage **132**

problem-finding stage **143**

pseudostupidity **140**

sensorimotor stage **132**

syncretism **133**

transductive reasoning **132**

THOUGHT QUESTIONS

1. If you give two children the same amount of ice cream but in different-sized bowls, what are they likely to do? Why?
2. Describe the characteristics of formal operational thinking.
3. What evidence do you have that adolescents are egocentric? According to Piaget, why are adolescents that way?
4. Do adolescents think logically? Why or why not?
5. How does the idealism of adolescents compare with that of adults?
6. What does it mean to move from egocentrism to sociocentrism?
7. What evidence is there that adolescents are hypocritical?
8. Give evidence of adolescents' belief in the personal fable.
9. Explain why some adolescents don't have an accurate perception of their own ability.

10. According to Piaget, does maturation or environment have more influence on the development of formal operational thinking?
11. Are there significant differences in formal operational abilities? Explain.
12. In what ways are modern schools stimulating formal operational thinking? In what ways are they not?
13. Comment on the statement, "Many adolescents are functioning at a cognitive level that renders them unable to practice most forms of birth control effectively."
14. What factors prevent adolescents from being more creative?
15. Why is it necessary to reach the formal operational stage before individuals can move on to the problem-finding stage?
16. What can parents do to encourage formal operational thinking? What sorts of influences do parents have that prevent their adolescent from doing formal operational thinking?

SUGGESTED READING

Elkind, D. (1981). *Children and Adolescents: Interpretive Essays on Jean Piaget.* 3rd ed. New York: Oxford University Press.

Flavell, J. H. (1977). *Cognitive Development.* Englewood Cliffs, NJ: Prentice Hall.

7

Intelligence, Information Processing, and Decision Making

There are three basic approaches to understanding cognition during adolescence. One is the *Piagetian approach*, discussed in Chapter 6, which emphasizes the qualitative changes in the way adolescents think. A second is the *psychometric approach*, which measures quantitative changes. This chapter begins with this approach, emphasizing the meaning of intelligence according to various measures and discussing the changes that take place as people mature. The third view is the *information-processing approach*, which examines the progressive steps, actions, and operations that take place when an adolescent receives, perceives, remembers, and utilizes information. This view is also presented in this chapter. It will help you understand why and how adolescents think in more advanced ways than when they were children and what abilities are developed when they become more efficient problem solvers.

Intelligence

Intelligence has almost as many definitions as experts who try to measure it (Ellison, 1984). It has been described as an innate capacity to learn, think, reason, understand, and solve problems.

According to Gardner, there are seven dimensions for assessing intelligence. One of these involves music and the ability to perceive and create pitch and rhythmic patterns.

Other definitions focus on mental abilities that are developed, almost without biological limit. Let's look at the various types of mental abilities that have been described.

Triarchic Theory of Intelligence

Sternberg (1981, 1985, 1990) and his colleagues at Yale University arranged abilities into the following three major groupings in his triarchic theory of intelligence:

1. *Componential intelligence:* Componential intelligence includes general learning and comprehension abilities, such as good vocabulary; high reading comprehension; the ability to do test items such as analogies, syllogisms, and series; and the ability to think critically. This is the traditional concept of intelligence as measured on tests.
2. *Experiential intelligence:* Experiential intelligence includes the ability to select, encode, compare, and combine information in meaningful ways to create new insights, theories, and ideas.
3. *Contextual intelligence:* Contextual intelligence includes adaptive behavior in the real world, such as the ability to size up situations, achieve goals, and solve practical problems (Sternberg and Wagner, 1986).

Seven Frames of Mind

Howard Gardner, an associate professor at the Boston University School of Medicine, objects to as-

sessing intelligence in only two dimensions: *linguistic* and *logical-mathematical abilities* (Gardner, 1989). His concept also includes five other dimensions:

1. *Linguistic intelligence.*
2. *Logical-mathematical intelligence.*
3. *Spatial intelligence:* Spatial intelligence is the ability to form spatial images and to find one's way around in an environment. The sailors in the Caroline Islands of Micronesia navigate among hundreds of islands using only the stars and their bodily feelings. Intelligence testers in Micronesia would have to come up with an entirely different list of intelligences and testing methods.
4. *Musical intelligence:* Musical intelligence is the ability to perceive and create pitch and rhythmic patterns. There are individuals who are otherwise classified as mentally retarded who can play a song on a piano after hearing it once, or who have an extraordinary talent as a trombonist yet not be able to read a newspaper.
5. *Body-kinesthetic intelligence:* Body-kinesthetic intelligence is the gift of fine motor movement, as seen in a surgeon or dancer.
6. *Interpersonal intelligence:* Interpersonal intelligence is the understanding of others, how they feel, what motivates them, and how they interact. Certain people interact well with others because of their empathetic understanding; others, such as politicians, are highly skilled at understanding others and manipulating them.

7. *Intrapersonal intelligence:* Intrapersonal intelligence centers on the individual's ability to know himself or herself and to develop a sense of identity.

Gardner insists that people have to develop completely different concepts of who is bright and how to measure brightness:

Gardner's concept is unique because he claims independent existence for different intelligences in the human neural system. He would like to stop measuring people according to some unitary dimension called "intelligence." Instead, he would like to think in terms of different intellectual strengths (Ellison, 1984; Lonner, 1990).

Intelligence Tests

The most well known intelligence tests are the Stanford-Binet and the Wechsler Scales. Let's review each in more detail.

Stanford-Binet   The first intelligence test was devised by Alfred Binet, a professor at the University of Sorbonne, in France. The members of the Paris Ministry of Education had been faced with a difficult problem. Their goal was to provide extensive education for all intelligent children and more practical, less academic kinds of schooling for less intelligent children. They wanted to be fair about choosing the children who would be given advanced academic training, so they asked Binet to devise a test to sort out children who were more intelligent from those who were less intelligent. Binet and his collaborators were able to construct a set of questions that could be answered by most children at a given age.

Revisions of Binet's test were made by Lewis Terman, of Stanford University, and the name was changed to Stanford-Binet test. It is used with individuals from age 2 through adulthood. The fourth edition of the Stanford-Binet was published in 1985 (Thorndike, Hagan, and Sattler, 1985). Terman used scores in four areas: verbal reasoning, quantitative reasoning, abstract/visual reasoning, and short-term memory. The test provides a composite score that can be interpreted as an *intelligence quotient (IQ).*

The Wechsler Scales   One of the most widely used measures of intelligence is the Wechsler Adult Intelligence Scale (WAIS-R), which may be used on people 16 years and older (Wechsler, 1981). Younger adolescents are usually given the Wechsler Intelligence Scale for Children (WISC-III). The WAIS-R divides intelligence into two components: verbal skills and performance/manipulation skills. Six subtests constitute the verbal component: Information, Comprehension, Arithmetic, Similarities, Digit Span, and Vocabulary. Five tests—Digit Symbol, Picture Completion, Block Design, Picture Arrangement, and Object Assembly—compose the performance scores. In the Wechsler Intelligence Scales and the 1985 revision of the Stanford-Binet, scores are converted into IQ by referring to tables in the test manuals.

Changes with Age

In the past, it was believed that IQ remained constant. Now, it is recognized that the IQ of an individual may vary considerably during his or her lifetime. The intelligence of the child depends partially on the degree of risk to which he or she is exposed during the developmental years (Sameroff, Seifer, Baldwin, and Baldwin, 1993). Pinneau (1961) reanalyzed the data from the Berkeley Growth Study and found that children tested at 5 years and at subsequent ages up to 17 years showed median changes from 6 to 12 points, with the range of individual changes from 0 to 40 points. The direction of the change is not always predictable. In general, predictability of test scores varies with the length of the interval between tests and with the age at the initial test. Test-retest correlations decrease as the interval between tests increases.

In summary, although most adolescents do not show gross changes in relative IQ placement, some do. Therefore, an IQ measurement should not be interpreted as a fixed attribute but rather as *a score on a test at a particular time.* The score may change as a result of a number of influences, creating the need for retesting over a period of years to make current judgments of IQ.

---

intelligence quotient (IQ)   calculated by dividing the mental age (MA) by the chronological age (CA) and multiplying by 100.

Any attempts to measure changes also depend on the tests used, when and how they are employed, and what they purport to measure. Figure 7.1 shows the curves on 11 Wechsler subtests (Bayley, 1968). It must be emphasized that the results obtained from the Berkeley Growth Study were longitudinal measurements, which tend to minimize intellectual decline (subjects who are less able drop out and are not available for testing). Cross-sectional measurements tend to maximize decline (older subjects are less educated). Both methods of measurement, however, show that verbal scores remain the most stable and performance scores decline the most.

Taken together, these findings show that the measurement of intelligence is a complex undertaking and that it is difficult to sort out age-related differences from other causes.

Factors Influencing Test Results

One reason for variations in IQ and other measures of intelligence is that it is sometimes difficult to get valid test results. Results vary not only because intelligence may vary but also because of factors influencing test scores (Hubble and Groff, 1982; Kerr and Colangelo, 1988). One of the most important influences is the presence

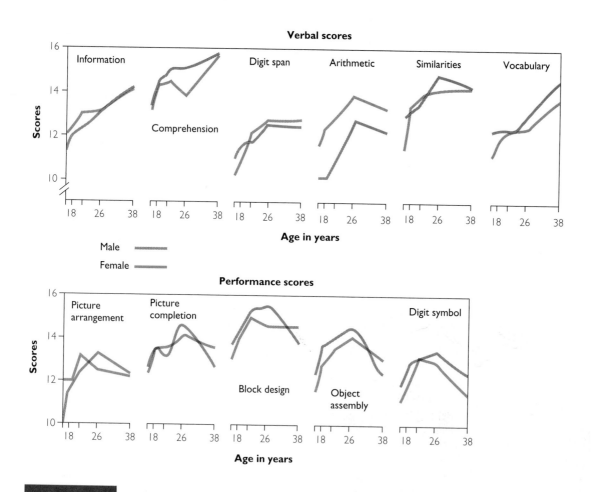

FIGURE 7.1   Curves of Mean Scores for Adolescents and Young Adults on the Eleven Wechsler Subtests, Berkeley Growth Study

Source: N. Bayley, "Behavioral Correlates of Mental Growth: Birth to Thirty-Six Years," American Psychologist, 23 (1968): 1–17. Copyright © 1968 by the American Psychological Association. Reprinted with permission.

of *anxiety* in the subjects tested. Anxious youths do not do as well on tests as those with greater emotional security.

Motivation also has a marked influence on test results (Wentzel, 1986). An otherwise bright student, poorly motivated to do well on a test, will not measure up to his or her capacity. Furthermore, the tests are not free of *cultural bias*. Tests to measure IQ were originally designed to measure "innate" general intelligence apart from environmental influences. But research over a long period has shown that sociocultural factors play a significant role in the outcome of the tests (Carmines and Baxter, 1986). Children reared in stimulus-rich environments may show superior intelligence capacities, whereas those reared under intellectually sterile conditions may become retarded in relation to their capabilities. The tests' language, illustrations, examples, and abstractions are designed to measure intelligence according to middle-class standards. Many adolescents from low-socioeconomic-status families grow up in a nonverbal world or in a world where words used are so different that understanding middle-class expressions on an intelligence test is difficult. Thus, some adolescents do poorly not because they are less intelligent but because they do not comprehend language foreign to their backgrounds and experiences (Berry and Bennett, 1992; Berry, Poortinga, Segal and Dasen, 1992).

Efforts to develop culturally unbiased tests have been very frustrating. The general approach has been to use language familiar to the particular minorities for which the test is designed. But the major problem with the tests so far developed is how to evaluate their accuracy, given that they continue to reflect a cultural bias (Miller-Jones, 1989).

A more promising approach of measuring intelligence, known as SOMPA (System of Multicultural Pluralistic Assessment), consists of the Wechsler IQ test, an interview in which the examiner learns the child's health history, a sociocultural inventory of the family's background, and an adaptive-behavior inventory that evaluates the child's nonacademic performance in school, at home, and in the neighborhood. A complete medical exam evaluates the child's physical condition, manual dexterity, motor skill, and visual and auditory ability. The final score on SOMPA is obtained not only from the IQ test but also through the other inventories. Thus, a child who receives 68 on the Wechsler may earn an adjusted IQ of 89 when scores on the sociocultural and the adaptive-behavior inventories are taken into account. Thus, SOMPA measures potential rather than current ability.

Limitations of IQ

One of the most important findings in the study of intelligence is that *IQ scores alone are not predic-*

The amount of anxiety and motivation are factors that influence test results. There is also the effect of cultural bias, where cultural standards and language favor the students from middle-class, nonminority backgrounds.

tive of occupational or personal success (Trotter, 1986). A follow-up of 52 superintelligent men from a study begun in 1921 at Stanford University by Lewis Terman revealed some interesting results (Hagan, 1983). Some 60 years after the initial study began, the men with the highest IQs could scarcely be distinguished from the general population in relation to marriage, family, and domestic relations. In terms of achievement, the majority had received advanced degrees and were successful, yet some were not, and those with IQs of 150 were just as successful as those with IQs of 180. Intelligence tests are, at best, only crude predictors of achievement. They tap only a few facets of intelligence and prerequisites for success.

Dangers of Labeling

Great caution must be used when interpreting test scores and labeling an individual "superior," "average," or "dull" on the basis of those scores, even over a period of time (Mehrens and Lehmann, 1985). This caution applies especially to African American and Mexican American children. The tests may not accurately measure the learning ability of these children. Also, the testers may be incompetent to interpret test results, ignorant of anxieties experienced by children having language problems, and insensitive to their cultural backgrounds. Yet, in some communities, IQ scores determine whether children are put into classes for the mentally retarded. Once these individuals are labeled "slow" or "mentally retarded," the social stigma may remain with them all of their lives.

Labels also have a way of becoming self-fulfilling prophecies, meaning that youths tend to try to live up to what is expected of them.

Scholastic Aptitude

Scholastic aptitude is the ability of individuals to do academic work, and to succeed in school. This ability may be evaluated by tests.

Scholastic Assessment Test

One of the most widely used tests in the United States is the *Scholastic Assessment Test (SAT)*, for-

merly called the Scholastic Achievement Test (see page 155). It is used by a majority of colleges as one basis for admission (Franco, 1983). Over one million high school seniors took the test in 1995. The combined verbal and math scores often determine eligibility not only for college admission but also for scholarships and financial aid. The Educational Testing Service (ETS), which produces the SAT, claims that in combination with high school records, the SATs have proved to be better predictors of students' first-year performances in college than any other measurement. Nevertheless, the protests against the use or misuse of this test grow louder (Robinson, 1983).

Objections to the test arise from the claim that it measures basic abilities acquired over a student's lifetime and is thus immune to last-minute cramming and is "coach-proof." However, a study by the Federal Trade Commission's Bureau of Consumer Protection showed that special coaching can improve SAT scores by an average of 25 points out of the possible 800. More than 80 coaching schools in one nationwide chain tutored 30,000 students in a recent year, in 10-week courses, and improved scores by an average of 25 points. The schools claim that in individual cases they can improve scores up to 100 points. I talked to a lawyer who had wanted to raise his verbal score on the LSAT (Law School Aptitude Test) for admission to law school before applying. He studied a vocabulary list of 5,000 most-used words and was able to raise his verbal score by 60 points.

If coaching can raise a student's score, should the SAT be relied on as a basic measure of scholastic aptitude? Should admission to college depend partly on a skill gained by those who can afford a coaching course? In all fairness, the College Entrance Examination Board has long issued warnings against making admissions decisions on the basis of the SAT score alone. The ETS itself has stated that an individual's score can vary plus or minus 30 to 35 points, a spread of 60 to 70 points. For these reasons, some of the best schools rely equally or more on student essays, interviews, and other admission procedures (Chance, 1988b). Even high marks from high school may be questioned, for they vary greatly from school to school, and the standards for good grades have been declining since the late 1960s. The number of students with A averages has increased so rapidly that there are now as many straight A students as there are those with C averages.

Test Scores

The SAT score averages for college-bound high-school seniors dropped until 1980, after which they increased until 1985. The math scores held steady from 1986 to 1992, after which they increased slightly. The verbal scores decreased from 1986 to 1994, after which they increased in 1995. Figure 7.2 shows score averages from 1963 through 1995. As you can see, average scores from the 1995 school year on the verbal section of the SAT averaged 428. Math scores averaged 482. Overall declining scores have led to increased criticism of the schools for relaxing teaching and learning standards and for not teaching the basics.

Revisions of the SAT

The College Board approved changes in the SAT that took effect in 1994. The test, called the Scholastic Assessment Test, has a mandatory section labeled SAT I. An essay was made optional in a separate part known as the SAT II, since educators could not agree to make it mandatory. Many thought such a section would discriminate against minorities, and all realized that scoring millions of essays would require enormous expense and time.

The new SAT I has both a math and a verbal section. The verbal part includes longer critical reading passages, which students must read and then answer relevant questions. The antonyms section has been omitted. The greatest changes are in the math section. Students may use calculators in solving problems rather than select from multiple-choice answers. There is a new emphasis on critical reasoning and "real-life" problem solving throughout the test. Proponents claim that the new test is less coachable than the old one. Maximum scores will still total 1600; 800 for each of the two parts, respectively.

Information Processing

In Chapter 6, we discussed the qualitative changes that take place in the way adolescents think. This *Piagetian approach* to cognitive development tells about the development of logical thinking and its implications as represented by adolescent thought and behavior. In the first section of this chapter, we discussed the *psychometric view* of intelligence as represented by a variety of mental abilities and as measured by "intelligence" tests.

These two views of cognition, however, really do not describe the *process* by which information is transmitted. The *information-processing approach*

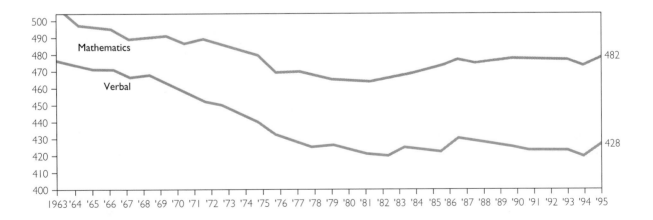

FIGURE 7.2   SAT Average Scores

to cognition emphasizes the progressive steps, actions, and operations that take place when the adolescent receives, perceives, remembers, thinks about, and utilizes information (Siegler, 1995). Studying the development of information-processing abilities provides additional insight into the growth of cognitive abilities during adolescence (Lapsley, 1990). Adolescents differ in the speed of processing information (just as different computers process information at different speeds). The processing speed continues to improve in early adolescence (Hale, 1990). For example, 10-year-olds are slower than 15-year-olds in processing information, but 15-year-olds process information about as fast as young adults.

Meaning

One way we can understand information processing in humans is to compare it with the actions of a computer. Information is coded and fed, in an organized way, into a computer, where it is stored in the memory banks. When any of that information is required, the computer is asked to produce it. The machine searches for the relevant information and reproduces or prints out the items requested.

Information processing by adolescents is similar in fashion but far more sophisticated. The adolescent receives information, organizes it, stores it, retrieves it, thinks about it, and combines it in such a way as to answer questions, solve problems, and make decisions. The most elaborate computer used in creating *artificial intelligence* cannot match the capacity of the human mind and nervous system in the input and output of information (Keating, 1990).

Steps in Information Processing

Figure 7.3 illustrates how information processing can be divided into a series of logical steps. The diagram shows information flowing in one direction only, from the time a stimulus is received until an action is begun. The general flow is in one direction, but there may be some flow backward as well as forward. For example, an adolescent may receive and select some information and take it in and out of memory to think about it over a long period of time before making a decision and in-

HIGHLIGHT

The American College Testing (ACT) Assessment Program

The American College Testing (ACT) Assessment Program (1995) is the second most widely used college admissions test, administered to more than a million students each year. It consists of three parts: (1) the Academic Tests, (2) the Student Profile Section (SPS), and (3) the ACT Interest Inventory. The Academic Tests are English Usage Tests, Mathematics Usage Tests, Social Studies Reading Tests, and the Natural Sciences Reading Test. Men consistently score higher than women on math and spatial abilities; the women consistently outscore men in English (Pearson and Ferguson, 1989). This is attributed partly to differences in education and socialization of boys and girls.

The Student Profile Section is a 192-item inventory of demographics, high school activities and accomplishments, and academic and extracurricular plans for college. The UNIACT is a survey of students' vocational preferences.

The ACT Academic Tests yield standard scores of 1 to 36, which are averaged to create the ACT Composite. The mean composite score in 1995 was 20.8 (U.S. Bureau of the Census, 1996). The SPS has been shown to be valid, with follow-up studies showing a 69 to 70 percent match between students' choices of major on the SPS and actual choices at the end of the freshman year (Laing, Valiga, and Eberly, 1986).

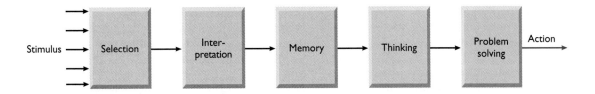

FIGURE 7.3   Steps in Information Processing

stituting action. Nevertheless, the flowchart helps us to understand the total process. Next we'll look at the steps in more detail.

Stimuli

Every person is constantly bombarded with stimuli—audible, visual, and tactile. As you walk down the street, for instance, you are exposed to sounds, sights, and even physical contact when someone bumps into you or touches you. Your senses are your *receptors,* your contacts with the world outside yourself. Through them, you receive all information.

Selection

People do not really hear, see, or feel all of the stimuli they are exposed to, primarily because they cannot focus attention on everything at once, and they may not be interested in much of what is happening. For example, you may dimly hear a horn honking, but you may not notice the color and make of the car from which the sound is emitted or care about who is doing the honking. However, if you hear someone call your name, your attention is directed immediately to the source, and you see that the person calling your name is your good friend, driving her blue car, which you have seen many times before. Your friend pulls over, you walk over to talk, and your attention is directed to the conversation rather than to the hundreds of other sights and sounds around you.

Thus, people are interested in some happenings but not others, so they are motivated to direct their attention to that which they select. Another name for this process is *cognitive monitoring.* Cognitive monitoring involves people thinking about what they are doing, what they are going to do

next, how the problem is going to be solved, and the approaches that they are going to take (Beal and Bonabitus, 1991; Brown, 1993; Lawton, Turner, and Paris, 1991).

Interpretation

People make judgments about everything to which they are exposed, partly according to their past experiences. The adolescent girl brought up by an alcoholic father may perceive her boyfriend as drunk when he has one beer. Another girl may not consider him inebriated at all. These two girls interpret information differently according to their perceptions of it. Adolescents, as well as adults, may sometimes make faulty judgments because of inaccurate perceptions or insufficient information. Therefore, there is often the need to make additional inquiry, to gain further information, or to check perception against fact to make sure the perception is accurate.

Memory

Information that is useful must be remembered long enough to undergo additional processing. The process of remembering involves a series of steps (Fitzgerald, 1991). The most widely accepted model is a three-stage one (Murdock, 1974): sensory storage, short-term storage, and long-term storage. Information is seen as passing

cognitive monitoring   thinking about what you are doing, what you are going to do next, how the problem is going to be solved, and the approaches that you are going to take.

from one compartment to another, with decreasing amounts passed on at any one time to the next stage. Figure 7.4 illustrates the three-stage model of memory.

Information is held only briefly (as little as a fraction of a second) in the mind before the image begins to decay and/or is blocked out by other incoming sensory information. Information that has not already faded from the sensory store is *read out* to **short-term storage.** Because of the limited capacity of the short-term store, information to be held longer must be further rehearsed and transferred to the relatively permanent **long-term storage.** For all practical purposes, long-term storage capacity is infinite. In the process of retrieval, stored information is obtained by searching, finding, and remembering, either through recall or recognition. Memory efficiency depends on all three of these processes and is usually at a maximum during adolescence and young adulthood.

Information received by the senses is held briefly in one of several specific **sensory storages.** Auditory information is held in an auditory sensory store, referred to as *echoic memory.* Visual information is held in a visual sensory store, called *iconic memory.* Other sensory stores include those for tactile information and for smell. Research evidence indicates that *the ability to retrieve information from the sensory store does not change much* as children and adolescents mature (Wickens, 1974).

There is some confusion about the difference between short-term and long-term memory. One helpful distinction was given by Waugh and Norman (1965). They used the terms *primary memory* and *secondary memory.* **Primary memory,** or short-term memory, involves information still being rehearsed and focused on in the conscious mind. **Secondary memory,** or long-term memory, is characterized by how deeply the information has been processed, not by how long the information has been held. Deep processing, in which perceived information has been passed into layers of memory below the conscious level, constitutes secondary memory. For example, when you memorize a word list, the words under immediate consideration are at the primary or short-term memory stage. Words already looked at, memorized, and tucked away are at the secondary or long-term memory level, though they were learned only a short time before. Specific words recalled several days or months later are recalled from secondary memory. Secondary memory can last for 30 seconds or for years. These two layers of memory are used synonymously in this discussion with short-term and long-term memory, though some secondary memory stores may be recalled after relatively short time intervals.

When measuring primary or short-term memory, the subject is presented with a short string of digits, letters, or words and then tested for the total that can be recalled immediately. When measured in this way, primary memory span is remarkably similar across a wide spectrum of ages, leading to the conclusion that *short-term memory also changes very little during adolescence.*

The most significant changes in memory storage occur in long-term ability or in the capacity to shift information from short- to long-term storage. *Adolescents are more efficient at deep processing than older adults and show superior ability in long-term memory.* Interestingly enough, subjects of all ages (20 to 79) can best remember sociohistoric events that occurred when they were 15 to 25 years old, indicating that these are the most impressionable years as far as memory is concerned.

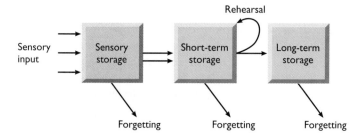

FIGURE 7.4 Three-Stage Model of Memory

Improving Memory Ability What factors influence memory ability? *Mental repetition or rehearsal* of information improves retention. Various *mnemonic techniques* (memory techniques) may be employed to improve memory. *Organizing material* into meaningful units is one such technique. This process, called *chunking*, enables a person to remember the material as a meaningful unit rather than its individual parts. For example, if you are presented with the letters NOTGNIHSAW, you would have difficulty remembering them, but when presented in reverse order—WASHINGTON—recalling them is easy.

Arranging material in a *logical order*, such as alphabetically, is another aid to memory. Material that is presented in *one category* (e.g., animals) is easier to remember than miscellaneous information that is not easily grouped. Material that is *meaningful and familiar* and in which the adolescent is interested is easier to remember than nonsense syllables. For example, an adolescent who is knowledgeable about and interested in music may remember a long list of composers of songs—a task an indifferent adolescent would find burdensome.

Anything is easier to remember if *cues are provided*. For example, let's say an adolescent girl is having trouble remembering the name of a math teacher she had in sixth grade. To jog her memory, you give her the following cues: The teacher is male, six feet tall, has brown eyes and hair, and speaks with a southern accent. This description may enable the student to visualize the teacher and to remember his name.

Information may be *coded* so that it is associated with something familiar. This technique is used by some to remember notes on the music staff (see Figure 7.5). The letters FACE refer to the notes between the lines. The letters EGBDF are the first letters of the words in the phrase *Every Good Boy Does Fine,* and represent the notes on the lines. Codes may be visual, such as a color code, with each color representing something different. A map, with its symbols, is a good illustration of a visual representation of roads, cities, railroads, rivers, highways, and so forth. A code may also be audible, such as the ringing of a timer bell to remind you to turn off the stove.

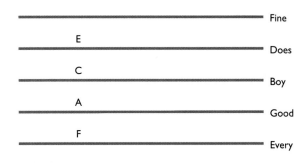

FIGURE 7.5   Codes to Remember Notes of a Music Staff

Another way to remember material is by *visualizing position or place*. The technique, called the *method of loci,* visualizes information, objects, or persons in particular locations. Thus, if you need to remember the objects of furniture in a room, you can visualize the room and each part of it, and you will be able to recall many of the things in it. Some students remember textbook information by visualizing the location of the material on the page.

short-term storage (short-term memory) the process by which information is still in the conscious mind, being rehearsed and focused on (also called primary memory).

long-term storage (long-term memory) The process by which information is perceived and processed deeply so it passes into the layers of memory below the conscious level (also called secondary memory).

sensory storage (Sensory memory) the process by which information is received and transduced by the senses, usually in a fraction of a second.

primary memory short-term memory that involves information still being rehearsed and focused on in the conscious mind.

secondary memory long-term memory of information that is processed deeply and passed into memory layers below the conscious level.

Thinking

Information processing also involves *thinking* about something after it has been retrieved from memory stores. Once facts are obtained, the relations between them and to other important information are noted so that inferences may be drawn and conclusions formulated. Actually, adolescents can be taught to think rationally, be critical of the first ideas that pop into their heads, examine evidence, and sort out the facts to discover truth from error (Baron, 1985).

Problem Solving

One of the end results of information processing is *problem solving*. This begins with *problem finding;* which means determining the problem so that the individual can determine what needs to be done. The second step is *evaluating the elements of the problem* so that the person knows the information and tasks with which he or she has to work. This step usually requires insightful reorganization and thinking about various facets of the problem. The third step is *generating a list of solutions and evaluating* them ahead of time by trying to foresee the effects or consequences each solution will produce. This will enable the individual to make a choice.

One of the differences between adolescents and children in problem-solving ability is the nature of adolescents' information processing. Adolescents are better able to remember more information, consider all possible relationships, think about them logically, and generate and evaluate different variables and solutions ahead of time before deciding on a solution and course of action. Children usually do not get sufficient information, remember enough of it, think about it logically enough, or consider all possible relations before arriving at solutions. Their information-processing ability is limited in relation to that of adolescents (Sternberg and Nigro, 1980).

Furthermore, researchers have found that when adolescents get together in groups to solve problems, more satisfactory solutions are found. Sometimes, the process takes longer than when an individual is solving a problem, but the problem is usually solved with greater understanding and results are more satisfactory. Research has docu-

mented the power of peer collaboration in problem solving (Ayman-Nolley and Church, 1993; Grannott, 1993; Tudge and Winterhoff, 1993).

The information-processing approach brings us closer to understanding why and how adolescents think in more advanced ways than when they were children. Such an approach sheds light on what abilities are developed when individual adolescents become more efficient problem solvers.

Decision Making

One of the characteristics of an intelligent, mature person is the ability to *make good decisions*. Some decisions made during adolescence may have life-long consequences. Important decisions may pertain to education, career, choice of mate, leisure activities, drug use, medical care, and health habits. Adolescence is a period of challenge and change—a time when both deliberate and unintentional decisions are made that affect the course of the adolescents' lives. Furthermore, adolescents begin to question parental authority and want to make some decisions on their own regarding choice of friends, leisure activities, curfews, and study habits. The consequences of these decisions depend partly on the degree to which good judgment is exercised (Mann, Harmoni, and Power, 1989).

The Process

Decision making is a complicated process involving information search and processing to understand available options (Moore, Jensen, and Hauck, 1990). It involves problem solving to find novel or creative solutions (Huber, 1986). Ross (1981) has taken an information-processing approach to decision competence. He proposed that decision makers must master five skills: identifying alternate courses of action, identifying appropriate criteria for considering alternatives, assessing alternatives by criteria, summarizing information about alternatives, and evaluating the outcome of the decision-making process (Mann, Harmoni, and Power, 1989).

One study of decision making during adolescence revealed that, in comparison with the early

One of the major decisions during adolescence is the choice of a college or a vocation, an important decision that has life-long consequences.

adolescent, the middle adolescent understands very well what is involved in the activity of decision making. The early adolescent has little recognition that decision-making activity involves clearly specifying goals, considering options, and checking before taking action to implement a decision. This conclusion is consistent with other research findings that young adolescents are less likely than older adolescents to generate options, to anticipate the consequences of decisions, and to evaluate the credibility of sources (Ormond, Luszez, Mann, and Beswick, 1991).

Other researchers found a relationship between age and decision-making ability. There is a significant increase with age among children 12 to 18 years old in the ability to handle sophisticated decision making. Older adolescents formulate more options, pay more attention to future outcomes, consult more with experts, and are more aware of the implications of advice received from someone with vested interest. Other studies of adolescents have identified such cognitive changes as improvement in memory and improved ability to process information and apply knowledge (Friedman and Mann, 1993).

The breadth of experience plays an important role in the quality of decisions that are made (Quadrel, Fischoff, and Davis, 1993; Jacobs and Potenza, 1990). Parents who involve their adolescents in family decision making are helping to

prepare them for mature adult life. So important is this skill that some schools have developed programs to help teach adolescents critical thinking skills (Ennis, 1990).

The Nine Cs of Decision Making

One of the most helpful decision-making models was developed by Mann and colleagues (1989). They listed nine elements of competent decision making (the nine Cs of decision making): choice, comprehension, creativity, compromise, consequentiality, correctness, credibility, consistency, and commitment.

Choice   Willingness to choose is an important prerequisite to decision making. Having high self-esteem gives adolescents the courage and confidence to make choices (Brown and Mann, 1991). If their locus of control is internal rather than external, their decision-making authority resides within themselves. In general, older adolescents (15 to 17 years old) have higher internality than young adolescents (12 to 14 years old) (Mann, Harmoni, Power, and Beswick, 1986). Some adolescents relinquish personal control in their desire to conform to peer groups. Peer pressures generally reach a peak at about 12 to 13 years of age, so group conformity is greatest during those years.

Comprehension   Comprehension refers to the understanding of decision making as a cognitive process. In one study, adolescents were asked "What makes someone a really good decision maker?" "What is the difference between a simple decision and a thinking decision?" and "You want to teach a younger student how to make decisions—what advice would you give?" The results showed that 15-year-olds evidenced significantly greater knowledge than 13-year-olds on all three questions (Ormond, Mann, and Luszez, 1987).

Creative Problem Solving   Creative problem solving involves defining the problem, recognizing different choices or alternative ways of solving the problem, combining choices to produce new alternatives, and conceptualizing the sequence of steps for moving toward the goal (Huber, 1986). One study found that only 14 percent of 13-year-olds and 24 percent of 15-year-olds referred to examining options when asked "What does a good decision maker do when making a decision?" However, 15-year-olds produced a greater number of choice options when presented with dilemmas (Mann, Harmoni, and Power, 1989).

Compromise   Decision making often involves a willingness to accept compromises—to negotiate a mutually acceptable solution in a dispute with family or friends. This includes the willingness to consider the other person's point of view as important.

Consequentiality   Competent decision making involves the willingness to think about the potential consequences of choosing actions for oneself and others. Research has found that seventh-, eighth-, and tenth-graders were less competent than twelfth-graders to imagine risks and consequences of medical decisions such as cosmetic surgery and acne experimentation (Lewis, 1981).

Correctness of Choice   Making a correct choice is the prime test of decision making (Klayman, 1985). However, the correctness of a choice may not be evident for years, or may depend on the decision maker's personal point of view or value system. However, in two studies in which the correctness of solutions to hypothetical medical dilemmas (Weithorn and Campbell, 1982) and custody dilemmas (Greenberg, 1983) was predetermined, 14-year-olds did not differ significantly from adults in choosing "reasonable outcomes." This outcome indicates that these adolescents had already developed considerable ability to choose correctly.

Credibility   Credibility involves the ability to accept the authenticity of the information relating to choice alternatives. Young adolescents are less able to recognize the vested interests of those who offer advice and are less likely to question the expertise or credibility of the source. Older adolescents are more likely to check new information against previous knowledge.

Consistency   A competent decision maker is expected to show some consistency and stability in patterns of choices.

Commitment   Commitment involves a willingness to follow through on decisions. Older students (ages 16 to 20) are more likely to follow through than younger students (ages 14 to 15) (Mann, Harmoni, and Power, 1989).

In summary, many adolescents are aware of the steps involved in systematic decision making and have the capacity for creative problem solving. Research has shown that late adolescents with more experience have greater competence than early adolescents. By age 15, adolescents who have achieved a reasonable degree of autonomy are competent in decision making. However, there is sometimes a gap between competence and involvement in decision making. Low self-esteem, peer pressure, structured family situations (Brown and Mann, 1988), and legal restraints may interfere with adolescents' involvement in making personal decisions. In order to develop this skill, adolescents must be taught how to make decisions and then given the opportunity to do so (Baron, 1989).

SUMMARY

1. There are three basic approaches to understanding cognition during adolescence: the Piagetian approach, the psychometric approach, and the information-processing approach.

2. Intelligence has been defined and described in many ways.

3. Sternberg groups intelligence into three categories: componential intelligence, experiential intelligence, and contextual intelligence.

4. Gardner includes seven facets of intelligence: linguistic intelligence, logical-mathematical intelligence, spatial intelligence, musical intelligence, body-kinesthetic intelligence, interpersonal intelligence, and intrapersonal intelligence. Gardner has purposed that educators stop measuring people according to one unitary dimension and instead think in terms of various intellectual strengths.

5. One approach to understanding adolescent cognition is the psychometric approach. Intelligence quotients are scores originally derived from the Stanford-Binet intelligence tests.

6. One of the most common tests is the Wechsler Adult Intelligence Scale (WAIS), which may be used on people 16 years and older. Scores are divided into two major components: verbal skills and performance/manipulation skills.

7. Intelligence scores may vary considerably during one's lifetime. Such scores should be considered only as a result on a test taken at a particular time and evaluated according to preestablished criteria. Cross-sectional measurements tend to maximize intellectual decline, whereas longitudinal measurements tend to minimize it. Scores on verbal portions of the WAIS remain the most stable as people age; performance scores decline the most. Fluid intelligence scores may show some decline with age (especially when measured cross-sectionally), but crystallized intelligence scores may increase.

8. Anxiety, the degree of motivation, and sociocultural factors, among others, may influence test results.

9. IQ cannot be used alone as a predictor of either occupational or personal success. Therefore, it is dangerous to label people as "average" or "dull" on the basis of intelligent test scores alone.

10. One of the most widely used tests is the SAT, which measures scholastic aptitude. The SAT score averages for college-bound seniors dropped until 1980, after which they increased until 1985. The math scores held steady from 1986 to 1992, after which they increased slightly. The verbal scores decreased from 1986 to 1994, after which they increased in 1995.

11. Proposed changes in the SAT took effect in 1994. The first part, which has both a verbal and a math section, is called the Scholastic Assessment Test (SAT I). The second part, known as SAT II, is an essay section and is optional. Both the verbal and math parts were changed.

12. The ACT is the second most widely used college admission test. It consists of three parts: (a) the academic tests, (b) the student profile section, and (c) the ACT interest inventory.

13. Another way of understanding adolescent cognition is through the information-processing approach, which describes the way information is transmitted. The process may be divided into a series of logical steps: selecting information from sensory stimuli, interpreting it, remembering it, thinking about it, using it in solving problems, and then making decisions.

14. Information is put into a series of memory storages: sensory storage, short-term storage, and long-term storage.

15. Information received by the senses is put into the sensory store, where it begins to decay in a fraction of a second. That which has not faded is passed on to the short-term store. Information that is held for a period of time is then transferred to the long-term store.

16. Stored information is retrieved by searching, finding, and remembering.

17. The capacity for sensory storage and short-term storage does not change much during adolescence, but adolescents are more efficient than children at deep processing, so they have superior long-term memory.

18. A number of factors improve memory ability: mental repetition and rehearsal, organizing material into meaningful units (chunking), arranging material into logical order or into categories, presenting material that is meaningful and familiar, and providing cues or codes so that what is remembered is associated with something familiar. Another way to remember is by visualizing position or place.

19. Information processing involves thinking about something after it has been retrieved from memory stores, and then solving problems after generating a list of solutions that can be evaluated using the information at hand so that a right answer is found.
20. One of the characteristics of an intelligent, mature person is the ability to make good decisions. Some decisions made during adolescence may have lifelong consequences.
21. Decision making is a complicated process involving information search and processing, problem solving, judgment in evaluating, learning about binding commitments, memory, knowledge in the areas about which decisions are made, and willingness to become involved in the process of decision making.
22. Ross says that the decision maker must master five skills: identify alternate courses of action, identify

appropriate criteria for considering alternatives, assess alternatives, summarize information about the alternatives, and self-evaluate the outcome of the decision-making process.
23. A helpful decision-making model was developed by Mann and colleagues. Their model listed nine elements of competent decision making (the nine Cs of decision making): choice, comprehension, creativity, compromise, consequentiality, correctness, credibility, consistency, and commitment.
24. Late adolescents, with more experience, have greater competence in decision making than early adolescents.
25. Low self-esteem, peer pressure, structured family situations, and legal restraints may interfere with adolescents becoming involved in making personal decisions. Adolescents need the opportunity to learn how to make decisions.

KEY TERMS

cognitive monitoring **157**

intelligence quotient (IQ) **151**

long-term storage **158**

primary memory **158**

secondary memory **158**

sensory storage **158**

short-term storage **158**

THOUGHT QUESTIONS

1. How would you describe an intelligent person? What factors distinguish a person who is intelligent from one who is not?
2. Have you ever known someone who is a genius in some ways and anything but a genius in other ways? Describe the person.
3. Are parents generally smarter than adolescents? Explain.
4. Do you think all students should be given intelligence tests and then given the test results? Why or why not? Should parents and teachers know the scores?
5. Have you ever taken IQ tests at different times, only to discover that your scores change? Why did they change? Explain.
6. What is the difference between cross-sectional and longitudinal measurements? Why do cross-sectional measurements accentuate intellectual

decline and longitudinal measurements minimize it?
7. What do you think of the SAT? Should it be used as a basis for admission to college? Why or why not? What criteria would you use for selection?
8. In what ways is the human mind similar and dissimilar to a computer?
9. Selective attention means each person notices something different, depending on interest and motivation. What sorts of things do you notice and remember most easily?
10. Are you more attracted by audible, visual, or tactile stimuli?
11. When you are studying for an exam, what techniques do you use to help you remember?
12. When you are faced with problems, what techniques do you find most helpful in making decisions or arriving at solutions?

SUGGESTED READING

Chipman, S. F., Segal, J. W., and Glaser, R. (Eds.). (1985). *Thinking and Learning Skills. Vol. 2: Research and Open Questions.* Hillsdale, NJ: Erlbaum.

Coles, G. (1987). *The Learning Mystique: A Critical Look at Learning Disabilities.* New York: Pantheon Books.

Marfo, K. (Ed.). (1988). *Parent-Child Interaction and Developmental Disabilities: Theory, Research, and Intervention.* New York: Praeger.

8

Gender,
Self-Concept,
Self-Esteem,
Ethnicity,
and Identity

An important consideration in any discussion of adolescents is the distinction between gender identity and gender role. *Gender* refers to a person's biological sex. *Gender identity* is the individual's internal sense or perception of being male or female. *Gender role,* or *sex role,* is the outward expression of maleness or femaleness in social settings. This chapter begins with a discussion of biological determinants of gender; it then goes on to discuss environmental influences. Changing concepts of masculinity, femininity, and gender role are examined, along with the trend toward

gender   a person's biological sex.

gender identity   a person's internal sense of being male or female.

gender role or sex role   the outward manifestation and expression of maleness or femaleness in a social setting.

167

androgyny. The implications of these changes are discussed. Another major subject in this chapter is the discussion of the importance of developing a positive self-concept and self-esteem. We will examine the relative stability of self-concept during adolescence—that is, determining whether the adolescent's self-conception changes. In the last part of the chapter, we will discuss identity: Marcia's four stages of identity status, women and identity, and ethnic identity.

Gender

Biological Basis

Biological gender is genetically and hormonally determined. The fetus becomes a male or female depending on whether it has XY or XX chromosomes and on the balance between the male and female hormones in the bloodstream. Hormones have a definite influence on physical characteristics. Male hormones can be administered to a woman, encouraging the growth of a beard, body hair, the clitoris, and the development of masculine muscles, build, and strength. Similarly, female hormones can be administered to a man, encouraging breast development, increasing voice pitch, and other female traits. Femaleness or maleness, then, is somewhat tenuous and may be partially altered.

Hormones alter physical characteristics, but do they influence sex-type behavior (Udry, 1990)? If human females are exposed to excessive androgenic (masculinizing sex hormones) influences prior to birth, they become more tomboyish, more physically vigorous, and more assertive than other females. They will prefer boys rather than girls as playmates and will choose strenuous activities over the relatively docile play of most prepubertal girls. Similarly, adolescent boys born to mothers who receive estrogen and progesterone during pregnancies tend to exhibit less assertiveness and physical activity, and may be rated lower on general masculine-type behavior (Rabin and Chrousos, 1991). This suggests that changes in prenatal, hormonal levels in humans may have marked effects on gender-role behavior; after birth, however, hormonal changes usually accentuate or minimize certain masculine/feminine characteristics already evident.

Cognitive-Developmental Theories

Cognitive-developmental theories suggest that sex-role identity has its beginning in the gender that is cognitively assigned to the child at birth and subsequently accepted by him or her while growing up. At the time of birth, gender assignment is made largely on the basis of genital examination. From that point on, the child is considered a boy or a girl. If genital abnormalities are present, gender assignment may prove to be erroneous if it is not in agreement with sex chromosomes and gonads that are present. However, even if erroneous, sex identification usually follows the sex in which the child is reared.

The cognitive assignment of gender influences everything that happens thereafter. The child's self-categorization as a boy or girl is the basic organizer of the sex-role attitudes that are developed. For example, the child who recognizes that he is a male begins to value maleness and to act consistently with gender expectations. He begins to structure his own experiences according to his accepted gender and to act out appropriate sex roles. He reflects sex-role differences and he fantasizes himself as a daddy with a wife and children. The same holds true for the girl, who pretends she is a grown-up woman with a husband and children. Sex differentiation takes place gradually as children learn to be male or female according to culturally established sex-role expectations and their interpretations of them (Trepanier-Street, Romatowski, and McNair, 1990).

Environmental Influences

Biological and cognitive characteristics are only part of the gender-role picture; environment also plays an important role. Certain qualities of maleness are defined and become "masculine," not only because of heredity and gender assignment but also in the way society describes that a man ought to be a man. Society prescribes how a male ought to look and behave, what type of personality he ought to have, and the roles he should perform. Similarly, a female is created not only by genetic conception but also by those psychosocial forces that mold and influence her personality.

Masculinity and *femininity* refer to those qualities of personality that are characteristic of a man

A child's sex-role identity begins with the cognitive assignment of gender made at birth. However, the environment also plays an important role, ascribing certain qualities of femininity or masculinity to the child.

or a woman. When an individual speaks of a masculine man, that person is expressing a value judgment based on an assessment of the personality and behavioral characteristics of the male. Similarly, a feminine woman is labeled according to culturally determined criteria for femaleness. In this sense, the development of masculinity or femininity is an education in human sexuality—in other words, what it means to be a man or a woman or what it means to be sexual, within the context of the culture in which one lives (Lopata, 1993).

Masculinity   Traditionally, masculine men were supposed to be aggressive, strong, forceful, self-confident, virile, courageous, logical, and unemotional. These stereotypes of masculinity are considered socially desirable by some people today. To be a man, a male must be a big wheel, have status, be successful, and be admired. Men who do not succeed in business feel they have to

prove themselves in other ways: perhaps by being stronger and tougher than anyone else or by being able to seduce and dominate women. To be a man, a male must be a sturdy rock with an air of toughness, confidence, and self-reliance. The great heros are John Wayne in *True Grit,* Clint Eastwood in *Dirty Harry,* or Sylvester Stalone in *Rocky.* He must never be emotional or reveal tenderness or weakness. Above all, men are never to express affection toward other men so as to avoid all suspicion of homosexuality (Rabinowitz, 1991; Salt, 1991).

These dimensions of the traditional masculine stereotypes can be readily seen in the three avenues by which adolescent boys gain admission to deviant peer groups (e.g., gangs) (Mosher and Tomkins, 1988):

1. They have to fight their way in and demonstrate their courage and toughness by being willing to fight.
2. They have to show fearlessness in deeds (e.g., climbing the water tower, racing the car) or demonstrate bravado and courage by some other means.
3. They have to engage in a callous sex act to prove their manhood by "scoring."

Femininity   What are the traditional concepts of femininity as taught by middle and upper-middle classes of U.S. society? In the past, women were supposed to be submissive, sensitive, tender, affectionate, sentimental, dependent, and emotional. A feminine female was never aggressive, loud, or vulgar in speech or behavior. She was expected to be soft-hearted, to cry easily, to get upset at times over small things, and to like frivolous things. She was expected to be dependent and submissive and to be interested primarily in her home. Today, few social groups hold these stereotypes of femininity, indicating that significant changes have taken place in people's concepts.

masculinity   personality and behavioral characteristics of a male according to culturally defined standards of maleness.

femininity   personality and behavior characteristics of a female according to culturally defined standards of femaleness.

However, some individuals hold stereotyped beliefs and attitudes regarding the rights and roles of women. They believe that, by nature, males are aggressive and females are passive, and that men and women should accept these roles that nature has intended for them (Murnen and Byrne, 1991).

Social Learning Theory Social learning theory suggests that a child learns sex-type behavior the same way he or she learns any other type of behavior: through a combination of indoctrination, observation, identification, and modeling. From the beginning, boys and girls are socialized differently. Boys are expected to be more active, hostile, and aggressive. They are expected to fight when teased and to stand up to bullies. When they act according to expectations, they are praised; when they refuse to fight, they are criticized for being "sissy." Similarly, girls are condemned or punished for being too boisterous and aggressive and are rewarded when they are polite and submissive. As a consequence, boys and girls grow up manifesting different behaviors.

Traditional gender roles and concepts are taught in many ways as a child grows up. For instance, television plays a significant role in the socialization process (for both young and old). Especially television commercials contain considerable gender bias and sexism (Beal, 1994). Another way of reinforcing gender roles is giving children gender-specific toys that may influence vocational choices. For example, boys might be persuaded to be scientists, astronauts, or football players, and girls might be inclined to be nurses, teachers, or flight attendants.

Without realizing it, many teachers still develop traditional masculine/feminine stereotypical behavior in school. Studies of teachers' relationships with boys and girls reveal that teachers, in general, encourage boys to be more assertive in the classroom (Sadker and Sadker, 1995). When the teacher asks questions, the boys call out comments without raising their hands, literally grabbing the teacher's attention. Most girls sit patiently with their hands raised, but when a girl calls out, the teacher reprimands her: "In this class, we don't shout out answers; we raise our hands." The message is subtle but powerful: Boys should be assertive academically; girls should be quiet.

Much has been done also to try to change school courses and programs that promote sex-type roles. Traditionally, physical education courses for boys emphasize contact sports and competition; those for girls promote grace, agility, and poise. Not so long ago, home economics was offered only to girls; shop and auto mechanics were offered only to boys. Guidance counselors urged girls to become secretaries and nurses; boys were influenced to become business managers and doctors. Females were usually prepared for marriage and parenthood; boys were on track for vocations. Gradually, these emphases are being eliminated so that both males and females are free to choose the programs they want.

Children also find appropriate gender roles through the processes of identification and modeling, especially with parents. Parental *identification* is the process by which a child adopts and internalizes parental values, attitudes, behavioral traits, and personality characteristics. Identification begins immediately after birth because of the child's early dependence on parents. This dependency, in turn, usually leads to close emotional attachment. Gender-role learning takes place almost unconsciously and indirectly in this close parent-child relationship. Children listen and observe how each parent behaves, speaks, dresses, and acts differently in relation to the other parent, to other children, or to people outside the family. Thus, children learn what a mother, a wife, a father, a husband, a woman, and a man *is* through example and through daily contacts and association.

The gender-role concepts the child learns depend not only on the intensity of parental relationships but also on the patterns of role models exemplified (Hansen and Darling, 1985). For example, daughters of rural mothers, especially those with large families, learn more traditional feminine roles than daughters from urban families where the mothers are likely to spend more time outside the family. It has also been found that high-status parents exert more influence than low-status ones, and that parents with more education are able to exert more influence. Not surprisingly, the girl who closely identifies with her masculine mother becomes only weakly identified with a typically feminine personality. One brought up by a mother with nontraditional, gender-role attitudes will learn a less stereotyped concept of femininity

Trying to be a macho man is sometimes harmful and has been associated with suicide, health and emotional problems, stress, and substance abuse. Do these adolescents fit the macho stereotype?

than one whose mother holds conservative attitudes. One study of the gender-role attitudes of early adolescents showed that daughters of mothers who were employed felt less traditional gender-role attitudes than did daughters of women who were not employed (Nelson and Keith, 1990). The happier the husband was with his wife's employment, the more nontraditional was the daughter. Sons' gender-role attitudes were not significantly influenced by their mothers' employment, at least in this study.

Problems with Stereotypes   One problem with gender stereotypes is that whenever written standards are applied to all members of one sex, individual personalities can be distorted. Everyone is expected to conform, regardless of individual inclinations or differences. Furthermore, gender identity and gender-role stereotypes place serious limitations on the relationships that people are capable of forming, as well as on career or personal achievements. For instance, traditionally, females were regarded as submissive, unaggressive, weak, and unable to stand up for herself at home, so her children and husband often took advantage of her. Basically, she was considered frivolous, illogical, and emotional, thus unworthy to assume positions of leadership in government or business. Today is a different story, however. Many

women—single, divorced, sole supporters of their children—must be breadwinners. Our daughters, then, need to learn the same assertiveness, independence, and rational thinking that we seek to develop in our sons. If women are to succeed, new roles require acceptance of different traits.

What about the traditional female traits of sensitivity and awareness of the feelings of others, tenderness, kindness, and soft-heartedness? These traits have always been needed in all types of human relationships. Traditionally, men were not supposed to exhibit these traits of showing feelings, crying, and being sensitive. Rather, they were supposed to be impervious to sorrow, pain, and tragedy and to be able to "take it like a man." As a result, some men considered it unmanly to tell their wives "I love you" or to give their children (especially boys) a big hug and a kiss. Men were encouraged to be interested in sex because "real men" were virile, but they were often encouraged to be indifferent to love. The result has been insensitive men and sensitive women trying to learn to live together in the same world. The very traits

---

identification   the process by which an individual ascribes to himself or herself the characteristics of another person.

that women were supposed to exhibit and men were expected to suppress exposed women to the hurts and upsets of intimate living and prevented men from understanding why their partners were upset in the first place. It was difficult for men and women to become real friends and companions.

Trying to be a supermasculine man has also been harmful to men themselves. Adherence to the traditional male role has been associated with suicide, health problems, stress, substance abuse, and emotional illness (Good and Mintz, 1990). Being openly dominant, aggressive, independent, and unemotional is self-destructive and dangerous. The over-aggressive male gets in trouble with family, friends, and society.

Modern men must learn to be less aggressive and more cooperative, expressive, and sensitive. Modern women need to learn to be more assertive and less passive. Both need to be sensitive and tender in their feelings and relationships with one another. Highly segregated gender roles result in lack of cooperation, companionship, and intimacy in the family. Cooperative sharing of roles results in greater commitment and companionship among all family members and to greater opportunity for meaningful relationships (Blair and Lichter, 1991).

Androgyny

A gradual mixing of male and female traits and roles seems to be emerging, thereby producing *androgyny* (male and female in one). Androgynous people are not sex-typed with respect to roles (although they are distinctly male or female in gender). They match their behavior to the situation rather than being limited by what is culturally defined as male or female. An androgynous male feels comfortable cuddling and caring for a young boy; an androgynous female feels comfortable pumping gas and changing the oil in her car. Androgyny expands the range of human behavior, allowing individuals to cope effectively in a variety of situations.

Although the concept of androgyny was an improvement over exclusive notions of femininity and masculinity, it has turned out to be less of a panacea than many of its early proponents envisioned (Doyle and Paludi, 1995). Some theorists believe androgyny should be replaced with gender-role transcendence—the belief that when an individual's competence is at issue, it should not be conceptualized on the basis of masculinity, femininity, or androgyny but rather on a person basis. Thus, rather than merging gender roles or stereotyping people as "masculine" or "feminine," we should begin to think about people as people.

Self-Concept and Self-Esteem

The *self* is that part of an individual's personality of which he or she is aware. *Self-concept* is a conscious, cognitive perception and evaluation by individuals of themselves; it is their thoughts and opinions about themselves. Self-concept has been called the individual's "self-hypothesized identity" (Wayment and Zetlin, 1989). Erikson (1968) refers to it as the individual's "ego identity," or the individual's self-perceived, consistent individuality. *Self-esteem* is a person's self worth.

Meaning

The first step in the development of a self-concept is when a person recognizes that he or she is a distinct, separate individual. This awareness begins in early childhood. Self-concept also implies a developing awareness on a person's part of who and what he or she is. It describes what individuals see when they look at themselves, in terms of their self-perceived physical characteristics, personality skills, traits, roles, and social statuses. It might be described as the system of attitudes they have about themselves. It is their ego identity or personal identity, which is the sum total of their self-definitions or self-images (Harter, 1990).

Self-concept is often described as a *global entity:* how people feel about themselves in general (DuBois, Felner, Brand, Phillips, and Lease, 1996). But it has also been described as made up of *multiple self-conceptions,* with concepts developed in relation to different roles (Griffin, Chassin, and Young, 1981). Thus, a person may rate himself or herself as a son or daughter, student, athlete, friend, and so forth. These conceptions of different aspects of the self may differ, which helps to explain how behavior varies in different roles.

Adolescents gather evidence that helps them evaluate themselves: Am I competent? Am I attractive to the opposite sex? Am I intelligent? From this evidence, they form postulates about themselves and check out their feelings and opinions through further experiences and relationships. They compare themselves with their own ideals and those of others.

Whether individuals have an accurate self-concept is significant. All people are six different selves: the people they are, the people they think they are, the people others think they are, the people they think others think they are, the people they want to become, and the people they think others want them to become. Self-concepts may or may not be close approximations of reality, and self-concepts are always in the process of change, particularly during childhood. A number of years ago, in *Becoming: Basic Considerations for a Psychology of Personality,* Allport (1950) emphasized that personality is less a finished product than a transitive process. It has some stable features, but at the same time it is undergoing change. Allport coined the word *proprium,* which he defined as "all aspects of personality that make for inward unity." This is the self or ego that has a core of personal identity that is developing in time.

Strang (1957) outlined four basic dimensions of the self. First, there is the *overall, basic self-concept,* which is the adolescent's view of his or her personality and "perceptions of his abilities and his status and roles in the outer world" (p. 68).

Next are the individual's *temporary or transitory self-concepts.* These ideas of self are influenced by the mood of the moment or by a recent or continuing experience. A recent low grade on an examination may leave a person with a temporary feeling of being stupid; a critical remark from parents may produce a temporary feeling of deflated self-worth.

Third, there are the adolescents' *social selves—* the selves that they think others see, which, in turn, influence how they see themselves. If they have the impression that others think they are stupid or socially unacceptable, they tend to think of themselves in these negative ways. Their perceptions of others' feelings color their views of themselves (Harter, Stocker, and Robinson, 1996; Street, 1988). Identity comes partly from an involvement of the self with others, in intimacy, group partici-

pation, cooperation, and competition. It evolves through social interactions, encompassing both continuity of self and identification with something beyond the self. Carlyle (1970) stated, "Show me the man who is your friend and I will know what your ideal of manhood is—and what kind of man you wish to be."

Part of self-concept is the sense of social status, the position in which individuals place themselves in the social system in the present or the future. For example, adolescents from low-socioeconomic-status groups who see themselves as not belonging there but as members of a higher socioeconomic class are molding new identities because of their higher aspirations.

The fourth dimension is the *ideal self,* which is the kind of people adolescents would like to be. Their aspirations may be realistic, too low, or too high. Ideal selves that are too low impede accomplishment; those that are too high may lead to frustration and self-depreciation. Realistic self-concepts lead to self-acceptance, mental health, and accomplishment of realistic goals.

Self-Esteem   Having built concepts of themselves, adolescents then must deal with the esteem with which they view themselves. When they perceive themselves, what value do they place on the selves they perceive? Does this appraisal lead to self-acceptance and approval, to a feeling of self-worth? If so, then they have enough self-esteem to accept and live with themselves. If people are to

---

androgyny   a blending of male and female characteristics and roles.

self   a person's personality or nature of which that person is aware.

self-concept   conscious, cognitive perception and evaluation by individuals of themselves; their thoughts and opinions about themselves.

self-esteem   a person's impression or opinion of himself or herself.

proprium   the self-identity that is developing in time.

ideal self   the kind of person an individual would like to be.

have self-esteem, there must be a correspondence between their *concepts of self* and their *self-ideals*.

With the onset of puberty, most young people begin to make a thorough assessment of themselves, comparing not only their body parts but also their motor skills, intellectual abilities, and social skills with those of their peers and their ideals or heroes. This critical self-appraisal is accompanied by self-conscious behavior that makes adolescents vulnerable to embarrassment. As a consequence, they are preoccupied with attempting to reconcile their selves as they perceive them with their ideal selves. By late adolescence, they may have managed to sort themselves out—to determine what they can most effectively be and to integrate their goals into their ideal selves.

Carl Rogers (1961) was one of the most important contemporary theorists in the development of a theoretical and practical structure of self-ideals. He pictured the end point of personality development as a basic congruence between the phenomenal field and experience and the conceptual structure of the self. This situation results in freedom from internal conflict and anxiety, when individuals discover who they are and what they perceive themselves to be and want to be begin to merge; they are then able to accept themselves, without conflict. Their self-perceptions and relationships with others elicit self-acceptance and self-esteem. Psychological maladjustment occurs when there is a divergence between the selves they

are being in relationship to others and the selves they perceive they are or want to be.

Importance of an Adequate Self-Concept and Self-Esteem

Self-esteem has been called the "survival of the soul"; it is the ingredient that gives dignity to human existence. It grows out of human interaction in which the self is considered important to someone. The ego grows through small accomplishments, praise, and success (Lazarus, 1991).

Mental Health   A positive self-perception, or high self-esteem, is a desired outcome of the human developmental process. It has been linked to long-term mental health and emotional well-being (Klein, 1995). Individuals whose identities are weak or whose self-esteem has never sufficiently developed manifest a number of symptoms of emotional ill health (Koenig, 1988). Such individuals may evidence psychosomatic symptoms of anxiety. Low self-esteem has also been found to be a factor in drug abuse and in unwed pregnancy (Blinn, 1987; Horn and Rudolph, 1987). In fact, unwed pregnancy is often an effort on the part of young women to enhance their self-esteem (Streetman, 1987). Low self-esteem is also associated with the eating disorders anorexia nervosa and bulimia (Button, 1990) and is a factor in ado-

Loving Ourselves and Others

Some theorists emphasize that by promoting or enhancing self-esteem alone, people focus attention on themselves, and this promotes a certain type of self-consciousness, self-preoccupation, and selfishness. When people focus their attention on others in order to enhance their own self-esteem, this is fundamentally a selfish type of attention, with the concern for others serving a secondary part of what is occurring. These theorists emphasize that the maxim "We cannot love others until we love ourselves" is actually 180 degrees wrong. Ironically and paradoxically, this idea would be more true, more relevant, and less harmful if we were to reverse it—"We cannot love ourselves until we love others." Theorists suggest that what we ought to do is to focus our attention on the welfare of others and establish intimate, emotional, and compassionate connections we humans have with others (Burr and Christensen, 1992).

lescent depression and anxiety (Greenberg et al., 1992; King, Akiyama, and Elling, 1996).

Sometimes, the adolescent with a weak identity and low self-esteem tries to develop a false front, or facade, with which to face the world. This is a compensating mechanism used to overcome the feeling of worthlessness by convincing others that one is worthy. The youth tries to put on an act to impress people. Putting on an act, however, is a strain. To act confident, friendly, and cheerful when one feels the opposite is a constant struggle. The anxiety that the person might make a false step and let the guard slip creates considerable tension.

Another reason for anxiety is that people with low self-esteem show a shifting and unstable identity. Adolescents with low self-esteem are self-conscious and overly vulnerable to criticism or rejection, which testifies to their inadequacy, incompetence, or worthlessness (Rosenthal and Simeonsson, 1989). They may be deeply disturbed when laughed at, when blamed, or when others have a poor opinion of them. The more vulnerable they feel themselves to be, the higher are their anxiety levels. Such adolescents report, "Criticism hurts me terribly" or "I can't stand to have anyone laugh at me or blame me when something goes wrong." As a result, they feel awkward and uneasy in social situations and avoid embarrassment whenever they can.

Interpersonal Competence and Social Adjustment

Those with poor self-concepts are often rejected by other people. Acceptance of others and acceptance by others, especially by best friends, are related to self-concept scores. Acceptance of self is positively and significantly correlated with acceptance of, and by, others. Thus, there is a close relationship between self-acceptance and social adjustment. One of the signs of possible disturbance during adolescence is an inability to establish friendships or to meet new people.

Poor social adjustment, which is related to low self-concept and self-esteem, manifests itself in a number of ways. Adolescents with low self-esteem tend to be outstanding in their social invisibility (see Chapter 17). They are not noticed or selected as leaders, and they do not participate often in class, clubs, or social activities. They do not stand up for their own rights or express their opinions on matters that concern them. These adolescents more often develop feelings of isolation and loneliness. One man wrote, "I used to be so shy that I first went out with a woman at 21. Words cannot express how excruciatingly, how desperately lonely I was in those days" (Zimbardo, 1978, p. 18).

Shy people often feel awkward and tense in social situations, which makes it more difficult for them to communicate with others. Because they want to be liked, they are more easily influenced and led and usually let others make decisions because they lack self-confidence.

Progress in School

Increasing evidence supports the theory that there is a correlation between self-concept and achievement in school. Successful students feel a greater sense of personal worth and somewhat better about themselves (Garzarelli, Everhart, and Lester, 1993). However, the relationship is reciprocal. Those who have high self-esteem tend to have higher academic achievement, and those who are academic achievers have higher self-esteem (Liu, Kaplan, and Risser, 1992). In general, the higher the grade averages, the more likely the student is to have a high level of self-acceptance (Mboya, 1989). One reason is that students who have confidence in themselves have the courage to try and are motivated to live up to what they believe about themselves. Students who have negative attitudes about themselves impose limitations on their own achievement. They feel they "can't do it anyhow" or are "not smart enough." (Fenzel, 1994).

Recently, attention has been focused on the strategies children use in school to portray themselves as unable to do schoolwork. By procrastinating, deliberately not trying, allowing others to keep them from studying, and using other self-defeating strategies, students can convey that circumstances, rather than lack of ability, are the reasons for poor performance. Survey data from 256 eighth-grade students indicated that boys used those strategies more so than girls, and low achievers more so than high achievers (Midgley and Urdan, 1995).

Other studies emphasize that participation in extracurricular activities is also related to increased self-esteem. Whether the participation is *because* of higher self-esteem or whether it *contributes* to higher self-esteem is sometimes questionable, but the two are nevertheless correlated. Also, participation in extracurricular activities is related to a higher grade-point average and lower absenteeism from school (Fertman and Chubb, 1992). This is in keeping with other research findings that participation in high school activities, especially athletic activities, is associated with higher self-esteem in both boys and girls (Steitz and Owen, 1992).

Boys from minority groups are less likely to develop positive self-concepts from high achievement because of the attitudes of the group toward good grades. Thus, to understand how academic achievement influences social self-image, we must consider the individual within the context of his or her peer group; that is, we must consider how peer attitudes toward achievement will affect an individual's social self-image. Peer influences may either encourage or discourage academic success, depending on the dominant value within the peer group. Peers who place a high value on academics influence each other to do well in school (Roberts and Petersen, 1992).

The positive attitudes and support of significant others—mothers, fathers, grandparents, older siblings, special friends, teachers, or school counselors—can have an important influence on students' academic self-concepts. Students who feel that others have confidence in their academic abilities have confidence in themselves.

Vocational Aspirations   For some people, the selection of an occupation is an attempt to fulfill the sense of self. The desire and expectation to get ahead vocationally also depend on self-esteem. Adolescents who have determined some career goals for themselves have higher self-esteem than do those without any career goals (Chiu, 1990; Munson, 1992). Women who have both a career and marriage tend to have higher self-esteem than those who are full-time homemakers. Boys who aspire to upward mobility also show a strong sense of self-esteem, whereas downwardly mobile boys more often wish for changes in self that are so extensive that they indicate self-rejection. Both those with low and high self-esteem consider it important to get ahead, but those with low self-esteem are less likely to expect they will succeed. They are

more likely to say, "I would like to get ahead in life, but I don't think I'll ever get ahead as far as I want." They do not believe that they possess those qualities essential for success.

Is there a difference in the types of positions desired by low and high self-esteem adolescents? In general, those with low self-esteem want to avoid positions in which they will be forced to exercise leadership and avoid jobs in which others dominate them; they want to be neither power wielders nor power subjects. Avoiding leadership or supervision by others is a way of avoiding criticism or judgment.

Educational and vocational aspirations depend partly on self-image, which in turn, may be derived from family background. In one study, adolescents' educational plans and self-image were consistently lower in a poor rural community than those of adolescents in a high or medium socioeconomic-status community (Sarigiani, Wilson, Petersen, and Vicary, 1990). Self-image and educational plans were related to the educational attainment of the parents in the rural sample. Also, within the rural sample, young adolescents with lower aspirations had lower self-images.

Delinquency   There is a close relationship between delinquency and self-concept. Delinquent youths tend to show lower self-esteem than do nondelinquent youths. Their delinquency may be a form of overcompensation for their inadequate self-concepts. One theory is that they have low self-esteem and therefore adopt deviant patterns of behavior to reduce self-rejecting feelings. If their behavior begins to match their low opinions of themselves, they decrease their own self-derogation and rejection. They seek to restore their self-respect by aligning themselves with deviant groups that accord them the approval denied by the rest of society. Thus, an adequate self-concept protects the adolescents from delinquency; those who see themselves as "good people" or "nondelinquents" have developed an inner containment against becoming delinquent. One effective form of treatment of delinquent youths is to place them in group homes where they can model appropriate behavior of houseparents and build the self-confidence necessary for changing undesirable behavior. As self-esteem improves, so does their behavior (Krueger and Hansen, 1987).

PERSONAL ISSUES

Perfectionism

Generally, the wish to excel is an admirable attribute. Normal perfectionists derive real pleasure from their accomplishments, but they feel free to be less precise if a situation permits. *Neurotic perfectionists* pursue excellence to an unhealthy extreme. They hold the irrational belief that they must be perfect to be accepted. Their standards are beyond reason—they strain toward impossible goals that are never reached. Plagued by self-criticism, their self-worth is further lowered. Because in their own eyes they never measure up, they become de-

fensive and angry when faced with possible criticism, a behavior that frustrates and alienates others and causes the very disapproval that they fear. Over time, they are filled with fear and emotional turmoil, and experience more pain than rewards. They avoid intimate relationships because they fear ultimate rejection. The end result is loneliness, a life devoid of closeness or intimacy. Even academic success, which many attain, does nothing to promote self-confidence (Halgin and Leahy, 1989).

Development of a Positive Self-Concept

How can a positive self-concept be developed? Let's look at several factors that contribute to its achievement.

Significant Others   The idea that self-concept is determined in part by others' views of us, or the way we think others view us, is generally accepted (Juhasz, 1989). However, not all people exert an equally strong influence. *Significant others* are those individuals who occupy a high level of importance. They are influential and their opinions are meaningful (Lackovic-Grgin and Dekovic, 1990). Their influence also depends on their degree of involvement and intimacy, the social support they provide (Blain, Thompson, and Whiffen, 1993), and the power and authority given to them by others.

Parental Relationships   A variety of researchers have found that the affective quality of family relations during adolescence is associated with high levels of self-esteem (Robinson, 1995). Adolescents with higher self-esteem report greater intimacy with their mothers and fathers; in other words, they feel close to and get along with their parents (Field, Lang, Yando, and Vendell, 1995). Adolescent self-esteem has been associated with parental willingness to grant autonomy (Gecas and Schwalbe, 1986), parental acceptance, flexibility

(Klein, 1992), communication (Barnes and Olson, 1985) and shared satisfaction, as well as parental support, participation, and control (Barber, Chadwick, and Oerter, 1992; Openshaw, Thomas, and Rollins, 1984; Robinson, 1995). We will discuss a number of these factors in more detail.

Maternal Relationship and Identification   The quality of parent-adolescent relationships is clearly an important factor in adolescent self-esteem (Demo, Small, and Savin-Williams, 1987; Gecas and Schwalbe, 1986; Hoelter and Harper, 1987). Older adolescent girls who feel close to their mothers see themselves as confident, wise, reasonable, and self-controlled. Those who feel distant from their mothers perceive themselves in negative terms: rebellious, impulsive, touchy, and tactless. These findings indicate that the degree of maternal identification influences self-concept.

Both boys and girls who identify closely with a parental model strive to be like the model in such a way that blending of self with the qualities of the model brings about a real likeness but not overidentification. Erikson (1968) felt that overidentification with parents cuts off a "budding identity" by stifling the ego. However, children with inadequate parental identification will also have poor ego identity. Ego identity of girls is weak with poor maternal identification and with overidentification. A moderate degree of identification seems to be the healthiest.

The Self's Development

The figure below shows that the beginnings of the self occur through four primary input channels: *auditory cues, physical sensations, body image cues,* and *personal memories.* These input channels provide the emotional medium that allows the self to grow (Hamachek, 1985). Self-awareness develops when young children begin to recognize the distinction between self and others, between their bodies and the remainder of their visible environment. When personal experience widens and intellectual functioning expands, the self differentiates further as the child gains increased ability both to understand the outside world more fully (to be the "knower" or "doer") and to see himself or herself as an object in the outside world (to be the "known"). The self-as-object involves attributes that are physical (how you look), social (how you relate), emotional (how you feel), and intellectual (how you think). These attributes interact with that aspect of the self that comes to know through its perceiving, performing, thinking, and remembering functions.

The component of the self that is the knower constitutes the "I" or the "agent of experience," and that dimension of the self that is the known constitutes the "me" or "the content of experience."

The interactive combination of these attributes and functions leads to the development of two core ingredients of the self—namely, self-concept (ideas about yourself) and self-esteem (feelings and evaluations about yourself). Self-concept can be more specifically differentiated into the perceived self (the way you see yourself) and into the "real" self (the way you really are, as measured more objectively through tests or clinical assessments) and the "ideal" self (the way you would like to be). Out of all this emerges personality, which, depending on who is describing it, can be either the sum total of (1) your own internal self-perceptions or (2) another person's external perceptions of you (Hamachek, 1985, pp. 138, 139).

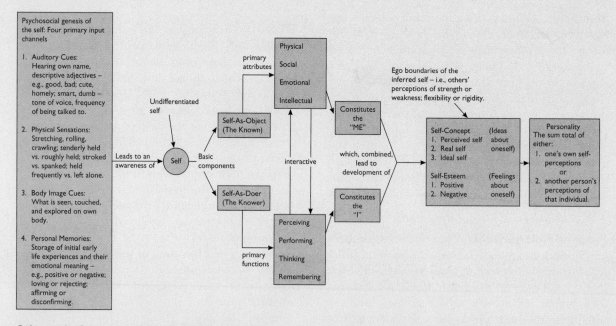

Schematic Overview of the Self's Development

Source: D. E. Hamachek, "The Self's Development and Ego Growth: Conceptual Analysis and Implications for Counselors," *Journal of Counseling and Development, 64* (1985): 136–142. Copyright © 1985 American Association of Counseling and Development. Reprinted by permission.

A positive relationship with his father will help the adolescent boy develop high self-esteem and a stable self-image. This is also true of the adolescent girl's relationship with her mother.

Paternal Relationship and Identification   Fathers are important, too, in an adolescent's development. Warm, rewarding father-daughter relationships play a vital role in helping a girl to value her femininity, to move toward a positive acceptance of herself as a woman, and to make easier and more satisfactory heterosexual adjustments. The same is true for the adolescent boy. If he identifies with his father but shares mutually warm feelings with his mother, his relationships with women are more likely to be comfortable and pleasant.

Parental Interest, Concern, and Discipline   A key factor in determining whether parents have a positive effect in helping their adolescents build a healthy ego identity is the warmth, concern, and interest they show them. Parents who care and show interest are more likely to have adolescents who have high self-esteem. Furthermore, high self-esteem adolescents have parents who are democratic but also less permissive than those of low

self-esteem adolescents (Bartle, Anderson, and Sabatelli, 1989). The parents of high self-esteem adolescents are strict but consistent, and they demand high standards, yet they are also flexible enough to allow deviations from rules under special circumstances. There seems to be a combination of warmth and firm discipline (Buri, 1989).

Divorced and Blended Families   What happens to the self-esteem of the growing child when a family is broken by divorce? It depends on a number of factors. If the mother is very young at the time of the marital rupture, the negative effect on the child is much greater than if the mother is older, because the younger mother is less able to cope with the upset of divorce. The effect also depends on the child's age. Young children are more adversely affected than are older children.

Remarriage also influences self-esteem. Children who do not get along with their stepfathers tend to be more disturbed than children whose mothers do not remarry. Students whose mothers were relatively young when they were widowed are less likely to have high self-esteem. Children from intact families tend to evaluate themselves the most positively of all.

A study of female high school seniors showed that two-thirds of those who were high in ego identity (identity achievers) came from homes broken by either divorce or death (St. Clair and Day, 1979). These findings indicate that broken homes do not necessarily have the adverse effects on adolescents that are sometimes supposed. Self-concept scores are significantly lower, however, for children who report higher levels of family conflict, regardless of family type. It is the quality and harmony of interpersonal relationships that are the important factors, not the type of family structure alone.

When children perceive conflict between parents or between themselves and their parents, lower self-esteem can be expected. Amato (1986) found lower self-esteem among adolescents from conflicting families and from those where the parent-adolescent relationship was poor. However, one of the significant findings was that loss of self-esteem when parents divorce is usually temporary. Amato (1988) also found no significant association between adult self-esteem and having experienced parental divorce or death as a child.

HIGHLIGHT

Self-Esteem and Symbolic Interaction

Symbolic interaction emphasizes that a child's self-esteem is a function of the parents' reflected appraisal of the child's worth. Parents who are supportive, warm, and nurturing and who show approval and other positive sentiments confirm in the adolescent's mind that his or her parents accept him or her as a competent, effective, and worthwhile individual. Thus, parental support is related positively to the adolescent's self-esteem.

The type of parental control attempts also influences self-esteem. There are two types of control: induction and coercion. *Induction* is the attempt to point out to the adolescent the consequences of behavior. Parents utilizing induction will attempt to avoid a direct contest of wills and seek to induce voluntary behavior in the adolescent. Induction transmits to the adolescent a recognition of his or her ability to evaluate the consequences of behavior and to make a decision based on the evaluation. The adolescent emerges with more confidence in the choices made and in the ability to make those choices. Thus, self-esteem is enhanced (Gecas and Seff, 1990).

Coercion involving parental control attempts utilizing physical strength or social status to elicit desired behavior. It utilizes punishment, which is negatively related to self-esteem.

The figure here illustrates the symbolic interaction model and its influence on a child's self-esteem.

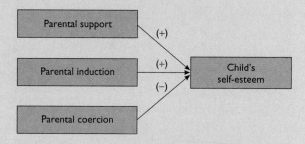

Source: D. K. Openshaw, D. L. Thomas, and B. C. Rollins, "Socialization and Adolescent Self-Esteem: Symbolic Interaction and Social Learning Explanations," *Adolescence, 18* (1983): 317–329. Used by permission.

The well-being of children can best be assessed by the adequacy of *nurturing, love, and training* they receive, rather than in terms of particular family structures (Hutchinson, Valutis, Brown, and White, 1989). One study found that adolescents who had experienced parental divorce were significantly more likely to have encountered parental hostility and/or lack of care, inadequate supervision when not in school, lack of concern by teachers, and greater financial hardship. In turn, lower self-concepts and/or social skills were found to be associated with these kinds of life experiences (Parish, 1993; Parish and Parish, 1991).

Socioeconomic Status The effects of socioeconomic status (SES) on self-esteem are variable. Generally, low SES students have lower self-esteem than high SES students. However, in their study of eleventh-grade students from three high schools in North Carolina, Richman, Clark, and Brown (1985) found that the higher SES girls had lower self-esteem than middle or low SES girls. Higher

SES girls felt under great pressure to excel in academics, physical attractiveness, social activities, and so on. Perceived failure in any one of these areas led to loss of self-esteem and feelings of inadequacy. Lower SES boys and girls were more accustomed to failure, so it was not as traumatic for them as for high SES girls.

Socioeconomic status of the parents, by itself, is not enough to produce low self-esteem children. Lower-class, low-income families produce high self-esteem children *if the parents' self-esteem is high*. This parental self-esteem depends, in turn, on the prestige of the parents' nationality or religious group or on the self-acceptance of the members within the group. The best example is that of Jewish adolescents, who, though they come from a religious group that is a minority in U.S. society, nevertheless usually have high self-esteem. This is probably due to the high self-esteem of the Jewish parents and the generally adequate parent-child relationship, measured by the degree of interest Jewish parents show in their children. Parental support lessens the impact of acute and chronic stress (Tinko, Stovel, Baumgartner, and Moos, 1995).

There is some relationship, however, between economic hardship and adolescent self-esteem. Economic hardship has an adverse effect on adolescents' self-esteem, and this effect is mediated primarily through the parent-adolescent relationship. Economic hardship reduces affective parental support and may thus convey a negative appraisal of the adolescent, thereby lowering his or her self-esteem (Ho, Lempers, and Clark-Lempers, 1995).

Race and Nationality   The influence of dissonance on self-esteem is felt among mixed racial groups (Fraser, 1994). In general, when African American adolescents attend White schools, they evidence a lower self-esteem than when attending predominantly African American schools (Dreyer, Jennings, Johnson, and Evans, 1994). African American students in segregated schools have higher self-esteem than African American students in integrated schools. The desegregated school may have certain advantages, but enhancing self-esteem is not one of them. Research findings suggest that with the increase of racial pride brought about by the civil rights movement, self-esteem among African Americans has risen. One study found that among a public high school sample of African American and White adolescents from Tennessee, the African American students had significantly higher levels of self-esteem than did the White students (Rust and McCraw, 1984). Another study reported the same findings in North Carolina (Richman, Clark, and Brown, 1985).

Overall, there is some evidence that African American youths have higher self-esteem when not exposed to White prejudices (Martinez and Dukes, 1991). When surrounded primarily by those with similar physical appearance, social-class standing, family background, and school performance, African Americans rate themselves much higher in self-esteem than when surrounded by Whites (Comer, 1993).

Research during late adolescence has revealed that multiple factors determine a student's self-esteem and self-image. One study showed that higher self-esteem scores were expected for youths, whether White or African American, who had graduated from high school, has positive experiences in school, were moving toward economic self-sufficiency, had positive relationships with their families, and perceived that their families approved of them and what they were doing. In other words, adolescents are more likely to have high self-esteem if they experience success in areas that are important to them and if they perceive that significant others, especially family members, hold them in high regard (Luster and McAdoo, 1995).

Birth Order   There is little correlation between the child's birth order in the family and self-esteem. An only child, however, is more likely to have higher self-esteem than a child with siblings. Also, those who are the first of their gender to be born in their family seem to have some advantage. Thus, a first-born boy in a family of all daughters enjoys high self-esteem, as does a first-born girl in a family of all sons. However, there are too many other variables—spacing of children, total number in the family, parent-child interactions, and so forth—to assume that birth order alone is a key to understanding self-concept (Steelman, 1985).

Physical Disabilities   As might be expected, adolescents with physical disabilities or negative body images have more difficulty developing positive self-concepts and self-esteem than do those who are more average (Koff, Rierdan, and Stubbs, 1990). (The importance of physical attractiveness and body image was discussed in Chapter 5.) It is certain that the degree of physical attractiveness and acceptance of one's physical self are influential factors in the development of a total self-concept (Padin, Lerner, and Spiro, 1981). Adolescents who think themselves "too short" or "too heavy" sometimes show not only lower self-concepts but also lower self-actualization, indicating that the fulfillment of their innermost potential may be greatly inhibited by their negative sense of self-worth.

Stress   One study of 2,154 North Dakota high school students between ages 14 and 19 revealed that as the number of negative life events increased, the level of self-esteem decreased (Youngs, Rathge, Mullis, and Mullis, 1990). Negative life events included the death of a close family member, failing an exam, change in school or residence, illness, work problems, problems in relationships, and family changes such as gaining a new family member or divorce. These findings are significant because if stress has a negative impact on self-esteem, this, in turn, affects many aspects of the adolescent's life, as we have seen.

Changes or Stability in Self-Concept

To what extent does self-concept change during adolescence? Overall, self-concept gradually stabilizes (Chiam, 1987). Adolescents are extremely sensitive, however, to important events and changes in their lives. One study found a lowered self-concept of high school juniors after they and their families had moved a long distance to another town. The more recent and frequent the move, the greater the negative effect on self-concept (Hendershott, 1989).

One study showed that self-esteem was lowest at around 12 years of age (Protinsky and Farrier, 1980). The researchers asked what factors were responsible for the sharp decline in a positive self-image. By applying careful statistical controls, they showed that the onset of puberty itself was not the determining factor, for 12-year-olds in junior high school had lower self-esteem, higher self-consciousness, and greater instability of self-image than did 12-year-olds in elementary school. When differences in race, socioeconomic class, or grades in school were considered, none of these variables was found to be determinative. The general findings held true for African American students as well as White students, for middle-class as well as working-class respondents, and for students with high as well as low grades. Nor was age itself significant. There was virtually no difference between the self-image ratings of 11- and 12-year-olds in the sixth grade or between 12- and 13-year-olds in the seventh grade.

The one determining factor was whether the student had entered junior high school. The move from a protected elementary school, where a child had few teachers and one set of classmates, to a much larger, more impersonal junior high, where teachers, classmates, and even classrooms were constantly shifting, was disturbing to the self-image. In addition, the students moved from a relatively safe elementary school environment to a

more hostile junior high school in which boys, particularly, were much more likely to experience victimization, such as being harassed or beaten up. This study clearly illustrates that self-image can be affected, at least for a while, by disturbing events. Others studies reinforce the finding that the transition from elementary to junior high or middle school can be a stressful event in the lives of early adolescents (Fenzel, 1989; Mullis, Mullis, and Normandin, 1992).

Educators can take into account the effect of different schools on self-concepts, and put pupils who are having difficulties into alternative schools to try to change the pupils' attitudes, behaviors, and self-concepts. Transferring pupils to different schools is particularly effective with junior high school students but less effective at the senior high level.

This also means, however, that self-image and self-esteem can be improved by helpful events (Markstrom-Adams and Spencer, 1994). For instance, summer-camp experiences have been found to be helpful in improving the self-concepts of young adolescents. Two studies reported good results with what was called *assertion training* of high school and college-level students who are timid, withdrawn, and incapable of dealing with other students, teachers, and relatives (Stake, De-Ville, and Pennell, 1983; Waksman 1984a, 1984b).

In summary, the concept of the self is not completely solidified by adolescence, although recognizable trends and traits persist. With increasing age, these recognizable traits become more stable. However, self-concepts are subject to change under the influence of powerful forces. Assisting the adolescent who has a negative identity to find a mature and positive image of self is a major undertaking, but it can be done in some cases. It is certain that the change is easier during adolescence than in adulthood.

Identity

Identity Status

The central developmental task of adolescence, according to Erik Erikson (1968), is the *formation of a coherent self-identity* (Berzonsky, Rice, and Neimeyer, 1990). This self-definition is formed as

According to Erikson, a coherent self-identity is formed as the adolescent chooses values, beliefs, and goals. These choices are made by exploring alternatives and committing to roles.

the adolescent chooses values, beliefs, and goals in life (Archer, 1989a). Society expects young people to decide on a college and/or a job, to become romantically involved, and to make choices regarding political philosophies and religious practices (Rotheram-Borus, 1989). Erikson described the task of identity formation as one of making choices by exploring alternatives and committing to roles (Adams, Gulotta, and Montemayor, 1992). Then, as one moves through adolescence, if these values, beliefs, goals, and practices are no longer appropriate, the individual can engage in a task of identity redefinition and refinement. Self-identity is clearly not stable, but is instead an ongoing process of self-reflection and change as one moves through life (Baumeister, 1991).

Since the mid-1960s, an extensive body of research has emerged and validated Erikson's psychosocial construct. Among the many studies of Erikson's concepts, those by James Marcia have been particularly influential (Bernard, 1981; Marcia, 1966, 1967, 1976, 1989, 1991, 1994). According to Marcia, the criteria used to establish the attainment of a mature identity are two variables: crisis and commitment, in relation to occupational choice, religion, and political ideology. "*Crisis* refers to the adolescent's period of engagement in choosing among meaningful alternatives,

commitment refers to the degree of personal investment the individual exhibits" (Marcia, 1966; emphasis added). A *mature identity* is achieved when the individual has experienced a crisis and has become committed to an occupation and ideology.

Marcia (1966) revealed four basic identity statuses: identity diffused, foreclosure, moratorium, and identity achieved. Numerous studies have shown the validity of these constructs (Marcia, 1980; Waterman, 1982). Table 8.1 shows the four identity statuses, which we will now examine in more detail.

Identity Diffused   *Identity-diffused* subjects have not experienced a crisis period, nor have they made any commitment to an occupation, a religion, a political philosophy, sex roles, or personal standards of sexual behavior (Archer and Waterman, 1990). They have not experienced an identity crisis in relation to any of these issues, nor have they gone through the process of reevaluating,

---

identity diffused   according to Marcia, those adolescents who have not experienced a crisis and explored meaningful alternatives nor made any commitments in finding an acceptable identity.

TABLE 8.1   The Four Identity Statuses as Derived from the Ego Identity Dimensions

| | COMMITMENT DIMENSION | |
EXPLORATION DIMENSION	Presence of Commitments	Absence of Commitments
Explored alternatives in the past	Identity achievement	Identity diffusion
Currently exploring alternatives	—	Moratorium
Never explored alternatives	Foreclosure	Identity diffusion

Source: S. L. Archer, "The Status of Identity: Reflections on the Need for Intervention," *Journal of Adolescence,* 12 (1989): 345–359. Reprinted by permission.

searching, and considering alternatives. Diffusion is developmentally the most unsophisticated identity status and is usually a normal characteristic of early adolescents. Given time and increasing pressure from parents, peers, and schools, most young people eventually begin to grapple with the issues. Adolescents who continue to express no interest in commitment may be masking an underlying insecurity about identity issues. Lacking self-confidence, they mask their feelings with an expression of apathy.

If an adolescent has tried to make identity commitments and has failed, the response may be anger directed against parents or religious, political, or corporate leaders. Older adolescents who become social dropouts, who are rebelling against all established values, and who have adopted a nihilistic attitude fall into this category. Identity-diffused adolescents who avoid anxiety, crisis, and commitment by using alcohol and drugs try to deny that any problem exists. Muuss (1988a) wrote, "Prolonged stagnation in the identity diffused stage without further development may lead to personality disintegration, thus becoming a diagnosis of psychopathology that may lead to schizophrenia or suicide" (p. 68).

Foreclosure   *Foreclosure* subjects have not experienced a crisis, but they have made commitments to occupations and ideologies that are not the result of their own searching but are ready-made and handed down to them, frequently by parents. They often have identified closely with same-sex parents (Cella, DeWolfe, and Fitzgibbon, 1987).

They become what others want them to become, without really deciding for themselves. An example of this type of identity status is the youth who wants to be a doctor because his or her parent is a doctor. Foreclosed adolescents are not able to distinguish between their own goals and the ones their parents plan for them. In one study, foreclosed adolescents reported a strong emotional foundation within the family, but it was such a close relationship that it reflected enmeshment. Foreclosed adolescents exhibited significantly lower levels of healthy separation (Papini, Mucks, and Barnett, 1989).

The foreclosure status of adolescents is often a symptom of neurotic dependence. Such subjects score high on authoritarianism and intolerance, show a high degree of conformity and conventionality (Berzonsky, 1989), and are usually satisfied with their college educations (Marcia, 1967). They seek security and support from significant others or familiar settings (Kroger, 1990). When put under stress, however, they perform poorly. Their security lies in avoiding change or stress. As one researcher observed, the "total lack of conflict during adolescence is an ominous sign that the individual's psychological maturity may not be progressing" (Keniston, 1971, p. 364).

It has been suggested also that foreclosure is a means of reducing anxiety. Persons who are too uncomfortable with uncertainty make choices without a lengthy process of consideration. They often marry while still in school, as well as make early decisions about vocations without lengthy consideration.

Some researchers suggest that identity statuses may not be comprised of homogeneous groups of people, raising the possibility of the need for subcategories (Kroger, 1995). For example, some research has discussed the possibility of distinguishing firm from developmental foreclosure individuals, based on an individual's willingness to respond to changing environmental circumstances. *Firm foreclosure* individuals are not likely to change statuses. *Developmental foreclosure* individuals could be expected to enter a moratorium phase at some future time, rather than remaining under the guidance of the parental examples. Current longitudinal and cross-sectional investigations of identity development in later adolescence and young adulthood indicate that fewer than one-half of foreclosed and diffused individuals would shift from those statuses over one- to six-year intervals. It seems desirable to distinguish those "likely to move" from those who are "likely to remain" arrested in their development over longer periods of time. One research study makes an initial step toward that goal by reliably differentiating those foreclosed individuals demonstrating some openness to possibilities to future change from those who are not. In other words, some foreclosure subjects began to look somewhat like moratorium and identity achieved individuals in their loosening of ties to the foreclosure category (Kroger, 1995).

Do individuals in cultures that neither encourage nor support identity crises have identities? Of course, but the identity is a foreclosed one. An identity does not have to be achieved in these cultures to be functional. Going through the decision-making process necessary to achieve an identity can be a painful, unrewarding experience if no cultural support is given for the crisis. It is certainly easier to remain foreclosed in a foreclosure society.

Moratorium   The word *moratorium* means a period of delay granted to someone who is not yet ready to make a decision or assume an obligation. During adolescence, it is a period of exploration of alternatives before commitments are made. Some moratorium subjects are involved in continual crises. As a consequence, they seem confused, unstable, and discontented. They are often rebellious and uncooperative and score low on authoritarianism. Some moratorium-status people avoid dealing with problems, and they may have a tendency to procrastinate until situations dictate a course of action (Berzonsky, 1989). Because they experience crises, they tend to be anxious. One study even showed that death anxiety is higher in moratorium-status adolescents than in those in the other three statuses (Sterling and Van Horn, 1989). Adolescents in this status category generally have fairly permissive parents, are uncertain they have selected the right major in college, and may be unhappy with their college experience and education. Others show a high level of authority conflict, so that part of their crisis is an attempt to disengage themselves from their parents. Archer (1989b) described a high school senior who said that deciding on a major was agony. Her favorite subject was chemistry but her friends had no interest in this area and her parents were encouraging her to major in business.

In contrast to this example, using adolescence as a period of moratorium can be a very positive experience:

> If adolescents, while experimenting with moratorium issues, have sufficient opportunity to search, experiment, play the field, and try on different roles, there is a very good chance that they will find themselves, develop an identity, and emerge with commitments to politics, religion, a vocational goal and a more clearly defined sex role and sex preference. These final commitments are frequently less radical than some of the tentative and exploratory commitments during the moratorium. According to Marcia, moratorium is truly an essential and necessary prerequisite for identity achievement. (Muuss, 1988b, p. 72)*

*R. E. Muuss, *Theories of Adolescence*, 5th ed. (New York: McGraw-Hill, 1988). Copyright © 1988 McGraw Hill Publishing Company. Used by permission of the McGraw-Hill Companies.

foreclosure   according to Marcia, establishing an identity without search or exploration, usually according to what has been handed down by parents.

moratorium   according to Marcia, a period of time in the life of adolescents who are involved in a continual crisis, who continue to search for an identity, and who have not made any commitments.

Even the process of selecting a major can be an exciting challenge. A female senior described the wonderful time she was having scouring through college catalogs, reviewing the course descriptions and requirements for several majors that interested her. She wanted to make a decision as soon as possible (Archer, 1989b). These types of moratorium females score high on measures of cognitive complexity, tolerance of ambiguity, intelligence, and social class. Such high-scoring girls are best able to explore alternatives and to use a moratorium period in a constructive way.

The number of adolescents in a state of moratorium increases after they enter college. This is because students in college are more actively and thoughtfully confronted with the crisis of making an occupational commitment and because they are stimulated to rethink their ideologies. As a result, many adolescents change their occupational plans during the college years (Arehart and Smith, 1990).

Identity Achieved *Identity-achieved* subjects have experienced a psychological moratorium, have resolved their identity crises by carefully evaluating various alternatives and choices, and have come to conclusions and decisions on their own. They have been highly motivated to achieve and are able to do so not so much because of great ability as because they have attained higher levels of intrapsychic integration and social adaptation. Once an identity has been achieved, there is self-acceptance, a stable self-definition, and a commitment to a vocation, religion, and political ideology. There is harmony within oneself and an acceptance of capacities, opportunities, and limitations. There is a more realistic concept of goals. Although these individuals are more advanced in their ego development, they are not necessarily free of all anxiety. Once committed to specific goals, they still worry about achieving them (Rothman, 1984).

Research with high school students indicates that few have achieved identity by the time of graduation. Living at home and possessing limited life and work experiences are not conducive to identity achievement. Some students miss out on a moratorium and have made commitments of a sort, which are often superficial:

I thought about various jobs when I was in grade 11. Now I know I want to be a nurse. No I can't imagine anything causing me to change my mind. (Raphael and Xelowski, 1980, p. 385)

I thought earlier this year about interior decorating, but now I want to be a secretary and will stay with that until I have a child. (Ibid.)

Are these individual identities achieved? It is doubtful. Even at the college level, 80 percent of students change their majors during their four years (Waterman, 1992). In general, however, the percentage of adolescents who are identity achievers increases with age (Fregeau and Barker, 1986).

Critique At this juncture, several comments need to be made about Marcia's model. Identity statuses do not always develop in exact sequence. It was originally believed that a developmental progression would be the norm. Most adolescents would enter the identity crisis from the foreclosure status, moving through a moratorium phase, out of which achievement status would be attained. The diffusion status during adolescence was seen as an aberration in this natural progression, hopefully a transient one.

Note that there are three important variations from this developmental sequence. First, a significant number of individuals enter adolescence in the diffusion status; some of them remain there. Second, some individuals seem never to make the transition to the moratorium and achievement statuses, remaining firmly entrenched within the foreclosure status. Third, certain individuals who attain an achievement status appear to regress to a lower status years later (Marcia, 1989). This suggests that individuals may go through the developmental sequence of identity more than once during a lifetime. A person may have found identity achievement at a certain period of life, then later in life go through another moratorium stage or stage of identity diffusion before identity achievement is accomplished (Stephen, Fraser, and Marcia, 1992).

Women and Identity

Traditionally, women found their identities through their roles in the family. Increasingly, many women seek identity achievement through their occupations and careers, some of which are traditionally held only by men (Mills and Mills, 1996).

Occupational Identity   There does seem to be some difference between males and females in occupational identity achievement. In spite of the increasing emphasis on careers for women, more females than males have trouble establishing occupational identities. One reason may be that college is still more conducive to ego development in men than in women, especially in terms of making vocational decisions and preparing for an occupation. Also, at this period when female roles are in a state of flux, women are experiencing conflict in gaining a sense of confidence and worthiness as women. However, a low level of anxiety about themselves and their roles indicates that increasing numbers are solving their identity crises. Those raised by mothers who encourage independence are most likely to find their identities apart from family living. One study found that high school girls whose parents were divorced were significantly more likely to be identity achievers than were those whose parents were not divorced. The authors concluded:

> These findings suggest that the security of the traditional family may not provide the optimal setting for the adolescent female to engage in the processes leading to identity achievement. In addition, the finding of higher identity achievement among girls from broken homes adds to the growing body of evidence that divorce does not necessarily have adverse effects on the adolescent, and, in fact, may be associated with better adjustment of the adolescent. (St. Clair and Day, 1979, p. 324)

Prior to the women's movement, identity-achieved females showed fewer positive traits than did males, primarily because of social prejudices. Identity-achieved females, for example, were lowest in self-esteem of all the four groups studied, with foreclosure females showing the highest self-esteem. Identity-achieved females also showed considerable anxiety, indicating that they were achieving identity status through an occupation (they were also majoring in more difficult subjects), but in opposition to stereotyped, cultural expectations, and with consequent feelings of anxiety and lowered self-esteem because of per-

ceived social stigmas. Later studies, however, indicated that this has slowly changed, with female identity achievers scoring higher in self-esteem and showing less anxiety.

There is some evidence that male-female differences in the process, domain, and timing of identity development are decreasing (Archer, 1989a; Dellas and Jernigan, 1990). There is perhaps a greater difference between individuals than there is between the sexes. A 1989 study found that women who exhibited a greater capacity for self-reflection achieved higher levels of identity development than those who were not self-reflective (Shain and Farber, 1989). This suggests that patterns of growth from less to more differentiated identity development are paralleled by corresponding changes in cognitive development, reflecting increasing maturity in the thinking process (Waterman, 1982).

Pathways to Identity   Some research (Gilligan, Ward, Taylor, and Bardige, 1988) indicates that the path of identity development for women may be different than that for men. The researchers suggested that women tended to define themselves through their relationships with others, whereas men followed "traditional masculine" lines of self-definition according to their own occupational selves (Streitmatter, 1993). Thus, identity development for women is quite different from that of men. Intimacy is a primary issue for women, but not for men (Enns, 1991).

Ethnic Identity

Ethnic identity is the sum total of group members' feelings about those symbols, values, and common histories that identify them as a distinct group. It is an individual's sense of self as a member of an ethnic group and the attitudes and behaviors associated with that sense (Helms, 1990). Ethnic development is the process of development from an unexamined ethnic identity through a period of exploration to arrive at an achieved ethnic identity

identity achieved   according to Marcia, those adolescents who have undergone a crisis in their search for an identity and who have made a commitment

Ethnic identity is an individual's sense of the attitudes and behaviors associated with being part of a particular ethnic group. It is an essential human need, which provides the adolescent with historical continuity and a feeling of belonging.

(Yeh and Huang, 1996). The development of an ethnic identity is an essential human need. It provides a sense of historical continuity and a sense of belonging (Smith, 1991).

Acculturation Options   *Acculturation* is the adjustment of minority groups to the culture of the dominant group (Sodowsky, Lai, and Plake, 1991). The problem for adolescents from ethnic minority families or from immigrant families is that the culture into which they were born is not always valued or appreciated by the culture in which they are raised (Feldman, Mont-Reynaud, and Rosenthal, 1992). In the early stages of forging an identity, ethnic minorities and immigrants often find conflict between their ethnic cultures and the values of the larger society in which they live. The central question is the way in which minority ethnic groups relate to the dominant cul-

ture and to one another. (Hiraga, Cauce, Mason, and Ordonez, 1993).

Let's review four possible ways in which ethnic group members can participate in a culturally diverse society. *Separation* involves exclusive focus on the cultural values and practices of the ethnic group and little or no interaction with the dominant society. *Assimilation* is the outcome when ethnic group members choose to identify solely with the culture of the dominant society and to relinquish all ties to their ethnic cultures. *Integration* is characterized by strong identification and involvement with both the dominant society's culture and the traditional ethnic culture. *Marginality* is defined by the absence or loss of one's culture of origin and the lack of involvement with the dominant society.

Which type of participation contributes most to the positive development of identity and self-esteem in adolescents? One study of high school and college students from a diverse, inner-city school sought an answer to this question. The students were from mixed backgrounds: Asians, African Americans, Hispanics, and Whites (Phinney, Chavira, and Williamson, 1992). Results indicated that among the four acculturation options, integration is the most adaptive, resulting in better psychological adjustment and higher self-esteem. A healthy relationship between endorsement of integration and self-esteem indicates that a more positive self-concept is associated with identification with a person's mainstream culture as well as his or her own culture. In contrast, endorsement of assimilation was found to be related to a lower self-esteem among the Asian and foreign-born subjects. Thus, giving up your ethnic culture can have a negative impact on your self-concept. The idea of separation (an ethnic group should keep to itself and not mix with mainstream society) was given little support by the students, with no difference among ethnic groups or by socioeconomic status. Of all four alternatives, marginality, in which a person identifies neither with his or her own ethnic group nor the dominant culture, is the least satisfactory alternative (Phinney, 1992).

Identity Statuses   In his book on adolescent identity, Erikson (1968) pointed out the likelihood of members of ethnic minorities internaliz-

CROSS-CULTURAL CONCERNS

Parental Ethnic Socialization

As the numbers of ethnic minority children continue to increase, the socialization of these children in adolescence has become a topic of growing interest and concern. On the basis of research, it appears that minority parents face three distinct challenges. Their children need to be socialized both to their own culture and the mainstream culture, and they need to understand prejudice and discrimination. The first challenge, the learning of one's own culture, would seem to be the least problematic, in that it is presumably learned naturally in the home. Yet, we know from several studies of African American families that some explicit cultural teaching is needed. A second socialization theme involves teaching children to get along in the mainstream culture or helping them to succeed in society at large. African American parents generally teach their children to be bicultural. Part of getting along in society involves developing the skills necessary to be successful; to accomplish this, children are encouraged to work hard and do well. The final theme common to all research on African American socialization is explicit teaching to prepare children to be aware of prejudice and discrimination. Racial barriers and blocked opportunities need to be emphasized.

In one study on ethnic socialization, parents were interviewed and given a series of questions:

1. Do you try to teach your son or daughter about the cultural practices of your ethnic group?
2. Have you tried to teach your son or daughter how to get along in mainstream American culture?
3. Have you talked to him or her about how to deal with experiences like name calling or discrimination?
4. Have you personally tried to prepare your daughter or son to live in a culturally diverse society? (Phinney and Chavira, 1995)

In-depth interviews with 60 American-born Japanese Americans, African Americans, and Mexican American high school students, ages 16 to 18, and one parent of each adolescent revealed significant ethnic group differences. Parental ethnic socialization with African American parents more frequently reported discussing prejudice with their child. Japanese American and African American parents emphasized adaptation to society more than Mexican American parents. Interestingly enough, youths who were socialized to be aware of racial barriers and cautioned about appropriate interracial behavior attained higher grades and a greater sense of personal efficacy (Phinney and Chavira, 1995).

---

ing the negative views of the dominant society, thereby developing negative self-identity and self-hatred. Such an internalization would be detrimental to psychological health, and has been the subject of much investigation (Rotheram-Borus, 1989).

Efforts have been made to apply Marcia's stages of ego identity development to the process of ethnic identity development. The stages are as follows:

Diffuse: Little or no exploration of ethnicity
Foreclosed: No exploration, but one is clear about one's ethnic identity; feelings about ethnicity may be positive or negative
Moratorium: Exploration, plus confusion about one's own ethnicity

Achieved: Exploration, plus a clear, secure understanding and acceptance of one's own ethnicity

Phinney (1989) studied the ethnic identity development of 91 American-born tenth-graders in two high schools in metropolitan Los Angeles. The group included Asian Americans, African Americans, Hispanics, and Whites. She found some interesting results.

1. Slightly over half the subjects were at the diffuse or foreclosed stage, characterized by lack of exploration of ethnicity as an identity issue. There was little evidence of negative attitudes about their own groups. Apparently, they had acquired positive attitudes from others.

2. About one-fourth of the subjects showed evidence of involvement in ethnic identity search and were in the moratorium stage. There was an increasing awareness of the importance of this issue.

3. About one-fourth of the subjects revealed a confident sense of self as a minority group member, after a search that indicated an achieved ethnic identity.

4. About one-fifth of all the subjects, including some from each stage, expressed a desire to change their ethnicity if they could. The subjects with the most negative attitudes were mainly Asian Americans, partly because they lacked participation in social movements that stress ethnic pride that were available to African Americans and Hispanics.

5. White students, even though in the minority, did not show evidence of these stages and were frequently unaware of their own ethnicity apart from being American.

SUMMARY

1. Gender is your sex—male or female. Gender identity is your internal perception of being male or female. Gender role is your outward expression of maleness or femaleness in social settings.

2. The biological basis of gender includes both heredity and hormonal influences. Both affect physical characteristics. Hormones usually accentuate or minimize certain masculine/feminine traits already in evidence.

3. Cognitive developmental theory suggests that sex-role identity has its beginnings in the gender cognitively assigned to the child at birth and subsequently accepted by him or her while growing up. Thus, girls model themselves after their mothers because they realize they are females.

4. Environmental influences are a major determinant of gender identity and roles. Concepts of masculinity and femininity vary from culture to culture and have undergone changes in the United States.

5. Social learning theory says that children learn sex-typed behavior through a combination of rewards and punishments, indoctrination, observation of others, and modeling. Boys and girls learn sex-typed behavior as defined by their culture and as taught and exemplified by significant others.

6. Parental identification says that children learn appropriate sex roles by identifying with parents and internalizing parental values, attitudes, traits, and personality characteristics. The extent to which identification takes place depends on the time parents spend with their children and the intensity of the contact. Sex-role concepts also depend on the patterns of role models exemplified.

7. One of the disadvantages of traditional concepts of masculinity in the United States has been the insistence that males not express emotions. This restriction prevents men from establishing close, affectionate relationships with others. Men are taught that it is unmanly to express tender feelings toward women.

8. Traditional concepts of females as being passive, meek, and dependent have kept them from accomplishment in their own right. Today, women are still not paid as much as men for the same work, education, and experience.

9. Traditional concepts are changing. Men are becoming more expressive and women more independent and assertive. What is emerging is a gradual mixing of male and female traits and roles to produce androgyny, which has advantages for both sexes.

10. Self-concept is the conscious, cognitive perception and evaluation by individuals of themselves. It is their ego identity; it defines who and what they are.

11. Self-concept is made up of multiple self-conceptions, with concepts developed in relation to different roles.

12. Strang outlined four basic dimensions of the self: the overall, basic self-concept; the temporary, transitory self-concepts; the social selves; and the ideal self.

13. Self-esteem is the value individuals place on the self they perceive.

14. The level of self-esteem influences mental health, interpersonal competence and social adjustment, progress in school, vocational aspirations, and delinquency.

15. Self-concept is determined partly by others' views of us, or the way we think others view us.

16. The affective quality of family relations is associated with high levels of self-esteem.

17. The adolescent's relationship with parents is important because the parents are role models with whom the adolescent identifies.
18. A healthy ego identity is developed through warm concern and interest on the part of parents, through loving, firm, and consistent discipline, and through induction rather than coercion.
19. Whether a family is intact, reconstituted, or divorced is not as important in developing positive self-esteem as whether the existing family is happy or unhappy, harmonious or conflicting.
20. In general, adolescents from lower SES families have lower self-esteem than those from higher SES families, but much depends on parental self-esteem, which is passed on to the children.
21. Race and nationality are not as important as having a strong sense of ethnic identity and social pride in one's cultural heritage.
22. Birth order shows little correlation with level of self-esteem.
23. Acceptance of one's physical self influences the development of self-concept.
24. The greater the stress (in adolescence), the greater the negative impact on self-esteem.
25. The number and type of problems experienced by adolescents influence their self-esteem. Schoolwork is a problem area for both adolescent boys and girls, girls are troubled by problems with health and with parents, and boys are troubled by social and psychological relations, according to one study.
26. Self-concept usually stabilizes during adolescence, but may be influenced temporarily by specific events.
27. The central developmental task of adolescence is the formation of a coherent self-identity.
28. Marcia revealed four basic identity statuses: identity diffused, foreclosed, moratorium, and identity achieved.
29. Adolescents who are identity diffused have not experienced a crisis, explored alternatives, or made a commitment in a given area.
30. Foreclosure status is typical of adolescents who have made a commitment without exploring alternatives. They are not able to distinguish between their own values and goals and those of their parents.
31. Adolescents in a moratorium status are exploring alternatives with the expectation of making a decision. Using adolescence as a period of moratorium can be a very positive or negative experience, depending on the outcome.
32. Adolescents who are identity achieved have experienced a crisis and moratorium, have evaluated various alternatives, and have come to conclusions and decisions on their own.
33. Individuals may go through the stages of identity more than once during a lifetime.
34. More women than men have trouble establishing occupational identities, but female identity achievers score higher in self-esteem and show less anxiety than nonachievers. There is some evidence that male-female differences in the process, domain, and timing of identity development are decreasing.
35. Women may find identity development through pathways different from those men choose. Significant relationships are one means by which some women find identity achievement.
36. Acculturation options for ethnic minorities include separation, assimilation, integration, and marginality. Assimilation is related to higher self-esteem more than are the other options.
37. One of the challenges for members of ethnic minorities is to develop positive ethnic identities. Those who are ethnic identity achievers have a clear, secure understanding and acceptance of their ethnic identities.

KEY TERMS

androgyny   **172**

femininity   **168**

foreclosure   **184**

gender   **167**

gender identity   **167**

gender role or sex role   **167**

ideal self   **173**

identification   **170**

identity achieved   **186**

identity diffused   **183**

masculinity   **168**

moratorium   **185**

proprium   **173**

self   **172**

self-concept   **172**

self-esteem   **172**

9

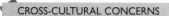

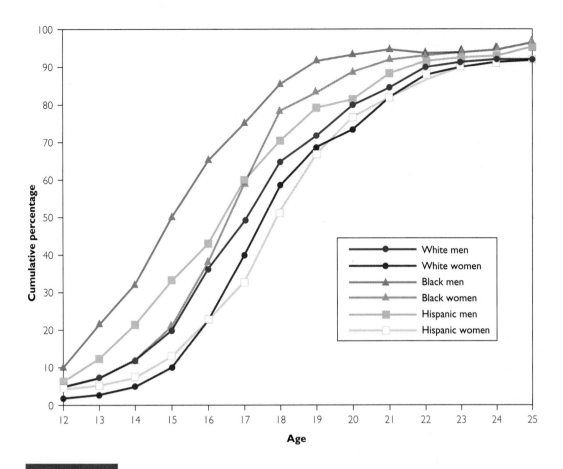

FIGURE 9.1   Cumulative Percentage Who Have Had Intercourse

Source: Sex in America by Robert Michael et al. Copyright © 1994 by CSG Enterprises, Inc., Edward O. Laumann, Robert T. Michael, and Gina Kolata. By permission of Little, Brown and Company.

sex because of a desire for physical pleasure. Most of the men said they were not in love with their first sexual partner; most of the women, in contrast, said they were.

Today, American teenagers are having sex earlier than their parents did, but they do not necessarily have more partners. About half of today's adolescents begin having intercourse with a partner sometime between the ages of 15 and 18, and at least four out of five have had intercourse by the time they are 21 years old. Since the average age of marriage is now in the mid-20s, few Americans are waiting until they marry to have sex, but most sexually active young people show no signs of having large numbers of partners. More than half the men and women between ages 18 and 24 in 1992

had had just one sex partner in the previous year, and 11 percent had had none.

Correlates

Let's examine the significant correlates with premarital sexual behavior (Bingham, Miller, and Adams, 1990; Day, 1992; Scott-Jones and White, 1990; Stanton, Black, Kaljee, and Ricardo, 1993):

1. *Age:* The older they are, the more likely adolescents are to have had premarital *coitus,* or sexual intercourse (Scott-Jones and White, 1990).

coitus   sexual intercourse.

2. *Race:* Other things being equal, African Americans report a higher incidence of premarital coitus than Whites (Juhasz and Sonnenshein-Schneider, 1987). When differences in socioeconomic status are taken into account, differences because of race become less significant (Bingham, Miller, and Adams, 1990).

3. *Religion:* Religiosity and a lower level of sexual permissiveness go together (Fisher and Hall, 1988). Church attendance is an important determinant of delayed sexual activity (Mott et al., 1996).

4. *Boyfriend or girlfriend:* Adolescents who report having a boyfriend or girlfriend are more likely to have premarital sexual intercourse than those who do not (Scott-Jones and White, 1990; Thornton and Camburn, 1989).

5. *Early dating and steady dating:* Adolescents who begin dating early and who develop steady relationships early are more likely to have more permissive attitudes concerning premarital sex, to be more sexually active, and to have sexual relations with more partners than are those who date and go steady at later ages (Thornton, 1990).

6. *Young age at first intercourse:* Those who are youngest at first intercourse tend to be more permissive subsequently than are those who report older ages at first intercourse.

7. *Liberality:* A high level of sexual and social liberalism is correlated with a high level of sexual permissiveness (Troiden and Jendrek, 1987); (Costa, Jessor, Donovan, and Fortenberry, 1995).

8. *Age at menarche:* The younger the age at menarche, the more likely premarital sexual intercourse will occur.

9. *Sexual attractiveness:* Those who feel they are the most sexually and socially attractive report the highest levels of sexual permissiveness.

10. *Parental standards and relationships:* Parents who are most liberal in their views of premarital sexual intercourse are those most likely to have adolescents whose views are also liberal (Baker, Thalberg, and Morrison, 1988; Thornton and Camburn, 1987). Mothers' attitudes and standards of behavior when they were adolescents are especially influential in forming adolescent attitudes (Newcomer and Udry, 1984). One study showed that high school females whose mothers had sex at an early age and were employed outside the home had a greater tendency to engage in sex relations than did those whose mothers stayed at home (Mott et al., 1996). This was attributed to their greater independence and lack of supervision. However, the influential factor is not that the mother works, but the fact that working mothers, especially if they are

CROSS-CULTURAL CONCERNS

Hispanic Female Sexual Activity

A study of 240 Hispanic and African American adolescent females from 12 to 18 years of age in New York City schools revealed some interesting differences between Hispanics and African Americans regarding sexual activity (Gibson and Kempf, 1990).

Hispanic adolescent females of all ages were more likely to be virgins than were African American adolescent females. Research shows that 80 percent of Hispanic females aged 12 to 15 were virgins, compared with 59 percent of African Americans; 54 percent of Hispanic females aged 16 to 18 were virgins, compared with 29 percent of African Americans. The average age of first coitus for Hispanic females was 15; for African Americans, age 14.

Both virgin and nonvirgin Hispanic females tended to come from single-parent households (virgins 79 percent, nonvirgins 67 percent), be Catholic (virgins 80 percent and nonvirgins 78 percent), and have mothers who did not graduate from high school (virgins 58 percent and nonvirgins 62 percent). Over half of all the households of both groups (virgins 54 percent, nonvirgins 60 percent) were on public assistance.

Among both African Americans and Hispanics, academically motivated adolescents were less likely to engage in sexual activities at an early age.

professionals, are likely to be more liberal in their sexual views (Fingerman, 1989).

Parental strictness, discipline, and control show a curvilinear relationship to sexual attitudes and behavior. Sexual permissiveness is highest among adolescents who view their parents as not strict at all, lowest among adolescents whose parents are moderately strict, and intermediate among those who perceive their parents as very strict (Miller, McCoy, Olson, and Wallace, 1986).

A survey of 751 African American youths showed that maternal disapproval of premarital sex, maternal discussions about birth control, and the quality of the parent-child relationship had an important influence on adolescents' sexual activity and the consistency of their contraceptive use (Jaccard, Dittus, and Gordon, 1996).

Another study showed that sexually active adolescent girls who were pregnant perceived their families as having low levels of family strength, classified communication with parents as closed, came from homes characterized by family fragmentation, came from low-income households, and were unlikely to use any method of birth control (Barnett, Papini, and Gbur, 1991). In a study of inner-city African American male adolescents, those who perceived their mothers as more strict than others reported less frequent coitus and with fewer women. Adolescents who perceived their fathers as more strict than did other adolescents reported using condoms more consistently in the previous year (Jemmott and Jemmott, 1992). Other research has shown that adolescent girls who are sexually active report less frequent and less supportive communication with parents than those who are not sexually active (Furman, Wehner, and Underwood, 1994).

The quality of parent-child relationships may affect adolescents' sexual behavior indirectly by decreasing the likelihood of depressed affect, making youths more vulnerable to the promised warmth and intimacy of early sexual activity. Poor parent-child relationships also are related to some types of adolescent deviant behavior, such as alcohol use, that are associated with adolescent sexual activity. Parental behaviors, then, may be associated with adolescent behaviors that, in turn, result in a greater likelihood of becoming sexually active (Crockett and Bingham, 1994; Whitbeck, Hoyt, Miller, and Kao, 1992).

Many variables correlate with adolescent premarital sexual behavior. Being able to discuss sexual matters with one's parent has the highest influence in early adolescence, whereas the influence of friends has a greater effect in later adolescence.

11. *Peer standards:* Adolescents tend to form sexual standards close to peer standards. Furthermore, they are more likely to engage in sex when peers make involvement seem thrilling and exciting (Billy and Udry, 1985). Also, adolescents who are members of deviant peer groups are more likely to engage in early sexual activity (Underwood, Kupersmidt, and Coie, 1996).

12. *Parents versus peer standards:* Adolescents whose parents are conservative and are their primary reference group are less likely to have premarital sexual intercourse than those who name peers as their primary reference (Wyatt, 1989). The opportunity to discuss sexual matters with parents has an important influence on sexual behavior (Treboux and Busch-Rossnagel, 1990). Adolescents with unrewarding primary relationships within the family are likely to compensate by establishing emotionally supportive relationships among their age group. Young women particularly seek sexual expression as one means of establishing emotionally supportive relationships (Whitbeck, Conger, and Kao, 1993). The influence of friends and parents on sexual behavior varies as a function of the age of the adolescent. Ninth- and tenth-grade adolescents are more affected by discussions with their mother than are adolescents who are older. Thus, parents exert the most influence in early adolescence. Effect of

friends on sexual behavior peaks in the early college years (Treboux and Busch-Rossnagel, 1995).

13. *Siblings:* Adolescents, particularly girls, are influenced by the attitudes and behavior of their same-sex siblings (Rodgers and Rowe, 1990). Younger siblings are systematically more sexually active at a given age than older siblings (Rodgers, Rowe, and Harris, 1992).

14. *Gender:* Girls tend to be less permissive than boys, although this double standard is being eliminated slowly (Miller and Olson, 1988). For example, the average age of first intercourse for girls has been declining. Girls do, however, place more emphasis on the quality of a relationship before intercourse takes place (Wilson and Medora, 1990). Among those who have experienced sexual intercourse, males and females are equally likely to be sexually active, as measured by having recent and frequent sexual intercourse (DeGaston, Weed, and Jensen, 1996).

15. *Drug usage:* Those who take drugs are more likely to have had premarital sexual intercourse than those who do not take drugs (Weinbender and Rossignol, 1996; Whitbeck, Conger, Simons, and Kao, 1993). One of the strongest predictors of high-risk sexual activity is alcohol use (Harvey and Spigner, 1995).

16. *Father absence:* Girls, in particular those who grow up in a father-absent home, are more likely to seek sexual relationships as a means of finding affection and social approval than are girls in father-present homes (Newcomer and Udry, 1987).

Single parenting has also been associated with greater loss of control over teenagers' activities (Miller and Bingham, 1989).

17. *Divorced and reconstituted families:* Adolescents from divorced and reconstituted families report more sexual experience than those from intact families (Kinnaird and Gerrard, 1986; Young, Jensen, Olsen, and Cundick, 1991).

18. *Parents' education:* Adolescents of parents with a high school education or less are more likely to have experienced intercourse and more permissive attitudes than those with more education (Miller and Olson, 1988).

19. *Educational expectations:* The higher adolescents' educational expectations, the less likely they are to have premarital sexual intercourse (Ohannessian and Crockett, 1993; Scott-Jones and White, 1990; Wyatt, 1989). Adolescent factory workers have a higher frequency of premarital intercourse than do adolescent students (Huerta-Franco, deLeon, and Malacara, 1996).

20. *Socioeconomic status:* There is a higher instance of early coital behavior among those of low socioeconomic status who have less-educated parents (Murry, 1996).

Masturbation

Masturbation refers to any type of self-stimulation that produces erotic arousal, whether or not arousal proceeds to orgasm. It is commonly practiced among both males and females in premarital, marital, and postmarital states. The reported

HIGHLIGHT

Virginity and Incidence of Divorce

Some research evidence shows that those who are virgins at the time of marriage face a slightly lower risk of divorce than nonvirgins, but the risk of divorce reflects neither a direct nor indirect causal relationship. Rather, it indicates that women who continue to hold traditional attitudes about marriage are less likely than other women to consider both premarital sex and divorce as acceptable options for themselves. It is likely that people who feel constrained by traditional expectations early in life will maintain this orientation throughout their lives, predisposing them to wait until marriage to begin sexual activity and to reject divorce as an option. Therefore, it is prior attitudes, and not sexual activity per se, that influence the risk of divorce (Kahn and London, 1991).

incidences of masturbation vary somewhat among studies.

In a recent study of female and male college students, twice as many males as females said they had masturbated, and of the males who masturbated, they did so more frequently than the females (Leitenberg, Detzer, and Srebnik, 1993). This and other studies indicate that a greater percentage of males than females masturbate. Among those who masturbate, males do so more often than females and more frequently fantasize erotic experiences (Jones and Barlow, 1990). According to one survey, teenage boys masturbate about five times a week (LoPresto, Sherman, and Sherman, 1985). By the end of adolescence, virtually all males and about three-fourths of females have masturbated to orgasm.

Practically all competent health, medical, and psychiatric authorities now say that masturbation is a normal part of growing up and does not have any harmful physical and mental effects, nor does it interfere with normal sexual adjustment in marriage. In fact, women who have never masturbated to orgasm before marriage have more difficulty reaching orgasm during coitus in the first year of marriage than do those who have masturbated to orgasm. Masturbation serves as a useful function in helping the individual learn about his or her body, learn how to respond sexually, and develop sexual identity, and achieve sexual release. The only ill effect from masturbation comes not from the act itself but from guilt, fear, or anxiety when the adolescent believes the practice will do harm or create problems. These negative emotions can do a great deal of psychological damage. Youths who continue to believe that masturbation is unhealthy or harmful, yet continue to practice it, will eventually feel anxiety.

Apparently, old myths die hard. One researcher reported that 15 percent of adolescents still believe that masturbation is wrong (Santrock, 1987). Some youths believe that masturbation causes mental illness, pimples, impotency, or other ills ascribed to it in the past. Much of the literature directed to adolescents or their adult leaders, teachers, or parents takes the viewpoint that masturbation is not harmful if it is not excessive. But what is excessive? There is no medical reason for limitation, and efforts to do so only shift the worry to what is too often. Masturbation should be considered excessive only in the same sense that reading or watching television can be excessive:

masturbation   self-stimulation for purpose of sexual arousal.

PERSONAL ISSUES

Changing Autoerotic Attitudes and Practices

One study sought to measure the overall effects that a college-level functional marriage and family course had on masturbatory attitudes and practices among college women two years after completion of the course (Davidson and Darling, 1988). The findings indicated that the experimental group respondents (those who had enrolled in the course) became substantially more accepting and tolerant of masturbation by their female and male acquaintances as compared with the control groups of those not having enrolled in the course. The experimental group subjects were also more likely to believe that masturbation was a healthy practice. There was also a significant increase in the percentage who had ever engaged in masturbation. During the first week of the class, 48 percent reported they had engaged in masturbation while alone. At the time of the two-year follow-up, 95 percent of the women who had taken the course reported they had engaged in masturbation while alone. The researchers felt that functional college courses have an important role in providing information about masturbation, and have liberating effects on masturbatory attitudes and behavior.

The activities themselves are not bad, but when they become all-consuming, they suggest the presence of problems that the individual is unable to handle. An adolescent who masturbates to the exclusion of normal friendships and social activities has a problem, not with masturbation, but with social relationships. The term *excessive* is vague, undefined, and subjective. Are adolescents who masturbate daily doing it to excess, especially if they seem to have made a happy and social adjustment? As a general rule, it is probably best for parents to disregard evidence of masturbation in children and adolescents.

Sex and Its Meaning

With an increasing number of adolescents having sexual intercourse at younger ages, the question arises regarding the meaning attached to these relationships.

Sex and Emotional Intimacy

Has the increase in premarital sexual intercourse been accompanied by emotional intimacy, development of loving feelings, and increasing com-

mitment? For years, research has shown that the preferred standard for youths is permissiveness with affection (Christopher and Cate, 1988). However, there are a significant number of adolescents today who engage in coitus without affection or commitment (Roche and Ramsbey, 1993). Figure 9.2 shows the results of a survey among 237 (male and female) undergraduate students enrolled in 1986 at Illinois State University (Sprecher, McKinney, Walsh, and Anderson, 1988). The subjects ranged in age from 18 to 47, with a mean age of 20. All four undergraduate classes were represented. Of the respondents, 90 percent were White, 8 percent African American, and 2 percent other; 49 percent were Catholic, 22 percent were Protestant, 3 percent Jewish, and the remainder were either another religion or no religion.

As you can see in Figure 9.2, 45 percent agreed that heavy petting was acceptable on a first date, 28 percent agreed that sexual intercourse was acceptable on a first date, and 22 percent found oral-genital sex acceptable on a first date. The comparable figures for casual dating showed that 61 percent approved of heavy petting, 41 percent approved of intercourse, and 28 percent approved of oral-genital sex. The largest increase in

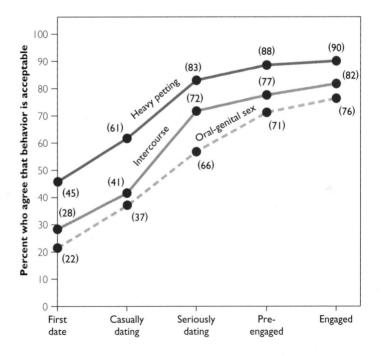

FIGURE 9.2   Acceptance of Sexual Activity by Relationship Stage

Source: S. Sprecher, K. McKinney, R. Walsh, and C. Anderson, "A Revision of the Reiss Premarital Sexual Permissiveness Scale," *Journal of Marriage and the Family, 50* (August 1988): 821–828. Copyrighted 1988 by the National Council on Family Relations, 3989 Central Ave. NE, Suite 550, Minneapolis, MN 55421. Reprinted by permission.

acceptability for sexual behavior occurred between the casual and serious dating stages. Surprisingly, there were no significant differences according to gender, although there were differences according to age. The 16-year-olds were less sexually permissive than those 21 years of age.

What Are Adolescents Seeking?

When adolescents say they want sex, what are their primary motives? It is easy to say that they want a quick fix to relieve biological drives. But often, adolescent sexuality is driven by emotional needs that have nothing to do with sex (Hajcak and Garwood, 1988). These emotional needs include the desire to receive affection, ease loneliness, gain acceptance, confirm masculinity or femininity, bolster self-esteem, express anger, or escape from boredom. Sex becomes a means of expressing and satisfying nonsexual needs.

When adolescents use sex as an effort to cope, other problems are created. When efforts do not result in emotional fulfillment, the result may be increased depression, lower self-esteem, decreased intimacy, hypersensitivity, and diminished sexual satisfaction. The danger is that adolescents develop immature, unsatisfactory relationships and sexual habits that carry into adulthood (Hajcak and Garwood, 1988).

Sexual Pluralism and the Individual Ethic

When questioning the meaning attached to present-day sexual practices, it is important to recognize that there are individual and social differences in sexual attitudes and behavior. We live in a *pluralistic society:* Our society accepts not one but a number of standards of sexual behavior. There have been many efforts to categorize these standards, but the work of Reis is particularly noteworthy (Reis, 1971). He outlined four standards of sexual permissiveness in our culture: abstinence, double standard, permissiveness with affection, and permissiveness without affection. A current analysis of the sexual behavior of today's adolescents would seem to require an expansion of Reis's categories to include the following:

Abstinence
Double standard
Sex with affection, commitment, and responsibility

pluralistic society   a society in which there are many different competing standards of behavior.

Often, an adolescent's sexuality is motivated by emotional needs that have nothing to do with sex. Desire for affection, easing of loneliness, acceptance, self-esteem, and expression of anger are some of these nonsexual needs.

Sex with affection and commitment but without responsibility

Sex with affection but without commitment

Sex without affection

Sex with ulterior motives

The exact meaning of *abstinence* may vary depending on the point at which sexual activity ceases and abstaining begins. Some adolescents allow kissing only with affection; others kiss without affection. Kissing can be perfunctory, whether light kissing, heavy kissing, or French kissing. Some adolescents feel that necking is allowed (all forms of kissing and embracing) but disallow petting (body caresses below the neck). Others allow caressing of the breasts but not of the genitals. Others engage in genital stimulation, even mutual masturbation to orgasm, but stop short of actual coitus. Some adolescents are technical virgins—meaning they never allow the penis to enter the vagina but engage in oral-genital, interfemoral stimulation (penis between the thighs), or other activity except intercourse itself.

The *double standard* refers to one standard of behavior for males, another for females. As will be seen in a later discussion, differences in standards between males and females are slowly being eliminated.

Some adolescents will engage in *sex only with affection, commitment, and responsibility.* They are in love; they are committed to each other and accept the responsibility and consequences of their actions. Responsibility in this case includes the use of dependable means of contraception to prevent unwanted pregnancies. In case of accidental pregnancy, they are willing to take full financial and other responsibility for whatever course of action they decide to pursue. But what does *commitment* mean? Interpretations vary. Some adolescents will have intercourse only if engaged, others only if they have an understanding to marry, others only if they are living together, and others if they are committed to exclusive dating and going steady. The distinguishing feature of this standard is that sex includes love and responsibility as well as a defined degree of commitment.

Some adolescents want *sex with affection and commitment but without responsibility.* They are in love, have committed themselves to one another, usually on a temporary basis only, but assume no real responsibility for their actions. Because they do not show real concern and care for one another, it's difficult to understand how they define *love.* They show evidence of immature sexual behavior.

Sex with affection but without commitment has become the standard of many adolescents. They would not think of making love unless they really loved (liked) and felt affection for each other. They may or may not show responsibility in the practice of birth control but have made no promises or plans for the future. They are affectionate, are having intercourse, and that's it, at least for the time being.

Sex without affection characterizes people having sexual intercourse without emotional involvement, without the need for affection. They engage in sex for sex's sake because they like it, enjoy it, and do so without any strings attached. Some may be having sex for subconscious reasons and motives they do not recognize or understand. Some who practice this standard have already had sex with a large number of partners. Some of these people see nothing wrong with this and enjoy it. Others are promiscuous but feel conflict and guilt that they have difficulty controlling. Some people who have sex without affection are responsible in the use of contraceptives; others are irresponsible.

Sex with ulterior motives may include a number of different motives:

1. *To punish:* "She made me mad, so just for spite, I did it." In this case, sex becomes an expression of hostility, anger, or revenge. Some adolescents have sex and strive for pregnancy to get even with parents or to punish a former lover.

2. *To win or return favors:* "I spent fifteen dollars on you tonight; now what do I get?" "I can't thank you enough for the coat." This is really the prostitution of sex: giving sex as payment.

3. *To control behavior:* "If I sleep with you, will you marry me?" "Let's have a baby; then our parents will have to give us permission to marry."

4. *To build up the ego:* "Wait until the others find out whom I slept with last night." "I bet you five dollars I can score." "I'll show you who's irresistible."

5. *To exploit selflessly:* The other person is used for physical satisfaction without regard for that person's well-being or for the consequences. "I don't care if you're not feeling well. You belong to me and I want sex now!"

The Exclusion of Intimacy

Some professionals feel that present-day teenage sexual relationships have no emotional meaning. Dr. W. Godfrey Cobliner of the Department of Gynecology/Obstetrics at the Albert Einstein School of Medicine, Bronx, New York, says that converging evidence from a variety of sources, including his own personal interviews, suggests that sexual involvement is often sporadic, episodic, without commitment, and accompanied by a deliberate effort to suppress tender, romantic feelings and intimacy. Cobliner finds an unmistakable disassociation from tenderness and love in the sexual involvement of some young people. The relationship between the sexes is goal-directed and lacking in tenderness. The primary goal is a casual encounter of individual sexual gratification without shared intimacy. He says we have established a mode in which sex precedes the development of sentiment. Relationships with partners are *expected* to be unstable and transient.

One college male explained:

> When I meet an attractive girl, I look for quick and easy pleasure. I make small talk, take her out to dinner—perhaps to a dance to make her come across. But they should not give too much warmth, should not become sentimental, and should not cry. That would upset me. I

stay cool. If any feelings well up in me, I check them at once. I am afraid of strong feelings of passion. (Cobliner, 1988, p. 103)

A college-aged female explains:

> As a woman, one has to be on guard if one has sex with a fellow one likes. One gets easily hurt if one gets involved. They make love to you, but then they leave. You never suspect it. . . . You can get upset if you care for him. It takes you quite some time to recover. . . . You can become the victim of your own strong feelings. I have to always be on guard. I have to curb my feelings. (Cobliner, 1988, pp. 103, 104)

Cobliner indicates that the restraint of feelings leads to diminished sexual gratification and to a rise of a type of psychiatric disturbance—***depersonalization,*** or ***derealization*** (separation of the self from feelings). Sex, then, acts as a barrier and inhibitor of enduring attachment and a sense of continuity. Instead of promoting inner peace and well-being, the partners are perturbed and anxious to suppress the feelings of affection toward one another that accompany sexual union (Cobliner, 1988).

All of these standards of behavior are being practiced in our culture. Most adolescents feel that what the other person does sexually is his or her own business; no one else has a right to interfere or judge. The only qualification they make is "as long as no one is hurt." Because intercourse involves two people, however, no ethic can be completely individualistic. At the very least, it must take into account one's sex partner. Of course, a person's actions may also affect many others: a child conceived out of wedlock, families and relatives, and others in the community if one needs to run to them for help or assistance. There is no such thing as behavior that does not affect someone else.

Not everyone who goes to bed with someone else does so out of love. Sex can mean "I love you," "I need you," "I don't care about you," or "I hate you and want to hurt you." Sex can therefore be

either loving or hateful, helpful or harmful, satisfying or frustrating. The outcome will depend partially on motives, meanings, and relationships. Sex is more than what a person does; it expresses what that person is and feels. Morality is defined by how one human being deals with another human being—responsibly or irresponsibly.

Sexual Aggression

In Los Angeles, 15 percent of a sample of sixth- through twelfth-graders reported that they had unwanted sexual experiences, which may or may not have ended in intercourse. This group included

depersonalization or **derealization** becoming detached emotionally from the self.

18 percent of the girls and 12 percent of the boys. High school students were more likely to report an unwanted sexual experience (17 percent) than were middle-school students (11 percent). Of the ethnic groups, Asian Americans were the least likely to report such an experience (7 percent), Hispanics and non-Hispanic Whites were equally likely to do so (16 percent), and African Americans were most likely to do so (19 percent) (Turner, 1991).

Both men and women can be victims of unwanted sexual aggression (Smith, Pine, and Hawley, 1988; Struckman-Johnson, 1988). One survey of 507 university men and 486 university women revealed that almost all (97.5 percent of the men and 93.5 percent of the women) had experienced unwanted sexual activity, such as kissing, petting, or intercourse (Muehlenhard and Cook, 1988). More men than women experienced unwanted intercourse. More women than men were likely to have engaged in unwanted kissing. The 10 most important reasons given for engaging in unwanted sexual activity were enticement by partners, altruism (desire to please partner), inexperience (desire to build experience), intoxication, reluctance (felt obligated, under pressure), peer pressure, sex-role concern (afraid of appearing unmasculine or unfeminine), threat to terminate

HIGHLIGHT

Date Rape

Date rape occurs on a voluntary, prearranged date, or after a woman meets a man on a social occasion and voluntarily goes somewhere with him (Koss, Gidyca, and Wisniewski, 1987). It has been an increasing problem in high schools and on college campuses (Klingman and Vicary, 1992). One student wrote:

> Charlie and I went parking after the movie. He asked me to get in the back seat with him, which I did, because I trusted him and felt safe with him. We necked and petted awhile and then he became violent. He ripped off my panties, pinned me down on the seat, and forced himself on me. I couldn't do anything about it. He had the nerve to ask me afterward if I enjoyed it. (from a student paper)

Men who rape women on a date are likely to have a history of repeated episodes of sexual aggression, where they use physical force to gain sexual ends. They are generally more aggressive than other men, and some are hostile to all women. Some exhibit symptoms of sexual sadism in which they experience arousal from a woman's emotional distress (Heilbrun and Loftus, 1986). Greendlinger and Byrne (1987) found that the likelihood of college men committing rape was correlated with their coercive fantasies, aggressive tendencies, and acceptance of the rape myth (i.e., that women like to be forced).

This is in keeping with other studies that show that belief in the rape myth is associated with assigning more blame to the victims (Blumberg and Lester, 1991). Denial of the validity of women's feelings about sexuality results in pro-rape attitudes by men (Feltey, Ainslie, and Geib, 1991; Kershner, 1996).

In one study, high school students viewed a photograph of a rape victim in provocative clothing and a photograph of a rape victim dressed conservatively. The students were more likely to indicate that the provocatively dressed victim was responsible for her assailant's behavior, that the assailant's behavior was justified, and that the act of unwanted sexual intercourse was not rape (Cassidy and Hurrell, 1995).

Rape is a traumatic experience for the victims as well as their families. A rape victim often becomes acutely disorganized and experiences much distress, which she shows through words and tears. As she tries to put her life back to normal, she may experience depression, fear, and anxiety for months or even years. About one-fifth of rape victims have made a suicide attempt—a rate eight times higher than that of women who have not been raped. A female's recovery is enhanced if she gains crucial support from parents, partners, and others. Professional counseling helps and is sometimes obtained through rape crisis centers (Koss, 1993).

Source: F. P. Rice, *Human Sexuality* (Dubuque, IA: Wm C. Brown, 1989). Used by permission.

the relationship, verbal coercion, and physical coercion. Whatever physical coercion existed was mostly of a nonviolent nature.

In another study of undergraduate men at a large state university, nearly half reported having verbally coerced women into engaging in sexual experiences (Craig, Kalichman, and Follingstad, 1989). In describing their accompanying feelings, they most commonly described themselves as "horny," "aroused," "seeking sex," "drunk," or "lustful."

In a completely different type of study of female college students with a mean age of 20 years, fully 33 percent had been subjected to unwanted male genital exposure by exhibitionists (Cox, 1988).

Another study of 275 undergraduate single women at Arizona State University revealed that over 50 percent of the participants reported being pressured into kissing, breast and genital manipulation, and oral contact with their partners' genitals (Christopher, 1988). The women rarely encountered either verbal threat of force or the use of physical force. The most common form of pressure was persistent physical attempts. The next most likely form of pressure was positive verbal statements that later proved to be untrue.

In other research, women reported on their rejection strategies (Perper and Weis, 1987). These include avoiding enticing behavior, avoiding intimate situations, ignoring sexual signals the man gives, using diversion and distraction, making excuses ("I have a big exam tomorrow"), saying no, and physical rejection. Women also use delaying themes ("I'm not ready yet" "I need an emotional relationship!") and threats ("I won't see you again if you don't stop" "I'll leave!").

---

date rape forced unwanted sexual intercourse while on a date.

PERSONAL ISSUES

Sexual Harassment in High School

Females encounter sexual harassment in many different forms, including sexist remarks, blatant propositions, actual physical contact (patting, brushing against the body), and sexual assaults (Paludi, 1992)

We hear a lot these days about sexual harassment in the workplace, but what about sexual harassment in the high school setting? In one study, 105 college students were asked to complete a survey to estimate the seriousness and frequency of such behaviors when they were in high school. According to this study, *sexual harassment* was defined as "any unwanted sexual leers, suggestions, comments, or physical contact that a person might find objectionable in the context of a teacher-student relationship." The results of this study indicated that most respondents did not think that sexual harassment by teachers was frequent or serious in their high schools, although half cited examples of such incidents happening to those they knew. Most of the examples involved unwanted comments or sexual looks, with touching and affairs the least frequent type of incidents. Although most of the incidents involved male teachers and females students, there were examples of female teachers behaving in a sexually inappropriate manner with male students. In addition, there were a few cases of male-to-male harassment.

Over one-third of the respondents said they had known of a sexual relationship between a teacher and a high school student. The majority of the students felt that both the student and the teacher were equally interested in the affair. Apparently, most students thought it was possible for high school students and their teachers to engage in mutually consenting sexual relationships despite differences in age and status. This finding, in conjunction with other comments, provides evidence that respondents often disclaim instances of sexual harassment in high school (Corbett, Gentry, and Pearson, 1993).

Sexual harassment can be especially damaging when the perpetrators are teachers and other adults who have considerable and authority over adolescents (Lee et al., 1995).

Some adolescents are able to say no to un-wanted sex easier than others. A study of almost 2,500 tenth-grade White, Hispanic, and African American adolescents found no racial or ethnic differences in the ability to say no. Females said they were more likely than males to believe they could say no to unwanted sex. Having a less per-missive attitude toward sex, giving low importance rating to peer influence, and, for females, having a generalized sense of self-efficacy, are predictors of the ability to say no (Zimmerman, Sprecher, Langer, and Holloway, 1995).

Contraceptives and Sexually Transmitted Diseases

With almost one-third of 16-year-old girls and over two-thirds of 17-year-old girls having premarital coitus, the rate of use of contraceptives is ex-tremely important.

Use of Contraceptives among Adolescents

What percentage of sexually active young people are using some form of protection against preg-nancy and sexually transmitted diseases (STDs)? According to one study, 70 percent of adolescent females under the age of 15, or their partners, did not use any contraceptive method at first inter-course (Johnson and Green, 1993). The result from the National Survey of Family Growth (NSFG) in 1988 revealed only 35 percent of 15- to 19-year-old females, or their partners, used any method of contraception (including withdrawal) at first intercourse (Forrest and Singh, 1990). Only 32 percent of 15- to 19-year-old females, or their partners, reported they were currently using contraceptives (Mosher, 1990). According to the 1988 National Survey of Adolescent Males (NSAM) who were 15 to 19 years old, 23 percent reported that they, or their partners, used no con-traceptive method, or that they used an ineffective method (withdrawal, douching, or rhythm) at last intercourse (Sonenstein, Pleck, and Ku, 1991).

These figures indicate large numbers who are not protected against unwanted pregnancy or STDs. As a result, 1 of every 10 women aged 15 to 19 becomes pregnant each year in the United States (Trussell, 1988); 4 out of 5 of these young women are unmarried. Among those who use con-traceptives, the most popular method is the birth control pill, followed by the condom (U S. Bureau of the Census, 1996). Withdrawal and rhythm, both relatively inefficient methods, are the next most commonly used methods. Only small per-centages of adolescents use the diaphragm, sponge, IUD, or foam.

Sexually active adolescents who value per-sonal achievement and have conventional life-styles are more likely to use contraceptives regu-larly than their peers who are less conventional (Hollander, 1996). One hopeful sign in relation to the possibility of transmitting AIDS or another sexually transmitted diseases is an increase in the use of condoms. According to the NSFG, 33 per-cent of the partners of 15- to 19-year-old females used condoms in 1988, compared with 21 percent in 1982 (Mosher, 1990). According to the NSAM, 58 percent of sexually active 17- to 19-year-old males, at last intercourse, used condoms alone or in combination with other methods in 1988, com-pared with only 21 percent in 1979 (Sonenstein, Pleck, and Ku, 1991).

The female condom (marketed under the brand name Reality) was approved by the Food and Drug Administration (FDA) in 1993 for re-ducing the risk of unwanted pregnancies and the transmission of sexually transmitted diseases, in-cluding HIV. The device is a six-inch long polyurethane sheath that is closed at one end. A free-moving pliable ring encased in the closed end of the female condom aids the user in insert-ing the device properly; an outer ring at the open end rests against the vulva during use. Effective-ness rates for the female condom have been de-termined for contraceptive trials and have ranged from a rate of 79 to 95 percent. Worldwide ac-ceptability data indicate that women are often eager to try the female condom because the de-vice is under their control. In the vast majority of studies, partners have acquiesced to its use and have sometimes preferred the device to a male condom (Gollub, Stein, and El-Sadr, 1995).

Despite dissatisfaction with condoms, both men and women report high rates of condom use. The method used, however, is dependent on the type of relationship involved, with condoms used

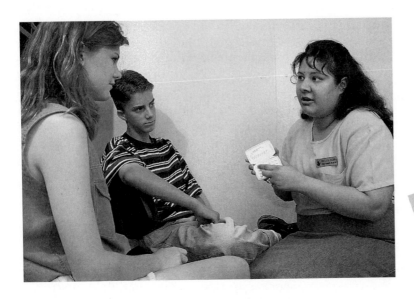

Family planning clinics are a good source of information about contraceptives for adolescents engaging in sexual intercourse. However, adolescents often do not go to clinics until after they are sexually active or even pregnant.

more frequently in casual sexual relationships than in long-term relationships. Both men and women in long-term relationships often switch from condoms to other methods once they have had time to assess, often by undesirable means, their partner's risk status (Landry and Camelo, 1994).

Why Contraceptives Are Not Used

Getting sexually active teenagers to use effective contraceptives is a challenge. Even sexually active teenagers who say they do not want pregnancy often do not use contraceptives. Users have to be knowledgeable of the method, be willing to admit that they are sexually active, and be willing and able to obtain contraceptives as needed. Some students are misinformed about "safe" times and the likelihood of pregnancy. Many do not believe pregnancy will happen to them. One young man remarked about his girlfriend, "She didn't look like the type" (Barret and Robinson, 1982, p. 350). There is a small percentage of unmarried adolescents who really want to get pregnant. Some believe they are in love and that pregnancy will ensure marriage. Because some have moral objections to intercourse, they deny the consequences of pregnancy or romanticize about the thrills of maternity, or they hesitate to obtain help for fear of parental disapproval (Milan and Kilmann, 1987).

One study of 1,200 young women 12 to 19 years of age sought to find out why they delayed so long in going to the family planning clinic for birth control help (Zabin and Clark, 1981). Only 14 percent sought protection *before* first intercourse. Some 50 percent were sexually active but not yet pregnant. The remaining 36 percent came to the clinic because they suspected pregnancy. Most of the sexually active women delayed coming to the clinic from three months to several years after first coitus. Only about half of the sexually active women had used any method of contraception at last intercourse before coming to the clinic.

When asked why they delayed coming to the clinic, a variety of answers were given. Table 9.1 lists the most common answers in order of decreasing frequency. Several factors in this list and from other studies stand out as particularly important.

1. Many of these adolescents showed anxieties and fears. They were afraid of parents, afraid of being examined, or feared that birth control was dangerous (Lowe and Radius, 1987; Scott et al., 1988). Others did not get contraceptives because of fear or embarrassment about sex itself.

2. They displayed widespread ignorance. They thought they had not had sex often enough to get pregnant, that they were too young, that birth control costs too much, that the method they were

TABLE 9.1   Reasons for Delaying Going to the Family Planning Clinic for Birth Control Help

Reason	Percentage Citing Contributing Reason
Just didn't get around to it	38.1
Afraid my family would find out if I came	31.0
Waiting for closer relationship with boyfriend	27.6
Thought birth control dangerous	26.5
Afraid to be examined	24.8
Thought it cost too much	18.5
Didn't think had sex often enough to get pregnant	16.5
Never thought of it	16.4
Didn't know where to get birth control help	15.3
Thought I had to be older to get birth control	13.1
Didn't expect to have sex	12.8
Thought I was too young to get pregnant	11.5
Thought birth control wrong	9.2
Partner opposed	8.4
Thought I wanted pregnancy	8.4
Thought birth control I was using was good enough	7.8
Forced to have sex	1.4
Sex with relative	0.7
Other	9.7

Source: Reproduced with the permission of The Alan Guttmacher Institute from Zabin, L. S., and Clark, S. D., Jr. "Why the Delay: A Study of Teenage Family Planning Clinic Patients," *Family Planning Perspectives*, 1981, *13* (5): 205.

using was all right, that they had to be older to get help, or they did not know where to get help.

3. They showed a lack of maturity and responsibility. They had not gotten around to it or never thought of it, so did not plan for it (Gruber and Chambers, 1987).

4. They were ambivalent in their feelings (Levinson, 1986). They wanted to wait until they were closer to their boyfriends, they did not expect to have sex, they thought birth control was wrong, they believed their partner opposed it, or they wanted to get pregnant.

5. A small number had delayed because sex had been forced on them against their will, or they had been sexually abused by a relative.

The median delay of nine months for these women who did eventually get to a family planning clinic involved a period of prolonged risk of pregnancy. This, of course, did not include those who never got to a clinic at all, thereby increasing the risk, unless they went to a private physician. It is clear that *widespread education is needed no later than junior high school–level if these youths are to avoid unwanted pregnancies* (Zabin and Clark, 1981; Zelnik and Kim, 1982).

Should Adolescents Have Contraceptives?

On June 9, 1977, the U.S. Supreme Court affirmed that no state could legally restrict the distribution of contraceptives to minors, that nonprescription devices could be dispensed by those other than registered pharmacists, and that such devices could be openly displayed and advertised (Beiswinger, 1979; *Carey,* 1977). The courts also ruled that clinics do not have to notify parents before prescribing contraceptives for adolescents, regardless of age.

Whether adolescents should have access to contraceptives has been a controversial subject. Some adults are worried that the availability of contraceptives will increase teen promiscuity. Nevertheless, about 80 percent of adults agree that contraceptive information should be made available to everyone, including teenagers (Rinck, Rudolph, and Simkins, 1983). Evidence indicates that even if they do not have contraceptives, youths who are so inclined will have sexual intercourse anyhow. Most youths usually seek contraceptive help after they have already been having intercourse. One study of African American and Hispanic adolescents revealed a two-year time lapse between the age at first intercourse and the age at which they first visited a family planning clinic (Schwartz and Darabi, 1986). Many were afraid they were already pregnant when they went

Condom Availability at Schools

A telephone survey was made of individuals who are involved in school programs that provide condoms to students. Data suggested that as of January 1995, at least 431 public schools in 50 U.S. school districts made condoms available—2.2 percent of all public high schools and 0.3 percent of high school districts. In about half of the schools that were surveyed, students obtained more than one condom per student per year, on average; 14 percent of the students obtained more than six. Students in alternative schools, in smaller schools, in schools that made condoms available in baskets, and in schools with health clinics obtained more condoms for students per year than did students in other schools (Kirby and Brown, 1996).

for help. Another study indicated that about one-third of the women being served in family planning clinics were in their teens (Furstenberg et al., 1983).

The availability of contraceptives, then, has almost no influence on whether youths have sex, but it may be a major determinant as to whether a particular girl gets pregnant. One of the major goals of sex education ought to be to provide information about contraception (Lincoln, 1984). Some who oppose sex education argue that they are afraid if teenagers "know too much," they will use their knowledge to "get into trouble." Evidence indicates, however, that sexual knowledge has no influence on sexual behavior. What really influences behavior are the values and morals accepted by individuals and the groups to which youths belong. The fact remains that contraceptives have become much more readily available to teenagers, but youths who have coitus use them only about half of the time.

Sexually Transmitted Diseases

People of all ages (children, youth, and adults) may be exposed to sexually transmitted diseases through sexual contact (Nevid and Gotfried, 1995). Essentially, all sexually active teens are at risk of contracting a sexually transmitted disease due to biological vulnerability and a variety of risk-taking behaviors (Rosenthal, Biro, Cohen, Succop, and Stanberry, 1995).

Currently, *chlamydial infections* are the most common of the STDs (Judson, 1985; Morris, War-

ren, and Aral, 1993). *Gonorrhea* is very common. Its incidence surpasses that of chicken pox, measles, mumps, and rubella combined (Alan Guttmacher Institute, 1993; Silber, 1982). About 1 in every 4 cases of gonorrhea involves an adolescent. As many as 1 in 35 adolescents has *genital herpes* (Oppenheimer, 1982). Other STDs, such as *syphilis,* are also found among adolescents. Youths in the 20- to 24-year-old bracket are hardest hit by STDs, followed by 15- to 19-year olds. There are more than 25 different infectious organisms that can be transmitted sexually. Chlamydia, gonorrhea, acquired immunodeficiency syndrome (AIDS), syphilis, and hepatitis B are among the country's 10 most frequently reported infections (Donovan, 1997).

AIDS

Authorities are becoming more concerned about the increase in AIDS among adolescents ("Kids and Contraceptives," 1987). The increased risk is due to heterosexually active adolescents who are inconsistent contraceptive users (Cox, 1994). Many have unrealistic attitudes. They feel "it won't happen to me," so they take no precautions. In addition, about one-third of an adult male sample and one-fifth of an adult female sample reported having had homosexual experiences during adolescence (Petersen et al., 1983). Furthermore, a small group of adolescents are intravenous drug users. Adolescents who are most heterosexually active, or who engage in homosexual contacts, or who are intravenous drug users comprise a high-

HIGHLIGHT

Talking about Contraception

The Alan Guttmacher Institute sponsored a series of group discussions to investigate some possible reasons for poor contraceptive practices among teenagers. The following are comments of teenagers attending the discussion (M = moderator, P = participants).

On Lack of Planning

M: Do you ever have sex without any [birth control] method?

P: Sometimes. Sometimes I have no alternative.

P: When you're our age, you can't always say when you're going to have sex ... because, you know. . . .

P: It just happens.

On Taking a Chance

P: There could be that casual guy you just met. You know it's going to be a big thing and you want to have sex with him, and you're not going to say, "Give me a few weeks. Let me get started on the pill" or "I'm going to run down to Planned Parenthood and get a diaphragm." . . . You take a chance.

On Ambivalent Feelings

P: If I did [use a contraceptive], then I'd have sex more. Then it would be too easy. The risk won't be there; the risk won't stop me.

M: Why do you need to stop? What's wrong with having sex?

P: I don't feel it's right. I haven't been raised that way.

On Using Withdrawal

P: You don't have to bother with putting on a rubber, bother with inserting foam, or taking a pill every day. It sounds like a cop-out, but you don't have to bother.

On Confusion about the Pill

P: She hears one thing, I hear something else. We don't travel in the same circles. She hears that she can't get pregnant for eight months after she goes off the pill. I hear I can't get pregnant 'til four months after I go off the pill. But I know someone who got pregnant a day after she stopped taking the pill.

On Putting the Responsibility on the Girl

P: You really can't tell [whether or not the girl is on the pill]. Why bring it up? You know sooner or later. You can ask if you want to, and she can ask or tell you, but why do it? The girl is smart. I really don't think she would go through with it if she wasn't prepared. So, hey, I wouldn't say nothing.

M: So you are assuming that [if] she doesn't say anything, she is on something?

P: I don't care if she [is] or not. That's her problem.

On Use of a Condom

P: It's inconvenient, of course. The guys don't like them. [They say] "It's unnatural, you know," [or] "I don't want to be cooped up," [or] "It's like having sex with a gym shoe."

Source: Reprinted with permission from E. E. Kisker, "Teenagers Talk about Sex, Pregnancy, and Contraception," *Family Planning Perspectives,* 17, March–April 1985, pp. 83–90.

risk group for contracting AIDS; they can easily become infected and transmit the disease to others.

One of the problems is that the incubation period for AIDS may be from a few years to up to 10 years (Wallis, 1987). The average latency time from viral infection to time of illness is about 5 to 7 years (Ahlstrom, Richmond, Townsend, and D'Angelo, 1992). An adolescent can be exposed to the human immunodeficiency virus (HIV), carry it for years without knowing it, and not come down with AIDS until after adolescence has passed. For this reason, only a small percentage of cases are reported during adolescence itself. However, increasing numbers of young adults who engaged in high-risk behavior during their adoles-

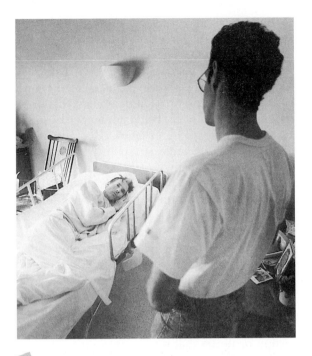

There is increased concern about the risk of AIDS among adolescents, since they are unrealistic and suffer from the "it can't happen to me" attitude. In addition, adolescents who contract HIV may not show any symptoms until adulthood.

cent years are reported to have AIDS (Anderson et al., 1990).

Acquired immunodeficiency syndrome is caused by the human immunodeficiency virus. When HIV gets into the bloodstream, it attacks particular white blood cells, called *T-lymphocytes*. T-lymphocytes stimulate the body's immune system and ability to fight disease. As HIV multiplies, more and more T-lymphocytes are destroyed. The immune system progressively weakens, leaving the body vulnerable to a variety of other "opportunistic" diseases. Not everyone who is exposed to the virus gets AIDS, however. A blood test has been developed to measure the presence of HIV antibodies in the bloodstream. A person is considered to have AIDS when symptoms develop.

Diagnosing AIDS can be difficult. Some people apparently remain well after being infected with the virus; they have no physical symptoms. Even at this stage, however, they can spread the virus to others without knowing that they are infected. It is important to note that abnormalities of the immune system may develop weeks or months before any symptoms develop. As the virus gradually destroys the body's immune system, other infections invade the body. It is these secondary diseases that eventually cause death. The AIDS patient not only experiences rapid swelling and soreness of the lymph glands in the neck, groin, and armpit, but also sudden loss of appetite, weight loss, persistent and unexplained diarrhea or bloody stools, night sweats, and/or fever, chronic fatigue, shortness of breath, severe headaches, persistent dry cough, reddish-purplish bumps on the skin, and chronic white coating on the tongue and throat. Physical manifestations may be divided into the following five major categories (Ognibene, 1984):

1. *Infectious:* Various infectious agents cause pneumonia, esophagitis, oral and anal ulcerations, mass lesions of the central nervous system, meningitis, encephalitis, peritonitis, and infections of the eyes, liver, spleen, lungs, and lymph nodes.
2. *Hematologic:* AIDS reduces both white and red blood cells, lowering the body's resistance to infections and causing anemia.
3. *Neurological:* AIDS patients may experience various infections of the central nervous system, which produce progressive dementia, seizures, aphasia, and other signs of neural deterioration.
4. *Nutritional and gastrointestinal:* Patients develop severe diarrhea, resulting in weight loss.
5. *Neoplastic:* Kaposi's sarcoma is a rare cancer that produces a proliferation in the cells lining the heart, blood vessels, and lymph glands. Violet lesions or lumps occur on the skin and mucous membranes.

To date, no patients have recovered from AIDS either spontaneously or with medical intervention once the full-blown disease develops (Rice, 1989).

HIV may be found in semen, blood, vaginal secretions, urine, saliva, tears, and breast milk of infected individuals. The disease may be transmitted from male to female, female to male, male to male, and female to female of any age. During sexual activity, the virus is passed from person to person in the exchange of body fluids, especially in the exchange of blood and semen. The skin itself is a barrier against the virus. However, small, unseen tears in the lining of the vagina or rectum may occur, thus providing an opening for the virus to enter directly into the bloodstream.

It is important to know that infected students can remain in school, as long as they feel well enough to attend and are not infectious with other diseases such as chicken pox. If an open cut or sore on one child is exposed to the blood or body fluids of a child infected with AIDS, there is a possible occurrence of infection. People who have AIDS can remain in virtually any occupation without special restriction as long as they do not have associated symptoms such as open sores. They can share telephones, typewriters, office equipment, desks, tools, papers, vehicles, toilets, showers, uniforms, eating facilities, coffee pots, and water fountains. Remember: *AIDS cannot be contracted by casual contact.*

Surgeons, dentists, and other health-care professionals who work inside the body need to take special precautions to avoid contact with blood and other body fluids. Care is needed to prevent needle-stick injuries, mucosal splashes, or contact with instruments contaminated by blood or body fluids from patients with AIDS. Workers with chronic dermatitis or wounds are asked not to have patient contact. Personal service workers such as hairdressers, cosmetologists, and manicurists need to handle sharp instruments with care and follow sanitary precautions. A razor, for example, should be used for only one client, then cleaned and disinfected or thrown away. The same recommendation applies to ear-piercing devices, tattoo needles, and other instruments that puncture the skin. It is recommended that such instruments be sterilized after each use. AIDS is not transmitted through preparation or service of food and beverages, so food-service workers known to be infected need not be restricted from work unless they have another infection or illness that may be transmitted to others. In case food is accidentally contaminated with

PERSONAL ISSUES

How Much Do You Know about AIDS?

Take the following quiz and find out how much you know about AIDS. Answer *yes* or *no* to each statement.

1. You can get AIDS from sharing needles.
2. You can infect another person with HIV during sex.
3. You can get AIDS from sex without a condom.
4. You can get AIDS from holding hands.
5. You can reduce your chance of HIV infection by using condoms.
6. Only gay men can get AIDS.
7. You can get AIDS from casual contact with students in class.
8. There is a cure for AIDS/HIV infection.
9. A pregnant women can infect her unborn baby.
10. You can reduce your chance of infection by abstinence.
11. You can reduce your chance of infection by not having sex with IV drug users.
12. You can reduce your chance of infection by taking birth control pills.
13. You can tell if a person is infected by their appearance.
14. You can get AIDS from public toilets.
15. You can get AIDS from donating blood.
16. You can get AIDS from insect bites.
17. You can transmit HIV to another person without knowing you are a carrier.
18. You can get AIDS from oral sex.
19. You can get AIDS from receiving a blood transfusion.
20. You can get AIDS from hugging an infected person.

Answers: 1. Yes, 2. Yes, 3. Yes, 4. No, 5. Yes, 6. No, 7. No, 8. No, 9. Yes, 10. Yes, 11. Yes, 12. No, 13. No, 14. No, 15. No, 16. No, 17. Yes, 18. Yes, 19. Yes, 20. No

blood from a cut, the food should be discarded, although food itself is not a vehicle for transmitting HIV. The Department of Health and Human Services recommends that all health and personal service workers be instructed in disease control, and that a licensure requirement should include evidence of such education ("Health Service Issues," 1985).

In one study, 218 adolescents from 15 residential centers received an intensive nine-session HIV prevention program. Results showed that discussion groups produced a long-term increase in knowledge about AIDS and an increase in reported intentions to cope with AIDS-risk situations. However, the discussion groups did not produce a long-term reduction in the level of engagement in high-risk behavior (Slonim-Nevo, Auslander, Ozawa, and Jung, 1996).

Other than total abstinence, condoms have been widely promoted as the best method of preventing the spread of AIDS. However, using condoms is not what people are talking about when they refer to *safe sex*. It may be safer sex, but it is a misnomer to say using condoms provides safe sex (Parachini, 1987). Before use, condoms should be inflated and held under water to see if they leak (if there are any air bubbles, leakage is indicated). If a condom does not have a hole in it, it can still rupture or slip off. Users are urged to hold on to the top of the condom when withdrawing the penis from the vagina or anus to prevent leakage and slippage. When used with a spermicidal foam, jelly, or cream, the contraceptive efficiency of condoms is increased. Spermicides are also damaging to any HIV that may be present.

With no medical procedure available to cure or prevent the spread of AIDS, it is imperative that people learn to recognize and change behaviors that place them at risk of contracting the disease. Individuals who recognize that their behavior places them at risk will be more likely to change than individuals who do not. Thus, if programs are to be effective in promoting change in individuals who engage in risky sexual behavior, sexual practices that decrease the likelihood of contracting AIDS need to be specified clearly, and participants must be encouraged to apply this information to themselves (Brown, Baranowski, Kulig, Stephenson, and Perry, 1996; Jurich, Adams, and Schulenberg, 1992).

Unwed Pregnancy and Abortion

The increase in premarital sexual intercourse accompanied by a lack of efficient use of contraceptives has resulted in an increase in out-of-wedlock pregnancies.

Incidence

The United States now has the highest rate of teen pregnancies among industrialized societies (Rodriquez and Moore, 1995). Adolescent pregnancy is widely recognized in our society as one of the most complex and serious health problems (Pete-McGadney, 1995). These pregnancies are now estimated at 1,065,000 each year among women less than 20 years of age. Of this number, 132,000 are

The United States has the highest rate of teen pregnancy among the industrialized nations. Each year, over 1 million girls younger than 20 years of age become pregnant. Most of these young mothers, such as this 18-year-old who gave birth at age 16, decide to keep their children.

miscarriages or stillbirths, 317,000 are induced abortions, and the remaining 616,000 babies are born alive. About 248,000 expectant mothers marry hastily before their babies are born, leaving 368,000 babies born out of wedlock in 1993 (Henshaw, 1997; U.S. Bureau of the Census, 1996).

Causes

Why does the United States rate so high in adolescent fertility rates and abortion rates among developing nations? Caldas (1993) offers these six explanations:

1. *Reproductive-ignorance hypothesis:* The elevated adolescent pregnancy rate is the result of a pervasive lack of knowledge regarding conception and contraception among the adolescent population. Unfortunately, providing information to adolescents on sexual and contraceptive matters does not necessarily assure that they will become users and alter their sexual behavior. Educational programs that focus on facts about reproduction and contraception do increase knowledge, but demonstrate inconsistent and inconclusive effects on sexual behavior and greater contraceptive usage (Levinson, 1995).

2. *Psychological needs hypothesis:* The causes of adolescent pregnancy and childbearing are rooted in the behavior that reflects the psychological state of the mother (e.g., an adolescent pregnancy and/or birth may fulfill a subconscious need). Some adolescents are not motivated to use adequate contraceptives because they want to become pregnant.

3. *Welfare hypothesis:* The cause of adolescent pregnancy and subsequent births to poor adolescents is the result of the desire to receive welfare payments.

4. *Parental role model/supervision hypothesis:* Parental behavior and/or lack of supervision is a cause of adolescent pregnancy and childbearing in single-parent families.

5. *Social norms hypothesis:* The cause of adolescent sexual and parenting behaviors is directly related to the strength of social norms received and internalized/acted on by adolescents. One survey of Latino, African American, and White students from an inner-city vocational high school revealed that most of the young women at this school desired their pregnancies; many of them preferred single parenthood to traditional family structure. Low academic skills and poverty often resulted in pregnancy, rather than pregnancy resulting in high school dropouts and a life of poverty (Gordon, 1996). Another study of high-risk inner-city African American and Caucasian adolescent girls (15 to 16 years of age) revealed that these girls experienced multiple pressures to engage in intercourse at young ages (Rosenthal, Lewis, and Cohen, 1996).

6. *Physiological hypothesis:* The act of coitus leading to adolescent pregnancy and childbearing is directly affected by hormonal influences.

Each of the six hypotheses focuses on only one, or perhaps a few, sometimes narrow explanations for the high rates. In reality, it is more likely that the complex interaction of the factors stressed by each hypothesis accounts for the high adolescent pregnancy and birthrates in the United States (Caldas, 1993).

Pregnancy-Resolution Decisions

One of the consequences of increased rates of adolescent sexual activity is the dramatic rise in teen pregnancies. Those who become pregnant and seek alternatives to childrearing have two options: abortion or adoption. One study investigated the pregnancy-resolution decisions of African American and Hispanic American adolescents, aged 15 to 21 years. African Americans who made a decision to terminate pregnancies had the following characteristics: They achieved higher levels of education, were at middle- or upper-income levels (at or above the poverty level), and had access to medically safe health-care clinics. Also, African Americans with adequate family resources and those with convenient access to family planning clinics were more apt to have abortions. Fewer adolescents would carry unplanned pregnancies to full term if they had adequate transportation and financial support to obtain abortions. Interestingly, those who reported a specific affiliation (Baptist) were more likely to decide not to carry their first pregnancies to full term. Apparently, adolescents who attended church were more intent on eliminating evidence of sexual involvement. They terminated their pregnancies so that they could continue attending church on a regular basis, without church members knowing their sexual activity or pregnancy status. African Americans who decided to abort were older when the pregnancy occurred.

Turning to the Hispanic Americans in the study, a greater proportion of them chose to abort, compared to their African American counterparts. Hispanic adolescents who terminated tended to be younger at the time of pregnancy. In addition, those who terminated were more likely to indicate that they had never used contraception or were quite inconsistent users. Hispanic females who aborted were younger when they first had sexual intercourse than those who maintained their pregnancies to full term. This study also provides evidence that Hispanic adolescents who decided to terminate pregnancies were more likely to have informed their mothers about the pregnancy. There was greater likelihood of pregnancy termination among Hispanic adolescents whose mothers had obtained high levels of education.

Regardless of race or ethnicity, early childbearing appears to be a function of poverty. In general, those who decide not to terminate their pregnancies report family incomes at or below poverty level (Murry, 1995).

Problems

About 95 percent of mothers decide to keep their babies (Donnelly and Voydanoff, 1991; Hanson, 1992; Namerow, Kalmuss, and Cushman, 1993). Those who decide to place their babies for adoption generally feel quite comfortable with this decision. Certainly, they fare somewhat better than parents who keep their babies on a set of social-democratic outcomes assessed some months after birth.

One study compared the coping responses and psychosocial adjustments of pregnant adolescents who intended to relinquish their infants with parenting adolescents who wanted to keep their infants. Pregnant adolescents who intended to relinquish their infants showed better overall levels of self-image than pregnant adolescents intending to parent. Parenting adolescents showed significantly more disruption in specific areas of

psychosocial adjustment than pregnant adolescents not intending to parent (Stern and Alvarez, 1992). The problem is made even worse if adolescents encounter lack of support from parents, teachers, and counselors (Gruskin, 1994).

Adolescent mothers who decide to keep their babies must have sufficient social support. One study of 75 African American mothers revealed that the adolescent mother's own mother was the most frequent provider of support. Friends were the second-most frequently identified source of support, followed by siblings. Studies indicate that a female kin system in African American families is adaptive and that family support is the most important type of support for African American females. The reliance on friends for support has also been shown to be related to positive well-being and adjustment among African American adolescent mothers (Nitz, Ketterlinus, and Brandt, 1995).

Some pregnant adolescents let their parents or other relatives adopt their babies, but the remainder want to raise their children themselves, assisted by whatever family or other help they can get. They usually have many motives for keeping their babies. One is to have someone to love. One mother said: "I planned on having this baby. She was no accident. I always wanted a baby so that I could have someone to care for. Now I can give her all the love that I never had myself." Another motive is for the young mother to fulfill herself through her child.

From most points of view, unmarried motherhood of a young teenage girl is a tragedy (Christmon, 1990; Moore and Stief, 1991; Ohannesian and Crockett, 1993). The single mother who decides to keep her baby may become entrapped in a self-destructive cycle consisting of failure to continue her education, repeated pregnancies (Kuziel-Perri and Snarey, 1991), failure to establish a stable family life, and dependence on others for support (Hanson, 1992). If she marries, the chances of her remaining married are only about one in five. Because few single mothers manage to complete their high school educations, they are unable to get good jobs to support themselves and their families and are likely to require welfare assistance for years (Ahn, 1994; Blau and Gulotta, 1993; Caldas, 1993; Klaw and Saunders, 1994).

The National Longitudinal Survey of Youth shows that early childbearing lowers the educational attainment of young women. Having a child before age 20 significantly reduces schooling—by almost 3.0 years among Whites, African Americans, and Hispanics. Having a child before age 18 has a significant effect only among African Americans, reducing years of schooling by 1.2 years (Klepinger, Lundberg, and Plotnick, 1995).

One study of 84 African American and Puerto Rican adolescent mothers were investigated to determine what happens to school attendance before pregnancy and 28 to 36 months after pregnancy. Mothers were classified as continuous attenders, returners, before-pregnancy dropouts, and after-pregnancy dropouts. By 12 months postpartum, 62 percent of the adolescent mothers were in school or had graduated. By 28 to 36 months postpartum, only 41 percent of Puerto Ricans and 57 percent of African Americans were in school or had graduated. Only 5 of the 84 mothers were pursuing postsecondary education. Compared to the dropout groups, mothers who were in school or who had graduated reported fewer repeat pregnancies and more of them sought postsecondary education. Others who returned to school reported fewer stressful life events, more family support, fewer depressive symptoms, and stronger career commitments than did mothers in the dropout groups (Leadbeater, 1996).

The costs of adolescent childbearing are enormous, and members of three generations share in these costs. First, there are direct costs to the young mothers in terms of loss or delayed education, abrupt changes in their developmental trajectories in relationships with peers, and lost economic opportunities. Many of the young fathers are negatively affected by early pregnancies and by family formation. Second, parents of these young parents are also affected: They usually feel immediate disappointment and shock, which precludes acceptance of the pregnancy, a disruption of their own life plans, often a large share of the child-care responsibilities for a child not their own, and the additional burden of cost of medical care, space for the new child, and a new mouth to feed. Third, for the children born to adolescent mothers, the cost often includes increased likelihood of life in poverty in a single-parent family, a poor educational prognosis, poor developmental prognosis, and increased probability of becoming adolescent parents themselves. In addition, those who are not directly impacted by adolescent parenting also experience the costs: Adolescent parenting (under age 18) cost U.S. taxpayers 30 billion dollars in 1992 for Aid to Families with Dependent Children (AFDC), Medicaid and food stamp payments, not including day-care costs, housing subsidies, and foster care (U S. Bureau of the Census, 1996). In fact, 59 percent of women receiving AFDC payments were teenagers at the birth of their first child (Roosa, 1991). Additional information on the adolescent mother may be found in Chapter 15.

Adolescent Fathers

Research suggests that there are five myths or stereotypes commonly believed about teenage fathers (Robinson, 1988):

1. *The Phantom Father myth:* He is basically absent and leaves the mother and child to fend for themselves.
2. *The Mr. Cool myth:* He has a casual relationship with the mother of his child and few feelings about the pregnancy.
3. *The macho myth:* He has an unnatural need to prove his masculinity because he feels inadequate.
4. *The Don Juan myth:* He exploits helpless and unsuspecting girls by taking advantage of them.
5. *The Super Stud myth:* He is "worldly wise"— knows more than most teenagers about sex.

In actuality, the most recent studies show that about one-fourth of adolescent fathers typically remain psychologically and physically involved throughout the pregnancy and do have feelings toward the mother and the baby (Robinson, 1988). About 10 percent of pregnant teenage couples marry, but the chances that the marriage will work out are very slim. Considering their financial conditions, it is usually difficult for teenage fathers to contribute much to the support of their children, although most express the intention of doing so before the baby is born. Most have less education and more children than men who postpone having children until age 20 or older. They feel overwhelmed at the responsibility and may doubt their ability to be good providers. Teenage fathers are often the sons of absent fathers themselves; they may or may not have a male parental model and, in fact, may have numerous models of pregnancy outside of marriage (Leadbetter, 1994; Leadbetter, Way, and Raben, 1994). Many adolescent fathers compound the problem by dropping out of school (Resnick, Wattenberg, and Brewer, 1992).

In light of these considerations, professionals need to increase their attempts to assist teenage fathers. Society can no longer demand that teenage fathers become responsible parents without providing them with the understanding and guidance needed to assist them in successfully managing the crisis of premature parenthood. There is documented evidence that teenage fathers respond favorably to appropriate outreach initiatives, and that such efforts enable teenage fathers to enhance their own lives and to contribute positively to society and to the well-being of their children (Kiselica and Sturmer, 1993).

Homosexuality

Homosexuality refers to sexual orientation in which one develops sexual interest in those of the same biological sex. Alfred Kinsey was one of the first social scientists to emphasize that there are degrees of *heterosexuality* (sexual orientation to those of the opposite sex) and homosexuality. Figure 9.3 shows Kinsey's six-point scale of sexual behavior (Weinberg and Williams, 1974). He found that some persons have a mixture of homosexuality and heterosexuality, and so are *bisexual*. Some of these persons live a typical heterosexual life with their mates and children and yet enjoy homosexual sex on the side.

Homosexuality does not describe physical appearance, sex roles, or personality any more than does heterosexuality. Many homosexual men are masculine in appearance and actions; some are outstanding athletes. Many lesbians are feminine in appearance and behavior. A person cannot tell by behavioral characteristics if someone is homosexual. Some may play stereotyped heterosexual sex roles in society and in their fam-

ilies, others exhibit some of the physical and personality characteristics of the opposite sex and assume opposite-sex roles.

Different types of people are homosexual. Some are poorly adjusted or even psychotic (as are some heterosexuals); others are psychologically well adjusted. Most are creative, contributing members of society. Homosexuality is considered deviant by some in U.S. culture, but is not so regarded in some other cultures. The American Psychiatric Association does not consider homosexuality a mental disorder. "For a mental condition to be considered a psychiatric disorder," a decision of the American Psychiatric Association read, "it should regularly cause emotional distress or regularly be associated with generalized impairment of social functioning; homosexuality doesn't meet these criteria" (McCary and McCary, 1982b, p. 457).

Causes

Considerable research has been done to find out what causes homosexuality. The research falls into three major categories: biological theories, psychoanalytic theories, and social learning theories.

Biological Theories   One theory is that homosexuality is inherited. The latest version of a genetic theory is proposed by Simon LeVay of the Salk Institute in San Diego (Begley and Gilman, 1991). He found that one bundle of neurons in the hypothalamus was three times larger in heterosexual men than in homosexual men and heterosexual women. LeVay (1991) ruled out AIDS as a confounding factor since he found smaller hypothalamus bundles in gay men than in straight men who had died of AIDS. Thus, the shrinkage was not due to AIDS. In 1978, experiments on male primates found that lesions in the hypothalamus left the monkeys' sexual drives vigorous, but that males had lost interest in females.

heterosexuality   sexual orientation to those of the opposite sex.

homosexuality   sexual orientation to those of the same sex.

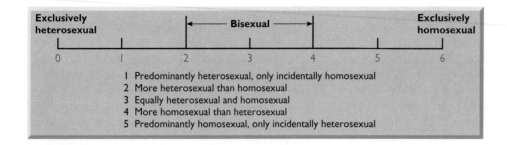

FIGURE 9.3   **Kinsey's Continuum of Heterosexuality-Homosexuality**

The question arises, however, regarding whether the smaller bundle of neurons causes homosexuality, or if a homosexual orientation causes that portion of the brain to shrink? Other research has shown that neurons change in response to experience. Another hypothesis asserts that an unknown factor might cause both homosexuality and the neuron differences. This factor might relate to the level of testosterone prenatally.

Furthermore, in one study, the homosexual orientations of pairs of twins were studied. The researchers found that two-thirds of the monozygotic twins (same eggs) had a homosexual orientation but less than one-third of dyzygotic twins (separate eggs) did. However, since not all of the monozygotic twins have a homosexual orientation, environmental factors might be partially involved also (Whitman, Diamond, and Martin, 1993).

Another biological theory relates the levels of male and female hormones in the body to homosexuality, but baseline hormonal levels of homosexuals and heterosexuals are only slightly dissimilar. However, in one study ("Medical First," 1984), a single injection of *Premarin*, an estrogen preparation, was given to 12 heterosexual women, 17 heterosexual males, and 14 homosexual males. The estrogen suppressed testosterone levels in both groups of men, but not in the women. However, 72 and 96 hours later, the homosexuals had significantly lower levels of testosterone than the heterosexuals. Apparently, the homosexuals were more influenced by the female hormone estrogen. Their bodies had less ability to recover from its influence and regain normal testosterone levels than did the heterosexual males. "This is the first study in this country clearly suggesting and presenting evidence of biological differ-

ences between homosexuals and heterosexuals as a group," said Dr. Brian Gladue, the chief researcher ("Medical First," 1984).

One implication is that people's bodies respond differently to changes in hormonal levels. These levels, in turn, may have differential effects on development and behavior. Part of sexual differentiation takes place in the hypothalamus of the brain (Kimura, 1985). Before birth, prenatal hormones can influence the brain so that a baby is born with a predisposition to develop behavior associated with the opposite sex (Ellis and Ames, 1987; Money, 1987). Many gay adolescents say that they felt differently from other boys when they were children (Savin-Williams and Rodriguez, 1993).

Psychoanalytic Theories   Traditionally, homosexuality was thought to be caused by problems in parent-child relationships in the family. The troubled relationships were thought to cause problems in identifying with the parent of the same sex. However, a study of 322 gay men and women from different sections of the country revealed that two-thirds perceived their relationships with their fathers as extremely satisfactory or satisfactory; three-fourths perceived their relationships with their mothers as extremely satisfactory or satisfactory (Robinson, Skeen, Flake-Hobson, and Herman, 1982). A total of 64 percent felt that they were always loved by their mothers, but only 36 percent felt that they were always loved by their fathers. Only 4 percent never or hardly ever felt loved by their mothers, and 11 percent did not feel loved by their fathers.

In summary, it can be said with certainty that negative family relationships may be significant factors in the backgrounds of some male and female homosexuals, but certainly not in all. There is not sufficient evidence to assert that parental relationships might be the primary cause of homosexuality.

Social Learning Theories   Behaviorists would emphasize that homosexuality is simply the result of learning. According to behavioral theories, psychological conditioning through reinforcement or punishment of early sexual thoughts, feelings, and behavior is what influences sexual preference. Thus, a person may lean toward homosexuality if he or she has unpleasant heterosexual experiences and rewarding same-sex experiences. A girl who is raped, or whose first attempts at heterosexual intercourse are quite painful, might turn to homosexuality. Parents who wanted a boy and who dress their girl in boys' clothing and encourage masculine interests and behavior might be encouraging lesbianism.

The behaviorist view explains why some people change their sexual orientation from heterosexual to homosexual and back again. A person in an unhappy heterosexual marriage may turn to a friend of the same sex for comfort. A positive sexual relationship may develop from this friendship. If that relationship sours, the person may enter into another heterosexual partnership (Masters and Johnson, 1979).

In another study, 686 homosexual men, 293 homosexual women, 337 heterosexual men, and 140 heterosexual women were interviewed intensively for three to five hours (Bell, Weinberg, and Hammersmith, 1981). The researchers tried to gain data that would uncover the causes of homosexuality. They then analyzed the data statistically through "path analysis" to establish cause and effect. *They could not find solid support for psychoanalytical, social learning, or various sociological theories, so they came to the conclusion that homosexuality must have a biological basis.*

The conclusion is that no one knows for certain the causes of homosexuality. There are a number of plausible causative factors, but no single factor emerges as a consistent reason. Perhaps one explanation may be that there are many different types of homosexuals. They are not a homogeneous group, so what contributes to one person's homosexuality may not contribute to another's (Robinson and Dalton, 1986). The tendency in some people seems to be there from

HIGHLIGHT

Homosexual Life-Styles

Not all homosexuals are alike or live alike, any more than do heterosexuals. Bell, Weinberg, and Hammersmith (1981) studied 979 homosexual men and women and found that about 75 percent of them could be assigned to one of the following categories based on established statistical criteria:

Close-coupled homosexuals had a close relationship with one partner, regarded themselves as "happily married," had few problems, and appeared to be the best adjusted of the group.

Open-coupled homosexuals lived in a stable relationship with one person but had many outside sexual partners. This is most prevalent among males.

Functional homosexuals were not coupled, had a high number of sexual partners, and little interest in settling down. They tended to be young, with a high degree of sexual interest.

Dysfunctional homosexuals were not coupled, had a large number of sexual partners, and were very active sexually, but had major problems with their sexual performance, and often had serious emotional and social problems and were sexually dissatisfied with their way of life.

Asexual homosexuals were loners, either by choice or because they could not find a partner, were "closet" homosexuals, seldom interacting with other homosexuals, and tended to be less exclusively homosexual.

childhood. In most cases, the children of homosexuals do not grow up to be homosexuals, indicating that modeling and imitation alone cannot account for individuals becoming homosexuals or heterosexuals. Most homosexuals do not choose their sexual preference. In fact, many deny it and fight against it for years because they are afraid of public and personal recrimination. In all probability, there is no single cause of homosexuality.

Adjustments

In one study of gay male adolescents, "coming out" was conceptualized in three stages: *sensitization; awareness of guilt, denial, confusion, and shame;* and *acceptance* (Newman and Muzzonigro, 1993). Some homosexuals accept their orientation fairly readily. Others go through a period of denial after which they accept their preferences, establish close friendships with their own sex, and are much happier and psychologically better adjusted because of it. The unhappiest are those who are never able to accept their condition, but lead separated, secretive life-styles, seeking anonymous sexual encounters in public restrooms or other places. They are often isolated, lonely, unhappy people—terribly afraid of rejection—even by other homosexuals. Lesbians are usually better able than male homosexuals to establish close friendships, because society is more tolerant of women living and being seen together.

Some adolescents are unable to move beyond labeling themselves as gay or lesbian and to become involved in the gay/lesbian community. Gay and lesbian adolescents negotiate the extent and nature of the costs and rewards associated with expressing a lesbian/gay identity. In other words, when the perceived benefits outweigh the perceived costs, identity expression is fostered. Alternatively, when the perceived costs of identity expression outweigh the perceived benefits, gay and lesbian youths will remain fixated, subject to identity confusion and otherwise psychologically disadvantaged (Waldner-Haugrud and Magruder, 1996).

Sex Knowledge and Sex Education

With the increase of out-of-wedlock pregnancies and of the incidence of HIV, it becomes even more important for adolescents to receive adequate sex education (Coleman, 1995; Hechinger,

Some adolescent homosexuals readily accept their sexual orientation. Others do so after a period of denial. Still others are never able to accept their preference. Becoming involved in the gay/lesbian community may help encourage the expression of their identity.

1992). Where do adolescents receive their information about sex?

Sources of Sex Information

Researchers surveyed 700 male and female respondents ranging in age from 9 to 73 years of age to determine, among other things, the source of their sexuality information. About a fourth of the respondents said their primary source of information was siblings; about 20 percent said their primary source was teachers; about 12 percent said their primary source was parents; about 5 percent said their primary source was relatives; and about a third of the respondents said they received their sexual information from other sources. (e.g., friends, mass media, literature, and miscellaneous sources) (Ansuini, Fiddler-Woite, and Woite, 1996).

In another study, 288 students from five public schools were surveyed to determine their sources of sexual information, their sexual knowledge, and sexual interests (Davis and Harris, 1982). The students ranged in age from 11 to 18 and were in grades 6 through 12. A little over one-third were White, a little over one-third were Hispanic, and about one-fourth were Native American (Navajo and Pueblo). Sixty-four percent were female and thirty-six percent male. A little over one-half were from rural schools in small communities, and the remainder were from urban schools in large communities. Table 9.2 shows the percentages of students receiving information from different sources.

As predicted, friends were the most frequently cited source of sexual information followed by schools, books and magazines, and parents. The majority of students received a little information from television and movies, but less than 8 percent received any information from church. Surprisingly, brothers and sisters and doctors and nurses were named by only half the students as sources of information about sex. Females reported receiving more information about sex from their parents and less from movies than did males. Older students were likely to receive more information from friends and less from movies, indicating a greater freedom among older students to discuss sexual topics.

TABLE 9.2   Percentages of Students Receiving Information from Different Sources

Source	A Lot	A Little	None
Friends	43.5	47.4	9.1
School	36.0	47.7	16.3
Books/magazines	25.5	51.0	23.4
Parents	26.1	50.2	23.7
Movies	18.6	51.9	29.5
Television	9.8	55.8	34.4
Brothers/sisters	20.3	32.9	46.9
Doctors/nurses	15.1	33.8	51.1
Church	2.8	4.6	92.6
Other	15.2	16.6	68.3

Source: S. M. Davis and M. B. Harris, "Sexual Knowledge, Sexual Interests, and Sources of Sexual Information of Rural and Urban Adolescents from Three Cultures," *Adolescence, 17* (Summer 1982): 478. Reprinted by permission.

Of the three ethnic groups, White students appeared to be the most knowledgeable and Native Americans the least. Females indicated a greater knowledge of sexual facts and terms than did males and a greater degree of interest than males in a number of terms. Older subjects scored higher on tests of sexual knowledge, indicating that formal or informal sex education was taking place. They also were more interested in terms such as *pregnancy* and *birth control,* reflecting their greater likelihood of having intercourse (Davis and Harris, 1982). These findings are in keeping with other studies that show students' interests are in intercourse, birth control, venereal disease, and pregnancy (McCormick, Folcik, and Izzo, 1985).

One study surveyed the role of physicians in counseling adolescents about sexuality, including abstinence. More than 60 percent of the physicians recorded regularly addressing the issues of contraception, menstruation, STD prevention, HIV prevention, and responsible sexual activity. About one-fourth of the surveyed physicians regularly counseled adolescents regarding sexual abstinence. One-fifth to one-third of the physicians rarely or never counseled adolescent patients regarding nocturnal emissions, ways of handling sexual pressure, normal sexual response, male sexual response, female sexual response, masturbation, sexual fantasies, homosexuality, rape prevention, incest, age at first intercourse, and the female menstrual cycle. However, most of these physicians were willing to counsel adolescent clients about these sexual topics and others if they were directly requested by the patient. None of the physicians felt very effective in their counseling and some agreed they would be helped by additional training themselves (Patton, Kolasa, West, and Irons, 1995).

The Role of Parents

If, as some people maintain, the place of sex education is in the home, then parents are not doing a very good job (Brock and Jennings, 1993). One study of over 500 adolescents and their mothers indicated that whatever parent-child communication about sex took place had no effect on the teenagers' subsequent sexual and contraceptive behavior (Newcomer and Udry, 1985). One reason may have been that some of the discussion was superficial. There was a need for more in-depth discussion. In one study, adolescents who reported open communication and satisfaction with family interactions indicated significantly more sex education in the home (Baldwin and Baranoski, 1990). In another study, college students who perceived their parents as friendly and attentive communicators reported less sexual activity in junior high school and in college than did students whose parents were contentious, argumentative, and dramatic communicators. Thus, the style of communication and the overall feelings between parents and adolescents are important in influencing adolescent sexual behavior (Mueller and Powers, 1990). Other research found that the influence of parents on adolescent sexual behavior was mixed (Sanders and Millis, 1988; Scales, 1986). Since these findings were inconsistent, there is a need for longitudinal studies to document the effects of early communication on later sexual behavior (Green and Sollie, 1989).

Most research reveals that parents are an important source of transmission of values and attitudes and do have an influence on adolescent attitudes and behavior, especially by way of example (Fisher, 1986). As far as providing formal sex education is concerned, however, many parents are deficient. There are a number of reasons for this.

1. *Some parents are too embarrassed to discuss the subject, or they deal with it in negative ways.* Many parents have been brought up to feel that all sex is wrong and dirty, and they become intensely uncomfortable any time the subject is mentioned. Some have an irrational fear of sex, generated by years of repressive and negative teaching. If they do discuss sex, the messages they give their children are negative ones, which interfere with sexual satisfaction. Some adolescents also feel embarrassed talking to their parents, so do not discuss the subject with them.

2. *Some parents have difficulty overcoming the incest barrier between themselves and their adolescents.* The taboo on parent-child sexual behavior may be so strong that any verbalization about sex in this relationship becomes almost symbolic incest. It has been found that even in families where there has been some communication about sex with young children, this communication drops as the children approach adolescence.

3. *Some parents are uninformed and do not know how to explain sexuality to their children.* In one study, 90 adolescents and 73 mothers were asked to define in their own words seven terms related to sexual development: *ejaculation, hormones, menstruation, copulation, puberty, semen,* and *wet dreams.* Results suggested that the mothers were not able to adequately define the sexual development terms and thus were poorly prepared to teach their children about sex or to reenforce information the adolescents learned in school (Hockenberry-Eaton, Richman, Dilorio, Rivero, and Maibach, 1996). One mother remarked, "I don't understand menstruation myself, so how can I explain it to my daughter?"

4. *Some parents are afraid that knowledge will lead to sexual experimentation; they do not tell their children because they want to keep them innocent.* The old argument, "Keep them ignorant and they won't get into trouble," couldn't be more wrong. Youths who are uninformed are more likely to get into

trouble. There is no evidence to show that sexual knowledge, per se, leads to sexual experimentation. There is a lot of evidence, however, to show that ignorance leads to trouble.

5. *Some parents tell too little too late.* Most parents are shocked to learn that the time to explain the basic physical facts about reproduction is *before* puberty. Most children ought to know about fertilization and how it takes place in humans by ages 7 to 9. For some children, this is too late; they ask questions during the preschool period that demand a simple, honest explanation. The parent who says "Wait until you are older" is running the risk of telling too little too late. The time to explain about menstruation is before the girl starts her menses, not after. As one boy said, "All the way through my childhood, whenever I asked questions about sex, my parents would say: 'Wait until you're older.' Now that I'm 18 and I ask them something, they remark. 'For Pete's sake, you're 18 years old, you ought to know that!' "

6. *Some parents set a negative example at home.* It is not just the words parents use that are important; it is also the lives they lead and the examples they set (Strouse and Fabes, 1985). One adolescent remarked, "My parents never came out and actually told me the facts of life. . . . But indirectly they told me plenty. They made me feel that sex was dirty and something to be ashamed of or embarrassed about."

Parents can do a better job by becoming better informed and more comfortable when talking about sexuality. Reading or attending classes in human sexuality will help parents tremendously. The schools can play an important role by teaching parents so they can do a better job of teaching their children (Alexander, 1984). Parents can also help start and support family life and sex education programs in the schools to supplement their own efforts.

The Role of Public Schools

Nationwide surveys indicate that about 85 percent of parents favor sex education in the schools (Kenney, Guardado, and Brown, 1989). Because so many parents do an inadequate job and adolescents need more reliable sources of information than peers, the public schools have a responsibility. There are several reasons why.

1. *Family life and sex education are natural parts of numerous courses already offered to adolescents.*

Sex education classes in the public schools provide adolescents with reliable information. Here, students cover a lesson on HIV and AIDS.

Biology courses should cover the reproductive system when other bodily systems are discussed; not to do so is hypocritical. It is difficult to study sociology or social problems without including a study of the family as the basic social unit or of social problems such as illegitimacy, early marriage, or divorce. Health education usually includes such topics as menstrual hygiene, masturbation, acne, venereal disease, and body odor. Home economics deals with parent-teen relationships, preparation for marriage, and child care and development. Literature courses may stimulate discussion about youths in today's world, moral values, interpersonal relationships, or other topics properly belonging to family life and sex education. Discussions of sex or sex behavior are hard to avoid in a course in the modern novel or in poetry. Even the study of the Bible as literature contains a sexual aspect. Thus, if existing courses are taught honestly, family life and sex education will have a place in many of them.

2. *Preparing youths for happy marriage and responsible parenthood is an important educational goal.* It is certain that having a happy marriage and being a good parent are among the most important personal goals of the average parent. If the school does not prepare youths for this goal, as well as for a vocation, is it preparing them for living as well as for making a living?

3. *The school is the only social institution that reaches all youths and therefore has a unique opportunity to reach youths who need family life and sex education the most* (Dryfoos, 1984). Some parents do an excellent job, but the majority of parents do not. Are their children to be deprived of proper information, attitudes, examples, and guidance? One would hope not. Other community youth-service organizations such as churches and scouts have a responsibility also, for family life and sex education of youths is a community responsibility. None of these groups, however, reaches as many youths, especially those of low socioeconomic status, as does the school.

4. *The school, as the professional educational institution, is or can be equipped to do a fine job.* This does not mean that all teachers are qualified to teach or that the individual school already has the expertise and resources to develop a program, but it does mean that the school is able to train teachers (Schultz and Boyd, 1984), develop curricula, and provide the necessary resources once priorities and needs are established. (For more information on sex education in the schools, see Arcus, 1986; Harriman, 1986; Leigh, Loewen, and Lester, 1986; Marsman and Herold, 1986; and Silverstein and Buck, 1986).

Availability in the Schools

Numerous public opinion polls have shown that sex education in the schools has strong support (Rosoff, 1989), but to what extent are schools providing programs? A national study of sex education at all grade levels in large school districts (cities over 100,000 population) revealed that 67 percent of districts with elementary grades, 75 percent of those with junior high school grades, and 76 percent of those with senior high school grades provided sex education to some portion of their students (Sonenstein and Pittman, 1984). Of those offering sex education, 61 percent of the districts offered sex education at all three levels. Of those elementary districts offering sex education, all said they integrated the material into other curriculum subjects, but 60 percent provided only five or fewer hours of instruction. Of those secondary districts offering sex education, 73 percent of junior high and 89 percent of senior high districts provided six or more hours of instruction. Of those offering sex education, 11 percent of junior high and 16 percent of senior high districts offered separate sex education courses. Of those with programs, over 40 percent made participation compulsory at all grade levels.

There is a difference, however, between offering *sex education* and *comprehensive sex education*. Table 9.3 indicates the total percentages of large city schools that include a particular topic in their sex education curriculum, by comprehensiveness of the program. Column 1 lists the proportions of

TABLE 9.3 Percentages of Large-City School Districts That Include a Particular Topic in Their Sex Education Curriculum, by Comprehensiveness of Program

Topic	1 Topic Discussed	2 75% Enrollment	3 In-Depth Discussion	4 Topic Introduced before Ninth Grade
Physiological				
Changes at puberty	71.5	43.7	36.8	36.6
Physical differences	72.1	45.4	32.2	31.4
Sexually transmitted diseases	71.5	44.3	37.4	27.3
Responsibilities of parenthood	69.3	43.7	32.8	17.4
Pregnancy and childbirth	67.0	42.0	31.0	23.3
Interpersonal issues				
Love relationships and commitment	65.4	41.4	28.7	16.9
Sexual feelings and attraction	68.2	42.0	26.4	20.3
Consequences of teen pregnancy	66.4	40.8	27.0	18.6
Communication with opposite sex	63.1	40.8	23.6	18.0
Intercourse and pregnancy probability	65.4	41.4	25.3	21.5
Teen marriage	65.9	40.8	25.3	7.6
Personal values	63.1	39.7	28.7	19.8
Sexual decision making	64.2	41.4	26.4	18.6
Contraception and family planning				
Most likely time in cycle for pregnancy	65.9	40.8	19.0	14.0
Family planning sources	63.7	41.4	19.0	7.0
Communication with parents	62.0	37.0	19.0	16.3
Resistance to peer pressure for sex	64.8	40.8	23.6	18.6
Contraceptives	62.0	39.1	24.7	11.0
Media messages about sex	61.5	40.8	18.4	11.0
Controversial issues				
Rape and sexual abuse	63.7	41.4	18.4	8.7
Masturbation	56.4	37.0	5.7	1.7
Abortion	54.7	34.5	8.0	2.3
Gynecologic examination	58.1	35.1	7.5	2.3
Homosexuality	52.0	35.1	6.3	2.9

Source: Reprinted with permission from F. L. Sonenstein and K. J. Pittman, "The Availability of Sex Education in Large City School Districts," *Family Planning Perspectives, 16,* 1984, pp. 19–25.

School Birth Control Clinics

Deeply disturbed by the rising tide of teenage pregnancies and the threat of AIDS, some high school administrators now offer contraceptive education programs and contraceptive services in birth control clinics right on the school premises. To many, the idea of a school-based clinic that deals with sex is shocking. Critics argue that to provide such services is condoning teenage sex, but proponents say that family planning programs in high schools are responses to desperate situations.

A clinic was established in DuSable High School in Chicago because more than one-third of 1,000 female students in the high school became pregnant each year (Plummer, 1985). The high rate of pregnancies resulted in a 50 percent dropout rate from school. One function of the clinic is to keep pregnant girls in school to continue their educations. The DuSable High School clinic is just one of many school-based clinics that have been estab-

lished across the United States. Dozens of other cities have established similar programs. This approach is pragmatic, because it is based on the realization that adolescents can at least be protected from unwanted pregnancy and from sexually transmitted disease, even if they are not going to reduce their sexual activity (Zellman, 1982).

Research is beginning to filter in to determine the extent to which such clinics are fulfilling their purposes. One investigation of six school-based clinics indicated that the presence of the clinics had little effect on the initiation or frequency of sexual activity, but they had some modest effect on reducing schoolwide pregnancy rates. Recommendations included the need to give priority to pregnancy and AIDS prevention, to reach more sexually active students, to make contraceptives available at the clinics, and to emphasize condom use and male responsibility (Kirby, Waszak, and Ziegler, 1991).

large city school districts discussing the topics at any grade. More than one-half of the districts discussed all of the topics. Column 2 gives the percentage discussing each topic, with 75 percent of the students enrolled. Using this criterion, 35 to 45 percent of the districts covered each topic. The third column shows the percentage of districts that discuss each topic, with 75 percent enrollment and for at least one class period. When this measure of comprehensiveness is used, only 6 to 37 percent of the districts discuss the topic. The fourth column shows the proportion of all districts discussing each topic, with 75 percent enrollment, for at least one class period, with the topics introduced before the ninth grade. Using this criterion, an average of 27 percent of districts cover topics in the physiological cluster, 18 percent cover interpersonal issues, 13 percent cover pregnancy avoidance, and only a few cover the most controversial topics. Thus, comprehen-

sive discussions before the ninth grade are quite rare.

Another nationwide study of sex education in public schools in grades 7 through 12 revealed a gap between what teachers thought should be taught at different grade levels and what was actually being taught (Forrest and Silverman, 1989). Virtually all teachers thought that sex education should cover sexual decision making, abstinence, birth control methods, prevention of pregnancy, and AIDS and other sexually transmitted diseases. Over 82 percent of the schools covered these topics but most not until the ninth or tenth grade. Teachers thought the topics should be covered by grades 7 or 8 at the latest. Only about half the schools provided information about sources of birth control. The major problems teachers faced in providing sex education were negative pressure from parents, the community, or the school administration (Reis and Seidly, 1989).

PERSONAL ISSUES

Education for Abstinence

Because of the seriousness and complexity of the teenage pregnancy problem and the problem of increase in transmission of AIDS, several programs have been developed to try to prevent adolescent pregnancy by teaching abstinence. Girls' Clubs of America developed a comprehensive model consisting of two components. Programs are designed for 12- to 14-year-old girls. The programs' two components were *Willpower/Won'tpower* and *Growing Together. Willpower/Won'tpower* addresses the social and peer pressures that lead girls into early sexual behavior and focuses on building skills that help young teens deal with these issues. This component was offered in cycles of six sessions.

Growing Together is designed to enable parents and daughters to communicate comfortably with each other about human sexuality. This component included five sessions, the first of which was for parents only.

In the case of *Growing Together*, during the year it was studied, nonparticipants were two and a half times more likely than the participants to initiate sexual intercourse. The weight of evidence indicated that participation in *Growing Together* delayed the initiation of sexual intercourse among these young teens. In the case of *Willpower/Won'tpower*, those who participated in the program for the longest period of time were less likely to

initiate sexual intercourse than those who participated in the program for a lesser period of time (Postrado and Nicholson, 1992).

Another review of five adolescent pregnancy-prevention programs showed that all five emphasized abstinence or delay of sexual initiation, training in decision-making and negotiation skills, and education on sexuality and contraceptives. Four of the five directly or indirectly provided access to contraceptive services. Four programs measured changes in sexual initiation among adolescents and had significant effects on that outcome, reducing the proportion of adolescents who initiated sexuality activity by as much as 15 percent; programs were most successful when they targeted younger adolescents. Three of these four programs also significantly increased rates of contraceptive use among participants. The most successful programs, which increased contraceptive use by as much as 22 percent, provided access to services targeted to adolescents who were younger and those who were not yet sexually experienced. Two programs significantly decreased the proportion of adolescents who become pregnant; these programs were the two that were most active in providing access to contraceptive services (Frost and Forrest, 1995).

SUMMARY

1. The latest survey of sexual behavior, called the National Health and Social Life Survey (NHSLS), was conducted in 1992. It shows that half of all African American men have had intercourse by age 15, half of all Hispanic men by age 16½, and half of all White men by age 17. Half of all African American women have had intercourse by about age 17, and half of White women and Hispanic women have had intercourse by about age 18. By age 22, about 90 percent of each group has had intercourse.

2. When asked why they had intercourse the first time, 51 percent of the men attributed it to curiosity and readiness for sex, and 25 percent answered affection for their partner. Among the women, it was the reverse: About half cited affection for their partner, and about 25 percent attributed it to curiosity and readiness for sex.

3. Most sexually active young people show no signs of having large numbers of partners. More than half the men and women between ages 18 and 24 in

1992 had had just one sex partner in the previous year, and 11 percent had had none.

4. Premarital sexual behavior may be correlated with age, race, religion, having a boyfriend or girlfriend, early dating and steady dating, age at first intercourse, liberality, age at menarche, sexual attractiveness, parental standards and relationships, peer standards, parent versus peer standards, sibling influence, gender, drug usage, father absence, divorce and reconstituted families, parents' education, education expectations, and socioeconomic status.

5. A study of 240 Hispanic and African American adolescent females from 12 to 18 years of age in New York City schools revealed that *Hispanic adolescent females of all ages were more likely to be virgins than were African American adolescent females.* The study showed that 80 percent of Hispanic females aged 12 to 15 were virgins, compared with 59 percent of African Americans; 54 percent of Hispanic females aged 16 to 18 were virgins, compared with 29 percent of African Americans. The average age of first coitus for Hispanic females was 15; for African Americans, age 14.

6. Both virgin and nonvirgin Hispanic females tended to come from single-parent households (virgins, 79 percent; nonvirgins, 67 percent), to be Catholic (virgins, 80 percent; nonvirgins, 78 percent), and to have mothers who did not graduate from high school (virgins, 58 percent; and nonvirgins, 62 percent). Over half of all the households of both groups (virgins, 54 percent; nonvirgins, 60 percent) were on public assistance. Among both African Americans and Hispanics, academically motivated adolescents were less likely to engage in sexual activities at an early age.

7. Almost all adolescent boys and at least twice as many males as girls masturbate regularly. The practice is not harmful and should be considered normal.

8. Although the preferred standard of sexual activity among youths is permissiveness with affection, many adolescents engage in coitus without affection or commitment. Generally speaking, women are less likely to have sex without affection than are men. There is some evidence that both men and women are preoccupied with the race toward sexual intercourse and achievement of orgasm, leaving affection and intimacy sidetracked.

9. Adolescent sexuality is often driven by emotional needs for affection, companionship, acceptance, confirmation of masculinity or femininity, bolstered self-esteem, expression of anger, or escape from boredom. There is a risk that adolescents suffer from increased depression, lower self-esteem, decreased intimacy, and diminished sexual satisfaction.

10. Not all adolescents have the same standards. Our society is pluralistic; it accepts not one but a number of different standards of sexual behavior. These standards may be grouped into different categories: abstinence, double standard, sex with affection, commitment and responsibility, sex with affection and commitment but without responsibility, sex with affection and without commitment, sex without affection, and sex with ulterior motives.

11. Both men and women can be victims of unwanted sexual aggression. Date rape is not uncommon.

12. Sexual harassment of pupils by high school teachers is not uncommon.

13. Data from the NSFG in 1988 revealed that only 35 percent of 15- to 19-year-old females, or their partners, used any method of contraception at first intercourse. About one-third were currently using contraceptives.

14. Getting sexually active teenagers to use effective contraceptives is a huge challenge. There are various reasons why contraceptives are not used: fear and anxiety, ignorance, lack of maturity and responsibility, ambivalent feelings about sex, a desire to get pregnant, and rape. The availability of contraceptives does not increase promiscuity—because, on the average, adolescents have been active for months before going to family planning centers—but it does decrease unwanted pregnancy.

15. Authorities are concerned with the spread of sexually transmitted diseases, especially AIDS, among adolescents who are at high risk because they are sexually active and poor contraceptive users.

16. With so many adolescents being sexually active and not using reliable means of birth control, the number of premarital pregnancies among 15- to 19-year-olds has skyrocketed to over 1 million a year. Slightly less than one-half are terminated by miscarriages, stillbirths, or therapeutic abortions. The remaining babies are born alive. About 248,000 of these mothers marry hastily before their babies are born, leaving 368,000 babies born out of wedlock each year.

17. There are six theories for why the rate of unmarried pregnancies among U.S. teenagers is so high: reproductive ignorance hypothesis, psychological needs, welfare hypothesis, parental-role/supervision hypothesis, social norms, and physiological hypothesis.

18. From most points of view, teenage pregnancy is a tragedy, creating a host of problems.

19. In one study, 95 percent of African American teenage mothers had their own mother or a surrogate mother involved in cases of unwed pregnancy and childbirth.

20. Contrary to common myths, many adolescent fathers remain involved during and after the pregnancy and have feelings toward the mother and baby.

21. There are three major categories of theories of the causes of homosexuality: biological theories, psychoanalytical theories, and social learning theories. One biological theory states that one bundle of neurons in the hypothalamus of homosexual men is smaller than in heterosexuals, thus resulting in loss of sexual interest in female partners. Another theory suggests that the levels of male and female hormones are different in homosexuals, or that their bodies respond differently to changes in hormonal levels. Homosexuality may have a hereditary base. Psychoanalytical theory says that homosexuality is caused by problems in parent-child relationships in the family. Social learning theory emphasizes that homosexuality is the result of learning. Many gays suffer painful conflict in accepting or not accepting their sexual orientation.

22. In all probability, there is no single cause of homosexuality.

23. Where do adolescents get their sex knowledge? Some 700 male and female respondents, ranging in age from 9 to 73 years, were surveyed to determine, among other things, the source of their sexuality information. About 25 percent of the respondents said their primary source of information was siblings; about 20 percent said their primary source was teachers; about 12 percent said their primary source was parents; about 5 percent said their primary source was relatives; and about one-third of the respondents said they received their sexual information from other sources (e.g., friends, mass media, literature, and miscellaneous sources). In another study, 288 students from five public schools were surveyed to determine their sources of sexual information, their sexual knowledge, and sexual interests (Davis and Harris, 1982). The students ranged in age from 11 to 18 and were in grades 6 through 12. As predicted, friends were the most frequently cited source of sexual information followed by schools, books, magazines, and parents. The majority of students received a little information from television and movies, but less than 8 percent received any information from church. Surprisingly, brothers and sisters and doctors and nurses were named by only half the students as sources of information about sex.

24. Students are interested in intercourse, birth control, sexually transmitted disease, and pregnancy.

25. Parents have an important role in sex education, but the style of communication and the overall feelings between parents and adolescents are important in influencing adolescent behavior.

26. Parents are not doing a good job of sex education for various reasons: they are too embarrassed, they have difficulty overcoming the incest barrier, they are uninformed, they are afraid knowledge will lead to sexual experimentation, they tell too little too late, or they set a negative example at home.

27. Some 85 percent of parents support sex education in the schools. National studies of large school districts indicate that between 67 and 76 percent of districts offer some sex education to some percentage of their students. Of those offering sex education, 61 percent offer it at all grade levels.

28. The programs in elementary school are usually integrated into other curriculum subjects, but 60 percent provide five or fewer hours of instruction. The higher the grade level, the more hours are offered and the more comprehensive the program becomes.

29. A minority of junior and senior high districts offer separate sex education courses. Only about one-fourth of large city school districts offer comprehensive programs, discussing each topic, with 75 percent enrollment, for at least one class period, earlier than the ninth-grade level. Research of exemplary programs reveals that they accomplish their objectives.

30. There is a gap between what teachers think should be taught at different grade levels and what is actually being taught. Most teachers feel that sex education should cover sexual decision making, abstinence, birth control methods, prevention of pregnancy, and AIDS and other STDs by the seventh or eighth grade at the latest.

31. Some schools have established birth control clinics at the high school as one means of helping to combat teenage pregnancies.

32. A number of schools have developed programs to teach abstinence as the best method of practicing safe sex.

KEY TERMS

coitus **197**

date rape **206**

depersonalization or derealization **205**

heterosexuality **219**

homosexuality **219**

masturbation **200**

pluralistic society **203**

THOUGHT QUESTIONS

1. What changes have you seen in sexual attitudes and behavior since you were in high school?
2. Do parents have any influence over the sexual behavior of their adolescents? Why or why not?
3. What are some myths about masturbation that you heard while you were growing up?
4. Has the increase in premarital sexual intercourse been accompanied by lessening of emotional intimacy, loving feelings, and decreasing commitment in relationships? Support your answer.
5. Among the seven categories of ethics mentioned in this chapter, which ones do you feel predominate in our society today, especially among adolescents?
6. Do you feel that unwanted sexual aggression has become a problem in dating relationships? Why or why not?
7. Was sexual harassment by teachers a problem in the high school that you attended? Explain.
8. Why don't more sexually active adolescents use effective contraceptives? What can be done to improve this situation?
9. What do you think about high schools offering family planning services, including distribution of condoms to students as a prevention of sexually transmitted disease and unwanted pregnancy?
10. Has the AIDS epidemic made any differences in the sexual behavior of your friends? Why or why not?
11. What can be done to reduce the risky sexual behavior of adolescents?
12. What can be done to reduce the number of unwed pregnancies?
13. Should adolescents marry because of pregnancy? Why or why not?
14. What are the alternatives to abortion for teenage pregnancy? What do you think of them?
15. What are your attitudes and feelings about homosexuality?
16. Do you know any gay men or lesbians? What are the most serious problems they face? What do you think about discharging individuals from the armed forces because of sexual orientation?
17. Comment on the statement: "Adolescents' primary source of sex information is their friends." How do you feel about this?
18. Did your parents tell you about sex when you were growing up? What did they tell you? How did they tell you?
19. Should the public school play a role in assisting parents with sex education? Why or why not? What role should the school play?
20. Should sex education in the school be compulsory? For what grade level? Who should teach it?
21. Did you have sex education in school? Comment on the program.
22. What do you think of trying to prevent adolescent pregnancy by teaching abstinence in public school programs of sex education?

SUGGESTED READING

D'Augelli, A. R., and Patterson, C. J. (Eds.). (1995). *Lesbian, Gay, and Bisexual Identities over the Lifespan*. New York: Oxford University Press.

Horowitz, R. (1995). *Teen Mothers: Citizens for Dependents?* Chicago: University of Chicago Press.

Leeming, F. C., Dwyer, W., and Oliver, D. P. (Eds.). (1996). *The Issues in Adolescent Sexuality: Readings from the* Washington Post *Writers' Group*. Boston: Allyn and Bacon.

Mathes, P. G., and Irby, B. J. (1993). *Teen Pregnancy and Parenting Handbook*. Champaign, IL: Research Press.

Millstein, S. G., Petersen, A. C., and Nightingale, E. O., (Eds.), (1993). *Promoting the Health of Adolescents: New Directions for the Twenty-First Century.*

Sander, J. (1991). *Before Their Time: Four Generations of Teen-age Mothers.* New York: Harcourt Brace Jovanovich.

Sugar, N. (Ed.). (1984). *Adolescent Parenthood.* New York: S. P. Medical and Scientific Books.

10

Adolescent Society, Culture, and Subculture

A careful sociological analysis of adolescents as an identifiable segment of the population makes a distinction between adolescent society and adolescent culture. *Adolescent society* refers to the structural arrangements of subgroups within an adolescent social system; in other words, it is the organized network of relationships and association among adolescents. *Adolescent culture* is the sum of the ways of living of adolescents; it refers to the body of norms, values, attitudes, and practices recognized and shared by members of the adolescent society as appropriate guides to action. Adolescent society consists of the interrelationships of adolescents within their social systems; their culture describes the way they think, behave, and live.

This chapter is concerned with both adolescent society and adolescent culture. We will focus on formal and informal adolescent societies but especially on the formal in-school groups and subsystems. Factors that influence the adolescent's social position in a formal group are outlined and discussed, along with the subculture that exists at the high school and college levels. The chapter

---

adolescent society structural arrangements of subgroups within an adolescent social system.

adolescent culture sum of the ways of living of adolescents.

concludes with a discussion of three important material aspects of adolescent culture—clothing, automobiles, and the telephone—and one non-material aspect of adolescent culture—music.

Culture and Society

Adolescent society is not one single, comprehensive, monolithic structure that includes all young people. There are usually numerous adolescent societies with wide variations among various age groups, socioeconomic levels, and ethnic or national backgrounds. Furthermore, adolescent societies are only vaguely structured. They exist without any formal, written codification and without traditions of organizational patterns. Individuals move into and out of each system within a few short years, contributing to structural instability. Each local group of adolescents is provincial, with few ties beyond school membership and the local clique. Although there are nationwide youth organizations, fan clubs, or competitive athletic events, most adolescent societies are primarily local, variably replicated in community after community.

The same cautions should be applied to adolescent culture. We cannot speak of U.S. adolescent culture as though it were a body of beliefs, values, and practices uniformly espoused by all youths throughout the country. Just as there are regional, ethnic, and class versions of the national adult culture, so are there variations in expression of adolescent culture among differing segments of the population. Adolescent culture is not homogeneous; the popular image of adolescent culture usually refers to urban, middle-class youths. Actually, there may be important deviations from this pattern. A more accurate description would convey that there are numerous versions of teenage culture expressed by various segments of youths who share some common elements of a general middle-class youth culture, but who participate selectively and in varying degrees in the activities of the organized adolescent society.

Before we can analyze adolescent society or culture, an important question needs to be answered: Are adolescent society and culture unique and different from those of the adult world?

The Adolescent Subculture

According to one point of view, *adolescent subculture* emphasizes conformity in the peer group and values that are contrary to adult values. This subculture exists primarily in the high school, where it constitutes a small society—one that has most of its important interactions within itself, maintaining only a few threads of connection with the outside adult society. This happens because children are set apart in schools, where they take on more and more extracurricular activities for longer periods of training. Segregated from the adult world, they develop subcultures with their own language, styles, and, most important, value systems that may differ from those of adults. As a result, the adolescent lives in a segregated society and establishes a subculture that meets with peer, but not adult, approval.

An opposite point of view is that the theory of an adolescent subculture, segregated and different from adult culture, is a myth. This view—that adolescents reflect adult values, beliefs, and practices—is substantiated by a number of studies. One study of 6,000 adolescents from 10 different nations revealed that, for the most part, adolescents are not alienated from their parents. Today's youths have great respect for their parents (Atkinson, 1988). When conflict *does* arise between the generations, it is usually centered in mundane, day-to-day issues such as noisiness, tidiness, punctuality, and living under the same roof, rather than on fundamental values such as honesty, perseverance, and concern for others.

A study examined the extent of agreement of adolescents' educational expectations with perceived maternal and paternal educational goals. Results showed that adolescents were more inclined to adopt the orientation if it was held by both parents than if it was supported by one parent but denied by the other (Smith, 1991). Consistency of parental expectations is an important factor in the socialization of adolescents and in their inclination to adopt the point of view of their parents.

From this point of view, the cultural norms shared by teenagers in the United States are not very different from those shared by adult Americans. (Were it otherwise, the indoctrinational efforts of parents, teachers, preachers, and others would constitute a pretty sorry record, and the theory of learning by imitation would be totally—instead of only partially—discredited.)

A False Dichotomy

The more studies that are conducted and the more closely these are analyzed, the more evident it becomes that adolescents choose to follow neither parents nor friends exclusively (Sebald, 1989). One explanation is that, in many instances, parents and friends are quite alike, so the peer group serves to reinforce rather than violate parental values. Adolescents tend to choose friends whose values are like their own (Whitbeck, Simons, Conger, and Lorenz, 1989); thus, there may be considerable overlap between the values of parents and peers because of commonalities in their backgrounds—social, economic, religious, educational, even geographic.

Also, there are considerable differences among adolescents, depending on their age and year in school, sex, socioeconomic status, and educational level. The younger adolescents are, the more likely they are to conform to parental values and mores and less likely to be influenced by peers. In one study of junior high school students, the students themselves said their parents were far more influential on their school adjustment than were peers (Berndt, Miller, and Park, 1989). A study of 272 9-, 10-, and 11-year-old boys and girls attending school in a large metropolitan area of the Southeast revealed a very high degree of conformity to parents (Thompson, 1985). The subjects were asked to indicate who was most likely to be influential on a variety of issues: parents, peers, or a best friend. Table 10.1 shows the results. As you can see, there were only four items on which parental opinions were not the major influence: choice of TV program to watch (8), choice of music (9), choice of reading material (10), and preference of sports (15). At the age of these adolescents, parents exerted the primary influence even on such matters as clothes and food. On those items in which there were significant sex differences, girls were more parent oriented than boys. However, peer influence increased for both sexes as the children got older.

Girls aged 12 to 15 are significantly more parent oriented than peer oriented. With increasing age, however, peer influence increases and parental influence declines. At the college level, freshmen show less disagreement with parents on certain social problems than do juniors or seniors. Apparently, increasing age and education widens the gap between parents and adolescents. One study found a considerable generation gap in values between 415 college students and 557 of their guardians, especially between youths who used marijuana and adults who did not (Traub and Dodder, 1988). College itself seems to have a liberalizing effect on students. It has also been found that adolescents with the highest IQs are more likely to be peer oriented than those with less intelligence.

Sex is also a significant variable in the degree of parent-peer orientation. Males tend to show more disagreement with parents than do females, but females who do disagree with parents tend to do so at younger ages, reflecting the earlier maturational age of females.

There are also socioeconomic status differences in parent-peer orientation. In general, upper-class adolescents are more closely supervised by parents and show less behavioral autonomy than lower-class adolescents. Low-socioeconomic-status adolescents are more likely to drop out of school to seek employment; they achieve earlier financial independence and are less subject to parental influence and control than their middle-class counterparts (Fasick, 1984).

Whether adolescents are more parent or peer oriented will depend partially on the degree of emotional closeness between parents and their children—that is, on the *affect* relationship. Youths who have a close emotional attachment to parents will more likely be parent oriented than will adolescents who are hostile toward parents or who reject them. In other words, the quality of adolescent-adult interaction is inversely related to peer-group involvement. Individual

adolescent subculture   values and way of life that are contrary to those found in adult society.

TABLE 10.1   Parent-Peer Influence on a Variety of Issues

Items	Parent (%)	Peer (%)	Best Friend (%)
1. Choice of clothes worn at school	72.2	25.9	1.9
2. Which clothes to buy	75.3	14.4	10.3
3. How late to stay out	95.9	3.0	1.1
4. Whether to attend party	85.3	8.5	6.2
5. Food preferences	93.4	5.1	1.5
6. How money is spent	69.4	14.0	16.6
7. How free time is spent	54.2	29.2	16.6
8. Which TV programs to watch	49.2	29.5	21.4
9. Choice of music	30.0	44.4	25.6
10. Choice of reading material	33.5	38.9	27.6
11. Manners of speech	70.9	14.0	15.1
12. Standards of conduct	83.0	13.7	3.3
13. Church attendance	92.4	4.4	3.2
14. Opinions of people	70.6	26.8	2.6
15. Preference of sports	46.0	31.6	22.4
16. Counsel of personal problems	70.6	7.3	22.1
17. Hairstyle	54.0	44.5	1.5
18. Choice of clubs	57.0	27.6	15.4

*Percentages of responses to categories parent, peer, and best friend by item.

Source: D. N. Thompson, "Parent-Peer Compliance in a Group of Preadolescent Youth," *Adolescence, 20* (1985): 501–508. Reprinted by permission.

adolescents differ markedly in their parent and peer orientations.

Distinctive Social Relationships and Culture

The adolescents' system of social relationships in which adolescents are involved is a highly distinctive one, not in the sense that it is the only world to which they are responsive but in the sense that it is a society over which adults exercise only partial control. Most modern teenagers are *both* typically confused adolescents in the adult world and relatively self-assured and status-conscious members of their peer groups—depending on the set of interactions being analyzed.

These same conclusions might be reached with respect to other aspects of adolescent cul-

ture, as well. Adolescents reflect many adult values and norms. One study of high school students revealed that they were primarily parent oriented in matters of finance, education, and career plans (Sebald, 1989). In contrast, activities that were intrinsic to peer life were heavily influenced by peer guidance. Certain aspects of their lives were distinguishable from U.S. adult culture because in these areas, adolescents can exercise some control and make their own decisions. Such matters as styles of dress, tastes in music, language, preference of popular movie and recording stars, dating customs and practices, and behavior at youth hangouts are particular to the adolescent subculture, for they may even sometimes run counter to adult preferences (Brown, 1982). It is therefore proper and possible to point to certain aspects of adolescent culture that are identifiable as separate, for they are developed and practiced predominantly by adolescents, sometimes in contradiction to adult norms. The further along adolescents are in school, the more likely they are to listen to peers rather than to parents in matters pertaining to social judgments.

Figure 10.1 shows that parent versus peer orientation has changed over the years. For both boys and girls, peer orientation was lowest in 1963, highest in 1976, and had declined by 1982. The year 1976 reflected the antiestablishment attitudes of the counterculture years when adult orientation was at an all-time low, and youth subculture orientation was at an all-time high. Since then, there has been a gradual lessening of the countercultural influence.

Two especially notable areas of adolescent-adult disagreement are drugs and sexual behavior (Brown, 1982). The primary reason adolescents and adults disagree in these matters is that cultural change has been so rapid and so great that youthful behavior *is* different from adult values. Take the attitude toward the smoking of mari-

juana, for example. In 1994, only 36 percent of adults aged 26 and over had ever used marijuana, in contrast to 43 percent of youths aged 18 to 25 (U.S. Bureau of the Census, 1996). This difference between adolescent and adult behavior indicates that youthful marijuana smoking is subcultural. Furthermore, those adolescents who are the most peer oriented are most likely to be users; those who are most parent oriented are less likely to use it.

Similarly, several attitude surveys have revealed that the sexual attitudes of adolescents are more liberal than those of adults (Thornton and Camburn, 1987). An attitude survey among 916 families in the Detroit area revealed that 65 percent of 18-year-old daughters and 77 percent of 18-year-old sons expressed approval of premarital sex for young people, but only 32 percent of the mothers approved (Thornton and Camburn, 1987). These youthful attitudes, therefore, may be regarded as subcultural. However, even though the study revealed that differences in attitudes existed, the mothers did exert some influence. Ado-

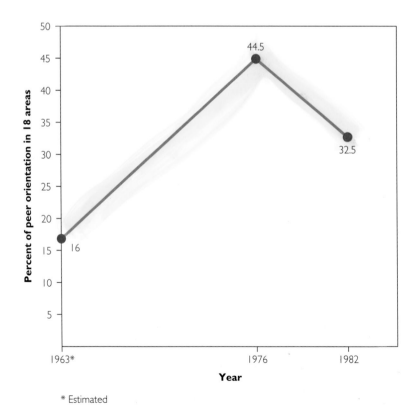

FIGURE 10.1   Average Percent of Peer Orientation Boys and Girls in Eighteen Areas, 1963, 1976, 1982

Source: Adapted from H. Sebald, "Adolescent Peer Orientation: Changes in the Support System during the Past Three Decades," *Adolescence, 25* (1989): 937–946. Used by permission.

lescents whose mothers were fundamentalist Protestants and those whose attended church regularly were significantly less likely than others to approve of premarital sexual intercourse.

Differences between parental and adolescent sexual attitudes vary somewhat according to age group and sex. Researchers have found that middle and late adolescents are more liberal in their sexual attitudes than early adolescents and also more liberal than their parents (Fisher and Hall, 1988). Early adolescents more likely reflect the sexual values of their parents. Boys are also more liberal than girls. Other studies have revealed that adolescents are more likely to incorporate the sexual values of their parents into their own value systems if there has been at least a moderate amount of parent-child dialogue about sex (Fisher, 1988).

Thus, whether a youthful subculture exists depends on what areas of concern are being examined. Overall, youth culture reflects adult culture. In specific areas, however, youth culture is a distinct subculture. The more rapid the social change, the more likely that youths' views become different from those of their parents. In this sense, certain aspects of adolescent life become subcultural—at least for a while.

Adolescent Societies

Like adult social structures, adolescent societies may be divided into two groups: formal and informal.

Formal Societies

Formal adolescent societies primarily include groups of in-school youths. Linkages with peers are determined by whether adolescents are enrolled in school, which school they are enrolled in, and which student organizations they join. The youth is identified with his or her particular school, team, and teachers. There are also out-of-school religious or youth groups, but, for the most part, only in-school youths participate in these activities. Therefore, any formal, well-defined social system to which adolescents belong is invariably related to in-school youth.

Informal Societies

Informal adolescent societies generally describe those loosely structured groups of out-of-school youths who get together socially but who have little opportunity to participate in a formally structured network of social relationships. These youths are too scattered and too involved in trying to find their places in adult society to be characterized as a separate adolescent society. One exception might be the adolescent street gang, which exists as a subsociety all its own.

This does not mean that all adolescents who remain in school are actively participating members of the organized adolescent society. Some adolescents remain in school but are really excluded from school life. Those who finally drop out of school have poor attendance records and rarely hold school office or have been active in school affairs. There are some who are socially outside "the society," though they may still be physically in it.

Age-Grade Societies

Adolescent societies are not only in-school but also *age-grade societies*—that is, adolescents are identified with a certain grade or class in school. This identification allows them to take certain courses, participate in certain school-sponsored activities (for which being a freshman or a senior, for instance, is a prerequisite for eligibility), or give or attend parent-permitted parties (for one's classmates). Freshmen compete with sophomores in sports or other events. Class membership is important in influencing friendship associations. Among pairs of friends, the one item that two members have in common far more often than any other—including religion, father's occupation, father's education, common leisure interests, grades in school, and others—is class in school.

Social Class and Status

Evidence continues to mount that an individual's acceptance by and active involvement in adolescent society are influenced by socioeconomic background (see Chapters 3 and 11). Social leadership scores of children in middle-class schools are higher than those of children in working-class schools, and the average scores for aggressive and withdrawn maladjustment are lower in middle-class than in working-class schools. Students from a higher social class far more often attend athletic events, dances, plays, and musical activities than those from the lower classes. Furthermore, youths who identify themselves with organized youth groups (e.g., Boy Scouts, Girl Scouts) and church or synagogue youth fellowship groups are predominantly from middle-class rather than lower-class homes.

This does not mean that every individual from a low-socioeconomic-status family is a social reject. Chapter 8 emphasizes that the youngster who has been given high self-esteem, even though from a poor home, will adjust more easily than another poor youngster with low self-esteem. Nevertheless, students whose fathers are college graduates (one clue to middle-class status) are far more likely than students whose fathers have only grade-school education to be identified as members of the leading crowd, to be chosen as friends, and to be viewed as people whom one would wish to be like.

In-School Subsystems

In-school adolescent societies also may be divided into distinct *subsystems* in which adolescents participate and in which they are assigned status positions. Furthermore, a particular student may be simultaneously involved in more than one of three distinct subsystems.

The Formal, Academic Subsystem

Adolescents are involved in a formal, academic subsystem shaped by the school administration, faculty, curriculum, classrooms, grades, and rules. Students in this group are concerned with intellectual pursuits, knowledge, achievement, and making the honor roll. In this system, seniors outrank freshmen, and the honor roll student outranks the D student, but the degree varies from school to school. In some schools, good students are rejected socially, especially if they also manifest undesirable personality traits; other students may refer to them as nerds, geeks, or losers. In re-

cent years, however, students have become increasingly aware of the emphasis on academic achievement in high schools and have been more willing to be identified with those getting good grades. The stereotypical bookworm is a social isolate who is still scorned. The very bright student who gets As without studying is admired and envied, especially if she or he also participates in extracurricular and athletic activities. Whether getting good grades has a positive value will depend on the particular social group. One reason for underachievement is negative peer pressure against studies.

The Semiformal, Activities Subsystem

Most youths are involved in a semiformal, activities subsystem, which includes all sponsored organizations and activities, such as athletics, drama, and departmental clubs. There are dozens of independent formal school organizations that may be subdivided further into subgroups, ranging from varsity basketball to the knitting club. Each group has a prestige ranking in the eyes of the students, which conveys a certain status rating to its members. Each group has specific offices, with the result that the individual's status is determined partly by which of these offices he or she holds. The amount of prestige that any position bestows depends on its rank within each respective group and the prestige standing of the group in relation to all other groups (Newman and Newman, 1987).

One study measured the effects of extracurricular activities on popularity in 6th, 7th and 8th grades. For males, basketball was strongly related to popularity in both large and small schools. In addition, football was strongly related to popularity in the large schools and track was moderately related in the small schools. There were also two nonathletic variables that were moderately related to popularity for males in the large schools: being on the honor roll and the level of the father's

---

age-grade society   adolescent societies composed of those at the same grade level.

subsystem   a smaller segment of adolescent society within the larger social system.

Involvement in extracurricular activities, such as athletics, can enhance the adolescent's development of sociability, popularity, competency, self-esteem, and commitment to goal achievement.

education. For females, cheerleading had the strongest relationship to popularity in both large and small schools. Several athletic activities also had significantly positive relationships to popularity. These activities included basketball, volleyball, and gymnastics. On the other hand, band and the mother's education had negative relationships to female popularity in the large schools. These findings provide strong evidence that certain school activities do contribute to significant gains in popularity. Male athletic activities and female cheerleading are the most visible activities at the middle school level and the ones most likely to have the strongest effect on students' popularity (Eder and Kinney, 1995).

Proponents of interscholastic sports competition for adolescents stress the many benefits, such as promotion of autonomy and self-definition, opportunities for sociability, and skill development. Teenagers who engage in athletic activities are more likely to be rated as competent and popular by peers. Adolescent boys consistently report that athletics are an important contributor to social status. Many studies have found positive associations between athletic participation and higher self-esteem, better grades, and higher vocational aspirations and success. One study examined the perceptions of social competence among adolescent participants in school-sponsored and independent sports (baseball and skateboarding). Subjects, aged 12 to 19 years, completed a ques-

tionnaire consisting of a social competence scale and miscellaneous items concerning school performance, sports commitment, and perceptions of adult attitudes. Perceptions of social competence were differentially related to the degree of sports involvement and perceived skill, but were not related to the social acceptability of the sport (Browne and Francis, 1993). Enjoyment in a sport is directly related to the years of participation in that sport and to the competence that developed. Mastery and high effort is conducive to enjoyment (Boyd and Yin, 1996).

Another study examined the educational effects of interscholastic athletic participation on a national, stratified, probability sample of African American and Hispanic boys and girls. In general, the study found that athletic participation enhanced popularity and contributed to greater involvement in extracurricular activities. Sports participation was generally unrelated to grades and standardized test scores. Depending on school location (i.e., urban, suburban, rural), athletic participation was significantly related to lower dropout rates for some minority youths. High school athletic participation was unrelated to educational expectations in the senior year. These findings show that high school athletic participation is a social resource for many minority youths but only a modest academic resource for others. Equally clear, however, is the fact that not all racial or ethnic groups reap the same benefits from sports. More importantly, the findings strongly suggest that high school sports should be considered only one of many institutional forces influencing the lives of minority youths in the United States (Melnick, Sabo, and Vanfossen, 1992).

Educators are not in complete agreement about the value of extracurricular activities and organizations in preparing students for adult life. Some feel that some students devote too much time to extracurricular activities or to sports participation, to the detriment of their academic work (Snyder and Spreitzer, 1992). The most common reason that students list for participation in out-of-school activities is entertainment. They also cite the need for self-assertion and for belonging to a group (Bergin, 1989). However, those who participate in extracurricular high school activities have also been found to be those most involved in adult voluntary organizations and most politically active 15 years after graduation. Many high school athletes have career ambitions to become professional athletes, but fewer than 2 percent of those participating in high school sports will become professional athletes (Lee, 1983). At any rate, participation in athletics is certainly one contribution to social acceptability in the average high school (Williams, 1983).

As students go through college, those who are able to make athletic teams begin to reap tangible benefits. Not only do they enjoy financial benefits and a superior social status while in college but they are also more socially mobile and achieve superior economic levels and business success when they get out. An investigation of adult males who had played football at Notre Dame revealed that "first team football players experienced greater income mobility in later life than second team and reserve players, and first team ballplayers were overrepresented as top ranking executives in their companies" (34 percent were top executives). This success was achieved despite the fact that fewer ballplayers earned graduate degrees than did other students (Sack and Thiel, 1979).

The Friendship Subsystem

Adolescent students may be involved in an informal network of friendship subsystems that operate primarily within the boundaries of the school world. Friendship choices are directed overwhelmingly to other students in the same school, and the majority of these choices are directed to members of the same grade and sex group.

Of the three subsystems, membership in the informal friendship system is most important in the eyes of other students. This is the only subsystem unencumbered by adult sponsorship. This is the adolescent's world, and the status an individual enjoys in this world is of major importance. Status in the academic and activities subsystems is coveted but primarily for the prestige, acceptance, and standing it gives one within the network of informal peer groupings.

Cliques are relatively small, tightly knit groups of friends who spend considerable and often exclusive time with each other. Virtually all observational studies of adolescents has shown that the clique is the most prevalent and important friendship structure for adolescents. Studies also have indicated that cliques are characterized by members being similar to one another in age, gender, race, and social status, as well as in the types of interest and activities of the members (Ennett and Bauman, 1996).

Students attach prestige rankings to being a member of one clique rather than another. Various descriptive titles convey the general reputation, central values, and activities shared by the group, such as the "leading crowd," "athletic crowd," "dirty dozen," "sexy six," and "beer drinkers." The adolescent's general social status within the student body appears to be a function of his or her combined rankings within each of the several subsystems. Furthermore, a student who scores high or low in one system is likely to hold a similar position within the others, but because the important system from the student's viewpoint is the informal one, it is more determinative of behavior than the other two.

Some friendship groups may be in active, open rebellion against the school's educational and social activities. Those in these groups reject the rules of the school system and flaunt authority.

Deviant Subcultures

Thus far, we have discussed the fact that adolescents seek comfort from those who welcome them and who reinforce their sense of belonging. Unfortunately, some youths turn to deviant subcultures, such as gangs and cults, to satisfy their need for approval, belonging, and self-worth.

Satanism

Satanism is a blatant attack on society's dominant value system. *Satan* in Hebrew means "adversary." Satanism is devil worship—the antithesis of the Judeo-Christian belief system. Adolescents who practice Satanism often make up rituals as they go along, learning their craft from their peers, occult books, album covers, movies, videos, and "heavy metal" rock bands that use Satanic lyrics in their music. Satanism is a destructive religion that advocates violence, death, and revenge. It has been described as a hole in the ground that some adolescents stumble into because they've been wandering, desperate, angry, and alone (Clark, 1992). Satanic practices, sometimes described as ritualized abuse, often involve the observation of, or the participation in, the physical or sexual abuse of animals and people. The traumatic impact of these rituals on both the victims and participants is profound, sometimes contributing to significant psychiatric disturbances (Belitz and Schacht, 1992).

Not all adolescents who are involved in Satanism are involved to the same degree. Their involvement can vary along the continuum from mild to severe. Reports from police and mental health practitioners suggest that most adolescents involved in Satanism are "dabblers"—they experiment with Satanic activities but are not fully committed to Satanism. They may experiment with ritualistic behaviors, display Satanic symbols, or be attracted to "heavy metal" music. For some adolescents, these activities may merely reflect normal youthful rebelliousness. Others may also engage in vandalism, theft, arson, substance abuse, or other illegal activities. For them, Satanism may provide a license for their sexual and antisocial urges, a way to express anger and frustration with family or hypocrisies they perceive in society. Still others become deeply involved in Satanism and may suffer from serious psychopathology that antedates any Satanic involvement. The Satanic ideology, which encourages belief in magical power

and sanctions aggressive behavior, can exacerbate these preexisting problems (Steck, Anderson, and Boylin, 1992).

Family conflicts and disruptions have been identified as precursors to Satanic cult involvement. Specific variables noted in families with a youth cult participant include parental abuse, disruption due to the absence of a parent, parental history of psychiatric illness, parental alcoholism, and the youth's experience of being rejected, unloved, or harshly criticized. Often, it is the family member who has been made the scapegoat of the family problem who engages in cult activities. These scapegoats, or "black sheep," tend to identify themselves as evil and seek the company of other "evil" persons.

Recent studies indicate that participants in Satanic or cult activities have poor social and psychological adjustment. They have been described as depressed, anxious, isolated, and alienated from others; as having low self-esteem and a history of substance abuse; and as engaging in antisocial behaviors. These adolescents are characterized as deviant, psychopathological, or poorly adjusted. A cult involvement is an effort to ameliorate a progressive feeling of powerlessness and inadequacy, and to achieve a sense of control and personal power. Many of these characteristics have also been noted in youths who, like many of these children, have been abused. Borderline personality organization, splitting, and the tendency to view the world in polarized good/bad terms also are observed to predispose individuals to cult involvement (Belitz and Schacht, 1992).

Youths probably become interested and involved with Satanic activities through the same type of learning experiences that produce other youthful deviance. Satanists are highly attached to and presumably influenced by their peers, and are likely to have friends involved in Satanism. Satanism participation is like all delinquency—a group phenomenon in which peers learn from and influence each other (Damphousse and Crouch, 1992).

Neo-Nazi Skinheads

The neo-Nazi *skinheads* are the most violent group of White supremacists this country has seen in a

Neo-Nazi skinheads, a violent group of White supremacists, espouse hatred, bigotry, and violence toward minorities. These gangs are composed primarily of adolescents, ages 16 to 19, who tend to come from broken homes and were often abused as children.

quarter century. They espouse hatred, bigotry, and violence toward minorities, and have been responsible for some of the worst racial assaults that have occurred in past years. The skinhead phenomenon originated in the 1970s in England, where gangs of menacing-looking, tattooed, headshaven youths wearing combat boots began to be seen in the streets (Clark, 1992).

Today, in the United States, skinheads resemble their British counterparts. They often shave their heads; wear black leather jackets, suspenders (called *braces*), rolled-up jeans and distinctive boots; and have tattoos and symbols that represent neo-Nazism, White supremacy, and racial violence. American skinheads are very dangerous. Most members are ages 16 to 19. The gangs are composed overwhelmingly of teenagers, many as young as 13 and 14 years of age, who bolster their courage with drugs. They tend to come from broken homes, and a high proportion were abused as children. Their weapons include baseball bats, knives, and steel-toed boots. Their crimes range from gang beatings to murder. They have carried on a campaign of reckless terrorism against minorities, Jews, and gays. White supremacy groups draw from skinhead gangs in an effort to recruit soldiers devoted to the cause (Clark, 1992).

Material Concerns of Adolescent Culture

Another way we can understand adolescent culture is by examining the material artifacts that youths buy, make, and use in their daily lives. Three items—adolescent clothing, automobiles, and the telephone—have been selected for discussion because they are so important in the adolescent's life.

Clothing

One of the most noticeable aspects of adolescent culture is the preoccupation with clothing, hairstyles, and grooming. (See also Chapter 5.) Adults often accuse adolescents of being rebellious nonconformists or, at the other extreme, of being superficial in their values. Sociologists and social

satanism   a devil-worshipping cult practicing ritualized abuse of animals and people.

skinheads   a neo-Nazi group of White supremacists that carry on campaigns of terrorism against Jews, gays, and minorities; they often shave their heads.

psychologists point out that neither accusation is true. Adolescents are conformists, especially when it comes to clothing and appearance within their own peer groups. Rather than showing superficiality because of their concern about appearance, youths are actually evidencing both their need to find and express their own individual identities and their need to belong to a social group.

Clothing is an important means by which individual adolescents discover and express their identities. As adolescent boys and girls search for self-images with which they can be comfortable, they are preoccupied with experimentation with their appearance (Littrell, Damhorst, and Littrell, 1990). Clothing and appearance are expressions of themselves as they strive to control the impressions that they make on others. Clothing is a visual means of communicating to others the kind of role a person wishes to play in life. Adolescents applying for jobs, for example, endeavor to communicate by the clothes they wear the kind of people they are and the type of job they expect to obtain. One study showed that adolescents preferred designer jeans to those not so labeled (Lennon, 1986). In selecting specific brands or more expensive jeans, they were portraying an image about themselves.

Appearance also plays an important role in social interaction, for it provides a means of identification. If a boy dresses like a tough delinquent, he is likely to be treated as one. Clothing enables one adolescent to discover the social identity of another person and to pattern his or her behavior and responses according to what is expected. As human beings within a society develop social selves, dress and adornment are intimately linked to their interacting with one another.

Clothing is one means by which adolescents express their dependence/independence conflicts or their conformity/individuality conflicts. Clothing can be a medium of rebellion against the adult world. Adolescents who are hostile or rebellious toward their parents may express their contempt by wearing clothes or hairstyles they know their parents dislike. The more fuss the parents make, the more determined adolescents are to stick to their own styles. However, the dominant motives in selecting the styles are the desire to be recognized by others as superior or the desire to depend on and be like others (Koester and May, 1985). Adolescents who buy clothes to show independence (from parents especially) wear clothes that will give them recognition or acceptance in their own peer groups.

Clothing and hairstyles have been used by some youths as an expression of rebellion against particular mores and values in adult society. Adult puritanical culture emphasized that cleanliness is next to godliness; therefore, some teenagers express their rejection of what they perceive as a hypocritical, materialistic, godless culture by choosing to remain unclean and unkempt. Youths of the 1960s chose various symbols of a youth culture that was predominantly antiwar and antiestablishment. Ban-the-bomb symbols; beads, flowers, and headbands; fringed leather, Native American–style jackets; granny dresses; moccasins or sandals; and beards and long, unkempt hair were an expression of independence, dissatisfaction with the status quo, and the determination of these youths to show solidarity against adult criticism. Such clothing symbolized their rejection of middle-class philosophy and values. Students of the 1980s who adopted punk-rock styles were expressing the same rebellion against middle-class society and conformity to their own peer groups. Youths of the 1990s who wear baggy, oversized clothing also seek to express their independence. Clothing remains a basic expression of personality, life-style, and political philosophy.

For adolescents, the most important function of clothing is to assure their identity and sense of belonging with peer groups. Clothing is used to enhance self-concept, to make adolescents feel good about themselves, and to make a favorable impression on others (Sweeney and Zionts, 1989). A number of studies have shown the relationship between adolescents' appearance and their social acceptance. Those who are defined by their peers as fashionable dressers have high status; well-dressed but not fashionable students occupy the middle ground; poorly dressed students have low status (Hinton and Margerum, 1984). Consciously or not, other students look down on those not dressed correctly.

Adolescents who are satisfied with the way they look also have more acceptable self-concepts and make more adequate personal adjustments. Preoccupations with clothing and appearance are

Clothing helps adolescents discover and express their identities as well as ensure their sense of belonging in their peer group. A number of studies have shown a positive correlation between adolescents' appearance and their social acceptance.

not superficial or unimportant to youths who are concerned about peer-group acceptance. They must either conform or be rejected. Research has shown that females are more concerned about clothes and more involved in shopping than males (Peters, 1989). This reflects differences in their socialization. Females are taught to place more emphasis on dress than are males.

One study of public high school students attending a large midwestern school divided students into social groups according to dress. Categories mentioned most frequently were "jocks," "freaks," "preppies," "nerds," and "punks." In this school, *jocks* encompassed both genders and played a prominent role. Description of male and female jocks typically included athletic clothing, such as leather jackets and jerseys, and casual items of dress.

Consensus existed about *nerds*, a contrasting social type. The emphasis was on out-of-style clothes: "flood" (pants that are too short and totally out of style), and ugly sweaters that looked like their parents' choice or hand-me-downs. One student commented, "They are in a different world, like striped shirts that don't match anything else." Unkempt hair was another characteristic of nerds: "They have messy hair, they don't comb their hair, their hair looks like they don't care."

There were similarities in the description of dress worn by punks and freaks, probably because both represent a visibly extreme social type that appears to be associated with rebellion. Some de-

scriptions of *punks* focused on distinctive makeup and hairstyles. One student said, "Their hair is all different, they have different-colored dyed hair. They wear strange makeup. One takes another person's hair, ties it to her hair. Another has shaved eyebrows, then draws zig-zag eyebrows. They look very pale."

Comments about *freaks* included the following: "Black and leather clothing and t-shirts. They wear black-everything, leather boots and coats. They wear black leather. Jackets are black leather, black ripped-up jeans. They wear hanging-cross earrings. They are a totally separate group." When hair was mentioned, it was identified as long for boys, teased or unkempt for girls. The characteristics that distinguish punks from freaks seemed to be the coloring and shaping of hair.

Observations of *preppies* seem to be contradictory. Some informants describe preppies as wearing "expensive, nice clothes" and "The boys wear brands like Guess" (Lawrence, Forbes, and Beall, 1993).

The Automobile

Another material aspect of adolescent culture is the automobile. It has become important in the lives of adolescents for a number of different reasons, such as the following:

1. *The automobile is a status symbol.* When boys are asked what impresses girls the most, they rank

being an athlete first, followed by being in the leading crowd, followed by having a nice car. Owning or having access to a car adds to one's prestige in the eyes of one's peers. The type of car one owns or drives is important, and the status attached to various types changes over the years. Not long ago, to drive the family car—especially if it was a new, large, and expensive one—added greatly to prestige. Later, the big car was out, and the small, fast, expensive sports car was in. Now, college students who cannot afford expensive sports cars are turning to compacts, primarily because of the lower price. For the majority of youths, owning a car is still one of the most coveted symbols of status.

2. *The automobile is a means of freedom and mobility.* A car allows adolescents the opportunity to get away from home and drive to the neighboring town, to the big city, or to Florida during the spring break from school. It provides adolescents with a home away from home. If particularly devoted to a car, an adolescent may spend hours in it each day, eating, talking with the gang, having sex in it.

3. *The automobile is a symbol of power and masculinity.* The insecure male especially finds that the automobile becomes a means of controlling an enormous amount of power and of gaining for himself a feeling of strength and virility. The more power in the engine, the faster the car will go; and the more daringly the adolescent drives it, the more manly he feels. Some young drivers become exhibitionists, primarily to impress girls.

4. *For a number of youths, an automobile has become a hobby.* Many adolescent boys share a love for power and speed. Drag-strip or stock-car races are opportunities to compete in socially sanctioned ways to see who can build the fastest engine or soup up an old car. Such races provide opportunities for boys to prove themselves as men and as expert mechanics.

PERSONAL ISSUES

The Automobile and Social Activity

Schlecter and Gump (1983) interviewed adolescents to determine the differences that access to a car made in their lives. They classified three groups of adolescent males:

Unrestricted drivers: Drives without any parental limitations

Limited drivers: Drives with parental limitations

Nondrivers: Drives without a license or drives infrequently

The unrestricted drivers explored by going from one friend's home to another and then "cruised" to a number of spots to "see what was happening." They went to a greater number of different settings, more frequently beyond their own neighborhood, and spent more time with friends, especially girlfriends or boyfriends. Certainly, driving helped these adolescents to achieve new and more solid relationships with peers of both sexes.

The limited drivers who drove with parental permission and limitations often used the car for specific social activities, to go to work, or to drive other family members. Driving with parental consent gave them a degree of independence and autonomy, so they were less childlike in relationships to the adult world than nondrivers.

Nondrivers were severely restricted in social activities. Their activities usually consisted of spending a limited amount of time at friends' homes or activities in outdoor settings. They spent significantly less time with friends than did the driving group. As one subject declared, "A teenager without a license is just not a teenager."

The researchers concluded by suggesting that driving seemed to have a positive influence on adolescents' social responsibility, freedom from parental controls, and engagement in work behavior.

5. *The automobile has become a symbol of glamour and sexuality, of romantic conquest and acceptability.* Madison Avenue has been quick to use not only snob appeal but also sex appeal in promoting automobiles. Advertisements imply that any man who drives a certain car will automatically fill it with beautiful women or that any girl who drives up in a car with plush upholstery will be considered as glamorous and beautiful as the model in the ad. The automobile has also become a favorite lovers' retreat. It allows for mobility, a fair degree of privacy, and even some degree of comfort and warmth.

6. *For some, the automobile has become a means of expressing hostility and anger.* Psychiatrists have hypothesized that driving a powerful automobile provides an outlet for expression of frustration and hostility. Immature people who jump into their cars when frustrated and angry and go careening down the highway are unintentionally using the automobile as a convenient weapon to kill, maim, or destroy. It has been widely publicized that hostile and explosive mental attitudes are major causes of injuries and deaths from automobiles and that the accident-prone driver rebels against authority. One study found that adolescents who were least likely to use seat belts were those who were most depressed, had decreased home support, had problems with school

and the law, had been on probation, or, in general, felt that their lives were not going well (Schichor, Beck, Bernstein, and Crabtree, 1990). The way adolescents use cars and the attitudes with which they drive are indications and tests of their emotional maturity. One investigator has pointed to the fact that some disturbed adolescents use the automobile as a means of committing suicide or murder and that after such a suicide is publicized, the number of similar automobile fatalities increases by almost one-third. Apparently, the behavior of young automobile drivers is affected by the processes of suggestion and modeling.

The Telephone

Adolescents love to use the telephone, as any parent will attest. They can be out all day with a good friend, only to come home and immediately call that same friend on the telephone. They can spend literally hours and hours talking about every conceivable subject on the telephone. Adolescents who receive a number of phone calls take this as an approval of their social standing. Those who don't get many phone calls experience feelings of rejection and sometimes loneliness.

In times gone by, it was socially acceptable for girls to call other girls, or for boys to call girls, but it seemed to be inappropriate for girls to call boys.

Talking on the phone takes up a large amount of time for most adolescents and is a very important pastime. Frequent phone calls are also an indication of one's social standing.

This pattern has changed as adolescent female gender roles in the United States have changed. Newspaper articles, television talk shows, and gossip all support the notion that teenage girls are now "sexually aggressive." Today, adolescent girls perceive their parents as approving of their calls to boys. In one study, a current sample of 578 men and women from a southern urban community university were interviewed to determine their telephone use patterns. Males' reports of receiv-

A Peer-Listening Phone Service

On May 1, 1987, a peer-listening phone service, called *Teen Line,* was established in northwest Ohio to discover the concerns of adolescents who have problems. Knowing which issues are important for adolescents better enables health-care providers to meet the needs of adolescents. Over a five-year period, 11,152 phone calls were logged in on an intake form. Over the entire period, 43 percent of the callers were male and 57 percent were female, although for the first three years there were twice as many calls from females as from males. More recently, it has been about half and half.

Volunteers answer the phones nightly from 6:00 P.M. to 10:00 P.M. A trained adult backup is always present but never answers the phone. The volunteers receive over 60 hours of training. Calls from males are more likely to be recorded under the category of "sexuality," "mental illness," or "just to talk." The sexuality category includes calls regarding sexual intercourse, homosexuality, and masturbation. The mental illness category is selected because the volunteer either discusses that issue or because the volunteer believes that the caller has some mental health problems. Some males may call just to talk, and when they feel more comfortable disclosing, go on to talk about other subjects. Other males may wish to hear a friendly voice and will talk about a variety of superficial subjects.

Females are more likely to call about family issues, peer relationships, abuse, pregnancy, and eating disorders than are males. Peer relationship categories include discussions about acquaintances, close friends, and dating relationships. The table here lists the issues identified during the calls.

There were some age variations in the subject matter of the call. Early adolescents (ages 11 to 13) were most likely to call regarding family problems, school problems, and peer relationships. Midadolescents (ages 14 to 16) were more likely to call regarding suicide, abuse, sexuality, or pregnancy. Late adolescents (ages 17 to 19) were more likely to call regarding drugs and alcohol, mental illness, death, spirituality, and just to talk. The results of this study support the need for peer-listening phone services that adolescents can use to discuss their concerns (Boehm, Schondel, Marlowe, and Rose, 1995).

Issues Identified during Calls

Issue	No. of Calls*	(%)*
Just to talk	4431	40
Peer relationships	4089	37
Family problems	2000	18
Sexuality	1563	14
Self esteem	1005	9
Other	804	7
Drugs & alcohol	746	7
Pregnancy	593	5
School problems	569	5
Suicide	441	4
Abuse	404	4
Mental illness	354	3
Death	190	2
Spirituality	157	1
Legal	43	0.4
Eating disorder	34	0.3
AIDS	27	0.2

*Callers may identify multiple issues per call.

Source: K. E. Boehm, C. K. Schondel, A. L. Marlowe, and J. S. Rose, "Adolescents Calling a Peer-listening Phone Service: Variations in Calls by Gender, Age, and Season of the Year," *Adolescence, 30* (1995): 863–871. Reprinted by permission.

ing calls from girls paralleled the females' reports of calling boys (Anderson, Arceneaux, Carter, Miller, and King, 1995).

Nonmaterial Aspects of Adolescent Culture

Music is an important part of adolescent culture. Popular music has taken many forms: pop, rhythm and blues, rap, folk, country western, jazz, and rock. Adolescents are drawn to a variety of types of popular music, perhaps due to the wide range of emotions expressed in today's songs.

Music

The most common themes in music are ballads of love. The love that is portrayed in modern music is often an ultraromantic, inevitable love. Love is a great miracle, it's a blessing, it can conquer all. It's like a beam of light shining on the edge of the universe (Keller and Keller, 1992, 1993). With a little faith, love can move mountains (Warren, 1992, 1993). In *The Right Kind of Love,* the singer says that everything will be alright if it's the right kind of love (Nevil, Golden, and Faragher, 1992, 1993).

Numerous songs deal with the subject of lovers breaking apart. The singer pleads with the lover to stay (Warren, 1993), to keep his or her promise of love (Boone, Williamson, and Lyras, 1992, 1993). In the song *I'll Never Get Over You Getting Over Me,* the singer recognizes the need to get over her love and to get on with her life. She recognizes that she ought to find someone new, but the tears just won't go away (Warren, 1992, 1993). Not all songs are about love. Some are about problems of everyday living. One couple has been *In 'n' Out* of debt almost from their conception. They can buy things now, but they know they will have to pay later and that they will be paying for the rest of their lives (Van Halen, Van Halen, Anthony, and Hagar, 1991).

The problem of spending time together is illustrated in a song entitled *Quality Time.* The singer repeatedly makes promises that he will spend quality time with his mate, but he makes excuses because he says he has got so much to do. He really wants to be with his mate, but he con-

tinues to ignore her (Kelly, 1992). Another song, entitled *Passionate Kisses,* reflects a philosophy of life that seems fairly simple. The singer wants a comfortable place to sleep, food, warm clothing, and passionate kisses (Williams, 1992, 1993). The singer of *Bad Girl* confesses that something is always missing, that she always seems to feel the need to hide her feelings from other people. She wonders what she is afraid of and why. Apparently, it's because she may believe that she is a bad person. She confesses that she was drunk by 6:00, that she is always kissing someone else's lips, that she smokes too many cigarettes in a day, and that she is not a happy person. In spite of herself, she continues to live like this, but she really is not happy when she acts this way (Ciccone and Pettibone, 1992).

Some songs are a commentary on the problems of youth. The song *Primal Scream,* talks about children and teenagers being suppressed by parents, teachers, and other authority figures. The singer is reaching inside himself to have the strength to fight back (Lee, Sixx, Mars, and Neil, 1991).

Other songs are blatantly sexual. One singer tells her lover that loving is what she's made for, that her lover takes her to heights above which she has been dreaming because he touches her in the right places, which feels so good (Barry, 1993).

In another song, entitled *Knockin' Da Boots,* a lover recalls how he and his partner made great love all night long. Their bodies were rockin' and boots were knockin' together. They made love until they were tired, until the break of dawn (Dino, Stick and Troutman, 1993). In *Freak Me,* the lover asks his partner to let him lick her up and down until she says to stop, then make her body real hot and let him do all the things that she really wants him to do. He wants to get freakie with her, if she knows what he means (Sweat and Murray, 1992, 1993).

Some of the pop songs reflect various problems of relationships. The song *Running Back to You* reveals the problem of infidelity. The singer's partner has been running around too long, and she's getting tired of it. He wants to jump in and out of her bed, and it's time for her to draw the line. She gives him an ultimatum: It's them or her (Hairston, Gale, and Davis, 1991). In another song, *Opposites Attract,* a couple seems to be very

Adolescents are drawn to a wide variety of popular music. Attending rock concerts, such as Woodstock '94, shown here, is a favorite form of entertainment.

attracted to one another but they never agree on anything. One likes the movies and the other likes television. One is serious and the other is light-hearted. One likes to party all night, the other wants to get to bed early. One wants to take two steps forward and the other takes two steps back. They are attracted to one another, but they can't get along. He's always broke, she's got money. One likes to smoke, the other doesn't like ciga-rettes. They don't have one thing in common, but when they get together, they have nothing but fun. They summarized the whole relationship by saying it doesn't really matter because they are perfectly matched (Leiber, 1988).

Some songs deal with the problems of the world. In the song *Heal the World,* the singer says that if we care enough, we could make the world a better place. Let's try to heal the world for you and for me. (Jackson, 1991, 1992). Another song, *Stand,* says that lives and money have become the White man's god. But the time has come to draw the line, to take a stand for what we believe.

One delightful song, called *Hat 2 Da Back,* is about a girl who is very independent. She's her own person and nobody can make her do what she doesn't want to do. She's proud of what she is and won't change for somebody else. She doesn't want to dress like anybody else; she wants to be free to do what pleases her. One of the symbols of her independence is wearing her hat backwards. She wears her pants down real low and puts her hat to the back because that's the kind of girl she is (Austin, Lopes, Wales, Casey, and Finch, 1992, 1993).

Heavy Metal Music

Some of the most controversial music today is hard rock, or *heavy metal* (defined as loud and he-donistic), which is direct and candid in its sensu-ality, emotionalism, or chagrin. Lyrics show stark realism and shocking sophistication.

Heavy metal groups seem to try to outdo one another in being as different as possible. Groups such as Twisted Sister emphasize a very weird ap-pearance, featuring unusual makeup and tattered clothing. Other groups, such as W.A.S.P., try to make their music as violent, sexy, and crude as possible. Bassist Mike Watson of the group Dan-gerous Toys explains, "We're not trying to save the world. Music is music, it shouldn't be a soapbox" (Flug, 1991, p. 34). Motley Crue is known as one of the most outrageous bands of the 1990s.

Rock groups are under criticism not only be-cause of what they sing but also because of what they do. W.A.S.P.'s Blackie Lawless appears on stage with "blood" streaming down his face and chest. On stage, mayhem runs through the entire show as feathers fly and chunks of raw meat are tossed into the crowd.

One result of recent trends has been the formation of adult groups opposed to "rockporn." A number of women have formed the Parents' Music Resource Center (PMRC). The PMRC's main criticism of heavy metal and rap music is the belief that the lyrics cause adolescents to display negative moods (e.g., depression, hostility) and to engage in negative behaviors (e.g., aggression, suicide, sexual activity, and drug use) that they would not participate in otherwise (Ballard and Coates, 1995).

The PMRC, PTA groups, and others have tried to get the Recording Industry of America and the National Association of Broadcasters not to record or air controversial songs or videos and to establish a rating system similar to the one used for movies. Some recording companies have given orders to identify cassettes and CDs that possess a blatant, explicit lyric content, and some stations are shying away from airing controversial music.

In the United Kingdom, a video company released two versions of Madonna's video *In Bed with Madonna (Truth or Dare)*. One is for people aged 15 and older; another is an uncut version for those 18 and older. The cuts include the singer performing a sex act with a bottle and referring to incest and anal and lesbian sex. In the United States, the video was released uncut under the title *Truth or Dare* (Dean, 1991).

In one study, adolescent boys 14 to 20 years of age were interviewed individually to find out why they liked heavy metal music and what effects they felt it had on them (Arnett, 1991). Heavy metal listeners report liking the music for a variety of reasons, but most of all for what they perceive as the talent and skill of the performers. They also favor heavy metal music because of the lyrical themes expressed in the songs—in particular, the dismal condition of the world as they see it. The songs they like best are those concerned with social issues, such as the nuclear arms race and environmental destruction. Heavy metal songs often lament the state of the world but do not provide even a hint for hope of the future. Hopelessness and cynicism pervade the songs. Most heavy metal songs are never played in a major key; the songs are nearly all in minor keys—the keys of melancholy.

It is not difficult to see why many adults object to the heavy metal songs listened to by their adolescents. In fact, the adolescents in this study most often mentioned *Fade to Black,* which describes suicidal despair, as their favorite song. It's remarkable that not even one subject reported that the music tended to make him feel sad or hopeless. Rather, heavy metal music served a purgative function, dissipating accumulative frustration and anger. Adolescents listened to it especially when they were angry, and it consistently had the effect of making them less angry and of calming them down.

The adolescent boys' enthusiasm for heavy metal music did not appear to be motivated by defiance or rebellion toward parents. Although most parents said they did not like the music, only in one case did a boy say his parents made any effort to stop or restrict him from listening to it.

In sum, the role of heavy metal music in the lives of adolescents who like and listen to it is complex, reflecting their concern with the condition of the world and a certain pessimism with regard to the future, but it is also used by them to assuage unpleasant and unruly emotions. Songs about suicide, murder, radical despair, and the destruction of the world are the result. But rather than being the cause of recklessness and despair among adolescents, heavy metal music is a reflection of these and of the socialization environment.

The popularity of heavy metal music among adolescents is, among other things, a symptom of their alienation. Even though the lyrics are despairing and the music is angry, listening to it does not cause them to despair but, in fact, dissolves their anger. Ultimately, there is something consoling in the bond they feel to others through the music, even if that bond is based on a shared alienation (Arnett, 1991).

A later study compared the relationship between preference for hard rock or heavy metal music and reckless behavior of adolescent boys and girls in the tenth and twelfth grades (Arnett, 1992). Adolescents who preferred heavy metal music reported higher rates of reckless behavior, including driving while intoxicated, driving over 80 miles per hour, sex without contraception, sex with someone known only casually, drug use, shoplifting, and vandalism. Preferences for hard rock or heavy metal music were also associated with higher levels of sensation seeking, negative family relationships, and, among girls, low self-esteem. It was concluded that adolescents who are high in sensation-seeking behaviors are attracted to hard rock and heavy metal music as well as to reckless behavior, perhaps because of the high intensity of sensation provided by these experiences (Arnett, 1992).

It is important to remember that preferences for hard rock or heavy metal music are associated with participation in reckless behavior but do not necessarily *cause* adolescents to behave recklessly. Rather, both reckless behavior and heavy metal or hard rock music appeal to adolescents who have an especially high propensity for sensation seeking.

Music Videos

With the advent of MTV (Music Television) in August 1981, an immensely popular new form of entertainment was spawned. After only 10 years, it was beamed into 55 million U.S. homes and continues to grow at a rate of 5 million homes a year. Moreover, MTV Europe is the fastest-growing foreign franchise, reaching 24 million homes in 27 countries. No one can dispute the huge commercial success of MTV and its residual impact on the music industry (Polskin, 1991).

Targeted at teenagers and containing more violence and sex than conventional television, the new music video industry has attracted a notable group of critics. For example, the American Academy of Pediatrics, Women against Pornography, National Coalition on Television Violence, Parents Music Resource Center, National Parent Teachers Association, and others have expressed concern about the possible harmful effects of music videos on youths. As a result, the U.S. Senate held hearings in 1985 to examine the rock music industry and its effect on youthful consumers, but there was insufficient research to support the allegation of the critics or to allay the anxieties of concerned parents. There are good reasons, however, why music videos have the potential to affect youths more than any other popular medium. Consider the following (Strouse, Buerkel-Rothfuss, and Long, 1995):

1. MTV is widely regarded as having revitalized the pop music industry, since it has had a huge influence on the commercial success of several low-talent performers.
2. Music can evoke very strong feelings; the mood-altering effects of music make people more susceptible to behavioral and attitudinal changes.
3. It is well known that a combined audio and visual presentation enhances learning and has a greater impact on attitudes and behavior than music alone.
4. Rock music has always contained rebellious, antisocial, and sexually provocative messages.
5. Concept music videos are frequently interspersed with unconnected segments of violence.
6. Some research reveals that a relatively short exposure to music videos can result in desensitization to violence and an increased acceptance of socially violent behavior.

The research on the effects of music videos on adolescents reveals some very interesting points. Females tend to listen to more music and prefer soft, romantic, danceable music, whereas males prefer hard rock, macho music. Females describe greater personal importance to music and pay more attention to lyrics. Therefore, they report more personal involvement and participation in music imagery and are more likely to recall the images of the videos than listening to a song on the radio. Survey research finds a stronger association between the amount of exposure to music videos to premarital sexual permissiveness for females than for males. Another important consideration is the environment of the family in which the youth dwells. Parental absence is associated with an increased use of television and radio by adolescents.

Furthermore, adolescents who are heavy consumers of rock music tend to be more involved with their peers and less with their families than are adolescents who are light users of rock music. Thus, the family environment is an important moderator of the impact of music videos on youth. Thus, adolescents' perceptions and feelings about their level of satisfaction with their family may be a better moderator of the potential effects of music video exposure than other more objective entices of actual family functions. Unsatisfactory conditions in a family promote an affective need for youthful members to select and attend to music programming that enables them to escape into the fantasies of a seductive video. In summary, the potential effects of music videos as a dynamic, interactional process has a greater impact on youths who are at risk. Adolescents from family environments with a high level of satisfaction may be relatively unaffected by the sexual messages of music videos (Strouse, Buerkel-Rothfuss, and Long, 1995).

SUMMARY

1. Adolescent society is the organized networks of associations among adolescents. Adolescent culture is the sum of their ways of living.

2. There are wide variations in adolescent societies and culture among various groups.

3. Some adults believe that adolescents have their own subculture; others believe that adolescent culture is a reflection of adult culture. Actually, both views are true. Certain aspects of adolescent culture (such as sexual behavior and use of marijuana) are subcultural because they run counter to adult culture. In general, however, adolescent culture reflects adult values, depending on parent versus peer orientation.

4. Adolescent societies may be divided into formal (primarily in-school) and informal (out-of-school) groups. Most in-school groups are also age-grade specific—that is, they are identified with a particular age and grade in school.

5. Active involvement in formal adolescent society is more prevalent among high-socioeconomic-status youths than among low-socioeconomic-status youths.

6. In-school subsystems may be divided into three groups: the formal, academic subsystem; the semiformal, activities subsystem; and the friendship subsystem. Of the three, membership in the friendship subsystem is the most important in the eyes of students.

7. Some youths turn to deviant gangs and cults to satisfy their needs.

8. Satanism is devil worship expressed by performing rituals, abusing animals and people, and engaging in a variety of illegal activities.

9. Neo-Nazi skinheads are violent gangs of youths who commit acts of violence against minority group members. Their efforts are aimed at establishing White supremacy.

10. To understand adolescent society, you must understand the material artifacts and the nonmaterial aspects that make up the lives of youths. Clothing is one of the most noticeable aspects of adolescent culture. It is an important means by which adolescents discover and express their identities; it expresses their dependence/independence conflict with adults; and it may even express a life-style and political philosophy, and assure their identity and sense of belonging with peer groups.

11. One study divides adolescents into social groups according to dress: jocks, freaks, nerds, punks, and preppies.

12. The automobile is another important material part of adolescent culture. It is a status symbol, a means of freedom and mobility, a symbol of power and independence, a hobby, a symbol of glamour and sexuality, and, for some, a means of expressing hostility and anger. Ready access to an automobile has a great influence on the adolescent's daily life, social activity, and freedom.

13. Talking on the telephone is a favorite pastime of adolescents.

14. Music is an important part of adolescent culture. Popular music takes many forms: pop, rhythm and blues, rap, folk, country western, jazz, and rock.

15. The most common themes of ballads relate to love. Others deal with the problems of everyday living: having enough money, spending time together, having the necessities of life, avoiding temptation, experiencing parental suppression, and so on. Various songs reflect different outlooks on life—some positive, others cynical. Some songs are blatantly sexual; others deal with relationships (infidelity, compatibility, being oneself, etc.), and

still others deal with social problems (materialism, homelessness, and other social evils).

16. Hard rock and heavy metal groups have come under fire for explicit lyrics relating to sex, violence, death, and suicide. These groups are also criticized for the bloody, shocking, deafening antics they create on stage.

17. Numerous adult groups have been formed to discourage "rockporn." Such music is thought by some to have a harmful effect on youth, especially on disturbed youngsters who might be pushed over the edge to commit suicide or otherwise follow the suggestions of the songs.

18. Youths listen to heavy metal music because the lyrics express the dismal conditions of the world, because it serves as a purgative function in dissipating their anger, and because it is a reflection of alienation. Listening to heavy metal music and reckless behavior are correlated, although the former does not *cause* the latter. Rather, those who do both have a propensity for sensation seeking.

19. Music videos are watched by millions of youths. Many professional organizations are critical of some of these videos because they portray much sex and violence.

KEY TERMS

adolescent culture   **235**

adolescent society   **235**

adolescent subculture   **236**

age-grade societies   **240**

Satanism   **244**

skinheads   **244**

subsystems   **241**

THOUGHT QUESTIONS

1. Is adolescent society subcultural? Explain.

2. In what ways are adolescent society and culture unique and distinctive from adult society and culture? In what ways does adolescent culture reflect adult culture?

3. Do parents or peers exert the greatest influence on the lives of youths?

4. Adolescents from low-socioeconomic-status families seem to be at a disadvantage. They are seen as nonparticipants in extracurricular activities and are not among the most popular students in school. Do you believe these statements are true? What was the situation in your high school?

5. Is there much snobbishness and socioeconomic class discrimination in high school?

6. This chapter presents the life and values of high school youths as quite superficial. Are adolescents more serious minded than these studies indicate? Are they less superficial, more concerned with world problems and academics? Explain.

7. Do extracurricular activities contribute to adolescent development? Explain.

8. Do you and your parents agree or disagree on important values? Is there a generation gap? Is the gap real? Is college alienating you from your parents and from the rest of society?

9. Have you ever known any young people who are members of Satanic groups? Describe them.

10. Have you ever known youths who were members of a Neo-Nazi skinhead group? Describe them.

11. Is clothing as important to the adolescent as this chapter claims? Why or why not?

12. What is your opinion of punk-rock clothing styles?

13. Should high school students be allowed to own cars? Why or why not?

14. Do you feel that some rock music has a negative influence on adolescents' behavior? Explain.

15. What is your opinion of college fraternities and sororities?

16. What factors determine popularity and prestige in high school?

SUGGESTED READING

Elder, D., with Evans, C. T., and Parker, S. (1995). *School Talk: Gender and Adolescent Culture*. New Brunswick, NJ: Rutgers University Press.

Furnham, A., and Stacey, B. (1991). *Young People's Understanding of Society*. New York: Routledge.

Langone, N. D. (Ed.). (1993). *Recovery from Cults: Help for Victims of Psychological and Spiritual Abuse*. New York: Norton.

Companionship

Need for Friends

> PERSONAL ISSUES
> Adolescent Relationships and Adjustments

Family and Peer Relationships

Early Adolescent Friendships

Broadening Early Friendships

Youth Culture Activities

> HIGHLIGHT
> Friendship Expectations

> HIGHLIGHT
> Factors Contributing to Adolescent Loneliness

Group Acceptance and Popularity

Conformity

Achievement

Participation

Personality and Social Skills

Shyness

> HIGHLIGHT
> Mall Rats and Bunnies

Deviance

Heterosociality

Psychosocial Development

Adolescent Love and Crushes

> PERSONAL ISSUES
> Questions Junior High Adolescents Ask about
> Social Development and Relationships

Loss of Love

Dating

Age Patterns for Dating

Common Problems

Going Steady

> PERSONAL ISSUES
> Questions Senior High Adolescents Ask
> about Dating

Nonmarital Cohabitation

Incidence

Meanings Attached to Cohabitation

Reactions to Cohabitation

> HIGHLIGHT
> Coed Dorms

Adjustments

Cohabiting and Marriage Differences

Effect on Subsequent Marriage

Cohabiting and Premarital Childbearing

Adolescent Marriage

Trends and Incidence

Prospects and Prognosis

A Profile of the Young Married

Reasons for Adolescent Marriage

Adjustments and Problems

Marriage and Public Schools

Social Development, Relationships, Dating, Nonmarital Cohabitation, and Marriage

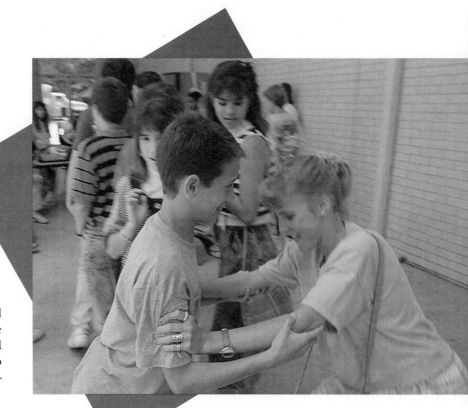

Analysis of the developmental tasks of adolescents that relate only to social development and relationships should take into consideration at least six important needs of youths:

1. The need to establish caring, meaningful, satisfying relationships with individuals
2. The need to broaden childhood friendships by getting acquainted with new people of differing backgrounds, experiences, and ideas
3. The need to find acceptance, belonging, recognition, and status in social groups
4. The need to pass from the homosocial interests and playmates of middle childhood to heterosocial concerns and friendships
5. The need to learn about, adopt, and practice dating patterns and skills that contribute to personal and social development, intelligent mate selection, and successful marriage

6. The need to find an acceptable masculine or feminine sex role and to learn sex-appropriate behavior

The content of this chapter has been selected primarily with these social needs of the adolescent in mind. (Masculine/feminine sex roles and appropriate sexual values and behavior were discussed in Chapters 8 and 9.)

In recent years, nonmarital cohabitation has become an extension of the social relationships developed among older youths. This trend needs to be better understood, along with some of its implications in the lives of participants.

A minority of adolescents also continue to enter into early marriage. We will discuss the reasons, adjustments, problems, and prognosis of success of early marriage in this chapter.

Companionship

The need for close friends becomes crucial during adolescence. Until adolescence, children's dependence on peers is rather loosely structured. Children seek out playmates of their own ages with whom they share common interests or activities. They engage them in friendly competition and win or lose some measure of their respect and loyalty, but emotional involvement with them is not been intense. Children do not depend primarily on one another for emotional satisfaction. They look to their parents for fulfillment of their emotional needs and seek their praise, love, and tenderness. Only if they have been unloved, rejected, and adversely criticized by parents will they turn to friends or parent substitutes for emotional fulfillment. During adolescence, this picture changes. Sexual maturation brings new feelings and needs for emotional fulfillment and for emotional independence and emancipation from parents. Adolescents now turn to their peers to find the support formerly provided by their families (Frankel, 1990; Sebald, 1986).

Need for Friends

The positive aspects of peer relationships among adolescents are well documented. One study found that the quality and stability of adolescents'

friendships are related to self-esteem (Keefe and Berndt, 1996). Involvement of peers has been found to be related positively to many indicators of psychological and social adjustment (Bishop and Inderbitzen, 1995). Numerous studies have indicated that social support is directly related to well-being and serves to buffer the effects of unusual stress. There is also reason to believe that adolescence is a time of life when the potential for stress arising from peer relationships is particularly high. Adolescents are oriented toward their peers and rely on them for a sense of self-worth. Peer conformity increases during the early adolescent years. Being neglected or rejected by peers during adolescence is linked to serious problems such as delinquency, drug abuse, and depression (Merten, 1996). Early adolescence may be an especially vulnerable time for experiences in social stress for peers (Moran and Eckenrode, 1991).

The first needs of adolescents are for relationships with others with whom they can share common interests (Hortacsu, 1989). As they grow older, they desire a closer, caring relationship that involves sharing mature affection, problems, and their most personal thoughts (Pombeni, Kirchler, and Palmonari, 1990). They need close friends who stand beside them and for them in an understanding, caring way. Friends share more than secrets or plans; they share feelings and help each other resolve personal problems and interpersonal conflicts (Werebe, 1987). As one boy said, "He is my best friend. We can tell each other things we can't tell anyone else; we understand each other's feelings. We can help each other when we are needed."

During adolescence, success in forming and maintaining peer relationships is positively implicated in social and psychological adjustment and achievement. An important element in success in peer relationships is the willingness of friends to be prosocial—that is, to help and provide emotional support, advice, and information (Estrada, 1995).

Overall, however, there are marked differences with respect to gender: Girls expect more from their friends than boys do, and their level of attachment and intimacy with friends is greater (Claes, 1992). Other research indicates that for girls, the major adolescent task is establishing and maintaining relationships and the development of intimacy, whereas boys are more concerned about independence. This view insists that girls have a "different world view," and boys value assertiveness, logic, and duty. Gilligan (1982) has asserted that girls value caring, responsibility, and interrelationships. There is strong evidence that this gender difference still exists during adulthood (Bakken and Romig, 1992).

Research has indicated that young adolescents prefer to disclose their emotional feelings to parents. Much depends on the openness of family communication. However, as they get older, adolescent self-disclosure to friends increases and becomes greatest among older adolescents. Females of all ages exhibit greater emotional disclosure to both parents and peers than do males. This finding is consistent with traditional masculine concepts that emphasize that males are not to express emotional concerns and feelings (Papini, Farmer, Clark, Micka, and Barnett, 1990).

One of the reasons friendships are crucial is that adolescents are insecure and anxious about themselves (Goswick and Jones, 1982). They lack personality definition and secure identities. Consequently, they gather friends around them from whom they gain strength and who help establish personal boundaries. From them, they learn the necessary personal and social skills and societal definitions that help them become part of the larger adult world. They become emotionally bound to others who share their vulnerabilities and their deepest selves. They become comrades in a hostile world.

One of the greatest problems of adolescents is the problem of loneliness (Roscoe and Skomski, 1989). One adolescent girl commented, "I'm really lonely. My mom and dad both work, so are not home a lot. My brother is six years older than I am, so we don't have too much in common. If it weren't for some friends, I wouldn't have anyone to talk to." Adolescents describe their loneliness as emptiness, isolation, and boredom. They are more likely to describe themselves as lonely when feeling rejected, alienated, isolated, and not in control of a situation (Woodward and Kalyan-Masih, 1990). Boys seem to have a greater problem with loneliness than do adolescent girls, probably because it is more difficult for boys to express their feelings.

Adolescents are lonely for a variety of reasons. Some have trouble knowing how to relate to others; they have difficulty reflecting on the appropriateness of their behavior and learning how to behave in different situations (Carr and Schellenbach, 1993). Some have a poor self-image and feel very vulnerable to criticism. They anticipate rejection and avoid actions that might cause them embarrassment. Adolescents who are depressed and emotionally disturbed have difficulty establishing close relationships (Brage, Meredith, and Woodward, 1993). Others have been conditioned to mistrust all people and are therefore cynical about relating to them (Mitchell, 1990). They avoid social contact and intimacy so others can't take advantage of them. Still other adolescents feel a lack of support from parents, which makes it harder to make friends. Whenever adolescents perceive the social risks of forming friendships to be greater than the potential benefits, they have difficulty establishing meaningful relationships (East, 1989).

For the most part, also, youths are lonelier than older people (Medora and Woodward, 1986). Part of loneliness is situational; it is socially conditioned because youth culture emphasizes that if you are alone on Friday night, you will be miserable, so adolescents end up feeling that way (Meer, 1985). Various research studies at the University of Nebraska have revealed that the loneliest group of students was low-income, single, adolescent mothers (Medora and Woodward, 1986).

Sometimes loneliness occurs even with others around, because it is difficult to communicate or get close. One adolescent expressed this in a poem:

> A void of nothingness
> Is where I sit
> I cannot come into your life
> Nor can you into mine
> And so we sit in a room
> Empty of all but ourselves
> And because we cannot or will not
> Touch each other's minds
> We cannot escape into ourselves
> Or into each other.*

*Caren Williams, "Do Not Enter, Do Not Exit." *High Grade*, Student Publication, Humanities Department, Colorado School of Mines, Golden, Colorado, Spring 1980, p. 3, quoted in E. G. Williams, "Adolescent Loneliness." *Adolescence, 18* (Spring 1983): 51–66. Reprinted by permission.

Adolescent Relationships and Adjustments

From a developmental perspective, the relative influence of peers depends on the child's age. Children evidence greater dependency on parents during middle through late childhood, which is followed by an increasing degree of dependency on peers during early to middle adolescence. During later adolescence, individuals exhibit greater resistance to peer pressure and greater capacity for autonomous behavior. For many adolescents, the shift toward a peer social orientation does not necessarily involve a rejection of parents' opinions and values.

The typical progression from family to peer to young adult can be upset when parental relationships fail to maintain a balance between supportive involvement and the encouragement of self-sufficiency. Adolescents who report less emotional support from their parents and less involvement in their families have been shown to be more susceptible to the influence of delinquent peers than adolescents who report more support from an involvement with their families. Similarly, excessive or premature autonomy from parental influence has been found to be related to adolescent girls' early initiation of sexual activity. Thus, it appears that the quality of both family and peer relations are related to adolescent development and adjustments (Sabatelli and Anderson, 1991).

Different adolescents cope with their loneliness in different ways. Those who are more independent engage in individual pursuits, keep busy, and readjust their thinking so they are more content. Those who are more dependent attempt to extend their social contacts, try to be with others more, rely on external sources of support, seek adult help, or resort to religion, physical activities, or professional help (Woodward and Kalyan-Masih, 1990). Most adolescents as well as adults experience loneliness at some time in their lives.

Family and Peer Relationships

The ability to form close friendships is partly learned in the family. There is a significant correlation between relationships with parents and adolescents' social adjustments (McCombs, Forehand, and Smith, 1988). One study of adolescent girls, 15 to 17 years old, showed that the degree of connectedness girls experienced in their family influenced the degree of connectedness they experienced in their relationship with peers (Bell, Cornwell, and Bell, 1988). Those who were close to their parents were most likely to have friendship choices that were reciprocal. Those who described family members as isolated and disconnected had a lower percent of friendship choices reciprocated. However, those girls whose families had an inordinate level of connectedness also had difficulty in establishing connectedness in reciprocal friendships, indicating that their families interfered in a general way with the daughter's development of friendships.

Early Adolescent Friendships

The need for companionship causes young adolescents to choose a best friend or two, almost always of the same sex. The adolescent will spend long hours conversing with this friend on the telephone; will attend school, club, and athletic events with him or her; and will strive to dress like, look like, and act like this person. Usually, this best friend is from a similar socioeconomic, racial, and home background; from the same neighborhood, school, and school grade; of the same age; and with numerous interests, values, and friends in common. Best friends usually get along well if they are well selected because they are similar and thus compatible. Successful friendships, like successful marriages, are based on each person's meeting the needs of the other (Zarbatany, Ghesquiere, and Mohr, 1992). If best friends meet each other's needs, the bonds of friendship may be drawn tightly.

These early adolescent friendships are intense, emotional, and sometimes stormy if needs are not met. Some adolescents make bad choices. Instead of their best friends meeting their needs,

Adolescents need close friends who will share secrets, plans, and feelings and who will help with personal problems. These best friends are usually quite similar, coming from the same type of socioeconomic and racial backgrounds, living in the same neighborhood, going to the same school, and sharing interests and values.

they stimulate frustration and anger. The more intense and narcissistic the emotions that drove adolescents to seek companionship, the more likely it is that sustained friendships will be tenuous, difficult, and tempestuous. Once thwarted, immature, rejected, unstable adolescents react with excessive emotion, which may disrupt their friendships temporarily or permanently.

Friendships during early adolescence are unstable. There is usually an increase in friendship fluctuations accompanying the onset of pubescence (at about age 13 for girls and age 14 for boys), followed by a decline in friendship fluctuations. After 18 years of age, friendship fluctuations increase because students leave home for college, jobs, the armed services, or marriage.

Broadening Early Friendships

When young adolescents leave the confines of their neighborhood elementary schools and transfer to district or consolidated junior high schools, they are immediately exposed to much broader and more heterogeneous friendships. They now have an opportunity to meet youths from other neighborhoods, social classes, and different ethnic and national origins. These youths may act, dress, speak, and think differently from those they have known before. One social task at this stage

of development is to broaden their acquaintances, to learn how to relate to and get along with many different types of people. During this early period, adolescents want many friends. Usually, there is an increase in the number of friends during early adolescence (until about age 15). After that, adolescents become more discriminating, and the number of reported friendships decreases. Two studies of 1,300 seventh- to twelfth-graders in three midwestern U.S. communities revealed that younger adolescents generally favored peer group (crowd) membership, but the importance of this affiliation declined after age 15. Figure 11.1 illustrates this trend (Brown, Eicher, and Petrie, 1986).

Youth Culture Activities

A sample of 2,074 male and female high school seniors, from three Canadian cities, was studied to determine the variety of cultural activities in which they engaged. Samples consisted of single high school students who were living at home. Some 82 percent of the youths lived at home in two-parent families; approximately 18 percent lived in a single-parent family. More than half of the students reported their family's financial situation to be about average, or, in other words, middle class.

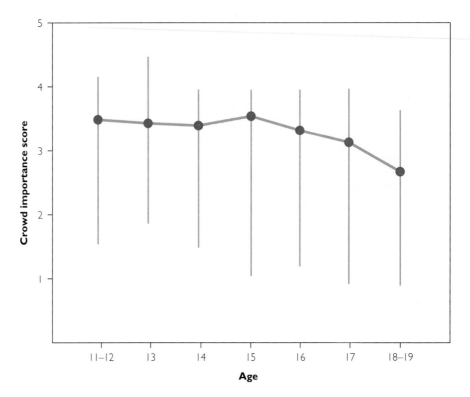

FIGURE 11.1   Age Differences in the Importance of Crowd Affiliation

Source: Adapted from B. B. Brown, S. A. Eicher, and S. Petrie, "The Importance of Peer Group ("Crowd") Affiliation in Adolescence," *Journal of Adolescence,* 9 (1986): 73–96. Used by permission.

One popular activity of these seniors was hanging around. When hanging around, some of the girls spent their time at their homes or at a friend's house. Also, when spending time just hanging around, they engaged in other activities at the same time. For example, on Saturday mornings, they hung around the house doing chores. Boys appeared to spend less time hanging around than girls.

Watching television was a common source of leisure for young people. Although they spent many hours in front of the television, it was not their first choice in leisure pursuits. Overall, the majority of young people spent less than 15 hours a week in front of the television. There were some gender differences in types of television viewing. Most female and male high school seniors spent much of their Saturday television viewing time watching cartoons. A greater proportion of males spent some time on Saturday watching sports. Few young women stated they watched sports on television.

Approximately 47 percent of the girls reported dating at least once a week. Not only were girls more involved in dating relationships than boys but they also spent greater amounts of time preparing for, organizing, and maintaining dating relationships. In general, females were more committed to the concept of dating relationships, whereas males were involved in casual, noncommitted dating patterns. Approximately half of the young people in this study spent moderate amounts of time (anywhere between one and five hours a week) cruising around in a car or on a motorbike. More males than females spent greater amounts of out-of-school hours "cruising around downtown," "just driving around," or cruising to pick up friends.

A larger proportion of females than males spent time at the mall or visiting or talking with friends. Young women were more likely to spend time "talking on the phone with my beau," "going downstairs to talk to mom and dad," "talking with my grandmother," "talking to my sister," or "just hanging around and talking with my friends." When boys spent time talking, they "talked with friends," they "drank beer and talked with friends," they "sat around and talked," or they had friends sleep over and in the morning "sat around and talked." They seemed to spend less time talking on

HIGHLIGHT

Friendship Expectations

Clark and Ayers (1993) studied friendship expectations during adolescence and came to the following conclusions:

1. Sharing mutual activities is important in friendships during early school years and remains an essential characteristic of friendships during adolescence. Mutual activities are perceived as rewarding and facilitate bonding between friends. Proximity and the sharing of activities facilitate interpersonal attraction.

2. Early adolescents felt that friends should be "morally good" and should be open and straightforward, especially about their feelings regarding the friendship. Early adolescents had high standards for conventional morality; however, they realized that many of their peers could not meet these idealized views, and, therefore, settled for those who had lower levels of conventional morality than they expected. They emphasized genuineness, which facilitated the growth of friendships, whereas the lack of genuineness, or phoniness, was one of the major reasons given by adolescents for the dissolution of adolescent friendships.

3. Early adolescents emphasized the importance of loyalty and commitment in the relationship.

4. Adolescents desired relationships in which there was empathetic understanding between them. However, there were some differences in expectations between boys and girls. The boys reported less empathetic understanding in their close friendships than did girls and indicated they required less understanding so that their expectations were still being met by their current relationships. In addition, boys did not require as much loyalty and commitment from their friends as girls did, so male friendships often surpassed their requirements for loyalty and commitment. In general, early adolescent friendships possess many of the qualities that adolescents believe are important for close friendships. Nevertheless, girls expected more from their friendships than they were getting. This emphasis on morality reinforces the view often expressed that early adolescents are more attached to friends who do not get into trouble (Gillmore, Hawkins, Day, and Catalano, 1992).

HIGHLIGHT

Factors Contributing to Adolescent Loneliness

A number of factors contribute to adolescent loneliness:

1. A sense of separation and alienation from parents*
2. Broken families
3. New cognitive abilities leading to an awareness of self
4. An increasing sense of freedom, which is frightening
5. The search for self-identity
6. The struggle for meaningful goals
7. Marginal status of adolescents in society
8. Fierce competitive individualism leading to feelings of failure and rejection

9. Excessive expectation of popularity
10. A low self-esteem and strong feelings of self-pity, pessimism regarding being liked and accepted by others
11. Apathy and aimlessness, low educational and occupational aspirations leading to a cycle of failure and withdrawal
12. Severe individual shyness and self-consciousness

*Other research has revealed that a lack of positive parental involvement in the life of the child contributes to the loneliness of the offspring (Lobdell and Perlman, 1986).

the phone than did girls and less time talking with family.

Part-time employment played a dominant role in the lives of Canadian young people. More than half of the students in the study held part-time jobs. A majority of these jobs required a time commitment involving anywhere between 10 and 20 hours a week. Equal proportions of males and females held part-time jobs while attending high school. Girls usually worked fewer hours per week than boys. Equal proportions of males and females held jobs in a restaurant or service industry. However, a larger proportion of males than females worked as laborers and a larger proportion of females than males did clerical/cashier type work. High school females were more likely than males to be expected to take on responsibility for household chores. Females were more likely to do indoor chores, and males were more likely to take responsibility for outdoor chores.

A greater proportion of young people overall reported regular participation in either sports or exercise rather than club participation. A large proportion of teens regularly participated in sports. A greater proportion of males than females spent time on hobbies. Hobbies for the teenage male included recording music, building model planes, and playing computer games. However, more often than not, teenage males spent time working on, fixing, and washing their cars. Males spent their time fixing cars; females cleaned them. Males fixed their own cars; females washed someone else's car. The overwhelming hobby of choice for young women was sewing.

A sizable majority of students consumed alcohol quite regularly. Of all the youths studied, 44 percent consumed alcohol at least once a week; 6 percent had never drunk alcohol. More males than females consumed alcohol and took drugs, although drinking is becoming more acceptable for girls. Young people perceived alcohol as helping them have more fun, especially when with their friends. (van Roosmalen and Krahn, 1996).

Group Acceptance and Popularity

As the number of acquaintances broadens, adolescents become increasingly aware of their need to belong to a group. One study emphasized that boys were more concerned with status or attributes that led to acceptance by a group than were girls. Girls were more interested in affiliation, in being close to a relatively small group of girls (Benenson, 1990). However, both boys and girls want to be liked by peers. By midadolescence, the goal toward which they strive is acceptance by members of a clique or crowd they strongly admire. At this stage, they are sensitive to criticism or to others' negative reactions to them. They are concerned about what people think because their concepts of who they are and their degree of self-worth are partly a reflection of the opinions of others.

The following questions are typically asked by adolescents in the seventh, eighth, or ninth grades who are worried about their social positions:

How should a boy who is very shy go about overcoming the problem?
How can you get other kids to like you?
How can you become more sociable?
Why do you feel left out when you're around a group of friends that don't even know you're there?
What do you do when a person hates you?
Why are some kids so popular and others not? How can you get popular?

Conformity

Adolescents choose their friends so as to maximize the congruency (similarity) within the friendship pair (Tolson and Urberg, 1993). If there is a state of imbalance such that the friend's attitude or behavior is incongruent, the adolescent will either break off the friendship and seek another friend or keep the friend and modify her or his own behavior.

Cliques and groups operate in the same way. Each group takes on a personality of its own: Members are characterized according to dress and appearance, scholastic standing, extracurricular participation, social skills, socioeconomic status, reputation, and personality qualifications (see Chapter 10). One way the individual has of being part of a particular group is to be like other members of the group. This may include using special slang, wearing a certain type of pin, hair ribbon, or different-colored socks on each foot. When a fad is in fashion, every person in the group adopts it. Those who are different are excluded. In one study of 200 high school students from two large suburban high schools, the students listed conformity (in activity, language, attitude, dress, and interest) as one of the most important requirements for popularity (Sebald, 1981).

Of course, conformity can be a helpful, positive social influence or a negative one, depending on the group and its values. The adolescent boy who wants to belong to a juvenile gang of delinquents and has to pull off a robbery to do so is obviously conforming, but to a peer code, that may get him into trouble.

Conformity needs also depend on adolescents' family adjustments. Youths with a good family adjustment and who are fond of their parents have less need to conform to peer demands, at least in some areas, so that when confronted with decisions, parental rather than peer opinions are accepted. The significant point is that total adjustment to parents influences the degree to which adolescents conform to parents versus peers.

Socioeconomic status also correlates with adolescent conformity. Higher-status adolescents conform more than ones from low-socioeconomic-status families. They more often like school, plan to continue their education, attend church or synagogue, and make higher-level vocational choices (see Chapter 10).

Adolescent girls show a greater degree of conformity than do adolescent boys. Members of girls' groups are more concerned with harmonious relations, social approval and acceptance, and living up to peer expectations than are members of boys' groups. In one study of peer pressure among high school students, this pressure was a more dominant and influential feature of life for girls than for boys. The pressures reported by girls were much more intense than for boys (Brown, 1982). However, for girls, the pressure was to be active in organizations and to maintain a "nice girl" image. For boys, the pressure was to be a "macho" athlete, to use drugs or alcohol, and to become sexually involved. The differences in expectations were part of the reason that boys were found to be relatively insensitive to their sexual partners.

Achievement

Another way of finding group acceptance and approval is through achievement—in sports, club membership, recreational activities, or academic subjects. The recognition and acceptance the individual achieves depends on the status accorded the activity by the peer group. Research indicates consistently that high school athletes are awarded higher social status (by several criteria of interpersonal popularity) than are scholars, but that athlete-scholars are the most popular of all, suggesting some positive status given to both academic and athletic achievements. Because of the negative status awarded to some activities (e.g., the knitting club), participation or achievement in these activities is a handicap to the adolescent seeking wider social acceptance.

Participation

Joining in-school clubs and participating in a variety of out-of-school social activities are other ways the adolescent has of finding social acceptance (Dubois and Hirsch, 1993). One study found that the desire to belong was the most important motive for participating in out-of-school activities (Bergin, 1989). The most popular students are the joiners, usually in multiple activities in schools, but also as members of out-of-school, community-sponsored youth groups and as participants in every conceivable type of social and recreational activity among friends. The group life of adolescents has been characterized as *herd life*. The herd assembles at the local hangout for refreshments and small talk. The herd goes joyriding in the car or to a movie, a dance, or a rock concert. The herd goes on a hayride, skiing, or to the beach. The herd hangs out at the local shopping mall (Anthony, 1985). To be part of the social scene, one has to join and be with the herd.

Efforts have been made to determine the criteria for popularity among adolescents. When boys were asked to rank the most important criteria for popularity with other boys and with girls, the results, in order of importance, were (1) being in athletics, (2) being in the leading crowd, (3) being a leader in activities, (4) having high grades, and (5) coming from the right family (Bozzi, 1986). When asked the same question, girls ranked, in order of importance, (1) being in the leading crowd, (2) being a leader in activities, (3) being a cheerleader, (4) having high grades, and (5) coming from the right family (Bozzi, 1986).

At the same time that student athletes enjoy high popularity, research indicates that there are considerable prejudices against them, particularly in relationship to their academic performance. Students simply do not believe that student athletes have the academic capabilities to obtain an A (Engstrom and Sedlacek, 1991).

In a later study, 496 college students who had graduated from high school were asked to list five ways in which male and female students could gain prestige in the high school from which they had recently graduated. The overall pattern showed that boys and girls acquire prestige through largely different means. Boys gained prestige primarily through (1) sports, (2) grades and intelligence, (3) access to cars, (4) sociability, (5) popularity with the opposite sex, (6) physical appearance, and (7) participation in school activities. In contrast, girls gained prestige primarily through (1) physical attractiveness, (2) sociability, (3) grades and intelligence, (4) popularity with the opposite sex, (5) clothes, (6) participation in school activities, and (7) cheerleading. Boys continue to acquire prestige primarily through sports, grades and intelligence, whereas girls continue to acquire prestige primarily through grades, intelligence and physical attractiveness. There was an increase in girls' participation in sports as a way of acquiring prestige, whereas the importance of cheerleading as a means of prestige had declined (Suitor and Reavis, 1995).

Personality and Social Skills

Personal qualities and social skills are important criteria for popularity and have been found to be very important in gaining social acceptance (Meyers and Nelson, 1986). Considerable evidence shows that personal qualities are the most important factors in popularity. According to 204 adolescents in the seventh, ninth, and twelfth grades, interpersonal factors were more important in friendship bonds than either achievement or physical characteristics. This was true of adolescents at all grade levels (Tedesco and Gaier, 1988). *Interpersonal factors* included character traits, per-

sonality, intimacy, and social conduct. *Achievement factors* included academic qualities and athletic prowess. *Physical characteristics* included physical appearance and material things such as money or autos. However, physical appearance has been found to play an important role in early attraction between the sexes. Even teachers have been found to rate physically attractive students more academically competent than less attractive students (Lerner, Delaney, Hess, Jovanovic, and von Eye, 1990). After getting to know less attractive students better, however, both adolescents and adults begin to place less emphasis on physical attractiveness and more emphasis on other qualities. The older they become, the more adolescents emphasize interpersonal factors and deemphasize achievement and physical characteristics in friendship bonds. Other research also emphasizes the importance of personal qualities as a criterion of popularity (East et al., 1992).

Thus, two principal ways adolescents find group acceptance is by *developing and exhibiting personal qualities that others admire* and by *learning social skills that ensure acceptance.* In general, popular youths are accepted because of their personal appearance, sociability, and character. They are neat, well-groomed, good-looking youths who are friendly, happy, fun-loving, outgoing, and energetic; they have developed a high degree of social skills; and they like to participate in many activities with others. They may be sexually experienced but are not promiscuous. Popular youths also have a good reputation and exhibit qualities of moral character that people admire. They usually have high self-esteem and positive self-concepts. Adolescents who are most popular with the same sex tend also to be most popular with the opposite sex (Miller, 1990).

Shyness

In a survey among tenth-grade boys and girls in a secondary school in Victoria, British Columbia, about one-half of the students rated themselves as "moderately shy" or "quite shy" (Ishiyama, 1984). Shyness usually increases during early adolescence because of increased self-awareness, the development of sexual interests, and the desire to be part of a social group (Hauck, Martens, and Wetzel, 1986). Shyness in social situations has been re-

HIGHLIGHT

Mall Rats and Bunnies

The Maine Mall in South Portland is the largest shopping mall in New England. A research team of observers studied adolescent visitation, social groups, and behavior in the mall over a six-week period during June and July of 1988 (Lewis, 1989). The observers found that the mall was an important place for teenagers to congregate. A small number of regulars visited the mall daily.

The boys call themselves "mall rats," the girls "mall bunnies." They wander around the different shops, playing video games in the arcade, smoking, showing off their latest hairstyles, makeup, and clothing, and waiting for something—anything—to happen. When tired of cruising, they usually migrate to the food court, sitting, talking, bumming change, smoking cigarettes, and trying to avoid the attention of the security personnel. They're supposed to eat something if they sit at the tables. Most have been kicked out at one time or another when not eating or for getting too boisterous. Most of the regulars stay until the mall closes at night.

The adolescents give various reasons for hanging out at the mall.

"It's a place to go before work."
"To play videos."
"It's something to do."
"You can come here anytime."
"I meet all these people here."
"Most of my friends I meet here at the mall."
"To get away from home."
"You can pick up anything—pot, acid, hash."

The mall acts as a social magnet, drawing adolescents to its neutral and safe territory. For youths with unresolved problems at home, the mall offers a haven where hassles are minimal (Lewis, 1989).

---

ferred to as *social-evaluative anxiety* (Warren, Good, and Velten, 1984). The person is anxious about being the center of attention, making mistakes in front of others, behaving, being expected to say something, or being compared with others. Shyness stems from a fear of negative evaluation of self by others, a desire for social approval, low self-esteem, and a fear of rejection (Connolly, White, Stevens, and Burstein, 1987). It may have its origins in childhood, in such problems as being teased, criticized, ridiculed, and compared with siblings. It may arise out of self-consciousness about appearance, weight, height, or some deficit. One researcher found that shy men often grew up in disharmonious, verbally abusive families (Gilmartin, 1985). They tended to be social isolates, growing up as only children without support from kin.

In extreme form, the shy adolescent may manifest physiological reactions to shyness: blushing, butterflies in the stomach, fast pulse, bodily shaking, heart palpitations, and nervous sweating. Shy people may become fidgety or nervous, avoid eye contact, stammer or stutter, or speak inaudibly. Shy adolescents are more likely to use illicit drugs than are those who are not shy (Page, 1990). This is one way of trying to overcome their feelings of social inferiority. They may feel that their problems are unique. They may have overlooked the possibility that others are equally shy but do not appear so. As a consequence, they attribute the cause of shyness to their own personalities; they lower their own self-confidence and avoid social situations, which reinforces their negative experience and expectations. They may experience considerable suffering over many years. Therapeutic intervention may help them to break this cycle and restore their self-confidence.

Deviance

Thus far, little has been said about achieving group acceptance through deviant behavior—that is, behavior different from that of the majority of youths (largely middle class) but considered acceptable in a particular group that itself deviates

---

social-evaluative anxiety   shyness.

from the norms. Whereas overtly aggressive, hostile behavior may be unacceptable in society as a whole, it may be required in a ghetto gang as a condition of membership. Likewise, what might be considered a bad reputation in the local high school (fighter, troublemaker, uncooperative, antisocial, sexually promiscuous, delinquent) might be a good reputation among a group of delinquents. One study of 12- to 16-year-old boys who were overaggressive and bullies toward younger, weaker youths showed that the bullies enjoyed average popularity among other boys (Olweus, 1994); those who were the targets of aggression were far less popular than the bullies. These findings illustrate that standards of group behavior vary with different groups so that popularity depends not so much on a fixed standard as on group conformity.

Sometimes, peer groups are formed because of hostility to family authority and a desire to rebel against it. When this happens, the peer groups may become delinquent gangs, hostile to all established authority yet supportive of the particular deviancy accepted by the group.

Heterosociality

Psychosocial Development

One of the most important social goals of mid-adolescence is to achieve heterosociality (Miller, 1990). In the process of psychosocial development, children pass through three stages:

1. *Autosociality:* The first stage, autosociality, is the early preschool period of development in which the child's chief pleasure and satisfaction is himself or herself. This is most typical of the 2-year-old who wants to be in the company of others but who plays alongside them, not with them. The adolescent who is still a loner, who does not have any friends, is still in this preschool period of development.

2. *Homosociality:* The second stage, homosociality, is the primary school period of development in which the child's chief pleasure and satisfaction are in being with others of the same sex (not for sexual purposes but for friendship and companionship) (Bukowski, Gauze, Hoza, and Newcomb,

1993). Every normal child passes through this important stage of forming same-sex friendships (Lempers and Clark-Lempers, 1993). Establishing same-sex friendships in preadolescence is crucial to identity formation and to subsequent heterosexual bonding. By establishing a "consensual exchange" with a same-sex friend, preadolescents are able to enrich their sense of self and validate their self-worth (Paul and White, 1990).

3. *Heterosociality:* The final stage, heterosociality, is the adolescent and adult stage of development in which the individual's pleasure and friendships are found with those of both sexes (Goff, 1990). The development of intimacy is one of the important challenges of late adolescence (Paul and White, 1990). Failure to achieve a close relationship with a member of the opposite sex may result in severe anxiety, fears about one's sexuality, and lower self-esteem. Older adolescents are particularly sensitive and vulnerable to feelings of heterosexual inadequacy.

Getting acquainted and feeling at ease with the opposite sex is a painful process for some youths. The following are some typical questions that worry the adolescent who is becoming attracted to new relationships:

> How do you go about talking to a girl?
> What can you do if you're chicken to ask a girl on a date?
> How can you attract the opposite sex?
> Does a girl wait for a boy to actually say he likes her? . . . [My] trouble is that I feel I don't hit it off exactly right with them—I'm more a friend than a boy.
> Why are we so self-conscious when we meet new boys?
> Should you worry if you don't have dates right away?
> How can you get a boy to notice you and like you?
> Why do boys shy away from being introduced?

With sexual maturity comes a biological-emotional awareness of the opposite sex, a decline in hostile attitudes, and the beginning of emotional responses. The girl who was looked upon before as a sissy, giggly, pain-in-the-neck kid now takes on a new allure. On the one hand, the now-maturing male is fascinated and mystified by this young woman; on the other hand, he is awed, terrified, and bewildered. No wonder he ends up asking "How do you go about talking to a girl?"

The boy's first effort is to tease by engaging in some sort of physical contact: swipe her books, pull her hair, hit her with a snowball. Her response is often a culturally conditioned, predictable one: scream, run (either away or after him), and pretend to be upset. The boy is not very good at talking to girls, but he knows how to roughhouse, so he uses this time-honored method of making his first emotionally charged heterosocial contacts.

Gradually, these initial contacts take on a more sophisticated form. Teasing is now kid stuff. To be "cool"—confident, poised, unemotional, a good conversationalist, and comfortable and mannerly in social situations—is the order of the day. The group boy/girl relationships change into paired relationships, and these deepen into affectionate friendships and romance as the two sexes discover each other. Table 11.1 lists the usual stages of psychosocial development

Overall, the average age for choosing opposite-sex companionship has been declining, probably because of earlier sexual maturity and changing social customs. A boyfriend/girlfriend relationship at early stages may not be reciprocal, and the object of affection may not be aware of the love affair. (I once knew a preadolescent boy who sold his girlfriend to another boy for 100 baseball cards, but the girl was never aware of the fact that she had been a girlfriend in the first place.) With advancing age, however, expected and actual reciprocity begin to converge.

Adolescent Love and Crushes

Along with the development of real or imagined reciprocal relationships comes the experience of "being in love." One survey indicated that love-prone people fell in love for the first time at the average age of 14 (Rubenstein, 1983). Falling in love serves as a positive need in the lives of most people. If the love is reciprocated, it is associated with fulfillment and ecstasy (Hatfield and Sprecher, 1986). College dating couples who report they are in love are also the ones who report the greatest happiness. Young adolescents may have an intense crush on someone they really do not know and will fantasize romantic encounters with this person. The fewer actual romantic contacts, the more likely they are to develop an intense emotional crush and to fantasize the involvement. Often, a crush is on an older person. It may even be a crush on an older person of the same sex.

---

autosociality period during which a child plays alongside other children, not with them.

homosociality period during which children prefer company of those of the same sex.

heterosociality period during which adolescents prefer company of both sexes.

TABLE 11.1 Ages and Stages in Psychosocial Development

Age	Stages
Infancy	Autosocial: Boys and girls are interested only in themselves.
About ages 2–7	They seek companionship of other children regardless of sex.
About ages 8–12	Homosocial: Children prefer to play with others of the same sex; some antagonism exists between the sexes.
Ages 13–14	Girls and boys become interested in one another.
Ages 15–16	Some boys and girls pair off.
Ages 17–18	Majority of adolescents are dating; some, particularly girls, marry.

Questions Junior High Adolescents Ask about Social Development and Relationships

The following questions were submitted to me by adolescents in family life education classes. They illustrate some of the concerns of junior high adolescents (grades 7, 8, and 9) about social development and relationships:

How can I get over being shy in groups?
Do you have to follow everybody else to be popular?

How can you get others to like you?
What do boys look for in a girl?
At what age can you begin dating?
Should seventh-graders be allowed to go to school dances?
What do you do if you're scared to ask a girl to go on a date?

In its extreme form, a fantasized romantic relationship is known as erotomania. **Erotomania** is the delusional belief of being loved by another person. The erotomaniac believes that the victim initiates the relationship and communicates in secret ways, interpreting everything as proof of love and rationalizing contradictory actions as timidity, pride, jealousy, or a test of love (Urbach, Khalily, and Mitchell, 1992).

Intense love can also be risky business. Success sparks delight and failure invites despair. Unrequited love is associated with emptiness and anxiety. Loss of love can be a devastating experience for the adolescent (Hatfield and Sprecher, 1986).

Loss of Love

Loss of a romantic relationship constitutes a major life change. However, it does not appear on stress or change scales. Although the concept of grief has been expanded to include many types of losses other than death, there are still significant losses that are minimized. One important example is the conclusion of a romantic relationship, especially by adolescents. Grief is often minimized for adolescents because they are erroneously perceived as incapable of experiencing both attachment and loss as intense emotional events.

Adults seek to make various types of comforting statements, such as "You're too young to understand what love is; this wasn't the real thing," "You'll feel better tomorrow," "You're young; you have plenty of time to find a relationship," and "You'll look back and wonder what you ever saw in this person."

In actuality, adolescents are especially vulnerable to loss because their egos are still evolving and their range of coping skills may not be fully developed. Adolescents are more vulnerable to loss because, when they enter a romantic relationship, they tend to fantasize about the future with their partner; this fantasy may include dreams of getting married, having children, or being together for the rest of their lives. Grief therapy has to identify and work through loss fantasies as well as loss realities.

Note that romance is an attachment process. An affectional bond between partners has been compared to that which develops between infants and parents. The very nature of feeling attached to someone makes one vulnerable to the loss of that significant other. To emotionally disengage from a relationship takes considerable time and effort. One of the symptoms of grief is depression. The number of symptoms and their duration indicate the severity of depression. Grief may result in reduced academic performance and health problems, as well as carelessness about home duties, employment responsibilities, schoolwork, or attire. Adolescents may withdraw and spend more time alone, even taking meals to their rooms. They may be thinking and fantasizing about the former partner while listening to sentimental music. They may express hopelessness of ever loving anyone else. They may also attempt to self-medicate with drugs or alcohol. Of equal concern are adolescents who exhibit no reaction to the loss, but who start living at a hectic pace and initiate new, intense relationships too quickly. The loss of a loved one has also been identified as a significant factor in adolescent suicide.

The following are some techniques, summarized from Kaczmarek and Backlund (1991), that can help adolescents survive a loss:

1. Help them to view the intense feelings as normal, to be expected. Adolescents need to be given permission to feel and to grieve.
2. Encourage them to express feelings and thoughts.
3. Teach them about the process of grief.
4. Encourage them to rely on a network of family and friends—those who will accept their pain and not offer comforting clichés. Friends who have also lost a love may prove empathetic and insightful.
5. Give them permission to slow down and allow the healing process to begin.
6. Encourage a balance between the need for connectiveness and the need for withdrawal.
7. Encourage them to take care of themselves physically through rest, diet, and exercise.
8. Suggest that they put away mementos. Doing this indicates that they relinquish some of the fantasy of being reunited.
9. Help them view themselves as survivors who understand that the hurt will become less intense with the passage of time.
10. Help them to understand that there will be up-days and down-days and to anticipate sadness occasionally.
11. Suggest that they postpone major decisions and avoid other significant changes in their lives, that the period of grief is not the time to make major changes.
12. Encourage them to find new ways to enjoy the extra time and new freedom. Propose ways to do this, such as taking up a hobby, making new friends, or engaging in additional work or activities. These can help rebuild confidence and self-esteem.

Dating

Sociologists have been careful to emphasize that dating in U.S. culture is not always equivalent to courtship, at least in the early and middle years of adolescence. If dating is not courtship, what are the primary reasons of dating in the eyes of adolescents (McCabe, 1984; Roscoe, Diana, and Brooks, 1987)? Following are some of the many purposes of dating:

1. *Recreation:* One major purpose of dating is to have fun. Dating provides amusement; it is a form of recreation and source of enjoyment. It can be an end in itself.

2. *Companionship without the responsibility of marriage:* Wanting the companionship of others is a strong motive for dating. Desiring the friendship, acceptance, affection, and love of others is a normal part of growing up.

3. *Status grading, sorting, and achievement:* Youths of higher socioeconomic levels date more frequently than do lower-class youths, and some use dating partly to achieve, prove, or maintain status. Membership in certain cliques is associated with the status-seeking aspects of dating. Although there has been a significant decline in dating as a means of gaining or proving status. There are still significant prestige dimensions to cross-sex socializing. However, this is not a major motive for dating.

4. *Socialization:* Dating is a means of personal and social growth. It is a way of learning to know, understand, and get along with many different types of people. Through dating, youths learn cooperation, consideration, responsibility, numerous social skills and matters of etiquette, and techniques for interacting with other people.

5. *Sexual experimentation or satisfaction:* Studies have shown that dating has become more sex oriented as more adolescents have sexual intercourse. Whether dating is used to have sex or sex

---

erotomania   the delusional belief of being loved by another.

Dating among adolescents ranges from platonic recreation, to companionship, to mate selection, to intense sexual and/or romantic involvement.

develops out of dating depends on the attitudes, feelings, motives, and values of the boys and girls. Most research, however, indicates that men want sexual intimacy in a relationship sooner than do women, with this discrepancy a source of potential conflict.

6. *Mate sorting and selection:* Whether this is a conscious motive or not, mate selection is eventually what happens, especially among older youths with prior dating experience. The longer a couple dates, the less they tend to overidealize each other and the greater are their chances of knowing each other. Also, dating provides an opportunity for two people to become a pair. If they are similar in role preferences, leisure interests, and personality characteristics, they are more likely to develop a compatible relationship than if they are dissimilar in physical attractiveness and psychological and social characteristics. Whether dating results in the selection of the most compatible pairs will depend on the total experience (Houts, Robins, and Huston, 1996). Not all dating patterns result in

wise mate selection, especially if dating partners are chosen on the basis of superficial traits. Also, some dating partners develop selfish, competitive, inconsistent, or other undesirable habits during dating that do not serve as good preparation for kind and cooperative marriage relationships (Laner, 1986). In this case, dating is a negative preparation for marriage.

7. *Achieving intimacy:* The development of intimacy is the primary psychosocial task of the young adult. *Intimacy* is the development of openness, sharing, mutual trust, respect, affection, and loyalty, so that a relationship can be characterized as close, enduring, and involving love and commitment (Roscoe, Kennedy, and Pope, 1987).

The capacity to develop intimacy varies from person to person. Research indicates that intimacy is more valued by females than by males, although gender differences decrease in later adolescence as males become closer to and more supportive of their partners (Eaton, Mitchell, and Jolley, 1991).

Men form the closest friendships with women, because they feel less anxiety with women and less competition with them than with men. Usually, women find it easier than men to talk intimately.

Age Patterns for Dating

The median age at which youths begin dating has decreased by almost three years since World War I, primarily because of peer pressure to date earlier. Parents also exercise less control at earlier ages than they used to. In 1924, the median age for girls beginning to date was 16 years. Today, it is about 13 years. In a study of White adolescents from the Detroit area, it was found that the median age for first going steady was about age 16 for both boys and girls (Thornton, 1990). Those who developed steady relationships early dated more frequently. The transition to sexual intercourse was fairly rapid after steady dating began.

There is also some evidence that adolescents from nonintact families begin dating earlier than those from intact, happy families. Dating sometimes apparently meets emotional and social needs not fulfilled in relationships with parents (Coleman, Ganong, and Ellis, 1985).

Common Problems

A study of 227 women and 107 men in a random sample of students at East Carolina University sought to identify dating problems (Knox and Wilson, 1983). Table 11.2 shows the problems experienced by the women. The most frequent problems expressed by the women were *unwanted pressure to engage in sexual behavior, where to go and what to do on dates, communication, sexual misunderstandings,* and *money.* An example of sexual misunderstandings was leading a man on when the woman did not really want to have intercourse. Some of the women complained that the men wanted to move toward a sexual relationship too quickly.

The problems most frequently mentioned by the men (see Table 11.3) were *communication, where to go and what to do on dates, shyness, money,* and *honesty/openness.* By honesty/openness, the men meant how much to tell about themselves and how soon, and getting their partner to open up (Knox and Wilson, 1983).

The problem of communication was mentioned by both men and women. Some students become anxious and nervous when the conversation starts to drag. One senior commented, "After a while you run out of small talk about weather and your classes. When the dialogue dies, it's awful."

Both college men and women look for honesty and openness in a relationship. Part of the problem is caused by the fact that both the man

TABLE 11.2 Dating Problems Experienced by 227 University Women

Problem	Percentage
Unwanted pressure to engage in sexual behavior	23
Places to go	22
Communication with date	20
Sexual misunderstandings	13
Money	9

Source: Adapted from D. Knox and K. Wilson, "Dating Problems of University Students," *College Student Journal, 17* (1983): 225–228.

TABLE 11.3 Dating Problems Experienced by 107 University Men

Problem	Percentage
Communication with date	35
Place to date	23
Shyness	20
Money	17
Honesty/openness	8

Source: Adapted from D. Knox and K. Wilson, "Dating Problems of University Students," *College Student Journal, 17* (1983): 225–228.

and woman strive to be on their best behavior. This involves a certain amount of pretense or play acting, called *imaging,* to present oneself in the best possible manner.

Going Steady

For many adults, particularly parents, adolescents going steady is equivalent to committing an unforgivable sin. As a result, steady dating probably receives more attention than any other aspect of dating, except perhaps sex and dating behavior. How widespread is going steady? Is it harmful or useful? Why do youths do it, often in spite of contrary pressures from their parents and leaders?

Because one of the worries of parents is that youths will make premature commitments, they urge their offspring to date a large number of partners. Research indicates, however, that those who date the greatest number of partners also have the greatest number of different steady relationships: The larger the number of casual partners, the greater the chances of going steady with them. Because marital success is positively correlated with the number of friends of both sexes one has before marriage, there is some advantage in going with large numbers of partners, though their chances of going steady with any one are greater. Steady dating for a long period can limit

imaging being on best behavior to make a good impression.

the number of dating partners, and a community that accepts steady dating as the norm for the group makes it harder for youths to avoid the pattern. In some cases, they either have to go steady or not date.

Going steady has advantages and disadvantages. The primary motive seems to be to enjoy the company of someone else; it is not often marriage-oriented. Steady dating also provides security for some adolescents. Apparently, they go steady because they need to, emotionally and socially. They try to find someone to love and be loved by, who understands and sympathizes. Steady dating may meet emotional needs. Those who go steady are also those who have the highest self-esteem (Samet and Kelly, 1987).

The disadvantages are many. Some youths feel "it's a drag," that they have more fun with different people. One girl said, "Instead of going steady, I wound up staying home steady. Ted didn't take me out." Some youths are not emotionally mature enough to handle such an intimate relationship and the problems that arise. Also, breaking up leads to hurt feelings. One boy asked, "How can I ditch Kathy without hurting her feelings?" This is a frequent remark from youths who are involved but who do not know how to get uninvolved. The problem of jealousy often arises. Boys tend to be jealous over sexual issues; girls complain of lack of time and attention.

The basic problem may be that neither person is ready for an intense, intimate relationship with one person over a long period of time. Most youths admit that steady dating becomes a license for increasing sexual intimacy. "You get to feeling married, and that's dangerous," is the way one adolescent expressed it. Others feel that going steady adds respectability to petting or even to intercourse and that this is an advantage rather than a disadvantage. Research indicates that those within a particular socioeconomic class who date the most frequently and who begin at the earliest ages are more likely to get married early as well; therefore, whenever steady dating pushes youths prematurely into early marriage, it is a serious disadvantage.

Nonmarital Cohabitation

To many older youths, nonmarital cohabitation is just an extension of steady dating (Thornton, 1990).

Incidence

In 1995, there were 3.7 million unmarried cohabiting couples in the United States. About 20 percent of these were under 25 years of age (U.S. Bureau of the Census, 1996). Studies of the incidence of cohabitation among college populations indicate that about 25 percent of students live with a dating partner at some point in their college careers (Risman, Hill, Rubin, and Peplau, 1981; Tanfer, 1987). However, the rates vary, de-

PERSONAL ISSUES

Questions Senior High Adolescents Ask about Dating

The following questions were submitted to me by adolescents in family life education classes. They reflect some of the concerns of senior high school adolescents (grades 10, 11, and 12):

Is it all right to date several boys at once?
How can you tell if you're really in love?
How should a girl refuse a date?

Will boys take you out if you're not willing to go all the way?
How can you break up without hurting the other person?
What do you do if your parents don't want you to go with your boyfriend because he's 3 years older (I'm 15; he's 18)?
What kind of boys do girls like best?

pending on the type of school, housing, parietal policies, sex composition, and ratio of the student body, as well as the researcher's sample and definition of cohabitation (Glick and Spanier, 1980). Of those who have cohabited, a great majority indicate that they would do so again (Newcomb, 1986).

The rise in nonmarital sex has been accompanied by an increase in cohabitation. The proportion of first marriages preceded by cohabitation has grown from 8 percent in the late 1960s to about 50 percent today. Thus, about half of all first marriages are now preceded by cohabitation (Bumpass, 1990).

Meanings Attached to Cohabitation

When couples decide to cohabit, the important questions are: What meaning do they attach to the relationship? Do they consider themselves in love? Are they committed to one another in an exclusive relationship? Are they testing their relationship? Are they preparing for marriage? Do they consider themselves married? There is a wide variety of patterns and meanings associated with cohabitation, which may be grouped as follows:

> Arrangements without commitment
> Intimate involvements with emotional commitment
> Living together as a prelude to marriage
> Living together as a trial marriage
> Living together as an alternative to marriage

Arrangements without Commitment Sometimes, cohabitation arrangements are hastily or informally decided. After a weekend of fun and a short acquaintance, for example, the young man decides to move into his girlfriend's apartment. He ends up staying the rest of the semester. Sometimes, the arrangement is carefully worked out over a period of time as desirable for the couple. They simply want to live, sleep, and have fun together. They are very good friends and lovers but want no permanent, intimate commitment. Their living together includes sharing expenses, housekeeping chores, and the other economic and material necessities that a married couple do, as well as sleeping together. This type of arrangement

usually is of short duration. Either it develops into a greater commitment or the couple breaks up ("Cohabiting Young Women Plan to Get Married," 1987).

Intimate Involvements with Emotional Commitment The majority of cohabiting college couples place themselves in this category. Couples describe themselves as having a strong, affectionate relationship. Although some permit dating and sexual relationships outside the relationship, monogamy is the rule (Newcomb, 1986). Although there is a strong emotional commitment, there are no long-range plans for the future or for marriage. Such couples intend to continue the relationship indefinitely, but most involvements are of fairly short duration. One study of cohabitation in college found no statistically significant association between cohabitation and the type of relation that eventually evolved (i.e., whether the couple married or not) (Risman, Hill, Rubin, and Peplau, 1981). Cohabiting couples were not less likely to have married or more likely to have broken up by the end of the two-year study in contrast to couples that had not cohabited.

Living Together as a Prelude to Marriage In this type of relationship, the couple has already committed themselves to legal marriage. They are engaged, formally or informally, but find no reason to live apart while they are waiting to be married or while they are making arrangements for their marriage. Many times, their living arrangements just develop over time, without conscious intent. Here is one student's story:

> My boyfriend and I never really *decided* we were going to live together before marriage. It just happened. He would come over to my apartment weekends. It would be late, so I'd put him up for the night. Then several weekends he stayed the whole time, it was easier than driving all that distance back home. After a while, we got thinking: "Isn't this silly, why should we be separated, why can't he just move in with me?" So he did. Finally, he gave up his own place, because it was cheaper for us to maintain only one apartment. Six months later we got married. If someone would ask: "What made you decide to live together before marriage?" my answer would be: "I don't know. It just happened."

Couples who cohabit attach many meanings to their relationships. It might be a temporary arrangement without commitment, an emotionally committed relationship without long-range plans, a prelude to marriage, a test trial for marriage, or an alternative to marriage.

Under these circumstances, there is never an intention that cohabitation will replace marriage or even be a trial period before marriage. It is just something the couple decides to do before they get married.

Living Together as a Trial Marriage   In this type of arrangement, the couple decides to live together to test their relationship—to discover if they are compatible and want to enter into legal marriage. This arrangement is "the little marriage before the big marriage that will last."

Living Together as an Alternative to Marriage   This arrangement has been called *companionate marriage, a covenant of intimacy,* or *a nonlegal voluntary association.* It is intended not as a prelude to marriage but as a substitute for it.

Reactions to Cohabitation

Generally, the majority of cohabiting couples report no regret at having cohabited. Among those who later married, one study reported that only 9 percent of the women and 4 percent of the men expressed regrets (Watson, 1983). The proportion of dissatisfied couples is higher for those who do

not marry. A few are devastated by relationships that do not work out. Some are very unhappy living together, experiencing much tension and frequent conflict, and even violence.

Some individuals are hurt, either because the relationship did not work out or because they expected that it would result in marriage and it did not. Several studies have shown that men and women have somewhat different reasons for cohabitation. For many men, cohabitation is no different from dating. Men most often cite their need for sexual gratification as the reason, whereas women state that marriage is their most important motive. When the relationship does not lead to marriage, some women feel used and exploited. The men expect them to pay half the expenses, do many of the household chores, and provide regular bed privileges without a commitment. As a result, many cohabiting women develop negative views of marriage and of the role of husband. They begin to see themselves as a source of sex, not as a source of affection. Then there is always their anxiety about pregnancy, in spite of contraception. If pregnancy occurs, some cohabiting couples say they would marry, yet marriage because of pregnancy is one of the worst possible motives in terms of subsequent chances for mari-

HIGHLIGHT

Coed Dorms

The arrangement of men and women in college living in adjacent rooms represents what is, to adults, a departure from tradition. In a few instances, men and women are allowed to share university apartments. But from a student's point of view, coed living is desirable because it is natural. As one woman said, "When you're separated, it's so unnatural. Your friends are all girls. You walk into a boy's dorm and they all stare at you. When you're all living together, the boys look at girls less as sex objects." Another remarked,

> The point is that we want to know boys as friends and companions, as well as dating objects. . . . It used to be, a guy kept trying to get the girl to bed, and she kept trying to stay out. Now they both want a good, honest relationship first. . . . And I'm not talking about promiscuity. Sometimes I think parents think so much dirtier than we do. I'm talking about the total relationship, as opposed to sex roles.

The primary objection from an adult point of view is that coed dorms lead to promiscuity. This fear of adults has little basis in fact. One advantage of coed dorms is that students form relationships other than those based ex-

clusively on sex. They go beyond sexual attraction to a more encompassing relationship. These students also participate less in structured, one-to-one dating and more in informal group activities. They plan more group activities and events. Administrators report that students spend as much time studying as those in single-sex residences, that the level of conversation is intellectually higher, and that there is less vandalism.

Not all students want or choose coed living when given the option. Some find it too much of a strain to "get dressed before walking down the hall" or "having to be on your best behavior all the time." Generally, the cautious or socially immature student (one who could benefit most from coed living) is most likely to choose a single-sex residence. When Lambda Nu, a fraternity at Stanford University, went coed, 4 men quit but 10 joined; 42 women applied, and 20 were picked by lot. The men and women live in separate sections of the house, but there are few rules. Students say there is little promiscuity.

Although coed living is not for everybody, it has many advantages in promoting natural heterosexual development and relationships.

---

tal success. All that can be said with certainty now is that cohabitation has been helpful to some and harmful to others. The effect depends on the individuals involved, on how they feel, and on what happens (Rice, 1993).

Still, the majority of college students who have cohabited indicate positive feelings about the experience. Students report the experience as "pleasant," "successful," "highly productive." Many students indicate that it fostered personal growth and maturity, resulting in a deeper understanding of themselves or of what marriage requires (Rice, 1993). In comparison with noncohabiting couples in the Boston area, cohabiting men and women were more likely to report satisfaction with their relationships (Risman, Hill, Rubin, and Peplau, 1981). Cohabiting men were more likely to say that having sexual intercourse with their partner was satisfying. Cohabiting cou-

ples reported seeing each other more often, having sexual intercourse more often, feeling greater love for each other, and disclosing more to their partner.

Adjustments

One major category of problems in cohabitation relates to the emotional involvement and feelings of the individuals concerned. A minority complain about overinvolvement, feeling trapped, losing identity, overpermissiveness of their partner, or the lack of opportunity to participate in activities with others. Without realizing it, these people became enmeshed in relationships for which they were not emotionally prepared. Once in, they did not know how to escape without hurting their partners. Others report being exploited or used by another person who did not care about them.

Jealousy of others' involvements is common. One major worry is concern and uncertainty about the future. This uncertainty pressures some into marriage, others into breaking off the relationship.

The other problems youths face while living together unmarried are similar to those of any other people sharing the same quarters. Arranging to do the housekeeping chores is a challenge to unmarried as well as married couples. Traditional sex-role concepts and role specialization in the division of labor are quite evident among couples. Far greater percentages of women than men report cooking, dusting, dishwashing, vacuuming, doing laundry, feeding pets, and planning menus, which are traditionally considered feminine chores. Men report major responsibility for cutting the lawn, washing the car, doing repairs, cleaning the garage, shoveling snow, which are traditionally considered masculine chores. More men than women report an equal sharing of traditionally feminine chores, indicating that men reported they helped with these tasks more often than women felt they did. It is obvious that nonmarital cohabitation is not a cure-all for sex-role inequality. Some tasks are shared, but generally the female partners do women's work and the male partners do men's work (as defined by traditional standards). This division leaves the women with most of the household duties regardless of whether they are going to school and are employed as well. A study of students from four colleges in the Boston area revealed that cohabiting men (in comparison with noncohabiting dating couples) were *not* more likely to say their relationship was egalitarian. Cohabiting women were more likely to report male dominance, and were more likely to see themselves at a power disadvantage (Risman, Hill, Rubin, and Peplau, 1981).

The more studies that are done of cohabitation, the more evidence there is that the couples behave like ordinary married couples. Learning to know and understand each other's personalities and adjusting to schedules, personal habits, and idiosyncrasies arise in unmarried relationships as well as in marriages. Many problems occur because couples are immature emotionally, socially, financially, and in other ways. They have to face most of the same problems that young married couples face as a result of their immaturities

and insecurities. The majority of couples, however, report that their sex life is satisfying ("Cohabitation by the Unmarried," 1986). Cohabiting couples generally have intercourse more frequently and are more faithful contraceptive users than either married couples or unmarried noncohabitants (Bachrach, 1987).

Cohabiting and Marriage Differences

Having said that cohabitation is similar to marriage in many ways, I hasten to add that there are also significant differences. People who cohabit are more prone to split up than are married couples, for several reasons. Normally, people who are cohabiting have lower levels of commitment than do those who are married. Those who cohabit eschew tradition and are less committed to a traditional life-style. Greater commitment is required in marriage and there are stronger social sanctions associated with deviation from tradition and marriage. Also, there is stronger social disapproval of deviant marital behaviors. This means that the relationship between a married couple is harder to dissolve. This is supported by stronger social norms than is true for cohabiting individuals. In marriage, there are more barriers that hold the relationship together (e.g., property interests). Therefore, lower levels of commitment are generally expected between cohabiting rather than married partners. The lack of social norms governing cohabitation contributes to higher dissolution rates in such relationships. Those in a relationship that is less socially recognized or governed by clear normative standards are less likely to be tightly integrated into networks of others who are in more traditional relationships.

Relationships with parents are potentially important for the overall quality of a partnership. Those who have poor relationships with their parents lack a basic emotional and possibly economic resource. Should the parent-child relationship suffer as a result of a cohabiting relationship, the quality of the partners' affectionate bonds may suffer.

Marriage has traditionally been viewed as the acceptable arrangement for the bearing and rearing of children. Even in the presence of higher rates of out-of-wedlock childbearing, nonmarital fertility is still viewed as less desirable than marital fertility. It has been argued that having or desiring a child is a fundamental difference between cohabiting and married couples. In the aggregate, we would expect that those who intend to have children will be more likely to marry than those who do not and that those who intend to remain childless will be more likely than those who desire children to enter a cohabiting relationship. The percentage of cohabiting people attempting to have a child is lower than the percentage of married people. Married individuals are predicted to express higher fertility intentions than cohabiting individuals.

Those who are cohabiting report significantly lower levels of happiness than married individuals. This is particularly noteworthy because very few people in relationships describe themselves as unhappy. Given the extremely small amount of variation in response to the question of happiness, a significant difference is particularly noteworthy. In summary, cohabiting individuals report lower levels of happiness with their partnerships, express lower degrees of commitment to their relationships, and have poorer quality relationships with their parents (Nock, 1995).

Another study evaluated cohabiting and marital relationships among African Americans and White Americans aged 19 to 48. Controlling for the relationship duration and demographic characteristics of the respondents, the study found that cohabiting respondents, in general, reported poorer relationship quality than their married counterparts. However, marriage plans largely explained the differences in relationship quality between cohabitors and marrieds. The majority of cohabitors reported plans to marry their partners; these cohabitors were involved in unions that were not significantly different from marriages. In fact, the relationship quality of marrieds and cohabitors with plans to marry is affected in the same way by the presence of potential sources of stress, such as biological children, children from past unions, and prior union experience (Brown and Booth, 1996).

Effect on Subsequent Marriage

What effect does premarital cohabitation have on subsequent marital adjustment? One of the argu-

ments used for cohabitation is that it weeds out incompatible couples and prepares people for more successful marriage. Is this true? No, according to several studies.

Those who cohabit prior to marriage have been significantly lower on measures of marital quality (Booth and Johnson, 1988) and have a significantly higher risk of marital dissolution at any given marital duration (Balakrishnan, Rao, Lapierre-Adamcyk, and Krotki, 1987; Bennett, Blanc, and Bloom, 1988; Booth and Johnson, 1988; Bumpass and Sweet, 1989; Gurak, Falcon, Sandefur, and Torrecilha, 1989; Teachman and Polonko, 1990; Trussell, Rodriquez, and Vaughan, 1988; Wu, 1995a). Data from the 1987–1988 National Survey of Families and Households show that couples who cohabited before marriage reported lower-quality marriages, lower commitment to the institution of marriage, more individualistic views of marriage (wives only), and a greater likelihood of divorce than couples who did not cohabit (Thomson and Colella, 1992). Effects were generally stronger for those who had cohabited for longer periods before marriage. Social and economic characteristics accounted for the higher perceived likelihood of divorce among those who had cohabited less than a year. Differences in marital quality and institutional commitment for those who had cohabited for longer periods of time were also evident.

Another study, which examined the data from the National Survey of Families and Households, found that cohabitation was generally associated with higher risk of marital dissolution. However, that differential was much smaller in recent cohorts where cohabitation was more common. Perhaps the differences in marital dissolution may largely disappear as cohabitation becomes more common (Schoen, 1992).

The results of studies seem to be affected partially by how long people have been married at the time of evaluation. Most research indicates that a period of disillusionment in relation to marriage occurs after the initial glow and excitement have worn off and couples have settled down to daily living. Presumably, the longer couples have lived together before marriage, the earlier in the relationship the period of disillusionment sets in. One study found that when marital duration was counted from the beginning of marriage for all couples, prior cohabitors indeed had the greater odds of dissolution at any given marital duration (Teachman and Polonko, 1990). When marital duration was counted for cohabitors from the beginning of the coresidential union, however, only those who cohabited more than once prior to marriage had higher odds for dissolution. For those who only cohabited with the future spouse, the odds of dissolution were not significantly different from those for noncohabitors. It is only among serial cohabitors that the cohabitation effect may be explained as less commitment to marital permanence. For others, the association of cohabitation with greater odds of marital dissolution is simply the artifact of the increased exposure to the risk of marital instability that is experienced during the cohabitating period.

This result comes as a simple explanation for cohabitors' higher likelihood of divorce. One such study found that cohabiting prior to marriage, regardless of the nature of that cohabitation, is associated with an enhanced risk of later marital dissolution (DeMaris and Rao, 1992). Contrary to the expectation of many couples, who envision that prior cohabitation is a hedge against marital failure, those who live together before marrying stand a higher chance of ending their marriages. Furthermore, the researchers found that the association of cohabitation with increased odds of dissolution persisted even after accounting for the extra time that cohabitors had been together. Other studies do not always substantiate this finding.

There are a number of important questions to be addressed before individual effects about cohabiting can be known. If, after living together, couples feel pushed into marriages for which they are not ready, the effect is detrimental. Studies at four colleges in the Boston area revealed that cohabiting couples were no less likely to marry or no more likely to break up than noncohabiting couples who were dating. Cohabitation appeared to be part of the courtship process rather than a long-term alternative to marriage (Risman, Hill, Rubin, and Peplau, 1981). However, those who were married by the end of the study reported a shorter interval between the time of first dating and the time they were married (22.8 months for cohabiting couples versus 35.8 months for noncohabiting couples). Those who had lived together before marriage had been under a great deal of pressure from parents either to marry or to end their cohabiting relationship. Cohabitation either speeded up their decision to marry, or the couples may have decided to live together only after they agreed to marry. Certainly, if cohabitation pushed couples into marriage when they were not ready, the result would be negative.

Cohabitating and Premarital Childbearing

The question arises of whether cohabitation is commonly a setting for procreation and care of the young. Research demonstrates that a nontrivial proportion of premarital pregnancies and births to U.S. women take place within cohabitation. Moreover, entry into motherhood is more likely among never-married women who are cohabiting than among those who are living alone. Premarital births to cohabiting women are less likely to be unplanned than premarital births to single (noncohabiting) women.

The rise of cohabitation has taken place in very different family contexts for various racial and ethnic groups. Cohabitation seems to operate differently for disadvantaged minorities than for Whites. One study documents sharp differences in the role of cohabitation across racial and ethnic groups. Cohabitation operates largely as a transitional stage before marriage for non-Hispanic Whites, but this is not the case for African Americans or Puerto Ricans. Nonmarital unions are a common family context for childbearing among Puerto Ricans; about half of the babies born premaritally have parents who live together. In contrast, African American women are much less likely to be in any union (cohabitation or marriage) when they become mothers. African Americans have markedly higher rates of premarital childbearing than Puerto Ricans. The historical prevalence of consensual unions among Puerto Ricans and their higher level of acceptance of cohabitation may partially explain why cohabitation plays a greater role in premarital childbearing for Puerto Ricans than for African Americans (Manning and Landale, 1996).

As the incidence of cohabitation continues to rise, the number of children born into these relationships is likely to increase. The question arises: Are cohabitational relationships likely to substitute for marriage as a setting for childbearing? The evidence suggests that this is unlikely to be the case in the years to come. A recent study in the United States (Manning, 1995) has shown that the majority of women bear their first child within marriages, and that many cohabiting women wait until their first marriage to have their first child (Wu, 1996). Cohabiting couples with children in the relationship are less likely to experience union disruption than are childless couples. Having children can encourage both married and unmarried couples to stay together. However, results show that the number, sex, and age of children appears to have virtually no effect on the risk of disruption. What is important is the presence of children in the relationship.

In addition, the transient nature of cohabitation relationships may cause both partners to work harder at maintaining the relationship and to expect clear gains from their continued involvement in the relationships. Cohabitors, particularly males, may be more eager to please their partners by assuming more responsibilities in the relationship, including child care (Wu, 1995b).

Adolescent Marriage

To evaluate whether adolescent marriage is wise or unwise, desirable or undesirable, we must ask how successful these marriages are. If they are strong, happy, satisfying marriages, there is no cause for complaint or alarm; but if they are weak, unhappy, frustrating marriages, causing much personal suffering and numerous social problems, there is ample cause for concern.

Trends and Incidence

Figure 11.2 gives a detailed picture of U.S. statistics on marriage ages between 1890 and 1993. The median age of first marriage stopped declining in 1956 for women and in 1959 for men, and has been increasing slowly since. The median age of first marriage in 1993 was 24.5 for women and 26.5 for men. It appears that the steady drop in median age of marriage that was especially noticeable in the 1940s has been arrested. However, there are still numbers of youths, especially girls, who are marrying young. Census figures for 1995 showed that 8.4 percent of girls and 2.3 percent of boys aged 18 to 19 are (or have been) married (U.S. Bureau of the Census, 1996). Data show that

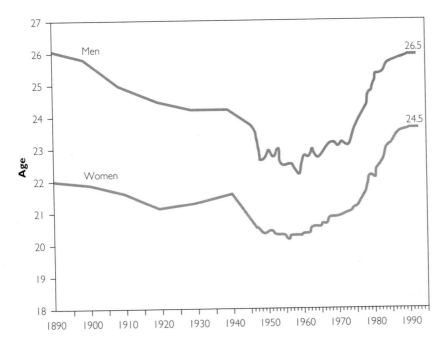

FIGURE 11.2   Median Age at First Marriage, by Sex: 1890 to 1993

Source: U.S. National Center for Health Statistics (U.S. Department of Health and Human Services), *Vital Statistics of the United States*, annual, 1890–1990 (Washington, DC: U.S. Government Printing Office); U.S. National Center for Health Statistics, *Monthly Vital Statistics Report*, monthly (Washington, DC: U.S. Government Printing Office); and U.S. Bureau of the Census, *Statistical Abstract of the United States, 1994* (Washington, DC: U.S. Government Printing Office, 1994).

33.3 percent of women and 19.3 percent of men aged 20 to 24 are or have been married.

Prospects and Prognosis

Divorce statistics are a means of measuring marriage success or failure. Using this measure, adolescent marriages do not work out well (Booth and Edwards, 1985). Numerous research studies indicate that the younger people are when married, the greater the chance of unhappy marriage and thus of divorce (Teti, Lamb, and Elster, 1987). The older the couple at first marriage, the greater is the likelihood the marriage will succeed. But this direct correlation between age at first marriage and marital success diminishes for men at about age 27, when the decline in divorce rates slows considerably. For women, the divorce rate declines with each year they wait to marry until a gradual leveling off occurs at about age 25. Therefore, strictly from the standpoint of marital stability, men who wait to marry until at least age 27 and women who wait until about age 25 have waited as long as practical to maximize their chances of marital success (Booth and Edwards, 1985).

Many couples marrying young may never get divorced, but some express deep dissatisfaction with their marriages. Here are some of their comments:

> "I don't think people should marry young. It's hard to get along when he is going to school. Our income is rather short. We probably should have waited."

> "We thought we were in love, we would get married and have good times. We had a very poor idea of what marriage was. We thought we could come and go, do as we pleased, do or not do the dishes, but it isn't that way."

> "I have missed several years of important living, the dating period, living with another girl, being away from home, working, maybe. I wouldn't get married so young again."

> "I would have waited to finish high school first. It has tied me down so. I've had no fun since I was married. I can't go to dances. I don't feel right there. . . . I guess I thought he was the only one in the world. I was badly mixed up."

A Profile of the Young Married

Early marriages primarily involve young wives and older husbands. Typically, a high school girl will marry a boy who is past high school age, usually from 3.5 to 5.5 years older. Usually, the younger the bride, the larger is the age difference between her and her husband. Early marriages disproportionately involve adolescents from lower socioeconomic backgrounds. Typically, their parents have less education and are of a lower occupational status.

There are several good reasons why low socioeconomic status correlates with early marriage. As a group, low SES youths are less interested in high school and post–high school education, so they see no need to delay marriage to finish their schooling, especially when marriage seems much more attractive than school. Less-skilled occupations require only a minimal amount of education. In some communities, marriage by age 18, especially for girls, is generally approved because the youths have reached a dead end in school and marriage seems to be the only attractive course. The parents are less likely to object to early marriage. Furthermore, premarital pregnancy, one of the principal causes of early marriage, is much more common among youths from low-socioeconomic-status families.

Similarly, adolescents who have lower intelligence and poorer grades in school more often marry early. Furthermore, those who marry during school are more likely to drop out of school. It becomes a vicious circle: The academically inferior marry earlier, and once married, are less likely to continue their educations (Lowe and Witt, 1984). This is especially true of those who have children soon after marriage (Haggstrom, Kanouse, and Morrison, 1986).

Place of residence seems to have some influence on age at marriage. Rural residents tend to marry a year earlier than urban residents. Those from the South tend to marry earlier than others, those from the Northeast later, with those from the central and western states somewhere in between. Youths of foreign parentage usually marry later than those of native-born parents. Foreign-born Irish men have the highest age at marriage (29.4 years), and those with Spanish surnames the earliest (25.6 years). The age is variable, depending on native customs.

There is some evidence that the less emotionally adjusted a boy or girl is, the more likely early marriage is to occur. Additionally, those who marry early are more socially maladjusted at the time of marriage than are others (Grover, Russell,

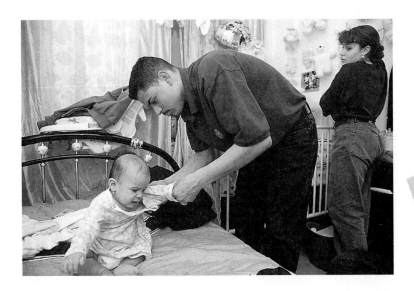

The number-one reason for early marriage, especially while still in school, is pregnancy. There are many problems associated with these early marriages, including financial worries, lack of maturity, and resentment at being tied down.

Schumm, and Paff-Bergen, 1985). However, young marrieds evidence the most personality improvement during the early years—more so than do the nonmarrieds—so that at the end of a few years, the personality differentials virtually disappear. If the marriage can survive, marriage itself seems to be a contributing factor in developing personal and social maturity.

Youths who marry early tend to have less satisfactory relationships with their parents. They have more disagreement with parents before marriage and less attachment to their fathers. Furthermore, wives who report problems with families in their childhood and adolescence report unhappiness, doubt, and conflict in early marriage.

Reasons for Adolescent Marriage

The most important causes or reasons for early marriage are the following:

Sexual stimulation; pregnancy
Early dating; acceleration of adult sophistication
Social pressure
Overly romantic, glamorous views of marriage
Escape; to resolve personal problems
Affluence and prosperity

Let's examine each of these reasons in greater detail.

The number-one reason for early marriage, particularly while still in school, is *pregnancy*. Preg-

nancy rates vary from study to study according to the age of the youths. The younger the adolescent is at the time of marriage, the more likely pregnancy is to be involved. Pregnancy rates may be as high as 50 percent when at least one of the partners is still in high school.

Research clearly indicates that within a social class, the earlier a boy or girl starts to date, the more likely early marriage is to occur. It is important to emphasize the phrase *within a social class*, for adolescents from higher-socioeconomic-status groups start *dating earlier* than those from lower-socioeconomic-status groups, yet the latter marry earlier. Why? Although higher-status youths start dating earlier, they proceed at a slower pace from dating to marriage. Lower-status youths start dating a little later but are more likely to become romantically involved, go steady, and proceed more rapidly from first date to marriage. Age when dating starts is not itself a deciding factor. What is important is the length of the person's dating experience before marriage—generally, the longer the better.

There are other correlates to these statements. The more dates a girl has, compared with others her age, the more likely early marriage is to occur. Also, the earlier a girl begins to go steady and the more steady boyfriends she has in high school, the more likely she is to marry early. But again, the emphasis should not be just on how young dating begins but on how rapidly the young person advances to serious dating, going steady, engagement, and other symbols of adult status.

Social pressure from parents, friends, and society pushes adolescents toward early marriage. Educators report a chain reaction of early marriages in their schools. When one couple marries, there is increased pressure on others to do the same. No one wants to be left out. Pressure also comes from parents who do not want their daughters to be wallflowers or spinsters or their sons to be thought different.

Adolescents often hold very *magical views of marriage.* Marriage is seen as a fairytale in which a man and woman fall in love, marry, and live in bliss for eternity. Even adolescents whose parents are divorced and/or remarried have idealized concepts of marriage. Being in love in our culture is held to be so romantic and wonderful that many youths do not want to wait to enter this blissful state. The concept of marriage for love leads youths to feel that the goal of life is to find love, and that once found, they must hurry up and marry, at all costs, before it escapes. Girls who marry early often feel that marriage is their goal in life.

Marriage is sometimes used as a means of *escape* from an unhappy home situation, lack of school achievement, personal insecurities or inadequacies, or unsatisfactory social adjustment with one's peers. The less attractive one's present situation is and the more attractive marriage seems, the more the emotionally insecure or socially maladjusted individual feels pushed toward marriage.

More early marriages occur in times of *economic prosperity* than in times of economic depression. The reason is obvious: Getting married costs money; therefore, when employment is readily available, young couples feel they can afford to get married.

Adjustments and Problems

Many of the adjustments young couples must make or the problems they must solve are no different from those of other couples, but they are aggravated by *immaturity.* It is essentially the problem of immaturity, then, that is the great obstacle to successful teenage marriage.

The less mature are less likely to make a wise choice of mate. When the time span between first date and marriage is shortened, youths have less chance to gain experience in knowing and understanding the kind of person with whom they are compatible. The young adolescent girl or boy in the throes of a first love affair is at a distinct disadvantage in making an intelligent choice of mate. Youths who marry young have spent insufficient time in the marital search process and tend to marry spouses who are relatively poor matches on a variety of unmeasured traits. Married at a young age signifies a failure to search adequately for a well-matched spouse; thus, early marriages are disproportionately composed of poorly matched spouses (South, 1995).

Immature individuals are less likely to evidence the ultimate direction of their personality growth. Youths change as they mature and may find they have nothing in common with their partners as they grow older. Two young people who might genuinely find common interests and a good reciprocal interaction at a particular point in time could easily grow away from each other in the ensuing two or three years as their personalities unfold.

The most common example is the young woman who drops out of school to work to put her husband through college only to discover afterward that he has grown away from her intellectually and they can no longer enjoy talking together. The same holds true of a boy who marries young. He may marry a girl who has not yet found herself in life and runs the risk of living with a girl different from the woman she will be several years later. Many girls marry only to discover later that they resent having to give up a promising career.

Difficult and complex adjustments and problems of marriage are not handled well by immature couples. There is ample evidence to show that emotional maturity and good marital adjustment go together (Booth and Edwards, 1985).

Many teenagers are still insecure, oversensitive, and somewhat tempestuous and unstable. Many are still rebelling against adult authority and seeking emotional emancipation from parents. If these youths marry, they carry their immaturities into marriage, making it difficult to adjust to living with their mates and making it harder to make decisions and solve conflicts as they arise. One study found that the principal sources of marital dissatisfaction among couples who married young were lack of faithfulness, presence of jealousy, lack of understanding, disagreement, and lack of communication (Booth and Edwards, 1985). Attempts to dominate or refusal to talk made communication difficult.

Most youths have not yet become responsible enough for marriage. The average teenage boy is not ready to settle down. He wants to go out, have fun, be with the gang, and be free to do as he pleases. He may resent being tied down and possibly having to support a wife and child. He may not yet evidence a "monogamous attitude." Nor are many teenage girls ready to be wives and probably mothers, to manage a family budget, or to handle their share of the responsibility for the homemaking tasks.

One of the real problems and disadvantages of early marriage is that it is often associated with early parenthood (Teti and Lamb, 1989). A majority of teenage couples have a baby within one year after marriage, if they have not already had a baby before marriage (Miller and Heaton, 1991; Moore and Stief, 1991). In one study of the best age for parenthood and marriage, both male and female African Americans indicated that the mean ideal age for first birth is less than the mean best age for marriage (Smith and Zabin, 1993).

The younger the bride and groom, the sooner they start having children. Also, the earlier the age at marriage, the greater is the percentage of brides who are premaritally pregnant. Those who get married because of pregnancy have the poorest prognosis of marital success. Because premarital pregnancy and early postmarital pregnancy are followed by a higher-than-average divorce rate, large numbers of children of early marriages grow up without a secure, stable family life or without both a mother and a father. Apparently, many young marrieds are not mature enough to assume the responsibilities of marriage and early parenthood, so the marriages often fail and the children suffer.

Adolescent married couples not only begin having children at an earlier age but they also have more children. The young women who are the least happily married are also the ones who experience unplanned pregnancies. Early motherhood creates many stresses in the lives of adolescents. Adolescent mothers are more likely to be out of school, unemployed, poor, and on welfare. They experience loneliness and isolation from friends, with little time for themselves. Many are able to cope only by asking family members and community agencies for assistance, and many live with their parents after the birth of the baby (Nathanson, Baird, and Jemail, 1986).

Another problem that often surfaces is a decrease in sexual satisfaction after marriage, especially after the first baby is born. Disagreements are common over the quality and frequency of sex relations. Physicians have emphasized the medical risks of early pregnancy. Children born to adolescent mothers are more likely to be born premature, with low birth weight and with physical and neurological defects, than are infants born to mothers in their twenties. Perinatal, neonatal, and infant mortality have been found to be higher for children of young mothers ("Substantially Higher," 1984).

The higher incidence of physical defects in children born to adolescent mothers is not due solely to the age of the mother. It is related also to the fact that these mothers may be pregnant out of wedlock and of low socioeconomic status and so receive inadequate nutrition and poor or inadequate prenatal care ("Social Factors," 1984). Early pregnancy is also a medical risk for the young teenage girl. If she becomes pregnant while her own body is still growing and maturing, the growing fetus imposes an additional strain on her system, and she is more prone to complications during pregnancy.

One of the major problems of early marriage is *financial worry* (Teti and Lamb, 1989). The primary difficulties are inadequate income and the fact that income has not reached the level expected. Little education, inexperience, and youth do not bring high wages (Grindstaff, 1988). Some couples marry without any income.

With little or no income, couples receive part or all of their financial assistance from parents. Families usually give some assistance to their children in the first year of marriage, such as wedding gifts, clothing, home furnishings and equipment, food, loans of household equipment and car, babysitting services, money, and other gifts.

Not only low income, but also inexperience in financial management and naively optimistic expectations get young marrieds into financial trouble. Teenagers usually expect to be able to purchase immediately many of the items that probably took their parents years to acquire.

One of the expensive obsessions of adolescent males is to have a car. The heavy outlay for cars and transportation is a major burden on the budgets of young families that need funds for current expenses or for household goods to begin marriage.

One of the most frequent complaints of immature wives is the husband who goes out with his friends and leaves her home alone. Also, in-law problems are more likely if young couples live with parents or accept financial help from them. When parents give assistance to married children, they often expect continual affectional response, inclusion in some of their children's activities, personal service and attention, and compliance with parental wishes. The more immature the young marrieds, the more likely parents are to try to "help"—to direct and interfere in their children's lives—and the more likely the young couple is to enact the residues of late adolescent conflicts over autonomy and dependence.

Marriage and Public Schools

Early marriage diminishes educational attainment among those attending high school. Not only do young marrieds make less educational progress during the four-year period of high school but they also tend to have lower educational aspirations for the future (Lowe and Witt, 1984). The converse is also true: Those with lower educational aspirations tend to marry earlier than those with higher aspirations.

Dropout rates among married high school couples are high. The rates reflect the fact that the great majority of the girls are pregnant before marriage, and school administrative policies and programs fail to keep the girl in school. Once she has dropped out, the chances of the adolescent mother returning to continue her education are relatively small, especially if she keeps her baby and receives little encouragement or help in returning. Boys who drop out most often do so for economic reasons. Figure 11.3 shows the mean educational attainment for women by the age at which they had their first child. If a girl is less than age 15 when she had her first child, her average

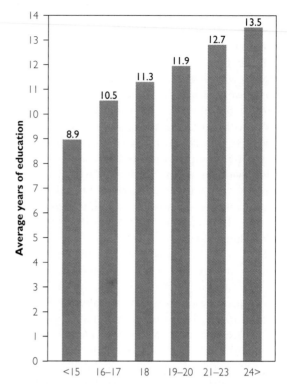

FIGURE 11.3 Mean Educational Attainment for Women by Age at Which They Had Their First Child

Source: K. D. Dillard and L. G. Pol, "The Individual Economic Costs of Teenage Childbearing," *Family Relations, 31* (April 1982): 255. Copyrighted 1982 by the National Council on Family Relations, 3989 Central Ave. NE, Suite 550, Minneapolis, MN 55421. Reprinted by permission.

years of education are only 8.9. If her first baby is born when she is 24 years old, her average years of education are 13.5 (Dillard and Pol, 1982).

What are high schools legally permitted to do when a student marries? What are they permitted to do when they discover a student is pregnant out of wedlock? What are the student's constitutional rights? What are the rights of the school board? What does the law say?

With the implementation of the regulations issued under Title IX of the Education Amendments of 1972, all married students and unmarried girls and young mothers are entitled to complete their education with full access to the resources and facilities provided by the public school system (Henderson, 1980). Specifically, these regulations require that any school system receiving federal funds shall not (1) apply any rule concerning a student's actual or potential parental, family, or marital status that treats students differently on the basis of sex; or (2) discriminate against or exclude any student from its education program or activity on the basis of such student's pregnancy or pregnancy-related condition. Assignment of a student to a separate portion of the program or activity of the school can be made only if the student voluntarily requests such assignment or if a physician certifies inability to continue in the normal program. Any separate instructional program for pregnant students must be comparable to that offered to nonpregnant students.

There are legally defensible reasons for a board to remove a pregnant girl from school, but these defenses sometimes are so difficult to prove that a board may wonder if it is all worth the effort. A school district may be able to justify in court the removal of a pregnant girl from the regular school program if one or more of the following conditions exist ("Pregnant," 1973):

1. The girl refuses to place herself under medical care.

2. The district is willing to claim and able to prove that the girl in question clearly is immoral. It is important to note that pregnancy outside of marriage is not in itself proof of promiscuity or immorality. As one court ruled, "The court would like to make manifestly clear that lack of moral character is certainly a reason for excluding a child from public education. But the fact that a girl has one child out of wedlock does not forever brand her as a scarlet woman undeserving of any chance for rehabilitation or the opportunity for further education" (*Perry* v. *Granada,* 1969).

3. The board is able to prove that the pregnant girl causes a substantial disruption in the operation of her school. Chances are that a pregnant girl will be the object of some whispering, giggling, and pointing, but a court may not rule that such attention adds up to a substantial disruption.

4. The board is able to prove that the pregnant girl presents a clear and present danger to the health, welfare, and safety of other students. Will other students run out and become pregnant because they see one of their classmates in that condition?

Generally, courts have said that the denial of regular academic education can be exercised in only the most severe cases and that marriage and pregnancy are not in themselves acceptable reasons for dismissal. This reasoning forces boards to rely on defenses such as the four just mentioned, and those defenses (except in the case of the girl who refuses to place herself under the care of a doctor) can become difficult.

If a school board is bent on restricting a pregnant student's activities, it may be able to keep her out of extracurricular activities. Courts have ruled that married students and pregnant students (married or not) can participate in extracurricular activities in those instances when:

> School officials are unable to prove that "any inconvenience or damage was suffered" (*Wellsand* v. *Valparaiso,* 1971).
>
> No disruption of or interference with school activities or threat of harm to other students can be linked to the appearance of a pregnant, unmarried student at extracurricular activities (*Ordway* v. *Hargraves,* 1971).
>
> Courts are unable to find a reasonable relationship between legitimate school purposes and rules that deny extracurricular activities to married and/or pregnant students.

It is evident that the courts are now clearly on the side of married and/or unmarried pregnant students who want to continue their education. Some schools make a real effort at rehabilitation. Others are relieved if the girl drops out of school voluntarily, and many of these schools make no effort to get her to return, even after the baby is born.

Probably the most successful approaches are those including special programs and services especially for expectant mothers (Holman and Arcus, 1987; MacGregor and Newlon, 1987; Roosa, 1986). The special services provided include the following:

Individual treatment plans for prenatal, obstetrical, and postnatal medical care are drawn up.

Social services include assignment of caseworkers to assist each girl.

Educational services include not only regular academic courses and assistance with these but also courses in reproductive health. Most important, the girls are helped in every way possible to continue their education during and after pregnancy.

Even if pregnant students are allowed to attend their regular schools and classes, they are often too embarrassed or uncomfortable to do so, so they drop out, never completing their education. For this reason, many schools have found it advisable to offer special classes and programs, usually away from the regular school building, to get the girls away from the scrutiny of other students. Often, other community health or youth service agencies cooperate with schools in offering a full range of classes, programs, and services to expectant mothers. These programs are expensive, but they have succeeded in keeping many girls in school, in giving them proper prenatal, obstetrical, and postnatal health care, and in providing counseling and guidance for a wide range of academic, vocational, family, social, and emotional problems with which they are confronted. (For a more complete discussion of the problems and adjustments of pregnant unwed mothers, see Chapter 9.)

SUMMARY

1. The need for close friends becomes crucial during adolescence. Adolescents seek to break the close dependency ties with parents and replace them with close, emotional attachments with friends with whom they can share common interests, find their identities, and overcome loneliness.

2. As adolescents get older, their self-disclosure with friends increases, with girls exhibiting greater emotional disclosure than boys.

3. One of the greatest problems of adolescents is loneliness.

4. Adolescents may be lonely because they have trouble relating to others, poor self-images, emotional disturbance, depression, cynicism about other people, or other situations.

5. Independent adolescents cope with loneliness by engaging in individual pursuits; dependent adolescents cope by relying on external sources of support.

6. The ability to form close friendships is partly learned in the family. There is a correlation between relationships with parents and social adjustments.

7. The need for companionship causes young adolescents to pair off, to choose a best friend or two, usually of the same sex.

8. Early adolescents feel that sharing mutual activities is important in friendships, and that friends should be morally good, loyal, and empathetic.

9. When adolescents leave the confines of their elementary schools, they broaden their friendships. Young adolescents want a lot of friends; as they get older, they become more discriminating and seek fewer but better friends.

10. By midadolescence, youths strive to be accepted by members of a clique or crowd they strongly admire.

11. Youths engage in a variety of leisure activities: just hanging around, watching television, dating, visiting and talking with friends, part-time employment, sports, computer games, cars, hobbies, and sometimes drinking.

12. Adolescents find group acceptance and popularity by conforming, achieving and participating in school activities, developing and exhibiting personal qualities that others admire, and learning social skills that ensure acceptance.

13. Shyness is a problem for some adolescents.

14. There is an association between parenting style (authoritative, authoritarian, indulgent, or uninvolved) and peer-group orientation.

15. Some adolescents find acceptance through deviant behavior that is acceptable in certain types of groups.

16. Psychosocial development takes place in three stages: autosocial, homosocial, and heterosocial. One of the chief tasks is to develop heterosociality wherein friendships are chosen from both sexes.

17. Some adolescents develop crushes on or fall in love with real or imagined partners. Unrequited love can cause much heartache.

18. Loss of love can be a major source of stress in the life of the adolescent.

19. Dating has several important purposes: to have fun; to provide companionship; as a means of status sorting, grading, and achievement; as a means of socialization; for sexual experimentation and satisfaction; as a means of mate sorting and selection; and as a means of developing intimacy.

20. The median age at which adolescents begin to date has decreased by almost three years since World War I, and is about age 13 for girls. One study found the median age for going steady was about 16 years old for boys and girls.

21. The most common dating problems for girls are unwanted pressure to engage in sexual behavior, where to go and what to do on dates, communication, sexual misunderstandings, and money. The most common problems for boys are communication, where to go and what to do on dates, shyness, money, and honesty/openness.

22. Going steady has both advantages and disadvantages.

23. Dating plays a central role in developing the self and the ability to be intimate with others. Adolescents learn what qualities they like in a partner.

24. Out of about 3.7 million unmarried cohabiting couples in the United States, about 20 percent are under 25 years of age. About 25 percent of college students will live with an opposite-sex partner some time during their college careers.

25. There are various meanings attached to the cohabitation decision. It may mean an arrangement without commitment, an intimate involvement with emotional commitment, living together as a prelude to marriage, living together as a trial marriage, and living together as an alternative to marriage.

26. The majority of cohabiting couples report no regret at having cohabited, but some individuals are hurt by an experience that did not work out or did not result in marriage when they expected it to.

27. Adjustment problems in cohabiting include over-involvement, not knowing how to escape without hurt, uncertainty about the future, sex-role responsibilities, learning to adjust to one another's moods and temperaments, and problems of immaturity, finances, sexual relations, and contraception.

28. Cohabitation is like marriage in some ways but there are significant differences between the two.

29. Cohabitation does not necessarily weed out incompatible couples so that it prepares for more successful marriages. Cohabitation may result in couples reporting less satisfaction early in marriage (they have already gone through a period of dissolutionment) but does not seem to have any long-term effects on marital adjustment, according to some research. However, the majority of studies show that couples who have cohabited run a greater risk of marital failure afterward.

30. If cohabitation pushes couples into marriage when they are not ready, the result may be negative.

31. Some women have babies while they are in cohabiting relationships. Such births are not likely to be planned, although nonmarital unions are a common family context for childbearing among Puerto Ricans. African American women who are single are less likely than Puerto Ricans to be cohabiting when they become mothers. Cohabitation that results in Whites bearing children often operates as a transitional stage before marriage. Cohabiting couples with children are less likely to break up than are couples without children.

32. About 10 percent of girls and 3.1 percent of boys age 18 to 19 are or have been married.

33. The younger people are when married, the greater is the chance of unhappy marriage and divorce. From the standpoint of marital stability, if couples wait until the man is age 27 and the woman is age 25, they have waited as long as practical to maximize their chances of marital success.

34. High school girls who marry are typically 3.5 to 5.5 years younger than their husbands. Typically, early marriages disproportionately involve adolescents who are from low-socioeconomic-status groups, are less interested in education, are premaritally pregnant, have lower intelligence and poorer grades, are rural residents, are less adjusted emotionally and socially, and have less satisfactory relationships with parents.

35. Important causes or reasons for early marriage include sexual stimulation and pregnancy, early dating and acceleration of adult sophistication, social pressure, overly romantic views of marriage, escape, an attempt to solve personal and social problems, and affluence and prosperity.

36. Many of the problems of young couples are due to their immaturity.

37. One of the real disadvantages of early marriage is that it is associated with early parenthood.

38. Other common problems of early marriage involve finances, disagreements over the quantity and quality of sexual relations, the husband going

out with friends and leaving the wife home alone, and in-law problems.

39. Early marriage diminishes educational attainment of those attending school. Dropout rates among married high school couples are high, but all married students and unmarried girls and young mothers are entitled to an education.

40. A school board must have legally defensible reasons for removal of a premaritally pregnant girl from a public school program. Marriage and pregnancy themselves are not grounds for dismissal.

KEY TERMS

autosociality **270**

erotomania **272**

heterosociality **270**

homosociality **270**

imaging **275**

social-evaluative anxiety **269**

THOUGHT QUESTIONS

Please answer the following questions, some of which are asked by adolescents.

1. A junior high school adolescent asks, "How do you go about making friends if you're new in school?"

2. A junior high adolescent asks, "How can you get others to like you?"

3. A junior high adolescent asks, "What do you do if your best friend talks about you behind your back?"

4. A junior high youth asks, "Do you have to follow everybody else to be popular?"

5. A junior high adolescent asks, "Should seventh-graders be allowed to go to school dances?"

6. A junior high adolescent asks, "What do boys look for in a girl?"

7. A junior high adolescent asks, "How do you attract the opposite sex?"

8. An adolescent asks, "How can I get over being shy in groups?"

9. A high school adolescent asks, "What can you do if you're chicken to ask a girl on a date?"

10. A high school adolescent asks, "What do you do if your parents don't want you to go with your boyfriend because he's three years older and has been in trouble with the police?"

11. An adolescent asks, "How do you know if you're really in love?"

12. A high school adolescent asks, "At what age can you begin dating?"

13. A high school adolescent asks, "How can you break up without hurting the other person?"

14. A junior high adolescent asks, "Why shouldn't a girl call a boy if she wants to?"

15. A high school adolescent asks, "What do you do if you're scared to ask a girl to go on a date?"

16. A high school adolescent asks, "When you go on a date, what do you talk about? I get so embarrassed by long periods of silence."

17. What are the pros and cons of going steady while in high school?

18. An adolescent asks, "Is it alright to date several boys at once?"

19. A high school adolescent asks, "Will boys take you out if you're not willing to go all the way?"

20. If you cohabited outside of marriage, or if you are cohabiting now, discuss your experiences.

21. If you have cohabited, what sort of commitment did you have? Were you engaged? Did you intend to get married? Did you have any special plans for the future?

22. If you have cohabited outside of marriage, and have now broken up or are still cohabiting, are you glad you did or are you sorry, and for what reasons?

23. If you had cohabited outside of marriage, what sort of arrangements did you make for finances? Housework? Cooking? Laundry? Other chores in and around your living quarters?

24. Does cohabiting help you in any way to select a mate? Or prepare for marriage? Do you think you have a better chance of having a happy marriage because you have cohabited, or do you have a worse chance?

25. Would you advise other young people to cohabit? Why or why not?

26. How old do you think people should be before getting married? Explain.

27. Should an adolescent girl ever get married because she is pregnant? Explain.

28. Why are some adolescents in such a hurry to get married?

29. What special problems do married adolescents face?

30. Should a high school girl remain in school if she is pregnant out of wedlock? Why or why not?

31. What responsibilities does a school have to a pregnant adolescent girl? What can the school do to help her?

SUGGESTED READING

Camerer, M. C. G. (1994). *A Parent's Guide to Coping with Adolescent Friendships: The Three Musketeer Phenomenon.* Springfield, IL: Charles C. Thomas.

Vurndt, T. J., and Ladd, G. W. (1989). *Peer Relationships in Child Development.* New York: Wiley.

Youniss, M., and Smollar, J. (1985). *Adolescent Relations with Mothers, Fathers, and Friends.* Chicago: University of Chicago Press.

12

Development of Moral Judgment, Character, Values, Beliefs, and Behavior

The process by which children and youths develop moral judgment is extremely interesting. A number of major theories, based on sound research findings, have been developed and will be discussed in this chapter. The work of Jean Piaget, Lawrence Kohlberg, and Carol Gilligan represents theories that emphasize the development of moral judgment as a gradual cognitive process stimulated by increasing, changing social relationships of children as they get older.

Other researchers have concentrated on an examination of various family correlates that influence moral development. In this chapter, we will discuss such factors as parental warmth, parent-teen interaction, discipline, parental role models, and independence opportunities outside the home in relation to their influence on moral learning. The transmission of religious beliefs and practices from parents to children is also an important consideration and depends on a number of religious and family variables. Finally, we will examine other social influences such as peer and reference groups, television, and schools. The effects of these influences on the development of values and behavior are important and need to be understood.

Cognitive-Socialization Theories of Development

The most important early research on the development of moral judgment of children is that of Piaget (1948) and Piaget and Inhelder (1969). Although some details of Piaget's findings have not been substantiated by subsequent research, his ideas formed the theoretical basis for later research. Piaget's work was with children, but the theoretical framework that outlines his stages of development may be applied to adolescents and adults, as well. It is important, therefore, to understand his discoveries.

Jean Piaget

Piaget's (1948) work is reported in four sections. The first section discusses the attitudes of children to the rules of the game when playing marbles. The second and third sections report the results of telling children stories that require them to make moral judgments on the basis of the information given. The last section reviews his findings in relation to social psychology, particularly to the work of Durkheim (1960), who argues that the sanctions of society are the only source of morality.

In studying children's attitudes to the rules of the game when playing marbles, Piaget concluded that there is first a *morality of constraint* and, second, a *morality of cooperation.* In the early stages of moral development, children are constrained by the rules of the game. These rules are coercive because children regard them as inviolable and because they reflect parental authority. Rules constitute a given order of existence and, like parents, must be obeyed without question. Later, as a result of social interaction, children learn that rules are not absolute; they learn that they can alter them by social consensus. Rules are no longer external laws to be considered sacred because they are laid down by adults but are social creations arrived at

through a process of free decision and thus deserving of mutual respect and consent. Children move from **heteronomy** to *autonomy* in making moral judgments (Piaget, 1948).

Piaget also discussed the motives or reasons for judgments. He said there are, first, judgments based solely on the consequences of wrongdoing (*objective judgments*) and, second, judgments that take into account intention or motive (*subjective judgments*). Piaget (1948) claimed there is a growing pattern of operational thinking, with children moving from objective to subjective responsibility as they grow older. Piaget would insist that although the two processes overlap, the second gradually supersedes the first. The first stage is superseded when children deem motive or intention more important than consequences.

> The child finds in his brothers and sisters or in his playmates a form of society which develops his desire for cooperation. Then a new type of morality will be created in him, a *morality of reciprocity* and not of *obedience.* This is the true morality of intention. (p. 133)

Piaget (1948) was careful to note that obedience and cooperation are not always successive stages but nevertheless are formative processes that broadly follow one another. "The first of these processes is the moral constraint of the adult, a constraint which leads to heteronomy and consequently to moral realism. The second is cooperation which leads to autonomy" (p. 193). (By *moral realism,* Piaget meant submitting meekly to the demands of law.)

Before moral judgment moves from the heteronomous to the autonomous stage, the self-accepted rules must be internalized. This happens when, in a reciprocal relationship and out of mutual respect, people begin to feel from within the desire to treat others as they themselves would wish to be treated. They pass from *preoperational* to *operational thinking,* from premoral to moral judgment, as they internalize the rules they want to follow.

In the third section of his report, Piaget discussed the child's concept of justice as the child moves from moral restraint to moral cooperation. Two concepts of punishment emerge. The first results from the transgression of an externally imposed regulation; this, Piaget called *expiatory punishment,* which goes hand in hand with constraint and the rules of authority. The second is self-imposed punishment, which comes into operation when the individual, in violation of his or her own conscience, is denied normal social relations and is isolated from the group by his or her own actions. Piaget (1948) called this the **punishment of reciprocity**, which accompanies cooperation. An ethic of mutual respect, of good as opposed to duty, leads to improved social relationships that are basic to any concept of real equality and reciprocity.

In the last section of his work, Piaget, following Durkheim, asserted that "society is the only source of morality" (p. 326). Morality, to Piaget, consisted of a system of rules, but such rules required a sociological context for their development. Thus, "whether the child's moral judgments are heteronomous or autonomous, accepted under pressure or worked out in freedom, this morality is social, and on this point, Durkheim was unquestionably right" (p. 344).

One of the important implications of Piaget's views is that the changes in moral judgments of children are related to their *cognitive growth* and to the changes in their *social relationships*. At first, children judge the severity of transgressions by their visible damage or harm. They also develop the concept of **immanent justice:** the child's belief that immoral behavior inevitably brings pain or punishment as a natural consequence of the transgression (e.g., "If you do wrong, you will certainly be punished"). Furthermore, the child judges the appropriateness of this punishment by its severity rather than by its relevance to the transgression. Only as children get older are they likely to recommend that the transgressor make restitution or that punishment be tailored to fit the wrong done. Gradually, they also come to see that the application of rules must be relative to people and situations and that rules are established and maintained through reciprocal social agreements.

As an example, if 6-year-olds are told the story of a little boy who has accidentally dropped a sweet roll in the lake, they are likely to respond, "That's too bad. But it's his own fault for being so clumsy. He shouldn't get another." For them, the punishment implies a crime, and losing a sweet roll in the lake is clearly a punishment in their eyes. They are incapable of taking extenuating circumstances into account. Adolescents, however, make moral judgments on the basis of what Piaget

called *equity,* assigning punishments in accordance with the transgressor's ability to take responsibility for his or her crime. Adolescents are as able to employ the same sort of reasoning in relation to moral dilemmas as they are in solving intellectual puzzles. Rather than being tied to concrete facts and a narrow range of possibilities (there is punishment; therefore there must be a crime), they are able to imagine a wide range of possibilities. (The sweet roll is lost; someone may or may not be to blame.) As a result, they are able to take into account the youthfulness of the child, many of the possible reasons why the sweet roll was lost, and to show more compassion (e.g., "It may not have been his fault; he should get another treat").

Another important implication of Piaget's view is that the changes in judgments of children must be related to the changes in their social relationships. As peer-group activity and cooperation increase and as adult constraint decreases, the child becomes more truly an autonomous, cooperative, moral person.

One of the best summaries of Piaget's conclusions has been given by Kay (1969, p. 157) in a series of simple propositions about the moral lives of children.

---

morality of constraint or morality of obedience conduct that is coerced by rules or authority.

morality of cooperation or morality of reciprocity conduct that is regulated by mutual respect and consent.

heteronomy control of conduct external to the self.

objective judgments judgments based solely on the consequences of wrongdoing.

subjective judgments judgments that take into account intention or motives.

expiatory punishment punishment that results from an externally imposed regulation.

punishment of reciprocity self-imposed punishment.

immanent justice the child's belief that immoral behavior inevitably brings pain or punishment as a natural consequence of the transgression.

equity assigning punishments in accordance with ability to take responsibility for a crime.

1. Human beings develop an intelligent and informed respect for law by experiencing genuine social relationships.
2. Social relationships are found in two basic forms. They are first characterized by child subordination and adult supremacy and then slowly change until the relationship is reciprocal. In this case, it can be based on equality or equity.
3. Social relationships are functionally linked with a system of moral judgment. When the relationship is one of subordination and supremacy, then the moral judgment exercised is based on authoritarian considerations that are objective and heteronomous. Equally, when the relationship is reciprocal, moral judgments are autonomous and reflect the subjective system of morality that now activates the child from within.
4. Judgment and conduct at the final stage of moral development are based not on subscription to an external code of law or even in the regulation of rigid reciprocity in human relationships. It consists of the recognition of the rights and needs of all individuals with due regard to the situational circumstances and the moral principles expressed in them.

Although Piaget's conclusions were deduced from research with children up to age 12, they have some relationship to the moral life of adolescents. It has been emphasized that Piaget said that children move from a morality of constraint (or obedience) to a morality of cooperation (or reciprocity); children pass from heteronomy to autonomy in making moral judgments; and they move from objective to subjective responsibility. Piaget has said that this second stage of moral development gradually supersedes the first as children grow older.

Some subsequent research questions this view. For example, it has been found that adolescents, as well as children, tend to seek justice in an authority person. There are adolescents, and even adults, who obey certain laws and rules only because of coercion and the threat of external punishment. They are constrained by authority, not by an inner conscience. If they break the rules, their concern is not remorse at doing wrong but at having been caught. In other words, they never move from heteronomy to autonomy, from objective judgment to subjective judgment, from a morality constraint to a morality of cooperation. They remain, like young children, at a preoperational, premoral stage of development, for the rules have never been internalized, and they never desire to do the right thing from mutual respect and concern for the feelings and welfare of others.

It is unreasonable, then, always to attach age categories to the stages of moral development. There are children, adolescents, and adults at any one stage of moral growth. This is one reason why Piaget's findings may be applied to adolescents as well as children. Researchers, such as Kohlberg, have confirmed some aspect of Piaget's conclusions, but they would not assign each step of development to a particular age group.

Lawrence Kohlberg

One of the principal deficiencies of Piaget's work was his exclusive concern with children under the age of 12. Kohlberg compensated for this deficiency by using adolescents in a series of studies (Kohlberg, 1963, 1966, 1969, 1970; Kohlberg and Gilligan, 1971; Kohlberg and Kramer, 1969; Kohlberg and Turiel, 1972); he confirmed Piaget's conclusions and showed their validity when applied to adolescents.

Kohlberg's (1963) initial study included 72 boys aged 10, 13, and 16. All groups were similar in IQ; half of each group was upper middle class. Data were collected through taped interviews in which 10 moral dilemmas were presented to each boy. In each dilemma, acts of disobedience to legal-social rules or the commands of authority figures conflicted with the human needs or welfare of others. Each boy was asked to select one of two acts as the more desired solution and was then questioned about the reasons for his choice. Kohlberg's material and technique were Piagetian in form. In this study, Kohlberg was concerned not with moral behavior but with moral judgment and the process of thought by which the individual made his judgment. There were no right or wrong answers expected; the individual was scored according to mode of reasoning, regardless of the direction of the given response.

From an analysis of the interviews, Kohlberg (1970), and then Kohlberg and Gilligan (1971), identified three major levels of moral development, each level having two types of moral orientation or judgment. The levels and subtypes are listed in Table 12.1. Kohlberg found that premoral thinking (Level I) declined sharply from the younger to the older age groups. Level II increased until age 13, then stabilized. Level III also increased markedly between 10 and 13 years of age, with some additional increase between ages 13 and 16.

In outlining his stages, however, Kohlberg was careful not to equate each type with a particular age. Within any one age group, individuals are at different levels of development in their moral thinking: Some are retarded and others are advanced. No person fits neatly into any one of the six types. Kohlberg and Gilligan (1971) indicated that the development of moral thought is a gradual and continuous process as the individual passes through a sequence of increasingly sophisticated moral stages.

TABLE 12.1   Kohlberg's Levels of Development of Moral Thought

Level I: Premoral Level

Type 1:   Punishment and obedience orientation (Motivation: To avoid punishment by others)

Type 2:   Naive instrumental hedonism (Motivation: To gain rewards from others)

Level II: Morality of Conventional Role Conformity

Type 3:   Good-person morality of maintaining good relations with and approval of others (Motivation: To avoid disapproval of others)

Type 4:   Authority-maintaining morality (Motivation: To maintain law and order and because of concern for the community)

Level III: Morality of Self-Accepted Moral Principles

Type 5:   Morality of democratically accepted laws (Motivation: To gain the respect of an individual or community)

Type 6:   Morality of individual principles of conduct (Motivation: To avoid self-condemnation for lapses)

Source: Kohlberg, Lawrence, "The Development of Children's Orientations toward a Moral Order. I. Sequence in the Development of Moral Thought," *Vita Humana,* 6: 11–33 (Karger, Basel 1963). Reprinted by permission.

At Level I, the ***premoral level,*** which comprises these two types, children are responsive to the definitions of *good* and *bad* provided by parental authority figures. Moral decisions are egocentric, based on self-interest; children interpret acts as good or bad in terms of physical consequences. A type 1 person obeys rules to avoid punishment. A type 2 person conforms in order to obtain rewards or to have favors returned.

Level II, the level of ***morality of conventional role conformity,*** comprising types 3 and 4, is less egocentric and more sociocentric in orientation, developing a conformity to social conventions that is based on a desire to maintain, support, and justify the existing social structure (Muuss, 1988b). A type 3 person is the good boy–nice girl orientation in which the child conforms to avoid disapproval and dislike by others, whereas a type 4 person conforms because of a desire to maintain law and order or because of concern for the larger community (Ward, 1991).

Level III is the level of ***morality of self-accepted moral principles.*** A type 5 person conforms in order to maintain the respect of an impartial spectator or to maintain a relation of mutual respect. At this stage, the individual defines morality in terms of general principles such as individual rights, human dignity, equality, contractual agreement, and mutual obligations. Because moral principles have been accepted by society as a whole, the individual is motivated to accept them because of a concern for human well-being and public welfare. This is the social-contract–legalistic orientation in which justice flows from a contract between the governors and the governed. Unjust laws must be changed, and individuals who are flexible in their

---

premoral level   according to Kohlberg, first level of development of moral thought, based on reward and punishments.

morality of conventional role conformity according to Kohlberg, second level of development of moral thought, based on desire to conform to social convention.

morality of self-accepted moral principles according to Kohlberg, third level of development of moral thought, based on adherence to universal principles.

approach to these laws seek to improve them through consensus. This type of person is represented by those who accept the official morality of the U.S. Constitution, which recognizes important moral principles.

Finally, a type 6 person conforms to avoid self-condemnation (Kay, 1969). The approach to moral issues is based not on egocentric needs or conformity to the existing social order but on autonomous, universal principles of justice that are valid beyond existing laws, social conditions, or peer mores. Thus, individuals governed by universal ethical principles may break unjust civil laws because they recognize a morality higher than existing law. Americans who avoided the draft and accepted the penalty, as a protest against the Vietnam War, practiced civil disobedience in the interest of what they felt was a higher moral good. They felt there were universal moral principles that should be followed, even though these challenged the existing official morality of their own government (Muuss, 1988b). Martin Luther King, Jr., (1964) wrote from a Birmingham jail:

> I do not advocate evading or defying the law. . . . That would lead to anarchy. One who breaks an unjust law must do so openly, lovingly, and with a willingness to accept the penalty. An individual who breaks the law that conscience tells him is unjust, and willingly accepts the penalty of imprisonment in order to arouse the conscience of the community over its injustice is, in reality, expressing the highest respect for the law. (p. 86)

Thus, Level III, the level of morality of self-accepted moral principles, is made up of individuals who accept democratically recognized principles or universal truths, not because they have to but because they believe in the principles or truths.

Kohlberg (1966) emphasized that a stage concept such as this implies sequence: Each child must go through each successive level of moral judgment before passing on to the next. Kohlberg also emphasized that a stage concept implies universality of sequence under varying cultural conditions (Jensen, 1995). That is, the development of moral judgment is not merely a matter of learning the rules of a particular culture; it reflects a universal process of development. In order to test this hypothesis, Kohlberg (1966) used his technique with boys 10, 13, and 16 years of age in a Taiwanese city, in a Malaysian (Atayal) aboriginal tribal village, and in a Turkish village, as well as in Great Britain, Canada, and the United States. The results for Taiwan and the United States indicate similar age trends in boys of both nationalities.

Kohlberg (1966) said that although his findings show a similar sequence of development in all cultures, the last two stages of moral thought do not develop clearly in preliterate village or tribal communities. It seems evident from the U.S. data

Parents need to understand that the development of moral thought and values is a gradual and continuous process. Adolescents must pass from an egocentric to a sociocentric level of operation.

also, however, that the great majority of American adults never reach Level III either, even by age 24. Only 10 percent of Kohlberg's middle-class urban male population had reached Level III, with another 26 percent at Level II. Although Kohlberg studied 10- to 16-year-olds, studies of students in Berkeley, California, showed that 72 percent were still at Level II (32 percent at stage 3, 40 percent at stage 4). Those who had arrived at stage 6 were active protestors on campus. This correlation led some writers to question the whole philosophical concept of moral maturity.

Kohlberg (1966) tested his hypothesis with children of both middle and working classes, Protestants and Catholics, popular and socially isolated children, and girls as well as boys. He found the same general stages of development among all groups but some differences in the *level* of moral development of middle- and working-class children, with the middle-class children, at all ages, in advance of the working-class children. Kohlberg emphasized that these differences were cognitive and developmental in nature, with middle-class children moving faster and farther. The explanation is not that lower-class children favor a different type of thought or hold values different from those of the middle class but that working-class children have less understanding of the broader social order and less participation in it; thus, their moral development is retarded. This explanation is further substantiated by the fact that children with extensive peer-group participation advance considerably more quickly through the successive stages of development or moral thinking.

However, whether social class has any influence must be related to culture to some extent (Corson, 1984). Research with Nigerian adolescents found no relationship to socioeconomic background, because all children, irrespective of background, were expected to be humble and obedient. In the United States, moral development is particularly dependent on the type of training children receive, and this may vary with class.

One other variable should be mentioned. Moral judgment also correlates highly with *IQ*, indicating that it is more cognitive in nature than either the "good habits" or "early experiences" views. As children participate more in social groups, they lose some of their cognitive naiveté and adopt a more sophisticated view of authority and social relationships. This does not necessarily

mean that they become better people; they do acquire a greater capacity for moral thinking, but whether such knowledge leads to better behavior depends on emotional and social influence in their backgrounds and relationships.

A central task of moral development theory is to explain the relation between moral judgment and moral behavior. For both Piaget and Kohlberg, judgment was essential to the determination of actions as moral. Thus, it is not unreasonable to assume that moral judgment has a positive association with moral behavior. However, researchers who have examined the relationship between both Piagetian-based and Kohlbergean-based moral reasoning and moral action have reported inconsistent results. In some cases, researchers have reported a positive association between reasoning and behavior. In many others, they have not. They have suggested that factors other than judgment may also be implicated in the production of moral behavior.

One construct that has received little attention in the moral development literature is **metacognition.** Metacognition, or knowing about knowing, refers to insights children have about their own cognitive processes. By analogy to the discussions of metacognition, moral metacognition would refer to the knowledge that children have about their own morality. One investigation described the relationship between metamoral knowledge, moral reasoning, and moral behavior in three age groups: adolescents in grades 7, 9, and 12 (Swanson and Hill, 1993). These researchers found that older children had more accurate understanding of moral judgmental processes than young children and that the higher levels of moral metacognition are closely tied to more advanced moral reasoning and behavior. In regard to moral judgment, the researchers assumed and found that children who were better able to think about their moral reasoning processes were more likely to be aware of inconsistencies in this reasoning and were also more likely to attempt to resolve these inconsistencies. Likewise, moral metacognition affected behavior in that children who were better able to reason about their actions were more likely to rec-

---

metacognition knowing about knowing; insight into one's own cognitive processes.

ognize moral aspects of their behavior and thus implore moral reasoning in formulating plans for that behavior. Finally, moral metacognition served as a correlate between moral action and moral reasoning and as a prerequisite to using moral judgment to direct one's actions.

According to developmental researchers, there is an increase in the sophistication of moral reasoning through adolescence due, in part, to an increase in perspective taking, intelligence, and the ability to think abstractly. Furthermore, perspective taking and intelligence have been found to be moderately and positively related to prosocial moral reasoning (Carlo, Eisenberg, and Knight, 1992). This finding is in keeping with other research that shows that those who are advanced in social perspective taking because of the experiences in university and employment settings are also advanced in moral judgment in late adolescence and childhood (Mason and Gibbs, 1993).

Kohlberg's theories have been tested by many researchers. Weinreich (1974) has shown that the rapidity and extent of progression through the sequence of stages are related to intelligence. This is in keeping with other research that shows that moral judgment is significantly and positively associated with chronological age and with IQ; older, brighter youngsters evidence greater maturity of moral judgment than do younger, less intelligent children. Achievement of a particular moral stage depends on reaching certain Piagetian levels and the ability to perform certain logical operations seems to be a prerequisite to performing certain moral operations. Parental attitudes toward children are significant, as in Gfellner's (1986) conclusion that children's egos and moral development are enhanced by parental warmth in the parent-child relationship (Walker and Taylor, 1991).

In fact, the *total family environment* has an influence on the moral development of adolescents (Eisenberg and Murphy, 1995). For example, family issues are more prominent in the moral dilemmas of early adolescents of divorce, as compared with early adolescents of intact families. Peer relationship issues are the focus of early adolescents of intact families. Early adolescents of divorce are more concerned about family issues and money, whereas early adolescents of intact families are more concerned about grades and friends (Breen and Crosbie-Burnett, 1993).

Later Developments and Critique of Kohlberg

One of the problems researchers have had in testing Kohlberg's theory has been the difficulty of determining at what stage an individual is (Boyes, Giordano, and Galperyn, 1993). In one study of 957 individuals, more than 45 percent could not be placed in one stage or another; most of the groups were in transition between two stages, and some gave responses that straddled three stages (Muson, 1979). Moreover, Kohlberg and his associate Kramer (1969) found that many who had been in stage 4 in previous interviews had regressed to stage 2, indicating that stage change was not always upward or in orderly sequence. Individuals may make moral judgments at one stage in one situation and at another stage in another situation. One circumstance may require a stage 4 response; another may require a more universally applicable response. Also, Kohlberg's scale evaluates the motivation for making judgments, which can vary under different circumstances.

Furthermore, Kohlberg's original scale for measuring stages lacked standardization in administration and scoring (Rest, 1983, 1986). In response, Kohlberg and colleagues completed a five-part manual that he promised would provide the consistency and reliability critics were looking for. Stage 6 (or type 6) was dropped from the new manual entirely, for Kohlberg estimated that only about 7 percent of 16-year-olds in the United States and Mexico and less than 1 percent of the same age group in Taiwan used stage 6 reasoning. None of those studied in Turkey or Yucatán had ever reached stage 5 (Muson, 1979).

Critics have also argued that it is not true or fair to say that the higher the stage, the greater the level of morality (Callahan and Callahan, 1981). Stage 6 reflects liberal and radical political reasoning. Does this mean that liberals are more advanced morally than conservatives? There is little basis in empirical fact to conclude that this is so. Also, there is some indication that more women end up in stage 3 and more men in stage 4. Women were more desirous of pleasing others, which enabled them to smooth tensions and bring people together. Men were more concerned about maintaining law and order. Why should stage 4 be considered superior to stage 3? This criticism led Kohlberg to emphasize stage 4 more

Emotions and Social Responsibility

Developing social responsibility involves more than having the intellectual capacity to make moral judgments. It also involves being motivated to make moral choices. In one study, 218 adolescents from San Francisco area high schools were given a Youth Decision-making Questionnaire (YDMQ) (Ford, Wentzel, Wood, Stevens, and Siesfeld, 1989). Respondents were asked to make hypothetical choices, each involving conflict between a socially responsible and a socially irresponsible course of action. They were asked to make choices under two different sets of conditions: (1) nothing bad would happen if they behaved irresponsibly and (2) negative social consequences would occur if they made an irresponsible choice.

After responding to the behavioral choice questions, the subjects were asked how much guilt, empathetic concern, fear, or pleasure they would feel if they made the socially irresponsible choice, or how much they would experience pride in themselves, worry about

peer or adult approval, or experience sadness or frustration (as a consequence of foregoing some personal gain) if they were to make the socially responsible choice. When the subjects were told that irresponsible behavior would result in negative consequences, their primary emotions associated with their behavior were guilt, pride, empathy, and fear. When told that nothing bad would happen if they behaved irresponsibly, self-interest emotions and worry about peer approval became more relevant to the decision-making process.

Adolescent social responsibility was largely a function of emotional responses such as anticipated guilt, empathetic concern, and fear of negative consequences. Irresponsible choices are fairly common under conditions of no social enforcement. This suggests that appropriate monitoring and some disciplinary control is necessary. This is especially true of adolescent boys who made more irresponsible choices than did girls in this study.

as concern for the larger community rather than concern for law and order. More and more, Kohlberg has suggested that an important goal of moral education should not be to reach stage 5, but rather "a solid attainment of the fourth stage commitment to being a good member of a community or a good citizen" (Muson, 1979, p. 57).

No evaluation of levels of moral judgment can be used to predict moral behavior; to know does not mean to do. Two people at the same level of reasoning might act differently under the pressure of circumstances. In fact, investigation of students at the University of California revealed large numbers of persons in stages 5 or 6, but also a large percentage of students who were in the relatively primitive stage 2 (Muson, 1979).

Gilligan's Theory of Sex Differences in Moral Reasoning

Carol Gilligan (1977), an associate of Kohlberg's, pointed out that Kohlberg conducted his research on moral development on male subjects. The scoring method was developed from male responses,

with the average adolescent female attaining a rating corresponding to stage 3 (the good boy–nice girl orientation). The average adolescent male was rated at stage 4 (the law-and-order orientation). To Gilligan, the female level of moral judgment is not "lower" than that of the male, but reflects the fact that females approach moral issues from a different perspective. Men emphasize justice—preserving rights, rules, and principles. Women emphasize concern and care for others and sensitivity to their feelings and rights. Women emphasize responsibility to human beings rather than to abstract principles. Thus, men and women speak with two different voices (Gilligan, 1982). In summarizing six studies, including four longitudinal, Gilligan (1984) revealed that men rely more heavily on a justice orientation, and women on an interpersonal network or care orientation (Muuss, 1988a).

This difference has been ascribed partially to differences in socialization experiences. Also, although the roles and opportunities for men and women are becoming increasingly equal, there are still more female models in the caregiving roles.

Gilligan based her theory of moral reasoning on the sex differences between women and men. Men concentrate on preserving justice. Women emphasize concern and care for others, as can be seen by the fact that more women than men are primary caregivers to children and elderly.

For example, it is more common for a women than a man to be the primary caregiver of children as well as the elderly, and there are typically more women than men working in nurseries and elementary schools (Skoe and Gooden, 1993).

As a result of the difference in the way men and women think, Gilligan proposed a female alternative to Kohlberg's stages of moral reasoning. Table 12.2 compares Kohlberg's and Gilligan's levels.

At Level I, women are preoccupied with self-interest and survival, which requires obeying restrictions placed on them. Gradually, they become aware of the differences between what they want (selfishness) and what they ought to do (responsibility). This leads to Level II, in which the need to please others takes precedence over self-interest. The woman becomes responsible for caring for others, even sacrificing her own preferences. Gradually, she begins to wonder whether she can fulfill the needs of others and still remain true to herself. Still, she does not give her own needs full equality with others. At Level III, which many never attain, the woman develops a universal perspective, in which she no longer sees herself as submissive and powerless, but active in decision making. She becomes concerned about the consequences for all, herself included, in making decisions.

Obviously, Kohlberg's and Gilligan's stages are parallel. Gilligan does not argue that her theory should replace Kohlberg's. She argues that her theory is more applicable to the moral reasoning of females and that the highest form of moral reasoning can utilize, combine, and interpret both the male emphasis on rights and justice and the female emphasis on responsibility and interpersonal care (Muuss, 1988a). This finding has been substantiated by a later study that found that early adolescents use a variety of modes to make moral decisions. These include the care mode, meaning they wish others not to suffer; the justice mode, where decisions are made according to principles (Golden Rule); and narrowly concerned or selfish mode. All three modes are used by males and females, but males are much more likely to choose the narrowly concerned modes than are females (Perry and McIntire, 1995).

Family Factors and Moral Learning

The Family's Role

Studies of family socialization have demonstrated repeatedly that parents have a tremendous impact on the development of their children. Parents play

TABLE 12.2   Kohlberg's versus Gilligan's Understanding of Moral Development

Kohlberg's Levels and Stages	Kohlberg's Definitions	Gilligan's Levels
Level I. Preconventional morality		*Level I. Preconventional morality*
Stage 1: Punishment orientation	Obey rules to avoid punishment	Concern for the self and survival
Stage 2: Naive reward orientation	Obey rules to get rewards, share in order to get returns	
Level II. Conventional morality		*Level II. Conventional morality*
Stage 3: Good boy/good girl orientation	Conform to rules that are defined by others' approval/disapproval	Concern for being responsible, caring for others
Stage 4: Authority orientation	Rigid conformity to society's rules, law-and-order mentality, avoid censure for rule-breaking	
Level III. Postconventional morality		*Level III. Postconventional morality*
Stage 5: Social-contract orientation	More flexible understanding that we obey rules because they are necessary for social order, but the rules could be changed if there were better alternatives	Concern for self and others as interdependent
Stage 6: Morality of individual principles and conscience	Behavior conforms to internal principles (justice, equality) to avoid self-condemnation, and sometimes may violate society's rules	

Source: J. S. Hyde, *Half the Human Experience* (Lexington, MA: D. C. Heath, 1985). Reprinted by permission.

a fundamental role in their children's transition from childhood to adulthood; in the development of their basic social, religious, and political values; and in encouraging them to adopt prosocial actions and empathetic responses to those in distress (McDevitt, Lennon, and Kopriva, 1991).

All the important research in the moral development of children and adolescents emphasizes the importance of parents and the family in the total process. A number of family factors correlate significantly with moral learning:

1. The degree of parental warmth, acceptance, mutual esteem, and trust shown the child
2. The frequency and intensity of parent-teen interaction and communication
3. The type and degree of discipline used
4. The role model parents offer the child
5. The independence opportunities the parents provide

Each of these factors needs elaboration, clarification, and substantiation. (For additional information on parent-adolescent relationships, see Chapters 13 and 14.)

Parental Acceptance and Trust

One important aid to moral learning is a warm, accepting relationship of mutual trust and esteem between parent and child. Young children who are emotionally dependent on their parents and have a strong emotional attachment to them develop strong consciences, whereas nondependent children grow up more lacking in consciences.

There are a number of explanations for the correlation between parental warmth and moral learning. In a warm, emotional context, respected parents are likely to be admired and imitated by youths, resulting in similar positive traits in the adolescents. Youths learn consideration for others by being cared for, loved, and trusted by their parents. In an atmosphere of hostility and rejection, youths tend to identify with the "aggressor," taking on the antisocial traits of a feared parent. In Sutherland and Cressey's (1966) theory of **differential association,** which outlines conditions that facilitate moral and criminal learning, the impact of a relationship varies according to its *priority, duration, intensity,* and *frequency.* The all-important parent-child relationship (high priority) over many years (long duration), characterized by close emotional attachment (high intensity) and a maximum amount of contact and communication (high frequency), has the maximum positive effect on the moral development of children. Similarly, a negative parent-child relationship existing for many years in an intense, repetitive way will have a disastrous and negative effect.

Frequency and Intensity of Parent-Teen Interaction

Role-modeling theory maintains that the degree of identification of the child with the parent varies with the amount of the child's interaction with the parent. For example, sons who have more frequent and intensive interactions with their fathers are more likely to be influenced by them. Similarly, daughters with frequent, close relationships with their mothers are more likely to identify with them. Frequent interaction offers opportunities for the communication of meaningful values and norms, especially if the exchange is democratic and mutual. A one-sided form of autocratic interaction results in poor communication and less learning for the adolescent. It is important, therefore, for the channels of communication between parents and youths to be kept open. Studies of father-absent homes, where there is a minimum of interaction with a male parent, show that paternal absence has an adverse effect on the moral development of adolescents (Parish, 1980).

Type of Discipline

Research on the influence of parental discipline on the moral learning of youths indicates that discipline has the most positive effect when it is (1) consistent rather than erratic; (2) accomplished primarily through clear, verbal explanations to develop internal controls rather than through external, physical means of control; (3) just and fair and avoids harsh, punitive measures; and (4) democratic rather than permissive or autocratic (Zelkowitz, 1987). Each of these factors needs to be examined.

One of the most important requirements is that discipline be consistent, both *intraparent* (within one parent) and *interparent* (between two parents). Erratic parental expectations lead to an ambiguous environment and thus to poor moral learning, anxiety, confusion, instability, disobedience, and sometimes hostility and delinquency in the adolescent.

Inconsistency alone is not the sole determinant, however. If accompanied by family cohesiveness and parental love, support, and warmth, it is less likely to produce antisocial behavior than if the parents are also rejecting. If parents are inconsistent, harsh, and rejecting, the effect is most damaging (see Chapter 13).

Parents who rely on clear, rational, verbal explanations to influence and control behavior have a more positive effect than those who use external controls. This is primarily because cognitive methods result in the internalization of values and standards, especially if explanations are combined with affection so that the adolescent is inclined to listen and to accept them. Reasoning or praise used to correct or reinforce behavior enhances learning, whereas physical means of discipline, negative verbal techniques such as belittling and nagging, or infrequent explanations are more often associated with antisocial behavior and delinquency.

Parents who rely on harsh, punitive methods are defeating the true purpose of discipline: to develop a sensitive conscience, socialization, and cooperation (Herzberger and Tennen, 1985). Cruel punishment, especially when accompanied by parental rejection, develops an insensitive, uncaring, hostile, rebellious, cruel person. Instead of teaching children to care about others, it deadens their sensitivities, so that they learn to fear and hate others and no longer care about them or want to please them. They may obey, but when the threat of external punishment is removed, they are antisocial. Many criminal types fit this description (Piaget and Inhelder, 1969).

Parents who are overly permissive also retard the socialization process and the moral development of their children, for they give the children no help in developing inner controls. Without external authority, the child will remain amoral. Adolescents want and need some parental guidance. Without it, they may grow up as spoiled brats, disliked by their peers because of their lack of consideration for others, and lacking self-discipline, persistence, and direction.

Parental Role Models

It is important for parents to be moral people themselves if they are to offer positive role models for their children to follow. A 30-year follow-up study of adults, mostly from lower-class homes, who as children were referred to a clinic because of antisocial behavior, found that antisocial behavior of the father correlated significantly with deviance of the subjects in adolescence and adulthood. Furthermore, the father's antisocial behavior was the most significant factor in predicting the consistent antisocial behavior of the individual between adolescence and the mid-40s (Robins, 1966). Adolescents who identify with and strongly value the esteem of parents and teachers are less likely either to cheat or to become delinquent than are nondependent boys who do not esteem parental teacher models.

Independence Opportunities

Peer influences are also important to the child's development, particularly in the lives of youths who are given maximum opportunity for varied social experiences outside the home. Social contacts with those from different cultural and socioeconomic backgrounds facilitate moral development (Kohlberg, 1966).

Numerous research studies show that the development of moral autonomy and judgment is faster among boys than among girls, apparently because boys are less dependent on parental controls: Parents give them more freedom than girls, and so they have greater opportunities for social experiences outside the home. However, though less independent, girls measure much higher on ratings of empathy, helping others, and being more caring, supportive, and sensitive to the needs of others. In this sense, they are more morally mature because they are "other-centered" (Gilligan, 1977). We will discuss some of the social influences outside the home in the next section.

Transmission of Religious Beliefs and Practices

A number of factors influence the transmission of religious beliefs and practices.

Religious Variables

Religious variables influencing beliefs and practices include the content of theological beliefs, consistency of parental religious beliefs, church or synagogue attendance, and frequency of discussions of religion within the family (Clark, Worthington, and Danser, 1988). These items constitute a religious salience, or a prominence of religious thought, behavior, or external stimuli within the family (Hoge and DuZuleta, 1988).

Family Variables

One study sought to determine the nature and extent of the relationship between the religiosity of mothers and their offspring, taking both the sex and the sexual orientation of the offspring into account. Religiosity was measured in terms of both intensity (importance of religion, frequency of church attendance) and denominational preference. Female offspring were found to be more religious than male offspring, and their religiosity tended to more closely resemble that of their mothers than did the religiosity of males. Offspring of both sexes who were not exclusively heterosexual in orientation tended to be less religious and less likely to emulate their mothers' religiosity, as compared with exclusively heterosexual offspring. In other words, religiosity was less likely to be transmitted by mothers to bisexual and homosexual offspring than to heterosexual offspring (Ellis and Wagemann, 1993).

Transmission of religious beliefs and practices is also facilitated by parental agreement (Clark and Worthington, 1987). Consistency promotes a value salience. When parents differ substantially, fathers usually influence their children's beliefs more than mothers. When parents agree,

differential association Sutherland's theory that outlines conditions that facilitate moral or criminal learning.

Parents who agree with one another are better at transmitting religious beliefs and practices to their children. This is especially true for fathers and their sons.

children usually adopt the same denominational membership as parents. High frequency of church attendance and family discussion of religion are influential in shaping religious beliefs and practices of adolescents (Ozorak, 1986). This is especially true in relation to sons. If fathers frequently attend church, discuss religion, and are committed to their religion, their sons will probably do likewise. If fathers do these religious activities infrequently, the sons and fathers will likely not agree on church attendance (Clark, Worthington, and Danser, 1988).

Furthermore, family relationships create a climate that promotes or inhibits adolescents' adoption of their parents' values. Parents who are highly supportive and controlling (authoritative) have children whose values are similar to their own. Parents high in support and low in control (permissive) and low in support and high in control (authoritarian) tend to have children whose values differ from their own (Clark, Worthington, and Danser, 1988). Marital and parent-child conflict can inhibit transmission of religious values to adolescents (Acock and Bengtson, 1980). One study of college students found that about 10 percent were more religious than the atmosphere in which they grew up (Zern, 1989). This was most true among those who were the most competent academically.

Social Reinforcement, Influences, Values, and Behavior

Moral development is subject to a variety of social influences. This section describes some of these influences and how they operate.

Social Reinforcement

One important requirement of moral development is to acquire knowledge and respect for the existing values and rules of one's social milieu. Once known, these values and rules must be internalized. According to Piaget (1948), this internalization brings about a qualitative transformation in character structure and a sense of "moral realism"; as a result, individuals follow the rules regardless of the difficulty in doing so. According to psychoanalytic theory, parents who are nurturant and responsive to children encourage identification and conscience development. As a result of this total "introjection" or "incorporation" of the parent, the child's superego becomes the internal construct that governs morality.

According to Bandura (1971) and other social learning theorists, internalization of values and rules comes through *identification* and *modeling*. Children observe a relevant adult model acting according to a social norm and discover that the adult is praised or otherwise rewarded (Norcini and Snyder, 1983). Being natural imitators, the children strive to do likewise, particularly because the parents are the chief source of love or hate, physical gratification or deprivation, comfort or pain, and security or anxiety, and the children desire rewards and satisfaction. Gradually, they become socialized to adopt the expected behavior themselves, even when the external rewards stop; compliance becomes a reward in itself.

Thus, social learning theory (see Chapter 2) emphasizes the acquisition of values through a process of identification, internalization, and reinforcement. Much has already been said about identification and internalization, but reinforcement needs to be discussed in more detail. *Reinforcement* is used in a particular context here to mean those social influences that parallel parental influences and enhance the learning and acceptance of particular values. When the peer group, school, church, or mass media emphasize values similar to those found in the family, learning of those values is enhanced. However, when the school, church, and other community agencies teach values different from those of the parents, the inconsistency of influence creates conflict. This is often the case with lower-class youths: The community teaches middle-class values, and the parents incompletely accept or cannot afford to accept these values and substitute their own. One outcome of this inconsistency is moral confusion. Another outcome may be rigidity or authoritarianism. Values must be adhered to rigidly if they are to be maintained at all.

Reference Groups

Studies of parent versus peer influence show that most parents will exert a tremendous influence over the moral development of their children (de-Vaus, 1983). However, these studies also show that peer influence has increased—especially in those families in which parental influence has declined. One study of 76 families in a rural county in a midwestern state showed that identification with parents weakly but consistently predicted endorsement of conventional values by adolescents (Whitebeck, Simons, Conger, and Lorenz, 1989). Conventional values indirectly influenced adolescent behavior by influencing peer-group affiliation. As described in Chapter 10, adolescents turn primarily to peers as a reaction against parental neglect and rejection. In such cases, the values of the peer group are particularly important in influencing adolescent behavior.

Youths may be members of many formal organizations, each of which has an influence, but they are just as likely to be influenced by neighborhood gangs or by the general cultural environment around them. Adolescents who are surrounded by deviant moral values may become delinquent because of their environment. Such delinquency has its origin in the values represented by the surrounding subculture. In a study

of individual values, peer values, and subcultural delinquency, six deviant value items common among male delinquents were identified (Lerman, 1968):

1. The ability to keep your mouth shut to the cops
2. The ability to be hard and tough
3. The ability to find kicks
4. The ability to make a fast buck
5. The ability to outsmart others
6. The ability to make connections with a racket

These values were basic elements of the delinquent subculture in which the boys grew up. Boys who scored high on these six values were more likely to engage in illegal behavior. Furthermore, these values were shared values; 50 percent of boys who chose a deviant value were associated with peers who also were high in deviant values. Attraction to these deviant values began early, increased especially at ages 12 to 13, and persisted as a counterattraction to school and work. But on an individual level, without the support of a delinquent peer group, deviant values were unstable and were likely to shift to a conforming value. Without the support of a peer group, individuals rarely held deviant values. If they were to maintain their values, they generally sought out those who could share and support their values. It has been shown also that boys who associate with greatest frequency, duration, and intensity with delinquent peers are more likely than other youths to report delinquent behavior. Also, a high rate of delinquency in a neighborhood provides numerous opportunities for youths to learn deviant skills and values and offers support for deviant activities.

Television

A survey in the mid-1980s indicated that the average child in the United States aged 2 to 11 viewed television 27.5 hours per week (Tooth, 1985). A survey of adolescents aged 12 to 17 in urban, two-parent families in southern Louisiana revealed that these youths viewed television an average of 17.25 hours per week (Lawrence et al., 1986). By age 18, children will have watched television approximately 22,000 hours, compared with 11,000 hours in the classroom. During 5,000 of these hours, they will have been exposed to about 35,000 commercials (LeMasters, 1974).

Television can have a significant impact on adolescents in the formation of value systems and behavior. In one survey, 1,043 adolescents, most under age 16, reported that they had seen between one and nine television shows in the previous week or so that pressured them about sex (stimulated them and motivated them to want sex) (Comstock, 1986; Howard, 1985).

One study of 50 11-year-old German boys measured the psychological, behavioral, and physiological effects associated with television viewing. The mean time spent watching TV was 123 minutes per day, during which the boys watched mostly entertainment and action shows. The heart rate of the boys, measured while they were watching television, was low for entertainment and high for action shows. The increase in heart rate also indicated that emotional arousal was highest for the action shows. Compared to school and leisure-time activities, the heart rates during television viewing was much higher. The programs most popular with children contained a considerable amount of emotionally laden information. As opposed to boys who watched little television, those with high TV consumption displayed lower heart rates and lower emotional arousal during TV viewing. This indicated that heavy television viewing resulted in some desensitization in relation to the material watched. Those who watched a lot of TV read fewer books and spent less time going to friends' houses or running errands. These boys also showed tendencies to stay at home more, do less school-related homework, and spend less time with hobbies (Myrtek, Scharff, Brugner, and Muller, 1996).

Public concern over the content of television shows has focused on the effect on children and youths of watching so much violence. By the time adolescents are 14 and in the eighth grade, they will have watched 18,000 human beings killed on television and violent assaults on thousands more. Thomas Radecki, a psychiatrist who is head of the National Coalition on Television Violence, reported a deluge of high-action, violent cartoon shows (Tooth, 1985). The coalition also reported that violent acts on television increased 65 percent from 1981 to 1985.

What effect does television violence have on the moral behavior of children and youth? A 1982 study by the National Institute of Mental Health concluded that "violence on television does lead to aggressive behavior by teenagers who watch the programs" (Tooth, 1985, p. 65). A study by the Task Force on Children and Television of the American Academy of Pediatrics stated that television contributes not only to violence but also to a high rate of drug and alcohol abuse (Tooth, 1985, p. 65). Another researcher found that adolescents who were heavy television viewers also consumed the most alcohol (Tucker, 1985).

Most of the classic studies on the relationship between television violence and aggression in children and adolescents support this correlation. (For more complete information, see the discussion of the research of Bandura and Walters in Chapter 2.)

Television violence not only increases aggressiveness in children but also influences moral values and behavior. The Great American Values Test was administered by television to millions of Americans. The researchers concluded that even a single 30-minute exposure to television could significantly alter basic beliefs, attitudes, and the behavior of large numbers of people for at least several months (Ball-Rokeach, Rokeach, and Grube, 1984). LeMasters (1974) listed six predominant values portrayed by the media that are in conflict with those of most parents attempting to prepare their children for the future:

1. *Sex:* Sex is usually presented in movies and TV on a physical level, both visually and verbally, yet is presented to viewers as "love."

2. *Violence:* By age 14, the average American child has seen 18,000 human beings killed on television.

3. *Idealization of immaturity:* Idols are not Abraham Lincolns but are often as juvenile and immature as is the viewer and seem to have gained "early wealth and fame . . . with a little talent and beauty and a hard-driving agent."

4. *Materialism:* The implication is that happiness comes with success, and success comes with houses and cars—and it all seems free. Television overrepresents and glamorizes the most prestigious jobs: those of doctors, lawyers, and other professional people. Viewers see relatively few bank tellers, shopkeepers, salespeople, factory workers, or laborers (Signorielli, 1993).

HIGHLIGHT

Sexual Violence in the Media

Donnerstein and Lint (1984) at the University of Wisconsin sought to discover how repeated exposure to films with sex and violence made viewers insensitive to real violence. Male subjects were asked to watch five feature-length films for ten hours (one a day for five days). The films were either R-rated, depicting sexual violence, or X-rated, showing consenting sex. After a week of viewing, the men watched another film of an actual rape trial and were asked to render judgments about how responsible the victim was for her rape and how much injury she suffered.

The men began to perceive the films differently as time went on. By the last day, after viewing graphic violence against women, the men rated the material as significantly less debasing and degrading to women and more humorous and more enjoyable, and they claimed a great willingness to see this type of film again. More significantly, the victim of rape was rated as significantly more worthless and her injury significantly less severe by men who had been exposed to filmed violence than by a control group who saw only the rape trial and did not view any of the films.

The researchers concluded that viewing the films resulted in the men becoming desensitized to violence, particularly against women. Other researchers have shown that even a few minutes of sexually violent pornography, such as rape, can lead to a viewer's acceptance of rape myths (that the woman wanted to be raped), to an increased willingness of a man to say he could commit rape, and to a decreased sensitivity to rape and the plight of a rape victim.

---

5. *Hedonism:* The viewer is exposed to an unreal world to which he or she can quickly escape and be entertained.

6. *Commercialism of the media:* Emphasis on making money is the prime value.

The corresponding parental values on these issues are sexual restraint (and association of sex with love); lifelong monogamy; avoidance of violence; development of responsibility, industriousness, and maturity; and planning for the future as opposed to enjoyment now.

One immediate criticism of LeMaster's analysis is that he presented television values as all negative and parental values as all positive, when, realistically, the lines cannot be so neatly drawn. Many parents, by their behavior and example, portray many of the negative values of which LeMasters speaks. There are some positive social values taught on television, along with the negative ones. Nevertheless, the analysis is partly true, though its findings cannot be applied to all television programs or to all parents.

Television advertising has also been criticized for portraying superficial views of social and personal problems and their solutions. Problems of romance, engagement, marriage, childrearing, employment, and neighborhood relations can be solved by chemical means: Use this headache remedy, nasal spray, deodorant, or toothpaste, and find happiness. Advertising in both television and other forms of mass media, such as magazines and newspapers, are powerful agents of socialization and attempt to tell adolescents how to dress, eat, and behave in order to attain and live "the good life" (Covell, 1992).

Daytime serial soap operas are watched by thousands of adolescents after school. These programs portray distorted and negative social images. The people portrayed are often upper-middle-class families with expensive tastes, comfortable or lavish homes, housekeepers and nannies for the children, expensive wardrobes, and extravagant vacations. The characters are constantly confronted with problems: rape, abortion, infertility, illegitimacy, divorce, death, extramarital lovers, drug addiction, juvenile delinquency, alcoholism, illnesses and operations, and mental illness. Certainly, the social values of these images that are presented to millions of viewers must be questioned.

Others have pointed to the fact that television puts children in an extremely passive position. They experience constant stimulation from the outside with little activity themselves. This may lead to the expectation that their needs will be met without effort and to a passive approach to life. Evidence has shown that watching television reduces the time that children spend reading and doing homework. Television watching also decreases family interaction and communication. Family members are able to avoid one another and tense family interactions by watching television. This may sometimes reduce overt conflict, but it does nothing to help solve family problems through personal communication

Some television programs have positive influences on youths, awakening social consciousness and encouraging social concern and reform (see Chapter 1). Television can be an important social influence for evil or for good.

Moral Education

According to one study, *morality* is prosocial behavior as manifested in private, interpersonal, and social spheres (Shelton and McAdams, 1990). Discussion has been going on for years about whether schools should or can teach moral values (Mills, 1987a). In recent years, increasing numbers of parents and politicians have been calling for schools to pay more attention to students' moral development. As a result, educators are developing programs to foster prosocial values, character development, and democratic virtues in schoolchildren. Educators in Baltimore, Maryland, chose to provide moral education by teaching 24 core values from the Constitution. Most programs attempt to develop student character through direct instruction in positive social values, school policies, student recognition for good citizenship, competitive activities, and firmly enforced discipline (Smith, 1989).

In one sense, it is almost impossible *not* to teach values. Schools emphasize sharing, cooperation, and punctuality, for example. Authors such as Allport (1961) advocate the deliberate inculcation of ideas and values as a goal of education:

> If the school does not teach values, it will have the effect of denying them. If the child at school never hears a mention of honesty, modesty, charity, or reverence, he will be persuaded that, like many of this parent's ideas, they are simply old hat. . . . If the school, which to the child represents the larger

outside world, is silent on values, the child will repudiate more quickly the lessons learned at home. He will also be thrown into peer values more completely, with their emphasis on the hedonism of teen-age parties or the destructiveness of gangs. He will also be more at the mercy of the sensate values peddled by movies, TV, and disc jockeys. (p. 215)

Allport felt that teachers should select those values from the whole of U.S. ethics, particularly those based on the "American creed" and Judeo-Christian ethics. He believed that teachers ought to teach what they themselves stand for, so that the teacher's enthusiasm and interest are ensured and "the teacher's self-disclosure leads the student to self-discovery" (p. 216).

One of the problems of moral education is that inculcating values does not necessarily result in moral behavior: There is a difference between *knowing* what is right and *doing it*. Traditional moral and religious education emphasized memorization of Bible verses, proverbs, and principles of conduct. This version of moral education constitutes what Kohlberg called a "bag of virtues"—honesty, service, self-control, friendliness, and other moral virtues. Aristotle proposed a list that included temperance, liberality, pride, good temper, truthfulness, and justice. The Boy Scouts added that a scout should be honest, reverent, clean, and brave.

As a result, some writers, including Kohlberg (1966), face the issue more flexibly. Kohlberg felt the proper role of the teacher is neither to moralize individual, personal principles nor to indoctrinate state-defined values, but to stimulate development of the individual's moral judgment by encouraging free discussion, participation, and thought about real-life issues (Santilli and Hudson, 1992).

Kohlberg viewed moral education, particularly during adolescence, as the stimulation of the natural developmental process that leads to mature, moral reasoning (Harding and Snyder, 1991). Kohlberg felt that a teacher ought to be able to evaluate the maturity of a child's moral judgment and, regardless of whether the child's values agree with his or her (or society's) own moral values, stimulate the child to develop a higher stage of moral judgment. (Kohlberg suggested his own stages of moral judgment as a basis for evaluation.) The effort would be made to help the child judge the rightness or wrongness of moral action based on "universal, consistent, objective, impersonal, ideal grounds." Kohlberg admitted that it is not certain that advanced moral judgment will automatically produce more moral action (the child may know what is right but not want to do it), so the teacher also has to teach the children to examine the pros and cons of their conduct on their own terms.

In this type of teaching, the primary method used is to present case studies, or moral dilemmas, for the students to solve (Mills, 1987a, 1987b, 1988). Here is one dilemma used to promote thinking and discussion:

> Joe is a 14-year-old boy who wanted to go to camp very much. His father promised him he could go if he saved the money for it himself. So Joe worked hard at his paper route and saved the $40 it cost to go to camp and a little more besides. But just before camp was going to start, his father changed his mind. Some of his friends decided to go on a special fishing trip, and Joe's father was short of the money it would cost, so he told Joe to give him the money he had saved from the paper route. Joe didn't want to give up going to camp, so he thought of refusing to give his father the money. (Pagliuso, 1976, p. 126)

The students are then presented with several questions (Pagliuso, 1976):

1. Should Joe refuse to give his father the money? Why? Why not?
2. What do you think of the father's asking Joe for the money?
3. Does giving the money have anything to do with being a good son?
4. Should promises always be kept?

Teachers need to invent other situations that relate to students' own lives and are meaningful to them.

There is considerable evidence to support the conclusion that public schools are not having much effect on the values of youths, at least during high school. As a result of the failure of moralizing as a method of teaching values, schools are now using an approach called **values clarification** (Arcus, 1980). The values clarification approach is not concerned with the *content* of values but with the *process* of valuing. It does not aim to instill any particular set of values; rather, the goal is to help students become aware of the beliefs and behaviors they prize and would be willing to stand up for, to learn to weigh the pros and cons and consequences of various alternatives, to choose freely after considerations of consequences, and to learn to match their actions with their beliefs in a consistent way. A limited amount of research and a lot of experience with this approach indicate that students who have been exposed to it become less apathetic, less flighty, less conforming, less overdissenting, more energetic, more critical in their thinking, and more likely to follow through on their decisions (Simon, 1972).

A number of authors have developed numerous exercises and strategies that may be used in the classroom to facilitate the process of values clarification.* Here are a few of the strategies that have been used (Rice, 1980).

1. *Either-or forced choice:* The teacher asks questions such as:

_____ "Are you more of a saver or a spender?"

_____ "Are you more of a loner or a grouper?"

_____ "Are you more physical or mental?"

2. *Values continuum:* Students are asked to arrange themselves in relation to an entire group of students to indicate their values position along a continuum. They might be asked, for example, "How far would you go to be popular with your group?" The students would place themselves anywhere along a continuum ranging from "Do anything, including risking safety" to "Do nothing at all."

3. *Listing and prioritizing:* Students are told to write down 20 things they would like to do, and to

---

*Much of the material in this section is from F. P. Rice, *Morality and Youth* (Philadelphia: Westminster Press, 1980). Used by permission.

---

values clarification a method of teaching values that helps students become aware of their own beliefs and values.

Adolescents who become involved in community service improve their moral development by learning through doing. One study found participation in community service by college students to be positively associated with spiritual and religious values.

indicate beside each the cost (in dollars and cents) of doing it, whether they like to do it alone or with other people, whether planning is required, and when they did it last. Then from the 20 items, they are to list the 5 most important. The students then discuss, as a class, their selections and the reasons they made them.

4. *Rank order:* Students are asked to rank various items in order of preference; for example:

Where would you rather be on a Saturday afternoon?

_____ at the beach

_____ in the woods

_____ in a discount store

What would you give the lowest priority to today?

_____ space

_____ poverty

_____ defense

_____ ecology

In *Advanced Value Clarification,* Kirschenbaum (1977) described the value clarification process in terms of five important dimensions:

1. *Thinking:* Focusing on value decisions

2. *Feeling:* becoming aware of your feelings so that you can achieve goals more readily

3. *Choosing:* considering alternatives and doing achievement planning

4. *Communicating:* listening and talking with others and resolving conflicts, which helps in establishing goals and values

5. *Acting:* Taking repeated, consistent, and skillful action in achieving one's goals

Values clarification has not been without its critics. For example, can anyone really be objective about what he or she values? Psychologists would say it is difficult. Does the act of clarifying personal values improve morality? Not if the values held are unworthy or superficial, and not if they remain unchanged. Other research, however, has emphasized that modern college students improve significantly in their ability to think critically, and become less dogmatic, less traditional in their morals, and more willing to accept new ideas over the four-year college span (White, 1980).

Another approach to moral education is to learn through doing—specifically, through community service. A study of 1,960 students enrolled in 11 colleges in one southeastern state found that community service was positively associated with spiritual/religious values and negatively associated with an emphasis on professional gratification (Serow and Dreyden, 1990). By encouraging community service, educational institutions can play a more active role in fostering the moral development of their students.

Academic Cheating

Evans and Craig (1990) asked 601 public school students in grades 7 through 12 and in college undergraduate classes about the problem of cheating in their school. Survey results showed that 64 percent of middle-school students (grades 7–8), 77 percent of high school students (grades 9–12), and 39 percent of college students said that cheating was a serious problem in their schools. When asked what constituted *cheating,* the older the students, the more insight they had. Active forms of cheating, such as using secret notes, copying from another student's paper, using signs to communicate during an examination, or altering grades, were clearly defined as cheating. Students were less clear about passive forms of cheating, such as allowing someone else to copy from a paper. Most students, including college students, were unclear about plagiarizing, such as failure to give credit to paraphrased material from a published source.

When asked why cheating occurred, students grouped causes into three categories pertaining to teachers, classrooms, and students. They complained about teachers who were unfriendly, boring, disorganized, did not provide supervision, were inaccessible to help students having problems, or held high academic expectations. They also mentioned having to take required courses that covered fairly large amounts of material, or tests that examined material not covered in class. The students mentioned that students who had a low opinion of their abilities, feared failure, had friends who cheated, worked part-time, or participated in athletics were more likely to cheat.

When asked how cheating could be discouraged or prevented, students mentioned using new tests, alternate test forms, different tests for makeups; giving ample advance notice of examinations; arranging seating, and providing close teacher supervision. Students also mentioned the need to clarify instructional objectives, having smaller, more personalized classes, enforcing penalties for cheating, and signing honor pledges. Interestingly, students rarely, if ever, reported cheating to their teachers or complained to peers who were observed cheating.

Another study compared the cheating activities of students in 1969, 1979, and 1989. Students were quizzed regarding the amount of cheating, who was the most guilty, the reasons for the cheating, the courses in which most cheating occurred, how to punish cheaters and who should do the punishing, beliefs regarding dishonesty in society, and confessions of their own dishonest behaviors in school.

Fear of failure remained the most common reason for cheating. Math and science were the courses in which cheating most often occurred. The home was considered the best place and school the worst place to inculcate honesty. Over the three decades covered by this study, dishonesty was viewed as increasingly necessary, more people believed advertising was suspect, and success in business was attributed to fraudulent activities. More students admitted to cheating on tests and homework. Also, more parents were aiding and abetting students in avoidance of school rules (Schab, 1991).

SUMMARY

1. This chapter has discussed four major aspects of moral development: (a) theories of development of moral judgment, represented by Piaget, Kohlberg, and Gilligan; (b) family correlates to moral development; (c) transmission of religious beliefs and practices; and (d) the social influences of peers, television, and education on moral values and behavior.

2. There are marked similarities among the theories of Piaget, Kohlberg, and Gilligan. Kohlberg's research and theory is actually Piagetian in method

and content and a substantiation of part of what Piaget said, though the number and titles of the stages of development of moral judgment are different. Piaget outlined only two stages of moral development: a morality of constraint (or obedience) and a morality of cooperation (or reciprocity). In between is a transitional stage during which rules become internalized as the individual moves from heteronomy to autonomy.

3. Kohlberg and Gilligan outlined three major levels of moral development: (a) a premoral (or precon-

ventional) level; (b) a morality of conventional role conformity; and (c) a morality of self-accepted moral principles (postconventional morality). Like Piaget, Kohlberg emphasized that the level of morality at which individuals operate depends on their *motives* for doing right. Piaget said that as children become more moral, they depend less on outside authority to constrain them and more on an inner, subjective desire to cooperate and to consider the rights and feelings of others. Essentially, Kohlberg said the same thing: Children's motives change gradually from a desire to avoid punishment, gain the reward of others, and avoid disapproval or censure, to a more positive motive of desire for individual and community respect and a desire to avoid self-condemnation. Amoral people do what is expected only if they have to avoid punishment or gain rewards. The most moral people depend on inner controls because certain principles and values have been incorporated into their cognitive structures through socialization with others. In between are people who maintain a morality of convention to avoid disapproval or censure. They are not immoral because they do conform, but they are not moral either, for their motives are selfish and their control is external.

4. Gilligan described the changes in women's motives. Their motives change from self-interest and survival to the desire to please and be responsible for others to a more universal perspective in which the woman becomes concerned about the consequences for all, including herself.

5. The moral progression is similar in all three theories: from amorality to outer control to inner control; from negative, selfish motivations to positive, altruistic motivations; from a desire to escape external punishment to a desire to escape self-condemnation. Also, according to all three theories, there are individuals of a particular age group in each of the stages of moral growth and development, although children tend to move to more ad-

vanced stages of development as they get older. All of the theories emphasize also the importance of the socialization process, peer-group participation, and the parent-child relationship in moral development.

6. Moral growth and development cannot be isolated from other aspects of the adolescent's life. They have many correlates in the parent-child relationship especially and, to a lesser extent, in the childhood peer relationship. What happens to children at home, with peers, and in the neighborhood will affect their moral development.

7. Moral growth and development begin in early childhood and are not as amenable during adolescence to outside influences and change as is sometimes thought. Such socializing influences as television, which can have a measurable effect on youths, begin very early, and these early influences can still be measured during adolescence. The public senior high school seems to exert little measurable influence on morals; values change little during four years. At college age, the situation is similar but not quite as static. The greater independence and autonomy of college students, especially of those away from home, makes them more amenable to school and peer influences; as a result, some of their basic values and moral principles are changed during these years. Essentially, however, even this stage of their moral growth and development is the culmination of years of socialization rather than the result of the influences of a few years of college.

8. Increasing numbers of people feel that schools ought to play a significant role in moral education. Some feel that the schools should teach selected moral values; others emphasize character development, values clarification, or learning through community service.

9. Cheating in school is widespread, and the practice seems to have gained more acceptance. Fear of failure is the most common reason given for cheating.

KEY TERMS

THOUGHT QUESTIONS

1. Give an example of morality of constraint and contrast it with an example of morality of cooperation.
2. Give examples of objective judgments versus subjective judgments.
3. Give an example of expiatory punishment versus punishment of reciprocity.
4. Contrast immanent justice versus equity, as described by Piaget.
5. Give an example of a child's behavior at the premoral level. Give an example of a child's behavior at Level 2, according to Kohlberg. Give an example of a child's behavior at Level 3 of morality of self-accepted moral principles, as outlined by Kohlberg.
6. Explain the difference between being able to make moral judgments and actually acting in a moral manner.
7. What are some criticisms of Kohlberg's model?
8. Do you agree or disagree with Gilligan's theory that women ought to be judged by different standards than men? Explain.
9. What family practice contributes positively to moral learning?
10. How does the type of discipline influence moral development?
11. How does modeling influence moral development?
12. Do adolescents always identify with their parents and model their behavior after him or her? Why or why not?
13. In U.S. culture, why do fathers and their sons go to church less frequently than mothers and their daughters?
14. Should adolescents be made to go to church or synagogue?
15. What factors determine whether peer influence is greater over adolescents than parental influence in regard to moral development?
16. What do you believe about the effect of television violence on children?
17. What do you believe about the effect of pornography on children?
18. What values are taught through television ads? Through soap operas?
19. Does the public school influence moral development? Values? Moral behavior? Explain.
20. Should schools teach moral values? Why or why not?
21. What do you think of the values clarification approach to moral education?
22. What should schools do about academic cheating?

SUGGESTED READING

Dosick, W. (1995). *Golden Rules: The Ten Ethical Values Parents Need to Teach their Children.* San Francisco: Harper.

Gibbs, J. C., Bassinger, K. S., and Fuller, D. (1992). *Moral Maturity: Measuring the Development of Sociomoral Reflection.* Hillsdale, NJ: Erlbaum.

13

Adolescents and Their Families

In this chapter, we will begin by discussing what youths expect of their parents in the way of interest and help, communication, love, approval, acceptance, trust, autonomy, guidance, home life, and parental example. The discussion will then continue with the subject of parent-adolescent tensions. We will first discuss the difficulties that parents have with adolescents. The next section will focus on adolescent-sibling relationships and the relationships of youths with other relatives in the family. Finally, discussion on maltreatment of adolescents will include the topics of child abuse, sexual abuse, incest, and neglect.

Adolescent-Parent Expectations

Adolescent-parent relationships and the role that parents play in adolescent development are important subjects.

What Kind of Parents Do Adolescents Want?

What kind of parents do adolescents want and need? A compilation of research findings indicates that youths want and need parents who display the following qualities (Newman, 1989):

> "Are interested in us and available to help us when needed."
>
> "Listen to us and try to understand us."
>
> "Let us know they love us."
>
> "Show approval of us."
>
> "Accept us as we are, faults and all."
>
> "Trust us and expect the best of us."
>
> "Treat us like grown-ups."

"Guide us."

"Are happy people with good dispositions and a sense of humor, who create a happy home, and who set a good example for us."

Let's examine these qualities in more detail.

Parental Interest and Help

Some of the ways adolescents know that their parents care about them is by the interest their parents show in them, by the amount of quality time spent with them, and by their willingness to stand beside them and help them as needed (Amato, 1990; Gecas and Seff, 1990; Northman, 1985). Positive parental support is associated with close relationships with parents and siblings, high self-esteem, academic success, and advanced moral development (Argyle and Henderson, 1985). Lack of parental support may have exactly the opposite effect: low self-esteem, poor schoolwork, impulsive behavior, poor social adjustment, and deviant and antisocial behavior or delinquency (Peterson and Rollins, 1987). For instance, consider this reaction expressed by a high school basketball player:

> I'm the star player on the school basketball team, but never once has either parent come to see me play. They're either too busy or too tired or can't get a baby sitter for my younger sister. The crowds cheer for me, the girls hang around my locker, some kids even ask me for my autograph. But it doesn't mean much if the two most important people in my life don't care. (Author's counseling notes)

Adolescents want attention and companionship from their parents (Henry, Wilson, and Peterson, 1989). They especially resent parents who have positions of responsibility that require them to work long hours or be away from home a great deal (Jensen and Borges, 1986). Many youths today are *latchkey children* who have to let themselves in the house after school because parents are not home.

Other parents overdo the companionship. Adolescents want to spend time with their own friends and do not want their parents to be pals. They need adult interest and help, not adults trying to act like adolescents. In one study, measures of maternal and parental demandingness, responsiveness, values toward achievement, involvement

in schoolwork, and involvement in school functions were obtained from both adolescents and their parents. Results showed that both adolescents and their parents perceived mothers to be more involved in parenting than were fathers in both ninth and twelfth grades. Additionally, both mothers and fathers perceived themselves to be higher in all aspects of parenting than their adolescents perceived them to be. In the longitudinal study, both adolescents and parents perceived levels of parenting to drop between ninth and twelfth grades—except values toward achievement, which did not change (Paulson and Sputa, 1996).

The attention adolescents get from their parents depends partially on the birth order and spacing of the children. Middle-born adolescents sometimes feel cheated of parental attention and support and express a sense of being "pushed around" in terms of family rules and regulations. Parents tend to be more punitive and less supportive when their children are spaced too closely together.

Listening and Empathetic Understanding

Empathy refers to the ability to identify with the thoughts, attitudes, and feelings of another person. It is *affective sensitivity* to others, the vicarious sharing of experiences of another person and the emotions associated with them (Kagan and Schneider, 1987). There are some parents who are completely insensitive to their adolescents' feelings and moods. They are unaware of what their adolescents are thinking and feeling and so act without taking those thoughts and feelings into account. When their adolescents are upset, they have no idea why. One possible consequence of this insensitivity is that children grow up as insensitive as the parents. The children's own feelings have never been considered, so they don't learn to consider other peoples' feelings.

Communication with parents deteriorates to some extent during adolescence. Adolescents have reported that they spend less time interacting with their parents compared to when they were younger. They disclose less information to their parents and communication with parents is often difficult (Beaumont, 1996). Perhaps one reason for this lack of communication is that many parents do not listen to their teens' ideas, accept their opinions as relevant, or try to understand their feelings and points of view. Adolescents want parents who will talk *with* them, not *at* them, in a sympathetic way.

> "We want parents we can take our troubles to and be sure they'll understand. Some parents won't listen or let their children explain. They should try to see things a little more from our point of view."
>
> "We wish our parents would lose an argument with us once in a while and listen to our side of problems." (Author's counseling notes)

Basically, adolescents are saying that they want sympathetic understanding, an attentive ear, and parents who feel that their children have something worthwhile to say (Noble, Adams, and Openshaw, 1989). Research indicates that the respect parents show for adolescent opinions contributes greatly to the climate and happiness of the home.

Some parents feel threatened when their adolescent disagrees, does not accept their ideas, or tries to argue. Parents who refuse to talk and close the argument by saying, "I don't want to discuss it; what I say goes," are closing the door to effective communication, just as are adolescents who get angry, stamp out of the room, refuse to discuss a matter reasonably, and go into their rooms to pout.

Communication is one key to harmonious parent-youth relationships (Masselam, Marcus, and Stunkard, 1990). Some families spend little time together. If families are to talk, they have to be together long enough to do so; they also have to develop an openness between the generations.

Love and Positive Affect

Affect, which refers to the emotions or feelings that exist among family members, may be positive or negative. *Positive affect* between family members refers to relationships characterized by emotional warmth, affection, love, and sensitivity (Felson and Zielinski, 1989). Family members show that they matter to one another, and are responsive to one another's feelings and needs. *Negative affect* is characterized by emotional coldness, rejection, and hostility. Family members don't seem to love one another—or even like one another. In fact, they may hate one another, be indifferent to one another's feelings and needs, and act as though they really don't care about the other members of the family. There is little affection, positive emotional support, empathy, or understanding.

Most adolescents need a great deal of love and demonstration of affection from parents (Barber and Thomas, 1986). Sometimes, however, parents themselves were brought up in unexpressive

---

empathy   the ability to identify with the thoughts, attitudes, and feelings of another person.

affect   feelings that exist among family members.

positive affect   relationships characterized by emotional warmth, affection, love, empathy, care, sensitivity, and emotional support.

negative affect   negative feelings of emotional coldness, rejection, hostility, anger, and insensitivity among family members.

▶ PERSONAL ISSUES

Parental Advice

A study of Caucasian students, some of middle-school age (average age 12.2) and others of high school age (average age 16.8), from both working-class and white-collar professional families revealed that adolescents in both age groups overwhelmingly preferred their mother's advice on self, social, family, school-related, and philosophical issues (Greene, 1990). The more distress in their relationship with their father, the more both male and female adolescents followed their mother's advice. The overwhelming preference for maternal advice is consistent with previous observations of greater intimacy characteristic of mother-adolescent as compared to father-adolescent dyads (Montemayor and Browler, 1987).

families where affection was seldom bestowed. As a consequence, the parents seldom hug their children, hold them, or kiss them. They don't express positive, warm feelings at all. As one girl expressed it: "I don't remember my parents ever telling me that they loved me. They just assumed I knew, but I wish they could have told me, and showed it once in awhile."

Two possibilities may result: Either the adolescents are so starved for love and affection that their needs become very great when they become adults, or they remain cold and aloof themselves, finding it difficult to express affection to their own spouses or children. Adolescents emphasize that they need both intrinsic support (encouragement, appreciation, being pleased with the child, trust, and love) and extrinsic support (external expressions of support, such as hugging and kissing, taking the child to dinner or a movie, and buying the child something special). Adolescents' perceptions of parental support, particularly intrinsic support and closeness, are positively correlated with life satisfaction for the adolescents (Young, Miller, Norton, and Hill, 1995).

Acceptance and Approval

An important component of love is unconditional acceptance. One way to show love is to know and accept adolescents exactly as they are, faults and all. Adolescents need to know they are valued, accepted, and liked by their parents. They also want parents to have tolerance for individuality, intimacy, and interpersonal differences in the family (Bomar and Sabatelli, 1996).

There must be a determined effort by parents both to show approval and to achieve enough objectivity to see the child as a human being, entitled to human attributes. Adolescents do not want to feel that their parents expect them to be perfect before they will love them, nor can they thrive in an atmosphere of constant criticism and displeasure.

Negative feelings between parents and adolescents may exist for a variety of reasons. Some children are resented, rejected, and unloved by parents from the time they are born, because they were unplanned and unwanted in the first place. One girl explained,

> My mother always tells me how upset she was when she found out she was pregnant with me. She had to give up a successful career when I was born. Carrying me destroyed her figure. Giving birth was painful. I was a fussy baby who cried a lot and kept her awake nights. Growing up, I was a pain in the butt most of the time, according to her. She's resented me all these years and she lets me know it. (Author's counseling notes)

Other parents may be very upset at the way their children have turned out. One father complained,

Most adolescents need a great deal of love and affection from their parents. Perceptions of parental support, both intrinsic and extrinsic, correlate positively with life satisfaction for adolescents.

I hate to admit it but I'm very disappointed in my son. He's not at all like me. When I was in school, I played football and other sports. My son prefers music and books. He has long hair, an earring in his left ear, and looks like a sissy. I wish I could be proud of him but I'm not. He really embarrasses me. (Author's counseling notes)

Trust

"Why are our parents always so afraid we are going to do the wrong thing? Why can't they trust us more?"

"Our parents could trust us more than they often do. They should tell us what we need to know about dating without being old-fashioned. Then they should put us on our own and expect the best of us so we have something to live up to." (Author's counseling notes)

One of the most annoying evidences of distrust are parents' opening the children's mail, reading their diaries, or listening in on their telephone conversations. One girl complained,

My mother is forever going through my room under the pretense of "cleaning." I don't like to have my desk straightened up (it's where I keep my diary) or my bureau rummaged through. . . . Don't you think a 16-year-old girl needs privacy? (Author's counseling notes)

Some parents seem to have more difficulty trusting their adolescents than others do. Such parents tend to project their own fears, anxiety, and guilt onto the adolescent. The most fearful parents are usually those who are the most insecure or who had difficulties themselves while growing up. Mothers who themselves have conceived or borne children out of wedlock are those most concerned about their own daughters' dating and sexual behavior. Most adolescents feel that parents should trust them completely unless they have given the adults reason for distrust.

Separation-Individuation and Autonomy

One goal of every adolescent is to be accepted as an autonomous adult. This is accomplished through a process called *separation-individuation,* during which the parent-adolescent bond is transformed but maintained (Fleming and Anderson, 1986; Josselson, 1988). The adolescent establishes individuality and connectedness with parents at the same time (Grotevant and Cooper, 1985). Thus, adolescents seek a differentiated relationship with parents, while communication, affection, and trust continue (Quintana and Lapsley, 1990). For example, they develop new interests, values, and goals and may develop points of view that are different from parents in order to experience distinctiveness. Nevertheless, the adolescents are still part of a family. Adolescents and their parents continue to expect emotional commitment from each other (Newman, 1989).

Individuation is a fundamental organizing principle of human growth (Gavazzi and Sabatelli, 1990). It involves the ongoing efforts of an individual to build self-understanding and identity in relation to other people. In making the transition from childhood to adulthood, the adolescent needs to establish a degree of *autonomy* and identity in order to assume adult roles and responsibilities. Adolescents who remain too dependent on their parents are not as able to develop satisfactory relationships with peers (Schneider and Younger, 1996).

There are two aspects of autonomy. *Behavioral autonomy* involves becoming independent and free enough to act on your own without excessive dependence on others for guidance. *Emotional autonomy* means becoming free of childish emotional ties with parents. Research indicates that behavioral autonomy increases sharply during adolescence. It is suggested in other parts of

---

separation-individuation the process by which the adolescent becomes separated from parents and becomes a unique individual.

autonomy independence or freedom

behavioral autonomy becoming independent and free enough to act on one's own without excessive dependence on others.

emotional autonomy becoming free of childish emotional dependence on parents.

this book (see Chapter 10 especially) that adolescents desire behavioral autonomy in some areas, such as clothing selection or choice of friends, but follow their parents' leads in other areas, such as formulating educational plans. Adolescents want and need parents who will grant them behavioral autonomy in slowly increasing amounts as they learn to use it, rather than all at once. Too much freedom granted too quickly may be interpreted as rejection. Youths want to be given the right to make choices, to exert their own independence, to argue with adults, and to assume responsibility, but they do not want complete freedom. Those who have it worry about it because they realize they do not know how to use it.

The shift to emotional autonomy during adolescence is not as dramatic as the shift to behavioral autonomy. Much depends on parental behavior. Some parents continue to encourage overdependency. Parents who have an unhappy marriage sometimes turn to their children for emotional satisfaction and become overly dependent on them. Parents who encourage dependency needs that become demanding and excessive, even into adulthood, are interfering with their child's ability to function as an effective adult. Some adolescents who have been dominated by their parents begin to accept and to prefer being dependent. The result is prolonged adolescence. Some adolescents, for example, may prefer to live with their parents after marriage, or may never achieve mature social relationships, establish a vocational identity of their own choosing, or develop a positive self-image as separate, independent people.

The opposite extreme from overdependence is emotional rejection by parents, so that the adolescent cannot depend on them at all for emotional satisfaction. As in so many other affairs of life, a middle ground should be established.

Cohesion refers to the degree to which family members are connected or separated from their family (Masselam, Marcus, and Stunkard, 1990; Papini, Sebby, and Clark, 1989; Wentzel and Feldman, 1996); it represents the emotional closeness or bonding of the family unit (Jackson, Dunham, and Kidwell, 1990).

Regarding adolescents and family cohesion, then, more is not necessarily better. Much depends on the adolescent's age and the stage of the family life cycle. Ordinarily, family cohesion is tightest in the early stages of marriage while the children are very young. Children like to feel that they are part of a closely knit family unit. As the children become adolescents, most families become less cohesive (Leigh and Peterson, 1986). When children leave home during the launching stage, family cohesion (at least as far as it involves youths) is usually at its lowest ebb (Larson and Lowe, 1990).

The lower level of family cohesion in adolescence is due to the adolescent striving to become autonomous, to carve out a life for himself or herself in the process of separation-individuation. At the same time, parents are separating from the adolescent in their increasing need for privacy as they create a new life for themselves (Leigh and Peterson, 1986). The result of these simultaneous separating processes is a lower level of cohesion at the adolescent stage of the family life cycle.

Furthermore, research indicates that the spatial distance in parental-adolescent dyads is greater for older adolescent families compared with younger adolescent families (Bulcroft, Carmody, and Bulcroft, 1996). This lends support to the idea that older adolescents strive for more autonomy and separateness, and for more personal space, compared with younger adolescents (Larson and Lowe, 1990). Thus, there is a clear and important relationship between the developmental stage of the family and the spatial distance in the family. This conclusion is even more evident in the research of Larson and Lowe (1990), who found that older adolescents and their parents maintained, on average, a 70 percent greater distance between themselves than did younger adolescents and their parents.

What degree of family cohesiveness is necessary for a functional family and what degree is necessary for a dysfunctional family? The most functional family situation seems to be that which is characterized by a high degree of family cohesiveness as children grow, with a gradual shift to a more balanced degree of closeness as children become adolescents, thus allowing formation of budding identities in adolescents who strive to become persons in their own right.

Guidance and Control

The methods by which parents seek to guide and control their adolescents vary. There are four basic patterns of family control:

HIGHLIGHT

Nontherapeutic versus Therapeutic Separation-Individuation

Jill Daniels (1990) makes a distinction between non-therapeutic and therapeutic separation-individuation. She views separation-individuation as a continuum (see figure). At the right end of the continuum, adolescents reach successful therapeutic separation-individuation—a sense of self—while remaining part of the family as a functioning member. To the left of the continuum is nontherapeutic, dysfunctional separation-individuation. These adolescents are characterized by alienation, disruptive behavior, rejection of family and societal norms, and potential suicide. Sometimes professional intervention is necessary to promote therapeutic separation-individuation in relation to all family members.

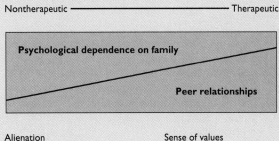

Nontherapeutic ———————————— Therapeutic

Psychological dependence on family

Peer relationships

Alienation	Sense of values
Disruptive behaviors	Sense of self
Rejection of family	Interdependent family
and societal norms	relationship
Social withdrawal	Autonomous individual
Suicide	

Source: J. A. Daniels, "Adolescent Separation-Individuation and Family Transitions," *Adolescence, 25* (1990): 105–116. Reprinted by permission.

1. *Autocratic:* The parent makes any decisions relevant to the adolescent.
2. *Authoratative but democratic:* Decisions are made jointly by the parent and the adolescent.
3. *Permissive:* The adolescent has more influence in making decisions than does the parent.
4. *Erratic:* Control is inconsistent, sometimes authoritarian, sometimes democratic, and sometimes permissive.

What effect does each method of control have on the adolescent? What methods are most functional?

The usual effect of *autocratic control* is to produce a combination of rebellion and dependency. Adolescents are taught to follow their parents' demands and decisions without question and not to try to make decisions themselves. Adolescents in such environments usually are more hostile to their parents, often deeply resent their control and domination, and less often identify with them. When they succeed in challenging parent authority, youths may become rebellious, sometimes overtly aggressive and hostile, especially if the parents' discipline has been harsh, unfair, or administered without much love and affection. Thus,

the effects on children growing up in autocratic homes differ. The meeker ones are cowed and remain codependent (Fischer and Crawford, 1992); the stronger ones are rebellious. Both usually show some emotional disturbances and have problems. Those who rebel often leave home as soon as they can; some become delinquent.

The effect of using punitive measures to exercise control is usually negative. Adolescents resist parental efforts to exact conformity through harsh means (Henry, Wilson, and Peterson, 1989). Furthermore, adolescent who grow up in homes where parents use harsh and physical punishment will usually model their parents' aggressive behavior (Johnson and O'Leary, 1987). Family violence seems to beget more violence in and outside the home (Martin et al., 1987; Peek, Fischer, and Kidwell, 1985; Roscoe and Callahan, 1985).

There is also a relationship between harsh discipline in the home and adolescents' relationships

cohesion the degree to which family members are connected to other family members.

Parental Control Techniques

In his research on parental control techniques in 1,109 parent-adolescent encounters, Smith (1988) outlined the following seven methods of control:

1. *Power assertion:* Physical punishment, deprivation, threats are doled out.
2. *Command:* Imperative statements are made, with or without the threat of punishment.
3. *Love withdrawal:* Behavior punishes or threatens to punish a child by means of temporary coldness or rejection.
4. *Self-oriented induction:* Parents suggest possible gains or costs the child might experience as a result of a choice made.
5. *Other-oriented induction:* Parents point to religion or ethical reasons, attraction to others, or personal obligations as reasons for a choice.
6. *Advice:* Suggestions are made to the child on how he or she may more efficiently, effectively, or easily accomplish what is desired by the parent.
7. *Relationship maintenance:* Appeals are made to the child to maintain a positive orientation toward the parent.

The subjects of the study were 109 mothers and 88 fathers, predominantly middle class, although of different income levels, in Columbia, South Carolina. The relative frequency of parental control techniques were

Command:	34 percent of parent-adolescent encounters
Self-oriented induction:	31 percent
Advice:	14 percent
Relationship maintenance:	10 percent
Power assertion:	8 percent
Other-oriented induction:	1 percent
Love withdrawal:	1 percent

These findings are important because research generally indicates that parental explanations and reasoning (**induction**) are strongly associated with the child internalizing ethical and moral principles. Parents and adolescents who exchange ideas and information are those who are most successful at conflict resolution (McCombs, Forehand, and Smith, 1988). Use of physical punishment, deprivation, and threats (power-assertive discipline) is associated with children's aggression, hostility, and delinquency. It impedes the development of emotional, social, and intellectual maturity (Portes, Dunham, and Williams, 1986). Harsh corporal punishment is associated with subsequent aggression of children. There is recent evidence that later in life this aggression includes physical assaults on spouses (Straus and Yodanis, 1996). Harsh physical punishment is especially damaging if punishment is seen by youths as a form of parental rejection (Rohner, Bourque, and Elordi, 1996).

Love withdrawal can have a devastating effect on adolescents if it is used frequently as a means of discipline. Adolescents begin to feel that they can't do anything right without displeasing their parents. They grow up feeling that their parents don't like them or approve of them, and this is threatening to their self-esteem and self-worth. Parents must somehow communicate the idea that they will always love their children but they don't love all the things that they do. This means parents have to learn to hate the sin but love the sinner.

with their peers. Adolescents who exercise little restraint in their social behavior, partly because they model the aggressive behavior of their parents, are not as well liked by peers as adolescents who have learned restraint from positive models at home (Feldman and Wentzel, 1990).

The other extreme is a *permissive* home, in which adolescents receive little guidance and direction, are given few restrictions from parents, and are expected to make decisions for themselves. The effects vary. If overindulged but not

guided or properly socialized, pampered adolescents will be ill prepared to accept frustrations or responsibility or show proper regard for others. They often become domineering, self-centered, and selfish, and get into trouble with those who will not pamper them the way their parents have. Without limits on their behavior, they feel insecure, disoriented, and uncertain. If adolescents interpret the parents' lack of control as disinterest or rejection, they blame the parents for not warning or guiding them. Lax discipline, rejection, and lack of parental affection also have been associated with delinquency.

The *authoritative but democratic* home has the most positive effect on adolescents (Kelly and Goodwin, 1983). Parents exercise authority, but concern expresses itself through guidance. Talking with adolescents is the most frequent discipline measure used and the one considered best for the age group (deTurck and Miller, 1983). Parents also encourage individual responsibility, decision making, and autonomy. Adolescents are involved in making their own decisions while listening to and discussing the reasoned explanations of their parents. Adolescents are also encouraged to detach themselves gradually from their families. As a result, the home atmosphere is likely to be one of respect, appreciation, warmth, acceptance, and consistent parenting (Necessary and Parish, 1995). This type of home is associated with conforming, trouble-free nondelinquent behavior for both boys and girls.

Erratic, inconsistent parental control, like lack of control, has a negative effect on adolescents. Parents who disagree about discipline are more likely to report that their children are aggressive, have control problems, and are disobedient (Kandel, 1990).

If children lack clear, definite guidelines, they will become confused and insecure. Such youths often demonstrate antisocial, delinquent behavior. They react by evidencing a great amount of rebellion against their parents. Fathers seem to exercise more authority over sons than do mothers, and mothers exercise more authority over daughters than do fathers. This is acceptable as long as parents don't openly disagree.

There are parents, however, who are too inflexible. Inflexible parents believe there is only one right way, and that is their way. Such parents are unyielding and refuse to change their ideas and behavioral responses. They won't discuss different points of view or allow disagreements, so they and their adolescents can never understand one another. They expect all of their children to fit narrow molds, to act, think, and be alike. They are usually prejudiced against minorities or children who are different.

Inflexible parents are often perfectionists, and thus are regularly critical and displeased with their adolescents' performances on most things. The results are the destruction of the adolescents' self-esteem and the creation of intolerable tension and stress. Many such adolescents grow up with a great deal of anxiety and fear they will be doing something wrong or not be able to measure up.

Parental Example

Youths say they want parents who "practice what they preach," "set a good example for us to follow," "follow the same principles they try to teach

---

induction   parental control through offering alternative choices.

PERSONAL ISSUES

Corporal Punishment

Corporal punishment or *physical punishment* refers to the use of physical force with the intention of causing a child pain, but not injury, for purposes of correction or control of the child's behavior. Corporal punishment of children by parents is a normative form of discipline in U.S. society. In fact, not only are spanking and slapping children considered acceptable but they are generally believed to be quite necessary and highly effective. One study found that 84 percent of the national sample of adults agreed that a good, hard spanking is sometimes necessary. Parents who refuse to use corporal punishment on children are viewed as too lenient and ineffective—in essence, poor parents. Although the prevalence of corporal punishment declines with the age of the child, it still remains high even during adolescence. Almost half of the children in early adolescence experience corporal punishment by a parent (Turner and Finkelhor, 1996).

us," and "make us proud of them." Adolescents want to feel proud of their parents, to feel they are the kind of people they can admire. Youths like adults who have a pleasant disposition and a good sense of humor, and who are as truthful and honest as they want their teenagers to be. Youths object to adults who nag about things they themselves do all the time or who are hypocritical in their beliefs and actions. As one adolescent expressed it, "It's good to feel our parents have a religion; they're sincerely trying to live right in the family and everywhere else. . . . It makes us feel we really belong and gives us something to build on."

Parent-Adolescent Tension

We will discuss some of the major causes of parent-adolescent tension.

Personality Differences

Parent-adolescent misunderstanding arises from the two different types of personalities of adults and youths. Table 13.1 shows a comparison of two possible personality types. Although not all adults or youths fit the types described, enough are similar to the two descriptions to make personality differences a major source of conflict.

Note that Table 13.1 reveals some significant differences between middle-aged parents and adolescent children. From a vantage point reached after many years of experience, parents feel that youths are irresponsible, reckless, and naive, too inexperienced even to recognize that they are foolish to take chances. Parents worry that their youths will have accidents, get hurt, or get in trouble with the law. Youths feel their parents are overly cautious and worry too much.

Middle-aged parents tend to compare today's youths and life-styles with their own past. Parents often suffer from a perennial "cultural lag"—a situation that renders them helpless and relatively poorly informed. Children and teenagers show a tendency to generalize the inefficiency of parents as instructors and have started to question their reliability as educators in general. In fact, there is some evidence that adolescents feel they have to socialize parents to bring them up to date on modern views (Peters, 1985).

Parents also become a little cynical about human character and somewhat disillusioned about trying to change the world and everybody in it; they realistically learn to accept some things as they are. Adolescents are still extremely idealistic and impatient with adults who are part of the establishment and accept and like things as they are. Adolescents want to reform the world overnight and become annoyed when their parents do not agree with their crusade (see Chapters 1 and 6).

Adolescents also grow to be wary of adults, primarily because they feel most adults are too critical and will not understand them. Youths feel

---

TABLE 13.1   Middle-Aged Adult and Adolescent Personalities

Middle-Aged Adult Generation	Adolescent Generation
Is careful/experienced	Is daring and adventurous; sometimes takes foolish chances
Holds to past; has tendency to compare present with yesterday	Considers past irrelevant; lives in present
Is realistic; sometimes skeptical about life and people	Is idealistic, optimistic
Is conservative in manners, morals, and mores	Is liberal; challenges traditional ideas; experiments with new customs
Is generally contented and satisfied; accepts status quo	Is critical with things as they are; desires to reform, change
Wants to stay youthful; fears age	Wants to be grown-up, but dislikes idea of ever being old
Tends to be restrictive on views of what is age-appropriate behavior	Tends to be more accepting than adults of actions that violate social expectations of age-appropriate behavior

they have good ideas, too, and know more about some things than their parents do, and, because they want to be grown-ups, they may scoff at parental suggestions or ideas. Adults react to criticism and rejection with anger and hurt.

Some aging adults become oversensitive about growing old or being considered aged. Because they hate to think of getting old, they focus more and more attention on staying young. If parents carry this insecurity to extremes in their dress and behaviors, they succeed only in attracting the embarrassed shame of their own teenagers and the amused ridicule of other youths as well.

Finally, adults tend to have more restricted ideas than adolescents about what constitutes age-appropriate behavior. With age and experience, adults tend to become more aware of age norms and social pressures. Adolescents are more tolerant of age-norm violations, partly because social change is so rapid (Roscoe and Peterson, 1989). Parents and youths view each other from prejudiced positions that do not help them to understand how to live with the other generation.

Focus of Conflict

In spite of personality differences, research indicates that parent-adolescent relationships are usually harmonious (Stefanko, 1984). When conflict occurs, the focus may be in any of five areas (Hall, 1987; Laursen, 1995; Leslie, Huston and Johnson, 1986; Noble, Adams, and Openshaw, 1989).

Social Life and Customs Adolescents' social lives and the social customs they observe probably create more conflict with parents than any other area. The most common sources of friction are the following:

Choice of friends or dating partners
How often they are allowed to go out, going out on school nights, and frequency of dating
Where they are allowed to go and the type of activity they can attend
Curfew hours
The age they are allowed to date, ride in cars, and participate in certain events
Going steady
Choice of clothes and hairstyles

One of the most common complaints of parents is that adolescents are never home and do not spend any time with the family.

Responsibility Parents become the most critical of adolescents who do not evidence enough responsibility. Parents expect adolescents to show responsibility in the following:

Performing family chores (Light, Hertsgaard, and Martin, 1985; Sanik and Stafford, 1985)
Earning and spending money
Caring for personal belongings, clothes, and room
Using the family automobile
Using the telephone
Doing work for others outside the home
Using family property or belongings (furniture, tools, supplies, equipment, etc.)

School Adolescents' school performance, behavior at school, and attitudes toward school receive much attention from parents. Specifically, parents are concerned about the following:

Grades and level of performance (whether the youths are performing according to their potential)
Study habits and homework
Regularity of attendance
General attitude toward school studies and teachers
Behavior in school

Sometimes, pressure on the adolescent to succeed in school is excessive, resulting in lowered self-esteem, deviant activity, and a feeling of failure in reaching goals set by families (Eskilson, Wiley, Muehlbauer, and Dodder, 1986).

Family Relationships Conflict arises over the following:

Immature behavior
General attitude and level of respect shown to parents
Quarreling with siblings
Relationships with relatives, especially aged grandparents in the home

Degree of orientation toward family or amount of autonomy from family (Jurich, Schumm and Bollman, 1987)

Values and Morals   Parents are concerned especially with the following:

Drinking, smoking, and using drugs
Language and speech
Basic honesty
Sexual behavior
Obeying the law, staying out of trouble
Going to church or Sunday school

Parents are particularly worried about adolescent sexual behavior. Interestingly, the quality of the mother-daughter relationship is the strongest predictor of the daughter's sexual experience. The more favorable the daughter's relationship with her mother, the less likely she is to have premarital sex (Inazu and Fox, 1980).

Variables Affecting Conflict

The focus of conflict in any one family will depend on a number of factors. The *age* of the adolescent is one variable. Girls are increasingly in conflict with their parents about boyfriends from age 12 on, with the peak years being 14 and 15. The same conflict for boys about girlfriends peaks at age 16. Autonomy-related issues tend to increase with age of the adolescent (Gehring, Wentzel, Feldman, and Munson, 1990).

The *sex* of the adolescent is another factor influencing conflict. Girls report a greater number of family problems than do boys, which is an indication of sex differences in the extent of difficulty. The sex of the parent also influences conflict. Most adolescents report more difficulties getting along with their fathers than with their mothers, and feel that they are closer to their mothers. As a result, their mothers exert more influence on them (Greene, 1990).

The total *atmosphere within the home* influences conflict. Conflict of all types is more frequent in authoritarian homes than in democratic homes. In authoritarian homes, there is more conflict over spending money, social life, activities outside the home, and home chores. Conflict between parents also affects the home atmosphere and has a detrimental effect on adolescents. The level of parent-

adolescent conflict is determined partially by family context. A family atmosphere of warmth and supportiveness promotes successful negotiation of disagreements between parents and adolescent children and thereby helps keep conflict at a low to moderate level. Under hostile, coercive conditions, however, parents and adolescents will be unlikely to resolve disagreements and conflict will escalate to dysfunctional levels (Rueter and Conger, 1995).

The *socioeconomic status* of the family is another variable affecting conflict. Low-socioeconomic-status families are more often concerned about obedience, politeness, and respect, whereas middle-income families are more concerned with developing independence and initiative. Low-socioeconomic-status families may also worry more about keeping children out of trouble at school; middle-class parents are more concerned about grades and achievement.

The *total environment* in which the child grows up will determine what parents worry about. An adolescent growing up in an area where there is high delinquency or considerable drug abuse will find parents more concerned with these problems.

Variations in *parental reactions* to adolescent behavior influence the extent and focus of conflict. Some parents show little concern about only a few specific problems. Others are greatly and generally dissatisfied with the overall behavior of their adolescents.

Family size has been found to be a significant variable, at least in middle-class families. The larger the middle-class family, the greater the degree of parent-youth conflict and the more often parents use physical force to control adolescents (Bell and Avery, 1985).

Another factor influencing conflict is *parental workloads.* Adolescent conflict is highest when both parents are stressed. This is particularly true in dual-career families, when both mother and father are stressed because of their jobs (Galambos, Sears, Almeida, and Kolaric, 1995). When both parents have to work to support the family, there is a reduction of parental attention and monitoring provided to the adolescent. This lack of proper supervision of the adolescent is the major cause of difficulty in some families. Some parents do a good job in parenting their adolescents even though both work; other parents virtually neglect this responsibility almost entirely, and their adolescents are left on their own to fend for themselves.

The variables influencing parent-adolescent conflict are almost countless, but the ones mentioned here indicate how many factors may be involved. Not all parents and adolescents quarrel about the same things or to the same extent.

Results of Conflict

Research with families of adolescents not under clinical treatment report that despite arguments with parents, adolescents characterize their family relationships by closeness, positive feelings, and flexibility (Barnes and Olson, 1985; Feldman and Gehring, 1988; Noller and Callan, 1986). However, studies focusing on the frequency and intensity of family conflict, including both marital conflict and parent-adolescent conflict, emphasize that high levels of conflict affect family cohesion and have an adverse effect on adolescent development. Adolescents in families with high levels of conflict are more likely to evidence antisocial behavior, immaturity, and low self-esteem than those in families with low levels of conflict (Montemayor, 1986).

Relationships with Other Family Members

In this section, we are concerned with the adolescent's relationships with siblings and other relatives.

Adolescent-Sibling Relationships

Research efforts have concentrated on exploring parent-adolescent relationships in the family, but little information is available, and some of it is contradictory, on adolescent-sibling relationships. Yet the relationships between brothers and sisters are vitally important because they may have a lasting influence on development and on the individual's ultimate adult personality and roles. Let's examine the number of ways in which sibling relationships are important.

First, older siblings are likely to serve as role models for younger brothers and sisters. This has a strong influence on the development of younger brothers and sisters.

Next, older siblings often serve as surrogate parents and caregivers. If older children feel useful, accepted, and admired because of the care they give younger children, this added apprecia-

tion and sense of usefulness contributes positively to their own sense of self-worth. Older brothers and sisters are often expected to protect younger siblings from the aggression of older children (Tisak and Tisak, 1996). Many adolescents learn adult roles and responsibilities by having to care for younger brothers and sisters while growing up.

Third, older siblings often provide companionship, friendship, and meet one another's needs for affection and meaningful relationships. Older brothers and sisters act as confidants, are able to help one another, and share many experiences.

If siblings are six or more years apart in age, they tend to grow up like single children. If there is less than six years' difference, however, they are often a threat to each other's power and command over their parents, rivalry is more pronounced, and conflicts tend to be more severe. One study of 274 high school junior and senior boys and girls explored the sources of conflict among siblings and the conflict resolution strategies that were used (Goodwin and Roscoe, 1990). The 10 most common sources of conflict were something the sibling said, teasing, possessions, duties and chores, name-calling, wearing other's clothing, invasion of privacy, special treatment by parents, embarrassment in front of friends, and conflict over privileges. The primary methods of resolving conflict between siblings involved yelling, arguing, ignoring, compromising, and talking about the conflict. More boys than girls used physical force or the threat of physical force as a means of conflict resolution.

Do relationships with siblings tend to be more frictional during early adolescence than later? As adolescents mature, they accept their siblings in a calmer, more rational manner, with the result that conflicting relationships generally subside and are replaced by friendlier, more cooperative ones.

Relationships with Other Relatives

Relationships with grandparents can have positive effects on adolescents. One study discussed three of these (Baranowski, 1982).

1. Grandparents may be the key agents in restoring a sense of continuity in an adolescent's life, in linking the past to the present, and in transmitting

Grandparents often have a positive effect in relationships with their adolescent grandchildren. A grandparent may help in the adolescent's search for identity by linking the past to the present and may serve as an arbiter in conflicts with the adolescent's parents.

knowledge of culture and family roots, and thus having a positive impact on the adolescent's search for identity.

2. Grandparents may have a positive impact on parent-adolescent relations by conveying information about the parents to the adolescent. Adolescents also turn to grandparents as confidants and arbiters when they are in conflict with their parents.

3. Grandparents help adolescents understand aging and accept the aged. Adolescents who see their grandparents frequently, and have a good relationship with them, are more likely to have positive attitudes toward the elderly.

During early adolescence, contact with older relatives may be frictional. Some grandparents assume an active role in the rearing and guidance of children in the family. Some interfere too much by nagging, ridiculing, or trying to control their grandchildren, often against the parents' wishes. Others take the adolescents' side against parents by pampering or overprotecting, thus undermining parental discipline. In either case, tension develops in the household, affecting all members negatively and stimulating adolescent rebellion and defiance. It is a rare grandparent who achieves the right degree of helping without interfering.

Gradually, as adolescents get older, they are able to accept grandparents and older relatives more graciously than before. Older relatives themselves usually are not as inclined to boss older adolescents as they are the younger ones. These two factors result in a gradual subsiding of tension between the generations.

Maltreatment

Maltreatment of children may include either child abuse or child neglect (Roscoe, 1990). *Child abuse* means nonaccidental physical injury and assault, sexual abuse, and/or mental and emotional injury of the child. The child may be physically attacked, burned, hit, beaten, banged against a wall or the floor, or battered, leading to fractures, lacerations, or bruises. *Sexual abuse* may include very suggestive language, use of pornography, fondling, petting, masturbation, exhibitionism, voyeurism, oral sex, or full vaginal or anal intercourse. *Emotional abuse* may include constant screaming at the child, calling him or her foul names, criticizing, making fun, comparing the child with siblings, or ignoring the child. *Child neglect* means failure to provide even minimal care of the child, including adequate food, clothing, shelter, and medical care, as well as failure to provide for a child's emotional, social, intellectual, and moral needs. Thus, maltreatment is a multidimensional concept that includes both attack and neglect.

Child Abuse

Parents who physically attack and hurt their children have a devastating effect on them both emotionally and physically. Some children die of the abuse; others are permanently maimed. The children are tortured and terrified and are deeply scarred emotionally by the rage and hatred directed against them. Pathological fear, shyness, passive dispositions, deep-seated hostility, sullenness, and a cold, indifferent inability to love others are often the results. Adolescents who are exposed to violence are more likely to use violence against their parents (Peek, Fisher, and Kidwell, 1985). Violence begets violence, which means it is passed on from generation to generation (Giles-Sims, 1985). The greater the frequency of the abuse, the greater the chance that the victims will be violent parents or partners.

Child abusers are not necessarily emotionally ill, but they exhibit more psychological problems than other parents do (Martin and Walters, 1982). They have low self-esteem, which they project onto the child. Their growing contempt for themselves and feelings of unworthiness make them even more violent out of anger and frustration. Usually, children who are hardest to take care of are most abused. Adolescent behavior is particularly annoying to some parents. Parents may use corporal punishment as a means of control, but such punishment gets out of hand. Drinking and drug use may also be a factor in child abuse.

Sexual Abuse

The effects of sexual abuse on children and adolescents have been well documented. Researchers in the area of child sexual abuse have noted that the constellation of symptoms observed among abuse survivors matches the diagnostic criteria for postraumatic stress disorder (PTSD) (Banyard and Williams, 1996).

Both clinical and community studies have found high levels of negative self-concept nervousness, depression, anxiety, sexual problems, and suicidal threats and behavior in sexual abuse victims (Briere and Runtz, 1986; Browne and Finkelhor, 1986; Herman, Russell, and Troiki, 1986; Sansonnet-Hayden, Haley, Marriage, and Fine, 1987). In addition, sexual abuse victims appear highly susceptible to substance abuse (Harrison, Hoffmann, and Edwall, 1989). Sexual abuse seems to be an important background factor in some patterns of adolescent antisocial behavior. People who are sexually abused, primarily female, have been found to score higher than controls on measures of hostility and aggression (Gomes-Schwartz, Norowitz, and Sauzier, 1985). They have also been reported to manifest elevated levels of school problems, including truancy and dropping out before completing high school. In addition, they are more likely than controls to run away from home during adolescence. There is evidence that many prostitutes have been sexual abuse victims, particularly those abused at relatively young ages and with greater violence. Females are more often sexually abused than males, but much sexual abuse of both males and females remains undetected and underreported (Finkelhor, 1984).

Incest

Much of child and adolescent sexual abuse is incestuous; that is, it takes place between persons who are closely related (Gordan and O'Keefe, 1984). We can only guess at the incidence. In a national survey of middle- to upper-class people, 15 percent of the males and 14 percent of the females reported incestuous contacts (Hunt, 1974). Girls reported incestuous contacts as follows:

---

child abuse may include not only physical assault of a child but also malnourishment, abandonment, neglect, emotional abuse, and sexual abuse.

sexual abuse may include very suggestive language, use of pornography, fondling, petting, masturbation, exhibitionism, voyeurism, oral sex, or full vaginal or anal intercourse.

emotional abuse may include constant screaming at the child, calling him or her foul names, giving constant criticism and put-downs, making fun, constantly comparing the child with siblings, ignoring the child, and refusing to talk or listen to him or her.

child neglect failure to provide even minimal care of a child, including adequate food, clothing, shelter, and medical care, as well as for the child's emotional, social, intellectual, and moral needs.

With male cousins: 35 percent
With brothers: 31 percent
With sisters: 8 percent
With uncles: 6 percent
With fathers: 5 percent

The females reported contact of less than 0.5 percent each with sons, grandfathers, female cousins, brothers-in-law, or stepfathers. One-half of the female contacts occurred prior to puberty. Most contacts with brothers or male cousins did not involve coitus.

As we have seen, most incest does not involve father-daughter, grandfather-granddaughter, or stepfather-stepdaughter contacts, as commonly supposed. The effects of incestuous abuse will depend on who is abused, for how long, and in what manner (Kirkpatrick, 1987). Long-term effects of forceful, hurtful, exploitative relationships can be severe (Kirkpatrick, 1986). The female victim may carry a burden of anger, bitterness, shame, guilt, and lower self-esteem for years. It becomes hard to trust any man or to let a man touch her.

The abusive father is often a shy, socially incompetent, dependent man. His sexual relationship with his wife is usually unsatisfactory, so he turns to his daughter for sex and affection. If the mother does not believe her daughter's stories, or knows what is happening and encourages it or does nothing, the girl becomes even more embittered.

From a mental health perspective, sexual abuse is most damaging when physical force is involved and when the offender is related to the victim. Over the long term, the victim may feel a sense of powerlessness and betrayal (Banyard and Williams, 1996).

Stepfather-stepdaughter incestuous relations are more common than between biological father and daughter, probably due to a lowered incest taboo and a more distant relationship between stepfather and stepdaughter (Giles-Sims and Finkelhor, 1984). The most common age at which stepdaughters become victims is in their early teens.

In the short term, the stepdaughter may feel used, trapped, confused, humiliated, angry, and fearful. The stepfather may try to prevent her from going out with boys and to restrict her social activities. He may become violent if the stepdaughter attempts to repel his advances.

Possible long-term effects may include antisocial and illegal behavior such as delinquency, running away from home, prostitution, and drug abuse. The girl may suffer from depression, try to commit suicide, and have difficulty functioning sexually or assuming a wife or mother role.

Neglect

Neglect is the most common form of maltreatment of children and adolescents. It may take many forms (Doueck, Ishisaka, and Greenaway, 1988). *Physical neglect* may involve failure to provide enough food or a proper diet, adequate clothing, health care, adequate shelter, or sanitary conditions in the home, or to require personal hygiene. *Emotional neglect* may include showing inadequate attention, care, love, and affection, or fail-

PERSONAL ISSUES

A Victim of Sexual Abuse

Diane, a woman of 23, was molested by two older brothers from the time she was age 6 until she was age 13. The molestation included intercourse with her older brother. When her brother told her father that Diane had had her clothes off, the father beat her. When she told her uncle at age 14, he began where the brother left off. Intercourse with him continued until she was 17 years old. Diane has been hospitalized in psychiatric wards five times since age 17. Her psychiatrist describes her as "devoid of all meaningful social relationships . . . helpless, empty, quite depleted, suicidal . . . depressed" (Siegall, 1977).

Neglect is the most common form of maltreatment of children and adolescents. The neglect may be physical, emotional, intellectual, social, or moral.

ing to provide for the child's need for approval, acceptance, and companionship. *Intellectual neglect* may include allowing the child to stay out of school frequently for no reason, failing to see that the child goes to school or does homework, or failing to provide intellectually stimulating experiences and materials. *Social neglect* may include inadequate supervision of social activities, lack of concern about the child's companions and playmates, unwillingness to get the child involved in social groups and activities, or failure to socialize the child to get along with others. *Moral neglect* may include the failure to provide a positive moral example for the child, or any type of moral education and guidance.

The stories of parental neglect are legion. One couple went on vacation for several weeks at a time and left their 12-year-old daughter alone in the house unsupervised. Another mother spent days with her boyfriend, leaving her 15-year-old son to care for himself. One mother let her daughter's teeth decay until they fell out without making any attempt to get dental care (Author's counseling notes).

Some cases of neglect are more subtle: The parents reject their children emotionally and fail to show that they love or care for them. Such situations can be just as devastating as actual abuse (Wolock and Horowitz, 1984).

SUMMARY

1. Adolescents want parents who are interested in them, help them, and spend quality time with them—who will provide companionship.
2. Adolescents want parents who will listen and understand, and with whom they can communicate.
3. *Empathy* is the ability to identify with the thoughts, attitudes, and feelings of another person; it is affective sensitivity to others.
4. Adolescents prefer their mother's advice to that of their father on self, social, family, school-related, and philosophical issues.

5. *Affect* refers to the feelings or emotions that exist among family members. It may be positive or negative. Some parents find it hard to express love and affection. Adolescents want parents who love them and have positive feelings of affection for them.
6. Adolescents want parents who will accept them as they are.
7. Adolescents want parents to trust them.
8. Adolescents want parents who will accept them as autonomous adults and let them establish individuality and independence through the process of

separation-individuation. Autonomy consists of two aspects: behavioral autonomy and emotional autonomy. The desire for behavioral autonomy arises during adolescence before the shift to emotional autonomy.

9. *Cohesion* refers to the degree to which family members are connected or separated. Families that are extreme—either completely disengaged or completely enmeshed—function less adequately than do families that are nearer the center of the scale. Family cohesion is greatest when children are young, and declines as adolescents grow up and seek to become autonomous adults. Spatial distance is greater for older adolescents than younger, and for males than females.

10. Separation-individuation may be nontherapeutic or therapeutic.

11. There are four basic patterns of family control: autocratic, authoritative but democratic, permissive, and erratic.

12. Autocratic control tends to produce a combination of rebellion and dependency. The effect of punitive measures is usually negative.

13. Permissive control results in lack of socialization and produces many negative effects.

14. The authoritative but democratic home has the most positive effect.

15. Erratic, inconsistent parental control has a negative effect and produces a great deal of rebellion and disobedience.

16. The most functional families are those in which the parents are flexible, adaptable, and tolerant in their ideas and behavior.

17. Inflexible parents refuse to change their ideas and to look at other points of view; they are intolerant, perfectionists, critical, and have inappropriate expectations of what children can do at different ages. As a result, they destroy the adolescents' self-esteem, eliminate individuality, and create stress between the parents and adolescents.

18. Adolescents want parents who will set a good example.

19. Parent-adolescent misunderstanding arises from their two different types of personalities.

20. Overall, parent-adolescent relationships are usually harmonious, but when conflict occurs, it may be in any one of the following five areas: social life and customs, responsibility, school, family relationships, and values and morals.

21. There are a number of variables that affect conflict: age and sex of the adolescent, the atmosphere within the home, the socioeconomic status of the family, the total environment in which the child grows up, parental reactions, and family size.

22. High levels of conflict affect family cohesiveness and have an adverse effect on adolescent development.

23. Older siblings affect the development of children: They serve as role models and surrogate parents, provide companionship, and meet one another's needs for affection and meaningful relationships.

24. Siblings also are sometimes jealous, compete for parental affection, and have conflict with one another.

25. Relationships with grandparents can have a positive effect on adolescents.

26. Relationships with older relatives are sometimes frictional, especially during early adolescence. As adolescents age, older relatives are not as inclined to tell them what to do, and the adolescents themselves are better able to accept older relatives graciously.

27. Maltreatment of children may include either child abuse or child neglect.

28. *Child abuse* means nonaccidental physical injury and assault, sexual abuse, and/or mental and emotional injury of the child. *Sexual abuse* may include suggestive language, pornography, fondling, petting, masturbation, exhibitionism, voyeurism, oral sex, or vaginal or anal intercourse. *Emotional abuse* may include screaming at the child, calling names, criticism and put-downs, making fun, unfavorable comparisons of the child, and refusal to talk or to listen. *Child neglect* means failure to provide even minimal care of the child; failure to provide adequate food, clothing, shelter, and medical care; and failure to provide for the child's emotional, social, intellectual, and moral needs.

29. Abused children not only are attacked and hurt but also are deeply scarred emotionally by the rage and hatred directed against them.

30. Sexual abuse may have many devastating psychological effects on children, depending on the abuse: its nature, the type of abuse, for how long, and by whom.

31. Much child and adolescent sexual abuse is incestuous—taking place between persons who are closely related.

32. There are many negative short-term and long-term effects of sexual abuse.

33. Neglect is the most common form of maltreatment. It may include physical, emotional, intellectual, social, or moral neglect.

KEY TERMS

affect **321**

autonomy **323**

behavioral autonomy **323**

child abuse **332**

child neglect **332**

cohesion **324**

emotional abuse **332**

emotional autonomy **323**

empathy **320**

induction **326**

negative affect **321**

positive affect **321**

separation-individuation **323**

sexual abuse **332**

THOUGHT QUESTIONS

1. What do adolescents expect of parents? What kind of parents do they prefer?
2. What keeps parents from listening to adolescents and understanding them?
3. Should parents try to give their adolescents advice? Explain.
4. What keeps some parents from trusting their adolescents?
5. What keeps some parents from granting autonomy and independence to their adolescents as they're growing up?
6. What do you think of the father who tells his adolescent son, "Now you're 18; you're on your own, you leave the house, make your own living, and do your own thing."
7. When you were an adolescent, what sort of discipline did your parents use on you? Was it effective? Why or why not?
8. Should adolescents be expected to obey their parents? Explain.
9. When you were growing up, what were the major problems between you and your parents?
10. What sorts of home responsibilities or family chores should be expected of adolescents? Should they be paid for performance? Why or why not?
11. If you have an adolescent brother or sister living at home, what are the major sources of conflict between him or her and your parents?
12. What are the major sources of conflict between the adolescent and siblings?
13. When you were living at home, did you have any grandparents living with you? How did you get along? Explain the situation.
14. Do you know any adult who was abused as a child? What have been some of the effects?
15. Do you know anyone who was sexually abused by their parents while growing up? Describe the situation and the outcome.

SUGGESTED READING

Ambert, Anne-Marie. (1992). *The Effect of Children on Parents.* Binghamton, NY: Haworth.

Barrish, I. J., and Barrish, H. H. (1989). *Surviving and Enjoying Your Adolescent.* Kansas City, MO: Westport.

Cath, S. H., Gurwitt, A., and Gunsberg, L. (Eds.). (1989). *Fathers and Their Families.* Hillsdale, NJ: Analytic Press.

Cicrelli, B. G. (1995). *Sibling Relationships across the Lifespan.* New York: Plenum.

Frude, N. (1991). *Understanding Family Problems: A Psychological Approach.* New York: Wiley.

Hauser, S. T., with Powers, S. I., and Noam, G. G. (1991). *Adolescents and Their Families: Paths of Ego Development.* New York: Free Press.

Larson, R., and Richards, M. H. (1994). *Divergent Realities: Emotional Lives of Mothers, Fathers, and Adolescents.* New York: Basic Books.

Newton, N. (1995). *Adolescence: Guiding Youth Through the Perilous Ordeal.* New York: Norton.

Noller, P., and Callan, V. (1991). *The Adolescent in the Family.* New York: Routledge.

Worden, N. (1991). *Adolescents and Their Family: An Introduction to Assessment and Intervention.* Binghamton, NY: Haworth.

14

Divorced, Parent-Absent, and Blended Families

In this chapter, we will discuss how adolescents are affected by divorce as well as being raised in a single-parent or blended household.

Divorce and Adolescents

As divorce becomes more common, the question arises as to the effects on adolescents.

Attitudes toward Divorce

Data indicate that slightly over half of ever-marrieds who wed between the ages of 25 to 29 will eventually end a first marriage by divorce (Norton and Moorman, 1987). The great majority of these couples have children, some of whom are adolescents. A growing number of mental health practitioners view these divorces as major, negative events that stimulate insecurity, confusion, and painful emotions. Some of these practitioners feel that most children are not permanently damaged by divorce. Others insist that the upset interferes with long-term emotional and social growth (Wallerstein and Kelly, 1980). The answers are difficult to pin down because there are so many variables to sort out.

Short-Term Emotional Reactions

Immediate emotional reactions to parents divorcing have been well documented. One is *shock and disbelief* if adolescents have not realized the extent of the marital problem. One female college student remarked, "My mother called me the other day to tell me she and daddy are getting divorced. I can't believe it. I didn't even know they were having problems" (Author's counseling notes). Another reaction is *fear, anxiety, and insecurity about the future:* "Will my father move away? Will I get to see him?" "Will I have to go to another school?" "Who am I going to live with?" "How am I going to be able to go to college?" (Author's counseling notes).

Anger and hostility are also common emotional reactions among adolescents, especially toward the parent they blame for the divorce. One girl asked her mother, "Why did you make daddy leave?" Another, age 12, asked, "Why did you leave my father all alone?" A son told his father, "I hate you for leaving mom for that other woman" (Author's counseling notes). Sometimes the anger is directed toward both parents: "You've ruined my whole life. I have to leave all my friends and my school." Other adolescents are concerned only with how their parents' divorce affects them, not with the pain their parents are experiencing.

Another common feeling is one of *self-blame and guilt.* If parental conflict has been about the children, they may feel partly responsible for their parents breaking up (Wallerstein and Kelly, 1980), or that the parent is leaving because he or she wants to get away from the children. They may also feel self-conscious and bewildered that their parents are getting divorced, and they try to hide that fact from their friends.

After separation occurs, adolescents have to adjust to the absence of one parent, often one on whom they have depended deeply for affection and help. One adolescent girl remarked, "The hardest thing for me was to get used to being without my father. I never realized how much I needed him until he left" (Author's counseling notes). Divorce is often followed by a period of *mourning and grief,* not unlike the feeling arising when one loses a parent by death. Feelings of sadness, dejection, and depression are common.

If parents begin to date again and get emotionally involved with another person, adolescents may become *jealous and resentful* because they have to share their parent with another adult. If parents remarry, as the majority do, the adolescents are confronted with a new adjustment to a stepparent.

Long-Term Effects

Many people believe that children whose parents divorce are scarred for life by the experience. This common conviction was reinforced by Judith Wallerstein's best seller, *Second Chances: Men, Women, and Children a Decade after Divorce* (Wallerstein and Blakeslee, 1989), based on a 15-year follow-up to a landmark clinical investigation. Wallerstein found that almost half of the children in her California study were, on reaching young adulthood, "worried, underachieving, self-deprecating, and sometimes angry young men and women. Many were involved in maladaptive pathways, including multiple relationships and impulsive marriages that ended in divorce" (Wallerstein, 1991, p. 354). However, there were among these young adults some who had seemed calm and untroubled at earlier ages. This led Wallerstein to remark that the long-term effects of divorce on children cannot be predicted from how they react earlier in life.

These rather pessimistic conclusions have been challenged partly because other studies have produced different results. Critics also note the limitations of the California study, such as its small size, the lack of a nondivorced control group, and the fact that the sample was not selected on a probability basis and was overrepresented by families that sought clinical help (Cherlin and Furstenberg, 1989).

Given continued high rates of marital disruption and continuing controversy over what impact it has on children (Gill, 1992), scholars have called for better evidence to test Wallerstein's and others' hypotheses about the long-term effects of parental divorce. One study provides such evidence based on a longitudinal study of a national sample of U.S. children born between 1965 and 1970. This study, based on the longitudinal data from the National Survey of Children, examines whether effects of parental divorce are evident in young adulthood. Among 18- to 22-year-olds from disrupted families, 65 percent had poor relationships with their fathers and 30 percent with their mothers, 25 percent had dropped out of high school, and 40 percent had received psychological help. Even after controlling for demographic and psychoeconomic differences, youths from disrupted families were twice as likely to exhibit these problems as youths from nondisrupted families. A significant effect of divorce on mother-child relationships was evident in adulthood, whereas none was found in adolescence. Youths experiencing disruption before 6 years of age showed poorer relationships with their fathers than those experiencing disruption later in childhood. Overall, remarriage did not have a protective effect, but there were some indications of amelioration among those who experienced early disruption (Zill, Morrison, and Coiro, 1993).

Using a subsample ($N = 850$), the data collected in the National Survey of Families and Households (Demo and Adcock, 1996) examined socioemotional adjustment, academic performance, and global well-being among adolescents (ages 12 to 18) living in the four most prevalent family structures in the United States: (1) intact first-married family units; (2) divorced, single-parent families; (3) stepfamilies; and (4) continuously single mothers and their children (one of the fastest growing types of households). These four family types vary dramatically on socioeconomic characteristics and measures of family relations. Compared to the other family types, families headed by continuously single mothers had the lowest income, whereas divorced families and stepfamilies reported the highest level of mother-

adolescent disagreements and the lowest levels of parental supervision and mother-adolescent interaction.

Analysis of adolescent well-being by family types showed a consistent pattern. Adolescents whose fathers and mothers were both in their first marriage had the fewest problems with socioemotional adjustment, academic performance, and global well-being. Adolescents whose mothers were divorced or remarried experienced more problems than their counterparts in first-married families, although these differences, in many cases, were not large.

What accounts for the lower well-being of adolescents who have experienced parental divorce? The findings give strong support for the *family-conflict hypothesis*. Multiple forms of family conflict—including frequent disagreements with parents, marital conflict, parental aggression, and conflict between nonresidential fathers and mothers—consistently and adversely affected adolescent outcome. For many adolescents in divorced families and stepfamilies, conflict had been a routine part of their lives. Many adolescents suffered lingering effects from sustained predivorce marital discord and accompanying family process, including inconsistent parenting, interspousal aggression, parent-child aggression, and deteriorating parent-child relationships. These problems are compounded by persistent postdivorce tensions and hostilities between parents as adolescents are

PERSONAL ISSUES

Living Together

Psychologist Marla B. Isaacs and sociologist George Lyon studied the adjustment of 87 custodial mothers in single-parent families over the first five years after divorce. By the end of the five-year period, 20 percent had remarried, 13 percent were living with a new partner, and 22 percent were seriously involved with a man. Almost half were not seriously involved. Isaacs and Lyon evaluated the children for behavioral problems and social competence by measuring how well they managed their friendships at school and in play.

The children whose mothers steered clear of romance were the best adjusted; the children whose mothers lived with a partner were the most poorly adjusted. Teenagers had a particularly hard time socially. Without the commitment that marriage signified, the children felt insecure about their mothers and their relationship with her new partner. Also, fathers who objected to their children residing in a live-in arrangement might communicate their disapproval to their children. Overall, teens felt embarrassed about the morality issues involved (King, 1989).

Until recently, the mother automatically was granted custody of the children, unless there were concerns about her competency. Today, the father's chances of custody are enhanced. Rallies, such as the one shown, have helped in this fight.

by higher educational levels of mothers, higher incomes for mothers, and support delinquency prior to final divorce judgments. It is not surprising that substantial policy debates concerning legal and custody arrangements at divorce are common (Fox and Kelly, 1995).

The greatest fear of adolescents who have good relationships with both parents is that divorce will result in their losing contact with a parent. For this reason, parents need to make it clear that they are not divorcing their children, and that they will continue to be active, concerned, and caring parents.

It is helpful if, after divorce, both parents are readily accessible (assuming that both parents have a positive influence). Of course, if a parent is poorly adjusted, extremely immature, or abusive in any way, tight restrictions on child visitation may be necessary (Warshak, 1986). Under the best circumstances, disturbance is minimized if the adolescent can see a parent any time he or she needs or wants to.

Divorce often results in reduced attachment to the noncustodial parent. Regular contact with the noncustodial parent is related to higher levels of adjustment. In one study, adolescents from intact families viewed themselves as more positively emotional attached to their fathers than did those from divorced and remarried families. Thus, divorce may have an impact on the emotional bonds adolescents have with their fathers, and remarriage does not seem to mediate this impact (McCurdy and Scherman, 1996).

In some instances, *joint custody* is awarded to the parents. The adolescent usually resides with one parent and visits the other often. Joint custody means both parents are responsible for caring for the adolescent and making decisions concerning his or her welfare. Research shows that joint custody fathers are more likely to be active in parenting than are noncustodial fathers (Bowman and Ahrons, 1985). The pressure is also off one parent to assume the total responsibility (Melli, 1986).

Such arrangements require a high degree of maturity and flexibility, or discussions will result in squabbles and a continuation of the marital stress. If desired by both parents, and if they are able to get along together, there is general agreement that joint custody is a helpful solution to a difficult problem (Kolata, 1988).

Sometimes, a vindictive spouse can turn the adolescent against the other parent, refuse to allow the adolescent to phone or to write, or manage to be away with the adolescent when it's time for the other parent to visit. One resident found that increased visitation is associated with a good noncustodial parent-child relationship, but the as-

After a divorce, it is important for the adolescent to know that each parent will continue to be active and caring. Since the adolescent's postdivorce adjustment is related to the relationship between the two parents, counseling to reduce parental conflict may be needed to help make the transition.

sociation depends on the quality of the postdivorce relationship (Koch, 1982).

Quality of Relationships after the Divorce

As indicated, adolescents' postdivorce adjustment is related to the relationship between the two parents (Lowery and Settle, 1985). Reduced conflict after divorce has a major positive effect on adolescents (Demo and Acock, 1988; Tschann, Johnston, and Wallerstein, 1989). Continued conflict has a negative effect (Kelly, 1988).

Maccoby and colleagues (1993) studied the postdivorce roles of mothers and fathers in the lives of their children to determine the effect of those roles on children's adjustments. These researchers found that the factors most powerfully associated with good adolescent adjustment were (1) having a close relationship with a residential parent who monitored well and remained involved in decisions regarding the young person's life and (2) not feeling caught in the middle of parental conflict. The effect on adolescents depended on how conflict was managed and the extent to which the child felt caught between parents as a result of the conflict. In this study, mothers carried the primary responsibility for residential care and economic support after the divorce, but fathers remained substantially involved in their children's lives. Adolescents did at least as well in joint physical custody as when living primarily with one parent.

Marriage and Divorce Behavior

Considerable evidence substantiates the fact that people whose parents are divorced are more likely to divorce than are people whose parents have stable marriages (Amato, 1988; Mueller and Cooper, 1986). In other words, divorce seems to run in families.

Researchers are trying to sort out causes for this phenomenon (Glenn and Kramer, 1987). One explanation is offered by social learning theory. Children tend to model their behavior after that of their parents. Thus, children may imitate parental behavior that is detrimental to successful marriage and prone to divorce.

Two other explanations have been offered. One is that when children of divorce marry, they are highly apprehensive about it and have a lower commitment to their marriages, so are more likely to fail than offspring from intact families. They tend to be hesitant and cautious about marriage, often saying they will not marry. However, they are just as likely to marry as are other people. They are strongly impelled toward marriage, but often hedge their bets against failure by withholding full

joint custody   legal custody shared between two parents, both of whom are responsible for childrearing and for making decisions regarding the child.

commitment to marriage (Glenn and Kramer, 1987).

Another explanation is that they marry at an earlier age than children from intact families. This may be because of emotional need or the desire to escape an unpleasant home situation. Marriage at early ages has been found to be significantly related to marital failure (Booth and Edwards, 1985).

Parent-Absent Families

As we have seen, divorce may have different effects on different adolescents, depending on a number of factors. What is the effect of parent absence, regardless of whether the parent is absent because of divorce, separation, death, desertion, neglect, or illegitimacy of the child (Edwards, 1987)? This is an important question, as 23 percent of all children under age 18 live with their mothers only, and 4 percent with their fathers. The figures are much higher for African American children: 52 percent live with their mothers only, and 4 percent with their fathers. Of all children under age 18, African American and White, who live in one-parent families, about 87 percent live with their mothers, and therefore lack a father figure in the home (see Figure 14.1) (U.S. Bureau of the Census, 1996).

Psychological Health

According to data from a nationally representative sample of 17,110 children under age 18, those living with single mothers or with mothers and stepfathers were more likely than those living with both biological parents to have repeated a grade of school, to have been expelled, to have been treated for emotional or behavioral problems in the year preceding the interview, and to have elevated scores for behavioral problems and health vulnerability. Compared to children living with both biological parents, children of divorce experience an increased risk of accidental injury, and those living with a single mother are at increased risk of asthma (Dawson, 1991).

There is some consensus among experts that the loss of a parent in childhood is associated with a higher incidence of emotional and personality problems (Bayrakal and Kope, 1990), high rates of psychiatric consultation, increased suicidal ideation and behavior, higher levels of alcohol and drug use (Burnside, Baer, McLaughlin, and Pickering, 1986; Newcomb, Maddahian, and Bentler, 1986; Thomas, Farrell, and Barnes, 1996), lower self-esteem or self-image, lower levels of perceived competence in school work (Saucier and Ambert, 1986), and negative evaluation regarding parents than those from intact families. One study generally substantiated many of these findings with

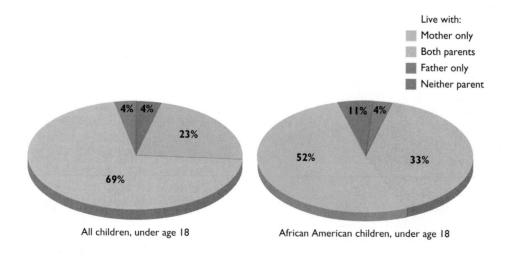

FIGURE 14.1 Living Status of Children Under Age 18, 1995

Source: U.S. Department of Commerce, Bureau of the Census, *Statistical Abstract of the United States, 1996* (Washington, DC: U.S. Government Printing Office, 1996), p. 65.

Australian adolescents (Raphael, Cubis, Dunne, Lewin, and Kelly, 1990). Let's look at these and other effects of parent absence on adolescents.

Development of Masculinity/Femininity

The common assumption has been that boys who lack an effective father figure and who are raised by their mothers are more likely to score lower on measures of masculinity, to have unmasculine self-concepts and sex-role orientations, and to be more dependent, less aggressive, and less competent in peer relationships than those whose fathers are present (Beaty, 1995). The younger a boy is when he is separated from his father and the longer the separation, the more the boy will be affected in his early years. As a boy gets older, however, the early effects of father absence decrease. By late childhood, lower-class father-absent boys may score as high as their father-present counterparts on measure of sex-role adoption and preference.

The effect of father absence depends partially on whether boys have male surrogate models (Klyman, 1985). Father-absent boys with a father substitute such as an older male sibling are less affected than those without a father substitute. Male peers, especially older ones, may become important substitute models for paternally deprived boys. Young father-absent male children seek the attention of older males and are strongly motivated to imitate and please potential father figures.

The effect of father absence on daughters seem to be just the opposite. Daughters are affected less when young but more during adolescence. Their lack of meaningful male/female relationships in childhood can make it more difficult for them to relate to the opposite sex later on. Case studies of father-absent girls are often filled with details of problems concerning interactions with males. During adolescence, girls of divorced parents who live with their mothers may be seductive and sometimes sexually promiscuous (Eberhardt and Schill, 1984). These girls may have ambivalent feelings about men because of the negative memories they have of their fathers, and pursue men in inept and inappropriate ways. They begin dating early and are likely to engage in sexual intercourse at an early age. Girls whose fathers are dead may be excessively shy and uncomfortable around men, probably because they do not have as much experience being around men as did girls who grew up with males at home.

Association with Delinquency

There seems to be a correlation between father absence and delinquency (Johnson and O'Leary,

In single-parent families, many children are faced with being on their own at home because their parents work. Although this is associated with many negative effects on the adolescent, the development of independence and autonomy may be one positive result.

1987; Thomas, Farrell, and Barnes, 1996). Adolescents from father-absent homes have a higher incidence of delinquency, but this does not mean that father absence causes delinquency. For one thing, children from father-absent families who get into trouble are more likely to be arrested and institutionalized when arrested than are those from intact families. Their mothers have fewer resources to fall back on when the children are in trouble. Furthermore, it may not be the family type (the one-parent family) but rather the family conflict that led to the disruption in the first place that causes the trouble. Levels of family conflict are better predictors of delinquency than family type. We do know that adolescents who become delinquent are more likely to have had fathers who were cold, rejecting, punitive, neglectful, and mistrusting. In these cases, having a father at home is a negative influence. Some adolescents get along better after their parents divorce (Bilge and Kaufman, 1983). Also, in groups such as low-income African Americans, wherein father absence is common, factors other than father absence are more important as determinants of delinquency (Weller and Luchterhand, 1983).

Mothers who go through separation or divorce usually suffer a significant reduction or loss of income. Many live in poverty and are forced to raise their children in poor sections of town under adverse conditions. Problems develop with the children, not because of father absence, as such, but as a by-product of poverty and low social status. Divorce or separation brings with it loss of environmental control. Mothers report being less able to discipline or influence their children after divorce, partly because the children are upset, partly because they put a lot of the blame for the absence of their father on the mother, partly because the mother feels guilty about the divorce and, in an effort to win their favor, is not as strict with them, and partly because the mother is working full time and therefore is not around to guide her children.

It is possible, too, that the children's upset may have been a causal factor in the divorce rather than the other way around. Temperamentally hard-to-handle children may be a factor in marital breakup. Once divorce has taken place, these disturbed children are usually placed in the custody of their mothers and continue to exhibit psychological problems. Children who are easy to handle and who get along well with their fathers encourage their fathers to stay home. Thus, though it appears that it is the intact family that has a more positive influence, in actual fact it is the best-adjusted children who have a positive influence on the marriage.

Influences on School Performance, Achievement, and Vocational Aspirations

A comparison of 559 youths in the seventh, eighth, and ninth grades showed that the children from the single-parent homes had the lowest grades and lowest occupational aspirations (Rosenthal and Hansen, 1980). Other research has suggested that parental divorce or separation delays cognitive development and cognitive functioning such as the development of moral judgment.

In another study of 530 students in grades 6 through 9 from two schools in Salt Lake City, Utah, it was found that students from intact two-parent families had fewer absences and tardies, higher grade-point averages, and fewer negative and more positive teacher behavioral ratings than did those from reconstituted and single-parent families (Featherstone, Cundick, and Jensen, 1992).

Here again, simple cause-effect relationships have not been clearly established. Certainly, some adolescents are deeply upset by parental divorce or separation, so their grades in school suffer as a result—at least during a period of readjustment. But this does not happen to all children. Usually, some remain unaffected as far as scholastic achievement is concerned. One study found a relationship between low school achievement and frequent conflict between the mother and her ex-spouse in front of the adolescent, and frequent arguments between the mother and her adolescent (McCombs and Forehand, 1989). According to this study, adolescents with high grade-point averages had mothers with low levels of depression, higher educational levels, less contact with their ex-spouses, and less intense levels of conflict between the mother and adolescent than those in the low grade-point average group. Thus, family factors may mediate scholastic achievement.

Lower vocational aspirations and achievement are often a result of the changed financial status of the family (Amato, 1988; Mueller and

Cooper, 1986). Adolescents in single-parent families have a lower level of educational attainment and consequent lower income as adults (Keith and Finlay, 1988; Mueller and Cooper, 1986). One study showed that the percentage of young men from single-parent families who did not finish high school was more than twice the percentage of those who always lived in two-parent families. The percentage from two-parent families who graduated from college and went on to do graduate work was almost double that of single-parent families (Krein, 1986).

Attitudes toward Self and Parents

One study in Canada indicated that adolescents from separated or divorced homes more often engaged in health-risk behavior (smoking, not fastening seat belts, and intemperate drinking) than those from intact families (Saucier and Ambert, 1983). Two major explanations were offered: (1) the health-risk behavior was an effort to improve self-esteem by adopting more daring attitudes and (2) the adolescents were less controlled by parents after parental breakup. This finding is in keeping with others that indicate that adolescents from father-absent homes have more problems with alcohol, marijuana, and sexual activity than those from intact homes (Stern, Northman, and Van Slyck, 1984).

One of the problems of divorce is what it does to the adolescents' attitudes toward themselves and their parents. Self-image seems to suffer, especially if adolescents blame themselves, feel guilty, or feel any social embarrassment because of what happens. Divorce is not the stigma it once was, but it is still a factor in social embarrassment.

Equally important is what it may do to the adolescents' feelings toward the parents. Feelings may range from concern or pity to anger or hostility. The adolescent will often feel sorry for a mother who is left against her will but be very hostile toward one who asks her husband to leave. An adolescent may have a good relationship with his divorced mother until she remarries—then suddenly become very jealous and angry at her. Much depends on the reasons for the breakup and the adolescent's perception of it. This means that it is important for adolescents to understand the reasons. Parents often have a difficult time explaining years of increasing alienation or falling out of love, but it is important to future parent-adolescent relationships that parents be honest and willing to explain.

There is a difference in effect also between father loss through divorce or separation and father loss because of death (Rozendal, 1983). Adolescents whose fathers have died are often brought up in families that are warm and accepting. In contrast, those who have lost fathers through divorce generally have to deal with their own guilt and their parents' guilt and negative feelings of rejection of one another.

Substance Abuse

An important longitudinal study examined substance use in a sample of adolescents from 508 families (Needle, Su, and Doherty, 1990). The adolescents were divided into three groups: those experiencing parental divorce during childhood, those experiencing parental divorce during their adolescent years, and those from intact families. The adolescents whose parents were divorcing were found to have greater overall drug involvement than the other two groups.

Another study of 2,102 young adolescents (ages 12 to 14) and their mothers in 10 southeastern cities was used to assess the relationship between family structure (intact, single-parent, or stepparent family) and whether cigarettes, alcohol, marijuana, and sexual intercourse had ever been tried (Flewelling and Bauman, 1990). The results showed higher levels of experience for adolescents from single-parent and stepparent families than from intact families. When controlled for age, race, gender, and mother's education, the results remained the same. The adolescents from disrupted families (both single-parent and stepparent) were at higher risk than adolescents from intact families. Table 14.1 shows the percentages in each category participating in each behavior.

Development of Autonomy

One of the effects of being brought up in a one-parent family is the encouragement of adolescent autonomy (Giles-Sims and Crosbie-Burnett, 1989). If the homes are financially, socially, and emotionally unstable, adolescents may question parental capabilities, such as the ability to provide emotional and financial support (Emery, 1988).

TABLE 14.1 Percentage of Adolescents in Each Category of Family Structure
Participating in Each Behavior

Family Structure	N	Ever Puffed Cigarette	Smoked Cigarette	Drank	Marijuana	Sexual Intercourse
Intact	1,230	36.1	11.2	47.3	5.5	11.4
Stepfather	245	45.8	19.2	53.4	12.3	20.6
Stepmother	51	56.9	16.3	66.7	16.0	28.0
Stepparents	47	51.1	15.4	54.3	4.3	20.0
Single mother	410	44.8	13.3	53.9	10.1	23.0
Single father	95	43.0	13.4	53.7	14.9	27.2
Total sample	2,078	40.3	12.9	50.3	7.9	16.1

Source: Adapted from R. L. Flewelling and K. E. Bauman, "Family Structure as a Predictor of Initial Substance Use
and Sexual Intercourse in Early Adolescence," *Journal of Marriage and the Family, 52* (1990): 171–181. Copyrighted 1990 by the National Council on Family Relations, 3989 Central Ave. NE, Suite 550, Minneapolis, MN
55421. Reprinted by permission.

Adolescents observe that parents have "a diminished capacity to parent" during the period of separation and the divorce process itself (Wallerstein,
1983). Diminished parenting is characterized by
decreased parental control, communication, and
affection and requires increased independence
and self-reliance from the adolescent (Sessa and
Steinberg, 1991). One result is that adolescents
from one-parent families have more responsibility,
independence, and decision-making power than
those in intact families (Brown and Mann, 1990;
Hetherington, 1987). Another result is that in
order to cope, adolescents may become more detached from their families, helping to expedite
the development of emotional and behavioral
autonomy.

Blended Families

Approximately 83 percent of divorced men and 76
percent of divorced women eventually remarry
(Fine, 1986). The high rate of divorce and remarriage means that 46 percent of marriages are now
second marriages for one or both of the partners.
The median age of spouses in these remarriages is
in the early or middle 30s, with children being of
elementary or preadolescent age at the time their
parents remarry (U.S. Bureau of the Census,
1996).

Family Combinations

There are many different combinations of
blended families. Family relationships in remarriage can become quite complicated. Children
may have natural parents and siblings, stepparents, stepsiblings, grandparents, and stepgrand-
parents plus other relatives. Adult spouses relate
to one another, to their own natural parents and
grandparents, and to their new in-laws, and they
may continue to relate to their former in-laws and
other family members (Berstein and Collins,
1985). It is understandable why family integration
is difficult (Ihinger-Tallman and Pasley, 1986).

Adolescents in remarried family households
who perceive their families to be more flexible
report greater satisfaction with both the overall
remarried family household and the parent-
stepparent subsystem. Flexibility allows households to adopt to the changing needs of households and individual family members (Henry and
Lovelace, 1995).

The probability of divorce is slightly greater in
remarriages than in first marriages (Aguirre and
Parr, 1982). However, divorce and redivorce rates
have started to decrease, and the data suggest that,
in the future, the incidence of redivorce may be similar to first divorce (Norton and Moorman, 1987).

The reasons for redivorce may be slightly different from those for first divorce. Remarrieds usually aren't as willing to stay in unhappy marriages

Children and Fathers in One-Parent, Stepparent, and Intact Families

A study of 399 children (192 primary-grade children and 207 secondary-grade children) in one-parent, stepparent, and intact families revealed the following relationship with fathers and stepfathers (Amato, 1987). Compared with children in intact families, children in one-parent families reported less father support, less father control, less father punishment, more autonomy, more household responsibility, more conflict with siblings, and less family cohesion. Stepfathers were said to provide less support, control, and punishment than biological fathers in intact families, although stepfather involvement was positively associated with the number of years stepfamilies had been together.

In another study, data from the 1987–88 National Survey of Families and Households was examined to determine family structure variations and parental socialization. All together, the data on 3,738 children aged 15 to 18 was examined. Male and female single parents reported less restrictive rules than did married parents, and stepmothers, stepfathers, and cohabiting male partners reported significantly less frequent activities with and responses to children than did original parents (Thomson, McLanahan, and Curtin, 1992).

as they were the first time around. Remarrieds are older, more experienced and mature, and often highly motivated to make their marriages work. Furstenberg and Spanier (1984) concluded that successful remarrieds stated that their new marriages were better than their first marriage. They felt they had married a person "who allows you to be yourself" (p. 83). They felt they handled problems more maturely and had learned to communicate and make decisions. They also believed that the division of labor was more equitable.

These evaluations came from those who had successful remarriages. For others, remarriage introduces some problems that were not present in first marriages. The biggest complication is children (Lagoni and Cook, 1985). Children from prior marriages increase the possibility of divorce among remarried couples (Fine, 1986). When remarrieds divorce, it is because they want to leave the stepchildren, not the spouse (Meer, 1986). In a majority of cases, at least one spouse has children when the remarriage begins. The mother most often gets custody, so her children are living with her and her husband, who becomes a stepfather (Fischman, 1988). The husband's children are usually living with his ex-wife, creating family ties with her household and the possibility of hostility and conflict. The wife's ex-spouse as noncustodial father usually comes to visit his children, so

he has contact with his ex-wife and her new husband, which may result in problems and tension. Being a stepparent is far more difficult than being a natural parent, because children have trouble accepting a substitute parent.

Stepmothers, more often than stepfathers, experience greater difficulties in rearing their stepchildren than in rearing their biological children. This is true regardless of whether their biological children are from a previous marriage or from the current marriage. The addition of new biological children (firstborn or otherwise) to the stepfamily has no effect on stepparents' perception of the relative difficulties of rearing their stepchildren (MacDonald and DeMaris, 1996).

The wife needs to adjust to her new husband's children as a noncustodial stepmother and try to develop a friendly relationship during infrequent visits—a difficult task at best (Ambert, 1986). All of the adults are coparenting, with three or four parent figures as opposed to two. The children are continually adjusting to those in two households— three or four adult figures and two or more models of relationship patterns with the opposite sex. Both children and adults must contend with the attitudes and influences of other family members (Rice, 1990). No wonder stepchildren score lower on academic achievement, evidence behavior problems at school, and score lower on child well-being

Because of the high rate of divorce and remarriage, there are many second marriages. In most blended families, it takes time and effort to work out problems and build good stepparent/ stepchildren relationships.

than do children from intact families (Hanson, McLanahan, and Thomson, 1996).

Adolescent stepchildren particularly have difficulty accepting their new stepfather or stepmother (Fine, 1986; Skeen, Covi, and Robinson, 1985). They may be jealous of the attention their own parent gives his or her mate (who is the stepparent). They may also feel their primary loyalty is toward their own parents and that the stepparent is an intruder (Pink and Wampler, 1985). This was dramatically illustrated in the case of a new wife who was greeting her husband's older daughter for the first time. The woman was anxious to make a good impression. "I'm your new mother," she cooed. "The hell you are," replied the daughter and stamped out of the room (Author's counseling notes). This case is not unusual. One of the typical reactions of a stepchild to a stepparent is rejection: "You're not my father" or "You're not my mother." This apparent rejection is hard for the stepparent to take and sometimes leads to a battle of wills. If children are infants when parents divorce and remarry, they usually grow up accepting the stepparent as a substitute mother or father (Papernow, 1984).

Research indicates that adjustments with stepmothers and noncustodial biological mothers are more difficult than stepfather-child relationships (Sauer and Fine, 1988). Adjustments with stepfathers are usually easier than with stepmoth-

ers primarily because stepmothers play a more active role in relation to the children and spend more time with them than do stepfathers (Ambert, 1986; Clingempeel, Brand, and Ievoli, 1984; Robinson, 1984). Stepdaughters especially have difficulties adjusting to stepmothers (Brand and Clingempeel, 1987). Also, fairytales and folklore have developed the stereotype of the cruel stepmother—a myth hard to overcome (Fine, 1986). Problems are greater if the parent without custody tries to get a child to dislike the stepparent.

Stepsibling relationships also become important (Amato, 1987). If there are stepsiblings living together, trouble may ensue if the natural parents show favoritism to their own children. If this happens, resentment and hostility are likely to occur. There is often competition between the spouse's own children and the children of the new partner. Children may each become jealous of the attention and time their own parent shows the stepchildren. A divorced mother and her children, especially a mother and her daughter, may become a *closed system* of social interaction, and it becomes difficult for a new stepfather to enter that system (Giles-Sims and Crosbie-Burnett, 1989). Single, previously unmarried women also have trouble finding their place in father-children relationships. The father's children may resent her efforts at becoming their new stepmother. She may have given up a

Stepparents versus Natural Parents

Many stepparents are disappointed, surprised, and bewildered when they find few similarities between being stepparents and natural parents (Mills, 1984; Skeen, Covi, and Robinson, 1985). Let's review important differences between the two (Rice, 1990).

Stepparents may have unrealistic expectations of themselves and of their stepchildren. After all, they have been parents before, so they anticipate that they will fit into the stepparent role very nicely. They are bewildered if their stepchildren don't accept them immediately and show them due respect. This creates anger, anxiety, guilt, and low self-esteem. They feel there is something wrong with the stepchildren or they blame themselves. They need to realize it may take several years before they accept one another and develop satisfactory relationships.

Parents and stepparents may enter into their new families with a great deal of regret and guilt over their failed marriages. They feel sorry that they have put their children through the trauma of divorce. As a result, parents tend to be overindulgent and not as strict as they would be otherwise, so they have more trouble controlling and guiding the children's behavior (Amato, 1987). Often, they try to buy the children's cooperation and affection.

Stepparents are faced with the necessity of dealing with children who have been socialized by another set of parents. They don't have a chance to bring them up from infancy as they see fit (unless a stepchild is quite young). The children resent the stepparent coming in and trying to change things.

Stepparent roles are not clearly defined. Stepparents are neither parents nor friends. In the beginning, efforts to take over the parental role may be rejected by older children. Stepparents can't be just friends, because they are confronted with parental responsibilities and hope to make a contribution to the lives of these children. They are required to assume many of the responsibilities of parents: support, physical care, recreational opportunities, and going to sports events and school functions. They may have the responsibilities of parents but few of the privileges and satisfactions.

Stepparents expect thanks and gratitude for all of the things they do, but may get criticism and rejection instead. They usually offer the same care as they give their own biological children, yet most biological children and stepchildren seem to take such help for granted. One stepfather complained, "I would like to have a little appreciation and thanks once in awhile" (Author's counseling notes).

Stepparents are faced with unresolved emotional issues from their prior marriages and divorces. Stepparents are still influenced by what happened in their previous families. They may still have a lot of anger, resentment, and hurt, which can come out in destructive ways in their new families. They may need therapy to resolve some of the negative feelings that were created by the separation and divorce.

Family cohesion tends to be lower in stepfamilies than in intact families. Life in reconstituted families tends to be stressful and chaotic during the years following remarriage (Wallerstein and Kelly, 1980). Fortunately, things usually settle down in time.

good job and a good deal of freedom and independence to marry and then finds out she is treated like an outsider in a closed family system.

In contrast to these, other examples might be given to show satisfactory stepchild-stepparent relationships. One mother spoke of her husband's relationship with her child: "He's always referred to her as his daughter rather than his stepdaughter. He never made any issue of her being a stepchild. There are times when I think she is closer to him than she is to me. He is more her father than her real father ever was or is now" (Duberman, 1973, p. 285).

Relationships between stepsiblings also can be quite harmonious: "Our boys are the same age to the day. They are just like brothers. His son and my son are more alike than the two real brothers are. They all refer to each other as brothers; they are like one family" (Duberman, 1973, p. 286).

Out of 88 couples who had remarried and had stepchildren, Duberman (1973) found that 64 percent of the families could be voted excellent as measured by a parent-child relationship score. In most families, however, working out problems and building good stepparent-stepchildren relationships takes time and effort (Mills, 1984).

SUMMARY

1. Slightly over half of ever-marrieds who wed between the ages of 25 to 29 will eventually end a first marriage by divorce.

2. Some experts feel that children are upset temporarily by divorce but are not permanently damaged psychologically. Others feel the negative effects are long-lasting.

3. Short-term emotional reactions include shock and disbelief, fear, anxiety, insecurity about the future, anger and hostility, self-blame and guilt, adjusting to the absence of one parent, mourning and grief, and jealously and resentfulness.

4. Wallerstein and other researchers found that the effects of parental divorce are long term—reaching into young adulthood.

5. Children and adolescents whose mothers live with another man following divorce are more poorly adjusted socially than are those offspring of mothers who steer clear of romance.

6. Family conflict before and/or after divorce is more harmful to children than is the divorce itself.

7. A number of factors influence the effects of divorce: family climate and parents' behavior, the quality of child care following the divorce, the circumstances and reasons for the divorce, whether the divorce is amicable or hateful, whether the adolescent feels caught between the parents, the effects on the parents, custody and living arrangements, and the quality of family relationships after the divorce.

8. People whose parents are divorced are more likely to divorce than are persons whose parents have a stable marriage. There are two reasons for this: (1) they are less sure and less committed to having a happy marriage and (2) they tend to marry at an earlier age than children from intact families.

9. The loss of a parent during childhood tends to have an adverse effect on psychological health: a higher incidence of emotional and personality problems, higher rates of psychiatric consultation, increased suicidal ideation and behavior, higher levels of alcohol and drug use, lower self-esteem or self-image, lower levels of perceived competence in school work, and negative evaluation of parents.

10. Boys in father-absent homes may have trouble in the development of masculinity; girls may have more trouble making heterosexual adjustments than adolescents from intact families.

11. There seems to be a correlation between father absence and delinquency, but definite cause and effect has not been established. It is family conflict that causes the problem, not father absence itself.

Furthermore, mothers who go through divorce may be forced to live under adverse financial and neighborhood conditions.

12. There is a relationship between parent absence and school performance, achievement, and vocational aspirations, but, here again, it is frequent conflict that seems to be the culprit. Lower vocational achievement and aspirations are often the result of the changed financial status of the family.

13. Adolescents from separated or divorced homes more often engage in health-risk behavior: smoking, greater involvement with drugs, and drinking. Such behavior seems to be an attempt to improve self-image and self-esteem, which has been damaged by the family breaking up, and to deal with family stress.

14. One of the effects of being brought up in a one-parent family is increased adolescent autonomy, because parents may have a "diminished capacity to parent."

15. Approximately 83 percent of divorced men and 76 percent of divorced women eventually remarry, which means large numbers of adolescents will grow up in blended families.

16. Married and female single parents report less restrictive rules than married parents, and stepparents report less frequent activity with the children than do natural parents.

17. Family relationships in remarriage may become quite complicated, requiring considerable readjustment.

18. The probability of divorce is slightly greater in remarriages than in first marriages, although successful remarrieds state that their new marriages are better than their first marriages.

19. The biggest complication in remarriage is children. Being a stepparent is far more difficult than being a natural parent because children have trouble accepting a substitute parent. Adolescents' perception of their families are related to their adjustments in stepfather families.

20. Stepsibling relationships are important and may cause trouble.

21. There are some important differences between being a natural parent and a stepparent. Stepparents may overindulge their children because they feel guilty about their divorce; stepparents have to deal with children who have been socialized by another set of parents; stepparent roles are not clearly defined; stepparents expect thanks and gratitude but get criticism and rejection instead; stepparents are faced with unresolved emotional

issues from their prior marriages and divorces—they must deal with a network of complex family relationships and they must deal with stepsibling relationships and feelings; and family cohesion tends to be lower in stepfamilies.

KEY TERMS

adversary approach   **342**   joint custody   **344**   no-fault divorce   **343**

THOUGHT QUESTIONS

1. Are your parents separated or divorced? How has this affected you? What upset you the most?
2. If your parents are divorced, how did you feel about their getting divorced at the time that it happened? What aspect of the divorce process was most difficult for you? How could the process have been improved?
3. From the point of view of a child of divorce, what are some dos and don'ts for parents getting a divorce?
4. From the point of view of a child of divorce, what is the worst thing that parents can do when they're getting divorced?
5. In the best interest of the child, what custody and living arrangements should be made when parents divorce?
6. Did you grow up in a parent-absent family? How did it affect you? Were your parents divorced, separated, or was one of them deceased? Is there a difference in terms of the effect on children growing up in a family in which the parents are divorced, separated, or one is deceased?
7. Is it possible to grow up emotionally mature and healthy in a parent-absent family? Explain your views.
8. How is the development of masculinity or femininity affected by growing up in a one-parent family? How might the effects be overcome?
9. Do other young people look down on adolescents in one-parent families? Explain.
10. Do you think that boys or girls are most affected by being brought up by their mothers? Explain.
11. Are your parents remarried, or do you have any friends whose parents are? How does everyone get along? What are the major problems and adjustments?
12. Is it easier to live with a stepmother or stepfather? Why? What might be some of the problems of living with each?
13. If your parents were divorced and you were brought up with stepsiblings in the family, how did you get along? What were the major problems and adjustments?

SUGGESTED READING

Booth, A., and Dunn, J. (Eds.). (1994). *Stepfamilies: Who Benefits? Who Does Not?* Hillsdale, NJ: Erlbaum.

Cummings, E. M., and Davies, P. (1994). *Children and Marital Conflict: The Impact of Family Dispute and Resolution.* New York: Guilford.

Furstenberg, F. F., Jr., and Cherlin, A. J. (1991). *Divided Families: What Happens to Children When Parents Part.* Cambridge, MA: Harvard University Press.

Ganong, L. H., and Coleman, M. (1994). *Remarried Family Relationships.* Thousand Oaks, CA: Sage.

Hodges, W. F. (1991). *Interventions for Children of Divorce: Custody, Access, and Psychotherapy,* 2nd ed. New York: Wiley-Interscience.

Martin, D. D., and Martin, M., with Jeffers, P. (1992). *Stepfamilies in Therapy: Understanding Systems, Assessment, and Intervention.* San Francisco: Jossey-Bass.

Stinson, K. M. (1991). *Adolescents, Family, and Friends: Social Support after Parents' Divorce or Remarriage.* Westport, CT: Praeger.

Visher, E. B., and Visher, J. S. (1991). *How to Win as a Stepfamily,* 2nd ed. New York: Brunner/Mazel.

Wolchik, S. A., and Karoly, P. (Eds.). (1988). *Children of Divorce: Empirical Perspectives on Adjustment.* New York: Gardiner.

15

Education
and School

Emphasis in education in the United States has shifted from traditionalism, focusing on basic education, to progressivism, focusing on life skills.

Trends in U.S. Education

Let's take a look at the evolution of educational trends in the United States, particularly during the last half of the twentieth century.

Traditionalists versus Progressives

Traditionalists argue that the purpose of education is to teach the basics—English, science, math, history, and foreign languages—to increase student knowledge and intellectual powers. *Progressives* urge that the purpose of education is to prepare students for life: citizenship, home and family living, a vocation, physical health, gratifying use of leisure time, effective personality growth.

The debate has continued partly because of the insistence that education has an important role in reforming society and solving social problems. Each time a social problem has arisen, a new school program has been designed to deal with it. When traffic fatalities rose, driver education was introduced. A rise in premarital pregnancies and in divorce rates was followed by courses in family life education. Demands for racial integration led

traditionalists educators who emphasize that the purpose of education is to teach the basics.

progressives educators who emphasize that the purpose of education is to prepare pupils for life.

to African American studies and school busing. Feminists' demands for equality and liberation resulted in women's studies. A rise in crime rates resulted in new social problems classes. Because social needs change from time to time, the educational pendulum has been pushed first in one direction and then another.

Rise of Progressive Education

Until the 1930s, traditionalism was the dominant emphasis in U. S. schools. Then came the Depression, which destroyed the job market for adolescents, so that many who would have gone to work stayed in school instead (Ravitch, 1983). Most of these youths were noncollege bound, uninterested in traditional academic subjects, and in need of different programs to deal with their own problems. Educational philosophers such as John Dewey felt the classroom should be a laboratory of living, preparing students for life. Under the progressive influence, many schools introduced vocational and personal service courses, restricting academic courses to the college-preparatory program. Life adjustment education centered around vocations, leisure activities, health, personal concerns, and community problems. Principals boasted that their programs adjusted students to the demands of real life, freeing them from dry academic studies. Developing an effective personality became as important as improving reading skills (Ravitch, 1983; Wood, Wood, and McDonald, 1988).

Sputnik and After

The United States was shocked when the Soviet Union launched *Sputnik,* the first space satellite, in the 1950s. Almost overnight, Americans became obsessed with the failure of the schools to keep pace with the technological advances of the Soviet Union. The schools were blamed for a watered-down curriculum that left U.S. youths unprepared to face the challenge of communism. As a result, Congress passed the National Defense Education Act and appropriated nearly $1 billion in federal aid to education, which supported the teaching of math, science, and foreign languages. Schools modernized their laboratories and courses in physical sciences and math were

rewritten by leading scholars to reflect advances in knowledge.

1960s and 1970s

By the mid-1960s, the so-called cold war with the Soviet Union had abated. The United States was swamped with the rising tide of social unrest, racial tension, and antiwar protests. Once again, society was in trouble, and the schools were called on to meet the challenge. Major school aid legislation was passed, primarily to benefit poor children, as part of the Johnson administration's War on Poverty. Once more, the educational clamor was for relevance. Educators claimed that schools were not preparing young people for adult roles and that adolescents needed to spend more time in community and work settings as well as in the classroom. Academic programs gave way to career and experimental education so that adolescents could receive "hands-on" experience. Elementary schools adopted open education, knocked down classroom walls, and gave students more choices as to what to do each day. High schools lowered graduation requirements. Enrollments in science, math, and foreign languages fell as traditional subjects gave way to independent study, student-designed courses, and a flock of electives. By the late 1970s, over 40 percent of all high school students were taking a general rather than college-preparatory or vocational course of study, and 25 percent of their educational credits came from work experience outside school, remedial course work, and classes aimed at personal growth and development (National Commission on Excellence in Education, 1983).

Soon, the nation became more alarmed at the steady, slow decline in academic indicators. *Scholastic Assessment Test (SAT)* scores showed a steady decline from 1963 to 1980. Verbal scores fell over 50 points and average math scores nearly 40 points. The College Entrance Examination Board administering the tests cited such in-school reasons as grade inflation, absenteeism, frivolous courses, absence of homework, and decline in reading and writing assignments as reasons for falling test scores. (Psychologists and educators cite other reasons also, such as family tensions, disorganization, and instability.) It became obvious that high school students were taking more nonacademic courses and fewer courses necessary for college preparation.

1980s

Parental and public outcry grew in the early 1980s, resulting in the appointment of the National Commission on Excellence in Education (1983). This commission found the following:

1. The number and proportion of students demonstrating superior achievement on the SATs (those with scores of 650 or higher) had declined.
2. Scores on achievement tests in such subjects as physics and English had declined.
3. There was a steady decline in science achievement scores of 17-year-olds by national assessments in 1969, 1973, and 1979.
4. The average achievement of high school students on most standardized tests was lower than when *Sputnik* was launched.
5. Nearly 40 percent of 17-year-olds could not draw inferences from written material; only one-fifth could write a persuasive essay; and only one-third could solve a mathematics problem requiring several steps.
6. About 13 percent of all 17-year-olds in the United States could be considered functionally illiterate. Functional illiteracy among minority youths ran as high as 40 percent.

This time, the reason given for demanding a back-to-basics education was not a threat from the Soviets but a fear that the nation was falling behind the economic competition from Japan and Western Europe and was losing its competitive edge in world markets. Educational reformers demanded more academic rigor in the schools; more required courses, particularly in math and science; longer school days; and tougher standards for graduation. Thus, the pendulum again swung back to a more traditionalist posture.

By the time the commission issued its report, however, the American Association of School Administrators (1983) pointed out the following:

1. The decline in SAT scores had stabilized and appeared to be reversing.

2. Students had been taking an increasing number of academic courses in each of the last six years.
3. Many states had already adopted stricter graduation requirements.
4. Many school districts had already raised expectations for students.
5. The percentage of adolescents enrolled in school continued to climb, and U. S. schools were educating a larger percentage of 17-year-olds than any other educational system in the world.
6. The average citizen was more literate and exposed to more math, literature, and science than the average citizen of a generation ago.
7. According to the United Nations, the United States had one of the highest literacy rates in the world.

1990s

The optimism of the American Association of School Administrators in the middle 1980s was short-lived. SAT scores did increase until 1986. However, since then, math scores declined slightly for males and rose slightly for females, producing an average of 478 in 1993. Verbal scores fell to 424 in 1993, the lowest since 1980. Once more, declining scores led to criticism of the schools for not teaching the basics. Partial blame was also placed on parents for not making their children do homework or for letting them pay more attention to video games than to their reading assignments.

How Adolescents View Their Schools

Some of the sharpest critics of school systems are the students themselves. Let's see how students view their schools as revealed in several surveys.

Scholastic Assessment Test (SAT) a test that measures aptitude to do academic work.

Students Grade Their Schools

A nationwide survey of 1,175 students from Maine to Alaska in grades 7 through 12 revealed some significant findings (Solorzano, 1984). Some 28 percent gave their schools an A rating; 57 percent gave a letter grade of B to the overall quality of education they were receiving. Just over 13 percent issued C grades. Hardly any gave their schools a D or F. Students who gave their schools an A felt that students had an excellent chance for a good education. They believed that there was a lot of academic pressure to succeed and that everyone was concerned that they get as good an education as possible.

Students who gave their schools a grade of B felt that not enough is expected of students. For example, there ought to be harder tests to help motivate students to learn, not all courses are as interesting or challenging as they should be, and there ought to be a stronger emphasis on the importance of education for the sake of excellence. Students felt that there should be stiffer regulations for participation in extracurricular activities such as sports and music events; 45 percent said participation should be limited to those maintaining at least a C average in their studies. Overall, students believed that schoolwork was most important but that extracurricular activities were also educational.

Quality of Teachers

In response to questions regarding how their education could be improved, half of the students surveyed said that the most important way would be to *upgrade the quality of teachers*. Only 14 percent gave their teachers a grade of A; 55 percent gave a B. One student commented,

> It's the minority of teachers who can't or don't try to give it their best who are destructive to the system. Some of the older teachers don't seem concerned if you learn their subject or not. Some teachers are not caring about kids, but just doing a job. I feel challenged in the majority of my classes, but there are those that are lacking and, in effect, are wasted time every day. (Solorzano, 1984, p. 50)

When asked what was the biggest problem with the quality of teaching, over half of the students said that teachers failed to make the subject matter interesting, 22 percent said teachers did not challenge students with work hard enough, and 11 percent complained about a lack of classroom discipline (Bear and Stewart, 1990). Many students felt that teachers' salaries were too low to attract the best teachers. One student remarked, "Your smarter students become doctors, lawyers, engineers, and other things with higher-paid salaries. If teachers were paid better, the quality of

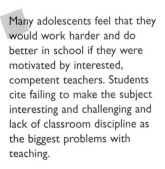

Many adolescents feel that they would work harder and do better in school if they were motivated by interested, competent teachers. Students cite failing to make the subject interesting and challenging and lack of classroom discipline as the biggest problems with teaching.

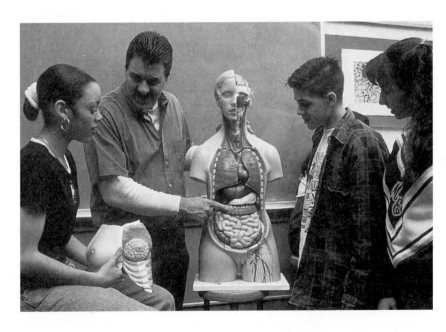

education might become better" (Solorzano, 1984, p. 50).

Youths blamed themselves, their schools, and their teachers for failing to earn an A for American education. Students stated that they want to work harder and to be challenged more, but most admitted that they will not do it without greater motivation from interested, competent teachers (Jussin and Eccles, 1992).

Teachers as Significant Others

The importance of teachers in the lives of adolescents cannot be overemphasized. Teachers represent the cumulative wisdom of our culture and are trained to transmit that wisdom. The way teachers are perceived by adolescents influences the attitudes youths hold toward the basic tenets of our society. Teachers exert a considerable influence if adolescents find them knowledgeable and caring. If the relationship between teacher and student is personal, and if communication is deep and ex-

tensive, there is strong evidence that teachers are significant others, are important role models, and can influence the formation of adolescents' identities, self-concepts, goals, and aspirations (Galbo, 1989).

Student Responsibility

Many teachers complain about the problem of getting students to be responsible for their own learning, but there's a difference between *being responsible* and *being held responsible*. Students who are being responsible will do the work without constant reminders or prodding. Students who are being held responsible will do the work only when someone is somehow forcing them to do so.

On the basis of a four-month participant/observation/interview study with sixth- and seventh-graders at a California middle school, six categories were found to be viewed by students as being their responsibility for learning: (1) do the work, (2) obey the rules, (3) pay attention,

HIGHLIGHT

Traditional versus Generative Instruction

Direct versus indirect methods of teaching have been an important area of study. *Direct instruction* is traditional: lecture oriented, teacher centered, in a highly controlled classroom in which expository textbooks play an important role. *Indirect teaching* is generative: dialogue oriented, student centered, with little structure and low control and in which self-direction and inquiry are essential to learning.

One study comparing the attitudes of eighth-graders toward these two methods of instruction revealed that traditional methods were rated much higher than generative (Maroufi, 1989). Those students who favored the traditional method took it seriously because it was structured and organized, with specific work assignments. Some students viewed the generative method as superficial and a waste of time because it was unstructured and disorganized. Typical remarks were: "Let's do some work," "Why do we waste so much time?" and "This is stupid." It was obvious that not all children were prepared for a debate-oriented, dialectical approach to

classroom instruction. Other students thrived on the generative method. Some children responded better to one method of instruction than to another.

Another study examined the effects of instruction on achievement in eighth-grade English and social studies. The findings of the study suggested that teacher-led activities and a strong academic focus raised achievement; but results also suggested that achievement was encouraged by building on students' ideas within the context of direct-instruction activities. The results showed modest but significant effects in both subjects with lecture, question-answer, and discussion activities; instructional coherence; and student participation. The results supported the prediction that when teachers work directly with students in an activity that encourages student input into academic content, such as discussion, the activities are more productive than those in which students have little or no input (Gamoran and Nystrand, 1991).

(4) learn or study, (5) try or make an effort, and (6) responsibility is something given or taken. It was concluded that the students did not perceive school as a place for learning. They saw school as neither challenging nor allowing them enough control to make the work challenging, and although they said they felt responsible for the learning, they were actually just being held responsible rather than being responsible (Bacon, 1993).

The researchers concluded that educators need to demonstrate to students that the primary reason for schools is learning, and then create appropriate, meaningful learning experiences, so that students can experience schoolwork as challenging (Bacon, 1993). This finding is in keeping with other studies that indicate that many students have a positive attitude toward school, but this attitude is seldom related to academic achievement. Students like school because it is a place to meet friends, to participate in activities, and to enjoy the companionship of others their own age (Anderson and Young, 1992).

The Secondary School Teacher

One of the important keys to fruitful secondary school education is having good teachers in the school system.

What Makes a Good Teacher?

What constitutes a "good" teacher? There is little agreement on the answer. Are good teachers those who are selected according to certain personality traits characteristic of mature, mentally healthy people? Are good teachers best defined by the degree of understanding, rapport, and warmth of the relationships they are able to establish with pupils, colleagues, and administrators? Or are good teachers best defined by their professional backgrounds, qualifications, and abilities to use appropriate materials and methods in motivating learning in students? Although various educators emphasize one category or another, there is sufficient evidence to justify emphasizing all three categories: (1) personality, (2) relationships, and (3) professional qualifications and performance.

Personality Traits and Character

Good teachers are emotionally secure people who are free from excessive fears, worries, and anxieties and who have good self-concepts. They do not rationalize or overcompensate for their own failures, nor do they need to protect their own egos by projecting their inadequacies on others or blaming others for their own failures. They are confident, accepting, trusting people who feel and act secure and mature. In one study of what

The characteristics of what make a "good teacher" fall into three categories: personality; quality of their relationships with pupils, colleagues, and administrators; and professional qualifications and performance.

high school dropouts thought of their teachers, the students listed self-confidence as the most important attribute of an effective instructor, because such teachers would not need to belittle others in order to feel secure themselves.

It is also beneficial to students' emotional development if teachers are emotionally stable people with high frustration tolerances and fairly even, pleasant dispositions and temperaments, free of excessive emotionalism and mood swings. They are usually patient and behave in a controlled manner.

Emotional security enables teachers to keep an open mind on questions and issues, to be willing to entertain different points of view, and to let students air their opinions and not pressure them to come up with the "right" answer (the teacher's answer). Such teachers can be flexible in scheduling, administering, and teaching their classes and not mind innovation or change if it makes a contribution to the learning process. They are relatively free of racial, ethnocentric, religious, political, and other prejudices and biases so that they can present issues honestly from different points of view. Thus, they are as tolerant, impartial, and fair as possible (Carter, 1984).

Emotional maturity also enables teachers to show kindness, love, and genuine warmth and regard for other people. This enables them to find close personal attachments in their own lives and to build rapport with adolescents. They can communicate that they like adolescents, understand them, and enjoy being with them. Students also like teachers who are generally happy, pleasant, cheerful people.

Although some good teachers are fairly self-centered, the better ones are unselfish and altruistic to the point of being pupil centered, with a genuine concern for them and their welfare. Good teachers are honest, sincere, caring, socially responsible people who strive to set a good example of personal conduct in their own lives and who are aware and sensitive to the social and ethical mores of the culture in which they live. This requires not only concern about individual ethics but also social morality.

Teaching is an exhausting profession, often requiring almost unlimited reservoirs of physical, emotional, and mental energy. It is not a profession for the sickly. Teachers need much drive and energy, backed up by a healthy constitution. Lethargic, apathetic, bored people in poor health can neither inspire students nor meet the vigorous demands of the profession.

Teachers' Relationships with Others

Good teachers enjoy satisfying social relationships outside of school, thus there is no need to work off negative feelings on their pupils or to use students to fulfill their own emotional and social needs. Teachers who get along well with their colleagues, who have satisfactory personal lives as individuals or members of a family, who are accepted and liked by others, and who have found social acceptance in adult society make better teachers.

Furthermore, teachers must like adolescents, be able to relate to them as growing people who are becoming adults, and treat them with admiration and respect as individuals. The teacher who hates youths and who is supercritical and rejecting of them has no business in the classroom. The best teachers evidence real understanding of youths, the developmental tasks of adolescence, and the particular problems, adjustments, and interests of young people (Lamport, 1993).

Professional Qualifications

One of the major criticisms of teacher candidates is that they are intellectually the poorest in the universities. This impression is commonly held among students outside colleges of education but can also be found among faculty members in universities across the nation. However, since the range of test scores overlaps among all college majors, there are some education majors scoring very high as well as low. Also, test scores vary from institution to institution.

Another criticism of teachers has been that they are too middle class and thus are not able to relate to lower-socioeconomic-class students. Although it is desirable from one point of view to employ more teachers from lower socioeconomic families, the likelihood of hiring teachers with lower scholastic ability becomes greater, for there is a positive correlation between performance on scholastic aptitude tests and the socioeconomic status of the family. However, a large number of those growing up in poor families are also of superior intelligence, so it is possible to find both brains and the ability to relate to all students in the same teacher.

It is important that teachers, once trained, keep abreast of the times in attitude, instructional knowledge, and skills. This means that teachers need to take advantage of numerous opportunities for professional improvement. They should participate in educational societies, attend workshops and conferences, take graduate courses, and keep up in their field by reading professional journals, new books, and research literature—not just in teaching methods but in subject matter, as well.

A good teacher is willing to spend necessary time in preparing the teaching of his or her subject matter. He or she understands and uses sound principles of learning through a variety of appropriate teaching methods and techniques. Students are highly critical of teachers who are never prepared, lazy, and uninterested in teaching and who don't care if students learn.

Curriculum Considerations

The *curriculum* of a school consists of the aggregate of the courses of study offered. Let's take a look at various curricula.

Three Curricula

Most comprehensive high schools today offer three basic curricula: college preparatory, vocational, and general.

College Preparatory Approximately half of high school students are enrolled in the college preparatory curriculum. Its goal is to prepare students for success in the type of college that leads to graduate school. Some high schools, particularly in middle- and upper-middle-class suburban communities, are particularly successful, boasting that 80 to 90 percent of their students go to college. Other schools, though enrolling large numbers of students in the "college prep" program, are unsuccessful because the majority of these students do not get into college. In such cases, the college prep program does not meet the needs of the majority of students; most do not go on to college, yet they are not employable without additional training.

Vocational The vocational curriculum is designed to prepare students for gainful employment. Students spend about half of their time in general education, the rest in specialized courses, and, in some cases, in on-the-job training. Vocational teachers usually have work experience in the vocation they are teaching. The quality of the program varies from superb to mediocre.

In order to prepare students for gainful employment, most high schools offer a vocational curriculum. This combines general education with specialized courses and possibly on-the-job training.

General Students in the general curriculum are often the castoffs from the other two curricula or are not committed either to college or to one of the vocations taught in the vocational curriculum. The curriculum has no goals other than to provide a general education for those who may be able to go onto some type of job or some type of vocational school after graduation. Most dropouts and unemployed youths come from the general curriculum. More of these youths might stay in high school and be employable if they were taught more specific vocational skills. (A student bulletin, put out by a large, well-known guidance firm, describes a general program as one teaching "what everybody should know." This, according to the bulletin, includes English, math, science, social studies, and a foreign language. No wonder this program does not meet all students' needs.)

Curriculum Improvement

Over the years, efforts at curriculum reform have consistently confronted two major problems. One is the rigidity of course requirements, grade demands, scheduling, and the lockstep structure of schools. When certain subjects are required, when carefully chosen subject-oriented content is obligatory in any one course, and when these subjects must be taught at particular grade levels for prescribed periods of time, with the student earning certain minimum ranks, any curriculum reform is difficult. To change would mean to overthrow the whole rigid system.

The second problem in instituting curriculum reform is the teacher and his or her methods. When teachers are required to cover so much material in a subject-centered course and when classes are overcrowded and budgets for hiring additional personnel are limited, teachers become conditioned to covering their vast subject matter in the most time-efficient way—lecturing. Some become so conditioned to "coverage" that new information or topics in their field are ignored because of time constraints.

In an effort to overcome these obstacles, considerable effort has gone into making some sweeping changes in curricular approaches. The new approaches emphasize student responsibility; individual study and growth at individual rates; and

flexibility of content, scheduling, and methods of teaching for each course.

Middle Schools

One of the problems of modern high schools stems partly from the size of some of the schools. Schools with large enrollments tend to become less personal, with less attention devoted to the needs of individual students. Ideally, the best schools seek to combine academic excellence with personalized attention and services, to achieve both intellectual rigor and intimacy. Most schools do not function at such a high level of performance (Lipsitz, 1991).

One of the answers has been the formation of schools in which older students are taken out of the upper elementary grades and put in middle schools, and eighth- and ninth-grade students are taken out of high schools and put in junior high schools (Wigfield and Eccles, 1995). There are all sorts of arrangements, depending on local facilities and policies. Grade divisions include the following variations:

> Grades K–3, 4–6, 7–9, 10–12
> Grades K–4, 5–8, 9–12
> Grades K–4, 5–6, 7–9, 10–12
> Grades K–4, 5–7, 8–9, 10–12
> Grades K–5, 6–9, 10–12
> Grades K–5, 6–8, 9–12
> Grades K–5, 6–7, 8–9, 10–12
> Grades K–6, 7–9, 10–12
> Grades K–6, 7–8, 9–12

Of course, in some remote or small areas, many grades are taught in the same building, or even in the same room.

Tremendous developmental and physical differences exit between older elementary-age pupils and those in lower grades. Separating older pupils from younger ones has some advantages on school buses, in school activities, and on playgrounds.

The transition from elementary school to junior high school is particularly traumatic to some pupils (see Chapter 8) (Lord, Eccles, and McCarthy, 1994). Other adolescents view the transition as desirable. Some students report difficulties in making new friends, others are worried about victimization by older students. High-achieving students who have been successful in elementary school are not sure they will be successful in their new schools. Despite their worries, adolescents with high grades generally enjoy junior high school. Adolescents who have the greatest difficulty adjusting to junior high school are usually those who have had behavioral or academic problems in elementary school. Since the problems are not treated before the adolescents leave elementary school, their adjustment to junior high school may be poor (Berndt and Mekos, 1995).

If a transition is made from elementary school to middle school to junior high school, the trauma of transition is reduced. Cotterell (1992b) found that school size has an effect on adjustments. If students move from a smaller to a much larger school, adjustments are more difficult (Costin and Jones, 1994; Estrada, 1992; Fenzel, Blyth, & Simmons, 1991).

Private versus Public Schools

The vast majority of pupils in the United States attend public schools. In spite of the rise of public education, however, there is still a wide variety of high schools in the United States. One study compared four types of secondary schools: *public, Catholic, elite private boarding schools,* and *elite high-performance private schools.* Among other things, the survey summarized the educational and pedagogical characteristics of the schools themselves and their pupils (Persell, Catsambis, and Cookson, 1992). The data comes from a National High School and Beyond (HSB) study, which was a national sample of public, Catholic, elite boarding, and other elite private schools.

There are considerable differences by high school type. The average school size of the private schools was smaller; the private schools had more volumes in their libraries and a greater percentage of teachers with masters degrees or higher. There was a teacher-student ratio of 13 teachers for each 100 students in both the elite private schools and the elite boarding schools, in contrast to 8 per 100 in public schools and 6 per 100 in Catholic schools. Fully 100 percent of students in both the elite private schools and the elite boarding schools were in academic programs, in contrast to only 34 percent of those in public schools.

Private schools also offered superior course programs in terms of academic difficulty. All (100 percent) of the private and boarding schools offered calculus; all offered French; and more private and boarding schools offered a variety of languages than public and Catholic schools.

It is also obvious that the students in the private schools had to work harder than those in the Catholic schools or in the public schools. Fully 86 percent of the students in the elite boarding schools said they spent 10 hours or more weekly on homework. Some 63 percent of the students in the elite private schools spent 10 hours or more weekly on homework. The students at both the elite private schools and the elite boarding schools were not able to watch TV very much each week.

A look at Catholic schools indicated that some 71 percent of the students in these schools surveyed were in the academic program, as compared with only 34 percent of students in the public schools. The greater percentage of Catholic schools offered advance courses in math, social sciences, art, drama, and languages. Interestingly enough, the Catholic schools showed a greater percentage of White students than either the public schools or the elite private schools. There were fewer percentages of African Americans than in other schools, especially public schools.

What do these facts mean in terms of practical implications? It is obvious for those families that can afford private education that they are more likely to get superior education for their adolescents than if they sent them to the average public school. The private schools are expensive; even Catholic schools cost a great deal of money in some locations (Persell, Catsambis, and Cookson, 1992).

Achievement and Dropping Out

In this section, we'll discuss school achievement and those factors that are related to dropping out of school.

Enrollment Figures

Education for all youths has not always been the philosophy of the American people. A famous Kalamazoo decision in 1874 established the now-

Tracking

Tracking or *ability grouping* is an organizational technique that permits schools to create homogeneous groupings of students within a heterogeneous student population in order to facilitate instruction of all students. Opponents view the practice as a means of perpetuating social class and societal values by providing greater learning opportunities for privileged students and fewer opportunities for less privileged ones. From this point of view, tracking hinders the attainment of the egalitarian goals associated with U.S. public education.

An administrator must make certain trade-offs in an effort to benefit all students. One administrator may believe that high-ability students benefit more from assignment to a small homogeneous group. Another administrator may believe that low-ability students might be stimulated by the academic diversity of their peers in a more heterogeneous group. Another administrator may feel that low-ability students have a greater need for homogeneous groupings, because of their more limited skills, and that high achievers learn regardless of their environments, making homogeneous grouping less critical for them. The problem of how to maximize learning benefits for both gifted and slow students when decisions are made regarding tracking is a difficult one (Hallinan, 1991).

One study examined the long-term correlates of being placed in an ability-group mathematics class upon entry into junior high school. Results of the study indicate that the long-term impact of ability grouping in mathematics at the seventh-grade level on students' achievement and on other outcomes at tenth grade depended on both the students' ability levels and the ability group into which they were placed. In terms of ability level, there were no positive long-term effects for low-ability students to be placed in low-group math classrooms when they were compared with low-ability students placed in the nongroup classrooms. In fact, in some instances, those placed in the low-group classroom appeared to fare worse. The medium- and high-ability students, however, placed at the seventh-grade level, generally showed more positive outcomes at the tenth-grade level than did students who were in heterogeneous class placement. In terms of ability-group level, results also showed that being placed in a group classroom in a level higher than one's ability resulted in some positive tenth-grade outcomes for both low- and medium-ability students (Fuligni, Eccles, and Barder, 1995).

---

accepted principle that public education need not be restricted to the elementary schools. Prior to that, in 1870, the country's youths could choose from among only 800 public high schools. Most youths who were preparing for college attended private secondary schools, often called *preparatory (or prep) schools*. In 1970, only 52 percent of those aged 25 and over had completed four or more years of high school; by 1995, the number was 82 percent. Figure 15.1 shows the rise since 1970. Figure 15.2 shows the percentage of dropouts from school by age and race during 1994. Until age 18, attendance figures are very high for Whites and African Americans but low for Hispanics. The dropouts occur during the high school years, especially after age 17, with a greater percentage of African Americans than Whites leaving school, and a much larger percentage of Hispanics leaving than African Americans (Goertz, Ekstrom,

and Rock, 1991; Romo and Falbo, 1995). The total number of dropouts is considerable, though the rate has been decreasing over the years (Bachman, 1991). During 1994, almost 4 million youths dropped out of school. The overall dropout rate in 1994 was 9.5 percent (U.S. Bureau of the Census, 1996).

Who Drops Out and Why

There is a constellation of causes for adolescents dropping out of school or underachieving (Zarb,

---

tracking an organizational technique that permits schools to create homogeneous groupings of students within a heterogeneous student population in order to facilitate instruction.

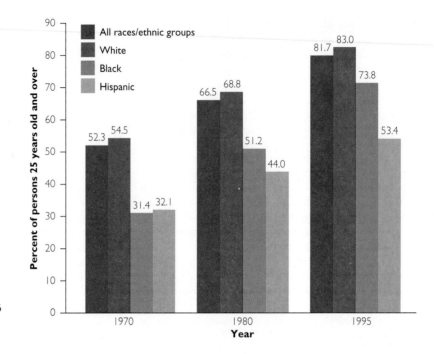

FIGURE 15.1 Percentage of Adults Who Have Completed Four Years of High School or More, 1970–1995

Source: U.S. Bureau of the Census, *Statistical Abstract of the United States, 1996* (Washington, DC: U.S. Government Printing Office, 1996) p. 159.

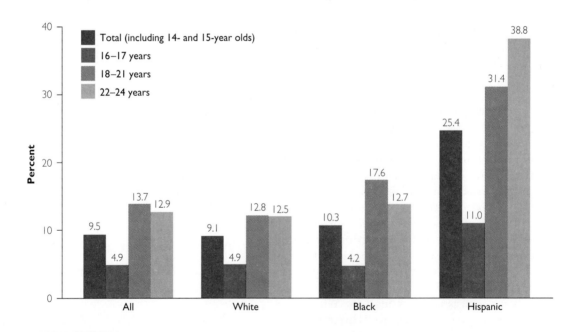

FIGURE 15.2 High School Dropouts from 14 to 24 Years Old, by Race and Age, 1994

Source: U.S. Bureau of the Census, *Statistical Abstract of the United States 1996* (Washington, DC: U.S. Government Printing Office, 1996), p. 176.

1984). The problem may begin before birth. Children who are born prematurely or with low birth weight, may be at high risk for both biological and social factors. It is known that low-birth-weight children are at risk for subtle defects that may appear in school functioning. Neurological problems are found more frequently in preterm children than in full-term children. Defective and neurological problems pay be seen throughout school achievement. Specific cognitive processes such as attention and short-term memory may be affected, and these, in turn, have an impact on reading and arithmetic ability and social adaptation. A number of studies of elementary schoolchildren indicate that low-birth-weight children have more learning problems, visual-motor deficits, and grade retention (Cohen, Beckwith, Parmelee, Sigman, Asarnow, and Espinosa, 1996).

Other important factors are socioeconomic status, racial and ethnic prejudice and discrimination, family background, parental influence and relationships, home responsibilities, personality problems, social adjustments, activities and associations, financial problems, health problems, pregnancy, marriage, intellectual difficulties or retardation, reading disability, school failure, misconduct, expulsion, low marks, and lack of interest in school (Tidwell, 1988; Connell, Halpern-Felsher, Clifford, Crichlow, and Usinger, 1995). Usually, problems accumulate over the years until withdrawal occurs, often after the legal requirement of age or number of years of schooling have been met. The actual event or circumstance that precipitates withdrawal may be minor: a misunderstanding with a teacher, a disciplinary action, difficulty with peers, misunderstanding at home, or other reasons. One boy withdrew in the last semester of his senior year because his foster parents would not buy him a suit for graduation. Another boy was a refused admittance to a class until a late excuse was obtained from his gym teacher in the prior period. The gym teacher would not give an excuse; the boy got angry, quit school, and never came back. In each incident like this, a whole series of prior events led to the final withdrawal: poor marks, grade retardation, conduct problems at school, strained family relationships, social maladjustment or isolation, and others. Here are some signs of possible early school withdrawal (Brooks-Gunn, Guo, and Furstenberg, 1993; Horowitz, 1992):

1. Consistent failure to achieve in regular schoolwork
2. Grade-level placement two or more years below average age for grade
3. Irregular attendance
4. Active antagonism to teachers and principals
5. Marked disinterest in school with feeling of not belonging, meaninglessness
6. Low scholastic aptitude
7. Low reading ability
8. Frequent changes of schools
9. Nonacceptance by school staff; estrangement
10. Nonacceptance by schoolmates
11. Friends much younger or older
12. Unhappy family situation
13. Marked differences from schoolmates with regard to size
14. Inability to afford the normal expenditures of schoolmates
15. Nonparticipation in extracurricular activities
16. Inability to compete with or ashamed of brothers and sisters
17. Performance consistently lower than potential
18. Serious physical or emotional disability
19. Discipline problems
20. Record of delinquency

We must interpret these signs cautiously; the presence of one or more of these symptoms of early school withdrawal may be a false alarm. At other times, only one symptom may be present but may be a real indication of possible withdrawal. When as many as eight of these symptoms appear together, a prognosis of school withdrawal is more reliable. Adolescents most at risk for dropping out need to be identified early in their school careers so that preventive measures can be taken (O'Sullivan, 1990). Large numbers of youths at risk need a lot more attention than they are getting in schools (Gregory, 1995).

Changing Schools

Changing schools is sometimes a factor in pupils dropping out. When an adolescent changes schools, the ability of the parents and the adolescent to make wise decisions about schooling is reduced. They have less information about the new school and its teachers and classes. Also, they may be less able to take advantage of resources that the

HIGHLIGHT

Push and Pull Factors

Using nationally representative high school student data, one study divided reasons why some adolescents drop out of school push factors and pull factors. *Push factors* are related to the school itself—when the school pushes students out. *Pull factors* are those reasons other than school that the student drops out.

There are several dimensions of school-related reasons for early withdrawal. School itself is defined as a push factor when the school becomes frustrating, punishing, or something a student wishes to avoid (and so is pushed toward quitting). There are three push dimensions in students' reasons for dropping out. First, is a general student alienation from school, which includes failing in schoolwork, not getting along with teachers, and not liking or feeling welcome at school. The second

push factor is school safety, meaning that the student is worried about attacks or hostile treatment from others at school or is having serious difficulties in getting along with schoolmates. The third push factor is having been expelled or suspended, which usually covers serious problems of discipline or confrontation with authorities by a student.

One important pull reason for dropping out is having to care for adult relatives, younger siblings, or one's own children. Clearly, this obligation mostly affects female dropouts. A second significant pull factor is employment—a reason given by female and male dropouts. Attraction of employment and the need to earn money definitely pulls many students away from school (Jordan, Lara, and McPartland, 1996).

new school and teachers can provide. Additionally, teachers may be less committed to a youth who has only recently moved into the system and may be less willing to devote additional time and energy to that youth. Such an adolescent may feel separated from the educational process and may be more likely to seek marginalized social contacts (Teachman, Paasch, and Carver, 1996).

Truancy

Those who drop out of school may have a high rate of truancy from school. Truants, in general, score lower in academic ability and achievement, are less likely to live with both parents, and have more siblings than those who are not truant (Sommer and Nagel, 1991). School officials are concerned about truancy because of its association with delinquency. Delinquents are often students of low ability who contribute little in school and are truant as well. Another study showed that students who were at risk for dropping out had significantly less positive attitudes toward their school experiences, lower self-concepts, more external control orientations, and viewed their parents as less demanding and more casual in their expectations (Browne and Rife, 1991).

Socioeconomic Factors

Research overwhelmingly indicates that low socioeconomic status correlates positively with early withdrawal from school (Manaster, 1977). Why is the dropout rate higher among students from low-socioeconomic families (Svec, 1986)? There are a number of considerations (Simons, Finley, and Yang 1991):

1. *Students from low socioeconomic families often lack positive parental influences and examples.* Many such parents want their children to have more education than they did. But if parents finished only fifth grade, they may consider graduating from junior high school sufficient. In general, sons of low socioeconomic status receive more encouragement to finish school than do daughters.

2. *Teachers are often prejudiced against youths from low socioeconomic families, showing preferential treatment to students from higher-status families.* Students of higher-social-class backgrounds are chosen more often for little favors (e.g., running errands, monitoring, chairing committees), whereas students from lower-status groups receive more than their share of discipline. Teachers are usually from middle-class backgrounds and therefore

often find it difficult to understand and accept the goals, values, and behavior of pupils from other social backgrounds.

3. *Low socioeconomic students receive fewer rewards for doing well and for staying in school than do students from higher-status families* (Taylor, Casten, and Flickinger 1993). Rewards may take the form of academic grades, favors by teachers, social acceptance by peers, offices in school government, participation in extracurricular activities, or school prizes and awards. Lower-status students receive these types of rewards less often than do higher-status students. Their grades are not as good nor do they enjoy as much social acceptance and prestige by peers; they seldom are elected to positions of leadership; they are nonjoiners in extracurricular activities; and they are not often given special prizes or awards by the school.

4. *Low socioeconomic students do not as often possess the verbal skills of their middle-class peers.* This in itself presents a handicap in learning to read or in almost all other academic work. Insofar as lack of verbal skills is associated with low socioeconomic status, lower-status youths do not do as well in school and are therefore more prone to drop out.

5. *Peer influences on low socioeconomic youths are often antischool and delinquency prone, emphasizing early marriage for girls and gang activities for boys.* Low socioeconomic youths often have severed their ties with adult institutions and values, becoming involved instead with groups composed of jobless dropouts.

Ethnic Considerations

Hispanic, African American, and other minority group students have a much higher dropout rate than White students do (U.S. Bureau of the Census, 1996) (Fenzel and Magaletta, 1993). The highest rates are among non-White students from inner-city high schools. The value orientation and the trying economic, social, and familial conditions are not conducive to continuing education. One researcher suggested that underachievement is best explained by numerous factors and circumstances. A variety of negative social, cultural, and psychological forces interfere with African American students' achievement and achievement orientation (Ford, 1992).

Family Relationships

The quality of interaction among members of the adolescent's family has a marked influence on school success (Hurrelmann, Engel, Holler, and Nordlohne, 1988; Masselam, Marcus, and Stunkard, 1990; Chavkin and Williams, 1993). Studies of the family relationships of bright, high-achieving versus underachieving high school students show that the high achievers more often than the underachievers describe their parents as typically sharing recreation and ideas, as understanding, approving, trusting, affectionate, and encouraging (but not pressuring) with respect to achievement, and as not overly restrictive or severe in discipline. One study of high school students found that too early autonomy in decision making in the family is associated with lower levels of effort and lower grades, whereas joint decision making is associated with more effort and higher grades for youths of both sexes, regardless of ethnicity and socioeconomic status (Dornbusch, Ritter, Mont-Reynaud, and Chen, 1990). Youths who come from conflicting family environments are more likely to be underachievers and school dropouts than those who come from cohesive, nonconflicting families (Wood, Chapin, and Hannah, 1988). One study of the school performance of early adolescents who lived with their recently divorced mothers found that those with high grade-point averages had mothers with a lower level of depression, a higher educational level, less conflict with their ex-spouse, and less intense levels of conflict between mother and adolescent than those in the low grade-point average group (McCombs and Forehand, 1989).

Another study found that ineffective discipline had a direct and negative effect on boys' seventh-grade academic engagement (parents failed to make the boys do their school work), and boys' academic engagement, in turn, had a direct and positive effect on eighth-grade academic achievement (DeBaryshe, Patterson, and Capaldi, 1993).

One study (Steinberg, Lamborn, Dornbusch, and Darling, 1992) measured the impact of parenting practices on adolescent achievement in school. The parenting practices studied were authoritative parenting, school involvement, and encouragement to succeed. As we have seen from previous studies, the researchers found that students who described their parents as authoritative—warm, firm, and democratic—reported better school performance and stronger school engagement than did their peers. The longitudinal analysis presented indicated that authoritative parenting actually led to school success.

This study also examined the mediating roles played by parent involvement in school and parent encouragement of academic success (Connors and Epstein, 1995; Ryan, Adams, Gullotta, Weissberg, and Hampton, 1995). As expected, parental authoritativeness was associated with higher levels of school involvement and more encouragement of academic success. A more important finding was that parental involvement accounted for the better school performance and stronger school engagement of adolescents from homes characterized as authoritative. The researchers were able to say with some confidence that parents' involvement in school actually led to improvements in school performance (Steinberg et al., 1992). This finding is in keeping with other research that demonstrates the connection between family and achievement, which shows that parental involvement plays a critical role in childrens' academic success (Snodgrass, 1991; Eccles et al., 1993).

A study of 347 seventh-graders and their parents examined the relation of types of parental behavior to academic performance. Parents who interacted with their children in an angry, irritating, and controlling manner exhibited behavior that disrupted effective parenting and adolescent academic competence. Conversely, parents who set appropriate standards, monitored children's activities, provided positive consequences for desired behaviors, promoted open communication, and shared in nurturing activities displayed behavior that helped facilitate effective parent-child relationships and adolescent academic competence (Melby and Conger, 1996).

Personality Characteristics

Dropouts are more likely to be emotionally immature and less well adjusted than high school graduates. They may manifest symptoms of defective ego functioning: rebellion, negativism and alienation, deep-seated feelings of hostility and resentment, low self-esteem, feelings of inferiority, excessive fear and anxiety, or emotional instability.

What is so often described as laziness or a lack of willpower may actually be sullen resentment toward punitive parents, social rejection, or unfair treatment at school, which causes such feelings of rebellion that the adolescent refuses to do anything demanded by authority. Some students develop a real phobia in relation to school (Paccione-Dyszlewski and Contessa-Kislus, 1987).

Five traits have been identified as common among underachievers: (1) negativism, (2) inferiority feelings, (3) high anxiety, (4) boredom, and (5) overprotectedness (Stevens and Pihl, 1987). When faced with obstacles to success, low-achieving adolescents are less likely to feel they can succeed (Elmen, 1991), are less likely to seek adequate help, and are more likely to display helplessness, to focus on their lack of ability, and to resort to inefficient strategies than are high achievers (Nelson-LeGall, 1990).

Psychologists have long recognized that individual students differ tremendously in their motivation to achieve. Almost from birth, some children seem to be highly motivated to succeed, whereas others are more laid back and do not care whether they excel.

Social Adjustment and Peer Associations

Peer influences often are a major factor in influencing a particular student to achieve in school. Most adolescents want to do what their friends are doing. If friends are dropping out of school to earn "big money" or to get married, the individual may be persuaded to do likewise. Similarly, the student who becomes acculturated into a lower-class pattern of life that rejects education or into a delinquent group rebelling against the established system of education is strongly influenced by his or her peers to drop out of school. In fact, in one study, boys' support from friends was negatively related to self-concept and educational plans (Cotterell, 1992a).

Developmental changes in relationships with peers are also likely to influence school motivation and engagement. The increased significance of friends during the transition to adolescence has been well documented. The inclusion, acceptance, and approbation of the peer group have a marked influence on achievement motivation.

Students need to feel that they belong. *Belonging* is defined here as a student's sense of being accepted, valued, included, and encouraged by others (teacher and peers) in the academic classroom setting and of feeling like an important part of the life and activity of the class (Goodenow, 1993).

Employment and Money

Financial considerations are important in an individual's decisions about whether to stay in school. One study pointed to a relationship between family financial stress and academic achievement in sixth-, seventh-, and eighth-graders (Clark-Lempers, Lempers, and Netusil, 1990). Even high school is expensive. This factor, plus financial pressures at home, force some adolescents to leave school to go to work. Sometimes, parents pressure youths to go to work to help support the family. At other times, there is the lure of being financially independent, having spending money for social activities or saving to buy a car. The desire for clothes, a car, and other symbols of status in an affluent society lures many youths to opt for early employment. If at-risk students are able to get fairly good jobs without an education, they're more likely to do so (Stallmann and Johnson, 1996).

School Stress

A large body of research has demonstrated that continual high levels of stress debilitate psychological well-being, physical health, and task performance. A number of studies have focused on the sources of students' stress while in school, which are many. One such source is safety. More and more students report that someone hit, kicked or pushed them, or threatened them with a knife or gun, and that they feel unsafe in the school. Being made fun of in front of the class or by friends is also a source of stress, as is being shouted at or screamed at by teachers. Being made to feel inferior and ashamed, not being able to finish classroom work, and doing worse on a test than one should and experiencing a change of teachers in one or more classes are sources of stress. Other stressful situations are having something stolen from your locker and seeing other students throwing things and fighting in the lunchroom. Anything that upsets the harmony and interferes with the classroom activities may be a source of stress and certainly affects academic functioning in the school situation (Ainslie, Shafer, and Reynolds, 1996; Grannis, 1992).

School Failure, Apathy, and Dissatisfaction

Many school factors have been associated with dropping out of school (Evans, Cicchelli, Cohen, and Shapiro, 1995). Among these are poor reading ability, grade retardation, repetition, misplacement, low or failing marks (Grande, 1988), inability to get along with teachers, misconduct, and low IQ or mental retardation. There is also a general, vague category that might be labeled apathy, lack of motivation, or a feeling that school is irrelevant. Some students are not necessarily emotionally or socially maladjusted—they simply lack interest in schoolwork, feel it is a waste of time, and would rather get married or go to work. Such youths may be capable of doing acceptable schoolwork but have no interest in doing so. Sometimes, such a student has been placed in the wrong type of program. A transfer to a vocational course that the student finds appealing and interesting is of help to the adolescent who has been wrongly placed in the college prep program. Many students do not drop out but are thrown out or given a temporary suspension, which they turn into a permanent absence.

Schools that establish effective intervention programs for potential dropouts can reduce the rate considerably. What is needed is a determined effort to correct the conditions that cause the student to drop out in the first place (Caliste, 1984).

Alienation

Student alienation—as manifested in a school context by poor academic performance, truancy, and rebellion—is a complex concept. One dimension of alienation is *powerlessness*. People feel powerless when they are controlled or manipulated by authority figures according to the rules of social institutions. In the school context, some students experience powerlessness when they can neither control nor change school policies, tracking, and their marginal academic positions. They choose not to compete for symbolic rewards such as praise and academic grades and, instead, play truant from classes, rebel against rules, or merely attend but not participate in classes.

Meaninglessness is a second dimension of student alienation. In a school context, students may be unclear on the connection between subjects taught at school and their future roles in society.

The third dimension of alienation, *normlessness,* occurs when individuals have little sense of their cohesive goals and norms through social institutions. Official school norms reward students who achieve academically and who intend to pursue higher education. Many students from low-socioeconomic-status and minority groups perceive official school norms as unfair. Alienated students may readily reject official school norms in favor of peer and/or counterschool norms (Mau, 1992).

Pregnancy and Marriage

Leaving high school to get married is seldom a reason boys drop out of school, but pregnancy and marriage are among the most common reasons for girls. One study found that pregnant girls who didn't drop out were more likely to be better students, to be 16 years of age or older, to be enrolled in vocational classes, to show improved grades in a special program, and to keep up their marks between grades 7 and 8, and were less frequently enrolled in special education classes (De-

Bolt, Pasley, and Kreutzer, 1990). Schools can play an important role in meeting the many needs of teenage parents (Kiselica and Pfaller, 1993).

Data from the National Longitudinal Survey of Youth (NLSY) (Center for Human Resource Research, 1987) demonstrate that there are significant differences between groups of girls: Girls from the most disadvantaged backgrounds are the most likely to drop out of school and/or to become teenage mothers. Adolescent mothers who graduate from high school most resemble women who graduate and delay childbearing, but are less likely to attend college than the latter (Aseltine and Gore, 1993; Rice, 1993; Upchurch, 1993).

Teenage Fathers

What about teenage fathers? An examination of the educational and labor market outcomes of young men in the United States finds that men who were teenage fathers completed fewer years of education and were less likely to finish high school compared to men who were not teen fathers. These educational deficits persist even after family and personal characteristics are taken into account. Teen fathers enter the labor market earlier and initially earn more money than do other men; but by the time teen fathers reach their mid-20s, they earn less. Teen fathers fare poorly in comparison to men who postpone having children until age 20 or later (Pirog-Good, 1996).

Pregnancy and marriage are among the most common reasons for girls to drop out of school. Schools that provide special programs to meet the needs of teen mothers play an important role in keeping them in school.

HIGHLIGHT

Middle-Class Parenting and Underachievement

Metcalf and Gaier (1987) studied patterns of parenting among middle-class parents of underachieving eleventh- and twelfth-graders and found the following four patterns that contributed to academic underachievement:

1. *Upward-striving parents* pressure adolescents to get good marks; they criticize and nag.
2. *Overprotective parents* are overrestrictive, overdirecting, domineering, compulsive perfectionists, constantly expecting their children to do better.

3. *Indifferent parents* set low standards, show little interest, and set no consistent limits.
4. *Conflicted parents* have blatantly inconsistent ideas on childrearing.

Apparently, excessive pressure, criticism, indifference, and conflict all contribute to academic underachievement.

SUMMARY

1. During the last half of the twentieth century, the emphasis in U. S. education shifted between traditionalism, emphasizing basic education, and progressivism, emphasizing education for life. Until the 1930s, traditionalism was the dominant emphasis. Then came the Depression and the introduction of life-adjustment education centered around vocations, leisure activities, health, personal concerns, and community problems.

2. Emphasis traditionalism changed after the Soviet Union launched *Sputnik* in the mid-1950s. Then the demand was for more emphasis in teaching math, science, and foreign languages. A billion-dollar aid-to-education program financed this change. By the mid-1960s, the cold war had abated, the nation was swamped with social problems and unrest, and so once more, the emphasis was on education to solve society's ills. The new progressivism emphasized work study, career and experiential education, open classrooms, independent study, and student-designed courses. Enrollments in basic education courses dropped.

3. By the mid-1970s, the nation became alarmed by the drop in SAT scores and other indicators of declining proficiency. As a result, the National Commission on Excellence in Education was created in the 1980s and made numerous recommendations to return to basic education.

4. SAT scores improved until 1985, but began to drop again, resulting in increased pressure in the 1990s to place more emphasis on basic education. The pendulum had swung full cycle.

5. Nationwide surveys among students reveal a general approval of their school programs. Suggestions for improvement include making courses more interesting and challenging, putting more emphasis on excellence, stiffening graduation requirements, and upgrading the quality of teachers. Students dislike other aspects of school; the emphasis on grades, the rigidity of requirements, the irrelevance of courses, the failure of the program to challenge brighter students, and the need for more emphasis on vocational education.

6. There is a difference between students being responsible for their own learning and being held responsible by teachers. Teachers need to instill in students a sense of responsibility and students need to learn that school is primarily a place for learning. Students like school because it is a place to meet friends and participate in activities.

7. One of the most important keys to superior secondary education is to have good teachers—those who have mature, well-adjusted personalities and are emotionally secure and stable. Teachers must be well adjusted socially and enjoy satisfying social relationships with others. They must be professionally qualified to teach: intelligent, well-trained, with a good grasp of subject matter, and willing to set aside time for preparation.

8. The average comprehensive high school offers three basic curricula: college preparatory, vocational, and general. Efforts at curriculum reform have consistently confronted two major problems: (a) the rigidity of course requirements, grades, de-

mands, and scheduling in the lockstep school structure and (b) the teacher and his or her methods, which emphasize content coverage and a lack of willingness to adopt new courses, emphases, and methods.

9. Tracking is an organizational technique that permits schools to create homogeneous groupings of students within a heterogeneous student population in order to facilitate instruction.

10. One of the problems of modern high schools is their size. Many are so large that instruction is too impersonal. Furthermore, older elementary pupils are far more mature than younger, and ninth-graders are generally too young for high school. One answer is to put older elementary pupils in middle schools and to put ninth-graders in junior high school. Such arrangements have many intellectual, emotional, and social advantages.

11. For those families that can afford them and wish to enroll their children, private schools offer education superior to that offered by public schools.

12. There are a number of reasons why pupils drop out of school: truancy, socioeconomic factors, racial and ethnic prejudices and discrimination, disturbed family situations and negative parental influences, emotional problems, negative social adjustments and peer associations, financial reasons, school failure, school stress, apathy, student alienation and dissatisfactions, pregnancy and marriage, and other reasons.

KEY TERMS

progressives **357**

Scholastic Assessment Test (SAT) **358**

tracking **367**

traditionalists **357**

THOUGHT QUESTIONS

1. Describe the type of high school you attended. Evaluate the good things about it.
2. What curriculum options were available in your high school? Did these meet the needs of the students?
3. What courses were offered in the high school that you attended that you feel were unnecessary? What courses were not offered that you feel should have been?
4. What types of vocational education were offered in your high school when you attended? Did these programs prepare students for jobs? What other types of vocational courses and programs should have been offered?
5. In what ways did your high school program prepare you for college? In what ways was it deficient in preparing you for college?
6. What did you think of the teachers in your high school? What qualities did you most admire? What qualities did you like the least?
7. Do you think students should have a voice in the organization and selection of the high school curriculum? How can the program become more relevant to student needs?
8. How much voice should students have in deciding the specific subjects to be studied as part of a course?

9. What are the most important attributes of a good teacher?
10. What training or preparation should be given to teachers to enhance their abilities and qualifications to teach?
11. Do you think high schools cater to college prep students while neglecting those in other programs? Explain.
12. What are the advantages and disadvantages of vocational education in high school? Should there be separate vocational schools? Comment on vocational education as it now exists. How could it be improved?
13. What subjects do you feel are most unnecessary in the average high school curriculum?
14. What sort of grade arrangements do you feel work best? That is, what classes should be placed in each building to achieve the maximum amount of learning and satisfactory adjustments of students?
15. What is your opinion of attending private versus public schools? Give examples from your own experience or the experience of others.
16. Did your high school have many dropouts? Why did these students leave school? What kept you in school when you sometimes felt you would rather leave and go to work?
17. Are high schools too strict or too lax in discipline?

18. What should schools do about such problems as drinking, smoking (cigarettes or marijuana), cheating, or vandalism in school?

19. For what reason should students be expelled from school?

20. Who should do the disciplining in school? Should parents be involved in school discipline?

21. What are the advantages and disadvantages of students having employment outside the home while attending high school?

22. What should the schools do about so many girls becoming pregnant while in school? About the boys who father children?

SUGGESTED READING

Csikszentmihalyi, M., Rathunde, K., Whalen, S., and Wong, M. (1993). *Talented Teenagers: The Roots Of Success and Failure.* New York: Cambridge University Press.

Dryfoos, J. G. (1994). *Full-Service Schools: A Revolution in Health and Social Services for Children, Youth, and Families.* San Francisco: Jossey-Bass.

Farrell, E. (1994). *Self and School Success: Voices and Lore of Inner-City Students.* Albany: University of New York Press.

Greenberg, D. (1992). *Education in America: A View from Sudbury Valley.* Framingham, MA: Sudbury Valley School Press.

Lipsitz, J. (1984). *Successful Schools for Young Adolescents.* New Brunswick, NJ: Transaction Books.

Natriello, G., McDill, E. L., and Pallas, A. M. (1990). *School and Disadvantaged Children: Racing against Catastrophe.* New York: Teachers College Press.

Newman, B. M., and Newman, P. R. (1992). *When Kids Go to College: Parents' Guide to Changing Relationships.* Columbus: Ohio State University Press.

Ryan, B. A., Adams, G. R., Gullotta, T. P., Weissberg, R. P., and Hampton, R. L. (Eds.). (1995). *The Family-School Connection: Theory, Research, and Practice.* Newbury Park, CA: Sage.

16

Work and Vocation

The choice of a vocation is one of the most important decisions that an adolescent has to make (O'Hare, 1987). In this chapter, we will examine the factors that influence that choice as well as other factors that should. We will also examine the major theories of vocational choice that have grown out of research discoveries and discuss the influence of parents, peers, school personnel, culture, sex-role concepts, intelligence, aptitudes, interest, job opportunities, job rewards and satisfactions, socioeconomic status, prestige factors, and race. The chapter concludes with a discussion of adolescent unemployment.

Motives for Choice

There are some basic psychological reasons why the task of vocational choice is important. All people need to meet their emotional needs for recognition, praise, acceptance, approval, love, and independence. One way individuals do this is by taking on a vocation identity, by becoming "some-

bodies" whom others can recognize and by which others grant them emotional fulfillment. By identifying with a particular vocation, people find selfhood, self-realization, and self-fulfillment. High career aspirations are both a consequence of high self-esteem and a contributor to superior self-images (Chiu, 1990). To the extent that adolescents succeed in their own and others' eyes, they gain self-satisfaction and recognition. In their search for identity and self-satisfaction, they are strongly motivated to make a vocational choice that will contribute to their fulfillment (see Chapter 8).

For adolescents who are of a philosophical frame of mind, their vocation is one channel through which their life goals and purposes might be fulfilled. It is the reason for their existence, the niche they feel compelled to fill in the world (Homan, 1986). If adolescents believe life has meaning and purpose, they strive to find and to live out that meaning and purpose by the way they spend their time, talents, and energy. One way is through the work they perform. Vocational choice not only involves asking How can I make a living?—it also involves asking What am I going to do with my life?

For adolescents whose concern is one of service—for meeting the needs of people or bettering the society in which they live—the choice of vocation will depend on the needs they recognize as most important and can best satisfy through their work. They thus seek a vocation in which they can be of service. For adolescents who try to be practical, the choice involves discovering the types of work in which there are the most vacant positions, in which the best money and benefits package are offered, in which they are most interested, and for which they are best qualified. Such choices are based primarily on economic motives, practical considerations, and personal interests and qualifications. For other youths, seeking a vocation becomes a means by which they show they are grown up, financially independent, emancipated from parents, and able to make it on their own. For them, going to work becomes a means of gaining entrance into the adult world.

Sometimes, however, no rational choice of vocation is made at all. Adolescents just go out and get the first job they can find that pays well, or they accept a job because a friend has recommended them for it or because it happens to be the only one that opens up and that they hear about. Under such circumstances, vocational choice is happenstance rather than a thoughtful process. Adolescents may temporarily enjoy economic and other benefits such employment brings. Only later do they discover they are unhappy, ill suited to the tasks, and sacrificing their freedom and lives for doubtful benefits. They need to back up, reassess their goals, talents, and opportunities, and discover the ways these might be combined in meaningful, rewarding work.

A minority of adolescents choose not to work at all, at least no more than they have to. Their rebellion against the values exemplified in the lives of adults and the values of their society has convinced them that they should reduce their need for money as much as possible and lead simple but impoverished lives to give them the freedom to do

as they please. Sometimes, this means doing absolutely nothing; at other times, it means engaging in what they feel are self-fulfilling activities, even though not remunerative. This kind of "dropping out" became almost epidemic during the 1960s, when adolescents began packing their bags and drifting around the country. This trend slowly abated during the 1970s.

Under the best of circumstances, choosing a vocation is an increasingly difficult task as society becomes more complex. *The Dictionary of Occupational Titles* now lists more than 47,000 different occupations, most of which are unfamiliar. If at all possible, adolescents need to make rational, considered choices of vocations. If they fail to identify themselves with the kind of work for which they are suited and in which they can find satisfaction and fulfillment, their vocational nonidentities will reflect their larger failure to discover their own identities. In a sense, they will have failed to discover what their own lives are all about.

Theories of Vocational Choice

A number of theorists have sought to describe the process of vocational development (Schulenberg, Vondracek, and Kim, 1993). The particular theories that we will discuss are those of Ginzberg (1988) and Holland (1985).

Ginzberg's Compromise with Reality Theory

In his *compromise with reality theory,* Eli Ginzberg (1988) emphasized that making a vocational choice is a developmental process that occurs not at a single moment, but over a long period. It involves a series of "subdecisions" that together add up to a vocational choice. Each subdecision is important because each limits the individual's subsequent freedom of choice and the ability to achieve his or her original goal. For example, a decision not to go to college and to take a commercial course in high school makes it difficult later to decide to go to college. Extra time, effort, and sometimes money must be expended to make up for deficiencies. As children mature, they gain

During the fantasy stage, young children imagine the type of work they want to do without regard to training, ability, opportunity, or other realistic considerations.

knowledge and exposure to alternatives; they learn to understand themselves and their environment; and they are better able to make rational choices. Most of these choices involve making comparisons between an ideal and a reality. Ginzberg divided the process of occupational choice into three stages: fantasy, tentative, and realistic.

Fantasy Stage   The fantasy stage generally occurs up to age 11. During this time, children imagine workers they want to be without regard to needs, abilities, training, employment opportunities, or any realistic considerations. They want to be airline pilots, teachers, quarterbacks, ballerinas, and so forth.

Tentative Stage   The tentative stage spans ages 11 through 17 and is subdivided into four periods or substages. During the *interest period,* from ages 11 to 12, children make their choices primarily based on their likes and interests. This stage represents a transition between fantasy choice and tentative choice. The second period, the *capacities period,* occurs between about 13 and 14 years of age. During this period, adolescents become aware of role requirements, occupational rewards, and different means of preparation. However, they are primarily thinking of their own abilities in relation to requirements. During the third period, the *value period,* from ages 15 to 16, adolescents attempt to relate occupational roles to their own in-

terests and values, to synthesize job requirements with their own values and capacities. They consider both the occupation and their own interests. The fourth and last stage, which occurs at around age 17, is a *transition period,* in which adolescents make transitions from tentative to realistic choices in response to pressures from school, peers, parents, colleges, and the circumstances of graduating from high school.

Realistic Stage   During the realistic stage, from age 17 on, adolescents seek further resolution of their problems of vocational choice. This stage is subdivided into a period of *exploration* (ages 17 to 18), during which they make an intensive search to gain greater knowledge and understanding; a period of *crystallization* (between ages 19 and 21), in which they narrowly define a single set of choices and commit themselves; and a period of *specification,* in which a general choice, such as physicist, is further limited to a particular type of physicist.

Ginzberg's interviews were conducted primarily with adolescents from upper-income families, who no doubt had a considerably great range of choices. The process would likely take longer for these youths than for others because their

compromise with reality theory   the theory of vocational choice proposed by Ginzberg.

extended education is more affordable. Lower-income youths often have an earlier crystallization of occupational choice, though their choices still seem to parallel those of the theoretical model. Also, Ginzberg's observations were primarily of boys, although he concluded that girls parallel the first two stages—fantasy and tentative. Other research indicates that the transition to realism applies to both boys and girls, but that girls tend to keep their vocational plans more tentative and flexible than do boys.

Ginzberg's theory suffers from rigidity with respect to the exact sequence, nature, and timing of the stages; thus, it may be too artificial and contrived. One study found no significant difference in career maturity between ninth- and twelfth-grade students (Post-Kammer, 1987). *Some research, however, generally supports the broad outlines of the hypothesis, but not always the chronological ages associated with Ginzberg's different stages.* For example, a study of 91 adolescent boys in a "potential scientist pool" showed that after eleventh grade, 34 moved out of the program and 17 moved in, but

only 5 of those who moved in after eleventh grade stayed in; 1 boy moved in after graduation and stayed in (Wattenberg, 1973). This finding indicates that some boys made relatively stable vocational choices before the eleventh grade, whereas others had not made up their minds even after high school. Thus, it is difficult to apply exact chronological ages to the periods Ginzberg outlines. Some relatively young adolescents show a high degree of maturity in making vocational choices; others evidence emerging maturity; and still others never seem to show the maturity necessary to match interests with capacities and training with job opportunities. Some people continue to change vocations throughout adulthood.

Ginzberg has made reformulations of his theory to take these factors into account. He now acknowledges that career choices do not necessarily end with the first job and that some people remain occupationally mobile throughout their work histories. He emphasizes that some people—the economically disadvantaged and minority races especially—do not have as many choices as

HIGHLIGHT

Developmental-Contextual Concepts

Research on career development emphasizes the dynamic interaction between individuals and their environment in their vocational quests. Specifically, there are three types of influences on development (Vondracek and Schulenberg, 1986, 1992):

1. *Normative, age-graded influences:* These influences, which vary with chronological time, might be biological or environmental. For example, certain types of careers, such as professional sports, require requisite physical characteristics.
2. *Normative history-graded influences:* These influences may be biological or environmental in nature, too. They could include such historical events as depression, war, famine, or even the launching of *Sputnik*.
3. *Nonnormative, life-event influences:* These influences might include an unexpected death of a family breadwinner, an illness, an injury, or a loss of scholarship, forcing alteration of career plans.

In other words, there may be significant influences on career choice over which the individual has minimal control. According to some researchers, *chance* plays a role in shaping career decisions (Cabral and Salomone, 1990). Such decisions are rarely purely rational, nor are they, in most instances, based purely on chance. Some combination of planning and happenstance seems to influence the decision. Individuals are most vulnerable to the effects of chance during life transitions, particularly those that occur early in one's career and that are not anticipated. However, the ability to cope with unforeseen events depends a great deal on the strength of the individual's self-concept and the sense of internal (or enabling) control. The accident theory of vocational choice emphasizes the effect of unexpected personal events on career development, but would still emphasize that some individuals are better able to overcome negative contingencies and to take advantage of positive developments than are others (Scott and Hatalla, 1990).

the upper classes do (Ginzberg, 1988). He also emphasizes that there is variability in choice patterns and in the timing of crystallization that is really a deviation from normal sequences and timing. He acknowledges that some people may make a stable choice from the time they are young. Others are never able to make a choice because of psychopathology or because of so much pleasure orientation that necessary compromises cannot be made (Ginzberg, 1988).

Holland's Occupational Environment Theory

According to Holland's (1985) *occupational environment theory* of vocational choice, people select occupations that afford environments consistent with their personality types; they are more likely to choose and remain in a field when personal and environmental characteristics are similar (Vondracek, 1991).

Holland outlined six personality types—*realistic, intellectual, social, conventional, enterprising,* and *artistic*—and occupational environments compatible with these types (Lowman, 1991). The personality types were measured with a *self-directed search system.* This system has six scales, each corresponding to one of Holland's personality types. Holland believes that responses to the lengthy inventory of items on each scale reveal individuals' vocational environmental preferences. Thus, individuals striving for a suitable career seek out those environments compatible with their patterns of personal orientations and exhibit these inclinations through their responses to the personality test items. According to Holland (1985), then, it is possible to ascertain occupational orientations by the scores on the personality scales.

Subsequent research offers only partial support to Holland's theory (Brown, 1987). Even though personality often influences vocational choice, individuals sometimes elect and stay in occupations even when their personalities do not match the vocational environment (Wallace-Broscious, Serafica, and Osipow, 1994). Thus, individuals may stay in a job because it offers more security, higher wages, or less travel; because it requires less education; because they are close to retirement; or because they don't want to move geographically. Many workers stay in jobs for which they are not perfectly fitted because of personal or family obligations (Salomone and Sheehan, 1985).

---

occupational environment theory   the theory of vocational choice proposed by Holland.

Highlight

Career Classes

Providing career assistance for college students through credit courses now seems to be quite common. Career classes reach large numbers of students by means of essentially rational techniques. In these classes, counselors generally try to help students gain accurate information about the world of work and about themselves, while also teaching decision-making skills. Textbooks emphasize abilities and values assessments, world-of-work exploration, option generation, decision making, and goal setting. Students are guided through self- and occupational exploration activities in an orderly process.

Overall effectiveness—as measured by self-reports, objective measures, and attitudinal measures—has been reported for these classes. Additionally, there is some evidence that group career treatments generally produce better treatment outcomes than one-on-one career counseling. It has been suggested that a substantial amount of time be spent in such classes and that thoroughness of content results in greater overall effectiveness than shorter group and individual counseling efforts. Other factors, such as modeling and peer support, may also contribute to the particular impact of career classes (McAuliffe, 1991).

There is a need also to formulate theories that can be applied specifically to women, who may behave differently vocationally than do men (Astin, 1984; Forrest and Mikolaitis, 1986).

People Influencing Choice

Parents

Parents influence their adolescent's choice of vocation in a number of ways (Lopez and Andrews, 1987; Young and Friesen, 1992). (Note that once married, people can be significantly influenced by their spouses as well as by their parents [Wilson, 1986].) One way is through direct inheritance: A son or daughter inherits the parents' business, and it seems easier and wiser to continue the family business than to go off on their own. Similarly, parents also exert influence by providing apprenticeship training. For example, a father who is a carpenter teaches his trade to his child by taking him or her along on the job or by arranging an apprenticeship with another carpenter. In the case of low-socioeconomic-status families, the adolescent may not have any other choices. Many mothers or fathers of such families have taught their skills to their children.

Parents influence children's interests and activities from the time they are young by the play materials provided, by the encouragement or discouragement of hobbies and interests, by the activities they encourage their children to participate in, and by the total experiences they provide in the family. Sibling influence also is important in stimulating masculine or feminine interests. A parent who is a musician exerts an influence on the child to take music lessons and to like music in a way that a nonmusician parent can never do. For instance, a mother who is a lawyer usually wants her child to be exposed to that profession from the time the child is little.

Parents provide role models for their children to follow. Although parents may not try to exert any conscious, direct influence, the influence by example is there, especially when the child identifies closely with one or both parents.

Parents sometimes direct, order, or limit the choices of their children by insisting they not go to school or go to a certain school, enroll in a particular major, or start out on a predetermined career. Parents who do so without regard for the talents, interests, and desires of their adolescent may be condemning the youth to a life of work to which she or he is unsuited. Often, an adolescent has no strong objections and accedes to parental wishes

One way that parents might influence their adolescent's choice of vocation is by acting as role models. "Take Your Children to Work" days give the adolescent the opportunity to see his or her parent on the job.

from a desire to please them and from not knowing what else to do. One of the motives of parents for taking such a course of action is to try to get the child to take up an occupation that the parents were always interested in but never got to do; the parents live vicariously through the child. Another motive is that the parents have a vocation in which they have found satisfaction, and so they urge the adolescent to share their goals because they are sure she or he would like it, too. Stories are legion of the father who insists his son attend his alma mater, join the same fraternity, play football as he did, and become a professional like himself. Some parents exert pressure by offering or withholding money or by getting their child into their alma maters. Other parents, of course, have very low educational and occupational expectations for their children, thus limiting the possible vocational choices (Galambos and Silbereisen, 1987).

It is also true, however, that of the one-third who do not choose an occupation in their parent's status category, a number circumvent the entire status structure through extensive education in order to rise far above their parents. In this way, adolescents move from blue-collar positions into professions. Others become socially mobile downward, never aspiring or able to succeed as their parents have.

One study found that when two parents agree on educational expectations and goals for their adolescents, their children are more inclined to adopt the orientations held by both parents than are those who are supported by one parent and denied by the other (Smith, 1991). This same study indicated that agreement with the perceived educational goal of the mother is positively associated with the mother's formal education. In the case of the father, high occupational status—professional, managerial, or substantial business ownership—appears to increase adolescent agreement with perceived paternal educational goals. In summary, when the mother's education or the father's occupational status is high enough, it promotes adolescent agreement with the perceived educational goals of the parents (Smith, 1991).

An additional study found that family functioning dimensions, as evaluated by eleventh-grade students and their parents, were more frequent and stronger predictors of career development than gender, socioeconomic status, and educational achievement (Penick and Jepsen, 1992). In this study, *family functioning* was defined as the ability of the family to achieve objectives. It was measured by such factors as cohesion, expression, degree of conflict, organization, sociability, democratic government, enmeshment, and other factors that had to do with the family system. For example, those families that showed a democratic family style and were able to resolve conflict exerted strong influences on career development of the adolescents in the family.

Peers

Studies of the relative influence of parents and peers on the educational plans of adolescents

---

PERSONAL ISSUES

Career Indecision and Family Enmeshment

Career development literature has largely ignored the role that family dynamics may play in the making of career decisions of individuals. Some adolescents are enmeshed and undifferentiated from their parents. In such situations, little individuation or differentiation has taken place, so adolescents have not extricated themselves from parental domination and have not developed autonomous self-identities. They suffer from low self-esteem, external locus of control, and anxiety, and have trouble making career decisions. Decisions that are made are emotionally based and are reactions to the perceived wishes of parents (Kimmier, Brigman, and Noble, 1990).

(relating to the level of vocation rather than to the particular job) reveal somewhat contradictory findings. Actually, the majority of adolescents hold plans in agreement with those of parents and their friends. Thus, friends reinforce parental aspirations because adolescents associate with peers whose goals are consistent with parental goals.

It has been found that the extent of upward mobility of working-class adolescents depends on the influences of both parents and peers. Working-class adolescents are most likely to aspire to high-ranking occupations if they are influenced in this direction by both parents and peers and are least likely to be high aspirers if they are subjected to neither of these influences.

School Personnel

To what extent do school personnel influence adolescents' vocational plans (Vinton, 1992)? A great deal, according to a study of college freshmen at the University of Maine (Johnson, 1967). Results showed that 39 percent felt that their high school teachers had been most influential in helping them make their decisions. This represented the highest percentage of any of the alternative choices, with "other adult acquaintances" next in rank order of influence, accounting for 19 percent of the responses. The other 42 percent of responses were variously distributed in lesser amounts among the following seven alternatives: father; mother; elementary school teacher or principal; high school counselor, dean, or principal; college teacher; college counselor, dean, or other nonteachers; and close friends.

Teachers exerted a major influence on the plans of college-bound students during the later part of their high school careers. These findings are in agreement with other research that shows the significant influence that school personnel and adult friends exert over vocational choice (Bachhuber, 1992; Saltiel, 1986).

Sex Roles and Vocational Choice

Adolescents are strongly influenced by societal expectations as to the type of work that men and

Adolescents have been strongly influenced by societal expectations of the type of work that men and women should do. Due to the breaking down of cultural expectations and barriers, women in the work force are entering more male-dominated fields and men are entering more female-dominated fields.

women should do (Jozefowicz, Barber, and Mollasis, 1994).

Cultural Expectations

One study measured the gender differences in adolescents' career interests. Overall, gender differences consistent with traditional sex-role stereotypes were found. That is, males scored higher on the Science/Technology scales and females scored higher on the Art/Service scales (Schulenberg, Goldstein, and Vondracek, 1991).

Another survey studied gender differences in childrens' and adolescents' career aspirations. This sample consisted of 148 children who were surveyed at two different times: when the participants were between 8 and 13 years of age, and approximately five years later, when they were between 13 and 18 years of age. Male and female respondents during both phases chose largely nonoverlapping careers. Boys' choices were heavily gendersstereotyped during both developmental periods. In contrast, over one-fourth of the girls during the initial study and close to one-half during the follow-up chose male-dominated occupations. This indicated that the occupations became less stereotyped as the girls became older (Sandberg, Ehrhardt, Ince, and Meyer-Bahlburg, 1991). Traditionally, women have been far more limited than men in the number and categories of jobs available to them. In spite of gains, women still outnumber men 1.5 to 1 in service occupations, 9 to 1 as bank tellers, and 5 to 1 in elementary level teaching. Some 93 percent of nurses, 84 percent of librarians, and 68 percent of social workers are women. Only 26 percent of lawyers and judges and 24 percent of physicians and surgeons are women (U.S. Bureau of the Census, 1996).

This picture is changing (Gerstein, Lichtman, and Barokas, 1988). Strict government enforcement of equal employment opportunity laws has ensured opportunities for women in hitherto restricted fields.

Cultural Barriers

One study was undertaken to determine students' perceptions of barriers to women in entering science and engineering fields. According to students who responded to the survey, fear of resentment from colleagues was a major barrier to womens' participation in science and engineering. This concern was consistent with the findings of studies that report that women in nontraditional fields may suffer the negative consequences of not being chosen as often as romantic partners or as friends. However, as there are more women engineers and scientists, the stigma of deviance will gradually diminish. Just as the negative stereotype of working mothers was removed when womens' labor was required during World War II, negative stereotypes of women engineers and scientists will be eliminated as the societal need for them becomes crucial (Morgan, 1992).

Another study of ninth-grade students in Pennsylvania schools asked them whether they would be willing to enroll in nontraditional occupations. Nontraditional occupations for women

were those occupations in which most of the workers were men. Nontraditional occupations for men were those occupations in which most of the workers were women. Most appealing nontraditional programs for girls statewide were drafting, electronics, auto mechanics, carpentry, and auto body repairs. The least appealing nontraditional programs for girls were brick laying, plumbing, and heating and air conditioning. The nontraditional vocational program choices for boys were medical lab technicians, retail sales, and dental assistants. The least appealing nontraditional programs for boys were cosmetology (hair styling), nursing, and secretarial work (McKenna and Ferrero, 1991).

Female Motivations

Some women, especially the less educated, are not highly motivated to succeed in a full-time, long-term career. Some want only to prepare for an occupation before and for a time after marriage and as financial insurance in case anything should happen to their husbands (Granrose, 1985). However, there is a rapidly increasing trend for women to work full time throughout much of their lives; therefore, an increasing percentage of adolescent girls choose occupations that indicate a permanent, major interest in a career. Most want to balance career ambitions with marriage and raising a family (Cook, 1985). One study measured the midlife career patterns and family status of women and men artists. There were no gender differences noted in midlife occupations; however, women experienced significantly more career discontinuity than did men, and women with discontinuous careers had significantly more children than did women in continuous patterns (Stohs, 1992).

Other Crucial Determinants of Vocational Choice

Mental ability has been shown to be important to vocational choice in several ways.

Intelligence

First, intelligence has been shown to be related to the decision-making ability of the individual.

Bright adolescents are more likely to make vocational choices in keeping with their intellectual abilities, interests, capacities, and opportunities to receive training. The less bright are more likely to make unrealistic choices. They more often choose glamorous or high-prestige occupations for which they are not qualified or even interested except for the prestige. They more often choose what they think parents want them to do or what peers consider desirable rather than what they are capable of doing.

Second, intelligence has been shown to relate to the level of aspiration. Students who show superior academic ability and performance tend to aspire to higher occupational choices than those with lesser ability.

Third, intelligence is related to the ability of the individual to succeed or fail in a given occupation. For this reason, the vocational counselor usually measures level of intelligence as a beginning in assessing the vocational qualifications of a given student, because some occupations require a higher ability than others. However, a high IQ is no guarantee of vocational success, nor is a low IQ a prediction of failure. The measurement may be in error (see Chapter 7). Interest, motivation, other abilities, and various personality traits determine success as much as intelligence does. A high IQ shows only that the individual has the capacity to succeed as far as intelligence is concerned, but actual achievement must also be taken into account. Bright, high-achieving students are generally superior to bright, under-achieving students in study habits, aspiration levels, and professionally oriented career expectations. A bright individual who is poorly motivated and indifferent may fail in an occupation, whereas an individual of average mental ability who is highly motivated, industrious, and conscientious may overachieve and far surpass the brighter person.

Furthermore, where do the IQ requirements for different occupations begin? There is actually a great deal of overlap in tested intelligence among workers in various jobs. How "smart" do you have to be to be a miner? an accountant? a physician? Some people who become physicians, teachers, engineers, or business executives show on tests that their intelligence is much below average for their professions.

Educational institutions are faced with a dilemma in deciding on the cutoff point below

HIGHLIGHT

Male and Female College Graduates—
Seven Months Later

A survey of 346 college graduates (51 percent men and 49 percent women) from an eastern university seven months after graduation revealed the following male/female differences (Martinez, Sedlacek, and Bachhuber, 1985):

> Similar percentages of men and women were employed or involved in further education.
> Men were more likely than women to report they were employed in their chosen fields or in satisfactory positions. Women were more likely in the process of seeking jobs in their chosen fields.

> Men were more likely than women to enter engineering and mathematics; women were more likely to hold jobs in education, the social sciences, and clerical fields.
> Men were more likely than women to have been hired by large corporations.
> About the same percentage of men and women held jobs in management or business administration.
> Men earned significantly more than women ($18,220 vs. $12,798).

which they will not admit students. Although, SAT scores are helpful in predicting possibilities of success or failure for groups of students, they are not sure indicators of the individual. Counselors must be extremely cautious in interpreting test results, particularly in predicting success or failure based on mental ability alone. Many individuals who are now successful in professional fields would not be admitted to the training programs if they had to pass the entrance exams today.

Aptitudes and Special Abilities

Different occupations require different aptitudes and special abilities. For example, mechanical ability tests may cover information required of mechanics, such as types of gears and wrenches, gauges, strength of materials, sizes of fasteners, and certain aptitudes such as manual and finger dexterity. Some occupations require strength, others speed, and still others good eye-hand coordination or good spatial visualization. Some require special talent such as artistic, musical, or verbal skills. Some fields require creativity, originality, and autonomy; others require conformity, cooperation, and ability to take direction. Possession or lack of certain aptitudes may be crucial in immediate job success or in the possibility of success with training and experience. Certainly, increasing technology requires more and more specialized training and abilities (Hoyt, 1987).

The measurement of some aptitudes, however, is not an exact science; therefore, it cannot always be determined which people are most likely to succeed in particular occupations. The fault lies generally with the tests used. Before relying too much on aptitude tests, counselors and students should be certain that the instruments used are valid measurements of the aptitudes tested.

Interests

Interest is another factor considered important to vocational success. The more interested people are in their work, the more likely they will succeed. To put it another way, the more their interests parallel those who are already successful in a field, the more likely they are to be successful, too, all other things being equal. Vocational interest tests are

based on this last principle: They measure clusters of interests similar to those of successful people in the field to predict the possibilities of success. The individual is counseled to consider vocations in the fields of greatest interest.

Intelligence, ability, opportunities, and other factors must be related to interests for success in a field (Prediger and Brandt, 1991). Factor analysis of the ***Strong Vocational Interest Blank*** (Strong, 1943) indicates that interests may be subdivided and grouped to some degree by level. There are professional-scientific, professional-technical, and subprofessional-technical groups, as well as others. Interests are related to both the field and level of occupational choice. Interests that are based on abilities are stronger and more realistic than those influenced primarily by such things as prestige factors and group values. However, there is only a low correlation between interests and aptitudes.

Job Opportunities

Being interested does not mean that jobs are available. Some employment fields, such as agricultural workers, are becoming smaller; others, such as clerical workers, are becoming larger. There has been a continued shift toward white-collar occupations. This means youths need to control interests as well as be controlled by them, for interests and job availability are not synonymous (Mitchell, 1988).

What are the employment opportunities in the professions? Table 16.1 shows increases from 1994 to 2005 in selected occupations (U.S. Bureau of the Census, 1996). The jobs showing the greatest percentage increase in employment from 1994 to 2005 are (in declining order) personal and home care aides, home health care aides, computer engineers, computer systems analysts, physical therapists, human services workers, and medical assistants. The jobs employing the greatest number of workers in the year 2005 will be general managers and executives, secretaries,

Strong Vocational Interest Blank a test that measures suitability for different vocations according to interests.

TABLE 16.1 Increase in Employment in Different Occupations, 1994 to 2005

OCCUPATION	TOTAL EMPLOYMENT (IN THOUSANDS)		PERCENT INCREASE
	1994	2005	(1994–2005)
Secretaries (except legal and medical)	2,842	3,109	9.4
Teachers, preschool and kindergarten	462	602	30.3
General managers, executives	3,046	3,512	15.3
Financial managers	768	950	23.6
Teachers, secondary	1,340	1,726	28.8
Accountants, auditors	962	1,083	12.6
Physicians	539	659	22.3
Child care workers	750	1,005	32.8
Food service, lodging managers	579	771	33
Social workers	557	744	33.5
Lawyers	656	839	27.9
Licensed practical nurses	702	899	28
Registered nurses	1,906	2,379	24.8
Electricians, electronics engineers	349	417	19.7
Human services workers	168	293	74.5
Computer programmers	537	601	12
Computer systems analysts	483	928	92.1
College & university faculty	823	972	29
Medical assistants	216	327	59
Physical therapists	102	183	80
Security and financial service workers	246	335	36.6
Computer engineers	145	372	101.9
Personal and home care aids	179	391	118.7
Home health aids	420	848	105.7

Source: U.S. Bureau of the Census, *Statistical Abstract of the United States, 1996* (Washington, DC: U.S. Government Printing Office, 1996), p. 408.

registered nurses, secondary teachers, and accountants and auditors.

Job Rewards and Satisfactions

One factor to consider when selecting a vocation is financial rewards. Table 16.2 shows an estimated starting pay for 1995 graduates with bachelor's degrees in different fields. Actual salaries vary in different parts of the country.

There is increasing evidence that student intentions and motivations in selecting college courses are changing. In the middle 1980s, more than half of high school students queried indicated they wanted to choose a humanities curriculum and people-oriented studies (e.g., social work), which emphasized nonmaterial values (Rosseel, 1985a, 1985b). Today, students choose options that have favorable professional opportunities and that are prestigious. (Engineering, com-

TABLE 16.2   Average Offered Salary to Start for 1995 Graduates with a Bachelor's Degree

Field	Average Salary, 1995
Engineering	$35,612
Computer science	33,712
Chemistry	29,340
Mathematics	30,271
Marketing, sales	25,400
Accounting	27,926
Humanities	22,811
General business administration	25,711
Social science	24,010

Source: U.S. Bureau of the Census, *Statistical Abstract of the United States, 1996* (Washington, DC: U.S. Government Printing Office, 1996), p. 190.

puter science, and business administration are popular options.)

Socioeconomic Status and Prestige Factors

There are a number of socioeconomic and prestige factors that influence vocational choice.

Choosing the Familiar

A study of the occupations chosen by over 1,000 boys and girls in a rural county in New York State and about 250 boys and girls from a school in Brooklyn showed that only 150 occupations were chosen by boys and even fewer by girls (Ramsey, n.d.). The occupations chosen could be grouped into two categories: those that were familiar to the rural community and those that were glamorous and prestigious.

HIGHLIGHT

Work, Military, or College?

One study took data from the Youth in Transition Study (YIT) directed by Jerald Bachman at the University of Michigan. The study attempted to identify those factors that led boys to enter the work force, the military, or college after graduation from high school.

Work was chosen by boys from large families who were in the lower socioeconomic strata, were enrolled in high school vocational tracks, and were working more hours in their senior year, as compared with those in the college group. Compared with members of any other context, workers tended to have the lowest intellectual ability and to have friends who were the least impressed by going to college. Boys who early on believed that their parents wanted them to enter the work force after high school were significantly more likely to enter work over the military context.

In relation to those who went into the *military*, this was chosen by boys who tended to express little desire to attend college, were generally from large families in

the lower socioeconomic strata, were enrolled in a vocational track, and were poor students when contrasted to the boys headed for college. The military bound, as opposed to those headed for one of the other choices, were most likely to come from nonfarm backgrounds, to have failed a grade, and to believe their parents would be happy if they served in the military. The military group tended to express more hawkish attitudes, but were not significantly more hawkish than the college-bound group.

College choice was accepted by boys who came from the smallest families and the highest socioeconomic-status backgrounds, had the highest grade-point averages and were in a college track, had a strong intention of going to college, and worked the least number of hours in twelfth grade. Boys with higher intellectual ability and friends who were impressed by going to college were more likely to go to college instead of to work (Owens, 1992).

On completion of high school, various factors determine whether an adolescent will enter the work force, attend college, or join the military. These high school ROTC cadets appear to have already made their choice.

Socioeconomic status tends to influence the knowledge and understanding youths have of different occupations. Middle-class parents are more able than working-class parents to develop broad vocational interests and awareness of opportunities beyond the local community. Socially disadvantaged adolescents have seen less, read less, heard less about, and experienced less variety in their environments in general and have fewer opportunities than the socially privileged. As a result, low-socioeconomic-status males and females are inclined to take the only jobs they know about at the time they enter the labor market. The socioeconomic and cultural backgrounds of youths influence their job knowledge and their job preferences.

Prestige and Value

Some adolescents want to go into an occupation simply because it sounds glamorous or has high prestige. There are at least five commonly accepted assumptions about occupational values in our culture: (1) white-collar work is superior, (2) self-employment is superior, (3) "clean" occupations are superior, (4) the importance of a business occupation depends on the size of the business, and (5) personal service is degrading (that is, it is better to be employed by an enterprise than to do the same work for an individual).

There have been other attempts at classifying values. One method has been to group values into three major value clusters: people oriented, extrinsic reward oriented, and self-expression oriented. Vocational selection will depend partly on which values are considered more important. Community values also influence youths. Jobs considered most prestigious and with the highest status are more desired by youths than those with lower prestige and status.

Social Class and Aspirations

Middle-class youths tend to choose occupations with higher status than do lower-class youths. There are a number of considerations in determining why this is so. To aspire to a position is one thing; to expect to actually achieve it is another. Lower-class youths more often than middle-class youths aspire to jobs they do not expect to achieve, but the fact that lower-class youths realize the remoteness of reaching their goal makes them lower their level of aspirations. Of course, sometimes guidance counselors, teachers, parents, or others try to persuade lower-status youths from aspiring to higher occupational levels, when—given sufficient incentives and help—they might be able to succeed at them (Yogev and Roditi, 1987). Many lower-socioeconomic-status youths are of superior ability and could succeed at high-status jobs if they had a chance.

Still another factor enters in: a correlation between academic ability and socioeconomic status.

The higher the status, the higher the academic performance; and the better the students' academic performances, the more prestigious the occupations to which they aspire. Apparently, students see their high academic ability as providing them access to high-prestige occupations. Occupational aspiration is related to both social class and academic aptitude.

Occupational Attainment

Across both educational and economic backgrounds, students in one study rated education, intelligence, and the type of occupation an individual applied for as the most important determinants of occupational attainment. Further, the higher the prestige level of the occupation, the more evident this effect was. Each of these influences was perceived as more important than other factors, such as race and gender (Klaczynski, 1991).

Race and Aspirations

When race is considered apart from social class, there is no conclusive evidence that race alone is the determinative factor in occupational aspirations. However, African American youths of lower socioeconomic status have lower aspirations, just as do White youths of lower status. Regardless of aspirations, there are fewer employment opportunities for youths than for adults and fewer opportunities for African Americans than for Whites.

One study did find differences between Asian Americans and White Americans in their occupational aspirations. Asian Americans place greater emphasis on extrinsic and security occupational value clusters (e.g., making more money and having a stable, secure future) in comparison with White Americans (Leong, 1991).

In another study, the career aspirations and expectations of African American, Mexican American, and White students were compared. Results suggested that (1) there seemed to be more gender than ethnic differences in students' career aspirations and expectations, (2) differences in career aspirations and expectations among Mexican American and White students followed traditional gender patterns, and (3) with some exceptions, the career expectations of students resembled the distribution of jobs in the labor market (Arbona and Novy, 1991).

Adolescents and Unemployment

One of the major social problems in the United States is unemployed youths.

Numbers

If youths, aged 16 to 19, who are in the labor force are considered, the unemployment rates in 1995 were 14.5 percent for Whites, 24 percent for

CROSS-CULTURAL CONCERNS

Occupational Stereotypes of Asian Americans

One study investigated the presence of occupational stereotyping in the ratings by 194 White college students of Asian Americans (Leong and Hayes, 1990). Asian Americans were perceived as being less likely to be successful as insurance salespersons and more likely to be successful as engineers, computer scientists, and mathematicians. In actual fact, these stereotypes were consistent with observations of other investigators that Asian Americans tend to gravitate toward scientific and theoretical careers, but avoid social and verbal-persuasive careers. In this case, their ethnic stereotype was based partly on their earned reputation.

There were some gender stereotypes revealed, however, that indicated clear prejudices. Men were seen to be more qualified to seek training as engineers, economists, and police officers, whereas women were seen as more qualified for training as secretaries and elementary teachers.

Hispanics, and 36 percent for African Americans (U.S. Bureau of the Census, 1996, p. 413). Figure 16.1 shows these figures plus comparable ones for young adults 20 to 24 years of age. Altogether, this means that 2.6 million young people, aged 16 to 24, were out of work. The highest unemployment is among African American teenagers, and this is true whether they are in school or not. Also, the jobless rate of Hispanic youths is above the rate for their White counterparts but much lower than that for African Americans. These statistics probably underestimate the extent of the problem, for many adolescents who get discouraged and stop looking for work are not counted as unemployed. This high rate of joblessness means more crime, more drug addiction, more social unrest, and less income for many poor families.

Causes of Unemployment

Why is the rate of unemployment among youths so high? One reason is that they have little train-ing and skill, little experience, and many are able to take only part time jobs while in school. They are confined to a narrower range of the less-skilled occupations, at which many can work only part time. Youths with high school diplomas have better chances in the labor market than do drop-outs, as is reflected by lower unemployment rates among graduates. Figure 16.2 shows the employ-ment status of high school graduates and drop-outs in the labor force. Many employers require educational degrees that have little relationship to job skills; dropouts are often denied work not be-cause they cannot do the job but because they do not have the necessary credentials.

Many unemployed youths are recent college graduates who are searching for first-time jobs. Some of these graduates have majored in social studies and other subjects that do not directly pre-pare them for employment. For some, it is fairly normative to be out of work for a while before they can find something that is compatible with their education.

State licensing boards often operate to re-strict entry into business. The Colorado Board of

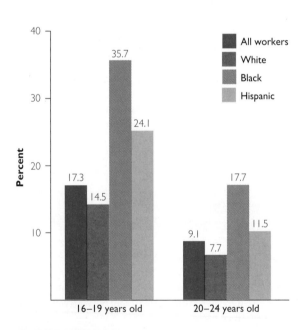

FIGURE 16.1   Civilian Labor Force Unemployment, by Race and Age, 1995

Source: U.S. Bureau of the Census, *Statistical Abstract of the United States, 1996* (Washington, DC: U.S. Government Printing Office, 1996), p. 413.

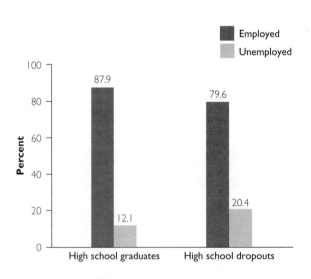

FIGURE 16.2   Employment Status of High School Graduates and School Dropouts Who Are in the Labor Force and Not Enrolled In School, 1993

Source: U.S. Bureau of the Census, *Statistical Abstract of the United States, 1996* (Washington, DC: U.S. Government Printing Office, 1996), p. 176.

Cosmetology, for example, requires that a prospective hairdresser take 1,650 hours of instruction, including 100 hours of supervised practice at shampooing. Such requirements hit the young hardest, especially those who seek to combine work with schooling. Union requirements also limit participation of the young. It takes time and experience to acquire membership in a union; therefore, adolescents are not able to accept jobs in the construction industry, for example, which could be an important source of part-time and summer employment. Many unions also limit the number of apprentices that can be trained. In cases of layoffs, seniority rules work in favor of the older, more experienced workers; youths are the first to lose their jobs.

Minimum wage legislation may sometimes affect unemployment. When the minimum wage goes up relative to the low productivity of inexperienced youths, employers hesitate to hire them, often preferring older people if they are available. Furthermore, job turnover among youths is higher than among older, more stable workers. Some employers will not hire anybody under age 21 for steady jobs; they want those who have a greater degree of maturity.

Many jobs in transportation, construction, manufacturing, and agriculture are closed even to youths available for full-time year-round work because of the legal minimum ages for hazardous work. Although state laws differ, the general standard is that all wage employment is barred to those under age 14, all employment during school hours is barred to those under age 16, and certain hazardous jobs and industries are barred to youths under age 18.

On the other hand, the average period of unemployment among youths is shorter than among older workers. Females average somewhat shorter periods of unemployment than males, and Whites shorter periods than non-Whites. The fact that half of all unemployed youths have no more than four weeks without work reflects the seasonal and intermittent nature of their unemployment and the rapid turnover of jobs.

Education and Employment

The educational backgrounds of youths continue to improve. Studies of dropouts consistently show that the high school graduate is superior to the early dropout in each of the following areas: (1) number of promotions and raises, (2) holding on to one job, (3) fewer and shorter periods of unemployment, (4) higher job satisfaction, (5) more recreational pursuits, (6) more hobbies, and (7) greater frequency of additional training.

One study investigated the relationship between early work experience among White and non-White youths and their implications for subsequent school enrollment and employment (Steel, 1991). What effect does early work experience have on youths' socioeconomic attainment and social mobility? Are today's youths better off for having worked during the high school years? The answer appears to be a qualified yes, at least for the White youths in this study. Early employment was associated with higher subsequent school enrollment for White youths, with the exception of White males working full time or nearly full time. Among White males and among African Americans, however, working longer hours was associated with lower subsequent school enrollment. Thus, there appears to be different mechanisms operating for Whites and non-Whites and, to a lesser extent, for White women and men. Early employment appears to be compatible with continued enrollment for White men earning low to moderate amounts. However, among non-Whites and White men working close to full time, early employment appears to represent a competing alternative to schooling. The more intense the work experience, the less likely that these youths are to continue their schooling. This suggests that early employment may indeed socialize some youths toward employment (as contrasted to schooling) and that non-White youths and White males working close to full time will be more likely to be affected (Steel, 1991).

SUMMARY

1. Choosing and preparing for a vocation is one of the most important development tasks of adolescence. Done wisely and realistically, it enables individuals to enter vocations for which they are well suited, in which they find satisfaction and fulfillment, and which are needed by society. Done haphazardly and foolishly, it leads to frustration, discontent, unhappiness, and social disapproval.

2. The process of choosing a job or career is often a complicated one. Ginzberg emphasized that it is a long-term process comprising many small decisions, each of which affects the next decision and further limits subsequent choices. Choices made early in high school affect the availability of later options. Thus, there is a fatalistic element to the process: Individuals do not have complete freedom but are limited by what they have already done and are also subject to many influences in the present. This is more true of low-socioeconomic-status adolescents, who are caught in a series of circumstances, some of which they are powerless to control. Adolescents from higher-socioeconomic-status groups are more fortunate because they have more options and more resources to use in taking advantage of options.

3. Ginzberg divides the process of occupational choice into three stages: fantasy stage (up to age 11), tentative stage (11 to 17 years), and realistic stage (from age 17 on). Research generally supports the broad outlines of this theory, though the sequence, nature, and timing of the stages may not always be the same. Also, career choices do not always end with the first job.

4. Influences on development have been divided into three categories: normative, age-graded influences; normative, history-graded influences; and nonnormative life-event influences.

5. Holland theorized that people select occupations that afford environments consistent with their personality types. He outlined six personality types: realistic, intellectual, social, conventional, enterprising, and artistic.

6. Career classes can help students make decisions about occupations.

7. There are numerous influences on an adolescent's vocational choice: parents, peers, and school personnel. Concepts of sex roles, cultural expectations and barriers, and female motivations also influence vocational choice. Other crucial determinants of vocational choice are intelligence, aptitude, and special abilities; interests; job opportunities; job rewards and satisfactions; socioeconomic status and prestige factors; social class; and race.

8. One of the major problems in the United States is unemployment among youths. Rates among African Americans and other minorities are higher than among Whites. There are numerous causes: the massive youth population; lack of training, skill, and experience of youths; restrictive licensing and union requirements; minimum wage legislation; and lack of education.

KEY TERMS

compromise with reality theory **380**

Strong Vocational Interest Blank **389**

occupational environment theory **383**

THOUGHT QUESTIONS

1. Why is making a wise vocational choice considered one of the most important developmental tasks of adolescence?

2. Why do so many adolescents make poor vocational choices?

3. Two theories of vocational choice have been outlined—those of Ginzberg and Holland. Explain the major emphasis of each. Which do you find most appealing? Which seems least true to life? Explain.

4. Have you ever attended a career education class? What was the result? In what ways was it helpful? In what ways was it not helpful?

5. Should parents have any voice about the vocation their adolescent chooses? What's the parental role in this regard?

6. How influential are peers over vocational choice?

7. Has any person at school been particularly influential in your choice of vocation? Discuss.

8. What role do gender stereotypes play in vocational choices? Which vocations are limited for women? Do you think that some vocations are unsuitable for women?

9. If a woman enters an occupation that has been traditionally masculine, such as science or engineering, does she suffer negative consequences for her vocational choice? What can be done to overcome stereotype prejudices in relation to vocational choice?

10. Is it possible for a woman to have a full-time career, raise two children, and be happily married? Explain. What are your feelings about entering into a dual-career marriage?

11. Just because a person is interested in a particular vocation, does this mean he or she should go into it? What other factors ought to be taken into consideration?

12. How do you go about finding out if you have an aptitude or special ability suitable for a particular vocation?

13. Should vocations be chosen on the basis of job rewards? What other factors are important?

14. Are job prestige and status valid considerations in choosing a vocation? Explain.

15. Is going into the military a suitable solution for the adolescent who does not know what he or she wants to do? Why or why not?

16. If you had an adolescent who did not know what he or she wanted to do in life, what role as a parent do you feel you should play? What can be done to help him or her find an answer to this dilemma?

17. If you had an adolescent whose only ambition in life was to get married, what would you do? What role do you feel you should play?

18. What can be done about the high unemployment rate among adolescents? Especially among African American adolescents?

19. Is a good education necessary to get a good job? Explain.

20. How great a part does chance play in the choice of a vocation?

SUGGESTED READING

Allatt, P., and Yeandle, F. (1992). *Youth Unemployment and the Family: Voices of Disordered Time*. New York: Routledge.

Carp, Frances M. (Ed.). (1991). *Lives of Career Women: Approaches to Work, Marriage, Children*. New York: Insight Books (Plenum Press).

Greenberger, E., and Steinberg, L. (1986). *When Teenagers Work*. New York: Basic Books.

Peterson, A., and Mortimer, J. (Eds.). (1994). *Youth Unemployment and Society*. New York: Cambridge University Press.

17

Adolescent Alienation

Sometimes, adolescents who are emotionally upset turn outward, expressing pent-up emotions through various forms of acting-out behavior: truancy, aggressive behavior, promiscuity, theft, assault, rape, even the destruction of one's own life or that of another. For the most part, such adolescents feel alienated from friends, family, and school. They do not function in the mainstream of adolescent and adult society. Their actions are an expression of their feelings of alienation, which they have found difficult to deal with in socially approved ways (Calabrese, 1987; Calabrese and Adams, 1990).

In this chapter, we will discuss three manifestations of disturbed, acting-out behavior: running away, suicide, and juvenile delinquency.

Running Away

National estimates indicate that the number of adolescents who run away from home each year range from one to two million (Rohr, 1996). In 1991, the National Network of Runaway Youth Services (NNRYS) reported that the current mean estimate of runaways per year is two million.

Problem Areas

Current research indicates that there are problems in the following areas: family relationships and parental problems, delinquent behavior, academic problems, social relationship difficulties, and problems symptomatic in psychopathology (Rohr, 1996). Problems in *family relationships* consist of such behavior as parental rejection, constant downgrading of the child, separation and divorce, intolerable and conflictual home conditions, sibling rivalry, problems in communicating with members of the family, family members not expressing love for each other, and a mutual lack of care for each other. *Parental problem areas* include behavior such as parents using excessive punishment, parents with a history of drug use, and inadequately managing children's behavior. *Delinquent problem behavior* includes such things as stealing, disobedience, legal difficulties, and having been arrested as a delinquent. *School problems* include such things as having a negative attitude toward school, poor problem-solving skills, and school behavior problems. *Poor social relationships* include difficulties with peers. Symptoms of *psychopathology* include problems such as anxiety, suicidal tendencies, physical and/or sexual abuse, and alcohol and drug usage (Rohr, 1996).

There does seem to be sufficient evidence to say that causal factors suggest a complex interaction among *family factors* (conflict), *school stress* (academic difficulties), and *interpersonal communication* as causal agents. Runaways often have strong egos, resent being "put down," and show impulsiveness and poor judgment. Unable to control their environment (whether at home, at school, or in the community) or to communicate with or relate to adults, they cannot tolerate sustained, close, interpersonal relationships. If runaways stay away, the negative effects, such as curtailment of schooling, may be long lasting, seriously limiting his or her future employment chances. Running away will likely compound their problems. Many turn to drugs, crime, prostitution, or other illegal activities.

Environmental Causes

Of all the background factors that relate to running away, a *poor home environment* is the central reason for leaving home. Typically, runaways report conflict with parents, the need for independence, rejection and hostile control, and problematic marital relationships with much internal conflict and family disorganization (Loeb, Burke, and Boglarsky, 1986). From one point of view, running away is viewed as a conflict-induced effort on the part of youths to evolve a differentiated self when imbedded within a family that inhibits freedom and the development of individuation (Crespi and Sabatelli, 1993).

Runaway girls generally view their parents as more controlling and punitive of their behavior in the home, whereas many runaway boys report minimal family control and supervision, which leads to outside forces, such as peers, becoming causal agents in running away. Thus, low levels of control of boys especially allows them opportunities to leave. Many parents of runaways are so absorbed with their own problems that they have little time to consider their children. Such youths report they are not wanted at home.

A study of 30 male and female adolescent runaways representing various ages, family structures, and ethnic groups emphasized problems with parents as a major reason for running away. Table 17.1 shows the replies when these adolescents were asked "What are some of the reasons for your leaving home?" When the parents were asked why their adolescents left home, they replied that their children did not want to listen to authority, were afraid of being punished, did

TABLE 17.1   Runaways' Reasons for Leaving Home

Reason	Number of Runaways Indicating Reason
Arguments with parents	7
Doesn't like stepfather	1
Doesn't like mother and father	1
Father raped me	1
Don't want a curfew	1
Father beat me when I was drinking	1
Mother beat me	1
Mother punishes me severely	1
Don't like it at home	1
Nobody understands me	1
No freedom	1
Fighting with siblings	4
Parents don't like boyfriend	1
Fighting with mother over boyfriend	1
To go with boyfriend	2
School problems	5

Source: E. Spillane-Grieco, "Characteristics of a Helpful Relationship: A Study of Empathetic Understanding and Positive Appeal between Runaways and Their Parents," *Adolescence, 19* (1984): 63–75. Reprinted by permission.

not want a curfew, or wanted to be free; or they left home because of boyfriends, arguments over friends, or problems at school. There were 14 parents who said they did not know why their adolescents left home (Spillane-Grieco, 1984).

Another study made a distinction between *adolescent runaways* and **throwaways** (Adams, Gullotta, and Clancy, 1985). Runaways left of their own volition because of personal family conflict, alienation, and poor social relations. Throwaways had been encouraged, asked, or were forced to leave home (Hier, Korboot, and Schweitzer, 1990). Throwaways, more often than runaways, reported that their parents did not get along with one another, said unpleasant things about them, called them names, and frequently punished and beat them.

Pressures, difficulties, and failures at school also contribute to running away. Children who are slow learners, left back to repeat grades, or ostracized by school personnel seek to escape the school environment that rejects them. An examination of the prevalence of arithmetic and reading difficulties in 16- to 21-year-old clients of a shelter for runaway and homeless street youths found that 52 percent had reading disabilities, 29 percent had trouble with arithmetic and written work, and only 20 percent were normal achievers. The groups did not differ in the reported history of substance abuse, maltreatment, or court involvement (Barwick and Siegel, 1996).

Typologies

Since all runaways are not alike, there have been numerous efforts to classify them according to type and motive. The simplest classification is to divide them into two groups: the *running from* and the *running to* (Roberts, 1982). The "running from" adolescents could not tolerate their home situation or one or both parents. The "running to" adolescents were pleasure seekers, running to places or people providing a wide variety of activities.

In a discussion of ungovernable and incorrigible girls, one study outlined three distinct types of runaway girls: the rootless, the anxious, and the terrified. The **rootless runaway** is a pleasure seeker who seeks immediate gratification. She has dropped out of school, quit a series of jobs, used drugs, and is sexually active. She was lavishly

praised by parents, but they never set limits on her. When the family began to get frightened and started to set limits, the girl rebelled and ran away.

The **anxious runaway** is from a multiproblem family and often had to do household chores, care for younger siblings, and worry about finances. If her father was at home, he might have drunk excessively and been physically and verbally abusive, so she left temporarily, usually for a few hours or overnight, seeking someone to talk to, often a friend's mother. The **terrified runaway** flees from her father's or stepfather's sexual advances toward her. She would invite friends to stay with her when she was home or stayed away as often as she could to avoid being alone with her sexually abusive father.

One of the most helpful classifications arranged runaways along a parent-youth conflict continuum (Roberts, 1982). Figure 17.1 illustrates its categories. The 0–1 category includes youths who want to travel but whose parents arranged a compromise so that the youths would not strike out alone. *Runaway explorers* wanted to travel for adventure and to assert their independence. They informed their parents where they were going, usually by note, and then left without permission. If not picked up by the police, they generally returned home on their own. *Runaway social pleasure seekers* usually had conflict with parents over what they felt was a major issue: dating a certain boy, an early curfew, or grounding that prevented them from attending an important event. They sneaked out of the house to engage in the forbidden activity and either sneaked back in or stayed in a friend's house overnight, usually telephoning the parents the next morning to ask to come home.

Runaway manipulators usually had more serious ongoing conflict with parents over home chores, choice of friends, and so forth, so they

---

throwaways adolescents who have been told to leave home.

rootless runaway one who runs away from home for fun and to seek pleasure and gratification.

anxious runaway a runaway who comes from a multiproblem family.

terrified runaway a runaway who is escaping sexual or physical abuse.

FIGURE 17.1
Formulation of the Degree of Parent-Youth Conflict Continuum

Source: A. R. Roberts, "Adolescent Runaways in Suburbia: A New Typology," *Adolescence, 17* (Summer 1982): 379–396. Reprinted by permission.

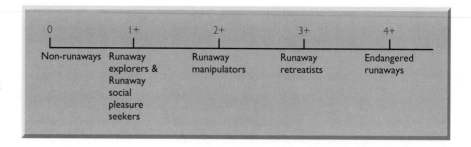

0	1+	2+	3+	4+
Non-runaways	Runaway explorers & Runaway social pleasure seekers	Runaway manipulators	Runaway retreatists	Endangered runaways

tried to manipulate parents by running away and then forcing a return on their own terms.

Runaway retreatists experienced even more conflict and tension at home, with frequent yelling, hitting, or throwing of objects. The majority of adolescents had one or more school problems and retreated into drugs or getting drunk daily prior to running away.

Endangered runaways left to escape recurring physical and/or sexual abuse inflicted on them by parents or stepparents, often while in a drunken state. These youths often used drugs and had drinking problems themselves. Usually, a beating or threat of a beating precipitated running away (Roberts, 1982). Physical and/or sexual abuse of both boys and girls is often a reason for running away (Janus, Burgess, and McCormack, 1987).

Youths who are both physically and sexually abused are distinctly different in many respects from other runaways. They experience the worst of both worlds. A large proportion encounter a wide range of personal problems and come from multiproblem families. These families involved in multiple forms of maltreatment have children who are significantly more likely than those in other families to experience a greater number of functional problems and stress (Kurtz, Kurtz, and Jarvis, 1991). It is quite obvious that not all runaways are the same or leave home for the same reasons.

The most recent survey by the NNRYS (1991) of 50,000 youths in 146 runaway facilities were surveyed. Results indicated that 46 percent of the youths had a substance abuse problem (with 14 percent being addicted), 31 percent reporting suffering physical abuse, and 21 percent reporting having been sexually abused; 61 percent reported being depressed (with 21 percent having had suicidal ideations). From this point of view, runaway

and homeless adolescents are considered at high risk for drug abuse, HIV infection, sexually transmitted diseases, and pregnancies. Studies document high rates of alcohol consumption and illicit drug use, infrequent condom use, multiple sexual partners, and frequent prostitution among runaway and homeless youths. However, virtually all of the research focuses on runaway street youths from New York City and California; it cannot be assumed that these runaway youths are representative of runaways from other parts of the country (Zimet et al., 1995).

Counterliterature rejects the psychopathology explanation for all youths and suggests that many have normal IQs, positive self-concepts, and are not particularly psychopathic, depressed, or emotionally disturbed. From this point of view, running away is seen as a function of normal adolescent development toward independence. It can be viewed as a positive psychological sign. The adolescent running away is generally not a cry for help but a search for adventure.

Help

Since 1978, the National Runaway Youth Program within the U.S. Youth Development Bureau has promoted assistance to youths who are vulnerable to exploitation and to dangerous encounters. Aid is now offered nationwide. This program also funds the National Toll-Free Communication System to enable youths to contact their families and/or centers where they can get help. Most of the individual programs throughout the country have developed multiple-service components to meet various needs of young people. Other community social service agencies and juvenile justice/law enforcement systems use their services. Although youths may be arrested

Consequences of Running Away

Much of the literature on runaways is devoted to analyzing the reasons for adolescents' departures from their homes. However, it is equally important to examine what happens to the young person, particularly the young woman, after she leaves. The most likely consequences are dropping out of school, sexual promiscuity, prostitution, and substance abuse. The runaway girl living on the street is likely to be exposed to others who engage in such behaviors (Perlman, 1980).

Once on the street, runaways tend to become involved in a social network composed of other runaways and street people who engage in deviant, often illegal, acts of various sorts to support themselves. If a girl has run away because of sexual abuse, the chances of her turning to prostitution or drug dealing to support herself increase (Simons and Whitbeck, 1991).

She has typically been neglected and deprived of love. She is in search of security and human attachments. Because she must fend for herself, she also finds the promise of food and a warm bed attractive, in exchange for sexual favors.

At the same time, she is unlikely to use effective birth control methods, as she is unable to admit to herself that she is sexually active. She also probably has difficulty in gaining access to reliable contraceptives. She uses typical excuses for not needing contraceptives (e.g., "I'm too young to get pregnant," "I don't have sex that often," or "It spoils spontaneity"). The likely consequences are pregnancy and disease.

Only about half of teenage pregnancies actually produce teenage mothers, with the remainder terminating in miscarriage or abortion. Nevertheless, motherhood is the option for the other half. Among these, poverty, inadequate nutrition, lack of prenatal care, and the abuse of drugs and alcohol have a negative impact on the pregnancies. After delivery, these young mothers lack the financial resources and help normally provided by family and other support systems. The future for both mother and child is not a promising one.

for running away, efforts are being made to abolish juvenile governance over runaway offenders. This will keep the courts from imprisoning children for noncriminal behavior.

Suicide

Adolescent suicide is an upsetting problem. How often does it occur? Who does it? What are the causes and motives? How might it be prevented?

Frequency

The incidence of suicide among children, especially among those under age 13, is rare. It is rare because children are still dependent on love objects for gratification; they have not yet completed the process of identification within themselves; thus, the thought of turning hostility toward themselves is too painful and frightening. Only as children find more self-identity can they be independent enough to commit suicide.

The suicide mortality rate increases with age, reaching a peak in males over 85 years of age and in females at ages 45 to 54 (U.S. Bureau of the Census, 1996). Figure 17.2 shows the trends. The rate per 100,000 among males aged 15 to 24 is 22.4; among females aged 15 to 24, the suicide rate is 4.1. The suicide rate in the 15- to 24-year age group has tripled over the past 40 years (Hepworth, Farley, and Griffiths, 1986). The suicide rate among college students varies considerably from school to school. The rate is extraordinarily high at a few schools such as Harvard and Yale, indicating there may be elements in some college environments conducive to suicide ("College Suicides," 1980). The suicide rate is higher in nonreligious youths than in those who are religious (Stein et al., 1992).

In the 1990s, suicide was second only to accidents as the leading cause of death among young

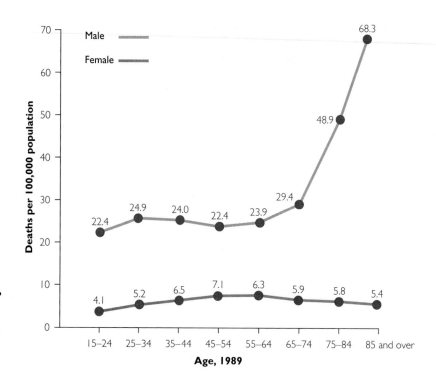

FIGURE 17.2   Suicide Mortality, by Sex and Age Groups, 1993

Source: U.S. Bureau of the Census, *Statistical Abstract of the United States, 1996* (Washington, DC: U.S. Government Printing Office, 1996), p. 97.

Americans (Gutstein and Rudd, 1990). Only a small percentage of attempted suicides succeed. Estimates of the ratio of suicide attempts to fatalities vary from as high as 120 to 1 in children to 5 to 1 in adults. About 5,000 young people between 15 and 24 years of age successfully commit suicide each year (Suicide Prevention Center, 1984). Females attempt suicide much more frequently than do males, but many more males than females are successful in completing the suicide. One of the reasons males more often succeed is that they frequently use more violent means—hanging, jumping from heights, single vehicle automobile accidents, or shooting or stabbing themselves—whereas females more often use passive and less dangerous methods, such as taking pills. Females more often make multiple threats but less often really want to kill themselves or actually do it (Peck and Warner, 1995).

Causes and Motives

Why do adolescents attempt to take their own lives? What are their motives? There are a variety of contributing factors. A significant body of empirical literature suggests that suicidal behavior in the teenage years is associated with family processes (Koopmans, 1995).

Suicidal adolescents tend to come from disturbed family backgrounds (Henry et al., 1993; Wright, 1985). There may have been much conflict between the parents and between the parents and children and considerable family violence, or the parents may have manifested negative, rejecting attitudes toward the children (Wade, 1987). Frequent unemployment and economic stress in the home may be a factor, as well as early parental physical or emotional deprivation, the absence or loss of one or both parents, or illness or abandonment by the father (Tishler, 1992).

Other studies relate adolescent suicide with frequent parental absence because of unemployment (Stack, 1985). As a consequence, there is often an absence of any warm, parental figure with whom to identify, and a sense of emotional and social isolation. Suicide attempters often state that they do not feel close to any adult. Many times, they have trouble communicating with significant others around them (Stivers, 1988). There is no one to turn to when they need to talk to someone. Lack of closeness to parents leads to a lack of emotional support when needed (Dukes and Lorch,

CROSS-CULTURAL CONCERNS

Suicide Rates of African Americans and Whites

Suicide frequency increases with age among all ethnic groups except Native Americans, but the rate peaks among African Americans in the 25 to 34 age group then decreases. Since 1970, the suicide rate has decreased for African American females and increased for African American males. Compared with White youths, ages 15 to 19, African Americans have a much lower suicide rate, but male/female differences exist in both groups, with males having a much higher rate than females.

	SUICIDE RATES (IN THOUSANDS)		
	1970	**1980**	**1993**
African American females	2.9	1.6	2.1
African American males	4.7	5.6	14.4
White females	2.9	3.3	4.2
White males	9.4	15.0	18.5

Source: U.S. Bureau of the Census, *Statistical Abstract of the United States, 1996* (Washington, DC: U.S. Government Printing Office, 1994), p. 102.

There are several explanations of why the rates for African Americans are lower than for Whites:

There is a general tendency to underreport rates for African Americans.

The religious families of African American youths view suicide as an intolerable social stigma, so the rates are lower.

African American youths, especially males, who have a history of confrontation with authorities and police, tend to respond with "retroflexed anger" toward external constraints, rather than turning inward on themselves with hopelessness and depression.

Several characteristics of the African American community—strong family ties, the church, fraternal and social organizations, community and social support networks—have promoted a sense of social cohesion and mutual support, mitigating high suicide rates among African Americans (Gibbs and Hines, 1989).

1989). One study found three common characteristics of college students who had thoughts of suicide (Dukes and Lorch, 1989). They had poor relationships with parents, poor relationships with peers, and a conviction of personal helplessness and a sense of helplessness regarding future. Where social integration is high, suicide rates for all age groups are lower (Lester, 1991).

The background of social isolation makes these adolescents particularly vulnerable to a loss of love object, which may trigger the suicide attempt. The loss of a parent in childhood makes any subsequent loss of a family member, mate, boyfriend, or girlfriend particularly hard to accept (Neiger and Hopkins, 1988). Depression may follow recent life stresses. One study found that loss and low family support were the best predictors of an adolescent's suicide attempt (Morano, Cisler, and Lemerond, 1993).

One frequent component of suicide is depression (Connell and Meyer, 1991; Lester and Gatto, 1989). The risk of suicide among adolescents increases with alcohol and drug abuse (Rogers, 1992). Under the influence of drugs or alcohol, adolescents are more likely to act on impulse (Sommer, 1984) or they sometimes overdose and kill themselves without intending to do so (Gispert, Wheeler, Marsh, and Davis, 1985).

Stress may also stimulate suicidal attempts (Peck, 1987). One study found that subjects who were high risks for suicide were found to have significantly poorer quality friendships, lower self-esteem, and more life stress in the previous year (Cole, Protinsky, and Cross, 1992). Another study, this one of Hispanic adolescents, found that those who had committed suicide the previous year had experienced significantly more school, personality, behavioral, and family stressors than had other adolescents (Queralt, 1993). A study of suicidal ideation in French-Canadian adolescents indicated that suicidal ideation was positively related to depression, negative stress, and drug and alcohol use, and was negatively related to self-esteem, satisfaction with social support, and school absenteeism (deMan, Leduc, and Labreche-Gauthier, 1993).

Lack of investment in the future is characteristic of suicidal adolescents. They are more likely to view their futures without hope, real plans, or expectations. They usually see only the discomfort and pain of the present situation.

Some suicidal adolescents have been categorized as immature personalities with poor impulse control. Suicidal adolescents have been found to lack a positive ego-identity development, which is needed to give them feelings of self-worth, meaningfulness, and purposefulness (Bar-Joseph and Tzuriel, 1990).

Other suicidal adolescents have been shown to be highly suggestible in following the directions or examples of others (Hazell, 1991). This factor of suggestibility has been borne out by studies of adolescent "suicide epidemics." Residents of Clear Lake City, Texas, home of the astronauts and the Johnson Space Center, were shocked by a wave of suicides of 6 teenagers within a 2-month period. Piano, Texas, had 8 youth suicides within 15 months after a high school student asphyxiated himself. The affluent counties north of New York City were shaken by a string of 12 deaths (Doan and Peterson, 1984). When one suicide occurs, it brings to the surface other suicidal adolescents who are vulnerable. Small groups of adolescents have even banded together to form a suicide subculture (Lester, 1987). Suicidal adolescents are likely to have a history of suicide within the family.

Some research shows that suicide may be a direct result of mental illness (Paluszny, Davenport, and Kim, 1991). Such adolescents experience hallucinations telling them to kill themselves. Others threaten suicide, in part, because of anticipated guilt caused by voices directing them toward external aggression. The vast majority of adolescents who commit suicide have relatively long histories of disturbed behavior and psychiatric signs and symptoms, especially depression and substance abuse (Rich, Sherman, and Fowler, 1990).

In cases of interpersonal problems (Lester, 1988), suicide becomes an act of aggression, expressed inwardly at the self, in contrast to homicide, which is an act of aggression expressed outwardly. The pregnant girl, for example, could try to get even with her boyfriend by killing herself (suicide) to make the boy feel sorry or by killing him directly (homicide). Of all the aggressive acts of which people are capable, suicide is one of the most extreme; it is a violent act directed at loved ones, at society, as well as at the self. The survivors are always left wondering how they failed.

Attempted suicide is a cry for help to get attention or sympathy or an attempt to manipulate other people. Attempted suicide is not necessarily an effort to die but rather a communication to others in an effort to improve one's life. As a matter of fact, desired changes in the life situation as a result of attempted suicide may be accomplished. However, many suicidal gestures for help misfire and lead to death.

Among 15 major predictors of suicide, depression and alcoholism are ranked first and second, and suicide ideation (the thought of suicide) and prior suicide attempts are ranked third and fourth. Since those making nonfatal suicide attempts talk about suicide and dying and explicit plans of preparation for dying or suicide, these findings can lead to more effective prevention (Ghang and Jin, 1996).

Contrary to common opinion, suicide attempts in a great majority of cases are considered in advance and weighed rationally against other alternatives. The attempter may have tried other means: rebellion, running away from home, lying, stealing, or other attention-getting devices. Having tried these methods and failed, the person turns to suicide attempts. Most adolescents who attempt suicide talk about it first (Pfeffer, 1987; Shafi, 1988). If others are alerted in time, if they pay attention to these developments and take them seriously enough to try to remedy the situation, a death may be prevented (Fujimura, Weis, and Cochran, 1985; Hamilton-Obaid, 1989).

Survivors

Adolescent suicide is particularly devastating for family and peers who are left behind. Survivors typically experience fear, rage, guilt, and depres-

HIGHLIGHT

Suicidal Risks

One of the ways of preventing suicide is to recognize symptoms in those who become suicide prone (Gispert, 1987). Some 80 school professionals were asked to list the most important indicators of suicidal risk in students. They listed the following:

Indicator	SCHOOL PROFESSIONALS REPORTING INDICATOR	
	Number	Percentage
Depression (sadness, despair, eating problems, indifference, sleeping problems)	56	70
Verbal or written cues (include comments about committing suicide, acknowledgment of the problem, requests for help, or indications of depressive, morbid, or suicidal themes in art, written work, or conversation)	48	60
Social isolation, withdrawal (absence of peer support)	45	56
Academic problems (low grades, truancy, lateness)	27	34
Self-destructive behavior (suicide attempts, self-mutilation, restlessness, proneness to accidents)	27	34
Drugs, alcohol	27	34
Other school problems	26	33
Acting out (running away, delinquency, pregnancy, sexual permissiveness)	25	31
Physical appearance (poor grooming, deterioration of dress)	17	21
Agitation	16	20
Somatic complaints	11	14

In addition to this list, other writers gave the following indicators (Allen, 1987):

Preoccupation with themes of death
Giving away prized possessions or making a will
Recent suicide of a friend or relative
Recent disappointment or loss
Violent or rebellious behavior

Radical change in personality
Persistent boredom
Loss of interest in previously pleasurable activities
Inability to tolerate praise or rewards (Henry, Stephenson, Hanson, and Hargett, 1993)
A lack of self-esteem (Choquet, Kovess, and Poutignat, 1993)

Source: M. S. Grob, A. A. Klein, and S. V. Eisen, "The Role of the School Professional in Identifying and Managing Adolescent Suicide Behavior," *Journal of Youth and Adolescence, 12* (April 1983): 162–173. Reprinted by permission.

sion. They feel responsible for not recognizing the signals that might have been given and preventing the suicide, and they feel angry at the victim for deserting them. Feelings of loss and emptiness and a sense of disbelief are often followed by bouts of self-doubt and recrimination. Survivors experience shock, disbelief, and numbness. Recovering from the loss may take one to two years, depending on the survivor's personality and the events surrounding the suicide. Intense feelings

Adolescent suicide is particularly difficult for the family and friends who are left behind. They suffer from loss and emptiness, as well as from feelings of responsibility for not recognizing the problem.

have to be worked through as survivors come to terms with the loss (Mauk and Weber, 1991).

Juvenile Delinquency

The term *juvenile delinquency* refers to the violation of the law by a juvenile, which in most states means anyone under eighteen years of age. The legal term *juvenile delinquent* was established for young lawbreakers to avoid the disgrace and stigma of being classified in legal records as criminals and to separate underage people and treat them differently from adult criminals. Most are tried in juvenile courts where the intent is to rehabilitate them.

A young person may be labeled a *delinquent* for breaking any of a number of laws, ranging from murder to truancy from school. Because laws are inconsistent, a particular action may be considered delinquent in one community but not in another. Furthermore, law enforcement officials differ in the method and extent of enforcement. In some communities, the police may simply talk to adolescents who are accused of minor crimes; in others, the police refer youths to their parents; and in still others, they may arrest them and refer them to juvenile courts. As with adults, many crimes adolescents commit are never discovered or, if discovered, are not reported or prosecuted.

Most statistics therefore understate the extent of juvenile crime.

Incidence

Statistics on juvenile delinquency include either the numbers of *persons* arrested, the number of *court cases* handled, or the number of *offenses* committed. Obviously, one adolescent may commit more than one offense, but not all cases are taken to court. During the period between 1992 and 1994, the number of arrests for crimes committed by those under age 18 rose (see Table 17.2 and

TABLE 17.2   Changes in the Number of Arrests for Serious Crimes* Committed by People under Age 18

1970	1980	1992	1994 Change Since 1992
523,677	750,800	1,027,000	42%

*Serious crimes include larceny, burglary, motor vehicle theft, robbery, aggravated assault, forcible rape, murder and nonnegligent manslaughter, and arson.

Source: U.S. Bureau of the Census, *Statistical Abstract of the United States, 1996* (Washington, DC: U.S. Government Printing Office, 1996), p. 206.

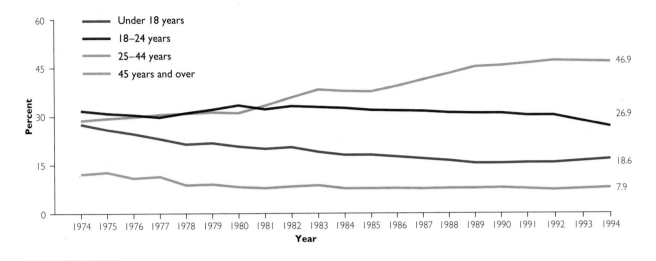

FIGURE 17.3   Persons Arrested: Percentage by Age, 1974–1994

Source: U.S. Bureau of the Census, *Statistical Abstract of the United States, 1996* (Washington, DC: U.S. Government Printing Office, 1996), p. 209.

Figure 17.3). This is partly due to the increase of the number of juveniles in the population (U.S. Bureau of the Census, 1996).

Of all persons arrested in 1994, 18.6 percent were under age 18; an additional 26.7 percent were aged 18 to 24. Figure 17.4 shows the percentages. This means that 45 percent of all arrests during 1994 were of people under age 25. The in-

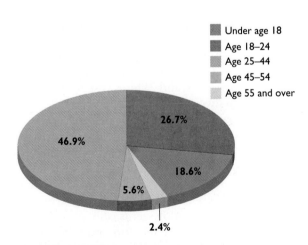

FIGURE 17.4   Age Distribution of All People Arrested, 1994

Source: U.S. Bureau of the Census, *Statistical Abstract of the United States, 1996* (Washington, DC: U.S. Government Printing Office, 1996), p. 209.

cidence of delinquency among males under age 18 is four times that among females in the same age group (U.S. Bureau of the Census, 1996). Boys are more likely to be referred for violations of the law, whereas girls are more likely to be referred for truancy, runaway behaviors, and social/personal problems. Boys tend to engage in serious delinquent behaviors, whereas the behaviors of girls tend to be more narrowly confined (Rhodes and Fisher, 1993). However, female delinquency is escalating, and according to annual reports from some of the larger U.S. police departments, a greater proportion of females are now involved in armed robbery, gang activity, and drug trafficking (Calhoun, Jurgens, and Chen, 1993).

The Census Bureau groups eight crimes together as "serious crimes"—larceny, burglary, motor vehicle theft, robbery, aggravated assault, forcible rape, murder and nonnegligent manslaughter, and arson—and gives totals for them. Table 17.2 shows that from 1992 to 1994, arrests for this group of crimes increased dramatically: 42 percent for those under age 18 (due partly to an increase in population of this age group).

juvenile delinquent   a juvenile who violates the law.

Causes of Delinquency

Antisocial behavior usually begins early in life (Pakiz, Reinherz, and Frost, 1992). The problem of delinquency has motivated research efforts to try to find its causes. In general, the causes may be grouped into three major categories: *Sociological factors* include influential elements in society and culture; *psychological factors* include the influences of interpersonal relationships and personality components; and *biological factors* include the effects of organic and physical elements.

Sociological Factors in Delinquency

The most important sociological factors that have been investigated in relation to juvenile delinquency are the following:

Socioeconomic status and class
Affluence, hedonism, and cultural values
Violence in our culture and in the media
Alcohol or drug usage
Peer-group involvement and influences
Neighborhood and community influences
Social and cultural change, disorganization, and unrest
School performance
Family background

Socioeconomic status and class have been found to be less important in relation to juvenile delinquency than was once thought (Tolan, 1988). Traditionally, delinquency was thought to be a by-product of poverty and low socioeconomic status. Delinquency is more common among youths who have fewer educational and occupational opportunities and who have become frustrated with the circumstances of their lives.

Studies show, however, that juvenile delinquency is becoming more evenly distributed through all socioeconomic-status levels. In fact, there is as great an incidence of some forms of delinquency among adolescents of the middle class as among those of other classes. One study found, for example, that high-socioeconomic-status (SES) youths were more likely to be involved in school vandalism than low SES youths (Tygart, 1988). The big difference is that middle-class adolescents who commit delinquent offenses are less often arrested and charged with them than are their lower-class counterparts. Many times, the son or daughter from a well-to-do family is let off with a warning, whereas those from poorer families are arrested and punished.

Affluence and hedonistic cultural values and lifestyles among modern youths are conducive to delinquent patterns of behavior. Today's youths, especially those of the middle class, have access to cars, alcoholic beverages, drugs, and pocket money. They are involved in a whirl of social activities: dating, dances, rock concerts, parking, and hanging out at their favorite meeting places. Their interests and attitudes lend themselves to late hours, getting into mischief and involvement in vandalism or delinquent acts just for fun. Other studies have shown that early age at first intercourse is associated with increased involvement in problem behaviors (Ketterlinus, Lamb, Nitz, and Elster, 1992). Thus, delinquency among contemporary adolescents is partly a by-product of participation in the legitimate youth culture.

There is some evidence also that violent youths have been influenced by the *violence they see in our culture and in the media* (Snyder, 1991). Research has found that youths who behave in a violent manner give more selective attention to violent cues (May, 1986). In other words, they imitate what they have seen and heard (see Chapter 12).

Research has been conducted regarding to what extent delinquency is related to *alcohol or drug usage* among adolescents (Watts and Wright, 1990). One study found that drinking was strongly associated with serious delinquency for both African Americans and Whites, especially when other factors were present, such as previous arrests, association with criminals or drug users, or heroin use by the adolescent (Dawkins and Dawkins, 1983). This is reinforced by further research that emphasizes the strong correlation between drug usage and criminal activity (Stuck and Glassner, 1985). Furthermore, there is a strong relationship between adolescents who are raised by substance-abusive parents and juvenile delinquency. Adolescents from substance-abusive homes have been found to suffer from low self-esteem, depression, anger, and a variety of acting-out behaviors (McGaha and Leoni, 1995).

Peer-group involvement becomes a significant influence in delinquency (Mitchell, Dodder, and

Not all adolescents become involved with gangs and the accompanying delinquency. Involvement in school and community organizations, such as the teen club shown here, is often a deterrent to gang and drug involvement.

Norris, 1990). There is a strong connection between peer relations and adolescent problem behaviors, especially delinquency and substance abuse (Pabon, Rodriguez, and Gurin, 1992). Adolescents become delinquent because they are socialized into it, particularly by peers (Kazdin, 1995). Youths who have a high degree of peer orientation are also more likely to have a high level of delinquency involvement. A girl's relationships with girlfriends are more important in determining gang membership and seriousness of delinquency than any other factor.

Various *neighborhood and community influences* are also important. Most larger communities can identify areas in which delinquency rates are high. Not all adolescents growing up in these areas become delinquent, but a larger than average percentage do because of the influence and pressures of their environment.

Today's adolescents are also living in a period of *rapid cultural change, disorganization, and unrest,* which tends to increase delinquency rates (see Chapter 1). Values that once were commonly accepted are now questioned. Social institutions such as the family that once offered security and protection may exert an upsetting influence instead. The specter of social, economic, and political unrest stimulates anxieties and rebellion.

School performance is also an important factor in delinquency (Grande, 1988). Dunham and Alpert (1987) studied school dropout behavior of 137 juvenile delinquents and found 14 factors that yielded a high level of prediction of whether they would drop out of school, such as misbehavior in school, disliking school, the negative influence of peers, and a weak relationship with parents. A lack of school success—poor grades, classroom misconduct, and an inability to adjust to the school program and to get along with administrators, teachers, and parents—is associated with delinquency.

Family background has an important influence on adolescent development and adjustment and hence on social conduct (Kroupa, 1988). Disrupted homes and strained family relationships have been associated with delinquent behavior. Lack of family cohesion and troubled family relationships are particularly important correlates of delinquency (Bischof, Stiph, and Whitney, 1995; Lytton, 1995; Tolan, 1988).

Psychological Factors in Delinquency Overall, *family environment* is a much more important factor in delinquency than is *family structure* (LeFlore, 1988). Relationships with parents are particularly important (Coughlin and Buchinich,

The juvenile correctional system includes boot camps, such as Camp Karl Holton, shown here. This form of incarceration is similar to the military boot camp in its rules, teaching of discipline, and rough physical training; it also includes an educational component.

pervision (JINS) who are wards of the court because their parents cannot, will not, or should not care for them. Some of the parents are ill or deceased; others have neglected, rejected, or abused the juveniles to the point where they have been taken out of the home. Some adolescents in detention facilities are those who have run away from home. Many are awaiting disposition by the court. Critics charge that these overcrowded detention centers are no place for juveniles. Sexual psychopaths and narcotics peddlers are detained with juveniles arrested for such (by comparison) innocuous offenses as curfew violations. At best, the centers are a bad influence.

The correctional system also includes *training schools, ranches, forestry camps,* and *farms.* About three-fourths of the juveniles in public custody are held in these types of facilities. (This does not include the juveniles in jail, privately operated facilities, foster homes, facilities exclusively for drug abusers, homes for dependent or neglected children, or federal correctional facilities.) Most authorities feel that, in their traditional forms, such training schools and correctional institutions do not correct or rehabilitate. While youths are being punished, "rehabilitated," or "corrected," they are exposed to hundreds of other delinquents who may be encouraging or modeling further antisocial and delinquent behaviors. The influence is therefore negative, not positive.

The system has been improved greatly by what has been called *token economy,* which places

the emphasis on a "twenty-four-hour positive learning environment" (Miller, Cosgrove, and Doke, 1990). In this system, students earn points for good behavior, with points convertible to money that can be used to purchase goods or privileges. Money can be spent for room rental, for fines for misconduct, in the commissary or snack bar, or for recreation. Students earn points for academic accomplishments and schoolwork, for proper social behavior, for doing chores or other jobs, or for social development. Under this system, they make great gains in academic achievement, on-the-job training, or eliminating assaultive, disruptive, and antisocial behavior.

One of the criticisms of these correctional institutions is that once the juveniles are released to the community, they often come under the same influences and face some of the same problems that led to detention in the first place. One suggestion has been to use *halfway houses* and *group homes* where youths may live, going from there to school or to work. In this way, some control can be maintained over the adolescents until they have learned self-direction. One of the most important needs is to prepare youths for employment after discharge (Weissman, 1985).

Sending adolescents to *prison* is the worst way to rehabilitate them. A percentage of inmates of a prison population are sociopaths who prefer antisocial behavior, have no regard for the interests of others, show little or no remorse, and are untreatable. For these people, prison is justified. They are in contrast to adolescents who are put in prison for relatively minor offenses. In spite of this, the average sentences of juveniles are greater than for adults who have committed the same crimes. Juvenile offenders tend to be passive, dependent youths who are easily bullied, try to maintain friendships with others, and then get into trouble trying to model their behavior after the group's expectations. They have had no adequate adult male role models with whom they could have had significant relationships. They are often school dropouts, unemployed, and without plans for the future. Left with no reasonable course of action, they engage in random activities with a gang that eventually gets them into trouble with the law. Once they have a prison record, their chances of finding a useful life are jeopardized.

When sent to prison, they learn that guards are arbitrary and unfair in the way they mete out punishment. One prisoner may be denied the privilege of one movie for a given offense, while another may be placed in solitary confinement for 10 days. They learn that fear, bribery, cheating, and sadism are ways of dealing with problems. When they compare their lot to that of the guards, they notice the complete lack of work activity of some of the guards and conclude it does not pay to work. In addition, many prisoners are harassed and bullied by fellow prisoners who may use them in any number of ways, including for homosexual activities. If adolescents were not antagonistic toward authority and the system on arrival in prison, they soon become so. They grow to hate the prison and vow never to return—not by becoming law abiding but by never again being caught.

Counseling and *therapy* both individually and in groups are important parts of any comprehensive program of treatment and correction of juvenile offenders. Individual therapy on a one-to-one basis is time consuming, with too few professionals and too many delinquents, but it can be effective in some instances. Some therapists feel that group therapy reaches a juvenile sooner than individual therapy because the delinquent feels less anxious and defensive in the group situation. Group therapy is sometimes offered to both juvenile offenders and their parents, in which case it becomes similar to other types of family therapy.

Work with parents is especially important in correcting family situations that contribute to the delinquency in the first place.

Critique of the Juvenile Justice System   The biggest criticism of the juvenile justice system is that it does not work. The present trend to try juveniles as adults has not helped. Neither juvenile nor adult crime has been reduced as a result of the juvenile court system, nor has the system reduced the rate of recidivism (Ashford and LeCroy, 1990; Benda, 1987). Almost all critiques of the system point out the lack of coordination and definition in the system; the defective delivery of services; the confusion of roles and responsibilities of the judges, social workers, and police; and the system's failure to protect either the child or society. As long as the emphasis is on punishing the juvenile offender, treatment and rehabilitation will be neglected (Wolff, 1987).

Knowledge of the Law   A neglected area of investigation has been the extent to which ignorance of the law has been a factor in juveniles getting into trouble or, once in trouble, of not getting full protection under the law. The assumption has always been that ignorance of the law is no excuse, but it is still a reason why some teenagers get arrested and are not able to utilize their legally permitted rights.

An investigation of the knowledge of the law of sophomore, junior, and senior students in six classes in a high school in a small industrial city in Oregon revealed widespread ignorance of it (Saunders, 1981). Lack of knowledge is often responsible for failure to seek many kinds of available help. All children in the public schools should be taught public law, definitions of crimes, their own rights, and the roles of professionals within the criminal justice system.

Private Community Programs

Private, community programs established to treat delinquency have taken many forms. One school-based program for ninth- to twelfth-graders in Oklahoma was designed to teach communication skills, which helped the students achieve positive peer support and enhance their self-esteem. The result was significantly fewer offenders among the trained students (Englander-Golden, Jackson, Crane, Schwarzkopf, and Lyle, 1989). Communities have established both resident and outpatient centers (Fairchild and Wright, 1984), drug abuse centers, coffeehouses, youth centers, boys' or girls' clubs, big brother or big sister programs, youth employment agencies, and psychoeducational programs (Carpenter and Sugrue, 1984). One five-year study of the effectiveness of a "Teen Ranch" 70-bed residential treatment program for adolescent boys in Michigan revealed startling improvement in intellectual scores, indicating an enhanced ability to deal with the world (Lorandos, 1990). There was also a dramatic decrease in pathology among the boys. The success of this program indicates that delinquent youths can be helped with the right kind of carefully designed program.

Prevention

Any effort to curb delinquency needs to focus on *prevention*. This means identifying children who may be predisposed to getting in trouble. Once identified, those who are emotionally disturbed can be enlisted in various types of psychotherapeutic treatment. Prevention also may mean enrolling others in a big brother/big sister program (Frecknall and Luks, 1992). It may mean focusing on adolescents' family environments and relationships and assisting parents in learning more effective parenting skills. It may mean putting antisocial youths into groups of prosocial peers, such as day camps, where their behavior is influenced positively. It may mean offering social-skills training for young offenders (Cunliffe, 1992). In all, *prevention* means providing various types of interventions as a means of altering the aggression in adolescents (Wells and Miller, 1993).

One researcher wrote, "A partial list of the proposed links to crime include television viewing, poor nutrition, eyesight problems, teenage unemployment, teenage employment, too little punishment, too much punishment, high IQ, low IQ, allergies and fluorescent lighting" (Hurley, 1985, p. 68). To root out the various links to crime and to correct these causes will take great commitment in the years ahead.

HIGHLIGHT

Reaffirming Rehabilitation

There has been a decline of rehabilitation in juvenile justice throughout much of the United States over the past 20 years. This decline was facilitated by the progressive community's abandonment of rehabilitation and their acceptance of the justice model as a means to restrict a growing number of youths in correctional institutions. The justice model was conceived as a means to impose confinement limitations to standardize sentencing while accommodating conservative demands for retribution and punishment. However, contrary to expectations, the justice model produced an unprecedented rise in the number of incarcerated youths and a deterioration in institutional conditions. This was occurring despite mounting evidence demonstrating the superior effectiveness of rehabilitation models in altering patterns of delinquency. This evidence showed that rehabilitation should be reaffirmed as the foundation for progressive agenda in juvenile justice (Macallair, 1993; Swenson and Kennedy, 1995).

SUMMARY

1. Alienated adolescents feel estranged from family, friends, and school. They turn away from the mainstream of youth and adult society and express their feelings through various types of acting-out behavior, including running away, suicide, and juvenile delinquency.

2. Adolescents run away from home for a number of reasons. The traditional view is that running away is a behavioral manifestation of psychopathology. Another view is that adolescents run away because of conflicts in the family, pressures and difficulties in school, or problems in the community. Runaways may have problems in the following areas: parental problems, delinquent behavior, academic problems, peer-relationship difficulties, and symptoms of psychopathlogy. Not all runaways suffer psychopathlogy. Some leave home in a search for adventure.

3. Some adolescents are throwaways, not runaways. "running from" adolescents seek to escape their home situations; whereas "running to" adolescents are pleasure seekers who run to other places or people to seek thrills and adventure.

4. One study classified runaway girls as rootless, anxious, or terrified. One researcher arranged runaways along a continuum as nonrunaways, runaway explorers, social pleasure seekers, runaway manipulators, runaway retreatists, and endangered runaways.

5. The consequences of running may be disastrous, especially for the teenage girl. She may drop out of school; become involved in sexual activity, prostitution, or substance abuse; and become pregnant and have a child.

6. The National Runaway Youth Program assists runaway adolescents.

7. The incidence of suicide increases with advancing age, reaching a peak in males over age 85 and in females at ages 45 to 54. The rate among males 15 to 24 years of age is six times that of females of the same age, and has tripled over the last 40 years. Only a small percentage of attempted suicides succeed.

8. The rate of suicide among Whites is much greater than among African Americans.

9. Adolescents commit suicide for a variety of reasons: disturbed family situations, emotional and social isolation, loss of a love object, depression, drug usage, stress, mental illness, guilt, or hostility, or as a cry for help. Adults ought to be alert to signs and symptoms that the adolescent is suicide prone.

10. Adolescent suicide is especially hard on survivors, who suffer fear, rage, guilt, and depression.

11. Juvenile delinquency is the violation of the law by anyone under legal age. From 1992 to 1994, the number of those under age 18 who committed serious crimes rose slightly, but this is due partly to the increase in the number of juveniles in the population. Still, 45 percent of all arrests in 1994 were of people under age 25. Arrests among males were over four times that among females of the same age.

12. The causes of delinquency may be grouped into three major categories: sociological, psychological, and biological. Sociological factors include family background, socioeconomic status, educational and occupational opportunities, affluence and hedonistic life-styles, alcohol or drug usage, peer-group pressures, neighborhood and community influences, rapid cultural change and conflicting values, and school performance.

13. Psychological factors of delinquency include relationships with parents, personality factors such as low self-esteem, deeper neuroses or psychopathology, and love deprivation.

14. Biological factors of delinquency include deficiencies in the development of the frontal lobe of the brain, retardation in autonomic nervous system responses, chromosomal aberrations, and inheritance of certain troublesome temperaments. Various other organic causes are abnormal blood-sugar level; hearing, vision, or speech impairment; hyperthyroidism; and abnormal brain-wave patterns or other neurological difficulties.

15. Adolescents often organize themselves into juvenile gangs for protection, companionship, excitement, or heterosexual contacts. Such gangs are a problem if they force members and some nonmembers to engage in antisocial and illegal acts that they would not participate in if acting on their own. In such cases, the only way to deal with delinquency is to dismantle or redirect the criminal activities of the group.

16. The juvenile justice system consists of the police, the juvenile court, and the correctional system (including the probation system, detention centers, training schools, ranches, forestry camps, farms,

halfway houses, group homes, treatment centers, and prisons). The largest criticism of the juvenile justice system is that it does not work.

17. Rehabilitation should be reaffirmed as the foundation for treating juvenile delinquency.

18. Various private and community programs are also offered: resident and outpatient treatment centers, drug abuse centers, coffeehouses, youth centers, boys' or girls' clubs, big brother/big sister programs, youth employment agencies, and psychoeducational programs. Any effort to curb delinquency needs to focus on prevention.

KEY TERMS

anxious runaway **401**

juvenile delinquent **408**

rootless runaway **401**

terrified runaway **401**

throwaways **401**

THOUGHT QUESTIONS

1. Do you know an adolescent who ran away from home? What were the circumstances?
2. Should runaways be forced to return home? When? When should they not?
3. What can or should be done to help parents of runaways?
4. What can or should be done to help runaways themselves?
5. Have you known an adolescent who committed suicide? What were the reasons?
6. How do you explain that a greater percentage of White adolescents than African American adolescents commit suicide?
7. What are the major symptoms of suicidal tendencies? What should you do if you realize someone is manifesting these symptoms?
8. Do you think that some rock music and performers influence some adolescents to commit suicide? Explain.
9. How do you account for the fact that the percentages of those under age 18 who are arrested are decreasing?
10. Why do far greater number of males than females become delinquent? What sociological, psycho-

logical, and biological factors may be exerting an influence?
11. Why do some adolescents who are brought up in crime-prone neighborhoods not become delinquent?
12. What should parents do if their adolescent is running around with a group whose members are known to be delinquent?
13. What is the role of the school in preventing delinquency?
14. How do adolescents' relationships with parents affect delinquency?
15. How do biological factors affect delinquency?
16. When you were growing up, were there any delinquent juvenile gangs in your area? Describe them.
17. What is your opinion of the juvenile justice system? How could it be improved? What do you think is needed to be able to reform known offenders?
18. Have you known a juvenile offender who was sent to a training school or correctional institution who became a productive, law-abiding citizen? What factors made the difference?
19. Is it possible to rehabilitate juvenile offenders?
20. How can juvenile delinquency be prevented?

SUGGESTED READING

Capuzzi, D. (1994). *Suicide Prevention in the Schools: Guidelines for Middle and High School Settings.* Alexandria, VA: American Counseling Association.

Goldstein, A. P. (1991). *Delinquent Gangs: A Psychological Perspective.* Champaign, IL: Research Press.

Goldstein, A. P., and Huff, C. R. (Eds.). (1993). *The Gang Intervention Handbook.* Champaign, IL: Research Press.

Klein, M. W. (1995). *American Street Gang: Its Nature, Prevalence, and Control.* New York: Oxford University Press.

Lester, D. (1990). *Understanding and Preventing Suicide: New Perspectives.* Springfield, IL: Charles C. Thomas.

Lester, D. (1992). *Why People Kill Themselves: A 1990s Summary of Research Findings on Suicidal Behavior,* 3rd ed. Springfield, IL: Charles C. Thomas.

Lester, D. (1993). *Cruelest Death: The Enigma of Adolescent Suicide.* Philadelphia: Charles Press.

Lundman, R. J. (1993). *Prevention and Control of Juvenile Delinquency,* 2nd ed. New York: Oxford University Press.

Nelson, R. E., and Galas, J. C. (1994). *The Power to Prevent Suicide: A Guide for Teens Helping Teens.* Minneapolis, MN: Free Spirit.

Patterson, G. R., Reid, J. B., and Dishion, T. J. (1992). *Antisocial Boys.* Eugene, OR: Castalia.

Quay, H. C. (Ed.). (1987). *Handbook of Juvenile Delinquency.* New York: Wiley.

Rothman, J. (1991). *Runaway and Homeless Youth: Strengthening Services to Families and Children.* New York: Longman.

Stavsky, L., and Mozeson, I. E. (1990). *The Place I Call Home: Voices and Faces of Homeless Teens.* New York: Shapolsky.

Straus. M. D. (1994). *Violence in the Lives of Adolescents.* New York: Norton.

Vito, G. F., and Wilson, D. G. (1985). *American Juvenile Justice System.* Vol. 5: Law & Criminal Justice Series. Beverly Hills, CA: Sage.

Walker, R. N. (1995). *Psychology of the Youthful Offender,* 3rd ed. Springfield, IL: Charles C. Thomas.

18

Substance Abuse, Addiction, and Dependency

This chapter focuses on three selected health problems of adolescents: drug abuse, smoking, and excessive drinking. These particular problems have been selected because of their frequency and their importance in the lives of adolescents (Wodarski, 1990). Drug abuse is considered by some to be the greatest social health problem relating to youths (Thorne and DeBlassie, 1985). It is also significantly related to delinquency and crime among youths (Watts and Wright, 1990). We will take a look at the problem and answer a number of questions: Which drugs are most commonly abused? Has the abuse of drugs been overestimated? Who is using drugs and for what reasons? Large numbers of youths also smoke tobacco. What can be done to prevent adolescents from starting? Drinking also becomes a problem for society as well as for the individual when it is excessive. We will also focus on alcohol as the drug of preference among adolescents.

Drug Abuse

By definition, a drug is a substance used as a medicine. As such, some drugs are used by virtually everyone. Aspirin is a very effective drug, but even aspirin is lethal if taken in excess. Drug abuse, therefore, is the use of a drug for other than a medicinal purpose or in improper quantities or administration. The problem is drug abuse, not drug use (Gullotta, Adams, and Montemayor, 1995).

Physical Addiction and Psychological Dependency

There is a distinction between *physical addiction, or physical dependency,* and *psychological dependency.* A **physical addiction** to a drug is physically habit forming because the body builds up a physical need for the drug, so that its sudden denial results in withdrawal symptoms. **Psychological dependency** is the development of a persistent, sometimes overpowering psychological need for a drug, resulting in a compulsion to take it. A well-established habit of psychological dependency may be more difficult to overcome than one involving physical dependency, especially if people become so deeply involved with a drug that they cannot function without it. Physical dependency on heroin, for example, may be broken, but individuals go back to it because of psychological dependence on it. It is a mistake, therefore, to assume that the only dangerous drugs are those that are physically addictive.

The drugs most commonly abused may be grouped into a number of categories: *narcotics, stimulants, depressants, hallucinogens, marijuana,* and *inhalants. Alcohol* and *nicotine* are also drugs, but because they are more widely used than any of the others, they will be discussed in separate sections of this chapter.

Narcotics

Narcotics include *opium* and its derivatives, such as *morphine, heroin,* and *codeine.* Opium is a dark, gummy substance extracted from the juice of unripe seed pods of the opium poppy. Opium is usually taken orally or sniffed—that is, it is heated and its vapor inhaled. *Morphine,* the chief active ingredient in opium, is extracted as a bitter, white powder with no odor. Each grain of opium contains about one-tenth of a grain of morphine. Morphine is used medicinally to relieve extreme pain because of its depressant effect on the central nervous system. Addicts refer to it as "M" or "monkey." It may be sniffed, but the powder is usually mixed with water and injected under the skin with a hypodermic needle ("skin popping"). For maximum effect, it is injected directly into a vein ("mainlined") (O'Brien and Cohen, 1984).

Heroin ("H," "horse," "Harry," or "smack") is produced from morphine by a simple chemical process. Like its relative, it is a white, odorless powder. If dirty needles or ingredients are used, the result may be blood poisoning or serious infections, such as AIDS or hepatitis, a leading cause of death among addicts. Heroin is the most widely used opiate, but is more addictive than morphine because it is stronger. Traditionally, more hardcore heroin addicts come from the ghettos of large cities than from any other area. A large percentage of all heroin addicts come from New York alone. If California, Illinois, and New Jersey are added, these four states contain more than three-fourths of the heroin addicts in the United States. Street supplies are diluted ("cut") with milk sugar to squeeze out maximum profits. Heroin is also often diluted with bitter-tasting quinine to make it impossible for addicts to gauge the heroin concentration by tasting the mixture. Pure quinine injected in sufficient quantity may be a leading cause of the deaths that are attributed to a heroin overdose. Addicts often die, also, if they shoot heroin while under the influence of alcohol or barbiturates, for the combination of drugs has a double depressive effect (O'Brien and Cohen, 1984).

Codeine is also a morphine derivative. Often used in cough syrups or to relieve mild body aches, it has the same but milder analgesic properties as other narcotics. *Paregoric,* a liquid preparation containing an extract of opium, is used medicinally to counteract diarrhea and abdominal pain. Codeine and paregoric are often used by young people who mistakenly think they are not addictive.

The synthetic opiates, *Demerol* (meperidine) and *Dolophine* (methadone), were created as chemical substitutes for the natural opiates and are used in medicine as pain relievers. They are addictive and restricted by law to medical use.

The consequences of morphine and heroin use are severe. They are the most physically addictive of all drugs. Users quickly develop tolerance and physical as well as psychological dependence and must therefore gradually increase the dosage. Because dependence becomes total and heroin is expensive (addicts spend several hundred dollars daily), many users turn to crime or prostitution to support their habits. Without the drug, withdrawal symptoms begin to appear. The first symptoms are running eyes and nose, yawning, sweating, dilation of the pupils, and appearance of goose pimples on the skin (from which the expression "cold turkey" originated). Within 24 hours, addicts develop leg, back, and abdominal cramps, violent muscle spasms, vomiting, and diarrhea. The expression "kicking the habit" developed as a result of the muscle spasms during withdrawal. Bodily functions such as respiration, blood pressure, temperature, and metabolism, which have been depressed, now become hyperactive. These symptoms gradually diminish over a period of a week or more. Women who have babies while addicted deliver infants who are addicts or who are born dead from drug poisoning.

Addiction may have other effects, too. Addicts usually lose their appetite for food, which leads to extreme weight loss and severe malnutrition. They neglect their health, suffer chronic fatigue, and are in a general devitalized condition. Sexual interest and activity decline; most marriages end in separation or divorce. Addicts become accident prone—they may fall frequently, drown, or even set themselves on fire if they drop off to sleep while smoking. They lose the willpower to carry on daily functions and they pay little attention to their appearance. Their whole lives center on getting the next "fix."

Because the prognosis for curing heroin addiction is so discouraging, methadone is now given as a substitute drug through medically recognized methadone maintenance programs. The drug blocks the hunger for heroin and the effects of it, with the result that the majority of addicts no longer have a constant desire to obtain heroin. Studies show outstanding success with methadone maintenance. The majority of patients who are regularly given medically prescribed doses of methadone become productive citizens, returning to work or school and avoiding any drug-related arrests (O'Brien and Cohen, 1984).

Stimulants

Cocaine ("coke," "snow," or "blow") is extracted from the leaves of the South American coca plant and is available as an odorless, fluffy, white powder. It is mistakenly classified as a narcotic and is therefore subject to the same penalties as opiates, but it is a stimulant rather than a depressant to the central nervous system. Even though it is expensive, it is widely used in the youth drug culture, as well as among more affluent groups (U.S. Bureau of the Census, 1996).

Cocaine depresses the appetite and increases alertness. It is not effective when taken orally, so users sniff or inject it intravenously into the bloodstream. Aside from financial depletion, the primary undesirable effects are nervousness, irritability, restlessness, mild paranoia, physical exhaustion, mental confusion, loss of weight, fatigue or depression when "coming down," and various afflictions of the nasal mucous membranes and cartilage. Taking large doses can lead to a severe psychosis while the person is still on the drug. Large doses can produce headaches, cold sweat, hyperventilation, nausea, tremors, convulsions, unconsciousness, and even death. Psychological dependence is severe; withdrawal is characterized by a profound depression for which cocaine itself appears to be the only remedy. One of the most famous cocaine addicts was Sigmund Freud, who escalated his use well into the twentieth century.

The newest form of cocaine, "crack," is smoked and is one of the most difficult drug habits to break. Crack is so potent that users develop a craving for the drug very quickly. The craving can be so demanding that users will resort to theft, deceit, and violence to procure the drug. The health consequences of use may be severe, because the drug has destructive effects on brain neurotransmitters, and acts as an excessive stimulant on the heart and other organs. Adolescent crack users are likely to make poor grades, be depressed, and be alienated from family and friends (Ringwalt and Palmer, 1989).

physical addiction or physical dependency a condition that develops from abusing a drug that forms a chemical dependency.

psychological dependency the development of a persistent, sometimes overpowering psychological need for a drug.

Amphetamines are stimulants that include such drugs as benzedrine, Dexedrine, Biphetamine, and methedrine ("speed"). They are used medically for treating obesity, mild depression, fatigue, and other conditions. The drugs are usually taken orally in the form of tablets or capsules. Because they are stimulants, they increase alertness, elevate mood, and produce a feeling of well-being. Large doses may produce a temporary rise in blood pressure, palpitations, headache, dizziness, sweating, diarrhea, pallor and dilation of the pupils, vasomotor disturbances, agitation, confusion, apprehension, or delirium. Regular amphetamine users do not develop physical dependence, but users soon develop an intense psychological need to continue taking the drug and require larger doses as their tolerance develops. Mental depression and fatigue are experienced after the drug has been withdrawn, so psychic dependence develops quickly because the "high" is so enticing and the "low" so depressing. Patients usually need to be treated in mental hospitals, especially patients who inject the drugs into their veins. Some users end up swallowing whole handfuls of tablets instead of only one or two. The outcome of this or injecting the drugs intravenously is an amphetamine psychosis (O'Brien and Cohen, 1984).

One of the amphetamines, called *methedrine* ("speed"), is particularly dangerous because it is commonly injected under the skin or directly into a vein, often causing rupturing of the blood vessels and death. Other hazards are infections such as tetanus, AIDS, syphilis, malaria, or hepatitis from dirty needles. The heavy user displays a potential for violence, paranoia, physical depiction, or bizarre behavior. Suicides are frequent during the periods of deep depression following withdrawal.

Depressants

Barbiturates are depressants that decrease the activity of the central nervous system, usually producing sedation, intoxication, and sleep. They include drugs commonly used in sleeping pills, such as *Quaalude, Nembutal, Seconal, Tuinal, Amytal,* and *phenobarbital*. Some of these drugs—Nembutal, Tuinal, and Seconal, for example—are short acting, meaning the effects set in sooner and wear off sooner. Others, such as phenobarbital, are long acting. Barbiturates are widely prescribed medicinally for insomnia, nervousness, or epilepsy. When taken as directed, in small doses, there is no evidence that the long-acting barbiturates are addictive. There is a greater chance of addiction with the short-acting drugs. All barbiturates are dangerous when abused because they develop total addiction: both physical and psychological dependence. Dosages must be increased as tolerance develops, and overdose may cause death.

Barbiturate users exhibit slurred speech, staggering gait, and sluggish reactions. They may be easily moved to tears or laughter, are emotionally erratic, and are frequently irritable and antagonistic. They are prone to stumble and drop objects and are often bruised or have cigarette burns on their bodies.

When the abuser has become physically dependent, withdrawal symptoms become severe in about 24 hours. Increasing nervousness, headache, muscle twitching, weakness, insomnia, nausea, and a sudden drop of blood pressure occur. Convulsions that can be fatal are an ever-present danger with barbiturate withdrawal. Delirium and hallucinations may develop. When barbiturates are taken in combination with alcohol or narcotics, the sedative effect is multiplied and can result in coma or death.

Tranquilizers such as *Miltown, Equanil, Placidyl, Librium,* and *Valium* are similar to barbiturates in their effects, for they, too, act on the central nervous system. The hazards of Valium are supplied to physicians by the manufacturer, Roche Laboratories. The product information supplied reads, in part:

> Warnings: . . . Patients receiving . . . Valium (diazepam) should be cautioned against engaging in hazardous occupations requiring complete mental alertness such as operating machinery or driving a motor vehicle. . . .
>
> Since Valium (diazepam) has a central nervous system depressant effect, patients should be advised against the simultaneous ingestion of alcohol and other central nervous system depressant drugs. . . .
>
> *Physical and Psychological Dependence:* Withdrawal symptoms (similar in character to those noted with barbiturates and alcohol) have occurred following abrupt discontinuance of diazepam (convulsions,

tremor, abdominal and muscle cramps, vomiting and sweating). . . . Particularly addiction-prone individuals (such as drug addicts or alcoholics) should be under careful surveillance when receiving diazepam. (Valium package insert, 1988)

In short, these products, when abused, have the same dangers as barbiturates. Drugs such as Valium and Librium have been called the "opium of the masses," particularly because one-half of the most commonly abused drugs may be classified as tranquilizers, barbiturates, or analgesics. *Analgesics,* such as *Darvon,* are pain killers.

Other common depressants sometimes used, but not as often abused, include bromides and sleep remedies such as Nytol. When used in excess, however, they produce psychological dependence.

Hallucinogens

Hallucinogens, or psychedelic drugs, include a broad range of substances that act on the central nervous system to alter perception and the state of consciousness. The best known psychedelic drug is *LSD (lysergic acid diethylamide),* a synthetic drug that must be prepared in a laboratory. Other hallucinogens include *peyote* and *mescaline* (derived from the peyote cactus plant), *psilocybin* (derived from a species of mushrooms), and four synthetics: *PCP* (*phencyclidine*), *STP* (also known as *DOM, dimethoxymethylamphetamine*), *DMT* (*dimethyl tryptomine*), and *MDA* (*methylene dioxyamphetamine*). DMT may also be prepared from natural plants that grow in the West Indies and parts of South America. STP and MDA share some of the same characteristics of the amphetamines. It is estimated that in 1994 approximately 12 percent of young adults 18 to 25 years of age and 4 percent of youths 12 to 17 years of age had used hallucinogens at some time (U.S. Bureau of the Census, 1996).

Each compound has users who claim unique effects from ingesting it. In general, the drugs produce unpredictable results, including distortions of color, sound, time, and speed. A numbing of the senses in which colors are "heard" and sounds are "seen" is common. Some people experience "bad trips" that are intensely frightening and characterized by panic, terror, and psychosis. A majority of those who experience a bad

trip report the feeling that no one anywhere can help, that they are no longer able to control their perceptions, or that they are afraid they have destroyed part of themselves with the drug. Users have been driven to suicide, violence, and murder, and have been permanently hospitalized as psychotic.

LSD, or "acid," must be viewed with extreme suspicion because the drug is so powerful, its strengths are often unknown, and its effects are so unpredictable. A dose of only 50 to 200 micrograms (no larger than a pinpoint) may take the user on a "trip" for 8 to 16 hours. Hallucinations and other psychotic reactions sometimes occur days or months after the last dose, indicating possible brain damage. Infants born of mothers who have taken LSD during pregnancy have shown abnormalities of chromosomal structure. But whether LSD causes pathological chromosomal deviations and genetic defects in users is not definitely known (O'Brien and Cohen, 1984). Users develop psychological but not physical dependence.

Peyote and mescaline are milder hallucinogens than LSD, as is psilocybin. Peyote has been used for years by Navajos, members of the Native American church, as part of their religion. DMT is a shorter-acting hallucinogen whose effects may come and go within the space of 2 hours, after a sudden and harsh onset. STP appeared in the early spring of 1967. Doses of more than 3 milligrams can cause hallucinations lasting 8 to 10 hours. It is said to be 200 times more powerful than mescaline but only one-tenth as potent as LSD. PCP seems to be used increasingly. PCP users tend to be antisocial, hostile, and violent. PCP causes hostility, paranoid symptoms, and prolonged psychotic or depressive states in many users. Its use is related to violent actions, including violence against the self (suicide).

Marijuana

Marijuana (cannabis; also "grass," "pot," or "weed") is made from the dried leaves of the wild hemp plant. The plant is hardy and useful: It thrives in virtually every country of the world and produces a strong fiber for making cloth, canvas, and rope. The oil serves as a fast-drying paint base. For these reasons, U.S. farmers grew cannabis, and as late as World War II, the federal government licensed production of cannabis in the South and the West. Federal law now forbids growing marijuana, but illegal production has skyrocketed in the United States in recent years.

The principal acting ingredient in cannabis is the chemical delta-9-THC, which will be referred to here as simply **THC.** The THC content of cannabis varies depending on the variety. In 1975, the THC content of "street" marijuana rarely exceeded 1 percent. More recently, new varieties have been produced, commonly containing THC content higher than 5 percent. These have more noticeable effects on users than did weaker strains. The THC content also varies with the part of the plant utilized. There is very little THC in the stem, roots, or seeds; the flowers and leaves contain more. *Ganja,* which comes from the flower tops and small leaves, ranges from 4 to 8 percent in THC content. *Hashish,* derived from the resin extracted from unfertilized female flowers, may have a THC content of 12 percent. *Hashish oil,* a concentration of resin, has been found to have a THC content as high as 28 percent, with typical samples containing 15 to 20 percent.

This variability in the THC content of different varieties of plants, and in the different parts and preparations made from them, has made it difficult for scientists to determine physical effects and psychological effects of marijuana use. Studies often yield conflicting results because of a lack of standardized procedures. What do research studies show concerning marijuana?

Tolerance to cannabis, diminished response to a given repeated drug dose, has now been well substantiated. Users are able to ingest ever larger quantities without disruptive effects.

Physical dependency, as indicated by withdrawal symptoms, does not occur in ordinary users ingesting small or weak amounts. However, withdrawal symptoms can occur following discontinuance of high-dose chronic administration of THC. These symptoms include irritability, decreased appetite, sleep disturbance, sweating, tremors, vomiting, and diarrhea. It should be emphasized that these symptoms occur only after unusually high doses of orally administered THC under researchlike conditions. Psychological dependency may develop over a period of time and may make it difficult for chronic users to break the marijuana habit.

An increase in heart rate and reddening of the eyes are the most consistently reported physiological effects of marijuana. The heart rate increase is closely related to dosage. Marijuana use decreases exercise tolerance of those with heart disease; therefore, use by those with cardiovascular deficiencies appears unwise. However, the drug produces only minimal changes in heart function of young, healthy subjects.

Clinical studies are beginning to point to various harmful effects of marijuana on the lungs and as a cause of lung cancer. The smoke contains much stronger tars and irritants than do regular cigarettes; one "joint" is the equivalent of smoking

Marijuana use remains popular with some adolescents. Although not as imminently destructive as other drugs, chronic heavy marijuana use may result in such negative outcomes as psychological dependency, damage to the lining of the lungs, and impairment of the immune system.

four cigarettes of tobacco, so heavy usage over a long period may harm the lungs. The tar from marijuana produces tumors when applied to the skin of test animals. Following exposure to marijuana smoke, the lung's defense systems against bacterial invasion have been shown to be impaired.

Because marijuana is an intoxicant, it impairs memory and concentration. It interferes with a wide range of intellectual tasks in a manner that impairs classroom learning among student users. Marijuana also alters time and space sense, impairs vision, and retards reaction time and performance abilities.

Research has also suggested that heavy marijuana use may impair reproductive functioning in humans. Chronic use is associated with reduced levels of the male hormone, testosterone, in the bloodstream, which, in turn, may reduce potency and sexual drive and diminish sperm count and motility. It is also associated with possible interference with fertility in females. These preliminary findings may have greater significance for the marginally fertile. Because the effects of marijuana on pregnant women and human fetuses have not been sufficiently established, most doctors strongly advise against smoking marijuana during pregnancy. Other questions of possible marijuana effects continue to be unresolved. Evidence concerning an effect on the body's principal defense against disease, the immune response, remains contradictory.

The long-term effects of chronic cannabis use on behavior are only partially known. It is certain, however, that the overall effect depends on the level and length of usage. Prolonged cannabis psychosis has been reported in Eastern literature under conditions of unusually heavy use. There is evidence that marijuana users may have more difficulty in deciding on career goals and may more often drop out of college to reassess their goals. There is some evidence that marijuana administration, coupled with monetary reward for work performance, results in a decline in productivity with heavier marijuana consumption.

Research is also revealing some positive and therapeutic uses of marijuana. The usefulness of cannabis in treating glaucoma by reducing internal eye pressures has been confirmed. The use of THC in reducing nausea and vomiting of cancer patients receiving chemotherapy shows unusual promise. Because THC dilates pulmonary air passages, its usefulness in treating asthmatics has been demonstrated. Marijuana is a lung irritant, however, so use of aerosolized THC seems prudent. In the years ahead, more important questions in relation to marijuana use will be answered.

Inhalants

Research findings have shown that solvent abusers are usually young children and adolescents, mainly male, with an average age of 13 years (Jansen, Richter, and Griesel, 1992). The solvent fumes from nail polish remover, plastic glue, gasoline, cleaning fluids, paint thinner, and other hydrocarbons are sometimes sniffed to produce intoxication. Impairment of orientation, memory, intellectual functions, and judgment are frequent, together with blurring of vision, ringing ears, slurred speech, headache, dizziness, dilated pupils, and staggering, followed by drowsiness, stupor, and even unconsciousness. On recovery, the individual usually does not recall what happened during the period of intoxication. Use of inhalants may cause permanent damage and impairment of brain tissue function (acute brain syndrome). The subject may die suddenly of asphyxia, become addicted, or develop inhalation psychosis. Accidental deaths while intoxicated from glue sniffing include suffocation from a plastic bag over the head (used to concentrate the fumes for inhalation) and falls from high places. Damage to the kidneys, liver, heart, blood, and nervous system, is possible from sniffing glue with a toluene base. Use of inhalants is dangerous and should be discouraged.

Patterns and Intensity of Use

Five patterns of drug use may be identified:

1. *Experimental use* is defined as the short-term, nonpatterned trial of one or more drugs, with a maximum frequency of 10 times per drug. It is motivated primarily by curiosity or by a desire to experience new feelings.

THC   the active ingredient in marijuana.

2. *Social-recreational use* occurs in social settings among friends or acquaintances who wish to share an experience. This type of use tends to vary in frequency, intensity, and duration but not to escalate in either frequency or intensity to patterns of uncontrolled use. Users typically do not use addictive drugs such as heroin; they are therefore able to exercise control over their behavior.

3. *Circumstantial-situational use* is motivated by the desire to achieve a known and anticipated effect. This would include the student who takes stimulants to stay awake or the person who takes sedatives to relieve tension and go to sleep. Four common psychological conditions may lead to illicit drug use by adolescents: a depressed mood, normlessness (not having definite values, opinions, or rules to live by), social isolation, and low self-esteem. The greatest danger from circumstantial use of marijuana is that the person will become accustomed to drug use to solve problems, and the habit will ultimately escalate to intensified use.

4. *Intensified drug use* is generally a long-term pattern of using drugs at least once daily to achieve relief from a persistent problem or stressful situation. Drug use becomes a customary activity of daily life, with people ordinarily remaining socially and economically integrated in the life of the community. Some change in functioning may occur, depending on the frequency, intensity, and amount of use.

5. *Compulsive drug use* is use at both high frequency and high intensity, of relatively long duration, producing physiological or psychological dependence, with disuse resulting in physiological discomfort or psychological stress. Motivation to continue comes from the physical or psychological comfort or relief obtained by using the drug. Users in this category include not only the street "junkie" or skid-row alcoholic but also the opiate-dependent physician, the barbiturate-dependent homemaker, or the alcohol-dependent business executive.

All research studies show that the most frequently used drugs in the United States are *alcohol, tobacco,* and *marijuana,* in that order. Table 18.1 shows the percentage of youths, aged 12 to 17, using various types of drugs in 1982, 1985, 1988, 1992, and 1994 (U.S. Bureau of the Census, 1996). These figures indicate an increase in adolescents' current use (use in the past month) of all the drugs except sedatives and tranquilizers.

TABLE 18.1 Percentage of Youths, Ages 12 to 17, Using Drugs

Drug	EVER USED					PAST MONTH				
	1982	1985	1988	1992	1994	1982	1985	1988	1992	1994
Marijuana	26.7	23.7	17.4	10.6	16.0	11.5	12.3	6.4	4.0	7.3
Inhalants	NA	9.1	8.8	5.7	6.2	NA	3.6	2.0	1.6	2.0
Hallucinogens	5.2	3.2	3.5	2.6	4.0	1.4	1.1	0.8	0.6	1.2
Cocaine	6.5	5.2	3.4	1.7	1.3	1.6	1.8	1.1	0.3	0.4
Heroin	<.5	<.5	0.6	0.2	0.4	<.5	<.5	NA	0.1	NA
Stimulants	6.7	5.5	4.2	2.1	2.6	1.3	1.8	1.2	0.2	0.4
Sedatives	5.8	4.0	2.4	1.5	3.2	0.9	1.1	0.6	0.4	0.3
Tranquilizers	4.9	4.8	0.2	1.6	2.0	0.7	0.6	0.2	0.2	0.2
Analgesics	4.2	5.9	4.2	3.9	4.7	2.6	1.9	0.9	0.8	1.3
Alcohol	65.2	55.9	50.2	39.3	41.2	26.9	31.5	25.2	15.7	16.3
Cigarettes	49.5	45.3	42.3	33.7	33.5	14.7	15.6	11.8	9.1	9.8

Source: U.S. Bureau of the Census, *Statistical Abstract of the United States, 1996* (Washington, DC: U.S. Government Printing Office, 1996), p. 144.

Youths are trying drugs at increasingly younger ages. It is not unusual for children 8 to 10 years old to use drugs. An elementary school official in Washington, DC, complained that he had not been able to keep one third-grader from smoking marijuana every day at recess. Threats of expulsion did not help because the child insisted he could not break the habit. He did refuse to share his cigarettes with classmates because, he said, "The habit is dangerous." One longitudinal study in the San Francisco area showed that socially precocious girls were more likely to become involved with drugs earlier than were boys, although for both boys and girls, the transition to junior high school played an important role in initiating drug use (Keyes and Block, 1984).

All drugs increased in lifetime use by 12- to 17-year-olds from 1992 to 1994 except cocaine and cigarettes. Figure 18.1 shows the changes from 1974 to 1994.

Why Drugs Are First Used

Why do adolescents first use drugs? The overwhelming majority try drugs out of *curiosity*—to see what they are like. If adolescents are more attracted by the promise of a drug than repelled by its potential harm, they may be led to experiment.

Other adolescents begin using drugs as a means of *rebellion, protest,* and *expression of dissatisfaction* with traditional norms and values. This group includes activists and protestors whose lifestyles include involvement with drugs (Pedersen, 1990).

Another reason for trying drugs is for *fun or sensual pleasure.* Users are seeking an exciting experience. Adolescents are growing up in a fun-oriented culture that emphasizes the need and value of having a good time. If smoking grass is thought to be fun, this becomes a strong motive for its use. Another aspect of having fun is to experience sensual pleasure. This pleasure may be sexual; many adolescents feel that pot makes the exploration of sex less inhibited and more enjoyable. The pleasure motive may involve seeking an increased sensitivity of touch or taste.

Another strong motive for trying drugs is the *social pressure* to be like friends or to be part of a social group. Whether friends use drugs or not is one of the most significant factors in determining adolescent drug usage (Hundleby and Mercer, 1987).

Research findings indicate that youths who use specific drugs almost invariably have friends who also use the same drugs (Dinges and Oetting, 1993). Adolescents say, "Many of my friends tried

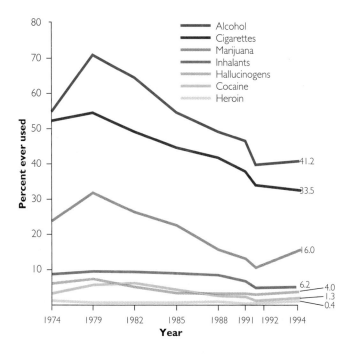

FIGURE 18.1   Lifetime Drug Usage among 12- to 17-Year-Old Americans, 1974–1994

Source: U.S. Bureau of the Census, *Statistical Abstract of the United States, 1996* (Washington, DC: U.S. Government Printing Office, 1996), p. 144.

CROSS-CULTURAL CONCERNS

Onset of Drug Use among Rural African American Youths

A sample of 363 African American students (grades 7 to 12) from a rural county in Alabama was surveyed to examine the age of onset and periods of risk for drug use, and patterns of multiple drug use (Okwumabua, Okwumabua, Winston, and Walker, 1989). As a group, these rural African American youths began drinking alcohol, smoking cigarettes and marijuana, and using smokeless tobacco and solvents by age 10. Initiation into cocaine use began by age 11. The period of risk for initiation of drug use was between the ages of 10 and 14. Approximately 65 percent of those who ever used drugs were single-drug users; 35 percent were multiple-drug users.

it and I didn't want to be different," or "Everybody is doing it." This motive is especially strong among immature adolescents who are seeking to belong to a crowd or gang. (McDonald and Towberman, 1993; Johnston, Bachman, and O'Malley, 1994).

One important motive for trying drugs is to *relieve tensions and anxieties,* to escape from problems, or to be able to deal with or face them (Eisen, Youngman, Grob, and Dill, 1992). Student have cited the following reasons for using drugs:

"I needed to get away from the problems that were bugging me."

"I felt tired and depressed and needed a lift."

"I had to stay awake to study for exams."

"When I'm on grass, I have more self-confidence and can do anything."

One study found that adolescents who were shy but sociable were more likely to use drugs than those who were not shy. Drugs became a means of feeling more comfortable in social situations (Page, 1990).

Those who use drugs as an escape from tension, anxiety, problems, or reality, or to make up for personal inadequacies are likely to find themselves dealing with a drug habit (Simons, Whitbeck, Conger, and Melby, 1991).

PERSONAL ISSUES

Drug Use and Pregnancy

Utilizing data from the National Longitudinal Survey of Youth (NLSY), researchers investigated the relationship between adolescent drug users and pregnancy. The researchers found that teenagers' use of hard drugs increased their risk of premarital pregnancy nearly fourfold. Nearly one-third (29 percent) of the sexually active, unmarried White respondents first interviewed at ages 14 to 16 became pregnant before their twentieth birthdays; the mean age at conception was 17 years. Not using contraceptives was an important factor related to premarital pregnancy; substance use was also significantly related to the probability of this outcome. The risk of pregnancy also increased with earlier initiation of substance use; for example, young White women who first used marijuana by age 14 were more than twice as likely to experience a premarital pregnancy as were those who did not start use until age 18. According to the researchers, indirect evidence suggests that greater frequency of sexual activity, rather than less effective contraceptive behavior, may explain why users of illicit drugs are at higher risk for premarital pregnancy than are nonusers (Remez, 1992).

There are those uses whose primary motive for trying a drug is to *gain self-awareness, increased awareness of others, or more religious insight* or to *become more creative.* The sense of increased awareness or greater creativity may be more imagined than real, but the person may truly believe that the drug provides this awareness. This is an especially strong motive for using the psychedelics.

There are some youths who begin selling drugs at an early age, prior to taking drugs. The bridge between drug dealing and drug using may eventually form. Motive for drug selling is obviously to make money, which may or may not, in the beginning, be spent on drugs for the seller (Feigelman, Stanton, and Ricardo, 1993).

Compulsive Drug Use

The reasons for adolescents to first use drugs and then to continue to use them are varied (Capuzzi and Lecoq, 1983). Those who continue to use nonaddictive drugs as a means of trying to solve emotional problems become psychologically dependent on them (Johnson and Kaplan, 1991). Drugs become a means of finding security, comfort, or relief (Andrews et al., 1993). When individuals become psychologically dependent on drugs that are also physiologically addicting—such as alcohol, barbiturates, and heroin—dependence is secondarily reinforced by the desire to avoid the pain and distress of physical withdrawal.

The need to use drugs excessively originates within the families in which children grow up. Drug abusers are not as close to their parents and are more likely to have negative adolescent-parental relationships and a low degree of supportive interaction with them than are nonusers (Smart, Chibucos, and Didier, 1990).

A study of public secondary school students from 18 high schools in New York State revealed the following correlations. Students who started to use illicit drugs

Lacked closeness to parents
Had parents who used authoritarian control in discipline
Had parents who used hard liquor and psychoactive drugs
Lacked intimate ties with a best friend
Had a history of marijuana use
Exhibited signs of depression

Were more often involved in delinquency than nonusers (Kandel et al., 1978)

Another study of the family relationships of adolescent drug users in comparison to nonusers revealed that the families of users

More often created the adolescent as a scapegoat for family problems
Showed inferior ability in arriving at decisions
Evidenced fewer positive communications among members
Allowed less freedom for open expression of opinions
Were less cooperative with one another (Gantman, 1978)

Overall, the family relationships of adolescents who abused drugs were similar to those of adolescents who were emotionally disturbed.

The net effect of these family situations is to create personality problems that cause individuals to be more likely to run to drugs. Numerous other studies correlate drug addiction and dependency with disturbed family relationships.

Treatment

There are various approaches in treating chemical dependency. These include the 12-step program of Alcoholics Anonymous (AA); professional counseling, medical treatment, and psychiatric care; family systems therapy; and therapeutic treatment. Let's look at these more in detail.

Alcoholics Anonymous The disease perspective of AA (also Narcotics Anonymous—NA) emphasizes the individual's inability to control drug consumption as a primary symptom. Willful attempts at stopping on one's own are seen as futile and counterproductive. Recovery is largely a spiritual awakening process that is achieved through working the 12 Steps. The 12-step program begins by accepting one's powerlessness over drugs and then developing a sense of one's higher power, which enables the individual to control the drug habit.

Professional Counseling, Medical Treatment, and Psychiatric Care Rather than viewing chemical dependency as a disease in and of itself,

Families of Drug Abusers

Several studies have delineated the relationship between family factors and drug abuse. The following family factors have an impact on drug use:

Family Closeness
Isolation of adolescent from family
Lack of closeness with parents
Little parental support
Lack of love
Need for recognition, trust, love not filled
Parental rejection, hostility
Closeness bordering on enmeshment
Father not actively involved with family

Conflict
Marital conflict
Husband irresponsible
Unhappy home
Wife unhappy
Disharmony in family
Children as pawns in marital discord
High degree of stress, trauma

Scapegoating
Adolescent as scapegoat for inadequacy

Role Model
Parents as inadequate role models
Parents as drug users
Parents as models of drug abuse
No emulation of parents by adolescent

Divorce, Family Breakup
Broken home
One or both parents absent much of time
Father absence especially harmful
Single-parent home

Discipline
Parents showing lack of coping skills
Inconsistent discipline

Discipline too autocratic or laissez-faire
Lack of clear rules, limits, guidance
Excessive use of punishment

Hypocritical Morality
Double standard of behavior: one for selves, another for adolescents
Denial of problems with self and of parental faults

Psychological Crutches
Parents lacking confidence in coping with life; using drugs as psychological crutch
No effective coping skills learned from parents; adolescent follows parental model of coping by using drugs, alcohol

Communication Gap
Lack of ability to communicate
Lack of parental understanding
Lack of communication by parents for fear of hearing anything negative
Unheard cries for help

Research suggests that adolescents who are able to talk openly with their parents use illicit substances to a lesser extent than those who aren't able to talk with their parents (Kafka and London, 1991).

Religiosity
Research has revealed a negative relationship between religiosity and alcohol and marijuana use. Similarly, religious conservatism has a similar effect on alcohol and marijuana use. It does appear that the influence of religiosity and religious conservatism on substance use is mainly confined to the less serious drugs (Free, 1993). Some scholars have maintained that the impact of religious involvement is small after other variables are controlled (Bahr, Hawks, and Wang, 1993).

Source: Data from Coombs and Landsverk, 1988; Jurich, Polson, Jurich, and Bates, 1985; Melby, Conger, Conger, and Lorenz, 1993; Volk, Edwards, Lewis, and Sprinkle, 1989.

traditional psychiatric and counseling approaches have tended to emphasize a host of emotional disorders as causal factors. Therefore, treatment is focused on understanding and resolving the emotional problems that underlie drug use, as well as medical treatment to restore health.

Family Systems Therapy This approach focuses on family-of-origin conflicts and issues as central in developing and maintaining chemical dependency. Drug abuse usually begins in adolescence and is the result of intense fears of separation. The family therapy approach seeks to help families address separation issues and to help the family system adapt more effectively as the addict gives up drug-using behavior. A central goal is to help parents address conflict between each other that may have been ignored because of their focusing on the drug-using and antisocial behavior.

Therapeutic Community Treatment The therapeutic community model of treatment strongly emphasizes both abstaining from alcohol consumption and addressing emotional factors associated with drug use. Emotional issues, however, are addressed primarily in terms of how they are reflected in behaviors and attitudes in the environment. There is less emphasis on resolving past developmental or family-of-origin issues. At the center of the therapeutic community philosophy is the critical importance of involvement with one's peer group. Clients are involved in process groups, confrontation groups, support groups, and community meeting groups.

The drug treatment field seems to be moving in the direction of using multimodal approaches, which incorporate several different models simultaneously. This shift may reflect the increasing recognition that chemically dependent clients require a broad-based approach because of the various needs presented by them.

One of the newer multimodal approaches is called *biopsychosocial*. This approach is being used to describe approaches that recognize and address psychological, biological, and social aspects of addictions. The factors related to successful outcome include the following: (1) the group-oriented approach to treatment, (2) interdisciplinary assessment and treatment, (3) a focus on psychiatric disorders in addition to alcoholism, (4) the judicious use of medications, (5) thorough medical evaluation, (6) involvement of clients in AA meetings, and (7) a strong focus on aftercare treatment (Polcin, 1992).

Tobacco and Smoking

Tobacco is the second most widely abused drug by youths age 12 to 17.

Incidence

Of all 12- to 17-year-old students, 34 percent have smoked cigarettes. About one-third of 18- to 25-year-olds are regular smokers. More than one-half of all youths who smoke have their first cigarette before the age of 12 (Bell and Battjes, 1985;

Treatment for chemical dependency is beginning to use multiple approaches simultaneously. A component of many of these multiple approaches is group counseling, such as the group shown here.

Since cigarette smoking is highly addictive and very difficult to stop, it is important to keep adolescents from starting to smoke. Antismoking programs should begin early and continue over a number of years. The 10-year-olds shown here at an antitobacco rally should continue to be exposed to antismoking programs throughout their adolescent years.

of consumer acceptance. This is probably fortunate, since the substance in these cigarettes is associated with increased oral cancer. Other long-term health risks are unknown (Dignan et al., 1986).

Keeping Adolescents from Starting

The ideal is to keep adolescents from starting to smoke in the first place. A number of studies have been conducted to determine the most effective way to keep adolescents away from this habit and to help more of them to stop once they have started. Some of the most important suggestions and proposals are discussed here.

First, antismoking education should *avoid extreme scare tactics* that attempt to frighten adolescents into stopping. It is all right to point to the facts, such as the relationship between smoking and lung cancer, respiratory illnesses, and cardiovascular disease, or the dangers of smoking during pregnancy or while taking oral contraceptives. Moderate anxiety can be especially useful in preventing adolescents from starting. But extreme scare tactics lead adolescents to deny that smoking will cause physical harm and to reject the teachings of the person who is trying to scare them. Teachers who are against smoking are more effective in antismoking education than are teachers who are neutral. Teachers need to take a stand

but not use extremely negative approaches, especially those that exaggerate.

Next, the *primary appeal should be positive.* The program should appeal to adolescents' vanity, their pride, their belief in themselves, and their sense of achievement. They should be encouraged to establish control over their own behaviors and not to blame others for their own habits (Sheppard, Wright, and Goodstadt, 1985). Appealing to their desire to maintain physical fitness has been proved to be an effective tactic.

Third, adolescents should be told *all the facts as honestly as possible.* A program should avoid half-truths and avoid creating a credibility gap. Even when adolescents have the facts about the hazards of smoking, some start or continue to smoke anyway because of the tendency to feel that lung cancer or other illnesses won't happen to them. Presenting factual information on the hazards does not often change behavior, but it usually has considerable influence on knowledge and attitudes.

Fourth, efforts should *enlist the help of student leaders* and of students themselves (Erickson and Newman, 1984). An antismoking campaign at Central High School in Great Falls, Montana, was sponsored by the student's cancer club. When the campaign ended, the whole cultural climate of the high school had changed from prosmoking to antismoking, and most of the students had pledged not to smoke. Nonsmokers suffer negative physiological and psychological symptoms from tobacco smoke pollution in public places, which suggests that schools have a responsibility to limit smoking.

Next, a *program should begin early,* when the child is young, and continue periodically over a span of years. A *recurring program* is more effective than a single mass exposure. Education laws in New York State require that antismoking education be started after grade 8. This is too late. Fourth or fifth grade is a better time to begin.

Sixth, students should be helped to *discover and analyze* their own inner, hidden, emotional, or social reasons for smoking and to deal with these problems so that the smoking crutch will not be needed.

Last, *no one teaching method can be considered best.* Antismoking education programs have been partly successful in changing smoking behavior among adolescents who already smoke.

Other measures are being taken to keep adolescents from starting smoking. States have passed laws making the smoking of cigarettes illegal before age 18. Also, cigarette taxes are being raised to make it harder for adolescents to afford cigarettes. Law suits against cigarette companies that use advertising to target youths or that distort the addictive power of nicotine seek to prevent companies from using false claims so they can sell tobacco products. Smoking is being banned in public places. Together, these measures should reduce the use of cigarettes.

Alcohol and Excessive Drinking

Alcohol is the drug of first choice among youths, yet it is often not recognized as a drug. We need a better understanding of its attraction to youths, its addicting qualities, and its effects.

Incidence

Studies of junior high, senior high, and college students reveal that a substantial proportion of adolescents drink. Findings from 1994 indicate that 41 percent of youths aged 12 to 17 and 87 percent aged 18 to 25 have had a drink (U.S. Bureau of the Census, 1996). Given that drinking is com-

Some 87 percent of youths ages 18 to 25 have had an alcoholic drink. One of the biggest problems with alcohol is the frequent drinking of large quantities—a problem that is especially prevalent on college campuses.

mon in the United States, it is no surprise that a vast majority of adolescents have been introduced to alcohol.

The problem is not so much in the drinking, per se, but in the frequent drinking of large quantities. In a nationwide sampling of students in grades 7 through 12, one in three said that alcohol was the "most serious social problem at my school" (Solorzano, 1984). Alcohol is also a major factor in crime (Dawkins and Dawkins, 1983). More than 50 percent of all arrests are for public drunkenness or driving under the influence. Alcohol is involved in half of all homicides; it is also a major factor in child abuse and family violence. In addition, the majority of pedestrians who are injured by cars have been drinking at the time of the accident. One can only guess the percentage of adolescents who have been drinking when unwed pregnancy occurs. One study found that drinking heavily prior to sex compromised adolescents' abilities to use contraceptives (Flanigan, McLean, Hall, and Propp, 1990). Alcohol abuse during pregnancy causes over 200,000 premature deaths a year.

Beer is the preferred beverage among boys of all ages, regardless of the frequency with which they drink, and among girls of all ages who drink once a week or more. Older girls who drink only once a month or more or once a year or more prefer distilled spirits to beer. The social contexts in which adolescents drink are subject to legal restrictions. Youths drink before they can legally buy alcoholic beverages or patronize licensed premises. Most who begin to drink do so at home under parental supervision. Much of this drinking occurs on holidays and other special occasions. As youths grow older, they tend to drink more often outside the home, until the most likely drinking places are those where adults are not present.

The prevalence of drinking among junior high and senior high youths has motivated many states to reexamine their laws regulating legal drinking ages. After the Vietnam War, many states lowered the drinking age to 18. The argument was: If they're old enough to fight, they're old enough to vote and to drink. But authorities complained that giving 18-year-olds the right to purchase alcoholic beverages also made alcohol available to their younger friends in junior and senior high school (the older seniors purchased it for the younger schoolmates). As a result, many states that lowered the drinking age raised it again to age 21 (Newman, 1987). Today, the drinking age in all 50 states is age 21.

It is clear that alcohol is the drug of choice for adolescents and young adults, just as it has been for decades. The frequency of regular drinking typically increases for men and women after graduation from high school, so that among those in the 18- to 25-year age group, 64 percent report they are current users of alcohol (past month) (U.S. Bureau of the Census, 1996).

Correlations with Drinking

There are wide variations in drinking habits among different ethnic groups. Some groups, such as Italian Americans and Jews, exhibit drinking habits that are well integrated into their cultures. The vast majority drink, but these groups have the lowest rates of alcoholism of any other groups in the United States, primarily because of the *patterns* of their drinking. For example, Italian Americans have strong sanctions against drunkenness, and the whole family usually drinks wine with meals. As a consequence, they have few alcohol-related problems, although second and later generations begin to show higher rates of heavy drinking as they begin to be less influenced by their cultural heritage and become more Americanized.

In contrast to these patterns, Irish Americans have more problem drinkers than do other Americans of the same social class. They often deliberately seek to get drunk, often drink distilled spirits rather than wine, and often take five or six drinks on a single occasion. Consequently, they have high rates of alcoholism, and their adolescents follow their example.

Drinking patterns among adolescents generally follow the adult models in their communities (Stevens, Mott, and Youells, 1996). Parents who drink or who sanction drinking are more likely to have adolescents who drink (Barnes, Farrell, and Banerjee, 1995); parents who do not drink or who disapprove of drinking are more likely to have youths follow their example. Parents who are moderate to heavy drinkers are more likely to have adolescents who are moderate to heavy drinkers (Barnes, Farrell and Cairns, 1986). Furthermore, chronic alcoholism is more likely to run in families. About one-third of any sample of alcoholics will have had at least one parent who was an alcoholic. Children who are exposed to drinking by their parents, however, do not necessarily grow up to be problem drinkers. The highest rates of alcoholism among adolescents are found in groups that are under pressure to refrain from drinking until age 21 or who are in families, such as the Irish or Native Americans, who themselves have high rates of alcoholism (Gfellner and Hundelby, 1994; Huston, Hoberman, and Nugent, 1994).

Alcohol consumption is also related to religious affiliation and church attendance. Jews have the lowest proportion of abstainers among the three major religions and the lowest proportion of heavy drinkers ("The Jewish Recipe," 1981). Catholics and liberal Protestants have a relatively

HIGHLIGHT

Alcohol Abuse and Alcoholism

Alcohol abuse is the use of alcohol to a degree that causes physical damage; impairs physical, social, intellectual, or occupational functioning; or results in behavior harmful to others. A person does not have to be an alcoholic to have problems with alcohol. The individual who drinks only once a month, but drives while intoxicated and has an accident, is an alcohol abuser—so is the man who gets drunk and beats up his children.

Alcoholism is dependence on alcohol—drinking compulsively and excessively, leading to functional impairment. Some alcoholics drink large amounts daily. Others drink heavily only on weekends. Still others may go through long periods of sobriety interspersed with binges of daily heavy drinking lasting for weeks or months. On some occasions, heavy drinking is limited to periods of stress, associated with periods of anxiety or strain.

The following are some warning signals that indicate a drinking problem is developing:

You drink more than you used to and tend to gulp your drinks.

You try to have a few extra drinks before or after drinking with others.

You have begun to drink alone.

You are noticeably drunk on important occasions.

You drink the "morning after" to overcome the effects of previous drinking.

You drink to relieve feelings of boredom, depression, anxiety, or inadequacy.

You have begun to drink at certain times, to get through difficult situations, or when you have problems.

You have weekend drinking bouts and Monday hangovers.

You are beginning to lose control of your drinking; you drink more than you planned and get drunk when you did not want to.

You promise to drink less but do not.

You often regret what you have said or done while drinking.

You are beginning to feel guilty about your drinking.

You are sensitive when others mention your drinking.

You have begun to deny your drinking or lie about it.

You have memory blackouts or pass out while drinking.

Your drinking is affecting your relationship with friends or family.

You have lost time at work or school due to drinking.

You begin to stay away from people who do not drink.

---

high proportion of drinkers and heavy drinkers. Conservative Protestants have the largest proportion of abstainers and the lowest proportion of heavy drinkers. Religiousness and frequency of church attendance are strongly related to abstinence. In many studies, problem drinkers among youths score lower than nonproblem drinkers on an index of religious participation.

There are a number of other significant correlations with drinking:

1. The highest proportion of abstainers (62 percent) in the general population is found among people with less than an eighth-grade education. The proportion of heavier drinkers increases

fairly steadily, from 6 percent of those with a grammar school education to 15 percent of college graduates (Harris and colleagues, 1974).

2. Proportionately more people on the lower socioeconomic levels are abstainers than are those on the upper levels. Both moderate and heavier drinking increases as social class rises (Harris and colleagues, 1974). Alcohol use among adolescents

alcohol abuse excessive use of alcohol so that functioning is impaired.

alcoholism chemical dependency on alcohol accompanied by compulsive and excessive drinking.

is highest when fathers are professionals or managers.

3. Youths from rural areas and small towns are more likely to be abstainers than are adolescents from cities and suburbs. The largest proportions of heavy drinkers live in urban and suburban areas; the smallest proportions of heavy drinkers live in rural communities and small towns (Gibbons, Wylie, Echterling, and French, 1986).

4. In one study, high school adolescents who abstained from drugs, alcohol, and tobacco generally claimed better health, better social relationships, and a happier state of mind than users. There was a lower incidence of the same problem in their parents and more reports of happier childhoods (Martson, Jacobs, Singer, Widaman, and Little, 1988).

5. The incidence of deviant drinking among juvenile delinquents is decidedly higher than in the general adolescent populations, suggesting that overdrinking is but one class of antisocial behavior among those who are maladjusted and who have the potential for getting into trouble (Farrow and French, 1986). Those who are the heaviest drinkers are those who are also most often involved in such crimes as shoplifting, breaking and entering, and auto theft.

6. There is a positive correlation between heavy television viewing and alcohol use. Although cause and effect cannot be inferred, it is plausible that adolescents are taught subtly by television that alcohol is good, healthy, and harmless (Tucker, 1985). Certainly, much youthful drinking is portrayed on television programs (DeFoe and Breed, 1988).

7. Loneliness increases alcohol risk, especially among late adolescent females (18 to 20 years of age). This means that these young women may turn to alcohol to cope with their feelings of loneliness (Page and Cole, 1991).

8. There's a strong and clear negative relationship between parental support and adolescent drinking. There's also a negative linear relationship between parental control and drinking behavior. Thus, low support and lack of control are associated with increased drinking (Foxcroft and Lowe, 1991).

9. In one study, the relationship between various risk factors and alcohol use among seventh-grade adolescents was examined (Webb et al., 1991). The researchers found three important factors related to a high risk of alcoholism:

    a. *Deviant behavior,* including tolerance for deviance and sensation seeking

    b. *Factors related to peer use* (peer use and peer approval of use)

    c. *Family-related risk factors* such as parental use and rejection of parental authority

The researchers cautioned that these risk factors were related to the use of alcohol and other drugs by early adolescents and that these may be different for older youths.

Why Adolescents Drink

Adolescents drink for a number of reasons. Because drinking is a widespread adult custom, drinking by adolescents reflects their perceptions of the attitudes and behavior of adults in our society (Halebsky, 1987). Adolescents use alcohol as an integral part of adult role playing, as a rite of passage into the adult community.

Youths drink also because of peer-group pressure and the need for peer identification, sociability, and friendship (Johnson, 1986). Drinking becomes a social custom of a particular group, therefore the adolescent who wants to be part of the group drinks, as well. Alcohol consumption is often a response to problems of loneliness and anxiety. It relieves shyness, social inhibitions, and anxiety (Mijuskovic, 1988). One way of avoiding drinking is associating with peers who do not drink (Brown and Stetson, 1988).

Another major reason why some youths drink is as a means of rebellion, indicated especially in studies of adolescents who are problem drinkers. Such youths evidence signs of rebellion and alienation from adults and adult institutions. They often experience greater stress in relationship to their parents and receive little social support from their families (Windle and Miller-Tutzauer, 1992). Their drinking is indicative of their estrangement from family and community. This is why adolescents who are excessive drinkers are also more likely to commit delinquent acts.

One study of personality characteristics of alcohol-abusing adolescents found them to have negative feelings about themselves and to be irresponsible, immature, defensive, undependable, self-centered, distrustful, and nonconformist (Mayer, 1988). Other studies show that the presence of psychological distress—for example, depression, anxiety, and psychophysiological symptoms—are positively related to alcohol use and cigarette smoking (Thorlindsson and Vilhjalmsson, 1991).

Not all adolescents who get drunk become problem drinkers. Problem drinkers start to drink in excess for psychological rather than social reasons. Heavy, escapist drinking is symptomatic of serious personality problems. Such youths do not get along at home or at school; they receive more failing grades, are more prone to delinquency, participate less often in extracurricular activities, spend more nights out away from home, and are not as close to their parents as nonproblem drinkers. Only a small percentage of youths are problem drinkers, but they are already evidencing the psychological imbalance that prompts them to rebel or to seek escape through alcohol (Ralph and Morgan, 1991).

Theories of Problem Drinking

Various theories have been developed regarding the causes of problem drinking. The first model is called the *moral model*, which attributes alcoholism to a controllable personal weakness. This theory assumes that people can stop drinking if they want, and the fact that they do not indicates moral weakness.

The second model is a *medical model*, which views alcoholism as a disease or illness. Of course, the medical model attributes less responsibility to the individual than does the moral model; adults who favor it are typically less likely to blame and stigmatize alcoholics.

A third model is a *psychological model*, which views alcoholism as a means of coping with stress, anxiety, and depression. In this model, alcoholism is viewed as a behavioral disorder rather than as a strictly physical condition.

Another model is a *genetic* or *heredity model*, which assumes that the tendency toward alcoholism is inherited (Sigelman, Gurstell, and Stewart, 1992).

The model that individuals accept determines their attitudes toward alcoholism and their interpretations of how it can be overcome. Problems caused by uncontrollable factors generally elicit more sympathy and willingness to help than do problems caused by controllable failings. Unfortunately, too many adults attribute alcoholism to a moral weakness or to an unfortunate means of coping with stress, anxiety, and depression. Many of these people, however, feel that individuals could overcome alcoholism if they would just try hard enough, if their wills were stronger. This is in contrast to medical models that consider alcoholism a disease or illness that is beyond the control of the individual without outside help. Similarly, a genetic model takes some of the personal responsibility away from the individual because, after all, the disease is inherited and the individual can't do anything to prevent it. However, the individual's own efforts are needed in order to overcome the illness, along with the help of significant others and professionals, as keys to recovery.

SUMMARY

1. A distinction needs to be made between *drug addiction* and *psychological dependency*. Some drugs are physically habit forming, meaning the body builds up a physical need for the drug. Psychological dependency is the development of an overpowering psychological need for a drug. Both physical addiction and psychological dependency are hard to break.

2. Abused drugs (in addition to alcohol and tobacco) may be grouped into a number of categories. The categories include the following drugs:

Narcotics—opium, morphine, heroin, codeine, and synthetic opiates (meperidine and methadone)

Stimulants—cocaine, amphetamines (benzedrine, Dexedrine, Biphetamine, and methedrine)

Depressants—barbiturates (Quaalude, Nembutal, Seconal, Tuinal, Amytal, or phenobarbital), tranquilizers (Miltown, Equanil, Placidyl, Librium, and Valium), and analgesics (Darvon)

Hallucinogens—LSD, peyote, mescaline, psilocybin, PCP, STP, DMT, and MDA

Marijuana—in various forms (the plant cannabis, ganja, hashish, hashish oil)

Inhalants—nail polish remover, plastic glue, gasoline, cleaning fluids, paint thinner, and other hydrocarbons.

3. The most frequently abused drugs in the United States are alcohol, tobacco, and marijuana, in that order. Current use of all drugs except tranquilizers and analgesics among youths ages 12 to 17 has been increasing. Alcohol continues to be the drug of choice of all age groups.

4. Teenagers' use of hard drugs increases their risk of premarital pregnancy.

5. Adolescents begin to use drugs for a number of reasons: curiosity; fun and sensual pleasure; social pressure to be like friends; relieve tensions, anxiety, and pressures; escape from problems; and trying to gain increased awareness, insight, and creativity. Those who continue to use drugs may build up a physical addiction and/or psychological dependency. Chronic abusers often have troubled family relationships and personal problems and turn to drugs to lessen pain and conflict and as a substitute for meaningful human relationships.

6. Treatment approaches to drug abuse include Alcoholics Anonymous, professional counseling and psychiatric care, family systems therapy, and therapeutic community treatment. Present approaches use several models simultaneously.

7. Of all 12- to 17-year-olds, 34 percent have smoked cigarettes. The incidence of smoking increases with age and reaches a peak of 34 percent of the population in the 26 to 34 age bracket. Adolescents are influenced to start smoking by cigarette advertising, by the model of adults who smoke, by peer-group pressure, and by their own need for status. Some smoke as an expression of rebellion and autonomy and a desire to be grown up. Once they start, they continue to smoke to relieve tension because it becomes an unconscious habit, because of compulsion for oral activity, and because of a physical addiction to nicotine. The best solution is to keep adolescents from starting in the first place by antismoking education.

8. Substantial portions of adolescents drink; in the 18- to 25-year age group, 87 percent have had a drink. Frequent drinking of large quantities is a major factor in crime, homicides, traffic accidents, child abuse and family violence, pedestrian injuries, unwed pregnancy, and premature deaths of babies.

9. *Alcohol abuse* is the use of alcohol to a degree that causes physical damage and impairs physical, social, intellectual, or occupational functioning. *Alcoholism* is compulsive alcohol dependence: excessive drinking, leading to functional impairment. Only a small percentage of youths are problem drinkers, but they are already evidencing the psychological imbalance that prompts them to rebel or seek escape through alcohol.

10. Drinking patterns among adolescents generally follow the adult models in their communities. Chronic alcoholism is likely to run in families. The amount of drinking is also related to religiosity, education, socioeconomic level, place of residence, health, social relationships, juvenile delinquency, television viewing, loneliness, parental support, deviant behavior, peer use, and family-related risk factors.

11. Adolescents also use alcohol as a part of adult role playing, the need for peer identification, as a means of rebellion, and because of personality problems and psychological distress.

12. There are four models to explain the causes of problem drinking: the moral model; the medical model; the psychological model; and the genetic, or heredity, model.

KEY TERMS

alcohol abuse **441**

alcoholism **441**

physical addiction or physical dependency **424**

psychological dependency **424**

THC **428**

THOUGHT QUESTIONS

1. Was drug abuse a problem in the high school you attended? Explain. What drugs were most commonly used? Was drug abuse limited to any particular type of student? From what type of family background did abusers generally come?

2. What effect did drug abuse have on the lives of adolescents in the school in which you were brought up?

3. What type of drug is most commonly used among students whom you know?

4. What should parents do if they discover their adolescent is using marijuana? Narcotics? LSD? Speed? Cocaine? Inhalants?

5. Discuss the current situation of drug abuse in college: its effects, consequences, and what, if anything, should be done about it.

6. Would you be willing to relate your experience with a particular drug? If you were able to break the habit, how did you do it?

7. Did your high school offer drug education? What type of program? With what effect?

8. What approaches should be taken to combat drug abuse among adolescents?

9. Do you smoke regularly? How old were you when you started? Why do you smoke? Have you ever tried to stop? With what effect?

10. Discuss ways and means of how to quit smoking, such as attending smoking clinics or joining anti-smoking campaigns. Which way works the best?

11. What are some of the best ways of keeping adolescents from starting to smoke?

12. Discuss drinking patterns that you know exist among adolescents and the effects and consequences in the lives of these youths.

13. Do you know any adolescents who are alcohol abusers or alcoholics? Discuss their situations.

14. Among adolescents you know who drink, why are some of them alcohol abusers?

15. What should an adolescent do who has a problem with alcohol? What should parents do?

SUGGESTED READING

Davies, J., and Coggans, N. (1991). *Facts about Adolescent Drug Abuse.* London: Cassell.

Gullotta, T. P., Adams, G. R., and Motemayor, R. (Eds.). (1995). *Substance Misuse in Adolescents.* Thousand Oaks, CA: Sage.

Newcomb, M. D., and Bentler, P. M. (1988). *Consequences of Adolescent Drug Use: Impact on the Lives of Young Adults.* Newbury Park, CA: Sage.

Wodarski, J. S., and Feit, M. D. (1995). *Adolescent Substance Abuse: An Empirical-Based Group Preventative Health Paradigm.* Binghamton, NY: Hayworth.

GLOSSARY

accommodation involves adjusting to new information by creating new structures to replace old.

acne pimples on the skin caused by overactive sebaceous glands.

adaptation including and adjusting to new information that increases understanding.

adolescence the period of growth from childhood to maturity.

adolescent culture sum of the way of living of adolescents.

adolescent society structural arrangements of subgroups within an adolescent social system.

adolescent subculture values and way of life that are contrary to chose found in adult society.

adrenal glands ductless glands, located just above the kidneys, that secrete androgens and estrogens in both men and women, in addition to the glands' secretion of adrenaline.

adversary approach legal approach to divorce whereby one party brings charges against the other, in an attempt to prove guilt of the other as a basis for the divorce.

affect feelings that exist among family members.

age-grade society adolescent society composed of those in the same grade level.

alcohol abuse excessive use of alcohol so that functioning is impaired.

alcoholism chemical dependency on alcohol accompanied by compulsive and excessive drinking.

anabolic steroids the masculinizing hormone testosterone taken by athletes to build muscle mass.

anal stage the second psychosexual stage in Sigmund Freud's theory of development: the second year of life, during which the child seeks pleasure and satisfaction through anal activity and the elimination of waste.

androgens a class of masculinizing sex hormones produced by the testes and, to a lesser extent, by the adrenals.

androgeny a blending of male and female characteristics and roles.

anorexia nervosa an eating disorder characterized by an obsession with food and with being thin.

anovulatory without ovulation.

anxious runaway a runaway who comes from a multiproblem family.

assimilation incorporating a feature of the environment into an existing mode or structure of thought.

autonomy independence or freedom.

autosociality Period during which a child plays alongside other children, not with them.

Bartholin's glands glands on either side of the vaginal opening that secrete fluid during sexual arousal.

behavioral autonomy becoming independent and free enough to act on one's own without excessive dependence on others.

bulimia an eating disorder characterized by binge-eating episodes and purging.

centering the tendency of children to focus attention on one detail and their inability to shift attention to other aspects of the situation.

Chicano (Chicana) term for Mexican American.

child abuse may include not only physical assault of a child but also malnourishment, abandonment, neglect, emotional abuse, and sexual abuse.

child neglect failure to provide even minimal care of a child, including adequate food, clothing, shelter, and medical care, as well as the child's emotional, social, intellectual, and moral needs.

clitoris a small shaft containing erectile tissue, located above the vaginal and urethral openings, that is highly responsive to sexual stimulation.

cognition the act or process of knowing.

cognitive monitoring thinking about what you are doing, what you are going to do next, how the problem is going to be solved, and the approaches that you are going to take.

cohesion the degree to which family members are connected to other family members.

coitus sexual intercourse.

colonias or barrios colonies or districts of Spanish-speaking people.

compromise with reality theory the theory of vocational choice proposed by Ginzberg.

concrete operational stage the third stage of cognitive development, according to Piaget, lasting from 7 to 11 or 12 years of age.

corpus luteum a yellow body that grows from the ruptured follicle of the ovary and becomes an endocrine gland that secretes progesterone.

Cowper's glands small twin glands that secrete a fluid to neutralize the acid environment of the urethra.

cultural determinism the influence of a particular culture in determining the personality and behavior of a developing individual.

cultural relativism variations in social institutions, economic patterns, habits, mores, rituals, religious beliefs, and ways of life from one culture to another.

date rape forced unwanted sexual intercourse while on a date.

deductive reasoning beginning with an hypothesis or premise and breaking it down to see if it is true.

defense mechanisms according to Sigmund Freud, unrealistic strategies used by the ego to protect itself and to discharge tension.

depersonalization and derealization becoming detached emotionally from the self.

developmental tasks the skills, knowledge, functions, and attitudes that individuals have to acquire at certain points in their lives in order to function effectively as mature persons.

differential association Sutherland's theory that outlines conditions that facilitate moral or criminal learning.

dysfunctional family one that does not function as it should so adolescents can grow into healthy, happy, secure mature, educated, and socially responsible adults.

ectomorph tall, slender body build.

ego according to Sigmund Freud, the rational mind that seeks to satisfy the id in keeping with reality.

egocentrism the inability to take the perspective of another or to imagine the other person's point of view.

emotional abuse may include constant screaming at the child, calling him or her foul names, giving constant criticism and put-downs, making fun, constantly comparing the child with siblings, ignoring the child, and refusing to talk or listen to him or her.

emotional autonomy becoming free of childish emotional dependence on parents.

empathy the ability to identify with the thoughts, attitudes, and feelings of another person.

endomorph short, heavy body build.

epididymis a system of ducts, running from the testes to the vas deferens, in which sperm mature and are stored.

equilibrium according to Piaget, achieving a balance between schemas and accommodation.

equity assigning punishments in accordance with ability to take responsibility for a crime.

erotomania the delusional belief of being loved by another.

estrogen feminizing hormone produced by the ovaries and, to some extent, by the adrenal glands.

exosystem that part of an ecological system that includes settings in which the adolescent does not have an active role as a participant but that influence him or her nevertheless.

expiatory punishment punishment that results from an externally imposed regulation.

expressive role a role that emphasizes fulfilling emotional needs.

fallopian tubes tubes that transport the ova from the ovaries to the uterus.

femininity personality and behavior characteristics of a female according to culturally defined standards of femaleness.

follicle-stimulating hormone (FSH) a pituitary hormone that stimulates the maturation of the follicles and ova in the ovaries and of sperm in the testes.

foreclosure according to Marcia, establishing an identity without search or exploration, usually according to what has been handed down by parents.

formal operational stage the fourth stage of cognitive development, according to Piaget, during which people develop abstract thought independent of concrete objects.

gender a person's biological sex.

gender identity a person's internal sense of being male or female.

gender role or sex role the outward manifestation and expression of maleness or femaleness in a social setting.

genital stage the last psychosexual stage in Sigmund Freud's theory of development, during which sexual urges result in seeking other persons as sexual objects to relieve sexual tension.

gonadotropic hormones   hormones that are secreted by the pituitary and that influence the gonads, or sex glands.

gonadotropin-releasing hormone (GnRH)   a hormone secreted by the hypothalamus that controls the production and release of FSH and LH from the pituitary.

gonads   the sex glands: testes and ovaries.

heteronomy   control of conduct external to the self.

heterosexuality   sexual orientation to those of the opposite sex.

heterosociality   period during which adolescents prefer company of both sexes.

homosexuality   sexual orientation to those of the same sex.

homosociality   period during which children prefer company of those of the same sex.

hormones   biochemical substances secreted into the bloodstream by the endocrine glands that act as an internal communication system that tells the different cells what to do.

human growth hormone (HGH)   a pituitary hormone that regulates body growth.

hymen   the tissue partly covering the vaginal opening.

hypocrisy   discrepancy between what people say and do.

hypothalamus   a small area of the brain that controls motivation, emotion, pleasure, and pain in the body; that is, it controls eating, drinking, hormonal production, menstruation, pregnancy, lactation, and sexual response and behavior.

id   according to Sigmund Freud, those instinctual urges that a person seeks to satisfy according to the pleasure principle.

ideal self   the kind of person an individual would like to be.

identification   the process by which an individual ascribes to himself or herself the characteristics of another person.

identity achieved   according to Marcia, those adolescents who have undergone a crisis in their search for an identity and who have made a commitment.

identity diffused   according to Marcia, those adolescents who have not experienced a crisis and explored meaningful alternatives nor made any commitments in finding an acceptable identity.

imaginary audience   the adolescents' belief that others are constantly paying attention to them.

imaging   being on best behavior to make a good impression.

immanent justice   the child's belief that immoral behavior inevitably brings pain or punishment as a natural consequence of the transgression.

individuation   the formation of personal identity by the development of the self as a unique person separate from parents and others.

induction   parental control through offering alternative choices.

inductive reasoning   gathering individual items of information and putting them together to form hypotheses or conclusions.

inhibin   a hormone produced in the testes to regulate FSH secretion and sperm production.

instrumental role   a role that emphasizes meeting physical needs.

intelligence quotient (IQ)   calculated by dividing the mental age (MA) by the chronological age (CA) and multiplying by 100.

Internet   thousands of interconnected computer networks that span the globe, allowing the exchange of information.

joint custody   legal custody shared between two parents, both of whom are responsible for childrearing and for making decisions regarding the child.

juvenile   one who is not yet considered an adult in the eyes of the law.

juvenile delinquent   a juvenile who violates the law.

labia majora   major or large lips of tissue on either side of the vaginal opening.

labia minora   smaller lips or tissue on either side of the vagina.

latency stage   the fourth psychosexual stage in Sigmund Freud's theory of development: from about 6 to 12 years of age, during which sexual interests remain hidden while the child concentrates on school and other activities.

long-term storage (long-term memory)   the process by which information is perceived and processed deeply so it passes into the layers of memory below the conscious level (also called secondary memory).

low socioeconomic status (low SES)   those persons who are of low social class and status, including cultural deprivation and low income.

luteinizing hormone (LH)   a pituitary hormone that stimulates the development of the ovum and estrogen and progesterone in females and of sperm and testosterone in males.

luteotropic hormone (LTH)   a pituitary hormone that contains the hormone prolactin, which stimulates milk production by the mammary glands of the female breast.

machismo   Spanish term for maleness or manhood.

macrosystem   the ideologies, attitudes, mores, customs, and laws of a particular culture that influence the individual.

marianismo   in Puerto Rican society, the implication that a woman finds her greatest satisfaction through motherhood.

masculinity   personality and behavioral characteristics of a male according to culturally defined standards of maleness.

masturbation   self-stimulation for purpose of sexual arousal.

matrilineal   descent through the mother's line.

maturation   the biological or generic components to development.

maturity   the time in life when one becomes an adult physically, emotionally, socially, intellectually, and spiritually.

menarche   first menstruation.

mesomorph   medium, athletic body build.

mesosystem   the reciprocal relationships among microsystem settings.

metabolism   the rate at which the body utilizes food and oxygen.

metacognition   knowing about knowing; insight into one's own cognitive processes.

microsystem   includes those persons with whom the adolescent has immediate contact and who influence him or her.

modeling   learning by observing and imitating the behavior of another.

mons veneris   mound of flesh (literally "mound of Venus") in the female located above the vagina, over which pubic hair grows.

morality of constraint or morality of obedience   conduct that is coerced by rules or authority.

morality of conventional role conformity   according to Kohlberg, second level of development of moral thought, based on desire to conform to social convention.

morality of cooperation or morality of reciprocity   conduct that is regulated by mutual respect and consent.

morality of self-accepted moral principles   according to Kohlberg, third level of development of moral thought, based on adherence to universal principles.

moratorium   according to Marcia, a period of time in the life of adolescents who are involved in a continual crisis, who continue to search for an identity, and who have not made any commitments.

negative affect   negative feelings of emotional coldness, rejection, hostility, anger, and insensitivity among family members.

nocturnal emissions   male ejaculation during sleep.

no-fault divorce   rejects fault grounds as a precondition for access to courts and recognizes the right of the individual to petition for divorce on the grounds of irretrievable breakdown of the marriage or irreconcilable differences.

obesity   overweight; excessively fat.

objective judgments   judgments based solely on the consequences of wrongdoing.

occupational environment theory   the theory of vocational choice proposed by Holland.

oral stage   the first psychosexual stage in Sigmund Freud's theory of development: from birth to one year, during which the child's chief source of pleasure and satisfaction comes from oral activity.

ovaries   female gonads or sex glands that secrete estrogen and progesterone and produce mature egg cells.

penis   the male organ for coitus and urination.

personal fable   adolescents' belief that they are invulnerable and that their feelings are special and unique.

phallic stage   the third psychosexual stage in Sigmund Freud's theory of development: from about the fourth to the sixth year during which the genital area is the chief source of pleasure and satisfaction.

physical addiction or physical dependency   a condition that develops from abusing a drug that forms a chemical dependency.

pituitary gland   master gland of the body located at the base of the brain.

pleasure principle   the motivation of the id to seek pleasure and avoid pain, regardless of the consequences.

pluralistic society   a society in which there are many different competing standards of behavior.

positive affect   relationships characterized by emotional warmth, affection, love, empathy, care, sensitivity, and emotional support.

premenstrual syndrome (PMS) typified by nervousness, irritability, anxiety, and unpleasant physical feelings and mood swings that occur just before menstruation.

premoral level according to Kohlberg, first level of development of moral thought, based on reward and punishments.

preoperational stage the second stage of cognitive development, according to Piaget, lasting from 2 to 7 years of age.

primary memory short-term memory that involves information still being rehearsed and focused on in the conscious mind.

problem-finding stage the fifth stage of cognitive development characterized by the ability to be creative, to discover, and to formulate problems.

progesterone a female sex hormone produced by the corpus luteum of the ovary.

progressives educators who emphasize that the purpose of education is to prepare pupils for life.

proprium the self-identity that is developing in time.

prostate glands two glands that secrete a portion of the seminal fluid.

pseudostupidity the tendency to approach problems at much too complex a level and to fail, not because the tasks are difficult, but because they're too simple. Adolescents appear stupid but they are, in fact, bright but not yet experienced.

Psychoanalytical theory Freud's theory that the structure of personality is composed of id, ego, and superego, and that mental health depends on keeping the balance among them.

psychological dependency the development of a persistent, sometimes overpowering psychological need for a drug.

psychosocial moratorium a socially sanctioned period between childhood and adulthood during which an individual is free to experiment to find a socially acceptable identity and role.

puberty the whole period during which a person reaches sexual maturity and becomes capable of reproduction.

pubescence the whole period during which physical changes related to sexual maturity take place.

punishment of reciprocity self-imposed punishment.

reinforcement positive reinforcements are influences that increase the probability that the preceding response will occur again. Negative reinforcements are influences that increase the probability that the preceding response will stop.

rootless runaway one who runs away from home for fun and to seek pleasure and gratification.

satanism a devil-worshipping cult practicing ritualized abuse of animals and people.

schema the original patterns of thinking; the mental structures that people use for dealing with what happens in the environment.

Scholastic Assessment Test (SAT) a test that measures aptitude to do academic work.

scrotum the pouch of skin containing the testes.

secondary memory long-term memory of information that is processed deeply and passed into memory layers below the conscious level.

secular trend the trend to mature sexually at earlier ages.

self a person's personality or nature of which that person is aware.

self-concept conscious, cognitive perception and evaluation by individuals of themselves; their thoughts and opinions about themselves.

self-esteem a person's impression or opinion of himself or herself.

self-reinforcement the act of learners rewarding themselves for activities or responses that they consider of good quality.

seminal vesicles twin glands that secrete fluid into the vas deferens to enhance sperm viability.

sensorimotor stage the first stage of cognitive development, according to Piaget, lasting from birth to about 2 years of age.

sensory storage (sensory memory) the process by which information is received and transduced by the senses, usually in a fraction of a second.

separation-individuation the process by which the adolescent becomes separated from parents and becomes a unique individual.

sexual abuse may include very suggestive language, use of pornography, fondling, petting, masturbation, exhibitionism, voyeurism, oral sex, or full vaginal or anal intercourse.

short-term storage (short-term memory) the process by which information is still in the conscious mind being rehearsed and focused on (also called primary memory).

skinheads A neo-Nazi group of White supremists that carry on a campaign of terrorism against Jews, gays, and minorities; they often shave their heads.

social cognition how people think and reason about their social world as they watch and interact with others; their understanding and ability to get along with other people.

social-evaluative anxiety   shyness.

social role taking   according to Selman, the social roles that individuals take on that reflect their understanding of themselves, their actions to others, and their abilities to understand others' points of view.

spermatogenesis   the process by which sperm are developed.

Strong Vocational Interest Blank   a test that measures suitability for different vocations according to interests.

subjective judgments   judgments that take into account intention or motives.

subsystem   a smaller segment of adolescent society within the larger social system.

superego   according to Sigmund Freud, that part of the mind that opposes the desires of the id by enforcing moral restrictions that have been learned to try to attain a goal of perfection.

syncretism   the act of trying to link ideas together.

teenager   in a strict sense, includes only the teen years: ages 13 to 19.

terrified runaway   a runaway who is escaping sexual or physical abuse.

testes   the male gonads that produce sperm and male sex hormones.

testosterone   a masculinizing sex hormone produced by the testes, and, to a lesser extent, by the adrenals.

THC   the active ingredient in marijuana.

throwaways   adolescents who have been told to leave home.

tracking   an organizational technique that permits schools to create homogeneous groupings of students within a heterogeneous student population in order to facilitate instruction.

traditionalists   educators who emphasize that the purpose of education is to teach the basics.

transductive reasoning   proceeding from particular to particular in thought, without making generalizations.

urethra   the tube carrying the urine from the bladder to the outside; in males, it also carries the semen to the outside.

uterus   the womb in which a baby grows and develops.

vagina   the canal from the cervix to the vulva that receives the penis during intercourse and acts as the birth canal through which a baby passes to the outside.

values clarification   a method of teaching values that helps students become aware of their own beliefs and values.

vas deferens   the tubes running from the epididymis to the urethra that carry semen and sperm to the ejaculatory duct.

vestibule   the opening cleft region enclosed by the labia minora.

vicarious reinforcement   learning from observing the positive or negative consequences of another person's behavior.

vulva   collective term referring to the external genitalia of the female.

World Wide Web   A system whereby users can connect to the Internet by use of software that gives information on specific subjects.

BIBLIOGRAPHY

Abell, E., Clawson, M. C., Washington, W. N., Bost, K. K., and Vaughn, V. E. (1996). "Parenting Values, Attitudes, Behaviors, and Goals of African American Mothers from a Low-Income Population in Relation to Social and Societal Context." *Journal of Family Issues,* 17, 593–613.

Abernathy, T. J., Massad, L., and Romano-Dwyer, L. (1995). "The Relationship between Smoking and Self-Esteem." *Adolescence,* 30, 899–907.

Abraham, K. G. (1986). "Ego-Identity Differences among Anglo-American and Mexican-American Adolescents." *Journal of Adolescence,* 9, 151–166.

Acock, A. C., and Bengtson, V. L. (1980). "Socialization and Attribution Processes: Active versus Perceived Similarity among Parents and Youth." *Journal of Marriage and the Family,* 42, 501–515.

Adam, K. S., Bouckams, A., and Streiner, D. (1982). "Parental Loss and Family Stability in Attempted Suicide." *Archives of General Psychiatry,* 39, 1081–1085.

Adams, G. R., Gullotta, T., and Clancy, M. A. (1985). "Homeless Adolescents: A Descriptive Study of Similarities and Differences Between Runaways and Throwaways." *Adolescence,* 22, 715–724.

Adams, G. R., Gullotta, T. T., and Montenayor, R. (Eds.). 1992. *Adolescent Identity Formation.* Newbury Park, CA: Sage.

Adams, G. R., and Jones, R. M. (February 1982). "Adolescent Egocentrism: Exploration into Possible Contributions of Parent-Child Relations." *Journal of Youth and Adolescence,* 11, 25–31.

Adcock, A. G., Nagy, S., and Simpson, J. A. (1991). "Selected Risk Factors in Adolescent Attempts." *Adolescence,* 26, 817–828.

Adegoke, A. (1992). "Relationship between Parental Socioeconomic Status, Sex, and Initial Pubertal Problems among School-going Adolescents in Nigeria." *Journal of Adolescence,* 15, 323–326.

Adeyanju, M. (1990). "Adolescent Health Status, Behaviors, and Cardiovascular Disease." *Adolescence,* 25, 155–169.

Agrawal, P. (March 1978). "A Cross-Cultural Study of Self-Image: Indian, American, Australian, and Irish Adolescents." *Journal of Youth and Adolescence,* 7, 107–116.

Aguirre, C. E., and Parr, W. C. (1982). "Husband's Marriage Order and the Stability of First and Second Marriages of White and Black Women." *Journal of Marriage and the Family,* 44, 605–620.

Ahlstrom, P. A., Richmond, D., Townsend, C., and D'Angelo, L. (1992). *The Course of HIV Infection in Adolescents.* Paper presented at the meeting of the Society for Adolescent Medicine, Washington, DC.

Ahn, N. (1994). "Teenage Childbearing and High School Completion: Accounting for Individual Heterogeneity." *Family Planning Perspectives,* 26, 17–21.

Ainslie, R. C., Shafer, A., and Reynolds, J. (1996). "Mediators of Adolescents' Stress in a College Preparatory Environment." *Adolescence,* 31, 913–924.

Akinboye, J. O. (Summer 1984). "Secondary Sexual Characteristics and Normal Puberty in Nigerian and Zimbabwian Adolescents." *Adolescence,* 19, 483–492.

Alan Guttmacher Institute. (1993). *National Survey of the American Male Sexual Habits.* Unpublished data.

Alexander, M. C., Moore, S., and Alexander, E. R., III. (1991) "What Is Transmitted in the Inter-generational Transmission of Violence?" *Journal of Marriage and the Family,* 53, 657–668.

Alexander, S. J. (April 1984). "Improving Sex Education Programs for Young Adolescents: Parents' Views." *Family Relations,* 33, 251–257.

Allen, B. P. (1987). "Youth Suicide." *Adolescence,* 22, 271–290.

Allport, G. W. (1950). *Becoming: Basic Considerations for a Psychology of Personality.* New Haven, CT: Yale University Press.

———. (1961). "Values and Our Youth." *Teachers College Record,* 63, 211–219.

Alsaker, F. D. (1992). "Pubertal Timing, Overweight, and Psychological Adjustment." *Journal of Early Adolescence,* 12, 396–419.

Altchek, A. (1988). "Abnormal Uterine Bleeding in Teenage Girls." *Medical Aspects of Human Sexuality,* 22, 82–88.

Amann-Gainotti, M. (1986). "Sexual Socialization during Early Adolescence: The Menarche." *Adolescence,* 83, 703–710.

Amato, P. R. (1986). "Marital Conflict, the Parent-Child Relationship, and Child Self-Esteem." *Family Relations,* 35, 403–410.

———. (1987). "Family Process in One-parent, Stepparent, and Intact Families: The Child's Point of View." *Journal of Marriage and the Family,* 49, 327–337.

———. (1988). "Long-term Implications of Parental Divorce for Adult Self-Concept." *Journal of Family Issues,* 9, 201–213.

———. (1988). "Parental Divorce and Attitudes toward Marriage and Family Life." *Journal of Marriage and the Family,* 50, 453–461.

———. (1990). "Dimension of the Family Environment as Perceived by Children: A Multidimensional Scaling Analysis." *Journal of Marriage and the Family,* 52, 613–620.

Ambert, A. (1986). "Being a Stepparent: Live-in and Visiting Stepchildren." *Journal of Marriage and the Family,* 48, 795–804.

American Association of School Administrators. (1983). *The Excellence Report: Using It to Improve Your Schools.* Arlington, VA: Author.

453

American College Testing Program. (1995). *The ACT Assessment Program.* Iowa City, IA: American College Testing Program.

American Psychiatric Association. (1987). *Diagnostic and Statistical Manual of Mental Disorders.* 3rd ed. Washington, DC: American Psychiatric Association.

Amos, R. J., Pingree, S., Ashbrook, S., Betts, N. M., Fox, H. M., Newell, K., Ries, C. P., Terry, R. D., Tinsley, A., Voichick, J., and Athens, S. (1989). "Developing a Strategy for Understanding Adolescent Nutrition Concerns." *Adolescence,* 24, 119–124.

Andersen, B. L., and LeGrand, J. (1991). "Body Image for Women: Conceptualization Assessment, and a Test of Its Importance to Sexual Dysfunction and Medical Illness." *Journal of Sex Research,* 28, 457–477.

Anderson, H. L., and Young, B. M. (1992). "Holistic Attitudes of High School Students towards Themselves and Their School Experiences." *Adolescence,* 27, 719–729.

Anderson, J. E., Kann, L., Holtzman, D., Arday, S., Truman, B., and Kolbe, L. (1990). "HIV/AIDS Knowledge and Sexual Behavior among High School Students." *Family Planning Perspectives,* 22, 252–255.

Anderson, P. B., Arceneaux, E. R., Carter, D., Miller, A. M., and King, B. M. (1995). "Changes in the Telephone Calling Patterns of Adolescent Girls." *Adolescence,* 30, 779–784.

Anderson, S. A., and Fleming, W. M. (1986). "Late Adolescents' Identity Formation: Individuation from the Family of Origin." *Adolescence,* 26, 785–796.

Andrews, J. A., Hops, H., Ary, D., Tildesley, E., and Harris, J. (1993). "Parental Influence on Early Adolescent Substance Use: Specific and Nonspecific Effects." *Journal of Early Adolescence,* 13, 285–310.

Anolik, S. A. (Fall 1983). "Family Influences upon Delinquency: Biosocial and Psychosocial Perspectives." *Adolescence,* 18, 489–498.

Ansuini, C. G., Fiddler-Woite, J., and Woite, R. S. (1996). "The Source, Accuracy, and Impact of the National Sexual Information on Lifetime Wellness." *Adolescence,* 31, 283–289.

Anthony, K. H. (1985). "The Shopping Mall: A Teenage Hangout." *Adolescence,* 20, 307–312.

Apfel, N. H., and Seitz, V. (1991). "Four Models of Adolescent Mother-Grandmother Relationships in Black Inner-City Families." *Family Relations,* 40, 421–429.

Aptekar, L. (Summer 1983). "Mexican-American High School Students' Perception of School." *Adolescence,* 18, 345–357.

"Aptitude-Test Scores: Grumbling Gets Louder." (May 14, 1979). *U.S. News & World Report,* pp. 76ff.

Arbona, C., and Novy, D. M. (1991). "Career Aspirations and Expectations of Black, Mexican American, and White Students." *The Career Development Quarterly,* 39, 231–239.

Archer, S. L. (1989a). "Gender Differences in Identity Development: Issues of Process, Domain, and Timing." *Journal of Adolescence,* 12, 117–138.

———. (1989b). "The Status of Identity: Reflections on the Need for Intervention." *Journal of Adolescence,* 12, 345–359.

Archer, S. L., and Waterman, A. S. (1990). "Varieties of Identity Diffusions and Foreclosures: An Exploration of Subcategories of the Identity Statuses." *Journal of Adolescent Research,* 5, 96–111.

Arcus, M. (1986). "Should Family Life Education Be Required for High School Students? An Examination of the Issues." *Family Relations,* 35, 347–356.

Arehart, D. M., and Smith, P. H. (1990). "Identity in Adolescents: Influences on Dysfunction and Psychosocial Task Issues." *Journal of Youth and Adolescence,* 19, 63–72.

Argyle, M., and Henderson, M. (1985). *The Anatomy of Relationships.* Harmondsworth, Middlesex, England: Penguin.

Arlin, P. K. (1975). "Cognitive Development in Adulthood: A Fifth Stage?" *Developmental Psychology,* 11, 602–606.

Armistead, L., Wierson, M., Forehand, R., and Frame, C. (1992). "Psychopathology in Incarcerated Juvenile Delinquents: Does It Extend beyond Externalizing Problems?" *Adolescence,* 27, 309–328.

Arnett, J. (1991). "Adolescents and Heavy Metal Music: From the Mouths of Metalheads." *Youth and Society,* 23, 76–98.

———. (1992). "The Soundtrack of Recklessness. Musical Preferences and Reckless Behavior among Adolescents." *Journal of Adolescent Research,* 7, 313–331.

Aseltine, R. H., and Gore, S. (1993). "Mental Health and Social Adaptation Following the Transition from High School." *Journal of Research on Adolescence,* 3, 247–270.

Ashford, J. B., and LeCroy, C. W. (1990). "Juvenile Recidivism: A Comparison of Three Prediction Instruments." *Adolescence,* 98, 441–450.

Asmussen, L., and Larson, R. (1991). "The Quality of Family Time among Adolescents in Single-Parent and Married-Parent Families." *Journal of Marriage and the Family,* 53, 1021–1030.

Astin, H. S. (1984). "The Meaning of Work in Women's Lives: A Sociopsychological Model of Career Choice and Work Behavior." *Counseling Psychologist,* 12, 117–128.

Atkinson, R. (1988). "Respectful, Dutiful Teenagers." *Psychology Today,* 22, 22–26.

Austin, D., Lopes, L., Wales, K., Casey, H., and Finch, R. (1992, 1993). *Hat 2 Da Back.* EMI April Music, Inc., Darp Music, Diva One Music, K. Wales Music, Inc., Tiz Biz Music, and Wind Swept Pacific Entertainment Company, d/b/a Longitude Business Company.

Avery, A. W. (December 1982). "Escaping Loneliness in Adolescence: The Case for Androgyny." *Journal of Youth and Adolescence,* 11, 451–459.

Axelson, L. J., and Dail, P. W. (1988). "The Changing Character of Homelessness in the United States." *Family Relations,* 37, 463–469.

Ayman-Nolley, S., and Church, R. B. (1993). *Social and Cognitive Mechanisms of Learning through Interaction with*

Peers. Paper presented at the biennial meeting of the Society for Research in Child Development, New Orleans.

Bachhuber, T. (1992). "Thirteen Ways to Pass Along Real Information to Students." *Journal on Career Planning and Employment, 27,* 67–70.

Bachman, J. B. (1991). "Dropouts, School." In R. M. Lerner, A. C. Petersen, and J. Brooks-Gunn (Eds.), *Encyclopedia of Adolescence.* Vol. 1. New York: Garland.

Bachman, J. G., and Schulenberg, J. (1993). "How Part-time Work Intensity Relates to Drug Use, Problem Behavior, Time Use, and Satisfaction among High-school Seniors: Are These Consequences or Merely Correlates?" *Developmental Psychology, 29,* 220–235.

Bachrach, C. A. (1987). "Cohabitation and Reproductive Behavior in the U.S." *Demography, 24,* 623.

Backover, A. (1991). "Native Americans: Alcoholism, FAS Puts a Race at Risk." *Guidepost, 33,* 1–9.

Bacon, C. S. (1993). "Student Responsibility for Learning." *Adolescence, 28,* 199–212.

Bahr, S. J., Hawks, R. D., and Wang, G. (1993). "Family and Religious Influences on Adolescent Substance Abuse." *Youth and Society, 24,* 443–465.

Baird, P., and Sights, J. R. (1986). "Low Self-Esteem as a Treatment Issue in the Psychotherapy of Anorexia and Bulimia." *Journal of Counseling and Development, 64,* 449–451.

Baker, C. D. (June 1982). "The Adolescent as Theorist: An Interpretative View." *Journal of Youth and Adolescence, 11,* 167–181.

Baker, E. R., Mathur, R. S., Kirk, R. F., et al. (1981). "Female Runners and Secondary Amenorrhea: Correlation with Age, Parity, Mileage and Plasma Hormonal and Sex Hormone-Binding Globulin Concentrations." *Fertility and Sterility, 36,* 183.

Baker, S. A., Thalberg, S. P., and Morrison, D. M. (1988). "Parents' Behavioral Norms as Predictors of Adolescent Sexual Activity and Contraceptive Use." *Adolescence, 23,* 265–282.

Bakken, L., and Romig, C. (1992). "Interpersonal Needs in Middle Adolescents: Companionship, Leadership, and Intimacy." *Journal of Adolescence, 15,* 301–316.

Balakrishnan, T. R., Rao, K. B., Lapierre-Adamcyk, E., and Krotki, K. J. (1987). "A Hazard Model Analysis of the Covariates of Marital Disillusion in Canada." *Demography, 24,* 395–406.

Baldwin, S. E., and Baranoski, M. V. (1990). "Family Interactions and Sex Education in the Home." *Adolescence, 25,* 573–582.

Balk, D. (April 1983). "Adolescents' Grief Reactions and Self-Concept Perceptions following Sibling Death: A Study of 33 Teenagers." *Journal of Youth and Adolescence, 12,* 137–161.

Ball-Rokeach, S. J., Rokeach, M., and Grube, J. W. (November 1984). "The Great American Values Test." *Psychology Today, 18,* 34–41.

Ballard, M. E., and Coates, S. (1995). "The Immediate Effects of Homicidal, Suicidal, and Nonviolent Heavy Metal and Rap Songs on the Moods of College Students." *Youth and Society, 27,* 148–168.

Bandura, A. (1971). *Social Learning Theory.* Morristown, NJ: General Learning Press.

———. (1973). *Aggression: A Social Learning Analysis.* Englewood Cliffs, NJ: Prentice-Hall.

———. (1986). *Social Foundations of Thought and Action: A Social Cognitive Theory.* Englewood Cliffs, NJ: Prentice-Hall.

———. (1989). "Human Agency in Social Cognitive Theory." *American Psychologist, 44,* 1175–1184.

Banks, I. W., and Wilson, P. I. (1989). "Appropriate Sex Education for Black Teens." *Adolescence, 24,* 233–245.

Banyard, B. L., and Williams, L. M. (1996). "Characteristics of Child Sexual Abuse as Correlates to Women's Adjustment: A Perspective Study." *Journal of Marriage and the Family, 58,* 853–865.

Bar-Joseph, H., and Tzuriel, D. (1990). "Suicidal Tendencies and Ego Identity in Adolescence." *Adolescence, 25,* 215–223.

Baranowski, M. D. (Fall 1982). "Grandparent-Adolescent Relations: Beyond the Nuclear Family." *Adolescence, 17,* 575–584.

Barber, B. K., and Thomas, D. L. (1986). "Dimensions of Fathers' and Mothers' Supportive Behavior: The Case for Physical Affection." *Journal of Marriage and the Family, 48,* 783–794.

Barber, B. K., Chadwick, B. A., and Oerter, R. (1992). "Parental Behaviors and Adolescent Self-Esteem in the United States and Germany." *Journal of Marriage and the Family, 54,* 128–141.

Barnes, G. M., and Farrell, M. P. (1992). "Parental Support and Control as Predictors of Adolescent Drinking, Delinquency, and Related Problem Behaviors." *Journal of Marriage and the Family, 54,* 763–776.

Barnes, G. M., Farrell, M. P., and Banerjee, S. (1995). "Family Influences on Alcohol Abuse and Other Problem Behaviors among Black and White Americans." In G. M. Boyd, J. H. Oward, and R. A. Ducker (Eds.), *Alcohol Problems among Adolescents.* Hillsdale, NJ: Erlbaum.

Barnes, G. M., Farrell, M. P., and Cairns, A. (1986). "Parental Socialization Factors and Adolescent Drinking Behavior." *Journal of Marriage and the Family, 48,* 27–36.

Barnes, H. L., and Olson, D. H. (1985). "Parent-Adolescent Communication and the Circumplex Model." *Child Development, 56,* 438–447.

Barnes, M. E., and Farrier, S. C. (Spring 1985). "A Longitudinal Study of the Self-Concept of Low-Income Youth." *Adolescence, 20,* 199–205.

Barnett, J. K., Papini, D. R., and Gbur, E. (1991). "Familial Correlates of Sexually Active Pregnant and Non-Pregnant Adolescents." *Adolescence, 26,* 456–472.

Baron, F. (1985). *Rationality and Intelligence.* Cambridge, England: Cambridge University Press.

Baron, J. (1989). *Teaching Decision-Making to Adolescents.* Hillsdale, NJ: Erlbaum.

Barret, R. L., and Robinson, B. E. (July 1982). "A Descriptive Study of Teenage Expectant Fathers." *Family Relations*, 31, 349–352.

Barry, J. (1993). *In All the Right Places*. Ensign Music Corporation, and Affirmed Productions, Inc. (BMI)/Big Life Music, Ltd. (BMI).

Barth, R. P. (1986). *Social and Cognitive Treatment of Children and Adolescents*. San Francisco: Jossey-Bass.

Bartle, S. E., Anderson, S. A., and Sabatelli, R. M. (1989). "A Model of Parenting Style, Adolescent Individuation, and Adolescent Self-Esteem: Preliminary Findings." *Journal of Adolescent Research*, 4, 283–298.

Barwick, N. A., and Siegel, L. S. (1996). "Learning Difficulties in Adolescent Clients of a Shelter for Runaway and Homeless Street Youths." *Journal of Research on Adolescence*, 6, 649–670.

Bauer, B. G., and Anderson, W. P. (1989). "Bulimic Beliefs: Food for Thought." *Journal of Counseling and Development*, 67, 416–419.

Bauman, R. P. (Spring 1978). "Teaching for Cognitive Development." *Andover Review*, 83–98.

Baumeister, R. F. (1991). "Identity Crisis." In R. M. Lerner, A. C. Petersen, and J. Brooks-Gunn (Eds.), *Encyclopedia of Adolescence*. Vol. 1. New York: Garland.

Baydar, N. (1988). "Effects of Parental Separation and Reentry into Union on the Emotional Well-Being of Children." *Journal of Marriage and the Family*, 50, 967–981.

Baydar, N., Brooks-Gunn, J., and Furstenberg, F. F. (1993). "Early Warning Signs of Functional Illiteracy: Predictors in Childhood and Adolescence." *Child Development*, 64, 815–829.

Bayley, N. (1968). "Behavioral Correlates of Mental Growth: Birth to Thirty-six Years." *American Psychologist*, 23, 1–17.

Bayrakal, S., and Kope, T. M. (1990). "Dysfunction in the Single-parent and Only-child Family." *Adolescence*, 25, 1–7.

Beal, C. R. (1994). *Boys and Girls: The Development of Gender Roles*. New York: McGraw-Hill.

Beal, C. R., and Bonitabitus, G. J. (1991). *Children's Developing Ability to Identify Alternative Interpretations and Narratives: The Role of Text Structure*. Paper presented at the Society for Research in Child Development meeting, Seattle.

Bear, G. G., and Stewart, M. (1990). "Early Adolescents' Acceptability of Interventions. Influence of Problem Severity, Gender, and Moral Development." *Journal of Early Adolescence*, 10, 191–208.

Beaty, E. A. (1995). "Effects of Paternal Absence on Male Adolescents' Peer Relations and Self Image." *Adolescence*, 30, 873–880.

Beaumont, S. L. (1996). "Adolescent Girls' Perceptions of Conversations with Mothers and Friends." *Journal of Adolescent Research*, 11, 325–346.

Begley, S., and Gilman, D. (Sept. 9, 1991). "What Causes People to Be Homosexual?" *Newsweek*, 118, p. 52.

Beilin, H. (1992). "Piaget's Enduring Contribution to Developmental Psychology." *Developmental Psychology*, 28, 191–204.

Beiswinger, G. L. (1979). "The High Court, Privacy, and Teenage Sexuality." *Family Coordinator*, 28, 191–198.

Belitz, J., and Schacht, A. (1992). "Satanism as a Response to Abuse: The Dynamics and Treatment of Satanic Involvement in Male Youths." *Adolescence*, 27, 855–872.

Bell, A. P., Weinberg, M. S., and Hammersmith, K. S. (1981). *Sexual Preference—Its Development in Men and Women*. Bloomington, IN: Indiana University Press.

Bell, C. S., and Battjes, R. (1985). *Prevention Research: Deterring Drug Abuse among Children and Adolescents*. NIDA Research Monograph 63. Rockville, MD: National Institute on Drug Abuse.

Bell, L. G., Cornwell, C. S., and Bell, D. C. (1988). "Peer Relationships of Adolescent Daughters: A Reflection of Family Relationship Patterns." *Family Relation*, 37, 171–174.

Bell, N. J., and Avery, A. W. (May 1985). "Family Structure and Parent-Adolescent Relationships: Does Family Structure Really Make a Difference?" *Journal of Marriage and Family Therapy*, 47, 503–508.

Bell, N. J., Avery, A. W., Jenkins, D., Feld, J., and Schoenrock, C. J. (1985). "Family Relationships and School Competence among Late Adolescence." *Journal of Youth and Adolescence*, 14, 109–119.

Belsky, J., Steinberg, L., and Draper, P. (1991). "Childhood Experience, Interpersonal Development, and Reproductive Strategies: An Evolutionary Theory of Socialization." *Child Development*, 62, 647–670.

Benda, B. B. (1987). "Predicting Juvenile Recidivism: New Method, Old Problems." *Adolescence*, 22, 691–704.

Benedict, R. (1938). "Continuities and Discontinuities in Cultural Conditioning." *Psychiatry*, 1, 161–167.

———. (1950). *Patterns of Culture*. New York: New American Library.

Benedikt, M. (1991). *Cyberspace: First Steps*. Cambridge, MA: MIT Press.

Benenson, J. F. (1990). "Gender Differences in Social Networks." *Journal of Early Adolescence*, 10, 472–495.

Bennett, N. T., Blanc, A. K., and Bloom, D. E. (1988). "Commitment and the Modern Union: Assessing the Length between Premarital Cohabitation and Subsequent Marital Stability." *American Sociological Review*, 53, 127–138.

Bergin, D. A. (1989). "Student Goals for Out-of-School Learning Activities." *Journal of Adolescent Research*, 4, 92–109.

Berkow, R., (Ed.), (1987). "Acne." *The Merck Manual*. 15th ed. Rahway, NJ: Merck and Co.

Bergman, S. J. (1995). "Men's Psychological Development: A Relational Perspective." In R. F. Levant and W. S. Pollack (Eds.), *A New Psychology of Men*. New York: Basic.

Berman, W. H., and Turk, D. C. (1981). "Adaptation to Divorce: Problems and Coping Strategies." *Journal of Marriage and the Family*, 43, 179–189.

Bernard, H. S. (Summer 1981). "Identity Formation during Late Adolescence: A Review of Some Empirical Findings." *Adolescence*, 16, 349–358.

Berndt, T. J., and Mekos, D. (1995). "Adolescents' Perceptions of the Stressful and Desirable Aspects of the

Transition to Junior High School." *Journal of Research on Adolescence, 5,* 123–142.

Berndt, T. J., Miller, K. E., and Park, K. (1989). "Adolescents' Perceptions of Friends and Parents' Influence on Aspects of Their School Adjustment." *Journal of Early Adolescence, 9,* 419–435.

Bernstein, B. E., and Collins, S. K. (1985). "Remarriage Counseling: Lawyer and Therapists' Help with the Second Time Around." *Family Relations, 34,* 387–391.

Berry, J. W., and Bennett, J. A. (1992). "Cree Conceptions of Cognitive Competence." *International Journal of Psychology, 27,* 73–88.

Berry, J. W., Poortinga, Y. H., Segall, M. H., and Dasen, P. R. (1992). *Cross-Cultural Psychology: Theories, Methods, and Applications.* Cambridge, England: Cambridge University Press.

Berzonsky, M. D. (Summer 1978). "Formal Reasoning in Adolescence: An Alternative View." *Adolescence, 13,* 279–290.

———. (1989). "Identity Style: Conceptualization and Measurement." *Journal of Adolescence, 4,* 268–282.

Berzonsky, M. D., Rice, K. G., and Neimeyer, G. J. (1990). "Identity Status and Self-Construct Systems: Process and Structure Interventions." *Journal of Adolescence, 13,* 251–263.

Bilge, B., and Kaufman, G. (January 1983). "Children of Divorce and One-Parent Families: Cross-Cultural Perspectives." *Family Relations, 32,* 59–71.

Billingsley, A. (1988). "The Impact of Technology on Afro-American Families." *Family Relations, 37,* 420–425.

Billy, J. O. G., and Udry, J. R. (Spring 1985). "The Influence of Male and Female Best Friends on Adolescent Sexual Behavior." *Adolescence, 20,* 21–32.

Bingham, C. R., Miller, B. C., and Adams, G. R. (1990). "Correlates of Age at First Intercourse in a National Sample of Young Women." *Journal of Adolescent Research, 5,* 18–33.

Bird, G. W., and Harris, R. L. (1990). "A Comparison of Role Strain and Coping Strategies by Gender: Family Structure among Early Adolescents." *Journal of Early Adolescence, 10,* 141–158.

Bischof, G. T., Stiph, S. N., and Whitney, M. L. (1995). "Family Environment in Adolescent Sex Offenders and Other Juvenile Delinquents." *Adolescence, 30,* 157–170.

Bishop, J. A., and Inderbitzen, H. M. (1995). "Peer Acceptance of Friendship: An Investigation of the Relation to Self-Esteem." *Journal of Early Adolescence, 15,* 476–489.

Black, C., and DeBlassie, R. R. (1985). "Adolescent Pregnancy: Contributing Factors, Consequences, Treatment, and Plausible Solutions." *Adolescence, 20,* 281–290.

Blain, M. D., Tompson, J. M., and Whiffen, V. E. (1993). "Attachment and Perceived Social Support in Late Adolescence. The Interaction between Working Models of Self and Others." *Journal of Adolescent Research, 8,* 226–241.

Blair, S. L., and Lichter, D. T. (1991). "Measuring the Division of Household Labor: Gender Segregation of Housework among American Couples." *Journal of Family Issues, 12,* 91–113.

Blash, R., and Unger, D. G. (1992). *Cultural Factors and the Self-Esteem and Aspirations of African-American Adolescent Males.* Paper presented at the meeting of the Society for Research on Adolescents, Washington, DC.

Blau, G. M., and Gulotta, T. P. (1993). "Promoting Sexual Responsibility in Adolescence." In T. P. Gulotta, G. R. Adams, and R. Montemayor (Eds.), *Adolescent Sexuality.* Newbury Park, CA: Sage.

Blinn, L. M. (1987). "Phototherapeutic Intervention to Improve Self-Concept and Prevent Repeat Pregnancies among Adolescents." *Family Relations, 36,* 252–257.

Block, J., Block, J. and Gjerde, P. F. (1986). "The Personality of Children Prior to Divorce: A Prospective Study." *Child Development, 57,* 827–840.

Block, J., and Robins, R. W. (1993). "A Longitudinal Study of Consistency and Change in Self-Esteem from Early Adolescence to Early Adulthood." *Child Development, 64,* 909–923.

Blos, P. (1979). *The Adolescent Passage: Developmental Issues.* New York: International Universities Press, 1979.

Blumberg, M. L., and Lester, D. (1991). "High School and College Students' Attitudes towards Rape." *Adolescence, 26,* 727–729.

Blyth, D. A., Hill, J. P., and Thiel, K. S. (December 1982). "Early Adolescents' Significant Others: Grade and Gender Differences in Perceived Relationships with Familial and Nonfamilial Adults and Young People." *Journal of Youth and Adolescence, 11,* 425–450.

Bode, J. (1987). "Testimony Before the U.S. House of Representatives Select Committee on Children, Youth, and Families." In *The Crisis of Homelessness: Effects on Children and Families.* G. Miller (Chairman). Washington, DC: U.S. Government Printing Office.

Boehm, K. E., Schondel, C. K., Marlowe, A. L., and Rose, J. S. (1995). "Adolescents Calling. A Peer-Listening Phone Service: Variation in Calls by Gender, Age, and Season of the Year." *Adolescence, 30,* 863–871.

Bomar, J. A., and Sabatelli, R. M. (1996). "Family System Dynamics, Gender, and Psychosocial Maturity in Late Adolescence." *Journal of Adolescent Research, 11,* 421–439.

Boone, C., Williamson, E., and Lyras, N. (1992, 1993). *Come In Out of the Rain.* W. B. Music Corporation, M. Squared Music, Square-Lake Music, Songs of Polygram International, Inc., Tiverton Music, and Deep N' Hard Music.

Booth, A., and Edwards, J. N. (1985). "Age at Marriage and Marital Instability." *Journal of Marriage and the Family, 47,* 67–75.

Booth, A., and Johnson, D. (1988). "Premarital Cohabitation and Marital Success." *Journal of Family Issues, 9,* 255–272.

Bourne, E. (September 1978a). "The State of Research on Ego Identity: A Review and Appraisal. Part I." *Journal of Youth and Adolescence, 7,* 223–251.

———. (December 1978b). "The State of Research on Ego Identity: A Review and Appraisal. Part II." *Journal of Youth and Adolescence, 7,* 371–392.

Bowen, G. L., and Chapman, M. V. (1996). "Poverty, Neighborhood Danger, Social Support, and the Individual Adaptation among At-Risk Youth in Urban Areas." *Journal of Family Issues,* 17, 641–666.

Bowman, M. E., and Ahrons, C. R. (1985). "Impact of Legal Custody Status on Fathers' Parenting Postdivorce." *Journal of Marriage and the Family,* 47, 481–488.

Boyd, M. P., and Yin, D. (1996). "Cognitive-Affective Sources of Sport Enjoyment in Adolescent Sport Participants." *Adolescence,* 31, 383–395.

Boyes, M. C., Giordano, R., and Galperyn, K. (1993). *Moral Orientation and Interpretative Contexts of Moral Deliberation.* Paper presented at the biennial meeting of the Society for Research in Child Development, New Orleans.

Boykin, A. W., and Toms, F. (1985). "Black Child Socialization: A Conceptual Framework." In H. McAdoo and J. McAdoo (Eds.), *Black Children: Social, Educational, and Parental Environments* (pp. 33–51). Newbury Park, CA: Sage.

Brack, C. J., Brack, G., and Orr, D. P. (1996). "Adolescent Health Promotion: Testing a Model Using Multi-Dimensional Scaling." *Journal of Research on Adolescence,* 6, 139–149.

Bozzi, V. (1985). "Body Talk." *Psychology Today,* 19, 20.

———. (1986). "Gotta Ring, Gotta Car!" *Psychology Today,* 20, 3.

Brage, D., Meredith, W., and Woodward, J. (1993). "Correlates of Loneliness among Midwestern Adolescents." *Adolescence,* 111, 685–693.

Brand, E., and Clingempeel, W. G. (1987). "Interdependencies of Marital and Stepparent-Stepchild Relationships and Children's Psychological Adjustment: Research Findings and Clinical Implications." *Family Relations,* 36, 140–145.

Breen, D. T., and Crosbie-Burnett, M. (1993). "Moral Dilemmas of Early Adolescents of Divorce and Intact Families: A Qualitative and Quantitive Analysis." *Journal of Early Adolescence,* 13, 168–182.

Briere, J., and Runtz, M. (1986). "Suicidal Thoughts and Behaviours in Former Sexual Abuse Victims." *Canadian Journal of Behavioural Science,* 18, 413–423.

Brill, H. Q., and Christie, R. L. (1974). "Marijuana Use and Psychological Adaptation: Follow-up Study of a Collegiate Population." *Archives of General Psychiatry,* 31, 713–719.

Brock, L. J., and Jennings, G. H. (1993). "What Daugthers in Their 30's Wished Their Mothers Had Told Them." *Family Relations,* 42, 61–65.

Brody, G. H., Stoneman, V., and Flor, D. (1995). "Linking Family Processes and Academic Confidence among Rural African American Youths." *Journal of Marriage and the Family,* 57, 567–579.

Broman, C. L. (1988). "Satisfaction among Blacks: The Significance of Marriage and Parenthood." *Journal of Marriage and the Family,* 50, 45–51.

Bromley, D. (1967). "Youth and Sex." In F. R. Donovan (Ed.), *Wild Kids.* Harrisburg, PA: Stackpole Co.

Brone, R. J., and Fisher, C. B. (1988). "Determinants of Adolescent Obesity: A Comparison with Anorexia Nervosa." *Adolescence,* 23, 155–169.

Bronfenbrenner, U. (1979). *The Ecology of Human Development.* Cambridge, MA: Harvard University Press.

———. (1987 August). *Recent Advances in Theory and Design.* Paper presented at the American Psychological Association, New York City.

Brooks-Gunn, J., Guo, G., and Furstenberg, F. F., Jr. (1993). "Who Drops Out of and Who Continues beyond High School? A Twenty-Year Follow-Up of Black Urban Youth." *Journal of Research on Adolescence,* 3, 271–294.

Brouwers, M. (1988). "Depressive Thought Content among Female College Students with Bulimia." *Journal of Counseling and Development,* 66, 425–428.

———. (1990). "Treatment of Body Image Dissatisfaction among Women with Bulimia Nervosa." *Journal of Counseling and Development,* 69, 144–147.

Brown, A. (1993). *Whither Cognitive Development in the 1990's?* Paper presented at the biennial meeting of the Society for Research in Child Development, New Orleans.

Brown, B. B. (April 1982). "The Extent and Effects of Peer Pressure among High School Students: A Retrospective Analysis." *Journal of Youth and Adolescence,* 11, 121–133.

Brown, B. B., Eicher, S. A., and Petrie, S. (1986). "The Importance of Peer Group ("Crowd") Affiliation in Adolescence." *Journal of Adolescence,* 9, 73–96.

Brown, B. R., Jr., Baranowski, M. D., Kulig, J. W., Stephenson, J. N., and Perry, B. (1996). "Searching for the Magic Johnson Effect: AIDS, Adolescents, and Celebrity Disclosure." *Adolescence,* 31, 253–264.

Brown, D. (1987). "The Status of Holland's Theory of Vocational Choice." *The Career Development Quarterly,* 36, 13–23.

Brown, J. D., and Lawton, M. (1986). "Stress and Well-Being in Adolescence: The Moderating Role of Physical Exercise." *Journal of Human Stress,* 12, 125–131.

Brown, J. E., and Mann, L. (1988). "Effects of Family Structure and Parental Involvement on Adolescent Participation in Family Decisions." *Australian Journal of Sex, Marriage, and Family,* 9, 74–85.

———. (1990). "The Relationship between Family Structure and Process Variables and Adolescent Decision Making." *Journal of Adolescence,* 13, 25–37.

———. (1991). "Decision-making Confidence and Self-esteem: A Comparison of Parents and Adolescents." *Journal of Adolescence,* 14, 363–371.

Brown, S. A., and Stetson, B. A. (1988). "Coping with Drinking Pressures: Adolescent versus Parent Perspectives." *Adolescence,* 23, 297–301.

Brown, S. L., and Booth, A. (1996). "Cohabitation versus Marriage: A Comparison of Relationship Quality." *Journal of Marriage and the Family,* 58, 668–678.

Browne, A., and Finkelhor, D. (1986). "Impact of Child Sexual Abuse: A Review of Research." *Psychological Bulletin,* 99, 66–77.

Browne, B. A., and Francis, S. K. (1993). "Participants in School-Sponsored and Independent Sports: Perceptions of Self and Family." *Adolescence,* 28, 383–391.

Browne, C. S., and Rife, J. C. (1991). "Social, Personality, and Gender Differences in At-Risk and Not-At-Risk Sixth-Grade Students." *Journal of Early Adolescence,* 11, 482–495.

Brownell, K. D. (1982). "Obesity: Understanding and Treating a Serious, Prevalent, and Refractory Disorder." *Journal of Consulting and Clinical Psychology,* 50, 820–840.

Bryant, Z. L., and Coleman, M. (1988). "The Black Family as Portrayed in Introductory Marriage and Family Textbooks." *Family Relations,* 37, 255–259.

Buchanan, C. M. (1991). "Pubertal Status in Early-Adolescent Girls: Relations to Moods, Energy, and Restlessness." *Journal of Early Adolescence,* 11, 185–200.

Buchanan, C. M., Maccoby, E. E., and Dornbusch, S. M. (1991). "Caught between Parents: Adolescents' Experience in Divorced Homes." *Child Development,* 62, 1008–1029.

———. (1992). "Adolescents and Their Families after Divorce: Three Residential Arrangements Compared." *Journal of Research on Adolescence,* 2, 261–291.

Buis, J. M., and Thompson, D. N. (1989). "Imaginary Audience and Personal Fable: A Brief Review." *Adolescence,* 24, 773–781.

Bukowski, W. M., Gauze, C., Hoza, B., and Newcomb, A. F. (1993). "Differences and Consistency between Same-Sex and Other-Sex Peer Relationships during Early Adolescence." *Developmental Psychology,* 29, 255–263.

Bulcroft, R. A., Carmody, D. C., and Bulcroft, K. A. (1996). "Patterns of Parental Independence Given to Adolescents: Variations by Race, Age, and Gender of Child." *Journal of Marriage and the Family,* 58, 866–883.

Bumpass, L. L. (1990). "What's Happening to the Family? Interactions between Demographic and Institutional Change." *Demography,* 27, 483–498.

Bumpass, L. L., and Sweet, J. A. (1989). "National Estimates of Cohabitation." *Demography,* 26, 615–625.

Buri, J. R. (1989). "Self-Esteem and Appraisals of Parental Behavior." *Journal of Adolescent Research,* 4, 33–49.

Burlew, A. K., and Johnson, J. L. (1992). "Role Conflict and Career Advancement among African-American Women in Non-Traditional Professions." *The Career Development Quarterly,* 40, 302–312.

Burnside, M. A., Baer, P. E., McLaughlin, R. J., and Pickering, A. D. (1986). "Alcohol Use by Adolescents in Disrupted Families." *Alcoholism: Clinical and Experimental Research,* 10, 272–278.

Burr, W. R., and Christensen, C. (1992). "Undesirable Side Effects of Enhancing Self-Esteem." *Family Relations,* 41, 460–464.

Burton, W. (1963). *Helps to Education* (pp. 38, 39). Boston: Crosby and Nichols.

Button, E. (1990). "Self-Esteem in Girls Aged 11–12: Baseline Findings from a Planned Prospective Study of Vulnerability to Eating Disorders." *Journal of Adolescence,* 13, 407–413.

Cabral, A. C., and Salomone, P. R. (1990). "Chance and Careers: Normative versus Contextual Development." *The Career Development Quarterly,* 39, 5–17.

Calabrese, L. H., Kirkendall, D. T., Floyd, M., et al. (1983). "Menstrual Abnormalities, Nutritional Patterns and Body Composition in Female Classic Ballet Dancers." *Physicians Sportsmedicine,* 11, 86.

Calabrese, R. L. (1987). "Adolescence: A Growth Period Conducive to Alienation." *Adolescence,* 22, 929–938.

Calabrese, R. L., and Adams, J. (1990). "Alienation: A Cause of Juvenile Delinquency." *Adolescence,* 25, 435–440.

Caldas, S. J. (1993). "Current Theoretical Perspectives on Adolescent Pregnancy and Childbearing in the United States." *Journal of Adolescent Research,* 8, 4–20.

Calhoun, G. (1987). "Enhancing Self-Perception through Bibliotherapy." *Adolescence,* 22, 929–943.

Calhoun, G., Jurgens, J., and Chen, F. (1993). "The Neophyte Female Delinquent: A Review of the Literature." *Adolescence,* 28, 461–471.

Caliste, E. R. (Fall 1984). "The Effect of a Twelve-Week Dropout Intervention Program." *Adolescence,* 19, 649–657.

Callahan, D., and Callahan, S. (April 1981). "Seven Pillars of Moral Wisdom." *Psychology Today,* 84ff.

Canabal, M. I. (1990). "An Economic Approach to Marital Dissolution in Puerto Rico." *Journal of Marriage and the Family,* 52, 515–530.

Canals, J., Carbajo, G., Fernandez, J., Marti-Henneberg, C., and Domenech, E. (1996). "Biopsychopathologic Risk Profile of Adolescents with Eating Disorder Symptoms." *Adolescence,* 31, 443–450.

Capuzzi, D., and Lecoq, L. L. (December 1983). "Social and Personal Determinants of Adolescent Use and Abuse of Alcohol and Marijuana." *Personnel and Guidance Journal,* 62, 199–205.

Carey v. *Population Services International.* (1977). 75–443.

Carey, M., and Walden, N. (1990). *I Don't Want to Cry.* Vision of Love Songs, Inc.

Carlo, G., Eisenberg, N., and Knight, G. P. (1992). "An Objective Measure of Adolescents' Prosocial Moral Reasoning." *Journal of Research on Adolescence,* 2, 331–349.

Carlson, M. (1996). *Childproof Internet: A Parent's Guide to Safe and Secure Online Access.* New York: Mis Press.

Carlyle, W. (1970). *You're My Friend So I Brought You This Book.* Edited by John Marvin. New York: Random House.

Carmines, E. G., and Baxter, D. J. (1986). "Race, Intelligence, and Political Efficacy among School Children." *Adolescence,* 22, 437–442.

Carpenter, P., and Sugrue, D. P. (Spring 1984). "Psychoeducation in an Outpatient Setting—Designing a Heterogeneous Format for a Heterogeneous Population of Juvenile Delinquents." *Adolescence,* 19, 113–122.

Carr, M., and Schellenbach, C. (1993). "Reflective Monitoring in Lonely Adolescents." *Adolescence,* 111, 737–747.

Carruth, B. R., and Goldberg, D. L. (1990). "Nutritional Issues of Adolescents: Athletics and the Body Image Mania." *Journal of Early Adolescence,* 10, 122–140.

Carruth, B. R., Goldberg, D. L., and Skinner, J. D. (1991). "Do Parents and Peers Mediate the Influence of Television Advertising and Food-Related Purchases?" *Journal of Adolescent Research,* 6, 253–271.

Carter, E. B. (June 1984). "A Teacher's View: Learning to Be Wrong." *Psychology Today,* 18, 35.

Case, R. (Ed.). (1992). *The Mind's Staircase.* Hillsdale, NJ: Erlbaum.

Casper, R. (1983). "On the Emergence of Bulimia Nervosa as a Syndrome: A Historical View." *International Journal of Eating Disorders,* 2, 3–17.

Caspi, A., Lynan, D., Moffitt, T. E., and Silva, P. A. (1993). "Unraveling Girls' Delinquency: Biological, Dispositional, and Contextual Contributions to Adolescent Misbehavior." *Developmental Psychology,* 29, 19–30.

Cassidy, L., and Hurrell, R. M. (1995). "The Influence of Victim's Attire on Adolescents' Judgements of Date Rape." *Adolescence,* 30, 319–323.

Cella, D. F., DeWolfe, A. S., and Fitzgibbon, M. (1987). "Ego Identity Status, Identification, and Decision-Making Style in Late Adolescents." *Adolescence,* 22, 849–861.

Center for Human Resource Research. (1987). *The National Longitudinal Survey Handbook.* Columbus: Ohio State University.

Chance, P. (1988a). "Fast Track to Puberty." *Psychology Today,* 22, 26.

Chance, P. (1988b). "Testing Education." *Psychology Today,* 22, 20–21.

Chassin, L. C., and Young, R. D. (Fall 1981). "Salient Self-Conceptions in Normal and Deviant Adolescents." *Adolescence,* 16, 613–620.

Chaucer, G. (1963). *Canterbury Tales.* (Translated by Vincent Hopper). New York: Barrons.

Chavkin, M. F., and Williams, D. W. (1993). "Minority Parents and the Elementary School: Attitudes and Practices." In N. F. Chavkin (Ed.), *Families and Schools in a Pluralistic Society.* Albany: State University of New York Press.

Cherlin, A. J., and Furstenberg, F. F. (March 19, 1989). "Divorce Doesn't Always Hurt the Kids." *The Washington Post,* p. C1.

Chiam, H. (1987). "Changes in Self-Concept during Adolescence." *Adolescence,* 85, 69–76.

Chiu, L. (1990). "The Relationship of Career Goals and Self-Esteem among Adolescents." *Adolescence,* 25, 593–597.

Chiu, M. L., Feldman, S. S., and Rosenthal, D. A. (1992). "The Influence of Immigration on Parental Behavior and Adolescent Distress in Chinese Families Residing in Two Western Nations." *Journal of Research on Adolescence,* 2, 205–239.

Choquet, M., Kovess, D., and Poutignat, M. (1993). "Suicidal Thoughts among Adolescents: An Intercultural Approach." *Adolescence,* 28, 649–659.

Christmon, K. (1990). "Parental Responsibility of African-American Unwed Adolescent Fathers." *Adolescence,* 25, 645–654.

Christopher, F. S. (1988). "An Initial Investigation into a Continuum of Premarital Sexual Pressure." *The Journal of Sex Research,* 25, 255–266.

Christopher, F. S., and Cate, R. M. (1988). "Premarital Sexual Involvement: A Developmental Investigation of Relational Correlates." *Adolescence,* 23, 793–803.

Ciccone, M., and Pettibone, S. (1992). *Bad Girl.* W. B. Music Corporation, Webo Girl Publishing, Inc., MCA Music Publishing.

Claes, M. E. (1992). "Friendship and Personal Adjustment during Adolescence." *Journal of Adolescence,* 15, 39–55.

Clark, C. A., and Worthington, E. V., Jr. (1987). "Family Variables Affecting the Transmission of Religious Values from Parents to Adolescents: A Review." *Family Perspectives,* 21, 1–21.

Clark, C. A., Worthington, E. L., Jr., and Danser, D. B. (1988). "The Transmission of Religious Beliefs and Practices from Parents to First Born Early Adolescent Sons." *Journal of Marriage and the Family,* 50, 463–472.

Clark, C. M. (1992). "Deviant Adolescence Subcultures: Assessment Strategies and Clinical Interventions." *Adolescence,* 27, 283–293.

Clark, M. L., and Ayers, M. (1993). "Friendship Expectations and Friendship Evaluations. Reciprocity and Gender Effects." *Youth and Society,* 24, 299–313.

Clark-Lempers, D. S., Lempers, J. D., and Netusil, A. J. (1990). "Family Financial Stress, Parental Support, and Young Adolescents' Academic Achievement and Depressive Symptoms." *Journal of Early Adolescence,* 10, 21–36.

Clingempeel, W. G., Brand, E., and Ievoli, R. (July 1984). "Stepparent-Stepchild Relationships in Stepmother and Stepfather Families: A Multinational Study." *Family Relations,* 33, 465–473.

Cobliner, W. G. (1988). "The Exclusion of Intimacy in the Sexuality of the Contemporary College-Age Population." *Adolescence,* 23, 99–113.

Codega, S. A., Pasley, B. K., and Kreutzer, J. (1990). "Coping Behaviors of Adolescent Mothers: An Exploratory Study and Comparison of Mexican-Americans and Anglos." *Journal of Adolescent Research,* 5, 34–53.

"Cohabitation by the Unmarried." (1986). *Medical Aspects of Human Sexuality,* 20, 63–69.

"Cohabiting Young Women Plan to Get Married." (1987). *Medical Aspects of Human Sexuality,* 21, 16.

Cohen, S. E., Beckwith, L., Parmelee, A. H., Sigman, M., Asarnow, R., and Espinosa, M. P. (1996). "Prediction of Low and Normal School Achievement in Early Adolescence Born Pre-Term." *Journal of Early Adolescence,* 16, 46–70 .

Cohen, Y. (1991). "Gender Identity Conflicts in Adolescents as Motivation for Suicide." *Adolescence,* 26, 19–29.

Cole, D. E., Protinsky, H. O., and Cross, L. H. (1992). "An Imperical Investigation of Adolescent Suicidal Ideation." *Adolescence*, 27, 813–818.

Coleman, J. S. (1995). *Adolescent Sexual Knowledge: Implications for Health and Health Risks.* Paper presented at the meeting of the Society for Research in Child Development, Indianapolis, IN.

Coleman, M., Ganong, L. H., and Ellis, P. (1985). "Family Structure and Dating Behavior of Adolescents." *Adolescence*, 20, 537–543.

Coleman, M., Ganong, L. H., Clark, J. M., and Madsen, R. (1989). "Parenting Perceptions in Rural and Urban Families." *Journal of Marriage and the Family*, 51, 329–335.

College Entrance Examination Board. (1979). *National College-Bound Seniors.* Princeton, NJ: Author.

"College Suicides: Exaggerated by Half." (August 1980). *Psychology Today*, p. 81.

Collins, J. D., and Propert, D. S. (Winter 1983). "A Developmental Study of Body Recognition in Adolescent Girls." *Adolescence*, 18, 767–774.

Comer, J. (1993). *African-American Parents and Child Development: An Agenda for School Success.* Paper presented at the biannual meeting of the Society for Research in Child Development, New Orleans.

Comerci, G. D. (1989). "Society/Community and the Adolescent: How Much the Problem, How Much the Solution." *Journal of Early Adolescence*, 9, 8–12.

Commons, M. L., Richards, F. A., and Kuhn, D. (1982). "Systematic and Metasystematic Reasoning: A Case for Levels of Reasoning Beyond Piaget's Stage of Formal Operations." *Child Development*, 53, 1058–1069.

Comstock, G. A. (1986). "Sexual Effects of Movie and TV Violence." *Medical Aspects of Human Sexuality*, 20, 96–101.

Conger, J. J. (1973). *Adolescence and Youth.* New York: Harper and Row.

Connell, J. P., Halpern-Felsher, B. L., Clifford, E., Crichlow, W., and Usinger, P. (1995). "Hanging in There: Behavioral, Psychological, and Contextual Factors Affecting Whether African-American Adolescents Stay in High School." *Journal of Adolescent Research*, 10, 41–63.

Connell, D. K., and Meyer, R. G. (1991). "Adolescent Suicidal Behavior and Popular Self-Report Instruments of Depression, Social Desirability, and Anxiety." *Adolescence*, 26, 113–119.

Connolly, J., White, D., Stevens, R., and Burstein, S. (1987). "Adolescents' Self-Reports of Social Activity: Assessment of Stability and Relations to Social Adjustment." *Journal of Adolescence*, 10, 83–95.

Connors, L. J., and Epstein, J. L. (1995). "Parent and School Partnerships." In M. H. Bornstein (Ed.), *Children and Parenting.* Vol. 4. Hillsdale, NJ: Erlbaum.

Cook, E. P. (1985). "Sex Roles and Work Roles: A Balancing Process." *The Vocational Guidance Quarterly*, 33, 213–220.

Cook, K. V., Reiley, K. L., Stallsmith, R., and Garretson, H. B. (1991). "Eating Concerns on Two Christian and Two Nonsectarian College Campuses: A Measure of Sex and Campus Differences in Attitudes towards Eating." *Adolescence*, 26, 273–293.

Coombs, R. H., and Landsverk, J. (1988). "Parenting Styles and Substance Use during Childhood and Adolescence." *Journal of Marriage and the Family*, 50, 473–482.

Cooney, R. S., Rogler, L. H., Hurrell, R. M., and Ortiz, V. (1982). "Decision Making in Intergenerational Puerto Rican Families." *Journal of Marriage and the Family*, 44, 621–632.

Cooney, T. M., and Hogan, D. P. (1991). "Marriage in an Institutionalized Life Course: First Marriage among American Men in the 20th Century." *Journal of Marriage and the Family*, 53, 178–190.

Cooney, T. M., Pedersen, F. A., Indelicato, S., and Paklovitz, R. (1993). "Timing of Fatherhood: Is 'On-Time' optimal?" *Journal of Marriage and the Family*, 55, 205–215.

Corbett, K., Gentry, C. S., and Pearson, W., Jr. (1993). "Sexual Harassment in High School." *Youth and Society*, 25, 93–103.

Corson, D. (Summer 1984). "Lying and Killing: Language and the Moral Reasoning of Twelve- and Fifteen-Year-Olds by Social Group." *Adolescence*, 19, 473–482.

Costa, F. M., Jessor, R., Donovan, J. E., and Fortenberry, J. D. (1995). "Early Initiation of Sexual Intercourse: The Influence of Psychosocial Unconventionality." *Journal of Research on Adolescence*, 5, 93–121.

Costantino, G., Malgady, R. G., and Rogler, L. H. (1988). "Folk Hero Modeling Therapy for Puerto Rican Adolescents." *Journal of Adolescence*, 11, 55–165.

Costin, S. E., and Jones, D. C. (1994). *The Stress-Protective Role of Parent and Friends' Support for Sixth and Ninth Graders Following a School Transition.* Paper presented at the meeting of the Society for Research on Adolescence, San Diego.

Cote, J. E. (1986). "Identity Crisis Modality: A Technique for Assessing the Structure of the Identity Crisis." *Journal of Adolescence*, 9, 321–335.

Cote, J. E., and Levine, C. G. (February 1983). "Marcia and Erikson: The Relationships among Ego Identity Status, Neuroticism, Dogmatism, and Purpose in Life." *Journal of Youth and Adolescence*, 12, 43–53.

———. (1992). "The Genesis of the Humanistic Academic. A Second Test of Erikson's Theory of Ego Identity Formation." *Youth in Society*, 23, 387–410.

Cotterell, J. L. (1992a). "The Relation of Attachments and Supports to Adolescent Well-Being and School Adjustment." *Journal of Adolescent Research*, 7, 28–42.

———. (1992b). "School Size as a Factor in Adolescents' Adjustment to the Transition to Secondary School." *Journal of Early Adolescence*, 12, 28–45.

Coughlin, T., and Buchinich, S. (1996). "Family Experience of Pre-Adolescents in the Development of Male Delinquency." *Journal of Marriage and the Family*, 58, 491–501.

Covell, K. (1992). "The Appeal of Image Advertisements: Age, Gender, and Product Differences." *Journal of Early Adolescence*, 12, 46–60.

Cox, D. J. (1988). "Incidence and Nature of Male Genital Exposure Behavior as Reported by College Women." *The Journal of Sex Research*, 24, 227–234.

Cox, F. D. (1994). *The AIDS Booklet*. 3rd ed. Madison, WI: Brown and Benchmark.

Craig, M. E., Kalichman, S. C., and Follingstad, D. R. (1989). "Verbal Coercive Sexual Behavior among College Students." *Archives of Sexual Behavior*, 18, 421–434.

Crawley, B. (1988). "Black Families in a Neo-Conservative Era." *Family Relations*, 37, 415–419.

Crespi, T. D., and Sabatelli, R. M. (1993). "Adolescent Runaways and Family Strife: A Conflict-Induced Differentiation Framework." *Adolescence*, 28, 868–878.

Crocker, J., Cornwell, B., and Major, B. (1993). "The Stigma of Overweight: Affective Consequences of Attributional Ambiguity." *Journal of Personality and Social Psychology*, 64, 60–70.

Crockett, L. J., and Bingham, C. R. (1994). *Family Influences on Girls' Sexual Experience and Pregnancy Risk*. Paper presented at the meeting of the Society for Research on Adolescents, San Diego.

Crystal, D. S., and Stevenson, H. W. (1995). "What Is a Bad Kid? Answers of Adolescents and Their Mothers in Three Cultures." *Journal of Research on Adolescence*, 5, 71–91.

Cummings, E. M., and Davies, P. (1994). *Children and Marital Conflicts: The Impact of Family Dispute and Resolution*. New York: Guilford Press.

Cunliffe, T. (1992). "Arresting Youth Crime: A Review of Social Skills' Training with Young Offenders." *Adolescence*, 27, 891–900.

Dalterio, S. L. (November 1984). "Marijuana and the Unborn." *Listen*, 37, 8–11.

Damphousse, K. R., and Crouch, B. M. (1992). "Did the Devil Make Them Do It? An Examination of the Etiology of Satanism among Juvenile Delinquents." *Youth and Society*, 24, 204–227.

Daniels, J. A. (1990). "Adolescent Separation-Individuation and Family Transitions." *Adolescence*, 25, 105–116.

Dare, C., Eisler, I., Russell, G. F. M., and Szmukler, G. I. (1990). "The Clinical and Theoretical Impact of a Controlled Trial of Family Therapy in Anorexia Nervosa." *Journal of Marriage and Family Therapy*, 16, 39–57.

Darling, C. A., and Davidson, J. K. (1986). "Coitally Active University Students: Sexual Behaviors, Concerns, and Challenges." *Adolescence*, 22, 403–419.

Darmody, J. P. (1991). "The Adolescent Personality, Formal Reasoning, and Values." *Adolescence*, 26, 732–742.

Davidson, J. K., Sr., and Darling, C. A. (1988). "Changing Autoerotic Attitudes and Practices among College Females: A Two-Year Follow-Up Study." *Adolescence*, 23, 773–792.

Davies, E., and Furnham, A. (1986). "The Dieting and Body Shape Concerns of Adolescent Females." *Journal of Child Psychology and Psychiatry*, 27, 417–428.

Davis, K. (1944). "Adolescence and the Social Structures." *Annuals of the American Academy of Political and Social Science*, 263, 1–168.

Davis, S. M., and Harris, M. B. (Summer 1982). "Sexual Knowledge, Sexual Interests, and Sources of Sexual Information of Rural and Urban Adolescents from Three Cultures." *Adolescence*, 17, 471–492.

Dawkins, R. L., and Dawkins, M. P. (Winter 1983). "Alcohol Use and Delinquency among Black, White, and Hispanic Adolescent Offenders." *Adolescence*, 18, 799–809.

Dawson, D. A. (1986). "The Effects of Sex Education on Adolescent Behavior." *Family Planning Perspectives*, 18, 162–170.

———. (1991). "Family Structure and Childrens' Health and Well-being: Data from the 1988 National Health Interview Survey on Child Health." *Journal of Marriage and the Family*, 53, 573–584.

Day, R. D. (1992). "Transition to First Intercourse among Racially and Culturally Diverse Youth." *Journal of Marriage and the Family*, 54, 749–762.

Dean, P. (October 5, 1991). "Madonna Vid in U.K. Daring Fare (or Not)." *Billboard*, p. 4.

DeBaryshe, B. D., Patterson, G. R., and Capaldi, D. M. (1993). "A Performance Model for Academic Achievement in Early Adolescent Boys." *Developmental Psychology*, 29, 795–804.

DeBlassie, A. M., and DeBlassie, R. R. (1996). "Education of Hispanic Youth: A Cultural Lag." *Adolescence*, 31, 205–216.

DeBolt, M. E., Pasley, B. K., and Kreutzer, J. (1990). "Factors Affecting the Probability of School Dropout: A Study of Pregnant and Parenting Adolescent Females." *Journal of Adolescent Research*, 5, 190–205.

Deci, E. L. (March 1985). "The Well-Tempered Classroom." *Psychology Today*, 19, 52–53.

DeFoe, J. R., and Breed, W. (1988). "Youth and Alcohol in Television Stories with Suggestions to the Industry for Alternative Portrayals." *Adolescence*, 23, 533–550.

DeGaston, J. F., Weed, S., and Jensen, L. (1996). "Understanding Gender Differences in Adolescent Sexuality." *Adolescence*, 31, 217–231.

Dellas, M., and Jernigan, L. P. (1990). "Affective Personality Characteristics Associated with Undergraduate Ego Identity Formation." *Journal of Adolescent Research*, 5, 306–324.

deMan, A. F., Leduc, C. P., and Labreche-Gauthier, L. (1993). "Correlates of Suicidal Ideation in French-Canadian Adolescents: Personal Variables, Stress, and Social Support." *Adolescence*, 28, 819–830.

DeMaris, A., and Rao, K. B. (1992). "Premarital Cohabitation and Subsequent Marital Stability in the United States: A Reassessment." *Journal of Marriage and the Family*, 54, 178–190.

Dembo, R., Dertke, M., LaVoie, L., Borders, S., Washburn, M., and Schmeidler, J. (1987). "Physical Abuse, Sexual Victimization and Illicit Drug Use: A Structural Analysis among High Risk Adolescents." *Journal of Adolescence*, 10, 13–33.

Demo, D. H., and Acock, A. C. (1988). "The Impact of Divorce on Children." *Journal of Marriage and the Family*, 50, 619–648.

———. (1996). "Family Structure, Family Process, and Adolescent Well-Being." *Journal of Research on Adolescence, 6,* 457–488.

Demo, D. H., Small, S. A., and Savin-Williams, R. C. (1987). "Family Relations and the Self-Esteem of Adolescents and Their Parents." *Journal of Marriage and the Family, 49,* 705–715.

deMoor, C., et al. (1992). "The Association between Teacher Attitudes, Behavioral Intentions, and Smoking, and the Prevalence of Smoking among 7th-Grade Students." *Adolescence, 27,* 565–578.

"The Denial of Indian Civil and Religious Rights." (1975). *Indian Historian, 8,* 43–46.

Dennison, B. A., Straus, J. H., Mellits, D., and Charney, E. (1988). "Childhood Physical Fitness Tests: Predictor of Adult Physical Activity Levels?" *Pediatrics, 82,* 324–330.

Denno, D. (Winter 1982). "Sex Differences in Cognition: A Review and Critique of the Longitudinal Evidence." *Adolescence, 17,* 779–788.

deRosenroll, D. A. (1987). "Creativity and Self-Trust: A Field of Study." *Adolescence, 22,* 419–432.

DeSantis, J. P., and Youniss, J. (1991). "Family Contributions to Adolescents' Attitudes towards New Technology." *Journal of Adolescent Research, 6,* 410–422.

Desmond, S. M., Price, J. H., Gray, N., and O'Connell, J. K. (1986). "The Etiology of Adolescents' Perceptions of Their Weight." *Journal of Youth and Adolescence, 15,* 461–474.

deTurck, M. A., and Miller, G. R. (August 1983). "Adolescent Perceptions of Parental Persuasive Message Strategies." *Journal of Marriage and the Family, 34,* 533–542.

deVaus, D. A. (Spring 1983). "The Relative Importance of Parents and Peers for Adolescent Religious Orientation: An Australian Study." *Adolescence, 18,* 147–158.

DiCindio, L. A., Floyd, H. H., Wilcox, J., and McSeveney, D. R. (Summer 1983). "Race Effects in a Model of Parent-Peer Orientation." *Adolescence, 18,* 369–379.

Dickens, C. (1959). *Oliver Twist.* London: Collins Publishers.

Dietrich, D. R. (1984). "Psychological Health of Young Adults Who Experienced Early Parent Death: MMPI Trends." *Journal of Clinical Psychology, 40,* 901–908.

Dignan, M., Block, G., Steckler, A., Howard, C., and Cosby, M. (1986). "Locus of Control and Smokeless Tobacco Use among Adolescents." *Adolescence, 82,* 377–381.

Dillard, D. D., and Pol, L. G. (April 1982). "The Individual Economic Cost of Teenage Childbearing." *Family Relations, 31,* 249–259.

Dinges, M. M., and Oetting, E. R. (1993). "Similarity in Drug Use Patterns between Adolescents and Their Friends." *Adolescence, 28,* 253–266.

Dino, S., Stick, G., and Troutman, R. (1993). *Knockin' Da Boots.* Pac Jam Publishing, Saja Music, and Troutman Music.

Doan, M., and Peterson, S. (November 12, 1984). "As 'Cluster Suicides' Take Toll of Teenagers." *U.S. News & World Report,* pp. 49, 50.

Dodge, K. A., and Somberg, D. (1987). "Hostile Attributional Biases among Aggressive Boys Are Exacerbated under Conditions of Threats to the Self." *Child Development, 58,* 213–224.

Doherty, W. J., and Harkaway, J. E. (1990). "Obesity and Family Systems: A Family FIRO Approach to Assessment and Treatment Planning." *Journal of Marriage and Family Therapy, 16,* 287–298.

Dolcini, M. M., Cohn, L. D., Adler, N. E., et al. (1989). *Journal of Early Adolescence, 9,* 409–418.

Domenech, E. (1996). "Biopsychopathologic Risk Profile of Adolescents with Eating Disorder Symptoms." *Adolescence, 31,* 443–450.

Donnelly, B. W., and Voydanoff, P. (1991). "Factors Associated with Releasing for Adoption among Adolescent Mothers." *Family Relations, 40,* 404–410.

Donnerstein, E., and Lint, D. (January 1984). "Sexual Violence in the Media: A Warning." *Psychology Today, 18,* 14, 15.

Donovan, F. R. (1967). *Wild Kids.* Harrisburg, PA: Stackpole Co.

Donovan, P. (1997). "Confronting a Hidden Epidemic: The Institute of Medicine's Report on Sexually Transmitted Diseases." *Family Planning Perspectives, 29,* 87–89.

Dornbusch, S. M., Ritter, P. L., Mont-Reynaud, R., and Chen, Z. (1990). "Family Decision Making and Academic Performance in a Diverse High School Population." *Journal of Adolescent Research, 5,* 143–160.

Doueck, H. J., Ishisaka, A. H., and Greenaway, K. D. (1988). "The Role of Normative Development in Adolescent Abuse and Neglect." *Family Relations, 37,* 135–139.

Doyle, J. A., and Paludi, M. A. (1995). *Sex and Gender: A Human Experience.* 3rd ed. Dubuque, IA: Brown and Benchmark.

Dreyer, T. H., Jennings, C., Johnson, F., and Evans, D. (1994). *Culture and Personality in Urban Schools: Identity Status, Self-Concepts, and Loss of Control among High School Students and Monolingual and Bilingual Homes.* Paper presented at the meeting of the Society for Research on Adolescents, San Diego.

Dreyfus, E. A. (1976). *Adolescence. Theory and Experience.* Columbus, OH: Charles E. Merrill.

Dryfoos, J. G. (July–August 1984). "A New Strategy for Preventing Teenage Childbearing." *Family Planning Perspectives, 16,* 193–195.

Duberman, L. (1973). "Step-Kin Relationships." *Journal of Marriage and the Family, 35,* 283–292.

DuBois, D. L., Felner, R. D., Brand, S., Phillips, R. S., and Lease, A. N. (1996). "Early Adolescent Self-Esteem: A Developmental-Ecological Frame Work and Assessment Strategy." *Journal of Research on Adolescence, 6,* 543–579.

DuBois, D. L., and Hirsch, B. J. (1993). "School/Non-School Friendship Patterns in Early Adolescence." *Journal of Early Adolescence, 13,* 102–122.

Duffy, J., and Coates, T. J. (1989). "Reducing Smoking among Pregnant Adolescents." *Adolescence, 24,* 29–37.

Dukes, R. L., and Lorch, B. D. (1989). "The Effects of School, Family, Self-Concept, and Deviant Behavior on Adolescent Suicide Ideation." *Journal of Adolescence,* 12, 239–251.

Duncan, G. J., and Rodgers, W. L. (1988). "Longitudinal Aspects of Childhood Poverty." *Journal of Marriage and the Family,* 50, 1007–1021.

Dunham, R. G., and Alpert, G. P. (1987). "Keeping Juvenile Delinquents in School: A Prediction Model." *Adolescence,* 22, 45–57.

Durbin, D. L., Darling, N., Steinberg, L., and Brown, B. B. (1993). "Parenting Style and Peer Group Membership among European-American Adolescents." *Journal of Research on Adolescence,* 3, 87–100.

Durkheim, E. (1960). *Moral Education.* New York: Free Press.

Dvorchak, R. (December 11, 1992). "Without Wampum or Buffalo, Indians Rely on Blackjack, Bingo." *Prescott Courier.*

Earl, W. L. (1987). "Creativity and Self-Thrust: A Field of Study." *Adolescence,* 22, 419–432.

Earle, J. R., and Perricone, P. J. (1986). "Premarital Sexuality: A Ten Year Study of Attitudes and Behavior in a Small University Campus." *The Journal of Sex Research,* 22, 304–310.

East, P. L. (1989). "Early Adolescents' Perceived Interpersonal Risks and Benefits: Relations to Social Support and Psychological Functioning." *Journal of Early Adolescence,* 9, 374–395.

East, P. L., Lerner, R. M., Lerner, J. B., Soni, R. T., Ohannessian, C. M., and Jacobson, L. B. (1992). "Early Adolescent-Peer Group Fit, Peer Relations, and Psycho-Social Competence: A Short-Term Longitudinal Study." *Journal of Early Adolescence,* 12, 132–152.

Eaton, Y. M., Mitchell, M. L., and Jolley, J. M. (1991). "Gender Differences in the Development of Relationships during Late Adolescence." *Adolescence,* 26, 565–568.

Eberhardt, C. A., and Schill, T. (Spring 1984). "Differences in Sexual Attitudes and Likeliness of Sexual Behaviors of Black Lower-Socioeconomic Father-Present vs. Father-Absent Female Adolescents." *Adolescence,* 19, 99–105.

Eccles, J. S., Midgley, C., Wigfield, A., Duchanan, C. M., Reuman, D., Flanagan, C., and MacIver, D. (1993). "Development during Adolescence: The Impact of Stage-Environment Fit on Young Adolescents' Experiences in Schools and Families." *American Psychologist,* 48, 90–101.

Eder, D., and Kinney, D. A. (1995). "The Effect of Middle School Extracurricular Activities on Adolescents' Popularity and Peer Status." *Youth and Society,* 26, 298–324.

Edwards, J. N. (1987). "Changing Family Structure and Youthful Well-being." *Journal of Family Issues,* 8, 355–372.

Edwards, S. (1994). "As Adolescent Males Age, Risky Behavior Rises and Condom Use Decreases." *Family Planning Perspectives,* 26, 45–46.

Edwards, W. J. (1996). "A Measurement of Delinquency Differences between Delinquent and Nondelinquent Youths between a Delinquent and Nondelinquent

Sample: What Are the Implications?" *Adolescence,* 31, 973–989.

Ehrhardt, A., and Meyer-Bahlburg, H. (1981). "Effects of Prenatal Sex Hormones on Gender-Related Behavior." *Science,* 211, 312–318.

Eisele, J., Hertsgaard, D., and Light, H. K. (1986). "Factors Related to Eating Disorders in Young Adolescent Girls." *Adolescence,* 82, 283–290.

Eisen, S. V., Youngman, D. J., Grob, M. C., and Dill, D. L. (1992). "Alcohol, Drugs, and Psychiatric Disorders. A Current View of Hospitalized Adolescents." *Journal of Adolescent Research,* 7, 250–265.

Eisenberg, N., and Murphy, B. (1995). "Parenting and Children's Moral Development." In M. H. Bornstein (Ed.), *Children and Parenting.* Vol. 4. Hillsdale, NJ: Erlbaum.

Eisenman, R. (1993). "Characteristics of Adolescent Felons in a Prison Treatment Program." *Adolescence,* 28, 695–699.

Elkind, D. (1967). "Egocentrism in Adolescence." *Child Development,* 38, 1025–1034.

———. (1970). *Children and Adolescents: Interpretive Essays on Jean Piaget.* New York: Oxford University Press.

———. (1975). "Recent Research on Cognitive Development in Adolescence." In S. E. Dragastin and G. H. Elder, Jr. (Eds.), *Adolescence in the Life Cycle.* New York: John Wiley and Sons.

———. (Spring 1978). "Understanding the Young Adolescent." *Adolescence,* 13, 127–134.

Ellis, L., and Ames, M. A. (1987). "Neurohormonal Functioning and Sexual Orientation: A Theory of Homosexuality-Heterosexuality." *Psychological Bulletin,* 101, 233–258.

Ellis, L., and Wagemann, B. M. (1993). "The Religiosity of Mothers and Their Offspring as Related to the Offspring's Sex and Sexual Orientation." *Adolescence,* 28, 227–234.

Ellis, N. B. (1991). "An Extension of the Steinberg Accelerating Hypothesis." *Journal of Early Adolescence,* 2, 221–235.

Ellison, J. (June 1984). "The Seven Frames of Mind." *Psychology Today,* 18, 21–26.

Elmen, J. (1991). "Achievement Orientation in Early Adolescence: Developmental Patterns and Social Correlates." *Journal of Early Adolescence,* 11, 125–151.

Emery, P. E. (Summer 1983). "Adolescent Depression and Suicide." *Adolescence,* 18, 245–258.

Emery, R. E. (1988). *Marriage, Divorce, and Children's Adjustment.* Newbury Park, CA: Sage.

Englander-Golden, P., Jackson, J. E., Crane, K., Schwarzkopf, A. B., and Lyle, P. S. (1989). "Communication Skills and Self-Esteem in Prevention of Destructive Behaviors." *Adolescence,* 24, 481–502.

Engstrom, C. A., and Sedlacek, W. E. (1991). "A Study of Prejudice toward University Student-Athletes." *Journal of Counseling and Development,* 70, 189–193.

Ennett, S. T., and Bauman, K. E. (1996). "Adolescent Social Networks: School, Demographics, and Longitudinal Considerations." *Journal of Adolescent Research,* 11,

194–215.

Ennis, R. H. (1991). "Critical Thinking: Literature Review and Needed Research." In L. Idol and D. S. Jones (Eds.), *Educational Values and Cognitive Instruction*. Hillsdale, NJ: Erlbaum.

Enns, C. Z. (1991). "The New Relationship Models of Women's Identity: A Review and Critique for Counselors." *Journal of Counseling and Development*, 69, 209–217.

Ephron, N. (1975). *Crazy Salad*. New York: Knopf.

Erickson, L., and Newman, I. M. (January 1984). "Developing Support for Alcohol and Drug Education: A Case Study of a Counselor's Role." *Personnel and Guidance Journal*, 62, 289–291.

Erikson, E. H. (1950). *Childhood and Society*. New York: W. W. Norton.

———. (1959). *Identity and the Life Cycle*. New York: International Universities Press.

———. (1968). *Identity: Youth, and Crisis*. New York: W. W. Norton.

———. (1982). *The Life Cycle Completed*. New York: W. W. Norton.

Erikson, J. (November 19, 1991). "LaFrontera, Its Indian AIDS Grant." *Arizona Daily Star*.

Eskilson, A., Wiley, M. G., Muehlbauer, G., and Dodder, L. (1986). "Parental Pressure, Self-Esteem and Adolescent Reported Deviance: Bending the Twig Too Far." *Adolescence*, 21, 501–515.

Estrada, P. (1992). *Socio-Emotional and Educational Functioning in Poor Urban Youth during the Transition to Middle School: The Role of Peer and Teacher Social Support*. Paper presented at the meeting of the Society for Research on Adolescence, Washington, DC.

———. (1995). "Adolescents' Self-Reports of Pro-Social Responses to Friends and Acquaintances: The Role of Sympathy-Related Cognitive, Affective, and Motivational Processes." *Journal of Research on Adolescence*, 5, 173–200.

Etringer, B. D., Altmaier, E. M., and Bowers, W. (1989). "An Investigation into the Cognitive Functioning of Bulimic Women." *Journal of Counseling and Development*, 68, 216–219.

Evans, E. D., and Craig, D. (1990). "Adolescent Cognitions for Academic Cheating as a Function of Grade Level and Achievement Status." *Journal of Adolescent Research*, 5, 325–345.

Evans, I. M., Cicchelli, P., Cohen, M., and Shapiro, M. (1995). *Staying in School*. Baltimore, MD: Paul Brookes.

Fairchild, H. H., and Wright, C. (Summer 1984). "A Social-Ecological Assessment and Feedback-Intervention of an Adolescent Treatment Agency." *Adolescence*, 19, 263–275.

Farrington, D. P. (1990). "Implications of Criminal Career Research for the Prevention of Offending." *Journal of Adolescence*, 13, 93–114.

Farrow, J. A., and French, J. (1986). "The Drug Abuse-Delinquency Connection Revisited." *Adolescence*, 21, 951–960.

Farrow, P. (Spring 1978). "The Presymposial State." *Andover Review*, 5, 14–37.

Fasick, F. A. (Spring 1984). "Parents, Peers, Youth Culture and Autonomy in Adolescence." *Adolescence*, 19, 143–157.

Faulkenberry, J. R., Vincent, M., James, A., and Johnson, W. (1987). "Coital Behaviors, Attitudes, and Knowledge of Students Who Experience Early Coitus." *Adolescence*, 22, 321–332.

Featherstone, D. R., Cundick, B. P., and Jensen, L. C. (1992). "Differences in School Behavior and Achievement between Children from Intact, Reconstituted, and Single-Parent Families." *Adolescence*, 27, 1–12.

Feigelman, S., Stanton, B. F., and Ricardo, I. (1993). "Perceptions of Drug Selling and Drug Use among Urban Youths." *Journal of Early Adolescence*, 13, 267–284.

Feiring, C. (1996). "Concepts of Romance in 15-Year-Old Adolescents." *Journal of Research on Adolescence*, 6, 181–200.

Feldman, N. A., and Ruble, D. N. (1988). "The Effect of Personal Relevance on Psychological Inference: A Developmental Analysis." *Child Development*, 59, 1339–1352.

Feldman, S. S., and Gehring, T. M. (1988). "Changing Perceptions of Family Cohesion and Power across Adolescence." *Child Development*, 59, 1034–1045.

Feldman, S. S., Mont-Reynaud, R., and Rosenthal, D. A. (1992). "When East Moves West: Acculturation of Values of Chinese Adolescents in the United States and Australia." *Journal of Research on Adolescence*, 2, 147–173.

Feldman, S. S., and Weinberger, D. A. (1994). "Self-Restraint as a Mediator of Family Influences on Boys' Delinquent Behavior: A Longitudinal Study." *Child Development*, 65, 195–211.

Feldman, S. S., and Wentzel, K. R. (1990). "The Relationship between Parenting Styles, Sons' Self Restraint, and Peer Relations in Early Adolescence." *Journal of Early Adolescence*, 10, 439–454.

Felson, R. B., and Zielinski, M. A. (1989). "Children's Self-Esteem and Parental Support." *Journal of Marriage and the Family*, 51, 727–736.

Feltey, K. M., Ainslie, J. J., and Geib, A. (1991). "Sexual Coercion Attitudes among High School Students. The Influence of Gender and Rape Education." *Youth and Society*, 23, 229–250.

Fennelly, K., Cornwell, G., and Casper, L. (1992). "A Comparison of the Fertility of Dominican, Puerto Rican, and Mainland Puerto Rican Adolescents." *Family Planning Perspectives*, 24, 107–110.

Fenzel, L. M. (1989). "Role Strain in Early Adolescence: A Model for Investigating School Transition Stress." *Journal of Early Adolescence*, 9, 13–33.

Fenzel, F. M. (1994). *The Perspective Study of the Effects of Chronic Strain on Early Adolescents' Self-Worth and School Adjustment*. Paper presented at the meeting of the society for Research on Adolescents, San Diego.

Fenzel, F. M., Blyth, D. A., and Simmons, R. G. (1991). "School Transitions, Secondary." In R. M. Lerner,

A. C. Petersen, and J. Brooks-Gunn (Eds.), *Encyclopedia of Adolescence*. Vol. 2. New York: Garland.

Fenzel, F. M., and Magaletta, P. R. (1993). *Predicting Intrinsic Motivation of Black Early Adolescents: The Roles of School Strain, Academic Confidence, and Self Esteem.* Paper presented at the biennial meeting of the Society for Research in Child Development, New Orleans.

Fernandez, M., Ruch-Ross, H. S., and Montague, A. (1993). "Ethnicity and Effects of Age Gap Between Unmarried Adolescent Mothers and Partners." *Journal of Adolescent Research,* 8, 439–466.

Ferreiro, B. W., Warren, N. J., and Konanc, J. T. (1986). "ADAP: A Divorce Assessment Proposal." *Family Relations,* 35, 439–449.

Fertman, C. I., and Chubb, N. H. (1992). "The Effects of a Psychoeducational Program on Adolescents' Activity Involvement, Self-Esteem, and Locus of Control." *Adolescence,* 27, 517–533.

Field, T., Lang, C., Yando, R., and Vendell, D. (1995). "Adolescents' Intimacy with Parents and Friends." *Adolescence,* 30, 133–140.

Fine, M. A. (1986). "Perceptions of Stepparents: Variations in Stereotypes as a Function of Current Family Structure." *Journal of Marriage and the Family,* 48, 537–543.

Fine, M. A., Donnelly, B. W., and Voydanoff, P. (1991). "The Relation between Adolescents' Perceptions of Their Family Lives and Their Adjustment in Stepfather Families." *Journal of Adolescent Research,* 6, 423–436.

Fingerman, K. L. (1989). "Sex and the Working Mother: Adolescent Sexuality, Sex Role Typing and Family Background." *Adolescence,* 24, 1–18.

Finkelhor, D. (1984). *Child Sexual Abuse: Theory and Research.* New York: Free Press.

Finkelstein, M. J., and Gaier, E. L. (Spring 1983). "The Impact of Prolonged Student Status on Late Adolescent Development." *Adolescence,* 18, 115–129.

Fischer, J. L., and Crawford, D. W. (1992). "Codependency and Parenting Styles." *Journal of Adolescent Research,* 3, 352–363.

Fischman, J. (1986). "Woman and Divorce: Ten Years After." *Psychology Today,* 20, 15.

———. (1988). "Stepdaughter Wars." *Psychology Today,* 22, 38–45.

Fisher, T. D. (1986). "Parent-Child Communication about Sex and Young Adolescents' Sexual Knowledge and Attitudes." *Adolescence,* 21, 517–527.

———. (1988). "The Relationship between Parent-Child Communication about Sexuality and College Students' Sexual Behavior and Attitudes as a Function of Parental Proximity." *Journal of Sex Research,* 24, 305–311.

Fisher, T. D., and Hall, R. G. (1988). "A Scale for the Comparison of the Sexual Attitudes of Adolescents and Their Parents." *The Journal of Sex Research,* 24, 90–100.

Fitzgerald, J. M. (1991). "Memory." In R. M. Lerner, A. C. Petersen, and J. Brooks-Gunn (Eds.), *Encyclopedia of Adolescence.* Vol. 2. New York: Garland.

Flanigan, B., McLean, A., Hall, C., and Propp, V. (1990). "Alcohol Use as a Situational Influence on Young Women's Pregnancy Risk-Taking Behavior." *Adolescence,* 25, 205–214.

Flannery, D. J., Rowe, D. C., and Gulley, B. L. (1993). "Impact of Pubertal Status, Timing, and Age on Adolescent Sexual Experience and Delinquency." *Journal of Adolescent Research,* 8, 21–40.

Flavell, J. H. (1992). "Cognitive Development: Past, Present, and Future." *Developmental Psychology,* 28, 998–1005.

Flavell, J. H., Miller, P. A., and Miller, S. A. (1993). *Cognitive Development.* 3rd ed. Englewood Cliffs, NJ: Prentice-Hall.

Fleck, J. R., Fuller, C. C., Malin, S. Z., Miller, D. H., and Acheson, K. R. (Winter 1980). "Father Psychological Absence and Heterosexual Behavior, Personal Adjustment and Sex-Typing in Adolescent Girls." *Adolescence,* 15, 847–860.

Fleischer, B., and Read, M. (Winter 1982). "Food Supplement Usage by Adolescent Males." *Adolescence,* 17, 831–845.

Fleming, W. M., and Anderson, S. P. (1986). "Individuation from the Family of Origin and Personal Adjustment in Late Adolescence." *Journal of Marriage and the Family,* 3, 311–315.

Flewelling, R. L., and Bauman, K. E. (1990). "Family Structure as a Predictor of Initial Substance Use and Sexual Intercourse in Early Adolescence." *Journal of Marriage and the Family,* 52, 171–181.

Flug, G. (1991). "Dangerous Toys: Hot N' Nasty." *Hit Parader,* 326, 34.

Flynn, T. M., and Beasley, J. (Winter 1980). "An Experimental Study of the Effects of Competition on the Self-Concept." *Adolescence,* 15, 799–806.

Folkenberg, J. (March 1984). "Bulimia: Not for Women Only." *Psychology Today,* 18, 10.

Ford, D. Y. (1992). "Self-Perceptions of Underachievement and Support for the Achievement Ideology among Early Adolescent African Americans." *Journal of Early Adolescence,* 12, 228–252.

Ford, M. E., Wentzel, K. R., Wood, D., Stevens, E., and Siesfeld, G. A. (1989). "Process Associated with Integrated Social Competence: Emotional and Contextual Influences on Adolescent Social Responsibility." *Journal of Adolescent Research,* 4, 405–425.

Forrest, J. D., and Silverman, J. (1989). "What Public School Teachers Teach about Preventing Pregnancy, AIDS, and Sexually Transmitted Diseases." *Family Planning Perspectives,* 21, 65–72.

Forrest, J. D., and Singh, S. (1990). "The Sexual Reproductive Behavior of American Women, 1982–1988." *Family Planning Perspectives,* 22, 206–214.

Forrest, L., and Mikolaitis, N. (1986). "The Relationship Component of Identity: An Expansion of Career Development Theory." *The Career Development Quarterly,* 35, 76–88.

Forste, R., and Tanfer, K. (1996). "Sexual Exclusivity among Dating, Cohabiting, and Married Women." *Journal of Marriage and the Family,* 58, 33–47.

Fowler, B. A. (1989). "The Relationship of Body Image Perception and Weight Status to Recent Change in Weight Status of the Adolescent Female." *Adolescence,* 95, 557–568.

Fox, G. L., and Inazu, J. K. (July 1980). "Mother-Daughter Communication about Sex." *Family Relations,* 29, 347–352.

Fox, G. L., and Kelly, R. F. (1995). "Determinants of Child Custody Arrangements at Divorce." *Journal of Marriage and the Family,* 57, 693–708.

Foxcroft, D. R., and Lowe, G. (1991). "Adolescent Drinking Behavior and Family Socialization Factors: A Meta-Analysis." *Journal of Adolescence,* 14, 255–273.

Franco, J. N. (January 1983). "Aptitude Tests: Can We Predict Their Future?" *Personnel and Guidance Journal,* 61, 263, 264.

Frankel, K. A. (1990). "Girls' Perceptions of Peer Relationship Support and Stress." *Journal of Early Adolescence,* 10, 69–88.

Franklin, D. L. (1988). "The Impact of Early Childbearing on Developmental Outcomes: The Case of Black Adolescent Parenting." *Family Relations,* 37, 268–274.

Fraser, K. (1994). *Ethnic Differences in Adolescents' Possible Selves: The Role of Ethnic Identity in Shaping Self-Concepts.* Paper presented at the meeting of the Society for Research on Adolescents, San Diego.

Frecknall, P., and Luks, A. (1992). "An Evaluation of Parental Assessment of the Big Brothers/Big Sisters Program in New York City." *Adolescence,* 27, 715–718.

Free, M. D., Jr. (1993). "Stages of Drug Use: A Social Control Perspective." *Youth and Society,* 25, 251–271.

Freeman, D. (1983). *Margaret Mead and Samoa: The Making and Unmaking of an Anthropological Myth.* Cambridge, MA: Harvard University Press.

Fregeau, D. L., and Barker, M. (1986). "A Measurement of the Process of Adolescence: Standardization and Interpretation." *Adolescence,* 21, 913–919.

Freud, A. (1946). *The Ego and the Mechanism of Defence.* New York: International Universities Press.

———. (1958). *Psychoanalytic Study of the Child.* New York: International Universities Press.

Freud, S. A. (1925). "Three Contributions to the Sexual Theory." *Nervous and Mental Disease Monograph Series,* No. 7.

———. (1953a). *A General Introduction to Psychoanalysis.* Translated by Joan Riviere. New York: Permabooks.

———. (1953b). *Three Essays on the Theory of Sexuality,* vol. 7. London: Hogarth Press.

Friedman, C. J., et al. (1976). "Juvenile Gangs: The Victimization of Youth." *Adolescence,* 11, 527–533.

Friedman, I. A., and Mann, L. (1993). "Coping Patterns in Adolescent Decision Making: An Israeli-Australian Comparison." *Journal of Adolescence,* 16, 187–199.

Friedman, J., and Rich, A. (1991, 1992). *Run to You.* PSO Ltd., Music by Candlelight, and Music Corporation of America.

Frisbie, W. P. (1986). "Variation in Patterns of Marital Instability among Hispanics." *Journal of Marriage and the Family,* 48, 99–106.

Frisch, R. E., Gotz-Welbergen, A. V., McArthur, J. W., et al. (1981). "Delayed Menarche and Amenorrhea of College Athletes in Relation to Age of Onset of Training." *Journal of American Medical Association,* 246, 1599.

Froman, R. D., and Owen, S. V. (1991). "High School Student's Perceived Self-efficacy in Physical and Mental Health." *Journal of Adolescent Research,* 6, 181–196.

Frost, J. J., and Forrest, J. D. (1995). "Understanding the Impact of Effective Teenage Pregnancy Prevention Programs. *Family Planning Perspectives,* 27, 188–195.

Fu, V. R., Hinkle, D. E., Shoffner, S., et al. (Winter 1984). "Maternal Dependency and Childbearing Attitudes among Mothers of Adolescent Females." *Adolescence,* 19, 795–804.

Fujimura, L. E., Weis, D. M., and Cochran, J. R. (June 1985). "Suicide: Dynamics and Implications for Counseling." *Journal of Counseling and Development,* 63, 612–615.

Fuligini, A. J., and Eccles, J. S. (1993). "Perceived Parent-Child Relationships in Early Adolescents' Orientation toward Peers." *Developmental Psychology,* 29, 622–632.

Fuligni, A. J., Eccles, J. S., and Barber, B. L. (1995). "The Long-Term Effects of Seventh-Grade Ability Grouping in Mathematics." *Journal of Early Adolescence,* 15, 58–89.

Fuller, J. R., and LaFountain, M. J. (1987). "Performance-Enhancing Drugs in Sport: A Different Form of Drug Abuse." *Adolescence,* 22, 969—976.

Furman, W., Wehner, E. A., and Underwood, S. (1994). *Sexual Behavior, Sexual Communications, and Relationships.* Paper presented at the meeting of the Society for Research on Adolescence, San Diego.

Furstenberg, F. F., Jr., Shea, J., Allison, P., Herceg-Baron, R., and Webb, D. (September–October 1983). "Contraceptive Communication among Adolescent's Attending Family Planning Clinics." *Family Planning Perspectives,* 15, 211–217.

Furstenberg, F. F., and Spanier, G. (1984). *Recycling the Family: Remarriage After Divorce.* Beverly Hills, CA: Sage.

Gainor, K. A., and Forrest, L. (1991). "African American Women's Self-Concept: Implications for Career Decisions and Career Counseling." *The Career Development Quarterly,* 39, 261–272.

Galambos, N. C., and Silbereisen, R. K. (1987). "Income Change, Parental Life Outlook, and Adolescent Expectations for Job Success." *Journal of Marriage and the Family,* 49, 141–149.

Galambos, N. L., Sears, H. A., Almeida, D. M., and Kolaric, G. C. (1995). "Parents' Work Overload and Problem Behavior in Young Adolescents." *Journal of Research on Adolescence,* 5, 201–223.

Galbo, J. J. (Summer 1983). "Adolescent's Perceptions of Significant Adults." *Adolescence,* 18, 417–427.

———. (Winter 1984). "Adolescent's Perceptions of Significant Adults: A Review of the Literature." *Adolescence,* 19, 951–970.

———. (1989). "The Teacher as Significant Adult: A Review of the Literature." *Adolescence,* 24, 549–556.

Galbo, J. J., and Demetrulias, D. M. (1996). "Recollections of Nonparental Significant Adults during Childhood and Adolescence." *Youth and Society,* 27, 403–420.

Gallagher, J. M., and Noppe, I. C. (1976). "Cognitive Development and Learning." In J. F. Adams (Ed.), *Understanding Adolescence.* 3rd ed. Boston: Allyn and Bacon.

Gamerman, E. (January 10, 1992). "State Blocks Gaming Pact, Indian Chairman Tells Panel." *Arizona Daily Star.*

Gamoran, A., and Nystrand, M. (1991). "Background and Instructional Effects on Achievement in Eighth-Grade English and Social Studies." *Journal of Research on Adolescence,* 1, 277–300.

Ganong, L. H., and Coleman, M. (1994). *Remarried Family Relationships.* Thousand Oaks, CA: Sage.

Ganong, L. H., Coleman, M., Thompson, A., and Goodwin-Watkins, C. (1996). "African American and European American College Students' Expectations for Self and for Future Partners." *Journal of Family Issues,* 17, 758–775.

Gantman, C. A. (December 1978). "Family Interaction Patterns among Families with Normal, Disturbed, and Drug-Abusing Adolescents." *Journal of Youth and Adolescence,* 7, 429–440.

Gardner, H. (1973). *The Arts and Human Development.* New York: John Wiley and Sons.

Gardner, H. (1989). "Beyond a Modular View of Mind." In W. Damon (Ed.), *Child Development Today and Tomorrow.* San Francisco: Jossey-Bass.

Garzarelli, P., Everhart, B., and Lester, D. (1993). "Self-Concept and Academic Performance in Gifted and Academically Weak Students." *Adolescence,* 28, 235–237.

Gavazzi, S. M., and Sabatelli, R. M. (1990). "Family System Dynamics, the Individuation Process and Psychosocial Development." *Journal of Adolescent Research,* 5, 500–519.

Gebhard, P. H., and Johnson, A. B. (1979). *The Kinsey Data.* Philadelphia: W. B. Saunders.

Gecas, V., and Pasley, K. (December 1983). "Birth Order and Self-Concept in Adolescence." *Journal of Youth and Adolescence,* 12, 521–533.

Gecas, V., and Schwalbe, M. L. (1986). "Parental Behavior and Adolescent Self-Esteem." *Journal of Marriage and the Family,* 48, 37–46.

Gecas, V., and Seff, M. A. (1990). "Families and Adolescents: A Review of the 1980s." *Journal of Marriage and the Family,* 52, 941–958.

Gehring, R. M., Wentzel, K. R., Feldman, K. R., and Munson, J. (1990). "Conflict in Families of Adolescents: The Impact on Cohesion and Power Structure." *Journal of Family Psychology,* 3, 290–309.

Gerstein, M., Lichtman, M., and Barokas, J. U. (1988). "Occupational Plans of Adolescent Women Compared to Men: A Cross-Sectional Examination." *The Career Development Quarterly,* 36, 222–230.

Gertner, J. M. (1986). "Short Stature in Children." *Medical Aspects of Human Sexuality,* 20, 36–42.

Gesell, Arnold, and Ames, L. B. (1956). *Youth: The Years from Ten to Sixteen.* New York: Harper and Row.

Gfellner, B. M. (1986). "Changes in Ego and Moral Development in Adolescents." *Journal of Adolescence,* 9, 281–302.

Gfellner, B. M., and Hundelby, J. D. (1994). *Patterns of Drug Use and Social Activities among Native Indians and White Adolescents.* Paper presented at the Society for Research on Adolescence, San Diego.

Ghang, J., and Jin, S. (1996). "Determinants of Suicide Ideation: A Comparison of Chinese and American College Students." *Adolescence,* 31, 451–467.

Gibbons, S., Wylie, M. L., Echterling, L., and French, J. (1986). "Patterns of Alcohol Use among Rural and Small-Town Adolescents." *Adolescence,* 84, 887–900.

Gibbs, J. R., and Hines, A. M. (1989). "Factors Related to Sex Differences in Suicidal Behavior among Black Youth: Implications for Intervention and Research." *Journal of Adolescent Research,* 4, 152–172.

Gibson, J. W., and Kempf, J. (1990). "Attitudinal Predictors of Sexual Activity in Hispanic Adolescent Females." *Journal of Adolescent Research,* 5, 414–430.

Gifford, V. D., and Dean, M. M. (1990). "Differences in Extracurricular Activity Participation, Achievement, and Attitudes toward School Between Ninth-Grade Students Attending Junior High School and Those Attending Senior High School." *Adolescence,* 25, 799–802.

Giles-Sims, J. (1985). "A Longitudinal Study of Battered Children of Battered Women." *Family Relations,* 34, 205–210.

Giles-Sims, J., and Crosbie-Burnett, M. (1989). "Adolescent Power in Stepfather Families. A Test of a Normative-Resource Theory." *Journal of Marriage and the Family,* 51, 1065–1078.

Giles-Sims, J., and Finkelhor, D. (1984). "Child Abuse in Stepfamilies." *Family Relations,* 33, 407–413.

Gilger, J. W., Geary, D. C., and Eisele, L. M. (1991). "Reliability and Validity of Retrospective Self-Reports of the Age of Pubertal Onset Using Twin, Sibling, and College Student Data." *Adolescence,* 26, 41–53.

Gill, R. T. (1992). "For the Sake of the Children." *The Public Interest,* 108, 81–96.

Gilligan, C. (1977). "In a Different Voice: Women's Conceptions of Self and of Morality." *Harvard Educational Review,* 47, 481–517.

———. (1982). *In a Different Voice: Psychological Theory and Women's Development.* Cambridge, MA: Harvard University Press.

———. (1984). "Remapping the Moral Domain in Personality Research and Assessment." Invited address presented to the American Psychological Association Convention, Toronto.

———. (1992). *Joining the Resistance: Girls' Development in Adolescence.* Paper presented at the Symposium on Development and Vulnerability in Close Relationships, Montreal, Quebec.

Gilligan, C., Ward, J. B., Taylor, J. M., Bardige, B. (1988). *Mapping the Moral Domain.* Cambridge, MA: Harvard University Press.

Gillmore, M. R., Hawkins, J. D., Day, L. E., and Catalano, R. F. (1992). "Friendship and Deviance: New Evidence of an Old Controversy." *Journal of Early Adolescence,* 12, 80–95.

Gilmartin, B. G. (1985). "Some Family Antecedents on Severe Shyness." *Family Relations,* 34, 429–438.

Ginsburg, S. D., and Orlofsky, J. L. (August 1981). "Ego Identity Status, Ego Development, and Loss of Control in College Women." *Journal of Youth and Adolescence,* 10, 297–307.

Ginzberg, E. (1988). "Toward a Theory of Occupational Choice." *The Career Development Quarterly,* 36, 358–363.

Giordano, P. C., Cernkovich, S. A., and DeMaris, A. (1993). "The Family and Peer Relations of Black Adolescents." *Journal of Marriage and the Family,* 55, 277–287.

Gispert, M. (1987). "Preventing Teenage Suicide." *Medical Aspects of Human Sexuality,* 21, 16.

Gispert, M., Wheeler, K., Marsh, L., and Davis, M. S. (1985). "Suicidal Adolescents: Factors in Evaluation." *Adolescence,* 20, 753–762.

Glenn, N. D., and Kramer, K. B. (1987). "The Marriages and Divorces of the Children of Divorce." *Journal of Marriage and the Family,* 49, 811–825.

Glick, P. C., and Spanier, G. B. (1980). "Married and Unmarried Cohabitation in the United States." *Journal of Marriage and the Family,* 42, 19–30.

Gnepp, J., and Chilamkurti, C. (1988). "Childrens' Use of Personality Attributions to Predict Other Peoples' Emotional and Behavioral Reactions." *Child Development,* 59, 743–754.

Goertz, M. E., Ekstrom, R. B., and Rock, D. (1991). "Dropouts, High School Issues: Issues of Race and Sex." In R. M. Lerner, A. C. Petersen, and J. Brooks-Gunn (Eds.), *Encyclopedia of Adolescence.* Vol. 1. New York: Garland.

Goff, J. L. (1990). "Sexual Confusion among Certain College Males." *Adolescence,* 25, 599–614.

Gold, S. R., and Henderson, B. B. (1990). "Daydreaming and Curiosity: Stability and Change in Gifted Children and Adolescents." *Adolescence,* 25, 701–708.

Gollub, E. L., Stein, D., and El-Sadr, W. (1995). "Short-term Acceptability of the Female Condom among Staff and Patients at a New York City Hospital." *Family Planning Perspective,* 27, 155–158.

Gomes-Schwartz, B., Norowitz, J., and Sauzier, M. (1985). "Severity of Emotional Distress among Sexually Abused Preschool, School-Age, and Adolescent Children." *Hospital and Community Psychiatry,* 36, 502–508.

Good, G. E., and Mintz, L. B. (1990). "Gender-role Conflicts and Depression in College Men: Evidence for Compounded Risk." *Journal of Counseling and Development,* 69, 17–21.

Goodenow, C. (1993). "Classroom Belonging among Early Adolescent Students: Relationships to Motivation and Achievement." *Journal of Early Adolescence,* 13, 21–43.

Goodenow, C., and Espin, O. M. (1993). "Identity Choices in Immigrant Adolescent Females." *Adolescence,* 28, 173–184.

Goodwin, M. P., and Roscoe, B. (1990). "Sibling Violence and Agonistic Interactions among Middle Adolescents." *Adolescence,* 25, 451–467.

Goossens, L., Seiffge-Krenke, I., and Marcoen, A. (1992). "The Many Faces of Adolescent Egocentrism. Two European Replications." *Journal of Adolescent Research,* 7, 43–48.

Gordon, C. P. (1996). "Adolescent Decision-making: A Broadly Based Theory and Its Application to the Prevention of Early Pregnancy." *Adolescence,* 31, 561–584.

Gordon, L., and O'Keefe, P. (1984). "Incest as a Form of Family Violence: Evidence from Historical Case Records." *Journal of Marriage and the Family,* 46, 27–34.

Gordon, M. (February 1981). "Was Waller Ever Right? The Rating and Dating Complex Reconsidered." *Journal of Marriage and the Family,* 43, 67–76.

Goswick, R. A., and Jones, W. H. (October 1982). "Components of Loneliness during Adolescence." *Journal of Youth and Adolescence,* 11, 373–383.

Graff, H. J. (1995). *Conflicting Paths: Growing Up in America.* Cambridge, MA: Harvard University Press.

Grande, C. G. (1988a). "Delinquency: The Learning Disabled Students' Reaction to Academic School Failure." *Adolescence,* 23, 209–219.

Grande, C. G. (1988b). "Educational Therapy for Failing and Frustrated Student Offenders." *Adolescence,* 23, 889–897.

Grannis, J. C. (1992). "Students' Stress, Distress, and Achievement in an Urban Intermediate School." *Journal of Early Adolescence,* 12, 4–27.

Granott, N. (1993). *Co-Construction of Knowledge: Interaction Model, Types of Interaction, and a Suggested Method of Analysis.* Paper presented at the biennial meeting of the Society for Research in Child Development, New Orleans.

Granrose, C. K. (1985). "Plans for Work Careers among College Women Who Expect to Have Families." *The Vocational Guidance Quarterly,* 33, 284–295.

Grant, C. L., and Fodor, I. G. (April 1984). "Body Image and Eating Disorders: A New Role for School Psychologists in Screening and Prevention." Mimeographed paper. New York University, School of Education, Health, Nursing, and Arts Profession.

———. (1986). "Adolescent Attitudes toward Body Image and Anorexic Behavior." *Adolescence,* 82, 269–281.

Green, J. J., Bush, D., and Sahn, J. (December 1980). "The Effects of College on Students' Partisanship: A Research Note." *Journal of Youth and Adolescence,* 9, 547–552.

Green, S. K., and Sollie, D. L. (1989). "Long-Term Effects of a Church-Based Sex Education Program on Adolescent Communication." *Family Relations,* 38, 152–156.

Greenberg, E. F. (1983). "An Empirical Determination of the Competence of Children to Participate in Child Custody Decision-Making." Doctoral dissertation, University of Illinois. *Dissertation Abstracts International,* 45, (0–1) 350–B.

Greenberg, J., et al. (1992). "Why Do People Need Self-Esteem? Converging Evidence that Self-Esteem Serves an Anxiety-Buffering Function." *Journal of Personality and Social Psychology*, 63, 913–922.

Greendlinger, V., and Byrne, D. (1987). "Coercive Sexual Fantasies of College Men as Predictors of Self-Reported Likelihood of Rape and Overt Sexual Aggression." *The Journal of Sex Research*, 23, 1–11.

Greene, A. L. (1990). "Age and Gender Differences in Adolescents' Preference for Parental Advice: Mum's the Word." *Journal of Adolescent Research*, 5, 396–413.

Greene, A. L., and Reed, E. (1992). "Social Context Differences in the Relation Between Self-Esteem and Self-Concept during Late Adolescence." *Journal of Adolescent Research*, 2, 266–282.

Greene, N. B., and Esselstyn, T. C. (1972). "The Beyond Control Girl." *Juvenile Justice*, 23, 13–19.

Gregory, L. W. (1995). "The 'Turn Around' Process: Factors Influencing the School Success of Urban Youth." *Journal of Adolescent Research*, 10, 136–154.

Griffin, N., Chassin, L., and Young, R. D. (Spring 1981). "Measurement of Global Self-Concept versus Multiple Role-Specific Self-Concept in Adolescents." *Adolescence*, 16, 49–56.

Grigg, D. N., and Friesen, J. D. (1989). "Family Patterns Associated with Anorexia Nervosa." *Journal of Marriage and Family Therapy*, 15, 29–42.

Grindstaff, C. F. (1988). "Adolescent Marriage and Childbearing: The Long-Term Economic Outcome, Canada in the 1980s." *Adolescence*, 23, 45–58.

Grob, M. C., Klein, A. A., and Eisen, S. V. (April 1983). "The Role of the High School Professional in Identifying and Managing Adolescent Suicidal Behavior." *Journal of Youth and Adolescence*, 12, 163–173.

Grotevant, H. D., and Cooper, C. R. (1985). "Patterns of Interaction in Family Relationships and the Development of Identity Exploration in Adolescence." *Child Development*, 56, 415–428.

———. (1986). "Individuation in Family Relationships." *Human Development*, 29, 82–100.

Grotevant, H. D., Thorbecke, W., and Meyer, M. L. (February 1982). "An Extension of Marcia's Identity Status Interview into the Interpersonal Domain." *Journal of Youth and Adolescence*, 11, 33–47.

Grover, K. M., Russell, C. S., Schumm, W. R., and Paff-Bergen, L. A. (1985). "Mate Selection Processes and Marital Satisfaction." *Family Relations*, 34, 383–386.

Gruber, E., and Chambers, C. V. (1987). "Cognitive Development and Adolescent Contraception: Integrating Theory and Practice." *Adolescence*, 22, 661–670.

Gruskin, E. (1994). *A Review of Research on Self-Identified Gay, Lesbian, and Bi-Sexual Youths from 1970–1993*. Paper presented at the meeting of the Society for Research on Adolescents, San Diego.

Guidubaldi, J., and Perry, J. D. (1985). "Divorce and Mental Health Sequelae for Children. A Two-Year Follow Up of a Nationwide Sample." *Journal of the American Academy of Child Psychiatry*, 24, 531–537.

Gullotta, T. P., Adams, G. R., and Montemayor, R. (Eds.). (1995). *Substance Misuse in Adolescence*. Newbury Park, CA: Sage.

Gurak, D. T., Falcon, L., Sandefur, G. D., and Torrecilha, R. (1989 March). "A Comparative Examination of the Link between Premarital Cohabitation and Subsequent Marital Stability." Paper presented at the meeting of the Population Association of America, Baltimore, MD.

Gurin, J. (1989a). "Leaner, Not Lighter." *Psychology Today*, 23, 32–36.

———. (1989b). "Exercise: Some Routines Burn Fat Better than Others." *Psychology Today*, 23, 34.

Gutierrez, J., Sameroff, A. J., and Carrer, B. M. (1988). "Acculturation and SES Effects on Mexican American Parents' Concepts of Development." *Child Development*, 59, 250–255.

Gutstein, S. E., and Rudd, M. D. (1990). "An Outpatient Treatment Alternative for Suicidal Youth." *Journal of Adolescence*, 13, 265–277.

Hafen, B. Q., and Frandsen, K. J. (1986). *Youth Suicide: Depression and Loneliness*. Provo, UT: Behavioral Health Associates.

Hafez, E. S. E. (Ed.), (1980). *Human Reproduction: Conception and Contraception*. Hagerstown, MD: Harper and Row.

Hagan, P. (May 1983). "Does 180 Mean Supergenius?" *Psychology Today*, 17, 18.

Haggstrom, G. W., Kanouse, D. E., and Morrison, P. A. (1986). "Accounting for the Educational Shortfalls of Mothers." *Journal of Marriage and the Family*, 48, 175–186.

Hairston, K., Gale, T., and Davis, J. (1991). *Running Back to You*. Zomba Enterprises, Inc./Hiss 'N' Tell Music/ Gale Warnings Music/Mideb Music.

Hajcak, F., and Garwood, P. (1988). "Quick-Fix Sex: Pseudosexuality in Adolescents." *Adolescence*, 23, 755–760.

Hale, S. (1990). "A Global, Developmental Trend in Cognitive Processing Speed." *Child Development*, 61, 653–663.

Halebsky, M. A. (1987). "Adolescent Alcohol and Substance Abuse: Parent and Peer Effects." *Adolescence*, 22, 961–967.

Halgin, R. P., and Leahy, P. M. (1989). "Understanding and Treating Perfectionistic College Students." *Journal of Counseling and Development*, 68, 222–225.

Hall, G. S. (1904). *Adolescence: Its Psychology and Its Relation to Physiology, Anthropology, Sociology, Sex, Crime, Religion and Education*. 2 vols. New York: D. Appleton.

Hall, G. S., and Lindzay, G. (1970). *Theories of Personality*. 2nd ed. New York: John Wiley & Sons.

Hall, J. A. (1987). "Parent-Adolescent Conflict. An Empirical Review." *Adolescence*, 22, 767–789.

Hallinan, M. T. (1991). "School Differences in Tracking Structures and Track Assignments." *Journal of Research on Adolescence*, 1, 251–275.

Halpern, C. T., and Udry, J. R. (1992). "Variation in Adolescent Hormone Measures and Implications for Behavioral Research." *Journal of Research on Adolescence*, 2, 103–122.

Hamachek, D. E. (1985). "The Self's Development and Ego Growth: Conceptual Analysis and Implications for Counselors." *Journal of Counseling and Development*, 64, 136–142.

Hamilton-Obaid, B. (1989). "Helping Adolescents in Crisis: A Care Study." *Adolescence*, 24, 59–63.

Hansen, S. L., and Darling, C. A. (1985). "Attitudes of Adolescents towards Division of Labor in the Home." *Adolescence*, 20, 61–72.

Hanson, S. L. (1992). "Involving Families and Programs for Pregnant Teens: Consequences for Teens and Their Families." *Family Relations*, 41, 303–311.

Hanson, T. L., McLanahan, S. S., and Thomson, E. (1996). "Double Jeopardy: Parental Conflict and Stepfamily Outcomes for Children." *Journal of Marriage and the Family*, 58, 141–154.

Harding, C. G., and Snyder, K. (1991). "Tom, Huck, and Oliver Stone as Advocates in Kohlberg's Just Community: Theory-Based Strategies for Moral Education." *Adolescence*, 26, 319–329.

Harper, J. F., and Marshall, E. (1991). "Adolescents' Problems and the Relationship to Self-Esteem." *Adolescence*, 26, 799–808.

Harriman, L. C. (1986). "Teaching Traditional versus Emerging Concepts in Family Life Education." *Family Relations*, 35, 581–586.

Harris, A. A., and Herrman, L. P. (1989). "Social Cognitive Skills and Behavioral Adjustment of Delinquent Adolescents in Treatment." *Journal of Adolescence*, 12, 323–328.

Harris, K. M., and Marmer, J. K. (1996). "Poverty, Paternal Involvement, and Adolescent Well-Being." *Journal of Family Issues*, 17, 614–640.

Harris, L., and Associates, Inc. (1974). *Public Awareness of the National Institute on Alcohol Abuse and Alcoholism Advertising Campaign and Public Attitudes toward Drinking and Alcohol Abuse*. Reports prepared for the National Institute on Alcohol Abuse and Alcoholism. Phase Four Report and Overall Summary.

Harrison, P. A., Hoffmann, N. G., and Edwall, G. E. (1989). "Sexual Abuse Correlates: Similarities between Male and Female Adolescents in Chemical Dependency Treatment." *Journal of Adolescent Research*, 4, 385–399.

Harter, S. (1990). "Self and Identity Development." In S. S. Feldman and G. R. Elliott (Eds.), *At the Thresholds: The Developing Adolescent*. Cambridge, MA: Harvard University Press.

Harter, S., Stocker, T., and Robinson, N. S. (1996). "The Perceived Directionality of the Link between Approval and Self-Worth: Reliabilities of a Looking Glass Self-Orientation among Young Adolescents." *Journal of Research on Adolescence*, 6, 285–308.

Harvey, S. M., and Spigner, C. (1995). "Factors Associated with Sexual Behavior among Adolescents: A Multivariate Analysis." *Adolescence*, 30, 253–264.

Haskett, M. E., Johnson, C. A., and Miller, J. W. (1994). "Individual Differences in Risk of Child Abuse by Adolescent Mothers: Assessment in the Perinatal Period." *Journal of Child Psychology and Psychiatry and Allied Disciplines*, 35, 461–476.

Hatfield, E., and Sprecher, S. (1986). "Measuring Passionate Love in Intimate Relationships." *Journal of Adolescence*, 9, 383–410.

Hauck, W. E., and Loughead, M. (1985). "Adolescent Self-Monitoring." *Adolescence*, 20, 567–574.

Hauck, W. E., Martens, M., and Wetzel, M. (1986). "Shyness, Group Dependence and Self-Concept: Attributes of the Imaginary Audience." *Adolescence*, 21, 529–534.

Haurin, R. J. (1992). "Patterns of Childhood Residence and the Relationship to Young Adult Outcomes." *Journal of Marriage and the Family*, 54, 846–860.

Havens, B., and Swenson, I. (1988). "Imagery Associated with Menstruation in Advertising Targeted to Adolescent Women." *Adolescence*, 23, 89–97.

———. (1989). "A Content Analysis of Educational Media about Menstruation." *Adolescence*, 24, 901–907.

Havighurst, R. J. (1972). *Developmental Tasks and Education*. 3rd ed. New York: David McKay.

Hazell, P. (1991). "Postvention after Teenage Suicide: An Australian Experience." *Journal of Adolescence*, 14, 335–342.

"Health Service Issues. AIDS Guidelines." (November 15, 1985). *Portland Press Herald*.

Heatherton, T. F., Herman, C. P., and Polivy, J. (1992). "Effects of Distress on Eating: The Importance of Ego-Involvement." *Journal of Personality and Social Psychology*, 62, 601–803.

Hechinger, F. (1992). *Faithful Choices: Healthy Youth for the 21st Century*. New York: Carnegie Corporation.

Heilbrun, A. B., Jr., and Loftus, M. P. (1986). "The Role of Sadism and Peer Pressure in the Sexual Aggression of Male College Students." *The Journal of Sex Research*, 22, 320–332.

Helms, J. E. (1990). *Black and White Racial Identity Theory and Professional Interracial Collaboration*. Paper presented at the meeting of the American Psychological Association, Boston.

Hendershott, A. B. (1989). "Residential Mobility, Social Support and Adolescent Self-Concept." *Adolescence*, 24, 217–232.

Henderson, B. B., and Gold, S. R. (1983). "Intellectual Styles: A Comparison of Factor Stuctures in Gifted and Average Adolescents." *Journal of Personality and Social Psychology*, 45, 624–632.

Henderson, G. H. (April 1980). "Consequences of School-Age Pregnancy and Motherhood." *Family Relations*, 29, 185–190.

Hendry, L. B., Roberts, W., Glendinning, A., and Coleman, J. S. (1992). "Adolescents' Perceptions of Significant Individuals in their Lives." *Journal of Adolescence*, 15, 255–270.

Henninger, D., and Esposito, N. (1971). "Indian Schools." In D. Gottlieb and A. L. Heinsohn (Eds.), *America's Other Youth: Growing Up Poor*. Englewood Cliffs, NJ: Prentice-Hall.

Henry, C. S., and Lovelace, S. G. (1995). "Family Resources and Adolescent Family Life Satisfaction in Remarried

Family Households." *Journal of Family Issues,* 16, 765–786.

Henry, C. S., Stephenson, A. L., Hanson, M. F., and Hargett, W. (1993). "Adolescent Suicide in Families: An Ecological Approach." *Adolescence,* 28, 291–308.

Henry, C. S., Wilson, S. M., and Peterson, G. W. (1989). "Parental Power Bases and Processes as Predictors of Adolescent Conformity." *Journal of Adolescent Research,* 4, 15–32.

Henshaw, S. K. (1997). "Teenage Abortion and Pregnancy Statistics by State, 1992." *Family Planning Perspectives,* 29, 115–122.

Hepworth, D. H., Farley, O. W., and Griffiths, J. C. (February 1986). "Research Capsule." *Social Research Institute Newsletter.* Salt Lake City, UT: Graduate School of Social Work.

Hepworth, J., Ryder, R. G., and Dreyer, A. S. (January 1984). "The Effects of Parental Loss on the Formation of Intimate Relationships." *Journal of Marital and Family Therapy,* 10, 73–82.

Herbert, W. (April 1984). "Freud under Fire." *Psychology Today,* 18, 10–12.

Herman, J., Russell, D., and Troiki, K. (1986). "Long-Term Effects of Incestuous Abuse in Childhood." *American Journal of Psychiatry,* 143, 1293–1296.

Hersch, P. (1988). "Coming of Age on City Streets." *Psychology Today,* 22, 28–37.

Hertzler, A. A., and Frary, R. B. (1989). "Food Behavior of College Students." *Adolescence,* 24, 349–356.

Herzberger, S. D., and Tennen, H. (1985). "The Effect of Self-Relevance on Judgments of Moderate and Severe Disciplinary Encounters." *Journal of Marriage and the Family,* 47, 311–318.

Hetherington, E. M. (1987). "Family Relations Six Years after Divorce." In K. Pasley and M. Ihinger-Tallman, (Eds.), *Remarriage and Stepparenting: Current Research and Theory* (pp. 185–205). New York: Guilford.

————. (1993). "An Overview of the Virginia Longitudinal Study of Divorce and Remarriage with a Focus on Early Adolescence." *Journal of Family Psychology,* 7, 39–56.

Hier, S. J., Korboot, P. J., and Schweitzer, R. D. (1990). "Social Adjustment and Symptomatology in Two Types of Homeless Adolescents: Runaways and Throwaways." *Adolescence,* 761–771.

Hilgard, E. R. (1949). "Human Motives and the Concept of Self." *American Psychologist,* 4, 374–382.

Hillman, S. B., and Sawilowsky, S. S. (1991). "Maternal Employment and Early Adolescent Substance Use." *Adolescence,* 26, 829–837.

Hines, S., and Groves, D. L. (1989). "Sports Competition and Its Influence on Self-Esteem Development." *Adolescence,* 24, 861–869.

Hinton, K., and Margerum, B. J. (Summer 1984). "Adolescent Attitudes and Values Concerning Used Clothing." *Adolescence,* 19, 397–402.

Hiraga, Y., Cauce, A. M., Mason, C., and Ordonez, N. (1992). *Ethnic Identity and the Social Adjustment of Biracial Youths.* Paper presented at the biennial meeting of the Society for Research on Child Development, New Orleans.

Hirch, B. J., and Rapkin, B. D. (1987). "The Transition to Junior High School: A Longitudinal Study of Self-Esteem, Psychological Symptomatology, School Life, and Social Support." *Child Development,* 58, 1235–1243.

Ho, C. S., Lempers, J. D., and Clark-Lempers, D. S. (1995). "Effects of Economic Hardship on Adolescent Self-Esteem: A Family Mediation Model." *Adolescence,* 30, 117–131.

Hockenberry-Eaton, M., Richman, M. J., Dilorio, C., Rivero, T., and Maibach, E. (1996). "Mothers and Adolescent Knowledge of Sexual Development: The Effects of Gender, Age, and Sexual Experience." *Adolescence,* 31, 35–46.

Hoelter, J., and Harper, L. (1987). "Structural and Interpersonal Family Influences on Adolescent Self-Conception." *Journal of Marriage and the Family,* 49, 129–139.

Hofferth, S., Kahn, J. R., and Baldwin, W. (1987). "Premarital Sexual Activity among U.S. Teenage Women over the Past Three Decades." *Family Planning Perspectives,* 19, 46–53.

Hoffman, V. J. (Spring 1984). "The Relationship of Psychology to Delinquency: A Comprehensive Approach." *Adolescence,* 19, 55–61.

Hogan, H. W., and McWilliams, J. M. (September 1978). "Factors Related to Self-Actualization." *Journal of Psychology,* 100, 117–122.

Hoge, D. R., and DuZuleta, E. (1988). "Salience as a Condition for Various Social Consequences of Religious Commitment." *Journal for the Scientific Study of Religion,* 24, 21–38.

Holcomb, W. R., and Kashani, J. H. (1991). "Personality Characteristics of a Community Sample of Adolescents with Conduct Disorders." *Adolescence,* 26, 579–586.

Hole, J. W. (1987). *Human Anatomy and Physiology.* 4th ed. Dubuque, IA: William C. Brown.

Holland, J. L. (1985). *Making Vocational Choices: A Theory of Vocational Personalities and Work Environments.* 2nd ed. Englewood Cliffs, NJ: Prentice-Hall.

Hollander, D. (1996). "Contraceptive Use Is Most Regular if Teenagers Have Conventional Lifestyles." *Family Planning Perspectives,* 28, 289–290.

Holleran, P. R., Pascale, J., and Fraley, J. (1988). "Personality Correlates of College-Age Bulimics." *Journal of Counseling and Development,* 66, 378–381.

Holman, N., and Arcus, M. (1987). "Helping Adolescent Mothers and Their Children: An Integrated Multi-Agency Approach." *Family Relations,* 36, 119–123.

Holmbeck, G. N., and Hill, J. K. (1991). "Conflictive Engagement, Positive Affect, and Menarche in Families with Seventh-Grade Girls." *Child Development,* 62, 1030–1048.

Homan, K. B. (1986). "Vocation as the Quest for Authentic Existence." *The Career Development Quarterly,* 35, 14–23.

Hooker, D., and Convisser, E. (December 1983). "Women's Eating Problems: An Analysis of a Coping Mechanism." *Personnel and Guidance Journal,* 62, 236–239.

Hopson, I., and Rosenfeld, A. (August 1984). "PMS: Puzzling Monthly Symptoms." *Psychology Today,* 18, 30–35.

Horn, M. E., and Rudolph, L. B. (1987). "An Investigation of Verbal Inter-Action, Knowledge of Sexual Behavior and Self-Concept in Adolescent Mothers." *Adolescence,* 87, 591–598.

Horowitz, R. (1983). *Honor and the American Dream.* Brunswick, NJ: Rutgers University Press.

Horowitz, T. R. (1992). "Dropout—Mertonian or Reproduction Scheme?" *Adolescence,* 27, 451–459.

Hortacsu, N. (1989). "Target Communication during Adolescence." *Journal of Adolescence,* 12, 253–263.

Houts, R. M., Robins, E., and Huston, T. L. (1996). "Compatibility and Development of Pre-Marital Relationships." *Journal of Marriage and the Family,* 58, 7–20.

Howard, M. (1985). "Postponing Sexual Involvement among Adolescents: An Alternative Approach to Prevention of Sexually Transmitted Diseases." *Journal of Adolescent Health Care,* 6, 271.

Hoyt, K. B. (1987). "The Impact of Technology on Occupational Change: Implications for Career Guidance." *The Career Development Quarterly,* 35, 269–278.

———. (1988). "The Changing Workforce: A Review of Projections—1986 to 2000." *The Career Development Quarterly,* 37, 31–39.

Huang, C., and Grachow, F. (n.d.). "The Dilemma of Health Services in Chinatown." New York: Department of Health.

Hubble, L. M., and Groff, M. G. (December 1982). "WISC-R Verbal Performance IQ Discrepancies among Quay-Classified Adolescent Male Delinquents." *Journal of Youth and Adolescence,* 11, 503–508.

Hubbs-Tait, L., and Garmon, L. C. (1995). "The Relationship of Moral Reasoning and AIDS Knowledge to Risky Sexual Behavior." *Adolescence,* 30, 549–564.

Huber, P. (1986). "Decision-Making as a Problem-Solving Process." In B. Brehmer, H. Jungerman, P. Lowrens, and G. Second (Eds.), *New Directions in Research on Decision-Making.* Amsterdam: North-Holland.

Hudson, L. M., and Gray, W. M. (1986). "Formal Operations, the Imaginary Audience and the Personal Fable." *Adolescence,* 84, 751–765.

Huerta-Franco, R., deLeon, J. D., and Malacara, J. M. (1996). "Knowledge and Attitudes towards Sexuality in Adolescence and Their Association with the Family and Other Factors." *Adolescence,* 31, 179–191.

Huffman, J. W. (1986). "Teenagers' Gynecologic Problems." *Medical Aspects of Human Sexuality,* 20, 57–61.

Hultsman, W. C. (1992). "Constraints to Activity Participation in Early Adolescence." *Journal of Early Adolescence,* 12, 280–299.

Humphrey, L. L., and Stern, S. (1988). "Object Relations and the Family System in Bulimia: A Theoretical Integration." *Journal of Marital and Family Therapy,* 14, 337–350.

Hundleby, J. D., and Mercer, G. W. (1987). "Family and Friends as Social Environments and Their Relationship to Young Adolescents' Use of Alcohol, and Marijuana." *Journal of Marriage and the Family,* 49, 151–164.

Hunt, M. (1974). *Sexual Behavior in the 1970s.* New York: Dell.

Hunt, W. A., and Matazarro, J. D. (1970). "Habit Mechanisms in Smoking." In W. A. Hunt (Ed.), *Learning Mechanisms in Smoking.* Chicago: Aldine.

Hurley, D. (March 1985). "Arresting Delinquency." *Psychology Today,* 19, 62–68.

Hurrelmann, K., Engel, U., Holler, B., and Nordlohne, E. (1988). "Failure in School, Family Conflicts, and Psychosomatic Disorders in Adolescence." *Journal of Adolescence,* 11, 237–249.

Huston, A. C., Donnerstein, E., Fairchild, H., Freshback, N. D., Katz, P. A., Murray, J. P., Rubenstein, E. A., Wilcox, B. L., and Zuckerman, D. (1992). *Big World, Small Screen: The Role of Television in American Society.* Lincoln: University of Nebraska Press.

Huston, L., Hoberman, H., and Nugent, S. (1994). *Alcohol Use and Abuse in Native American Adolescents.* Paper presented at the meeting of the Society for Research on Adolescence, San Diego.

Hutchinson, R. L., Valutis, W. E., Brown, D. T., and White, J. S. (1989). "The Effects of Family Structure on Institutionalized Children's Self-Concepts." *Adolescence,* 94, 303–310.

Hyde, J. S. (1985). *Half the Human Experience.* Lexington, MA: D. C. Heath.

Ieit, D. (February 1985). "Anxiety, Depression, and Self-Esteem in Bulimia: The Role of the School Psychologist." Paper presented at the annual meeting of the Eastern Educational Research Association, Virginia Beach, VA.

Ihinger-Tallman, M., and Pasley, K. (1986). "Remarriage and Integration within the Community." *Journal of Marriage and the Family,* 48, 395–405.

Inazu, J. K., and Fox, G. L. (1980). "Maternal Influence on the Sexual Behavior of Teen-Age Daughters." *Journal of Family Issues,* 1, 81–102.

Information Please Almanac, Atlas and Yearbook: 1992. (1992). 45th edition. Boston: Houghton Mifflin.

Inhelder, B., and Piaget, J. (1958). *The Growth of Logical Thinking from Childhood to Adolescence.* New York: Basic Books.

Jaccard, J., Dittus, P. J., and Gordon, B. B. (1996). "Maternal Correlates of Adolescent Sexual and Contraceptive Behavior." *Family Planning Perspectives,* 28, 159–165.

Jackson, E. P., Dunham, R. M., and Kidwell, J. S. (1990). "The Effects of Gender and Family Cohesion and Adaptability on Identity Status." *Journal of Adolescent Research,* 5, 161–174.

Jackson, M. (1991, 1992). *Heal the World.* Mijac Music. Jacobs, J. B. (1988). "Families Facing the Nuclear Taboo." *Family Relations,* 37, 432–436.

Jacobs, J. B. (1988). "Families Facing the Nuclear Taboo." *Family Relations,* 37, 432–436.

Jacobs, J. E., and Potenza, M. (1990). *The Use of Decision-Making Strategies in Late Adolescence.* Paper presented at the meeting of the Society for Research in Adolescence, Atlanta.

Jacobs, S. B., and Wagner, M. K. (1984). "Obese and Nonobese Individuals: Behavioral and Personality Characteristics." *Addictive Behaviors,* 9, 223–226.

James, W. (1890). *The Principles of Psychology.* New York: Holt.

Jamison, W., and Signorella, M. L. (1980). "Sex-Typing and Spatial Ability: The Association between Masculinity and Success on Piaget's Water-Level Task." *Sex Roles,* 6, 345–353.

Jansen, P., Richter, L. M., and Griesel, R. D. (1992). "Glue Sniffing: A Comparison Study of Sniffers and Non-Sniffers." *Journal of Adolescence,* 15, 29–37.

Janus, M., Burgess, A. W., and McCormack, A. (1987). "Histories of Sexual Abuse in Adolescent Male Runaways." *Adolescence,* 22, 405–417.

Jarrett, R. L. (1995). "Growing Up Poor: The Family Experiences of Socially Mobile Youth in Low-Income African American Neighborhoods." *Journal of Adolescent Research,* 10, 111–135.

Jemmott, L. S., and Jemmott, J. B., III. (1992). "Family Structure, Parental Strictness, and Sexual Behavior among Inner City Black Male Adolescents." *Journal of Adolescent Research,* 7, 192–207.

Jenkins, M. E. (1987). "An Outcome Study of Anorexia Nervosa in an Adolescent Unit." *Journal of Adolescence,* 10, 71–81.

Jensen, L. (1995). *The Moral Reasoning of Orthodox and Progressivist Indians and Americans.* Paper presented at the meeting of the Society for Research in Child Development, Indianapolis, IN.

Jensen, L., and Borges, M. (1986). "The Effect of Maternal Employment on Adolescent Daughters." *Adolescence,* 21, 659–666.

Jessop, D. J. (February 1981). "Family Relationships as Viewed by Parents and Adolescents: A Specification." *Journal of Marriage and the Family,* 43, 95–106.

"The Jewish Recipe for Moderate Drinking." (March 15, 1981). *Psychology Today,* pp. 78–80.

Johnsen, K. P., and Medley, M. L. (September 1978). "Academic Self-Concept among Black High School Seniors: An Examination of Perceived Agreement with Selected Others." *Phylon,* 39, 264–274.

Johnson, C., Lewis, C., Love, S., Lewis, L., and Stuckey, M. (February 1984). "Incidence and Correlates of Bulimic Behavior in a Female High School Population." *Journal of Youth and Adolescence,* 13, 15–26.

Johnson, E. G. (1967). "The Impact of High School Teachers on the Educational Plans of College Freshmen." Testing and Counseling Service Report No. 32. Orono: University of Maine. Mimeo.

Johnson, J. H. (1986). *Life Events as Stressors in Childhood and Adolescence.* Beverly Hills, CA: Sage.

Johnson, K. A. (1986). "Informal Control Networks and Adolescent Orientation toward Alcohol Use." *Adolescence,* 21, 767–784.

Johnson, P. L., and O'Leary, D. (1987). "Parental Behavior Patterns and Conduct Disorders in Girls." *Journal of Abnormal Child Psychology,* 15, 573–581.

Johnson, R. E. (1987). "Mother's versus Father's Roles in Causing Delinquency." *Adolescence,* 22, 305–315.

Johnson, R. J., and Kaplan, H. B. (1991). "Developmental Processes Leading to Marijuana Use: Comparing Civilians and the Military." *Youth and Society,* 23, 3–30.

Johnson, S. A., and Green, B. (1993). "Female Adolescent Contraceptive Decision Making and Risk Taking." *Adolescence,* 28, 81–96.

Johnson, T. R., and Troppe, M. (1992). "Improving Literacy and Employability among Disadvantaged Youth: The Job Corp. Model." *Youth and Society,* 23, 335–355.

Johnston, L., Bachman, J., and O'Malley, P. (1994). *Drug Use Rises among American Teenagers.* News Release, Institute of Social Research, University of Michigan, Ann Arbor.

Johnston, L. D., O'Malley, P. M., and Bachman, J. G. (1985). *Use of Licit and Illicit Drugs by America's High School Students, 1975–1984.* Rockville, MD: National Institute on Drug Abuse.

———. (1987). *National Trends in Drug Use and Related Factors among American High School Students and Young Adults, 1975–1986.* Washington, DC: U.S. Government Printing Office.

Jones, J. C., and Barlow, D. H. (1990). "Self-Reported Frequency of Sexual Urges, Fantasies, and Masturbatory Fantasies in Heterosexual Males and Females." *Archives of Sexual Behavior,* 19, 269–279.

Jordan, N. (1989). "Spare the Rod, Spare the Child." *Psychology Today,* 23, 16.

Jordan, W. J., Lara, J., and McPartland, G. M. (1996). "Exploring the Causes of Early Drop Out among Race-Ethnic and Gender Groups." *Youth and Society,* 28, 62–94.

Jorgensen, S. R., and Adams, R. P. (1988). "Predicting Mexican-American Family Planning Intentions: An Application and Test of a Social Psychological Model." *Journal of Marriage and the Family,* 560, 107–119.

Josephs, R. A., Markus, H. R., and Tafarodi, R. W. (1992). "Gender and Self-esteem." *Journal of Personality and Social Psychology,* 63, 391–402.

Josselson, R. (August 1982). "Personality Structure and Identity Status in Women as Viewed through Early Memories." *Journal of Youth and Adolescence,* 11, 293–299.

———. (1987). *Finding Herself: Pathways to Identity Development in Women.* San Francisco: Jossey-Bass.

———. (1988). "The Embedded Self: I and Thou Revisited." In D. K. Lapsley and F. C. Power (Eds.), *Self, Ego, and Identity: Integrative Approaches* (pp. 91–106.) New York: Springer-Verlag.

Jovanovic, J., Lerner, R., and Lerner, J. V. (1989). "Objective and Subjective Attractiveness and Early Adolescent Adjustment." *Journal of Adolescence,* 12, 225–229.

Jozefowicz, D. M., Barber, B. L., and Mollasis, C. (1994). *Relations between Maternal and Adolescent Values and Be-*

liefs: Sex Differences and Implications for Vocational Choice. Paper presented at the meeting of the Society for Research on Adolescence, San Diego.

Judson, F. (1985). "Assessing the Number of Genital Chlamydial Infections in the United States." *Journal of Reproductive Medicine,* 30 (Supplement), 269–272.

Juhasz, A. M. (1989). "Significant Others and Self-Esteem: Methods of Determining Who and Why." *Adolescence,* 24, 581–594.

Juhasz, A. M., and Sonnenshein-Schneider, M. (1987). "Adolescent Sexuality: Values, Morality, and Decision Making." *Adolescence,* 22, 579–590.

Jurich, A. P., Polson, C. J., Jurich, J. A., and Bates, R. A. (Spring 1985). "Family Factors in the Lives of Drug Users and Abusers." *Adolescence,* 20, 143–159.

Jurich, A. P., Schumm, W. R., and Bollman, S. R. (1987). "The Degree of Family Orientation Perceived by Mothers, Fathers, and Adolescents." *Adolescence,* 22, 119–128.

Jurich, J. A., Adams, R. A., and Schulenberg, J. E. (1992). "Factors Related to Behavior Change in Response to AIDS." *Family Relations,* 41, 97–103.

Jussin, L., and Eccles, J. S. (1992). "Teacher Expectations II: Construction and Reflection of Student Achievement." *Journal of Personality and Social Psychology,* 63, 947–961.

Kacerguis, M. A., and Adams, G. R. (April 1980). "Erikson Stage Resolution: The Relationship between Identity and Intimacy." *Journal of Youth and Adolescence,* 9, 117–126.

Kaczmarek, M. G., and Backlund, V. A. (1991). "Disenfranchised Grief: The Loss of an Adolescent Romantic Relationship." *Adolescence,* 26, 253–259.

Kafka, R. R., and London, P. (1991). "Communication in Relationships and Adolescent Substance Use: The Influence of Parents and Friends." *Adolescence,* 26, 587–598.

Kagan, N., and Schneider, J. (1987). "Toward the Measurement of Affective Sensitivity." *Journal of Counseling and Development,* 65, 459–464.

Kahn, J. R., and London, K. A. (1991). "Premarital Sex and the Risk of Divorce." *Journal of Marriage and the Family,* 53, 845–855.

Kalmuss, D. (1992). "Adoption in Black Teenagers: The Viability of a Pregnancy Resolution Strategy." *Journal of Marriage and the Family,* 54, 485–495.

Kalmuss, D., Namerow, P. B., and Cushman, L. F. (1991). "Teenage Pregnancy Resolution: Adoption versus Parenting." *Family Planning Perspectives,* 23, 17–23.

Kandel, D. B. (1990). "Parenting Styles, Drug Use, and Children's Adjustment in Families of Young Adults." *Journal of Marriage and the Family,* 52, 183–196.

Kandel, D. B., et al. (March 1978). "Antecedents of Adolescent Initiation into Stages of Drug Use: A Developmental Analysis." *Journal of Youth and Adolescence,* 7, 13–40.

Kane, M. J. (1988). "The Female Athletic Role as a Status Determinant within the Social System of High School Adolescents." *Adolescence,* 23, 253–264.

Kanin, E. J., and Parcell, S. R. (1977). "Sexual Aggression: A Second Look at the Offended Female." *Archives of Sexual Behavior,* 6, 67–76.

Kaplan, H. S. (1979). *Disorders of Sexual Desire.* New York: Simon and Schuster.

Katchadourian, H. (1977). *The Biology of Adolescence.* San Francisco: W. H. Freeman.

Kay, A. W. (1969). *Moral Development.* New York: Schocken Books.

Kazdin, A. E. (1995). *Conduct Disorders in Childhood and Adolescence.* 2nd ed. Newbury Park, CA: Sage.

Keating, D. P. (1990). "Adolescent Thinking." In S. S. Feldman and G. R. Elliott (Eds.), *At the Threshhold: A Developing Adolescent.* Cambridge, MA: Harvard University Press.

Keefe, K., and Berndt, T. J. (1996). "Relations of Friendship Quality to Self-Esteem in Early Adolescence." *Journal of Early Adolescence,* 16, 110–129.

Keelan, J. P. R., Dion, K. K., and Dion, K. L. (1992). "Correlates of Appearance Anxiety in Late Adolescence and Early Adulthood among Young Women." *Journal of Adolescence,* 15, 193–205.

Keesey, R. E, and Pawley, T. L. (1986). "The Regulation of Body Weight." *Annual Review of Psychology,* 37, 109–133.

Keith, V. M., and Finlay, B. (1988). "The Impact of Parental Divorce on Children's Educational Attainment, Marital Timing, and Likelihood of Divorce." *Journal of Marriage and the Family,* 50, 797–809.

Keller, J., and Keller, K. T. (1992, 1993). *Love Is.* Warner-Tamerlane Publishing Company, Checkerman Music, Pressmancherryblossom, W. B. Music Corporation, N. Y. M., and Pressmancherry Music.

Kelly, C., and Goodwin, G. C. (Fall 1983). "Adolescents' Perceptions of Three Styles of Parental Control." *Adolescence,* 18, 567–571.

Kelly, J. B. (1988). "Longer-term Adjustment in Children of Divorce: Conveying Findings and Implications for Practice." *Journal of Family Planning,* 2, 119–140.

Kelly, R. (1992). *Quality Time.* Willesden Music/R. Kelly Publishing Inc. (Administered by Willesden Music) (BMI).

Keniston, K. (1971). "Youth: A New Stage of Life." *American Scholar,* 39, 4.

————. "The Tasks of Adolescence." *In Developmental Psychology Today.* Del Mar, CA: CRM Books.

Kenney, A. M., Guardado, S., and Brown, L. (1989). "Sex Education and AIDS Education in the Schools: What States and Large School Districts are Doing." *Family Planning Perspectives,* 21, 56–64.

Kerr, B. A., and Colangelo, N. (1988). "The College Plans of Academically Talented Students." *Journal of Counseling and Development,* 67, 42–48.

Kershner, R. (1996). "Adolescent Attitudes about Rape." *Adolescence,* 31, 29–33.

Keshna, R. (1980). "Relevancy of Tribal Interests and Tribal Diversity in Determining the Educational Needs of American Indians." In *Conference on the Education and Occupational Needs of American Indian Work.*

Washington, DC: U.S. Department of Education, National Institute of Education.

Ketterlinus, R. D., Henderson, S., and Lamb, M. E. (1991). "The Effects of Maternal Age-at-Birth on Children's Cognitive Development." *Journal of Research on Adolescence,* 1, 173–188.

Ketterlinus, R. D., Lamb, M. E., Nitz, K., and Elster, A. B. (1992). "Adolescent Nonsexual and Sex-related Problem Behaviors." *Journal of Adolescent Research,* 7, 431–456.

Keye, W. R. (Fall 1983). "Update: Premenstrual Syndrome." *Endocrine and Fertility Forum,* 6, 1–3.

Keyes, S., and Block, J. (February 1984). "Prevalence and Patterns of Substance Use among Early Adolescents." *Journal of Youth and Adolescence,* 13, 1–13.

Kidwell, J. S., Dunham R. M., Bacho, R. A., Pastorino, E., and Portes, P. R. (1995). "Adolescent Identity Exploration: A Test of Erikson's Theory of Transitional Crisis." *Adolescence,* 30, 785–793.

"Kids and Contraceptives." (February 16, 1987). *Newsweek,* pp. 54–65.

Kifer, E. (1985). "Review of the ACT Assessment Program." In J. V. Mitchell (Ed.), *Ninth Mental Measurement Yearbook* (pp. 31–45). Lincoln: Buros Mental Measurement Institute, University of Nebraska Press.

Kimmier, R. T., Brigman, S. L., and Noble, F. C. (1990). "Career Indecision and Family Enmeshment." *Journal of Counseling and Development,* 68, 309–312.

Kimura, D. (1985). "Male Brain, Female Brain: The Hidden Difference." *Psychology Today,* 19, 50–58.

King, C. A., Akiyama, M. M., and Elling, K. A. (1996). "Self-perceived Competencies and Depression among Middle School Students in Japan and the United States." *Journal of Early Adolescence,* 16, 192–210.

King, M. L. (1964). *Why We Can't Wait.* New York: Harper and Row.

King, P. (1989 March). "Living Together: Bad for Kids." *Psychology Today,* 23, 77.

Kinnaird, K. L., and Gerrard, M. (1986). "Premarital Sexual Behavior and Attitudes toward Marriage and Divorce among Young Women as a Function of Their Mothers' Marital Status." *Journal of Marriage and the Family,* 48, 759–765.

Kinsey, A., Pomeroy, W. B., and Martin, C. E. (1948). *Sexual Behavior in the Human Male.* Philadelphia: W. B. Saunders.

Kinze, J. D., Frederickson, R. H., Ben, R., Fleck, J., and Karls, W. (1984). "Post-Traumatic Stress Disorder among Survivors of Cambodian Concentration Camps." *American Journal of Psychiatry,* 141, 645–650.

Kirby, D. D., and Brown, N. L. (1996). "Condom Availability in Programs in U.S. Schools." *Family Planning Perspectives,* 28, 196–202.

Kirby, D., Waszak, C., and Ziegler, J. (1991). "Six School-Based Clinics: Their Reproductive Health Services and Impact on Sexual Behavior." *Family Planning Perspectives,* 23, 6–16.

Kirkpatrick, A. C. (1986). "Some Correlates of Women's Childhood Sexual Experiences: A Retrospective Study." *The Journal of Sex Research,* 22, 221–242.

———.(1987). "Childhood Sexual Experiences: Problems and Issues in Studying Long-Range Effects." *The Journal of Sex Research,* 23, 173–196.

Kirschenbaum, H. (1977). *Advanced Value Clarification.* La Jolla, CA: University Associates.

Kiselica, M. S., and Pfaller, J. (1993). "Helping Teenage Parents: The Independent and Collaborative Roles of Counselor Educators and School Counselors." *Journal of Counseling and Development,* 72, 42–48.

Kiselica, M. S., and Sturmer, P. (1993). "Is Society Giving Teenage Fathers a Mixed Message?" *Youth and Society,* 24, 487–501.

Kisker, E. E. (March–April 1985). "Teenagers Talk about Sex, Pregnancy, and Contraception." *Family Planning Perspectives,* 17, 83–90.

Klaczynski, P. A. (1990). "Cultural-Developmental Tasks and Adolescent Development: Theoretical and Methodological Considerations." *Adolescence,* 25, 811–823.

———. (1991). "Sociocultural Myths and Occupational Attainment. Educational Influences on Adolescents' Perceptions of Social Status." *Youth and Society,* 22, 448–467.

Klaw, E., and Saunders, M. (1994). *An Ecological Model of Career Planning in Pregnant African-American Teens.* Paper presented at the biennial meeting of the Society for Research on Adolescents, San Diego.

Klayman, J. (1985). "Children's Decision Strategies and Their Adaptation to Talk Characteristics." *Oganizational Behavior and Human Decision Processes,* 35, 179–201.

Klebanob, P. K., and Brooks-Gunn, J. (1992). "Impact of Paternal Attitudes, Girls' Adjustment and Cognitive Skills upon Academic Performance in Middle and High School." *Journal of Research on Adolescence,* 2, 81–102.

Klein, H. A. (1992). "Temperament and Self-Esteem in Late Adolescence." *Adolescence,* 27, 689–694.

———. (1995). "Self-perception in Late Adolescence: An Interactive Perspective." *Adolescence,* 30, 579–591.

Klepinger, D. H., Lundberg, S., and Plotnick, R. G. (1995). "Adolescent Fertility and the Educational Attainment of Young Women." *Family Planning Perspectives,* 27, 23–28.

Klingman, L., and Vicary, J. R. (1992). *Risk Factors Associated with Date Rape and Sexual Assault of Young Adolescent Girls.* Paper presented at the meeting of the Society for Research on Adolescents, Washington, DC.

Klitsch, M. (1991). "Hispanic Ethnic Groups Face a Variety of Serious Health, Social Problems." *Family Planning Perspectives,* 23, 186–188.

Klos, D. S., and Loomis, D. F. (June 1978). "A Rating Scale of Intimate Disclosure between Late Adolescents and Their Friends." *Psychological Reports,* 42, 815–820.

Klyman, C. M. (1985). "Community Parental Surrogates and Their Role for the Adolescent." *Adolescence,* 20, 397–404.

Knapp, M., and Shields, P. (1990). "Recovering Academic Instruction for the Children of Poverty." *Phi Delta Kappan,* 71, 753–758.

Knox, D., and Wilson, K. (1983). "Dating Problems of University Students." *College Student Journal,* 17, 225–228.

Koch, M. P. (1982). *The Visitation Experience of Divorced Noncustodial Fathers.* Unpublished doctoral dissertation, University of Kentucky.

Koenig, L. J. (1988). "Self-Image of Emotionally Disturbed Adolescents." *Journal of Abnormal Child Psychology,* 16, 111–126.

Koester, A. W., and May, J. K. (1985). "Profiles of Adolescents' Clothing Practices: Purchase, Daily Selection, and Care." *Adolescence,* 20, 109–113.

Koff, E., and Rierdan, K. (1995). "Preparing Girls for Menstruation: Recommendations from Adolescent Girls." *Adolescence,* 30, 795–811.

Koff, E., Rierdan, J., and Stubbs, M. L. (1990). "Gender, Body Image, and Self-Concept in Early Adolescence." *Journal of Early Adolescence,* 10, 56–68.

Kohlberg, L. (1963). "The Development of Children's Orientations toward a Moral Order." *Vita Humana,* 6, 11–33.

———. (1966). "Moral Education in the Schools: A Developmental View." *School Review,* 74, 1–30.

———. (1969). *Stages in the Development of Moral Thought and Action.* New York: Holt, Rinehart and Winston.

———. (1970). "Moral Development and the Education of Adolescents." In R. F. Purnell (Ed.), *Adolescents and the American High School.* New York: Holt, Rinehart and Winston.

Kohlberg, L., and Gilligan, C. (Fall 1971). "The Adolescent as a Philosopher: The Discovery of the Self in a Postconventional World." *Daedalus,* 1051–1086.

Kohlberg, L., and Kramer, R. (1969). "Continuities and Discontinuities in Childhood and Adult Development." *Human Development,* 12, 93–120.

Kohlberg, L., and Turiel, E., (Eds.). (1972). *Recent Research in Moral Development.* New York: Holt, Rinehart and Winston.

Kolata, G. (1988). "Child Splitting." *Psychology Today,* 22, 34–36.

Koniak-Griffin, D., Lominska, S., and Brecht, M. (1993). "Social Support during Adolescent Pregnancy: A Comparison of Three Ethnic Groups." *Journal of Adolescence,* 16, 43–56.

Koopmans, M. (1995). "A Case of Family Dysfunction and Teenage Suicide Attempt: Applicability of a Family System's Paradigm." *Adolescence,* 30, 87–94.

Koss, M. P. (1993). "Rape: Scope, Impact, Interventions, and Public Policy Responses." *American Psychologist,* 48, 1062–1069.

Koss, M. P., Gidyca, C. A., and Wisniewski, N. (1987). "The Scope of Rape: Incidence and Prevalence of Sexual Aggression and Victimization in a National Sample of Higher Education Students." *Journal of Consulting and Clinical Psychology,* 55, 162–170.

Kramer, L. R. (1991). "The Social Construction of Ability Perceptions: An Ethnographic Study of Gifted Adolescent Girls." *Journal of Early Adolescence,* 11, 340–362.

Kratzert, W. F., and Kratzert, M. Y. (1991). "Characteristics of Continuation of High School Students." *Adolescence,* 26, 13–17.

Krein, S. F. (1986). "Growing Up in a Single-Parent Family: The Effect on Education and Earnings of Young Men." *Family Relations,* 35, 161–168.

Krieshok, S. I., and Karpowitz, D. H. (1988). "A Review of Selected Literature on Obesity and Guidelines for Treatment." *Journal of Counseling and Development,* 66, 326–330.

Kroger, J. (1990). "Ego Structuralization in Late Adolescence as Seen through Early Memories and Ego Identity Status." *Journal of Adolescence,* 13, 65–77.

———. (1995). "The Differentiation of 'Firm' and 'Developmental' Foreclosure Identity Statuses: A Longitudinal Study." *Journal of Adolescent Research,* 10, 317–337.

Kroupa, S. E. (1988). "Perceived Parental Acceptance and Female Juvenile Delinquency." *Adolescence,* 23, 171–185.

Krueger, R., and Hansen, J. C. (1987). "Self-Concept Changes during Youth-Home Placement of Adolescents." *Adolescence,* 86, 385–392.

Kuhn, D. (1979). "The Significance of Piaget's Formal Operations Stage in Education." *Journal of Education,* 161, 34–50.

Kuperminc, G. P., Allen, J. P., and Arthur, M. W. (1996). "Autonomy, Relatedness, and Male Adolescent Delinquency." *Journal of Adolescent Research,* 11, 397–420.

Kurdek, L. A., and Fine, M. A. (1993). "The Relation between Family Structure and Adolescents' Appraisals of Family Climate and Parenting Behavior." *Journal of Family Issues,* 14, 279–290.

Kurtz, P. D., Kurtz, G. L., and Jarvis, S. D. (1991). "Problems of Maltreated, Runaway Youths." *Adolescence,* 26, 543–555.

Kuziel-Perri, P., and Snarey, J. (1991). "Adolescent Repeat Pregnancies: An Evaluation Study of a Comprehensive Service Program for Pregnant and Parenting Black Adolescents." *Family Relations,* 40, 381–385.

Lachenmeyer, J. R., and Muni-Brander, P. (1988). "Eating Disorders in a Nonclinical Adolescent Population: Implications for Treatment." *Adolescence,* 23, 303–312.

Lackovic-Grgin, K., and Dekovic, M. (1990). "The Contribution of Significant Others to Adolescents' Self-Esteem." *Adolescence,* 25, 839–846.

LaFromboise, T. D., and Bigfoot, D. S. (1988). "Cultural and Cognitive Considerations in the Prevention of American Indian Adolescent Suicide." *Journal of Adolescence,* 11, 139–153.

Lagoni, L. S., and Cook, A. S. (1985). "Stepfamilies: A Content Analysis of the Popular Literature, 1961–1982." *Family Relations,* 34, 521–525.

Laing, J., Valiga, M., and Eberly, C. (1986). "Predicting College Freshmen Major Choices from ACT Assessment Program Data." *College and University,* 61, 198–205.

Lamke, L. K., Lujan, B. M., and Showalter, J. M. (1988). "The Case for Modifying Adolescents' Cognitive Self-Statements." *Adolescence,* 23, 967–974.

Lamport, M. A. (1993). "Student-Faculty Informal Interaction and the Effect on College Student Outcomes: A Review of the Literature." *Adolescence,* 28, 971–990.

Landale, M. S., and Hauan, S. M. (1992). "The Family Life Course of Puerto Rican Children." *Journal of Marriage in the Family,* 54, 912–924.

Lowman, R. L. (1991). *The Clinical Practice of Career Assessment.* Washington, DC: American Psychological Association.

Lowney, J. (Winter 1984). "Correspondence between Attitudes and Drinking and Drug Behavior: Youth Subculture over Time." *Adolescence, 19,* 875–892.

Lundholm, J. K., and Littrell, J. M. (1986). "Desire for Thinness among High School Cheerleaders: Relationship to Disordered Eating and Weight Control Behavior." *Adolescence, 21,* 573–579.

Luster, T., and McAdoo, H. M. (1995). "Factors Related to Self-Esteem among African American Youths: A Secondary Analysis with a High/Scope Perry Preschool Data." *Journal of Research on Adolescence, 5,* 451–467.

Lytton, H. (1995). *Child and Family Predictors of Conduct Disorders and Criminality.* Paper presented at the meeting of the Society for Research in Child Development, Indianapolis, IN.

Macallair, D. (1993). "Reaffirming Rehabilitation in Juvenile Justice." *Youth and Society, 25,* 104–125.

Maccoby, E. E., Buchanan, C. M., Mnookin, R. H., and Dornbusch, S. M. (1993). "Postdivorce Roles of Mothers and Fathers in the Lives of their Children." *Journal of Family Psychology, 7,* 24–38.

MacDonald, W. L., and DeMaris, A. (1996). "Parenting Step-Children and Biological Children." *Journal of Family Issues, 17,* 5–25.

MacGregor, J., and Newlon, B. J. (1987). "Description of a Teenage Pregnancy Program." *Journal of Counseling and Development, 65,* 447.

Malamuth, N. M., and Check, J. B. P. (1985). "The Effects of Aggressive Pornography on Beliefs and Rape Myths: Individual Differences." *Journal of Research of Personality, 19,* 299–320.

Mallick, M. J., Whipple, T. W., and Huerta, E. (1987). "Behavioral and Psychological Traits of Weight Conscious Teenagers: A Comparison of Eating Disordered Patients and High- and Low-Risk Groups." *Adolescence, 22,* 157–167.

Manaster, G. J. (1977). *Adolescent Development and the Life Tasks.* Boston: Allyn and Bacon.

Manaster, J., Chan, J., and Safady, R. (1992). "Mexican-American Migrant Students' Academic Success: Sociological and Psychological Acculturation." *Adolescence, 27,* 123–136.

Mann, L., Harmoni, R. V., and Power, C. N. (1989). "Adolescent Decision-Making: The Development of Competence." *Journal of Adolescence, 12,* 265–278.

Mann, L., Harmoni, R. V., Power, C. N., and Beswick, G. (1986). *Understanding and Improving Decision-Making in Adolescents.* Unpublished manuscript, Flinders University of South Australia.

Manning, M. L. (Winter 1983). "Three Myths Concerning Adolescence." *Adolescence, 18,* 823–829.

Manning, W. D. (1995). "Cohabitation, Marriage, and Entry into Motherhood." *Journal of Marriage and the Family, 57,* 191–200.

Manning, W. D., and Landale, N. S. (1996). "Racial and Ethnic Differences in the Role of Cohabitation and Premarital Childbearing." *Journal of Marriage and the Family, 58,* 63–77.

Marcia, J. E. (1966). "Development and Validation of Ego Identity Status." *Journal of Personality and Social Psychology, 3,* 551–558.

———. (1967). "Ego Identity Status: Relationship to Change in Self-Esteem, 'General Maladjustment,' and Authoritarianism." *Journal of Personality, 35,* 118–133.

———. (1976). "Identity Six Years After: A Follow Up Study." *Journal of Youth and Adolescence, 5,* 145–160.

———. (1980). "Identity in Adolescence." In J. Adelson (Ed.), *Handbook of Adolescent Psychology* (pp. 159–187). New York: Wiley.

———. (1989). "Identity and Intervention." *Journal of Adolescence, 12,* 401–410.

———. (1991). "Identity and Self Development." In R. M. Lerner, A. D. Petersen, and J. Brooks-Gunn (Eds.), *Encyclopedia of Adolescence.* Vol. 1. New York: Garland.

———. (1994). "The Empirical Study of Ego Identity." In H. A. Bosma, T. L. G. Graafsma, H. D. Grotebanc, and D. J. DeLivita (Eds.), *The Identity and Development.* Newbury Park, CA: Sage.

Marcia, J. E., and Friedman, M. L. (1970). "Ego Identity Status in College Women." *Journal of Personality, 38,* 249–263.

Marcus, R. F. (1996). "The Friendships of Delinquents." *Adolescence, 31,* 145–158.

Marin, P. (July 1983). "A Revolution's Broken Promises." *Psychology Today, 17,* 50–57.

Markstrom-Adams, C. (1990). "Coming-of-Age among Contemporary American Indians as Portrayed in Adolescent Fiction." *Adolescence, 25,* 225–237.

Markstrom-Adams, C., and Spencer, N. B. (1994). "A Model for Identity Intervention with Minority Adolescents." In S. A. Archer (Ed.), *Intervention for Adolescent Identity Development.* Newbury Park, CA: Sage.

Maroufi, C. (1989). "A Study of Student Attitudes towards Traditional and Generative Models of Instruction." *Adolescence, 24,* 65–72.

Marsiglio, W. (1989). "Adolescent Males' Pregnancy Resolution Preferences and Family Formation Intentions: Does Family Background Make a Difference for Blacks and Whites?" *Journal of Adolescent Research, 4,* 214–237.

Marsiglio, W., and Mott, F. L. (1986). "The Impact of Sex Education on Sexual Activity, Contraceptive Use and Premarital Pregnancy among American Teenagers." *Family Planning Perspectives, 18,* 151–162.

Marsman, J. C., and Herold, E. S. (1986). "Attitudes toward Sex Education and Values in Sex Education." *Family Relations, 35,* 357–361.

Marston, A. R., Jacobs, D. F., Singer, R. D., Widaman, K. F., and Little, T. D. (1988). "Characteristics of Adolescents at Risk for Compulsive Overeating on a Brief Screening Test." *Adolescence, 89,* 59–65.

Martin, M. J., Schumm, W. R., Bugaighis, M. A., Jurich, A. P., and Bollman, S. R. (1987). "Family Violence and Adolescents' Perceptions of Outcomes of Family

Conflict." *Journal of Marriage and the Family*, 49, 165–171.

Martin, M. J., and Walters, J. (1982). "Family Correlates of Selected Types of Child Abuse and Neglect." *Journal of Marriage and the Family*, 44, 267–275.

Martinez, A. C., Sedlacek, W. E., and Bachhuber, T. D. (1985). "Male and Female College Graduates—7 Months Later." *The Vocational Guidance Quarterly*, 34, 77–84.

Martinez, E. A. (1988). "Child Behavior in American/ Chicano Families: Maternal Teaching and Child-Rearing Practices." *Family Relations*, 37, 275–280.

Martinez, R., and Dukes, R. L. (1991). "Ethnic and Gender Differences and Self-Esteem." *Youth and Society*, 3, 318–338.

Martson, A. R., Jacobs, D. F., Singer, R. D., Widaman, K. F., and Little, T. D. (1988). "Adolescents Who Apparently Are Invulnerable to Drug, Alcohol, and Nicotine Use." *Adolescence*, 23, 593–598.

Mason, M. G., and Gibbs, J. C. (1993). "Social Perspective Taking and Moral Judgment among College Students." *Journal of Adolescent Research*, 8, 109–123.

Masselam, V. S., Marcus, R. F., and Stunkard, C. L. (1990). "Parent-Adolescent Communication, Family Functioning, and School Performance." *Adolescence*, 25, 725–737.

Masters, W. H., and Johnson, V. (1966). *Human Sexual Response*. Boston: Little, Brown.

———. (1979). *Homosexuality in Perspective*. Boston: Little, Brown.

Matthews, L. J., and Ilon, L. (July 1980). "Becoming a Chronic Runaway: The Effects of Race and Family in Hawaii." *Family Relations*, 29, 404–409.

Mau, R. Y. (1992). "The Validity and Devolution of a Concept: Student Alienation." *Adolescence*, 27, 731–741.

Mauk, G. W., and Weber, C. (1991). "Peer Survivors of Adolescent Suicide: Perspective on Grieving and Postvention." *Journal of Adolescent Research*, 6, 113–131.

May, J. M. (1986). "Cognitive Processes and Violent Behavior in Young People." *Journal of Adolescence*, 9, 17–27.

Mayer, J. E. (1988). "The Personality Characteristics of Adolescents Who Use and Misuse Alcohol." *Adolescence*, 23, 383–404.

Mayer, J. E., and Ligman, J. D. (1989). "Personality Characteristics of Adolescent Marijuana Users." *Adolescence*, 24, 965–976.

Mayfield-Brown (1989). "Family Status of Low-Income Adolescent Mothers." *Journal of Adolescent Research*, 4, 202–213.

Mazor, A., and Enright, R. D. (1988). "The Development of the Individuation Process from a Social-Cognitive Perspective." *Journal of Adolescence*, 11, 29–47.

Mboya, M. M. (1986). "Black Adolescents: A Descriptive Study of Their Self-Concepts and Academic Achievement." *Adolescence*, 21, 689–696.

———. (1989). "The Relative Importance of Global Self-Concept and Self-Concept of Academic Ability to Predicting Academic Achievement." *Adolescence*, 24, 39–46.

McAuliffe, G. J. (1991). "Assessing and Treating Barriers to Decision Making in Career Classes." *The Career Development Quarterly*, 40, 82–92.

McCabe, M. P. (Spring 1984). "Toward a Theory of Adolescent Dating." *Adolescence*, 19, 159–170.

———. (1987). "Desired and Experienced Levels of Premarital Affection and Sexual Intercourse during Dating." *The Journal of Sex Research*, 23, 23–33.

McCary, J. L., and McCary, S. P. (1982). *McCary's Human Sexuality*. 4th ed. Belmont, CA: Wadsworth.

McCombs, A., and Forehand, R. (1989). "Adolescent School Performance Following Parental Divorce: Are There Family Factors That Can Enhance Success?" *Adolescence*, 24, 871–880.

McCombs, A., Forehand, A., and Smith, K. (1988). "The Relationship between Maternal Problem-Solving Style and Adolescent Social Adjustment." *Journal of Family Psychology*, 2, 57–66.

McCormick, N., Folcik, J., and Izzo, A. (1985). "Sex Education Needs and Interests of High School Students in a Rural New York County." *Adolescence*, 20, 581–592.

McCreary, M. L., Slavin, L. A., and Berry, E. J. (1996). "Predicting Problem Behavior and Self-Esteem among African American Adolescents." *Journal of Adolescent Research*, 11, 216–234.

McCurdy, S. J., and Scherman, E. (1996). "Effects of Family Structure on the Adolescent Separation-Individuation Process." *Adolescence*, 31, 307–319.

McDevitt, T. M., Lennon, R., and Kopriva, R. J. (1991). "Adolescents' Perceptions of Mothers' and Fathers' Pro-Social Actions and Empathic Responses." *Youth and Society*, 22, 387–409.

McDonald, R. M., and Towberman, D. B. (1993). "Psychosocial Correlates of Adolescent Drug Involvement." *Adolescence*, 28, 925–936.

McElroy, T., and Foster, D. (1992). *Love Don't Love You*. 2 Tuff-E-Nuff Songs (BMI).

McGaha, J. E., and Leoni, E. L. (1995). "Family Violence, Abuse, and Related Family Issues of Incarcerated Delinquents of Alcoholic Parents Compared with those of Nonalcoholic Parents." *Adolescence*, 30, 473–482.

McGoldrick, M. (1982). "Ethnicity and Family Therapy." In M. McGoldrick, J. Pearce, and J. Giordana (Eds.), *Ethnicity and Family Therapy*. New York: Guilford.

McGrory, A. (1990). "Menarche: Responses of Early Adolescent Females." *Adolescence*, 25, 265–270.

McKenna, A. E., and Ferrero, G. W. (1991). "Ninth-Grade Students' Attitudes towards Non-Traditional Occupations." *The Career Development Quarterly*, 40, 168–181.

McKenry, P. C., Kotch, J. B., and Browne, D. H. (1991). "Correlates of Dysfunctional Parenting Attitudes among Low-Income Adolescent Mothers." *Journal of Adolescent Research*, 6, 212–234.

McLeod, B. (1986). "The Oriental Express." *Psychology Today*, 20, 48–52.

McLoyd, V. C. (1990). "Minority Children: Introduction to the Special Issue." *Child Development*, 61, 260–263.

McManus, M. J. (1986). "Introduction." In *Final Report of the Attorney General's Commission on Pornography.* Washington, DC: U.S. Government Printing Office. Reprint. Nashville, TN: Rutledge Hill Press.

McMurran, M. (1991). "Young Offenders and Alcohol-Related Crime: What Interventions Will Address the Issues?" *Journal of Adolescence,* 14, 245–253.

McShane, D. (1988). "An Analysis of Mental Health Research with American Indian Youth." *Journal of Adolescence,* 11, 87–116.

Mead, M. (1950). *Coming of Age in Samoa.* New York: New American Library.

———. (1953). *Growing Up in New Guinea.* New York: New American Library.

———. (1970). *Culture and Commitment: A Study of the Generation Gap.* Garden City, NY: Doubleday.

———. (1974). "Adolescence." In H. V. Kraemer (Ed.), *Youth and Culture: A Human Development Approach.* Monterey, CA: Brooks/Cole.

"Medical First: Physical Link Found in Homosexuality." (September 1984). *Portland Press Herald.*

Medora, N., and Woodward, J. C. (1986). "Loneliness among Adolescent College Students at a Midwestern University." *Adolescence,* 21, 391–402.

Meer, J. (March 1984). "Psychotherapy for Obesity." *Psychology Today,* 18, 10, 11.

———. (July 1985). "Loneliness." *Psychology Today,* 19, 28–33.

———. (1986). "Yours, Mine, and Divorce." *Psychology Today,* 20, 13.

Mehrens, W. A., and Lehmann, I. J. (January 1985). "Testing the Test. Interpreting Test Scores to Clients: What Score Should You Use?" *Journal of Counseling and Development,* 5, 317–320.

Melby, J. N., and Conger, R. D. (1996). "Parental Behaviors and Adolescent Academic Performance: A Longitudinal Analysis." *Journal of Research on Adolescence,* 6, 113–137.

Melby, J. N., Conger, R. D., Conger, K. J., and Lorenz, F. O. (1993). "Effects of Parental Behavior on Tobacco Use by Young Male Adolescents." *Journal of Marriage and the Family,* 55, 439–454.

Melli, M. S. (1986). "The Changing Legal Status of the Single Parent." *Family Relations,* 35, 31–35.

Melnick, M. J., Sabo, D. F., and Vanfossen, B. (1992). "Educational Effects of Interscholastic Athletic Participation on African-American and Hispanic Youth." *Adolescence,* 27, 295–308.

Merrit, R. (Spring 1983). "Comparison of Tolerance of White Graduates of Racially Integrated and Racially Segregated Schools." *Adolescence,* 18, 67–70.

Merten, D. E. (1996). "Visibility and Vulnerability: Responses to Rejection by Nonaggressive Junior High School Boys." *Journal of Early Adolescence,* 16, 5–26.

Metcalf, K., and Gaier, E. L. (1987). "Patterns of Middle-Class Parenting and Adolescent Underachievement." *Adolescence,* 23, 919–928.

Meyers, J. E., and Nelson, W. M., III. (1986). "Cognitive Strategies and Expectations as Components of Social Competence in Young Adolescents." *Adolescence,* 21, 291–303.

Michael, G. (1989). *Praying for Time.* Morrison Leahy Music, Ltd.

Michael, R. T., Gagnon, J. H., Laumann, E. O., and Kolata, G. (1994). *Sex in America.* Boston: Little, Brown.

Michaels, B., Dall, B., Rockett, R., and Kotzen, R. (1993). *Stand.* Cyanide Publishing (Administered by Willesden Music/Richie Kotzen Music) (Administered by Zomba Enterprises, Inc.).

Michelman, J. D., Eicher, J. B., and Michelman, S. O. (1991). "Adolescent Dress, Part I: Dress and Body Markings of Psychiatric Outpatients and Inpatients." *Adolescence,* 26, 375–385.

Midgley, C., and Urdan, T. (1995). "Predictors of Middle School Students' Views of Self-Handicapping Strategies." *Journal of Early Adolescence,* 15, 389–411.

Mijuskovic, B. (1988). "Loneliness and Adolescent Alcoholism." *Adolescence,* 23, 503–516.

Milan, R. J., Jr., and Kilmann, P. R. (1987). "Interpersonal Factors in Premarital Contraception." *The Journal of Sex Research,* 23, 289–321.

Milgram, R. M. (June 1978). "Quantity and Quality of Creative Thinking, in Children and Adolescents." *Child Development,* 49, 385–388.

Miller, A. T., Eggertson-Tacon, C., and Quigg, B. (1990). "Patterns of Runaway Behavior within a Large Systems Context: The Road to Empowerment." *Adolescence,* 25, 271–289.

Miller, B. C., and Bingham, C. R. (1989). "Family Configuration in Relation to the Sexual Behavior of Female Adolescents." *Journal of Marriage and the Family,* 51, 499–506.

Miller, B. C., Christopherson, C. R., and King, P. K. (1993). "Sexual Behavior in Adolescence." In T. P. Gullota, G. R. Adams, and R. Montemayor (Eds.), *Adolescent Sexuality.* Newbury Park, CA: Sage.

Miller, B. C., and Heaton, T. B. (1991). "Age at First Sexual Intercourse and the Timing of Marriage and Childbirth." *Journal of Marriage and the Family,* 53, 719–732.

Miller, B. C., McCoy, J. K., Olson, T. D., and Wallace, C. M. (1986). "Parental Discipline and Control Attempts in Relation to Adolescent Sexual Attitudes and Behavior." *Journal of Marriage and the Family,* 48, 503–512.

Miller, B. C., and Moore, K. A. (1990). "Adolescent Sexual Behavior, Pregnancy, and Parenting: Research through the 1980s." *Journal of Marriage and the Family,* 52, 1025–1044.

Miller, B. C., and Olson, T. D. (1988). "Sexual Attitudes and Behavior of High School Students in Relation to Background and Contextual Factors." *The Journal of Sex Research,* 24, 194–200.

Miller, D. (1974). *Adolescence: Psychology, Psychopathology, and Psychotherapy.* New York; Jason Aronson.

———. (1980). "The Native American Family: The Urban Way." In E. Corfman (Ed.), *Families Today* (pp. 441–484). Washington, DC: U.S. Government Printing Office.

Miller, K. E. (1990). "Adolescents' Same-Sex and Opposite-Sex Peer Relations: Sex Differences in Popularity, Perceived Social Competence, and Social Cognitive Skills." *Journal of Adolescent Research,* 5, 222–241.

Miller, P. H., and Aloise, P. A. (1989). "Young Children's Understanding of the Psychological Causes of Behavior: A Review." *Child Development,* 60, 257–285.

Miller, R. L. (1989). "Desegregation Experiences of Minority Students: Adolescent Coping Strategies in Five Connecticut High Schools." *Journal of Adolescent Research,* 4, 173–189.

Miller, R. P., Cosgrove, J. M., and Doke, L. (1990). "Motivating Adolescents to Reduce Their Fines in a Token Economy." *Adolescence,* 25, 97–104.

Miller-Jones, D. (1989). "Culture and Testing." *American Psychologist,* 44, 360–366.

Mills, D. M. (July 1984). "A Model for Stepfamily Development." *Family Relations,* 365–380.

Mills, R., and Mills, R. (1996). "Adolescents' Attitudes towards Female Gender Roles: Implications for Education." *Adolescence,* 31, 741–745.

Mills, R. K. (1987a). "Traditional Morality, Moral Reasoning and the Moral Education of Adolescents." *Adolescence,* 22, 371–375.

———. (1987b). "The Novels of S. E. Hinton; Springboard to Personal Growth of Adolescents." *Adolescence,* 22, 641–646.

———. (1988). "Using Tom and Huck to Develop Moral Reasoning in Adolescents: A Strategy for the Classroom." *Adolescence,* 23, 325–329.

Mitchell, C. E. (1988). "Preparing for Vocational Choice." *Adolescence,* 23, 331–334.

———. (1990). "Development or Restoration of Trust in Interpersonal Relationships during Adolescence and Beyond." *Adolescence,* 25, 847–854.

Mitchell, C. M., O'Nell, T. D., Beals, J., Dick, R. W., Keane, E., and Manson, S. M. (1996). "Dimensionality of Alcohol Use among American Indian Adolescents: Latent Structure, Construct Validity, and Implications for Developmental Research." *Journal of Research on Adolescence,* 6, 151–180.

Mitchell, J., and Dodder, R. A. (August 1983). "Types of Neutralization and Types of Delinquency." *Journal of Youth and Adolescence,* 12, 307–318.

Mitchell, J., Dodder, R. A., and Norris, T. D. (1990). "Neutralization and Delinquency: A Comparison by Sex and Ethnicity." *Adolescence,* 25, 487–497.

Mitchell, J. E., Pyle, R. L., and Eckert, E. D. (1981). "Frequency and Duration of Binge-Eating Episodes in Patients with Bulimia." *America Journal of Psychiatry,* 138, 835, 836.

Moffitt, T. E., Caspi, A., Belsky, J., and Silva, T. A. (1992). "Childhood Experience and the Onset of Menarche: A Test of the Sociobiological Model." *Child Development,* 63, 47–58.

Money, J. (1987). "Sin, Sickness, or Status? Homosexual Gender Identity and Psychoneuroendocrinology." *American Psychologist,* 42, 384–399.

Montemayor, R. (1986). "Family Variation in Parent-Adolescent Storm and Stress." *Journal of Adolescent Research,* 1, 15–31.

Montemayor, R., and Browler, J. R. (1987). "Fathers, Mothers, and Adolescents' Gender Based Differences in Parental Roles During Adolescence." *Journal of Youth and Adolescence,* 16, 281–291.

Moore, D., and Hotch, D. F. (April 1982). "Parent-Adolescent Separation: The Role of Parental Divorce." *Journal of Youth and Adolescence,* 11, 115–119.

Moore, D., and Schultz, N. R. (1983). "Loneliness at Adolescence: Correlates, Attributions, and Coping." *Journal of Adolescence,* 12, 95–100.

Moore, J. W., Jensen, B., and Hauck, W. E. (1990). "Decision-Making Processes of Youth." *Adolescence,* 25, 583–592.

Moore, J., and Pachon, H. (1985). *Hispanics in the United States.* Englewood Cliffs, NJ: Prentice-Hall.

Moore, K. A., and Stief, T. M. (1991). "Changes in Marriage and Fertility Behavior: Behavior versus Attitudes of Young Adults." *Youth and Society,* 22, 362–386.

Moran, P. B., and Eckenrode, J. (1991). "Gender Differences in the Costs and Benefits of Peer Relationships during Adolescence." *Journal of Adolescent Research,* 6, 396–409.

Morano, C. D., Cisler, R. A., and Lemerond, J. (1993). "Risk Factors for Adolescent Suicidal Behavior: Loss, Insufficient Family Support, and Hopelessness." *Adolescence,* 28, 851–865.

Moreno, A. B., and Thelen, M. H. (1995). "Eating Behavior in Junior High School Females." *Adolescence,* 30, 171–174.

Morgan, C. S. (1992). "College Students' Perceptions of Barriers to Women in Science and Engineering." *Youth and Society,* 24, 228–236.

Morris, G. B. (1992). "Adolescent Leaders: Rational Thinking, Future Beliefs, Temporal Perspective, and Other Correlates." *Adolescence,* 105, 173–181.

Morris, L., Warren, C. W., and Aral, S. O. (1993). "Measuring Adolescent Sexual Behaviors and Related Health Outcomes." *Public Health Reports,* 108, 31–36.

Morrow, K. B., and Sorell, G. T. (1989). "Factors Affecting Self-Esteem, Depression, and Negative Behaviors in Sexually Abused Female Adolescents." *Journal of Marriage and the Family,* 51, 677–686.

Mortimer, J. T., Finch, M., Shanahan, M., and Ryu, S. (1992). "Work Experience, Mental Health, and Behavioral Adjustment in Adolescents." *Journal of Research of Adolescence,* 2, 25–57.

Mosher, D. L., and Tomkins, S. S. (1988). "Scripting the Macho Man: Hypermasculine Socialization and Enculturation." *The Journal of Sex Research,* 25, 60–84.

Mosher, W. D. (1990). "Contraceptive Practice in the United States, 1982–1988." *Family Planning Perspectives,* 22, 198–205.

Mott, F. L., Fondell, M. M., Hu, P. N., Kowaleski-Jones, L., and Menaghan, E. G. (1996). "The Determinants of First Sex by Age 14 in a High-Risk Adolescent Population." *Family Planning Perspectives,* 28, 13–18.

Muehlenhard, C. L., and Cook, S. W. (1988). "Men's Self-Reports of Unwanted Sexual Activity." *The Journal of Sex Research,* 24, 58–72.

Mueller, D. P., and Cooper, P. W. (1986). "Children of Single-Parent Families: How They Fare as Young Adults." *Family Relations,* 35, 169–176.

Mueller, K. E., and Powers, W. G. (1990). "Parent-Child Sexual Discussion: Perceived Communication Style and Subsequent Behavior." *Adolescence,* 25, 469–482.

Mullis, A. K., Mullis, R. L., and Normandin, D. (1992). "Cross-Sectional and Longitudinal Comparisons of Adolescent Self-Esteem." *Adolescence,* 27, 51–61.

Mullis, R. L., and McKinley, K. (1989). "Gender-role Orientation of Adolescent Females: Effects on Self-Esteem and Locus of Control." *Journal of Adolescent Research,* 4, 506–516.

Mulsow, M. H., and Murry, V. M. (1996). "Parenting on Edge." *Journal of Family Issues,* 17, 704–721.

Munson, W. W. (1992). "Self-Esteem, Vocational Identity, and Career Salience in High School Students." *The Career Development Quarterly,* 40, 361–368.

Murdock, B. B., Jr. (1974). *Human Memory: Theory and Data.* MD: Lawrence Erlbaum.

Murnen, S. T., and Byrne, D. (1991). "Hyperfemininity: Measurement and Initial Validation of the Construct." *The Journal of Sex Research,* 28, 479–489.

Murry, B. M. (1992). "First Pregnancy among Black Adolescent Females over Three Decades." *Youth and Society,* 23, 478–506.

Murry, B. M. (1995). "An Ecological Analysis of Pregnancy Resolution Decisions among African American and Hispanic Adolescent Females." *Youth and Society,* 26, 325–350.

Murry, B. M. (1996). "An Ecological Analysis of Coital Timing among Middle-Class African-American Adolescent Females." *Journal of Adolescent Research,* 11, 261–279.

Muson, H. (February 1979). "Moral Thinking: Can It Be Taught?" *Psychology Today,* 48ff.

Muuss, R. E. (Fall 1982). "Social Cognition: Robert Selman's Theory of Role Taking." *Adolescence,* 17, 499–525.

———. (1985). "Adolescent Eating Disorder: Anorexia Nervosa." *Adolescence,* 20, 525–536.

———. (1986). "Adolescent Eating Disorder: Bulimia." *Adolescence,* 22, 257–267.

———. (1988a). "Carol Gilligan's Theory of Sex Differences in the Development of Moral Reasoning during Adolescence." *Adolescence,* 23, 229–243.

———. (1988b). Theories of Adolescence. 5th ed. New York: McGraw-Hill.

Myers, W. C., and Burket, R. C. (1992). "Current Perspectives on Adolescent Conduct Disorder." *Adolescent Medicines,* 3, 61–70.

Myrtek, M., Scharff, C., Brugner, G., and Muller, W. (1996). "Physiological, Behavioral, and Psychological Effects Associated with Television Viewing in School Boys: An Exploratory Study." *Journal of Early Adolescence,* 16, 301–323.

Namerow, P. B., Kalmuss, D. S., and Cushman, L. F. (1993). "The Determinants of Young Women's Pregnancy-Resolution Choices." *Journal of Research on Adolescence,* 3, 193–215.

Nathanson, M., Baird, A., and Jemail, J. (1986). "Family Functioning and the Adolescent Mother: A Systems Approach." *Adolescence,* 21, 827–841.

National Commission on Excellence in Education. (1983). *A Nation at Risk: The Imperative for Educational Reform.* Washington, DC: U.S. Government Printing Office.

National Network of Runaway and Youth Services. (1991). *To Whom Do They Belong?* Washington, DC: Author.

Neapolitan, J. (Winter 1981). "Parental Influences on Aggressive Behavior: A Social Learning Approach." *Adolescence,* 16, 831–840.

Necessary, J. R., and Parish, T. S. (1995). "Relationships of Parents' Perceived Actions toward Their Children." *Adolescence,* 30, 175–176.

Needle, R. H., Su, S. S., and Doherty, W. J. (1990). "Divorce, Remarriage, and Adolescent Substance Use: A Prospective Longitudinal Study." *Journal of Marriage and the Family,* 152, 157–159.

Neiger, B. L., and Hopkins, R. W. (1988). "Adolescent Suicide: Character Traits of High-Risk Teenagers." *Adolescence,* 23, 469–475.

Neighbors, B., Forehand, R., and Armistead, L. (1992). "Is Parental Divorce a Critical Stressor for Young Adolescents? Grade Point Average as a Case in Point." *Adolescence,* 27, 639–646.

Nelson, C., and Keith, J. (1990). "Comparisons of Female and Male Early Adolescent Sex-Role Attitudes and Behavior Development." *Adolescence,* 25, 183–204.

Nelson, W. L., Hughes, H. M., Handal, P., Katz, B., and Searight, H. R. (1993). "The Relationship of Family Structure and Family Conflict to Adjustment in Young Adult College Students." *Adolescence,* 28, 29–40.

Nelson-LeGall, S. (1990). "Academic Achievement Orientation and Help-Seeking Behavior in Early Adolescent Girls." *Journal of Early Adolescence,* 10, 176–190.

Nevid, J. S., and Gotfried, F. (1995). *Choices: Sex in the Age of STD.* Boston: Allyn and Bacon.

Nevil, R., Golden, L., and Faragher, T. (1992, 1993). *The Right Kind of Love.* W. B. Music Corporation, Dresden China Music, MCA Music Publishing.

Newcomb, M. D. (1986). "Sexual Behavior of Cohabitators: A Comparison of Three Independent Samples." *The Journal of Sex Research,* 22, 492–513.

Newcomb, M. D., Maddahian, E., and Bentler, P. M. (1986). "Risk Factors for Drug Use among Adolescents: Concurrent and Longitudinal Analysis." *American Journal of Public Health,* 76, 525–531.

Newcomer, S. F., and Udry, J. R. (May 1984). "Mothers' Influence on the Sexual Behavior of Their Teenage Children." *Journal of Marriage and the Family,* 46, 477–485.

———. (July–August, 1985). "Parent-Child Communication and Adolescent Sexual Behavior." *Family Planning Perspectives,* 17, 169–174.

———. (1987). "Parental Marital Status Effects on Adolescent Sexual Behavior." *Journal of Marriage and the Family,* 49, 235–240.

Newell, G. K., Hammig, C. L., Jurick, A. P., and Johnson, D. E. (1990). "Self-Concept as a Factor in the Quality of Diets of Adolescent Girls." *Adolescence,* 25, 117–130.

Newman, B. M. (1989). "The Changing Nature of the Parent-Adolescent Relationship from Early to Late Adolescence." *Adolescence,* 96, 915–924.

Newman, B. M., and Newman, P. R. (1987). "The Impact of High School on Social Development." *Adolescence,* 22, 525–534.

Newman, B. S., and Muzzonigro, P. G. (1993). "The Effects of Traditional Family Values on the Coming Out Process of Gay Male Adolescents." *Adolescence,* 28, 213–226.

Newman, J. (1987). "Psychological Effects on College Students on Raising the Drinking Age." *Adolescence,* 22, 503–510.

Newman, P. R., and Newman, B. M. (Summer 1978). "Identity Formation and the College Experience." *Adolescence,* 13, 311–326.

———. (1988). "Differences between Childhood and Adulthood: The Identity Watershed." *Adolescence,* 91, 551–557.

Nitz, K., Ketterlinus, R. D., and Brandt, L. J. (1995). "The Role of Stress, Social Support, and Family Environment in Adolescent Mother's Parenting." *Journal of Adolescent Research,* 10, 358–382.

Noble, P. S., Adams, G. R., and Openshaw, D. K. (1989). "Interpersonal Communication in Parent-Adolescent Dyads." *Journal of Family Psychology,* 2, 483–494.

Nock, S. L. (1995). "A Comparison of Marriages and Cohabiting Relationships." *Journal of Family Issues,* 16, 53–76.

Noller, P., and Callan, V. J. (1986). "Adolescent and Parent Perception of Family Cohesion and Adaptability." *Journal of Adolescence,* 9, 97–106.

Norcini, J. J., and Snyder, S. S. (April 1983). "The Effects of Modeling and Cognitive Induction on the Moral Reasoning of Adolescents." *Journal of Youth and Adolescence,* 12, 101–115.

Northman, J. E. (1985). "The Emergence of an Appreciation for Help during Childhood and Adolescence." *Adolescence,* 20, 775–781.

Norton, A. J., and Moorman, J. E. (1987). "Current Trends in Marriage and Divorce among American Women." *Journal of Marriage and the Family,* 49, 3–14.

Nwadiora, E., and McAdoo, H. (1996). "Acculturative Stress among Amerasian Refugees: Gender and Racial Differences." *Adolescence,* 31, 477–487.

O'Brien, R., and Cohen, S. (1984). *The Encyclopedia of Drug Abuse.* New York: Facts on File.

O'Brien, S. (1989). *American Indian Tribal Governments.* Norman, OK: University of Oklahoma Press.

Offer, D., Ostrov, E., and Howard, K. I. (August 1982). "Family Perceptions of Adolescent Self-Image." *Journal of Youth and Adolescence,* 11, 281–291.

Office of Refugee Resettlement. (1982, 1985). *Refugee Resettlement Program: Report to the Congress.* Washington, DC: U.S. Government Printing Office.

Ogbu, J. (1981). "Origins of Human Competence: A Cultural-Ecological Perspective." *Child Development,* 52, 413–429.

Ognibene, F. P. (October 1984). "Complications of AIDS." *Medical Aspects of Human Sexuality,* 18, 9.

Ogundari, J. T. (Spring 1985). "Somatic Deviations in Adolescence: Reactions and Adjustments." *Adolescence,* 20, 179–183.

Ohannesian, C. M., and Crockett, L. J. (1993). "A Longitudinal Investigation of the Relationship between Educational Investment and Adolescent Sexual Activity." *Journal of Adolescent Research,* 8, 167–182.

O'Hare, M. M. (1987). "Career Decision-Making Models: Espoused Theory vs. Theory-In-Use." *Journal of Counseling and Development,* 65, 301–303.

Okum, M. A., and Sasfy, J. H. (Fall 1977). "Adolescence: The Self-Concept, and Formal Operations." *Adolescence,* 12, 373–379.

Okwumabua, J. O., Okwumabua, T. M., Winston, B. L., and Walker, H., Jr. (1989). "Onset of Drug Use among Rural Black Youth." *Journal of Adolescent Research,* 4, 238–246.

Olson, D. H. (1986). Circumplex Model VII: Validation Studies and FACES III. *Family Process,* 25, 337–351.

Olson, D. H., Portner, J., and Lavee, Y. (1985). "FACES III." In D. H. Olson, H. McCubbin, H. Barnes, A. Larsen, M. Muxen, and M. Wilson (Eds.), *Family Inventories* (pp. 7–42). St. Paul: Family Social Science, University of Minnesota.

Olweus, D. (December 1977). "Aggression and Peer Acceptance in Adolescent Boys: Two Short-Term Longitudinal Studies of Ratings." *Child Development,* 48, 1301–1313.

Openshaw, D. K., Thomas, D. L., and Rollins, B. C. (1984). "Parental Influences of Adolescent Self-Esteem." *Journal of Early Adolescence,* 4, 259–274.

Oppenheimer, M. (October 1982). "What You Should Know about Herpes." *Seventeen,* pp. 154–155, 170.

Ordway v. *Hargraves.* (1971). 323 F. Supp. 1115.

Orlofsky, J. L., and Ginsburg, S. D. (Spring 1981). "Intimacy Status: Relationship to Affect Cognition." *Adolescence,* 16, 91–99.

Ormond, C. L., Mann, L., and Luszez, M. (1987). *A Metacognitive Analysis of Decision-Making in Adolescence.* Unpublished manuscript, Flinders University of South Australia.

Ormond, C., Luszez, M. A., Mann, L., and Beswick, G. (1991). "Metacognitive Analysis of Decision Making in Adolescence." *Journal of Adolescence,* 14, 275–291.

Oropesa, R. S. (1996). "Normative Beliefs about Marriage and Cohabitation: A Comparison of Non-Latino Whites, Mexican Americans, and Puerto Ricans." *Journal of Marriage and the Family,* 58, 49–62.

Orr, M. T. (November–December, 1982). "Sex Education and Contraceptive Education in U.S. Public High Schools." *Family Planning Perspectives,* 14, 304–313.

Ortman, P. E. (1988). "Adolescents' Perceptions of and Feelings about Control and Responsibility in Their Lives." *Adolescence,* 23, 913–924.

O'Sullivan, R. G. (1990). "Validating a Method to Identify At-Risk Middle School Students for Participation in a Dropout Prevention Program." *Journal of Early Adolescence,* 10, 209–220.

Overton, W. F., and Byrnes, J. C. (1991). "Cognitive Development." In R. M. Lerney, A. C. Petersen, and J. Brooks-Gunn (Eds.), *Encyclopedia of Adolescence.* Vol. 1. New York: Garland.

Overton, W. F., and Montangero, J. (1991). "Piaget, Jean." In R. M. Lerner, A. C. Petersen, and J. Brooks-Gunn (Eds.), *Encyclopedia of Adolescence.* Vol. 2. New York: Garland.

Owens, T. J. (1992). "Where Do We Go from Here? Post-High School Choices of American Men." *Youth and Society*, 23, 452–477.

Ozorak, E. W. (August 1986). *The Development of Religious Beliefs and Commitment in Adolescence*. Paper presented at the meeting of the American Psychological Association, Washington, DC.

Pabon, E., Rodriguez, O., and Gurin, G. (1992). "Clarifying Peer Relations and Delinquency." *Youth and Society*, 24, 149–165.

Paccione-Dyszlewski, M. R., and Contessa-Kislus, M. A. (1987). "School Phobia: Identification of Subtypes as a Prerequisite to Treatment Intervention." *Adolescence*, 22, 277–384.

Paddack, C. (1987). "Preparing a Boy for Nocturnal Emissions." *Medical Aspects of Human Sexuality*, 21, 15, 16.

Padilla, A. M., and Lindholm, K. J. (1992). *What Do We Know about Culturally Diverse Children?* Paper presented at the meeting of the American Psychological Association, Washington, DC.

Padin, M. A., Lerner, R. M., and Spiro, A., III. (Summer 1981). "Stability of Body Attitudes and Self-Esteem in Late Adolescents." *Adolescence*, 16, 271–384.

Page, R. M. (1990). "Shyness and Sociability: A Dangerous Combination for Illicit Substance Use in Adolescent Males?" *Adolescence*, 25, 803–806.

Page, R. M., and Cole, G. E. (1991). "Loneliness and Alcoholism Risk in Late Adolescence: A Comparative Study of Adults and Adolescents." *Adolescence*, 26, 925–930.

Pagliuso, S. (1976). *Understanding Stages of Moral Development: A Programmed Learning Workbook*. New York: Paulist Press.

Patton, D., Kolasa, K., West, S., and Irons, T. G. (1995). "Sexual Abstinence Counseling of Adolescents by Physicians." *Adolescence*, 30, 963–969.

Pakiz, B., Reinherz, H. Z., and Frost, A. K. (1992). "Antisocial Behavior in Adolescents: A Community Study." *Journal of Early Adolescence*, 12, 300–313.

Palenski, J. E., and Launer, H. M. (1987). "The 'Process' of Running Away: A Redefinition." *Adolescence*, 22, 347–362.

Paluszny, M., Davenport, C., and Kim, W. J. (1991). "Suicide Attempts and Ideation: Adolescents Evaluated on a Pediatric Ward." *Adolescence*, 26, 209–215.

Papernow, P. L. (July 1984). "The Stepfamily Cycle: An Experimental Model of Stepfamily Development." *Family Relations*, 33, 355–363.

Papini, D. R., Farmer, F. F., Clark, S. M., Micka, J. C., and Barnett, J. K. (1990). "Early Adolescent Age and Gender Differences in Patterns of Emotional Self-Disclosure to Parents and Friends." *Adolescence*, 25, 959–976.

Papini, D. R., Mucks, J. C., and Barnett, J. K. (1989). "Perceptions of Intrapsychic and Extrapsychic Functioning as Bases of Adolescent Ego Identity Statuses." *Journal of Adolescent Research*, 4, 462–482.

Papini, D. R., Sebby, R. A., and Clark, S. (1989). "Affective Quality of Family Relations and Adolescent Identity Exploration." *Adolescence*, 24, 457–466.

Parachini, A. (August 19, 1987). "Condoms Fail Government Tests." *Portland Press Herald*.

Parish, J. G., and Parish, T. S. (Fall 1983). "Children's Self-Concepts as Related to Family Structure and Family Concept." *Adolescence*, 18, 649–658.

Parish, T. S. (Fall 1980). "The Relationship between Factors Associated with Father Loss and Individuals' Level of Moral Judgment." *Adolescence*, 15, 535–541.

———. (1991). "Ratings of Self and Parents by Youth: Are They Affected by Family Status, Gender, and Birth Order?" *Adolescence*, 26, 105–112.

———. (1993). "The Relationships between Support System Failures and College Students' Ratings of Self and Family: Do They Vary across Family Configuration?" *Adolescence*, 28, 422–424.

Parish, T. S., and Dostal, J. W. (August 1980). "Evaluations of Self and Parent Figures by Children from Intact, Divorced, and Reconstituted Families." *Journal of Youth and Adolescence*, 9, 347–351.

Parish, T. S., and Parish, J. G. (1991). "The Effects of Family Configuration and Support System Failures during Childhood and Adolescence on College Students' Self-Concept and Social Skills." *Adolescence*, 26, 441–447.

Parrott, C. A., and Strongman, K. T. (Summer 1984). "Locus of Control and Delinquency." *Adolescence*, 19, 459–471.

Paul, E. L., and White, K. M. (1990). "The Development of Intimate Relationships in Late Adolescence." *Adolescence*, 25, 375–400.

Paul, M. J., and Fischer, J. L. (April 1980). "Correlates of Self-Concept among Black Early Adolescents." *Journal of Youth and Adolescence*, 9, 163–173.

Paulson, S. E. (1994). "Relations of Parenting Style and Parental Involvement with Ninth-Grade Students' Achievement." *Journal of Early Adolescence*, 2, 250–267.

Paulson, S. E., and Sputa, C. L. (1996). "Patterns of Parenting during Adolescence: Perceptions of Adolescents and Parents." *Adolescence*, 31, 369–381.

P.C. Games. (January 1997). Volume 4, Number 1.

Pearlman, M. (1995). "The Role of Socioeconomic Status in Adolescent Literature." *Adolescence*, 30, 223–231.

Pearson, J. L., and Ferguson, L. R. (1989). "Gender Differences in Patterns and Spatial Ability, Environmental Cognition, and Math and English Achievement in Late Adolescence." *Adolescence*, 24, 421–431.

Peck, D. L. (1987). "Social-Psychological Correlates of Adolescent and Youthful Suicide." *Adolescence*, 22, 863–878.

Peck, D. L., and Warner, K. (1995). "Accident or Suicide? Single-Vehicle Car Accident and the Intent Hypothesis." *Adolescence*, 30, 463–472.

Pedersen, W. (1990). "Adolescents Initiating Cannabis Use: Cultural Opposition or Poor Mental Health?" *Journal of Adolescence*, 13, 327–339.

Peek, C. W., Fisher, J. L., and Kidwell, J. S. (1985). "Teenage Violence toward Parents: A Neglected Dimension of Family Violence." *Journal of Marriage and the Family*, 47, 1051–1058.

Penick, N. I., and Jepsen, D. A. (1992). "Family Functioning and Adolescent Career Development." *The Career Development Quarterly*, 40, 208–222.

Penner, M. J. (Summer 1982). "The Role of Selected Health Problems in the Causation of Juvenile Delinquency." *Adolescence*, 17, 347–368.

Peretti, P. O. (Fall 1980). "Perceived Primary Group Criteria in the Relational Network of Closest Friendships." *Adolescence*, 15, 555–565.

Perlman, S. B. (1980). "Pregnancy and Parenting among Runaway Girls." *Journal of Family Issues*, 1, 262–273.

Perper, T., and Weis, D. L. (1987). "Proceptive and Rejective Strategies of U.S. and Canadian College Women." *The Journal of Sex Research*, 23, 455–480.

Perry v. Granada. (1969). 300 F. Supp. 748 (Miss.).

Perry, C. L., Telch, M. J., Killen, J., Burke, A., and Maccoby, N. (Fall 1983). "High School Smoking Prevention: The Relative Efficacy of Varied Treatments and Instructions." *Adolescence*, 18, 561–566.

Perry, C. N., and McIntire, W. G. (1995). "Modes of Moral Judgement among Early Adolescents." *Adolescence*, 30, 707–715.

Persell, C. H., Catsambis, S., and Cookson, P. W., Jr. (1992). "Family Background, School Type, and College Attendance: A Conjoint System of Cultural Capital Transmission." *Journal of Research on Adolescence*, 2, 1–23.

Pestrak, V. A., and Martin, D. (1985). "Cognitive Development and Aspects of Adolescent Sexuality." *Adolescence*, 22, 981–987.

Pete, J. M., and DeSantis, L. (1990). "Sexual Decision Making in Young Black Adolescent Females." *Adolescence*, 25, 145–154.

Pete-McGadney, J. (1995). "Differences in Adolescent Self-concept as a Function of Race, Geographic Location, and Pregnancy." *Adolescence*, 30, 95–105.

Peters, J. F. (1985). "Adolescents as Socialization Agents to Parents." *Adolescence*, 20, 921–933.

———. (1989). "Youth Clothes-Shopping Behavior: An Analysis by Gender." *Adolescence*, 24, 575–580.

Petersen, J. R., Kretchner, A., Nellis, B., Lever, J., and Hertz, R. (March 1983). "The Playboy Reader's Sex Survey, Part 2." *Playboy*, p. 90.

Peterson, G. W., and Rollins, B. C. (1987). Parent-Child Socialization: A Review of Research and Applications of Symbolic Interaction Concepts. In M. B. Sussman and S. K. Steinmetz (Eds.), *Handbook of Marriage and the Family* (pp. 471–507). New York: Plenum.

Peterson, G. W., Stiver, M. E., and Peters, D. F. (1986). "Family versus Nonfamily Significant Others for the Career Decisions of Low-Income Youth." *Family Relations*, 35, 417–424.

Peterson, J. L., and Zill, N. (1986). "Marital Disruption, Parent-Child Relationships and Behavior Problems in Children." *Journal of Marriage and the Family*, 48, 295–307.

Peterson, K. L., and Roscoe, B. (1991). "Imaginary Audience Behavior in Older Adolescent Females." *Adolescence*, 26, 195–200.

Pett, M. A., and Vaughan-Cole, B. (1986). "The Impact of Income Issues and Social Status in Post-Divorce Adjustment of Custodial Parents." *Family Relations*, 35, 103–111.

Pfeffer, C. (1987). "Suicidal Children Announce Their Self-Destructive Intentions." *Medical Aspects of Human Sexuality*, 21, 14.

Phelps, L. A., Johnston, L. S., Jimenesez, D. P., Wilczenski, F. L., Andrea, R. K., and Healy, R. W. (1993). "Figure Preference, Body Dissatisfaction, and Body Distortion in Adolescence." *Journal of Adolescent Research*, 8, 297–310.

Philliber, S. G., and Tatum, M. L. (Summer 1982). "Sex Education and the Double Standard in High School." *Adolescence*, 17, 272–283.

Phinney, J. S. (1989). "Stages of Ethnic Identity Development in Minority Group Adolescents." *Journal of Early Adolescence*, 9, 34–49.

———. (1992). "The Multigroup Ethnic Identity Measure. A New Scale for Use with Diverse Groups." *Journal of Adolescent Research*, 7, 156–176.

Phinney, J. S., and Chavira, V. (1995). "Parental Ethnic Socialization and Adolescent Coping with Problems Related to Ethnicity." *Journal of Research on Adolescence*, 5, 31–63.

Phinney, J. S., Chavira, V., and Williamson, L. (1992). "Acculturation Attitudes and Self-Esteem among High-School and College Students." *Youth and Society*, 23, 299–312.

Phinney, J. S., Dupont, S., Landin, J., and Onwughalu, M. (1994). *Social Identity Orientation, Bicultural Conflicts, and Coping Strategies among Minority Adolescents.* Paper presented at the meeting of the Society for Research on Adolescents, San Diego.

Phinney, V. G., Jensen, L. C., Olsen, J. A., and Cundick, B. (1990). "The Relationship between Early Development and Psychosexual Behaviors in Adolescent Females." *Adolescence*, 25, 321–332.

Piaget, J. (1948). *The Moral Judgment of the Child.* Glencoe, IL: Free Press. (Originally 1932).

———. (1950). *The Psychology of Intelligence.* London: Routledge and Kegan Paul.

———. (1967). *Six Psychological Studies.* Translated by A. Tenzer and D. Elkind. New York: Random House.

———. (1971). "The Theory of Stages in Cognitive Development." In D. R. Green (Ed.), *Measurement and Piaget.* New York: McGraw-Hill.

———. (1972). "Intellectual Evolution from Adolescence to Adulthood." *Human Development*, 15, 1012.

———. (1980). "Intellectual Evolution from Adolescence to Adulthood." In R. E. Muuss (Ed.), *Adolescent Behavior and Society: A Body of Readings.* 3rd ed. New York: Random House.

Piaget, J., and Inhelder, B. (1969). *The Psychology of the Child.* Translated by Helen Weaver. New York: Basic Books.

———. (Winter 1976). "The Development of Formal Thinking and Creativity in Adolescence." *Adolescence*, 11, 609–617.

Pillemer, D. B., Koff, E., Rhinehart, E. D., and Rierdan, J. (1987). "Flashbulb Memories of Menarche and Adult Menstrual Distress." *Journal of Adolescence*, 10, 187–199.

Pink, J. E. T., and Wampler, K. S. (1985). "Problem Areas in Stepfamilies: Cohesion, Adaptability, and the Stepfather-Adolescent Relationship." *Family Relations*, 34, 327–335.

Pinneau, S. R. (1961). *Changes in Intelligence Quotient.* Boston: Houghton Mifflin.

Pipher, M. (1996). *The Shelter of Each Other: Rebuilding Our Families.* New York: Grosset/Putnam Book.

Pirog-Good, M. A. (1996). "The Education and Labor Market Outcomes of Adolescent Fathers." *Youth and Society*, 28, 236–262.

Pittman, F. S. (1991). "The Secret Passions of Men." *Journal of Marital and Family Therapy*, 17, 17–23.

Plake, B. S., Kaplan, B. J., and Steinbrunn, J. (1986). "Sex Role Orientation, Level of Cognitive Development, and Mathematics Performance in Late Adolescence." *Adolescence*, 83, 607–613.

Plummer, L. C., and Koch-Hattern, A. (1986). "Family Stress and Adjustment to Divorce." *Family Relations*, 523–529.

Plummer, W. (October 28, 1985). "A School's Rx for Sex." *People*, pp. 39–41.

Polaneczky, M., et al. (1994). "The Use of Levonorgestrel Implants (Norplant) for Contraception in Adolescent Mothers." *New England Journal of Medicine*, 331, 1201–1206.

Polcin, D. L. (1992). "A Comprehensive Model for Adolescent Chemical Dependency Treatment." *Journal of Counseling and Development*, 70, 376–382.

Polskin, A. (1991). *T.V. Guide.* Radnor, PA: News America Publications.

Pombeni, M., Kirchler, E., and Palmonari, A. (1990). "Identification with Peers as a Strategy to Muddle through the Troubles of the Adolescent Years." *Journal of Adolescence*, 13, 351–369.

Portes, P. R., Dunham, R. M., and Williams, S. (1986). "Assessing Child-Rearing Style in Ecological Settings: Its Relation to Culture, Social Class, Early Age Intervention, and Scholastic Achievement." *Adolescence*, 21, 723–735.

Post-Kammer, P. (1987). "Intrinsic and Extrinsic Work Values and Career Maturity of 9th- and 11th-Grade Boys and Girls." *Journal of Counseling and Development*, 65, 420–423.

Postrado, L. T., and Nicholson, H. J. (1992). "Effectiveness in Delaying the Initiation of Sexual Intercourse in Girls Aged 12–14." *Youth and Society*, 23, 356–379.

Powers, P. S. (1980). *Obesity: The Regulation of Weight.* Baltimore: Williams and Wilkins.

Prediger, D. J., and Brandt, W. E. (1991). "Project CHOICE: Validity of Interest and Ability Measures for Student Choice of Vocational Program." *The Career Development Quarterly*, 40, 132–144.

"Pregnant Schoolgirls and Pregnant Teachers: The Policy Problem School Districts Can Sidestep No Longer." (1973). *American School Board Journal*, 160, 23–27.

Prince, F. (1995). "The Relative Effectiveness of a Peer-Led and Adult-Led Smoking Intervention Program." *Adolescence*, 30, 187–194.

Pritchard, M. E., Myers, B. K., and Cassidy, D. J. (1989). "Factors Associated with Adolescent Saving and Spending Patterns." *Adolescence*, 24, 711–723.

Protinsky, H. (1988). "Identity Formation: A Comparison of Problem and Nonproblem Adolescents." *Adolescence*, 23, 67–72.

Protinsky, H., and Farrier, S. (Winter 1980). "Self-Image in Pre-Adolescents and Adolecents." *Adolescence*, 15, 887–893.

Pryor, D. W., and McGarrell, E. F. (1993). "Public Perceptions of Youth Gang Crime: An Exploratory Analysis." *Youth and Society*, 24, 399–418.

Ptacek, C. (1988). "The Nuclear Age: Context for Family Interaction." *Family Relations*, 37, 437–443.

Quadrel, M. J., Fischoff, B., and Davis, W. W. (1993). "Adolescent (In)vulnerability." *American Psychologist*, 48, 102–116.

Queralt, M. (1993). "Risk Factors Associated with Completed Suicide in Latino Adolescents." *Adolescence*, 28, 831–850.

Quintana, S. M., and Lapsley, D. K. (1990). "Rapprochement in Late Adolescent Separation-Individuation: A Structure Equations Approach." *Journal of Adolescence*, 13, 371–385.

Rabin, D. F., and Chrousos, G. P. (1991). "Androgens, Gonadal." In R. M. Lerner, A. C. Petersen, and J. Brooks-Gunn (Eds.), *Encyclopedia of Adolescence.* Vol. 1. New York: Garland.

Rabinowitz, F. E. (1991). "The Male-to-Male Embrace: Breaking the Touch Taboo in Men's Therapy Groups." *Journal of Counseling and Development*, 69, 574–576.

Ralph, N., and Morgan, K. A. (1991). "Assessing Differences in Chemically Dependent Adolescent Males Using the Child Behavior Check List." *Adolescence*, 26, 183–194.

Ramsey, C. E. "A Study of Decision-Making of Adolescence." Unpublished data.

Randolph, E. M., and Dye, C. A. (Winter 1981). "The Peter Pan Profile Development of a Scale to Measure Reluctance to Grow Up." *Adolescence*, 16, 841–850.

Rank, M. R. (1987). "The Formation and Dissolution of Marriages in the Welfare Population." *Journal of Marriage and the Family*, 49, 15–20.

Raphael, B., Cubis, J., Dunne, M., Lewin, T., and Kelly, B. (1990). "The Impact of Parental Loss on Adolescents' Psychosocial Characteristics." *Adolescence*, 25, 689–700.

Raphael, D., and Xelowski, H. G. (October 1980). "Identity Status in High School Students: Critique and a Revised Paradigm." *Journal of Youth and Adolescence*, 9, 383–389.

Raschke, H. J., and Raschke, V. J. (May 1979). "Family Conflict and Children's Self-Concepts: A Comparison of Intact and Single-Parent Families." *Journal of Marriage and the Family*, 41, 367–374.

Rathus, S. A., Nevid, J. S., and Fichner-Rathus, L. (1997). *Human Sexuality in a World of Diversity*. Boston: Allyn and Bacon.

Ravitch, D. (October 1983). "The Educational Pendulum." *Psychology Today*, 17, 62–71.

Ray, W. J., Georgiou, S., and Ravizza, R. (1979). "Spatial Abilities, Sex Differences, and Lateral Eye Movements." *Developmental Psychology*, 15, 455–457.

Read, M. H., Harveywebster, M., and Usinger-Lesquereux, J. (1988). "Adolescent Compliance with Dietary Guidelines: Health and Education Implications." *Adolescence*, 23, 567–575.

Reardon, B., and Griffing, P. (Spring 1983). "Factors Related to the Self-Concept of Institutionalized, White, Male, Adolescent Drug Abusers." *Adolescence*, 18, 29–41.

Reis, I. L. (1971). *The Family System in America*. New York: Holt, Rinehart and Winston.

Reis, J., and Seidly, A. (1989). "School Administrators, Parents, and Sex Education: A Resolvable Paradox?" *Adolescence*, 24, 639–645.

Remez, L. (1991). "Rates of Adolescent Pregnancy and Childbearing are High among Mexico-Born Americans." *Family Planning Perspectives*, 23, 88–89.

———. (1992). "Adolescent Drug Users More Likely to Become Pregnant, Elect Abortion." *Family Planning Perspectives*, 24, 281–282.

Resnick, M. D., Wattenberg, E., and Brewer, R. (1992). *Paternity of Avowal/Disavowal among Partners of Low Income Mothers*. Paper presented at the Meeting of the Society for Research on Adolescence, Washington, DC.

Rest, J. (1986). *Moral Development: Advances in Research and Theory*. New York: Praeger.

Rest, J. R. (1983). "Morality." In P. H. Mussen (Ed.), *Handbook of Child Psychology*, III. 4th ed. New York: Wiley.

Rhodes, J. E., and Fisher, K. (1993). "Spanning the Gender Gap: Gender Differences in Delinquency among Inner-City Adolescents." *Adolescence*, 28, 879–889.

Rice, F. P. (1980). *Morality and Youth*. Philadelphia: Westminster Press.

———. (1989). *Human Sexuality*. Dubuque, IA: Wm. C. Brown.

———. (1993). *Intimate Relationships, Marriages, and Families*. Mountain View, CA: Mayfield.

———. (1996). *Intimate Relationships, Marriages, and Families*. Moutain View, CA: Mayfield.

Rice, K. G. (1993). "Separation-Individuation and Adjustment in College: A Longitudinal Study." *Journal of Counseling Psychology*, 39, 203–213.

Rich, C. L., Sherman, M., and Fowler, R. C. (1990). "San Diego Suicide Study: The Adolescents." *Adolescence*, 25, 855–865.

Rich, Y., and Golan, R. (1992). "Career Plans for Male-Dominated Occupations and Female Seniors in Religious and Secular High Schools." *Adolescence*, 27, 73–86.

Richards, M. H., and Larson, R. (1993). "Pubertal Development in the Daily Subjective States of Young Adolescents." *Journal of Research on Adolescence*, 3, 145–169.

Richman, C. L., Clark, M. L., and Brown, K. P. (1985). "General and Specific Self-Esteem in Late Adolescent Students: Race x Gender x SES Effects." *Adolescence*, 20, 555–566.

Rierdan, J., Koff, E., and Stubbs, M. L. (1989). "A Longitudinal Analysis of Body Image as a Predictor of the Onset and Persistence of Adolescent Girls' Depression." *Journal of Early of Adolescence*, 9, 454–466.

Rinck, C., Rudolph, J. A., and Simkins, L. (Winter 1983). "A Survey of Attitudes Concerning Contraception and the Resolution of Teenage Pregnancy." *Adolescence*, 18, 923–929.

Ringwalt, C. L., and Palmer, J. H. (1989). "Cocaine and Crack Users Compared." *Adolescence*, 24, 851–859.

Risman, B. J., Hill, C. T., Rubin, Z., and Peplau, L. A. (February 1981). "Living Together in College: Implications for Courtship." *Journal of Marriage and the Family*, 43, 77–83.

Robbins, D. (1983). "A Cluster of Adolescent Suicide Attempts: Is Suicide Contagious?" *Journal of Adolescent Health Care*, 3, 253–255.

Roberto, L. G. (1986). "Bulimia: The Transgenerational View." *Journal of Marital and Family Therapy*, 12, 231–240.

Roberts, A. R. (Summer 1982). "Adolescent Runaways in Suburbia: A New Typology." *Adolescence*, 17, 379–396.

Roberts, E., and DeBlossie, R. R. (Winter 1983). "Test Bias and the Culturally Different Early Adolescent." *Adolescence*, 18, 837–843.

Roberts, L. R., and Petersen, A. C. (1992). "The Relationship between Academic Achievement and Social Self-Image during Early Adolescence." *Journal of Early Adolescence*, 12, 197–219.

Roberts, L. R., Sarigiani, P. A., Petersen, A. C., and Newman, J. L. (1990). "Gender Differences in Relationship between Achievement and Self-Image during Early Adolescence." *Journal of Early Adolescence*, 10, 159–175.

Robertson, E. B., Skinner, M. L., Love, M. M., et al. (1992). "The Pubertal Development Scale: A Rural and Suburban Comparison." *Journal of Early Adolescence*, 12, 174–186.

Robertson, J. F., and Simons, R. L. (1989). "Family Factors, Self-Esteem, and Adolescent Depression." *Journal of Marriage and the Family*, 51, 125–138.

Robins, L. N. (1966). *Deviant Children Grown Up*. Baltimore: Williams & Wilkins.

Robinson, B. (1988). "Teenage Pregnancy from the Father's Perspective." *American Journal of Orthopsychiatry*, 58, 46–51.

Robinson, B. E. (July 1984). "The Contemporary American Stepfather." *Family Relations*, 33, 381–388.

Robinson, B. E., Skeen, P., Flake-Hobson, C., and Herman, M. (1982). "Gay Men's and Women's Perceptions of Early Family Life and Their Relationships with Parents." *Family Relations*, 31, 79–83.

Robinson, I. E., and Jedlicka, D. (February 1982). "Change in Sexual Attitudes and Behavior of College Students from 1965 to 1980: A Research Note." *Journal of Marriage and the Family,* 44, 237–240.

Robinson, L. H., and Dalton, R. (1986). "Homosexuality in Adolescence." *Medical Aspects of Human Sexuality,* 20, 106–114.

Robinson, N. S. (1995). "Evaluating the Nature of Perceived Support in Its Relation to Perceived Self-Worth in Adolescents." *Journal of Research on Adolescence,* 5, 253–280.

Robinson, S. E. (January 1983). "Nader versus ETS: Who Should We Believe?" *Personnel and Guidance Journal,* 61, 260–262.

Roche, J. P., and Ramsbey, T. W. (1993). "Premarital Sexuality: A Five-Year Follow-up Study of Attitudes and Behavior by Dating Stage." *Adolescence,* 28, 67–80.

Rodgers, J. L., and Rowe, D. C. (1990). "Adolescent Sexual Activity and Mildly Deviant Behavior." *Journal of Family Issues,* 11, 274–303.

Rodgers, J. L., Rowe, D. C., and Harris, D. F. (1992). "Sibling Differences in Adolescent Sexual Behavior: Inferring Process Models from Family Composition Patterns." *Journal of Marriage and the Family,* 54, 142–152.

Rodriquez, C., Jr., and Moore, M. B. (1995). Perceptions of Pregnant/Parenting Teens: Reframing Issues for an Integrated Approach to Pregnancy Problems." *Adolescence,* 30, 685–706.

Rogers, C. R. (1961). *On Becoming a Person: A Therapist's View of Psychotherapy.* Boston: Houghton Mifflin.

Rogers, E., and Lee, S. H. (1992). "A Comparison of the Perceptions of the Mother-Daughter Relationship of Black Pregnant and Nonpregnant Teenagers." *Adolescence,* 27, 555–564.

Rogers, J. R. (1992). "Suicide and Alcohol: Conceptualizing the Relationship from a Cognitive-Social Paradigm." *Journal of Counseling and Development,* 70, 540–543.

Rogler, L. H., and Procidano, M. E. (1989). "Egalitarian Spouse Relations and Wives' Marital Satisfaction in Intergenerationally Linked Puerto Rican Families." *Journal of Marriage and the Family,* 51, 37–39.

Rogow, A. M., Marcia, J. E., and Slugoski, B. R. (October 1983). "The Relative Importance of Identity Status Interview Components." *Journal of Youth and Adolescence,* 12, 387–400.

Rohner, R. P., Bourque, S. L., and Elordi, C. A. (1996). "Children's Perceptions of Corporal Punishment, Caretaker Acceptance, and Psychological Adjustment in a Poor, Biracial Southern Community." *Journal of Marriage and the Family,* 58, 842–852.

Rohr, N. E. (1996). "Identifying Adolescent Runaways: The Predictive Utility of the Personality Inventory of Children." *Adolescence,* 31, 604–613.

Roll, E. J. (Fall 1980). "Psychologists' Conflicts about the Inevitability of Conflict during Adolescence: An Attempt at Reconciliation." *Adolescence,* 15, 661–670.

Romo, H. D., and Falbo, T. (1995). *Against the Odds: Latino Youth and High School Graduation.* Austin: University of Texas Press.

Roosa, M. W. (1986). "Adolescent Mothers, School Drop-Outs and School Based Intervention Programs." *Family Relations,* 35, 313–317.

———. (1991). "Adolescent Pregnancy Programs Collection: An Introduction." *Family Relations,* 40, 370–372.

Roscoe, B. (1990). "Defining Child Maltreatment: Ratings of Parental Behavior." *Adolescence,* 24, 517–528.

Roscoe, B., and Callahan, J. E. (1985). "Adolescents' Self-Report of Violence in Families and Dating Relations." *Adolescence,* 20, 545–553.

Roscoe, B., Diana, M. S., and Brooks, R. H., II. (1987). "Early, Middle, and Later Adolescents' Views on Dating and Factors Influencing Partner Selection." *Adolescence,* 22, 59–68.

Roscoe, B., Kennedy, D., and Pope, R. (1987). "Adolescents' Views of Intimacy: Distinguishing Intimate from Nonintimate Relationships." *Adolescence,* 87, 511–516.

Roscoe, B., and Peterson, K. L. (1989). "Age-Appropriate Behaviors: A Comparison of Three Generations of Females." *Adolescence,* 214, 167–178.

Roscoe, B., and Skomski, G. G. (1989). "Loneliness among Late Adolescents." *Adolescence,* 24, 947–965.

Rosenthal, D. A., and Feldman, S. S. (1991). "The Influence of Perceived Family and Personal Factors on Self-Reported School Performance of Chinese and Western High School Students." *Journal of Research on Adolescence,* 1, 135–154.

Rosenthal, D. A., Moore, S. M., and Taylor, M. J. (April 1983). "Ethnicity and Adjustment: A Study of the Self-Image of Anglo-, Greek-, and Italian-Australian Working Class Adolescents." *Journal of Youth and Adolescence,* 12, 117–135.

Rosenthal, D., and Hansen, J. (October 1980). "Comparison of Adolescents' Perceptions and Behaviors in Single- and Two-Parent Families." *Journal of Youth and Adolescence,* 9, 407–417.

Rosenthal, R., and Jacobson, L. (1968). *Pygmalion in the Classroom: Teacher Expectation and Pupil's Intellectual Development.* New York: Holt, Rinehart and Winston.

Rosenthal, S. L., Biro, F. N., Cohen, S. S., Succop, P. A., and Stanberry, L. R. (1995). "Strategies for Coping with Sexually Transmitted Diseases by Adolescent Females." *Adolescence,* 30, 655–666.

Rosenthal, S. L., Lewis, L. M., and Cohen, S. S. (1996). "Issues Related to the Sexual Decision-Making of Inner-City Adolescent Girls. *Adolescence,* 31, 731–739.

Rosenthal, S. L., and Simeonsson, R. J. (1989). "Emotional Disturbances and the Development of Self-Consciousness in Adolescence." *Adolescence,* 24, 689–698.

Rosoff, J. I. (1989). "Sex Education in the Schools: Policies and Practice." *Family Planning Perspectives,* 21, 52, 64.

Ross, J. A. (1981). "Improving Adolescent Decision-Making Skills." *Curriculum Inquiry,* 11, 279–295.

Rosseel, E. (1985a). "Work Ethic and Orientation to Work of the Young Generation: The Impact of Educational Level." *Social Indicators Research,* 17, 171–187.

———. (1985b). *Riders and Knights in the Empty Dawn: Evolution in the Work Ethic of the Youth.* Brussels: Free University Press.

————. (1989). "The Impact of Attitudes toward the Personal Future in Study Motivation and Work Orientations of Nonworking Adolescents." *Adolescence*, 24, 73–93.

Rotheram-Borus, M. J. (1989). "Ethnic Differences in Adolescents' Identity Status and Associated Behavior Problems." *Journal of Adolescence*, 12, 361–374.

Rotherarm, M. J., and Armstrong, M. (Summer 1980). "Assertiveness Training with High School Students." *Adolescence*, 15, 267–276.

Rothman, K. M. (Fall 1984). "Multvariate Analysis of the Relationship of Personal Concerns to Adolescent Ego Identity Status." *Adolescence*, 19, 713–727.

Rowe, D. C., Rodgers, J. L., and Meseck-Bushey, S. (1992). "Sibling Delinquency and the Family Environment: Shared and Unshared Influences." *Child Development*, 63, 59–67.

Rozendal, F. G. (Winter 1983). "Halos vs. Stigmas: Long-Term Effects of Parents' Death or Divorce on College Students' Concepts of the Family." *Adolescence*, 18, 947–955.

Rubenstein, C. (July 1983). "The Modern Art of Courtly Love." *Psychology Today*, 17, 40–49.

Rubin, Z., Hill, C. T., Peplau, L. A., and Dunkel-Schetter, C. (May 1980). "Self-Disclosure in Dating Couples: Sex Roles and the Ethic of Openness." *Journal of Marriage and the Family*, 42, 305–317.

Rueter, M. A., and Conger, R. D. (1995). "Antecedents of Parent-Adolescent Disagreements." *Journal of Marriage and the Family*, 57, 435–448.

Rumbaut, R. G., and Weeks, Jr. (1985). *Fertility and Adaptation among Indochinese Refugees in the United States*. Research Paper No. 3. San Diego: University of California, San Diego, Indochinese Health and Adaptation Research Project.

Russell, J., Halasz, G., and Beumont, P. J. V. (1990). "Death Related Themes in Anorexia Nervosa: A Practical Exploration." *Journal of Adolescence*, 13, 311–326.

Russell, M. A. H. (1971). "Cigarette Smoking: Natural History of a Dependence Disorder." *British Journal of Medical Psychology*, 44, 9.

Rust, J. O., and McCraw, A. (Summer 1984). "Influence of Masculinity-Femininity on Adolescent Self-Esteem and Peer Acceptance." *Adolescence*, 19, 357–366.

Ryan, B. A., Adams, G. R., Gullotta, T. P., Weissberg, R. P., and Hampton, R. L. (Eds.). (1995). *The Family-School Connection*. Newbury Park, CA: Sage.

Sabatelli, R. M., and Anderson, S. A. (1991). "Family System Dynamics, Peer Relationships, and Adolescents' Psychological Adjustment." *Family Relations*, 40, 363–369.

Sack, A. L., and Thiel, R. (January 1979). "College Football and Social Mobility: A Case Study of Notre Dame Football Players." *Sociology of Education*, 52, 60–66.

Sadker, M., and Sadker, M. (1985). "Sexism in the School of the 80s." *Psychology Today*, 19, 54–57.

Salomone, P. R., and Sheehan, M. C. (1985). "Vocational Stability and Congruence: An Examination of Holland's Proposition." *The Vocational Guidance Quarterly*, 34, 91–98.

Salt, R. E. (1991). "Affectionate Touch between Fathers and Preadolescent Sons." *Journal of Marriage and the Family*, 53, 545–554.

Saltiel, J. (1986). "Segmental Influence: The Case of Educational and Occupational Significant Others." *Adolescence*, 21, 615–622.

Sameroff, A. J., Seifer, R., Baldwin, A., and Baldwin, C. (1993). "Stability of Intelligence from Preschool to Adolescence: The Influence of Social and Family Risk Factors." *Child Development*, 64, 80–97.

Samet, N., and Kelly, E. W. (1987). "The Relationship of Steady Dating to Self-Esteem and Sex-Role Identity among Adolescents." *Adolescence*, 22, 231–245.

Sandberg, D. E., Ehrhardt, A. A., Ince, S. E., and Meyer-Bahlburg, H. F. L. (1991). "Gender Differences in Childrens' and Adolescents' Career Aspirations: A Follow Up Study." *Journal of Adolescent Research*, 6, 371–386.

Sanders, G. F., and Millis, R. L. (1988). "Family Influences on Sexual Attitudes and Knowledge as Reported by College Students." *Adolescence*, 23, 837–846.

Sanik, M. M., and Stafford, D. (Spring 1985). "Adolescents' Contributions to Household Production: Male and Female Differences." *Adolescence*, 20, 207–215.

Sansonnet-Hayden, H., Haley, G., Marriage, K., and Fine, S. (1987). "Sexual Abuse and Psychopathology in Hospitalized Adolescents." *Journal of the American Academy of Child and Adolescent Psychiatry*, 26, 753–757.

Santilli, N. R., and Hudson, L. M. (1992). "Enhancing Moral Growth: Is Communication the Key?" *Adolescence*, 27, 145–160.

Santrock, J. W. (1987). *Adolescence*. Dubuque, IA: Wm. C. Brown.

Sarigiani, P. A., Wilson, J. L., Petersen, A. C., and Vicary, J. R. (1990). "Self-Image and Educational Plans of Adolescents from Two Contrasting Communities." *Journal of Early Adolescence*, 10, 37–55.

Saucier, J. F., and Ambert, A. M. (1983). "Adolescents' Self-Reported Mental Health and Parents' Marital Status." *Psychiatry*, 46, 363–369.

————. (1986). "Adolescents' Perceptions of Self and of Immediate Environment by Parental Marital Status: A Controlled Study." *Canadian Journal of Psychiatry*, 31, 505–511.

Sauer, L. E., and Fine, M. A. (1988). "Parent-Child Relationships in Stepparent Families." *Journal of Family Psychology*, 1, 434–451.

Saunders, L. E. (Fall 1981). "Ignorance of the Law among Teenagers: Is It a Barrier to the Exertion of Their Rights as Citizens?" *Adolescence*, 16, 711–726.

Savin-Williams, R. C., and Rodriguez, R. G. (1993). "A Developmental, Clinical Perspective on Lesbian, Gay Male, and Bisexual Youths." In T. P. Gullota, G. R. Adams, and R. Montemayor (Eds.), *Adolescent Sexuality*. Newbury Park, CA: Sage.

Scales, P. (1986). "The Changing Context of Sexuality Education: Paradigms and Challenges for Alternative Futures." *Family Relations*, 35, 265–274.

————. (1990). "Developing Capable Young People: An Alternative Strategy for Prevention Program." *Journal of Early Adolescence*, 10, 420–438.

Schab, F. (1991). "Schooling without Learning: Twenty Years of Cheating in High School." *Adolescence, 26,* 839–847.

Scheer, S. D., Unger, D. G., and Brown, M. P. (1996). "Adolescents Becoming Adults: Attributes for Adulthood." *Adolescence, 31,* 127–131.

Schichor, A., Beck, A., Berstein, B., and Crabtree, B. (1990). "Seat Belt Use and Stress in Adolescents." *Adolescence, 25,* 773–779.

Schlecter, T. M., and Gump, P. V. (1983). "Car Availability and the Daily Life of the Teenage Male." *Adolescence, 18,* 101–113.

Schmidt, J. A., and Davison, M. L. (May 1983). "Helping Students Think." *Personnel and Guidance Journal, 61,* 563–569.

Schneider, B. H., and Younger, A. K. (1996). "Adolescent-Parent Attachment in Adolescents' Relations with their Peers." *Youth and Society, 28,* 95–108.

Schoen, R. (1992). "First Unions and the Stability of First Marriages." *Journal of Marriage and the Family, 54,* 281–284.

Schoen, R., and Weinick, R. M. (1993). "Partner Choices in Marriage and Cohabitations." *Journal of Marriage and the Family, 55,* 408–414.

Schulenberg, J., Asp, E., and Petersen, A. C. (1984). "School from the Young Adolescents' Perspective: A Descriptive Report." *Journal of Early Adolescence, 4,* 107–130.

Schulenberg, J., Goldstein, A., and Vondracek, F. W. (1991). "Gender Differences in Adolescents' Career Interests: Beyond Main Effects." *Journal of Research on Adolescence, 1,* 37–61.

Schulenberg, J., Vondracek, F. W., and Kim, J. (1993). "Career Certainty and Short-Term Changes in Work Values during Adolescence." *The Career Development Quarterly, 41,* 268–284.

Schultz, J. B., and Boyd, J. R. (October 1984). "Sexuality Attitudes and Secondary Teachers." *Family Relations, 33,* 537–541.

Schvaneveldt, J. D., and Adams, G. R. (1983). "Adolescents and the Decision-making Process." *Theory into Practice, 22,* 98–104.

Schwartz, D. B., and Darabi, K. F. (1986). "Motivations for Adolescents' First Visit to a Family Planning Clinic." *Adolescence, 21,* 535–545.

Schwartz, R. C. (1987). "Working with 'Internal' and 'External' Families in the Treatment of Bulimia." *Family Relations, 36,* 242–245.

Schweinhart, L. J., and Weikert, D. P. (1985). "Evidence That Good Early Childhood Programs Work." *Phi Delta Kappan, 66,* 545–551.

Scott, C. S., Shifman, L., Orr, L., Owen, R. G., and Fawcett, N. (1988). "Hispanic and Black American Adolescents' Beliefs Relating to Sexuality and Contraception." *Adolescence, 23,* 667–688.

Scott, J., and Hatalla, J. (1990). "The Influence of Chance and Contingency Factors on Career Patterns of College-Educated Women." *The Career Development Quarterly, 39,* 19–30.

Scott-Jones, D., and White, A. B. (1990). "Correlates of Sexual Activity in Early Adolescence." *Journal of Early Adolescence, 10,* 221–238.

Sebald, H. (Spring 1981). "Adolescents' Concept of Popularity and Unpopularity, Comparing 1960 with 1976." *Adolescence, 16,* 187–193.

———. (1986). "Adolescents' Shifting Orientation toward Parents and Peers: A Curvilinear Trend over Recent Decades." *Journal of Marriage and the Family, 48,* 5–13.

———. (1989). "Adolescent's Peer Orientation: Changes in the Support System during the Past Three Decades." *Adolescence, 24,* 937–946.

Seebach, E. E., and Norris, R. C. (1989). "A Brunsickian Model for Body Image Research in Patients with Eating Disorders." *Journal of Adolescence Research, 3,* 299–318.

Segal, S. D., and Fairchild, H. H. (1996). "Polysubstance Abuse—A Case Study." *Adolescence, 31,* 797–805.

Seide, F. W. (Spring 1982). "Big Sisters: An Experimental Evaluation." *Adolescence, 17,* 117–128.

Seitz, V., and Apfel, N. H. (1994). "Parent-Focused Intervention: Diffusing Effects on Siblings." *Child Development, 65,* 677–683.

Selman, R. L. (1977). "A Structural-Developmental Model of Social Cognition: Implications for Intervention Research." *Counseling Psychologist, 6,* 3–6.

———. (1980). *The Growth of Interpersonal Understanding: Development and Clinical Analysis.* New York: Academic Press.

Serow, R. C., and Dreyden, J. I. (1990). "Community Service among College and University Students: Individual and Institutional Relationships." *Adolescence, 25,* 552–566.

Sessa, F. M., and Steinberg, L. (1991). "Family Structure and Development of Autonomy during Adolescence." *Journal of Early Adolescence, 11,* 38–55.

Seydlitz, R. (1991). "The Effects of Age and Gender on Parental Control and Delinquency." *Youth and Society, 23,* 175–201.

Seydlitz, R. (1993). "Perplexity in the Relationships among Direct and Indirect Parental Controls and Delinquency." *Youth and Society, 24,* 243–275.

———. (1988). "Suicidal Children." *Medical Aspects of Human Sexuality, 22,* 63.

Shain, L., and Farber, B. A. (1989). "Female Identity Development and Self-Reflection in Late Adolescence." *Adolescence, 24,* 381–392.

Shakespeare, W. (1974). *Plays: The Riverside Shakespeare.* Boston: Houghton Mifflin.

Shapiro, S. H. (1973). "Vicissitudes of Adolescence." In S. L. Cope (Ed.), *Behavior Pathology of Childhood and Adolescence.* New York: Basic Books.

Sharlin, S. A., and Mor-Barak, M. (1992). "Runaway Girls in Distress: Motivation, Background, and Personality." *Adolescence, 27,* 387–405.

Sharp, J. G., and Graeven, D. B. (December 1981). "The Social, Behavioral, and Health Effects of Phencyclidine (PCP) Use." *Journal of Youth and Adolescence, 10,* 487–499.

Sheinberg, M., and Penn, P. (1991). "Gender Dilemmas, Gender Questions, & the Gender Mantra." *Journal of Marriage and the Family Therapy,* 17, 33–44.

Shelton, C. M., and McAdams, D. P. (1990). "In Search of an Everyday Morality: The Development of a Measure." *Adolescence,* 25, 923–943.

Sheppard, B. J. (1974). "Making the Case for Behavior as an Expression of Physical Condition." In B. L. Kratonile (Ed.), *Youth in Trouble.* San Rafael, CA: Academic Therapy Publications.

Sheppard, M. A., Wright, D., and Goodstadt, M. S. (1985). "Peer Pressure and Drug Use—Exploding the Myth." *Adolescence,* 20, 949–958.

Sherrod, L. R., Haggerty, R. J., and Featherman, D. L. (1993). "Introduction: Late Adolescence and the Transition to Adulthood." *Journal of Research on Adolescence,* 3, 217–226.

Shilts, L. (1991). "The Relationship of Early Adolescent Substance Use to Extracurricular Activities, Peer Influence, and Personal Attitudes." *Adolescence,* 26, 613–617.

Shreve, B. W., and Kunkel, M. A. (1991). "Self-Psychology, Shame, and Adolescent Suicide: Theoretical and Practical Considerations." *Journal of Counseling and Development,* 69, 305–311.

Shure, M. B., and Spivak, G. (1980). "Interpersonal Problem Solving as Mediator of Behavioral Adjustment in Preschool and Kindergarten Children." *Journal of Applied Developmental Psychology,* 1, 29–44.

Siegall, B. (August 21, 1977). "Incest: An American Epidemic." *Los Angeles Times.*

Siegler, R. S. (1991). *Children's Thinking.* 2nd ed. Englewood Cliffs, NJ: Prentice-Hall.

Sigelman, C. K., Gurstell, S. A., and Stewart, A. K. (1992). "The Development of Lay Theories of Problem Drinking: Causes and Cures." *Journal of Adolescent Research,* 7, 292–312.

Signorielli, N. (1993). "Television and Adolescents' Perceptions about Work." *Youth and Society,* 24, 314–341.

Silverberg, D., and Sternberg, L. (1987). "Adolescent Autonomy, Parent-Adolescent Conflict and Parental Well-Being." *Journal of Youth and Adolescence,* 16, 293–311.

Silverstein, C. D., and Buck, G. M. (1986). "Parental Preferences Regarding Sex Education Topics for Sixth Graders." *Adolescence,* 21, 971–980.

Simmons, R., and Blyth, D. (1987). *Moving into Adolescence: The Impact of Pubertal Change and Social Context.* New York: Adine de Greyter.

Simon, S. B., et al. (1972). *Values Clarification.* New York: Hart Publishing.

Simons, J. M., Finley, R., and Yang, A. (1991). *The Adolescent and Young Adult Fact Book.* Washington, DC: Children's Defense Fund.

Simons, R. L., and Robertson, J. F. (1989). "The Impact of Parenting Factors, Deviant Peers, and Coping Style among Adolescent Drug Users." *Family Relations,* 38, 273–281.

Simons, R. L., and Whitbeck, L. B. (1991). "Sexual Abuse as a Precursor to Prostitution and Victimization among Adolescent and Adult Homeless Women." *Journal of Family Issues,* 12, 361–379.

Simons, R. L., Whitbeck, L. B., Conger, R. D., and Melby, J. N. (1991). "The Effect of Social Skills, Values, Peers, and Depression on Adolescent Substance Use." *Journal of Early Adolescence,* 11, 466–481.

Singh, K., and Hernandez-Gantes, B. M. (1996). "The Relation of English Language Proficiency to Educational Aspirations of Mexican-American Eighth Graders." *Journal of Early Adolescence,* 16, 253–273.

Skandhan, K. P., Pandya, A. K., Skandhan, S., and Mehta, Y. B. (1988). "Menarche: Prior Knowledge and Experience." *Adolescence,* 89, 149–154.

Skeen, P., Covi, R. B., and Robinson, B. E. (1985). "Stepfamilies: A Review of the Literature with Suggestions for Practitioners." *Journal of Counseling and Development,* 64, 121–125.

Skoe, E., and Gooden, A. (1993). "Ethic of Care and Real-Life Moral Dilemma Content in Male and Female Early Adolescents." *Journal of Early Adolescence,* 13, 154–167.

Slater, E. J., Stewart, K. J., and Linn, M. W. (Winter 1983). "The Effects of Family Disruption on Adolescent Males and Females." *Adolescence,* 18, 931–942.

Slonim-Nevo, V. (1992). "First Premarital Intercourse among Mexican-American and Anglo-American Adolescent Women." *Journal of Adolescent Research,* 7, 332–351.

Slonim-Nevo, V., Auslander, W. F., Ozawa, M. N., and Jung, K. G. (1996). "The Long-Term Impact of AIDS—Preventative Interventions for Delinquent and Abused Adolescents." *Adolescence,* 31, 409–421.

Smart, L. S., Chibucos, T. R., and Didier, L. A. (1990). "Adolescent Substance Use and Perceived Family Functioning." *Journal of Family Issues,* 11, 208–227.

Smith, E. (May 1989). "The New Moral Classroom." *Psychology Today,* 23, 32–36.

Smith, E. A., and Caldwell, L. L. (1989). "The Perceived Quality of Leisure Experiences among Smoking and Nonsmoking Adolescents." *Journal of Early Adolescence,* 9, 153–162.

Smith, E. A., and Zabin, L. S. (1993). "Marital and Birth Expectations of Urban Adolescents." *Youth and Society,* 25, 62–74.

Smith, E. J. (1991). "Ethnic Identity Development: Toward the Development of a Theory within the Context of Majority/Minority Status." *Journal of Counseling and Development,* 770, 181–188.

Smith, R. E., Pine, C. J., and Hawley, M. E. (1988). "Social Cognitions about Adult Male Victims of Female Sexual Assault." *The Journal of Sex Research,* 24, 101–112.

Smith, S. P. (1996). "Dating-Partner Preferences among a Group of Inner-City African-American High School Students." *Adolescence,* 31, 79–90.

Smith, T. E. (1988). "Parental Control Techniques." *Journal of Family Issues,* 2, 155–176.

———. (1990). "Parental Separation and the Academic Self-Concepts of Adolescents: An Effort to Solve the Puzzle of Separation Effects." *Journal of Marriage and the Family,* 52, 107–118.

———. (1991). "Agreement of Adolescent Educational Expectations with Perceived Maternal and Paternal Educational Goals." *Youth and Society,* 23, 155–174.

Snodgrass, D. M. (1991). "The Parent Connection." *Adolescence,* 26, 83–87.

Snow, J. T., and Harris, M. B. (1989). "Disordered Eating in South-Western Pueblo Indians and Hispanics." *Journal of Adolescence,* 12, 329–336.

Snyder, E. E., and Spreitzer, E. (1992). "Social Psychological Concomitants of Adolescents' Role Identities as Scholars and Athletes." *Youth and Society,* 23, 507–522.

Snyder, S. (1991). "Movies and Juvenile Delinquency: An Overview." *Adolescence,* 26, 121–132.

———. (1995). "Movie Portrayals of Juvenile Delinquency: Part I—Epidemiology and Criminology." *Adolescence,* 30, 53–64.

Sobal, J. (1984). "Group Dieting, the Stigma of Obesity, and Overweight Adolescents: Contributions of Natalie Allon to the Sociology of Obesity." *Marriage and Family Review,* 7, 9–20.

———. (1987). "Health Concerns of Young Adolescents." *Adolescence,* 87, 739–750.

"Social Factors, Not Age, Are Found to Affect Risk of Low Birth Weight." (May–June, 1984). *Family Planning Perspectives,* 16, 142, 143.

Sodowsky, G. R., Lai, E. W. M., and Plake, B. S. (1991). "Moderating Effects of Sociocultural Variables on Acculturation Attitudes of Hispanics and Asian Americans." *Journal of Counseling and Development,* 70, 194–204.

Solorzano, L. (August 27, 1984). "Students Think Schools Are Making the Grade." *U.S. News & World Report,* pp. 49–51.

Sommer, B. (1984). "The Troubled Teen: Suicide, Drug Use, and Running Away." *Women's Health,* 9, 117–141.

Sommer, B., and Nagel, S. (1991). "Ecological and Typological Characteristics in Early Adolescent Truancy." *Journal of Early Adolescence,* 11, 379–392.

Sonenstein, F. L., and Pittman, K. J. (January–February, 1984). "The Availability of Sex Education in Large School Districts." *Family Planning Perspectives,* 16, 19–25.

Sonenstein, F. L., Pleck, J. H., and Ku, L. C. (1991). "Levels of Sexual Activity among Adolescent Males in the United States." *Family Planning Perspectives,* 23, 162–167.

South, S. J. (1995). "Do You Need to Shop Around?" *Journal of Family Issues,* 16, 432–449.

Special Issue: Mental Health Research and Service Issues for Minority Youth. (June 1988). *Journal of Adolescence,* 11.

Spencer, M. B., Dobbs, B., and Swanson, D. P. (1988). "African American Adolescents: Adaptational Processes and Socioeconomic Diversity in Behavioral Outcomes." *Journal of Adolescence,* 11, 117–137.

Spillane-Grieco, E. (Spring 1984). "Characteristics of a Helpful Relationship: A Study of Empathetic Understanding and Positive Regard between Runaways and Their Parents." *Adolescence,* 19, 63–75.

Sprecher, S., McKinney, K., Walsh, R., and Anderson, C. (1988). "A Revision of the Reiss Premarital Sexual Permissiveness Scale." *Journal of Marriage and the Family,* 50, 821–828.

Spring-Mills, E., and Hafez, E. S. (1980). "Male Accessory Sexual Organs." In E. S. Hafz (Ed.), *Human Reproduction* (pp. 60–90). New York: Harper and Row.

St. Clair, S., and Day, H. D. (September, 1979). "Ego Identity Status and Values among High School Females." *Journal of Youth and Adolescence,* 8, 317–326.

Stacey, B. G., Singer, M. S., and Ritchie, G. (1989). "The Perception of Poverty and Wealth among Teenage University Students." *Adolescence,* 24, 193–207.

Stack, S. (May 1985). "The Effect of Domestic/Religious Individualism in Suicide, 1954–1978." *Journal of Marriage and the Family,* 47, 431–447.

Stager, J. M. (1984). "Reversibility of Amenorrhea in Athletes: A Review." *Sports Medicine,* 1, 337.

———. (1988). "Menarche and Exercise." *Medical Aspects of Human Sexuality,* 22, 118, 133.

Stager, J. M., Ritchie, B. A., and Robertshaw, D. (1984). "Reversal of Oligo/Amenorrhea in Collegiate Distance Runners." *New England Journal of Medicine,* 310, 51.

Stake, J. E., DeVille, C. J., and Pennell, C. L. (October 1983). "The Effects of Assertive Training on the Performance Self-Esteem of Adolescent Girls." *Journal of Youth and Adolescence,* 12, 435–442.

Stallmann, J. I., and Johnson, T. G. (1996). "Community Factors in Secondary Educational Achievement in Appalacia." *Youth and Society,* 27, 469–484.

Stanton, B. F., Black, M., Kaljee, L., and Ricardo, I. (1993). "Perceptions of Sexual Behavior among Urban Early Adolescents: Translating Theory through Focus Groups." *Journal of Early Adolescence,* 13, 44–66.

Stanton, W. R., and Silva, P. A. (1992). "A Longitudinal Study of the Influence of Parents and Friends on Childrens' Initiation of Smoking." *Journal of Applied Developmental Psychology,* 13, 423–434.

Steck, G. M., Anderson, S. A., and Boylin, W. M. (1992). "Satanism among Adolescents: Imperical and Clinical Considerations." *Adolescence,* 27, 901–914.

Steel, L. (1991). "Early Working Experience among White and Nonwhite Youths: Implications for Subsequent Enrollment and Employment." *Youth and Society,* 22, 419–447.

Steelman, L. C. (February 1985). "The Social and Academic Consequences of Birth Order: Real, Artifactual, or Both?" *Journal of Marriage and the Family,* 47, 117–124.

Stefanko, M. (Spring 1984). "Trends in Adolescent Research: A Review of Articles Published in Adolescence—1976–1981." *Adolescence,* 19, 1–14.

Stein, D., Witztum, E., Brom, D., DeNour, A. K., and Elizur, A. (1992). "The Association between Adolescents' Attitudes towards Suicide and Their Psychosocial Background and Suicidal Tendencies." *Adolescence,* 27, 949–959.

Stein, D. B., and Smith, E. D. (1990). "The 'Rest' Program: A New Treatment System for the Oppositional Defiant Adolescent." *Adolescent,* 25, 891–904.

Stein, D. M., and Reichert, P. (1990). "Extreme Dieting Behaviors in Early Adolescence." *Journal of Early Adolescence,* 10, 108–121.

Stein, R. F. (1987). "Comparison of Self-Concept of Nonobese and Obese University Junior Female Nursing Students." *Adolescence,* 22, 77–90.

Stein, S. L., and Weston, L. C. (Winter 1982). "College Women's Attitudes toward Women and Identity Achievement." *Adolescence,* 17, 895–899.

Steinberg, L., Fegley, S., and Dornbusch, S. M. (1993). "Negative Impact of Part-time Work on Adolescent Adjustment: Evidence from a Longitudinal Study." *Developmental Psychology,* 29, 171–180.

Steinberg, L., Lamborn, S. D., Dornbusch, S. M., and Darling, N. (1992). "Impact of Parenting Practices on Adolescent Achievement: Authoritative Parenting, School Involvement, and Encouragement to Succeed." *Child Development,* 63, 1266–1281.

Steitz, J. A., and Owen, T. P. (1992). "School Activities and Work: Effects on Adolescent Self-Esteem." *Adolescence,* 27, 37–50.

Stephen, J., Fraser, E., and Marcia, J. E. (1992). "Moratorium Achievement, (Mama) Cycles in Life Span Identity Development: Value Orientations and Reasoning Systems' Correlates." *Journal of Adolescence,* 15, 283–300.

Sterling, C. M., and Van Horn, K. R. (1989). "Identity and Death Anxiety." *Adolescence,* 24, 321–326.

Stern, M., and Alvarez, A. (1992). "Pregnant and Parenting Adolescents. A Comparative Analysis of Coping Response and Psychosocial Adjustment." *Journal of Adolescent Research,* 7, 469–493.

Stern, M., Northman, J. E., and Van Slyck, M. R. (Summer 1984). "Father Absence and Adolescent 'Problem Behaviors': Alcohol Consumption, Drug Use, and Sexual Activity." *Adolescence,* 19, 301–312.

Sternberg, R., and Nigro, G. (1980). "Developmental Strategies in the Solution of Verbal Analogies." *Child Development,* 51, 27–38.

Sternberg, R. J. (Spring 1981). "The Nature of Intelligence." *New York University Education Quarterly,* 12, 10–17.

———. (1985). *Beyond IQ.* Cambridge, England: Cambridge University Press.

———. (1990). *Academic and Practical Cognition Has Different Aspects of Intelligence.* Paper presented at the 12th West Virginia Conference on Life-span Developmental Psychology, Morgantown.

Sternberg, R. J., and Wagner, R. K. (Eds.). (1986). *Practical Intelligence: Nature and Origins of Competence in the Everyday World.* Cambridge, England: Cambridge University Press.

Stevens, N. M., Mott, L. A., and Youells, F. (1996). "Rural Adolescent Drinking Behavior: Three-Year Follow-Up on the New Hampshire Substance Abuse Prevention Study." *Adolescence,* 31, 159–166.

Stevens, R., and Pihl, R. O. (1987). "Seventh-Grade Students at Risk for School Failure." *Adolescence,* 22, 333–345.

Stivers, C. (1988). "Parent-Adolescent Communication and Its Relationship to Adolescent Depression and Suicide Proneness." *Adolescence,* 23, 291–295.

Stohs, J. H. (1992). "Career Patterns and Family Status of Women and Men Artists." *The Career Development Quarterly,* 40, 223–233.

Story, M. D. (Winter 1982). "A Comparison of University Student Experience with Various Sexual Outlets in 1974 and 1980." *Adolescence,* 737–747.

Strang, R. (1957). *The Adolescent Views Himself.* New York: McGraw-Hill.

Strang, S. P., and Orlofsky, J. L. (1990). "Factors Underlying Suicidal Ideation among College Students: A Test of Teicher and Jacob's Model." *Journal of Adolescence,* 13, 39–52.

Straus, M. A., and Yodanis, C. L. (1996). "Corporal Punishment in Adolescence and Physical Assaults on Spouses in Later Life: What Accounts for the Link?" *Journal of Marriage and the Family,* 58, 825–841.

Street, S. (1988). "Feedback and Self-Concept in High School Students." *Adolescence,* 23, 449–456.

Streetman, L. G. (1987). "Contrasts in Self-Esteem of Unwed Teenage Mothers." *Adolescence,* 23, 459–464.

Streitmatter, J. (1993). "Gender Differences in Identity Development: An Examination of Longitudinal Data." *Adolescence,* 28, 55–66.

Stringer, D. M., and Duncan, E. (1985). "Nontraditional Occupations: A Study of Women Who Have Made the Choice." *The Vocational Guidance Quarterly,* 33, 241–248.

Strong, E. K. (1943). *Vocational Interests of Men and Women.* Palo Alto, CA: Stanford University Press.

Strouse, J., and Fabes, R. A. (1985). "Formal versus Informal Sources of Sex Education: Competing Forces in the Sexual Socialization of Adolescents." *Adolescence,* 20, 251–263.

Strouse, J. S., Buerkel-Rothfuss, N., and Long, E. C. J. (1995). "Gender and Families as Moderators of the Relationship between Music Video Exposure and Adolescent Sexual Permissiveness." *Adolescence,* 30, 505–521.

Struckman-Johnson, C. (1988). "Forced Sex on Dates: It Happens to Men, Too." *The Journal of Sex Research,* 24, 234–241.

Stubbs, M. L., Rierdan, J., and Koff, E. (1989). "Developmental Differences in Menstrual Attitudes." *Journal of Early Adolescence,* 9, 480–498.

Stuck, M. F., and Glassner, B. (1985). "The Transition from Drug Use and Crime to Noninvolvement: A Case Study." *Adolescence,* 20, 669–679.

"Substantially Higher Morbidity and Mortality Rates Found among Infants Born to Adolescent Mothers." (March–April, 1984). *Family Planning Perspectives,* 16, 91, 92.

Suicide Prevention Center. (1984). *Suicide Statistics*. Los Angeles, CA.

Suitor, J. J., and Reavis, R. (1995). "Football, Fast Cars, and Cheerleading: Adolescent Gender Norms, 1978 through 1989." *Adolescence*, 30, 265–272.

Sullivan, M. L. (1993). "Culture and Class as Determinants of Out-of-Wedlock Childbearing and Poverty during Late Adolescence." *Journal of Research on Adolescence*, 3, 295–316.

Sutherland, E. H., and Cressey, D. R. (1966). *Principles of Criminology*. 7th ed. New York: J. B. Lippincott.

Svec, H. (1986). "School Discrimination and the High School Dropout: A Case for Adolescent Advocacy." *Adolescence*, 21, 449–452.

———. (1987). "Anorexia Nervosa: A Misdiagnosis of the Adolescent Male." *Adolescence*, 87, 617–623.

Swanson, H. L., and Hill, G. (1993). "Metacognitive Aspects of Moral Reasoning and Behavior." *Adolescence*, 28, 711–735.

Sweat, K., and Murray, R. (1992, 1993). *Freak Me*. WB Music Corporation, E/A Music Inc., Keith Sweat Publishing, Inc., EMI Blackwood Music, Inc., and Saints Alive Music.

Sweeney, M. M., and Zionts, P. (1989). "The Second-Skin Perceptions of Disturbed and Nondisturbed Early Adolescents on Clothing, Self-Concept, and Body Image." *Adolescence*, 24, 411–420.

Swenson, C. C., and Kennedy, W. A. (1995). "Perceived Control and Treatment Outcome with Chronic Adolescent Offenders." *Adolescence*, 30, 565–578.

Swenson, I. E., Foster, B., and Asay, M. (1995). "Menstruation, Menarche, and Sexuality in the Public School Curriculum: School Nurses' Perceptions." *Adolescence*, 30, 677–683.

Tanfer, K. (1987). "Patterns of Premarital Cohabitation among Never-Married Women in the United States." *Journal of Marriage and the Family*, 49, 483–497.

Tanner, J. M. (1962). *Growth of Adolescence*. Springfield, IL: Charles C. Thomas.

———. (1968). "Earlier Maturation in Man." *Scientific American*, 218, 21–27.

———. (September 1973). *Scientific American*, p. 8.

Taylor, L. T. (1994). *Winning Combinations: The Effects of Different Parenting Style Combinations on Adolescent Adjustment*. Paper presented at the biennial meeting of the Society for Research on Child Development, San Diego.

Taylor, R. D., Casten, R., and Flickinger, S. M. (1993). "Influence of Social Support on the Parenting Experiences and Psychosocial Adjustment of African-American Adolescents." *Developmental Psychology*, 29, 382–388.

Teachman, J. D., Paasch, K., and Carver, K. (1996). "Social Capital and Dropping Out of School Early." *Journal of Marriage and the Family*, 58, 773–783.

Teachman, J. D., and Polonko, K. A. (1990). "Cohabitation and Marital Stability in the United States." *Social Forces*, 69, 207–220.

Tedesco, L. A., and Gaier, E. L. (1988). "Friendship Bonds in Adolescence." *Adolescence*, 89, 127–136.

"Teenage Pregnancy and Birth Rate—United States, 1990." (1993). *Morbidity & Mortality Weekly Report*, 42, 733–737.

Terrell, F., Terrell, S. L., and Miller, F. (1993). "Level of Cultural Mistrust as a Function of Educational and Occupational Expectations among Black Students." *Adolescence*, 28, 573–578.

Teti, D. M., and Lamb, M. E. (1989). "Socioeconomic and Marital Outcomes of Adolescent Marriage, Adolescent Childbirth, and Their Co-occurrence." *Journal of Marriage and the Family*, 51, 203–212.

Teti, D. M., Lamb, M. E., and Elster, A. B. (1987). "Long-Range Economic and Marital Consequences of Adolescent Marriage in Three Cohorts of Adult Males." *Journal of Marriage and the Family*, 49, 499–506.

Thelen, E., and Adolph, K. E. (1992). "Arnold L. Gesell: The Paradox of Nature and Nurture." *Developmental Psychology*, 28, 368–380.

Thomas, G., Farrell, M. P., and Barnes, G. M. (1996). "The Effects of Single-Mother Families and Nonresident Fathers on Delinquency and Substance Abuse in Black and White Adolescents." *Journal of Marriage and the Family*, 58, 884–894.

Thomas, T. (1992, 1993). *Mr. Wendal*. EMI Blackwood Music, Inc., and Arrested Development Music.

Thompson, D. N. (1985). "Parent-Peer Compliance in a Group of Preadolescent Youths." *Adolescence*, 20, 501–508.

Thompson, L., Acock, A. C., and Clark, K. (1985). "Do Parents Know Their Children? The Ability of Mothers and Fathers to Gauge the Attitudes of Their Young Adult Children." *Family Relations*, 34, 315–320.

Thompson, W. E., and Dodder, R. A. (1986). "Containment Theory and Juvenile Delinquency: A Reevaluation Through Factor Analysis." *Adolescence*, 21, 365–376.

Thomson, E., and Colella, U. (1992). "Cohabitation and Marital Stability: Quality or Commitment?" *Journal of Marriage and the Family*, 54, 259–267.

Thomson, E., McLanahan, S. S., and Curtin, R. B. (1992). "Family Structure, Gender, and Parental Socialization." *Journal of Marriage and the Family*, 54, 368–378.

Thorlindsson, T., and Vilhjalmsson, R. (1991). "Factors Related to Cigarette Smoking and Alcohol Use among Adolescents." *Adolescence*, 26, 390–418.

Thorndike, R. L., Hagen, E. P., and Sattler, J. M. (1985). Stanford-Binet. 4th ed. Chicago, IL: Riverside.

Thorne, C. R., and DeBlassie, R. R. (1985). "Adolescent Substance Abuse." *Adolescence*, 20, 335–347.

Thornton, A. (1990). "The Courtship Process and Adolescent Sexuality." *Journal of Family Issues*, 11, 239–273.

Thornton, A., and Camburn, D. (1987). "The Influence of the Family on Premarital Sexual Attitudes and Behavior." *Demography*, 24, 323.

———. (1989). "Religious Participation and Adolescent Sexual Behavior and Attitudes." *Journal of Marriage and the Family*, 51, 641–653.

Thornton, B., and Ryckman, R. M. (1991). "Relationship Between Physical Attractiveness, Physical Effectiveness, and Self-Esteem: A Cross-Sectional Analysis among Adolescents." *Journal of Adolescence*, 14, 85–98.

Thornton, L. P., and DeBlassie, R. R. (1989). "Treating Bulimia." *Adolescence*, 24, 631–637.

Tice, D. M., Buder, J., and Baumeister, R. F. (1985). "Development of Self-Consciousness: At What Age Does Audience Pressure Disrupt Performance?" *Adolescence*, 20, 301–305.

Tidwell, R. (1988). "Dropouts Speak Out: Qualitative Data in Early School Departures." *Adolescence*, 23, 939–954.

Tierno, M. J. (Fall 1983). "Responding to Self-Concept Disturbance among Early Adolescents: A Psychosocial View for Educators." *Adolescence*, 18, 577–584.

Timnick, L. (August 1982). "How You Can Learn to Be Likeable, Confident, Socially Successful for Only the Cost of Your Present Education." *Psychology Today,* 42ff.

Tinko, C., Stovel, K. W., Baumgartner, M., and Moos, R. H. (1995). "Acute and Chronic Stressors, Social Resources, and Functioning among Adolescents with Juvenile Rheumatic Disease." *Journal of Research on Adolescence*, 5, 361–385.

Tisak, M. S., and Tisak, J. (1996). "My Sibling's but Not My Friend's Keeper: Reasoning about Responses to Aggressive Acts." *Journal of Early Adolescence*, 16, 324–339.

Tishler, C. L. (1992). "Adolescent Suicide: Assessment of Risk, Prevention, and Treatment." *Adolescent Medicine*, 3, 51–60.

Tobin, J. J., and Friedman, J. (1984). "Intercultural and Developmental Stresses Confronting Southeast Asian Refugee Adolescents." *Journal of Operational Psychiatry*, 15, 39–45.

Toder, N. L., and Marcia, J. E. (1973). "Ego Identity Status and Response to Conformity Pressure in College Women." *Journal of Personality and Social Psychology*, 26, 287–294.

Tolan, P. (1988). "Socioeconomic, Family, and Social Stress Correlates of Adolescent Antisocial and Delinquent Behavior." *Journal of Abnormal Child Psychology*, 16, 317–331.

Tolson, J. M., and Urberg, K. A. (1993). "Similarity between Adolescent Best Friends." *Journal of Adolescent Research*, 8, 274–288.

Tomlinson-Keasey, C. (1972). "Formal Operations in Females from Eleven to Fifty-four Years of Age." *Developmental Psychology*, 6, 364.

Tooth, G. (February 18, 1985). "Why Children's TV Turns Off So Many Parents." *U.S. News & World Report*, p. 65.

Toray, T., Coughlin, C., Buchinich, S., and Patricelli, P. (1991). "Gender Differences Associated with Adolescent Substance Abuse: Comparisons and Implications for Treatment." *Family Relations*, 40, 338–344.

Torres, R., Fernandez, F., and Maceira, D. (1995). "Self-esteem and Value of Health as Correlates of Adolescent Health Behavior." *Adolescence*, 30, 403–412.

Toufexis, A. (1992). "When Kids Kill Abusive Parents." *Time*, 140, 60–61.

Traub, S. H., and Dodder, R. A. (1988). "Intergenerational Conflict of Values and Norms: A Theoretical Model." *Adolescence*, 23, 975–989.

Traver, N. (October 26, 1992). "Children without Pity." *Time*, 140, 46–51.

Treboux, C., and Busch-Rossnagel, N. A. (1990). "Social Network Influences on Adolescent Sexual Attitudes and Behaviors." *Journal of Adolescent Research*, 5, 175–189.

Trepanier-Street, M. L., Romatowski, J. A., and McNair, S. (1990). "Development of Story Characters in Gender-Therapeutic and Non-Therapeutic Occupational Roles." *Journal of Early Adolescence*, 10, 496–510.

Trevoux, D., and Busch-Rossnagel, N. A. (1995). "Age Differences in Parents and Peer Influences on Female Sexual Behavior." *Journal of Research on Adolescence*, 5, 469–487.

Troiden, R. R., and Jendrek, M. P. (1987). "Does Sexual Ideology Correlate with Level of Sexual Experience? Assessing the Construct Validity of SAS." *The Journal of Sex Research*, 23, 256–261.

Trotter, R. J. (1986). "Three Heads Are Better Than One." *Psychology Today*, 20, 56–62.

Trotter, R. T. (Summer 1982). "Ethical and Sexual Patterns of Alcohol Use: Anglo and Mexican-American College Students." *Adolescence*, 17, 305–325.

Trussell, J. (1988). "Teenage Pregnancy in the United States." *Family Planning Perspectives*, 20, 262–272.

Trussell, J., Rodriguez, G., and Vaughan, B. (1988). "Union Disillusion in Sweden." Paper presented at the *Seminar on Event History Analysis* sponsored by the International Union for the Scientific Study of Population, Paris, France.

Tschann, J. M., Johnston, J. R., and Wallerstein, J. S. (1989). "Resources, Stressors, and Attachment as Predictors of Adult Adjustment after Divorce: A Longitudinal Study." *Journal of Marriage and the Family*, 51, 1033–1046.

Tucker, L. A. (1983). "Muscular Strength and Mental Health." *Journal of Personality and Social Psychology*, 45, 1355–1360.

———. (1985). "Television's Role Regarding Alcohol Use among Teenagers." *Adolescence*, 20, 593–598.

Tudge, J., and Winterhoff, P. (1993). *The Cognitive Consequences of Collaboration: Why Ask How?* Paper presented at the biennial meeting of the Society for Research in Child Development, New Orleans.

Turner, H. A., and Finkelhor, D. (1996). "Corporal Punishment as a Stressor among Youth." *Journal of Marriage and the Family*, 58, 155–166.

Turner, R. (1991). "One in Seven 6th–12th Graders had an Unwanted Sexual Encounter, Including One in Five Females." *Family Planning Perspectives*, 23, 286–287.

Tygart, C. (1988). "Public School Vandalism: Toward a Synthesis of Theories and Transition to Paradigm Analysis." *Adolescence*, 23, 187–200.

Udry, J. R. (1990). "Hormonal and Social Determinants of Adolescent Sexual Initiation." In J. Bancroft and J. M. Reinisch (Eds.), *Adolescence in Puberty*. New York: Oxford University Press.

Umberson, D. (1989). "Relationship with Children: Explaining Parents' Psychological Well-Being." *Journal of Marriage and the Family*, 51, 999–1012.

Underwood, N. K., Kupersmidt, J. B., and Coie, J. D. (1996). "Childhood Peer Sociometric Status and

Aggression as Predictors of Adolescent Childbearing." *Journal of Research on Adolescence,* 6, 201–223.

U.S. Bureau of the Census. Department of Commerce. (1994). *Statistical Abstract of the United States, 1994.* Washington, DC: U.S. Government Printing Office.

U.S. Bureau of the Census. Department of Commerce. (1996). *Statistical Abstract of the United States, 1996.* Washington, DC: U.S. Government Printing Office.

U.S. Department of Agriculture and United States Department of Health and Human Services. (1985). *Dietary Guidelines for Americans.* Home and Garden Bulletin, No. 232. Washington, DC: U.S. Government Printing Office.

U.S. Department of Health and Human Services, Office of Human Development. (August 1980). *Status of Children, Youth, and Families (1979).* DHHS Publication No. (OHDS) 80-30274.

U.S. Department of Justice, Attorney General's Commission on Pornography. (1986). *Final Report of Attorney General's Commission on Pornography.* Washington, DC: U.S. Government Printing Office.

Upchurch, D. M. (1993). "Early Schooling and Childbearing Experiences: Implications for Post Secondary School Attendance." *Journal of Research on Adolescence,* 3, 423–443.

Urbach, J. R., Khalily, C., and Mitchell, P. P. (1992). "Erotomania in an Adolescent: Clinical and Theoretical Considerations." *Journal of Adolescence,* 15, 231–240.

Utter, J. (1993). *American Indians. Answers to Today's Questions.* Lake Ann, MI: National Woodlands.

Valium Package Insert. (1988). Roche Laboratories.

Van den Broucke, S., and Vandereycken, W. (1986). "Risk Factors for the Development of Eating Disorders in Adolescent Exchange Students: An Exploratory Study." *Journal of Adolescence,* 9, 145–150.

Van Halen, E., Van Halen, A., Anthony, M., and Hager, S. (1991). *In 'N' Out.* Yessup Music.

Van Roosmalen, E., and Krahn, H. (1996). "Boundaries of Youth." *Youth and Society,* 28, 3–39.

Van Roosmalen, E. H., and McDaniel, S. A. (1989). "Peer Group Influence as a Factor in Smoking Behavior of Adolescents." *Adolescence,* 24, 801–816.

———. (1992). "Adolescent Smoking Intentions: Gender Differences in Peer Context." *Adolescence,* 27, 87–105.

Van Thorre, M. D., and Vogel, F. X. (Spring 1985). "The Presence of Bulimia in High School Females." *Adolescence,* 20, 45–51.

Vartanian, L. R., and Powlishta, K. K. (1996). "A Longitudinal Examination of the Social-Cognitive Foundations of Adolescent Egocentrism." *Journal of Early Adolescence,* 16, 157–178.

Vega, W. A. (1990). "Hispanic Families in the 1980s: A Decade of Research." *Journal of Marriage and the Family,* 52, 1015–1024.

Vicary, J. R., and Lerner, J. V. (1986). "Parental Attributes and Adolescent Drug Use." *Journal of Adolescence,* 9, 115–122.

Vinton, D. (1992). "Helping Students Find Time for the Job Search." *Journal of Career Planning and Employment,* 27, 71–74.

Violato, C., and Wiley, A. J. (1990). "Images of Adolescence in English Literature: The Middle Ages to the Modern Period." *Adolescence,* 25, 253–264.

Vischof, G. P., Stith, S. M., and Wilson, S. M. (1992). "A Comparison of the Family Systems of Adolescent Sexual Offenders and Nonsexual Offending Delinquents." *Family Relations,* 41, 318–323.

Vodanovich, S. J., and Kramer, T. J. (1989). "An Examination of the Work Values of Parents and Their Children." *The Career Development Quarterly,* 37, 365–374.

Volk, R. J., Edwards, D. W., Lewis, R. A., and Sprinkle, D. H. (1989). "Family Systems of Adolescent Substance Abusers." *Family Relations,* 38, 266–272.

Vondracek, F. W. (1991). "Vocational Development and Choice in Adolescence." In R. M. Lerner, A. C. Petersen, and J. Brooks-Gunn (Eds.), *Encyclopedia of Adolescence.* Vol. 2. New York: Garland.

Vondracek, F. W., and Schulenberg, J. E. (1986). "Career Development in Adolescence: Some Conceptual and Intervention Issues." *The Vocational Guidance Quarterly,* 34, 247–254.

———. (1992). "Counseling for Normative and Nonnormative Influences on Career Development." *The Career Development Quarterly,* 40, 291–301.

Voorhees, J. (Spring 1981). "Neuropsychological Differences between Juvenile Delinquents and Functional Adolescents: A Preliminary Study." *Adolescence,* 16, 57–66.

Wade, N. L. (1987). "Suicide as a Resolution of Separation—Individuation among Adolescent Girls." *Adolescence,* 22, 169–177.

Waite, B., Foster, H., and Hillbrand, M. (1992). "Reduction of Aggressive Behavior after Removal of Music Television." *Hospital and Community Psychiatry,* 43, 173–175.

Waksman, S. A. (Spring 1984a). "Assertion Training with Adolescents." *Adolescence,* 73, 123–130.

———. (Summer 1984b). "A Controlled Evaluation of Assertion Training with Adolescents." *Adolescence,* 19, 277–282.

Waldner-Haugrud, L. K., and Magruder, B. (1996). "Homosexual Identity Expression among Lesbian and Gay Adolescents." *Youth and Society,* 27, 313–333.

Walker, D. K., Cross, A. W., Heyman, P. W., Ruck-Ross, H., Benson, P., and Tuthill, J. W. G. (1982). "Comparison's Between Inner City and Private School Adolescents' Perceptions of Health Problems." *Journal of Adolescent Health Care,* 3, 82–90.

Walker, L. J., and Taylor, J. H. (1991). "Family Interaction and the Development of Moral Reasoning." *Child Development,* 62, 264–283.

Wall, J. A., Power, T. G., and Arbona, C. (1993). "Susceptibility to Antisocial Peer Pressure and Its Relation to Acculturation in Mexican-American Adolescents." *Journal of Adolescent Research,* 8, 403–418.

Wallace-Broscious, A., Serafica, F. C., and Osipow, S. H. (1994). "Adolescent Career Development: Relationships to Self-Concepts and Identity Status." *Journal of Research on Adolescence*, 4, 127–150.

Wallerstein, J. S. (1983). "Children of Divorce: Stress and Developmental Tasks." In N. Garnezy and M. Rutter (Eds.), *Stress, Coping and Development in Children* (pp. 265–302). New York: McGraw-Hill.

———. (1991). "The Long-Term Effects of Divorce on Children: A Review." *Journal of the Academy of Child Adolescence Psychiatry*, 30, 349–360.

Wallerstein, J. S., and Blakeslee, S. (1989). *Second Chances: Men, Women, and Children a Decade after Divorce.* New York: Ticknor & Fields.

Wallerstein, J. S., and Kelly, J. B. (1980). *Surviving the Breakup: How Children and Parents Cope with Divorce.* London: Grant McIntyre.

Wallis, C. (February 16, 1987). "You Haven't Heard Anything Yet." *Time.*

Walsh, A., and Beyer, J. A. (1987). "Violent Crime, Sociopathy, and Love Deprivation among Adolescent Delinquents." *Adolescence*, 22, 705–717.

Walsh, R. N., et al. (1981). "The Menstrual Cycle, Sex, and Academic Performance." *Archives of General Psychiatry*, 38, 219–221.

Ward, S. L. (1991). "Moral Development in Adolescence." In R. M. Lerner, A. C. Petersen, and J. Brooks-Gunn (Eds.), *Encyclopedia of Adolescence.* Vol. 2. New York: Garland.

Warren, D. (1992, 1993). *I'll Never Get Over You Getting Over Me.* Real Songs.

———. (1992, 1993). *Love Can Move Mountains.* Real Songs.

———. (1993). *Don't Take Away My Heaven.* Real Songs.

Warren, R., Good, G., and Velten, E. (Fall 1984). "Measurement of Social-Evaluative Anxiety in Junior High School Students." *Adolescence*, 19, 643–648.

Warshak, R. A. (1986). "Father-Custody and Child Development: A Review of Analysis of Psychological Research." *Behavioral Science and the Law*, 4, 185–202.

Washburn, W. E. (Ed.). (1988). *Handbook of North American Indians—History of Indian-White Relations.* Washington, DC: Smithsonian Institution.

Waterman, A. S. (1992). "Identity as an Affect of Optimal Psychological Functioning." In G. R. Adams, T. P. Gullota, and R. Montemayor (Eds.), *Adolescent Identity Formation.* Newbury Park, CA: Sage.

Watkins, B. (1992). "Youth Beliefs about Health and Physical Activity." *Journal of Applied Developmental Psychology*, 13, 257–269.

Watson, M. F., and Protinsky, H. O. (1988). "Black Adolescent Identity Development: Effects of Perceived Family Structure." *Family Relations*, 37, 288–292.

Watson, R. E. L. (January 1983). "Premarital Cohabitation vs. Traditional Courtship: Their Effects on Subsequent Marital Adjustment." *Family Relations*, 32, 139–147.

Watson, R. E. L., and DeMeo, P. W. (1987). "Premarital Cohabitation vs. Traditional Courtship and Subsequent Marital Adjustment: A Reflection and Follow-Up." *Family Relations*, 36, 193–196.

Wattenberg, W. W. (1973). *The Adolescent Years.* 2nd ed. New York: Harcourt Brace Jovanovich.

Watts, W. D., and Wright, L. S. (1990). "The Relationship of Alcohol, Tobacco, Marijuana, and Other Illegal Drug Use to Delinquency among Mexican-American, Black, and White Adolescent Males." *Adolescence*, 25, 171–181.

Waugh, N. C., and Norman, D. A. (1965). "Primary Memory." *Psychological Review*, 72, 89–104.

Wayment, H., and Zetlin, A. G. (1989). "Theoretical and Methodological Considerations of Self-Concept Measurement." *Adolescence*, 24, 339–349.

Webb, J. A., Baer, P. E., Caid, C. D., McLaughlin, R. J., and McKelbey, R. S. (1991). "Concurrent and Longitudinal Assessment of Risk for Alcohol Use among Seventh Graders." *Journal of Early Adolescence*, 11, 450–465.

Webb, R. A. (1974). "Concrete and Formal Operations in Very Bright 6- to 11-Year-Olds." *Human Development*, 17, 292–300.

Weber, T. E. (January 16, 1997). "Mainstream Sites Accept Ads Selling X-Rated Fare." *The Wall Street Journal.*

Wechsler, D. (1955). *Manual for the Wechsler Adult Intelligence Scale.* New York: Psychological Corporation.

———. (1981). WAIS-R Manual: Wechsler Adult Intelligence Scale—Revised. San Antonio, TX: Psychological Corporation.

Wehr, S. H., and Kaufman, M. E. (1987). "The Effects of Assertive Training on Performance in Highly Anxious Adolescents." *Adolescence*, 85, 195–205.

Weinbender, M. L. M., and Rossignol, A. M. (1996). "Lifestyle and Risk of Premature Sexual Activity in a High School Population of Seven-Day Adventists: Valuegenesis, 1989." *Adolescence*, 31, 265–281.

Weinberg, M. S., and Williams, C. J. (1974). *Male Homosexuals.* New York: Oxford University Press.

Weinreich, H. E. (1974). "The Structure of Moral Reason." *Journal of Youth and Adolescence*, 3, 135–143.

Weissman, S. (April 1985). "Preparing Incarcerated Youth for Employment." *Journal of Counseling and Development*, 63, 524–525.

Weithorn, L. A., and Campbell, S. B. (1982). "The Competency of Children and Adolescents to Make Informed Treatment Decisions." *Child Development*, 53, 1589–1598.

Weller, L., and Luchterhand, E. (Spring 1983). "Family Relationships of 'Problem' and 'Promising' Youth." *Adolescence*, 1, 93–100.

Wells, B., and Miller, M. K. (1993). "Adolescent Affective Aggression: An Intervention Model." *Adolescence*, 28, 781–791.

Wellsand v. *Valparaiso Community Schools Corporation et al.* (1971). U.S.C.C., N.D., 71 Hlss (2) (Ind.).

Welte, J. W., and Barnes, G. M. (1987). "Youthful Smoking: Patterns and Relationships of Alcohol and Other Drug Use." *Journal of Adolescence*, 10, 327–340.

Wentzel, K. R. (1996). "Social and Academic Motivation in Middle School: Concurrent and Long-Term Relations to Academic Effort." *Journal of Early Adolescence*, 16, 390–406.

Wentzel, K. R., and Erdley, C. A. (1993). "Strategies for Making Friends: Relations to Social Behavior and Peer Acceptance in Early Adolescence." *Developmental Psychology*, 29, 819–826.

Wentzel, K. R., and Feldman, S. S. (1996). "Relations of Family Cohesion and Power in Family Dyads to Social and Emotional Adjustment during Adolescence." *Journal of Research on Adolescence*, 6, 225–244.

Wentzel, K. R., Feldman, S. S., and Weinberger, D. A. (1991). "Parental Child Rearing and Academic Achievement in Boys: The Mediational Role of Social-Emotional Adjustment." *Journal of Early Adolescence*, 11, 321–339.

Werebe, M. J. G. (1987). "Friendship and Dating Relationships among French Adolescents." *Journal of Adolescence*, 10, 269–289.

West, C. K., Jones P. A., and McConahay, G. (Fall 1981). "Who Does What to the Adolescent in the High School: Relationships among Resulting Affect and Self-Concept and Achievement." *Adolescence*, 16, 657–661.

Westney, O. I., Jenkins, R. R., Butts, J. D., and Williams, I. (Fall 1984). *Adolescence*, 19, 557–568.

Whitbeck, L. B., Conger, R. D., and Kao, M. (1993). "The Influence of Parental Support, Depressed Affect, and Peers on the Sexual Behaviors of Adolescent Girls." *Journal of Family Issues*, 14, 261–278.

Whitbeck, L. B., Conger, R. D., Simons, R. L., and Kao, M. (1993). "Minor Deviant Behaviors in Adolescent Sexual Activity." *Youth and Society*, 25, 24–37.

Whitbeck, L. B., Hoyt, D. R., Miller, M., and Kao, M. (1992). "Parental Support, Depressed Affect and Sexual Experience Among Adolescents." *Youth and Society*, 24, 166–177.

Whitbeck, L. B., Simons, R. L., Conger, R. D., and Lorenz, F. (1989). "Value Socialization and Peer Group Affiliation among Early Adolescents." *Journal of Early Adolescence*, 9, 436–453.

White, K. M. (Spring 1980). "Problems and Characteristics of College Students." *Adolescence*, 15, 23–41.

White, R. H. (1990). *Tribal Assets: The Rebirth of Native America*. New York: Henry Holt.

White, S. H. (1992). "G. Stanley Hall: From Philosophy to Developmental Psychology." *Developmental Psychology*, 28, 25–34.

Whitman, F. L., Diamond, M., and Martin, J. (1993). "Homosexual Orientation in Twins: A Report on 61 Pairs and 3 Triplet Sets." *Archives of Sexual Behavior*, 22, 187–206.

Wickens, C. D. (1974). "Limits of Human Information Processing: A Developmental Study." *Psychological Bulletin*, 81, 739–755.

Wierson, M., Long, P. J., and Forehand, R. L. (1993). "Toward a New Understanding of Early Menarche: The Role of Environmental Stress and Pubertal Timing." *Adolescence*, 28, 913–924.

Wigfield, A., and Eccles, J. S. (1995). "Middle School Grades, Schooling, and Early Adolescent Development." *Journal of Early Adolescence*, 5–8.

Wilkins, R., and Lewis, C. (1993). "Sex and Drugs and Nuclear War: Secular, Developmental, and Type A Influences upon Adolescents, Fears of the Nuclear Threat, AIDS, and Drug Addiction." *Journal of Adolescence*, 16, 23–41.

Williams, E. G. (Spring 1983). "Adolescent Loneliness." *Adolescence*, 18, 51–66.

Williams, J. W., and White, K. A. (1983). "Adolescent Status Systems for Males and Females at Three Age Levels." *Adolescence*, 18, 381–389.

Williams, K. (1988). "Parents Reinforce Feminine Role in Girls." *Medical Aspects of Human Sexuality*, 22, 106–107.

Williams, L. (1992, 1993). *Passionate Kisses*. Warner-Tamerlane Publishing Corporation, Lucy Jones Music, and Noman Music.

Williams, M., Himmel, K. F., Sjoberg, A. F., and Torrez, D. J., (1995). "The Assimilation Model, Family Life, & Race and Ethnicity in the United States." *Journal of Family Issues*, 16, 380–405.

Wilson, J. B. (1986). "Perceived Influence of Male Sex Role Identity on Female Partner's Life Choices." *Journal of Counseling and Development*, 65, 74–77.

Wilson, P. M., and Wilson, J. R. (1992). "Environmental Influences on Adolescent Educational Aspirations. A Logistic Transform Model." *Youth and Society*, 24, 52–70.

Wilson, S. M., and Medora, N. P. (1990). "Gender Comparisons of College Students' Attitudes toward Sexual Behavior." *Adolescence*, 25, 615–627.

Windle, M., and Miller-Tutzauer, C. (1992). "Confirmatory Factor Analysis and Concurrent Validity of the Perceived Social Support-Family Measure among Adolescents." *Journal of Marriage and the Family*, 54, 777–787.

Wodarski, J. S. (1990). "Adolescent Substance Abuse: Practice Implications." *Adolescence*, 99, 667–688.

Wolff, S. (1987). "Antisocial Conduct: Whose Concern?" *Journal of Adolescence*, 10, 105–118.

Wolock, I., and Horowitz, B. (1984). "Child Maltreatment as a Social Problem: The Neglect of Neglect." *American Journal of Orthopsychiatry*, 54, 530–543.

Wood, J., Chapin, K., and Hannah, M. E. (1988). "Family Environment and Its Relationship to Underachievement." *Adolescence*, 23, 283–290.

Wood, N. L., Wood, R. A., and McDonald, T. D. (1988). "Integration of Student Development Theory into the Academic Classroom." *Adolescence*, 23, 349–356.

Woodward, J. C., and Kalyan-Masih, V. (1990). "Loneliness, Coping Strategies and Cognitive Styles of the Gifted Rural Adolescent." *Adolescence*, 25, 977–988.

Wright, J. E. (Ed.). (1990). *The Universal Almanac, 1990*. Kansas City, MO: Andrews and McMeel.

Wright, L. S. (1985). "Suicidal Thoughts and Their Relationship to Family Stress and Personal Problems among High School Seniors and College Undergraduates." *Adolescence*, 20, 575–580.

Wright, R. (1937). "The Ethics of Living Jim Crow." In *American Stuff*. New York: Harper and Row.

Wu, Z. (1995a). "Premarital Cohabitation and Postmarital Cohabiting Union Formation." *Journal of Family Issues*, 16, 212–232.

———. (1995b). "The Stability of Cohabitation Relationships: The Role of Children." *Journal of Marriage and the Family,* 57, 231–236.

———. (1996). "Childbearing and Cohabitational Relationships." *Journal of Marriage and the Family,* 58, 281–292.

Wyatt, G. E. (1989). "Reexamining Factors Predicting Afro-American and White American Women's Age at First Coitus." *Archives of Sexual Behavior,* 18, 271–298.

Yacoubian, J. H., and Lourie, R. S. (1973). "Suicide and Attempted Suicide in Children and Adolescents." In S. L. Copel (Ed.), *Pathology of Childhood and Adolescence.* New York: Basic Books.

Yau, J., and Smetna, J. G. (1993). "Chinese-American Adolescents' Reasoning about Cultural Conflicts." *Journal of Adolescent Research,* 8, 419–438.

Yeh, C. J., and Huang, K. (1996). "The Collectivistic Nature of Ethnic Identity Development among Asian-American College Students." *Adolescence,* 31, 645–661.

Yogev, A., and Roditi, H. (1987). "School Counselors as Gatekeepers: Guidance in Poor versus Affluent Neighborhoods." *Adolescence,* 22, 625–639.

Young, E. W., Jensen, L. C., Olsen, J. A., and Cundick, B. P. (1991). "The Effects of Family Structure on the Sexual Behavior of Adolescents." *Adolescence,* 26, 977–986.

Young, M. H., Miller, B. C., Norton, M. C., and Hill, E. J. (1995). "The Effect of Parental Supportive Behaviors on Life Satisfaction of Adolescent Offspring." *Journal of Marriage and the Family,* 57, 813–822.

Young, R. A., and Friesen, J. D. (1992). "The Intentions of Parents in Influencing the Career Development of Their Children." *The Career Development Quarterly,* 40, 198–207.

Youngs, G. A., Jr., Rathge, R., Mullis, R., and Mullis, A. (1990). "Adolescent Stress and Self-Esteem." *Adolescence,* 25, 333–341.

Zabin, L. S., and Clark, S. D., Jr. (September–October, 1981). "Why They Delay: A Study of Teenage Family Planning Clinic Patients." *Family Planning Perspectives,* 13, 205ff.

Zambrana, R. E., and Silva-Palacios, V. (1989). "Gender Differences in Stress among Mexican Immigrant Adolescents in Los Angeles, CA." *Journal of Adolescent Research,* 4, 426–442.

Zarb, J. M. (Summer 1984). "A Comparison of Remedial Failure, and Successful Secondary School Students across Self-Perception and Past and Present School Performance Variables." *Adolescence,* 19, 335–348.

Zarbatany, L., Ghesquiere, K., and Mohr, K. (1992). "A Context Perspective on Early Adolescents' Friendship Expectations." *Journal of Early Adolescence,* 12, 111–126.

Zelkowitz, P. (1987). "Social Support and Aggressive Behavior in Young Children." *Family Relations,* 36, 129–134.

Zellman, G. L. (January–February, 1982). "Public School Programs for Adolescent Pregnancy and Parenthood: An Assessment." *Family Planning Perspectives,* 14, 15–21.

Zelnik, M., and Kim, Y. J. (May–June, 1982). "Sex Education and Its Association with Teenage Sexual Activity, Pregnancy, and Contraceptive Use." *Family Planning Perspectives,* 14, 117.

Zern, D. S. (1989). "Some Connections between Increasing Religiousness and Academic Accomplishment in a College Population." *Adolescence,* 24, 141–153.

Zill, N., Morrison, D. R., and Coiro, M. J. (1993). "Long-Term Effects of Parental Divorce on Parent-Child Relationships, Adjustment, and Achievement in Young Adulthood." *Journal of Family Psychology,* 7, 91–103.

Zimbardo, P. G. (June 1978). "Misunderstanding Shyness: The Counterattack." *Psychology Today,* 17ff.

Zimet, G. D., Sobo, E. J., Zimmerman, T., Jackson, J., Mortimer, J., Yanda, C. P., and Lazebnik, R. L. (1995). "Sexual Behavior, Drug Use, and AIDS Knowledge among Mid-Western Runaways." *Youth and Society,* 26, 450–462.

Zimmerman, R. S., Sprecher, S., Langer, L. M., and Holloway, C. D. (1995). "Adolescents' Perceived Ability to Say 'No' to Unwanted Sex." *Journal of Adolescent Research,* 10, 383–399.

Zuckerman, D. (January 1985). "Too Many Sibs Put Our Nation at Risk?" *Psychology Today,* 19, 5, 10.

INDEX

and music videos, 254
on television, 310
in video and computer games, 20
Violent adolescents, 19–21, 245
Virginity and incidence of divorce, 200
Visual imagery, 141–142
Vocation (*see* Work and vocation)
Vocational aspirations:
and fulfillment of self, 176
and single-parent homes, 348–349
Vocational curriculum, 364
Voice changes, 91, 103, 105
Vulva:
definition of, 96
development of, 97

Wechsler Adult Intelligence Scale (WAIS-R), 151
Wechsler Intelligence Scale for Children (WISC-III), 151, 152
Weight, 116–118
loss, 121, 122
physiological contributors, 116–118
psychological contributors, 118

Welfare dollars and teen pregnancy, 216
Wet dreams, 96
White supremacists, 244–245
Whites, suicide rates, 405
Williams, C., 261
Withdrawal from school (*see* Dropping out of school)
Women:
and career choices, 387
and identity, 186–187
in work force, 7, 12
Work and vocation, 379–396
and education, 395
and people influencing choice, 384–386
and prestige, 391–393
and sex roles, 386–387
and socioeconomic status, 391–393
theories of vocational choice, 380–384
unemployment, 393–395
Working vs. college or military, 391
Working in the community, 142
Working mothers and low socioeconomic status, 56
World Wide Web, 4
Worthlessness and self-esteem, 175